Igbo Nation: history, challenges of rebirth and development — vol. 2

Igbo Nation:
History, Challenges of Rebirth and Development

Igbo Nation:
History, Challenges of Rebirth and Development

Edited by

By

S. Okechukwu Mezu
& T. Uzodinma Nwala

Igbo Nation:
History, Challenges of Rebirth and Development

Edited by

S. Okechukwu Mezu
& T. Uzodinma Nwala

Igbo Nation, Ala Igbo,
Biafra, Nigeria, African Society

All Rights Reserved
Including the right of reproduction
in whole or in part in any form

Copyright©2014 by Black Academy Press, Inc.

ISBN 0-87831- 033-9 978-0-87831-033-3 Cloth

**BLACK ACADEMY PRESS, INC.
4015 OLD COURT ROAD
PIKESVILLE, MARYLAND 21208 USA**

Cover concept from Engr. Karl Uzodinma Nwala

ALAIGBO DEVELOPMENT FOUNDATION (ADF)
Suite B04 Gouba Plaza, Plot 171 Ekukinam Street
Utako District, FCT ABUJA
Enugu Office: No 1 Idemili Street, Ind. Layout, Enugu
Phone: 08033497985; 08023455681
Email: alaigbocongress@yahoo.com
Website: www.alaigbodf.com   Date: December 5, 2014

Alaigbo Development Foundation (ADF) is a body of intellectuals, clergy, elders, public figures women and youth and some pan-Igbo Associations working for the immediate and long-term Socio-cultural and Economic Rebirth and Development of Igbo-land, on the basis of a comprehensive National Charter.

ADF Working Committee and Standing Committees

Prof. T. Uzodinma Nwala, *President*
Prof. Elochukwu Amucheazi, *Vice President*
Prof. Nath Aniekwe , *Secretary*
Dr Jerry Chukwuokolo, *Financial Secretary*
Prof. Chinyere Ohiri-Aniche, *Treasurer*
Col Justin Ezeoke, *Publicity Secretary*
Bar Ukpai Ukairo, *Legal Adviser*
Dr. Onyemauchechi, *Asst. Secretary*
Mazi Sam Ohuabunwa, OFR, *Ex-Officio*
Prof. Martin Aghaji, *Ex-Officio*
Prince Emeka Onyesoh, *Ex-Officio*
Hon. Mrs. Maria Okwor, *Ex-Officio*
Prof. Dennis Odionyenfe Balogu, *Ex-Officio*

Standing Committees

Research and Documentation
Dr Chinweizu, *Chairman*
Dr Luke Aneke, *Secretary.*

Finance and Budget
Elder (Dr) Kalu Uke Kalu, *Chairman*
Dr Jerry Chukwuokolo, *Secretary*

Planning/Projects Committee
Dr Kalu Idika Kalu, *Chairman*
Dr Onyemauchechi Gbujie, *Secretary*

Publicity and Information
Hon. Abia Onyike, *Chairman*
Col Justino Ezeoke, *Publicity Secretary*

Igbo National Integration
Prof. Emmanuel A. C. Nwanze, *Chairman*
Bishop Chris Dr Asadu, *Secretary*

Religious Affairs
Prof. Bishop David Eberechukwu, *Chairman*
Evang. G. O. Gbujie, *Secretary*

Diaspora & International Relations
Dr. S. Okechukwu Mezu, *Chairman*
Chief Emmanuel Nwankwo, *Vice-Chair*
Prof. Ngozichukwu Ugo, *Member* - Dr Jerome Okolo, *Secretary*

Legal Affairs
Bar Ukpai Ukairo, *Legal Adviser*
Chief Debe Odumegwu Ojukwu, *Secretary*

Security
Chairman
Prof. Onyi Nwagbara, *Secretary*

Contact and Mobilization
Bishop Obi Onubogu, *Church Front*
Prince Emeka Onyesoh, *Secular Front*
Bar. Maxwell Alaeto, *Secretary*.

Editorial Committee
Prof. 1. Uzodinma Nwala – Dr. S. Okechukwu Mezu
Dr Chinweizu Chinweizu - Prof Chima Korieh
Prof, Chinyere Aniche-Ohiri - Prof Nath Aniekwu - Dr Jerry Chukwuokolo
Princess Alu Ibiam - Dr Ibeneche Gbujie - Dr Ugorji Okechukwu Ugorji

The Board of Trustees of ADF
Dr Dozie Ikedife, *Chairman*
Elder (Dr) Kalu Uke Kalu, *Vice Chairman*
Prof. 1. Uzodinma Nwala, *President*
Members
Prof. Barth Nnaji, Chief Innocent Nwoga, Princess Alu Ibiam, Prof. Chimah Korieh
Prof Ngozichukwuka Ugo, Chief Okey Nwankwor, Bishop Obi Udemezue Onubogu

Igbo Nation:
History, Challenges of Rebirth and Development

Edited by

**S. Okechukwu Mezu
& T. Uzodinma Nwala**

CONTENTS VOLUME ONE

Contents

Preface by Professor Uzodinma Nwala 15

Call to Service: *Oke Okpa Ebela* 20

Nseputa Mba di iche iche n'Ala Ndi Igbo 21

Foreword by S. Okechukwu Mezu 22

Commerce and Industry in Igbo Land by Chief Ralph Obioha 26

Economic Blueprint for Attracting Business
and Commerce in Igbo land by Felix Oti 34

Bringing Back the Focus on Agriculture by
Mazi Sam Ohuabunwa 40

Ogbemudia's Regime and Post-civil War
Reconstruction in Western Igboland, 1970-1975
by Daniel Olisa Iweze 47

A Revolutionized Agricultural Development in Southeast and South-
South (SESS) Geo-political Zones of Nigeria
by Prof. Dennis Odionyenfe Balogu 65

Infrastructure and Education as
the Basis for Industrialization by Prof. Bath Nnaji 81

Educational Challenges in Igbo Land: Today and Tomorrow

by Obiageli Ezekwesili 91

Prof. Gordian Ezekwe: The Hall of Fame Medalist for Scientific and Technological Development

by Alex O. E. Animalu 101

Security of the Ndi Igbo in Nigeria: The Way Forward

by Col. JMO Ezeoke 118

In Defence of the January 15 Revolution,

Chinua Achebe, Ndigbo and Biafra

by Mazi Chike Chidolue 122

Igbo Security: Making Igbo Life too expensive to Expend

by Dr. Luke N. Aneke 132

Securing the South-East and Igbo Economic Interest

by AU Max Gbanite 143

AlaIgbo Development Foundation (ADF)

Rebuilding the Igbo Hearth by Dr. Kalu Idika Kalu, *OFR* 152

Addressing Social, Moral and Spiritual Decay in Igboland

by Professor Vincent C. Anigbogu 162

The Concept of *"Igbo enwe eze"*

and its Implications for Ndi Igbo Development

by Dr. J. Chidozie Chukwuokolo 178

Morality and Igbo Cohesion on the Igbo Question in Nigeria

by Albert O. M. Ogoko 196

Igbo Nation: A Diasporean Perspective

by Holden Anele 204

The Potentials of Diaspora Igbo in the Making of a Powerful Igbo Nation in a Fast Degenerating Nigeria

by Professor Anthony Ejiofor 212

Media Ownership and Control in Nigeria:

The Dialectics of Political Hegemony

by Abia Onyike 220

Mass Media in the Spectrum of War Propaganda

during Nigeria's civil war years

by Ray A. Udeajah.. 226

Ajo Onudu Asusu Igbo na ihe a ga-eme ya

nke Okammuta (Prof.) Pita Ejiofor.. 249

Preserving Igbo Ancestral Language and Upholding the Linguistic Human Rights of Igbo Children

by Professor Chinyere Ohiri-Aniche 260

Igbo Language before, during and after the Biafra War

by Dr. Crescentia Ugwuona 269

Mammy Water in Igbo Culture: *Ogbuide of Oguta Lake*

by Dr. Sabine Jell-Bahlsen... 279

Ofo in Igbo Culture by Professor Richard C. Okafor 286

The Youth in the Posterity of Igboland: Victims or Villains?

by A. N. Aniekwu 298

The Nigeria-Biafra War and the Igbo Question:

Travails of the Biafran Woman

by Ada Agbasimalo and Godwin Okaneme 309

The Ndi-Igbo Interest in Nigeria

by Dr. Chinweizu Chinweizu 321

Nigeria's National Integration and the Dilemma of *Ndigbo:*

A sober reflection by Prof. Michael O. Maduagwu 329

Draft Igbo Agenda in Nigeria Project

by Nze Professor M A C Odu 336

Ndi Igbo in Nigeria: Challenges and the Future

by Dr. Dozie Ikedife 342

The Road Map to Igbo Restoration and Reconstruction

by Dr. Uduma Idika 346

Charting a New Political Direction for Ndigbo

by Dr Uma Eleazu 361

The Igbo Nation in the 21st Century

by Professor Umelo Ojinmah 381

The Psycho-theoretic substrate for the Economic and

Technological Resurgence of Ala Igbo

by Goddyn Ehiogu-Nwosu 385

Research, Planning and Development:

The Future of the Igbo Nation by Prof. Ukachukwu A. Awuzie 389

About the Contributors to volumes one and two 415

Index 423

Igbo Nation: history, challenges of rebirth **and development — vol. 2**

Preface
by Professor Uzodinma Nwala

The First International Colloquium on the **The Igbo Question in Nigeria** was held on March 11-14, 2014 at Igbozurume Unity Centre, Emene, Enugu, Enugu State, Nigeria. Organized by Igbo intellectuals, elders, clergy, women and youth from within and outside Nigeria, the Colloquium was convened as a global platform involving Igbo citizens, at home and abroad, with two major objectives, namely: (a) To mobilize active and effective involvement of Ndigbo in the National Conference set up by the Federal Government of Nigeria to review and renegotiate an enduring rationale for the Nigerian Federation; (b) To critically examine the historical roots of the predicament of Ndigbo, the assault on their psyche, the challenges in the domestic sphere as well as in the contemporary world, and to search for measures for rebuilding the Igbo hearth.

It is paramount that Ndigbo overcome their disadvantaged position in Nigeria, so that they can live a life of dignity, self-confidence and peaceful coexistence with their neighbors. Furthermore, their individual and collective interests must be secured so they can apply, without let or hindrance, their God-given talents and endowments for the betterment of themselves and all humanity, do honor to the spirit of their ancestors and serve their God Almighty. The Colloquium attracted many of the best minds in the Igbo nation, many of whom came from the United States of America, Canada, the United Kingdom, Germany, Australia, South Africa, Ghana, etc.

Issues examined at the three-day event ranged from Ndigbo in prehistory, the colonial era, the First Republic, the Nigeria/Biafra War to events since the end of the war. Chinua Achebe's epic novel, *Things Fall Apart*, showed the richness and complexity of Igbo culture during its resistance to British conquest at the beginning of the 20th century. In the life and works of Olaudah Equiano, the Igbo ex-slave and a noted abolitionist in 18th century Britain, the freedom-fighting spirit and character of Igbos are evident. In the life and struggles of King Jaja, the founder of Opobo Kingdom in the Niger Delta, it is the same. The 1929 Oloko Womens' Tax Resistance that rapidly spread beyond Igbo-land to their neighbors in Ibibio-land, Efik-land and Ijaw-land, (and which the British dubbed the "Aba Women's Riot") manifested the same unquenchable thirst for freedom that has remained a hallmark of Igbos.

Challenges and Predicament of Ndigbo

The participants extensively x-rayed critical issues that influence the socio-economic, political and cultural conditions and development in Igboland. Thus, issues of politics, governance, self-determination and internal autonomy; economics, commerce and industry; infrastructure, agriculture and natural resources; education, science and technology; security, national character, the international system; media, IT and communications; language and culture; women, youth, children and health; etc. were discussed. Issues relating to the ongoing National Conference were also discussed and proposals were harvested for forwarding to the Igbo delegates. Lastly, the participants dwelt on the critical question of the way forward and how to reposition Ndigbo in Nigeria and in the contemporary World.

The participants noted that due to years of neglect and to punitive federal policies since the end of the Nigeria-Biafra War, development in Igboland has been seriously handicapped. If the Igbo people had been left in control of their natural resources and social space after the Nigeria-Biafra War, the story today would have been different. Igbos would have been able to build on the foundations laid by the Azikiwe-Okpara regimes in the areas of infrastructure, agriculture, industry and commerce, education and manpower development, cooperatives and culture. Unemployment and the crimes that go with it (armed robbery, kidnapping, 419, etc.) would have been reduced to the barest minimum, if not totally eliminated, if Igboland had been allowed to develop at its own pace.

The Way Forward

The participants dwelt on the critical question of the way forward and how to reposition Ndigbo in Nigeria and in the Contemporary World. There was strong unanimity in the view that the time has come to restore the developmental trajectory in Igbo-land that has been distorted since the end of the Nigeria-Biafra war. To this end, the following were adopted as fundamental principles, tasks and agenda for Igbo National Rebirth:-

- Igbo renaissance/restoration/rebuilding the Igbo hearth.
- Recapture of Igbo values, culture, language, lore and literature.
- Youth--their education, employment, protection.
- Coexistence, with mutual respect in all interactions between Ndigbo and their neighbors.
- Federalism--The Nigerian Federation must become a Federation of the willing and not a Federation of the conquerors and the conquered.
- Autonomy, political and cultural, to enable Igbo development of their domain and at their pace.
- Doing honor to the Spirit of their icons and ancestors, and
- Serving their God without let or hindrance.

In considering concrete measures, it was noted that the dilapidated social, economic and political conditions in Igbo-land require urgent attention. To fast-track this process of repair requires unity of purpose by all--Government, non-governmental forces and individuals. Special attention is needed in the key areas of

Security: The problems of poverty and unemployment are the root of the security challenges within Igbo-land. Solving this security problem requires commitment from the State Governments as well as the Federal Government. The Igbo nation should devise all possible measures to ensure the protection of their citizens whose lives are being wasted all over Nigeria, and at the same time make the life of any Igbo person too expensive to waste.

Agriculture: Ndigbo must reconnect with the vision and legacy of the Azikiwe-Okpara era.

Language, cultural and spiritual rebirth: The participants called for the establishment of a **Centre for Igbo Studies** in every University in Igboland. These will engage in research and studies of the various aspects of Igbo life and interests including philosophy, history, politics, economics, religion, art, literature, science and technology. They should be equipped with Professorial Chairs, endowments and scholarships for the study of Igbo culture and Igbo language. In addition, a Department of Igbo Language should be established in every tertiary institution in Igbo-land.

Good Governance: Accountability, as well as prudent and efficient management of the resources of Igbo-land must be insisted upon. Finally, the Participants adopted the following resolutions: -
- To call on Ndigbo, wherever they are, to always endeavor to cultivate and promote their communal spirit as well as their general internal cohesion and unity (*Umunna bu ike*) as these are the first steps in reversing their troubled position in Nigeria and the contemporary world.

- To call on Ndigbo to demand that as long as the Igbo nation remains part of the Federal Republic of Nigeria, her citizens shall be accorded equal political and economic rights and privileges, and that

Igbo-land be treated on equal terms in matters of resource and power sharing. Henceforth, Ndigbo will not tolerate organized conspiracy against the Igbo nation and her people. The sanctity of human life guaranteed under the Nigerian constitution as well as by International law must be respected.

- To enjoin Ndigbo to apply all possible self-help to protect themselves and their property whenever the authorities in Nigeria are incapable of doing so.

- To call on Igbo politicians and other leaders, as servants of the Igbo nation, to make the collective interests of Ndigbo paramount in all their activities - paramount especially over religious, political party or personal interests.

- To articulate agreed positions which are relevant for the Igbo position at the National Conference and to make same available to Igbo delegates from the South-East zone and other Igbo-speaking areas. This was done immediately after the Colloquium as contained in booklet published by Alaigbo Development Foundation captioned **Memorandum to the Igbo Delegates at the National Conference Abuja, 2014.**

For all intents and purposes, the National Conference has eventually become an exercise in futility as no meaningful outcome is expected from it . Four things are responsible for this:-

i. The forces in control of the Nigerian Federation do not want any meaningful change in the status quo.

ii. The forces that are on the receiving end are so incapacitated that they are unable to liberate themselves from such a tragic state of hegemony. Ndigbo are at the center of this question of which way Nigeria.

iii. The Government of the day is weak and held hostage by the same forces.

iv. Ndigbo, who are the most affected victims of this situation, are internally disorganized and even colonized by the same forces of hegemony.

- A number of Action Plan was decided upon by the participants:-

i. To publish the outcome of the Colloquium, hence this publication, *Igbo Nation: History, Challenges af Rebirth and Development.*

ii. To generate an **Igbo National Charter** from the proceedings and deliberations of the Colloquium, and in consultation with all relevant stakeholders in Igbo-land. To this end sub-committees are being set up to draft the document.

iii. To ensure that Ndigbo will hold future Colloquia in and outside Nigeria at given intervals.

iv. Finally, it was decided to set up an International Platform charged with working with all Pan-Igbo organizations, Governments and the International Community on the Rebirth and development of the Igbo nation.

v. This is the genesis of the birth of **ALAIGBO DEVELOPMENT FOUNDATION (ADF),** which has been officially registered with its basic structures in place.

PROF. T. UZODINMA NWALA
President (ADF).
Enugu, November 29, 2014

Call to Service: *Oke Okpa Ebela*

Ndi Igbo teeta nu

Ndi Igbo bilie Nu

Were nu otu obi

Mezie onodi unu

Ndi Igbo kweko nu

Ndi Igbo bilie nu

Mesie nu obi ike

Were onodi unu

Chi anyi o, Lee anyi o

Gbaghara anyi,

Nonyere anyi o

Bia dube anyi

Maka umu anyi o

Ndi Igbo kele nu

Ndi Igbo bilie nu

Soro nu Chi unu

Gbanwo onodi unu

Unu anugo!

Unu anugo!

Unu anugo!

By Isaac Akuchie

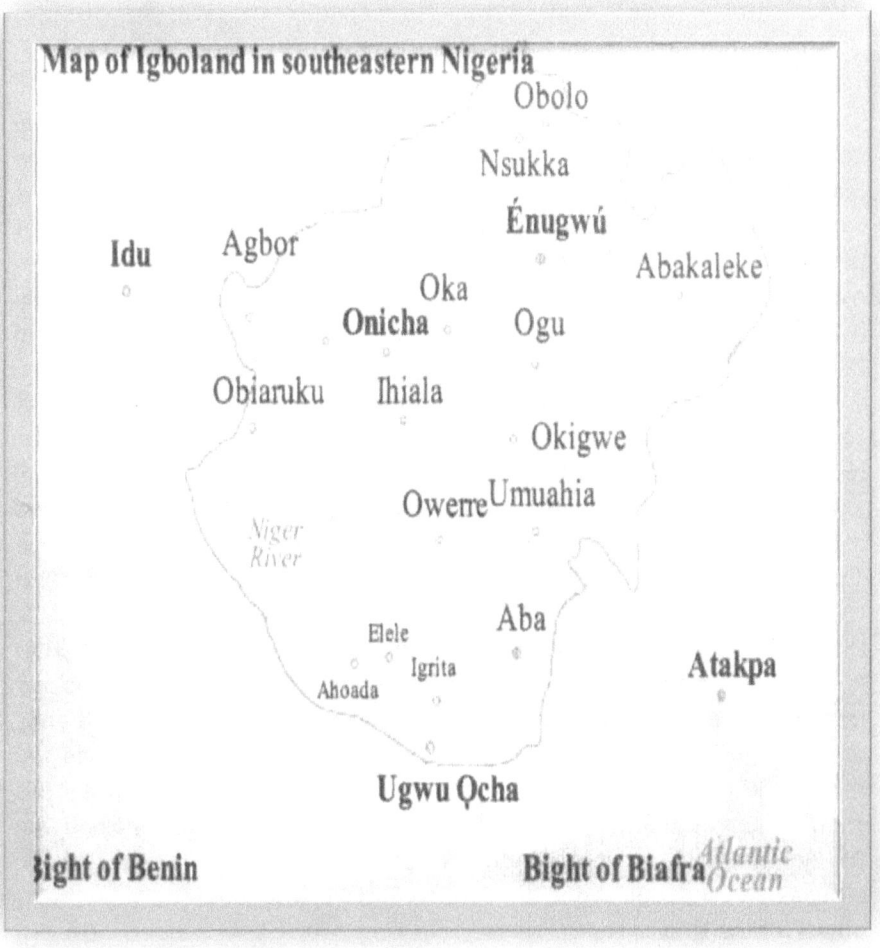

Nseputa Mba di iche iche n'Ala Ndi Igbo
Ebe esi weputa ya bu na http://en.wikipedia.org/wiki/Igboland

Foreword
by S. Okechukwu Mezu

Igbo Nation: History, Challenges of Rebirth and Development

The papers in this collection were presented at the **First International Colloquium on the Igbo Question in Nigeria before, during and after the Biafra War** held in Enugu from 10-14 March 2014 greatly facilitated by a number of Igbo organizations and groups including The Conference of Democratic Scholars (CODES), Aka Ikenga, Izu-Umunna, Igbo Studies Association (ISA-USA), World Igbo Congress (WIC), Igbo World Assembly (IWA), Council for National Coordination, Ofobuike Intellectual Union, and Council for Intellectual Cooperation of Nigeria (COFICON) among others. Immeasurable thanks go to several individuals and organizations that contributed generously to the funding of the conference, to the Organizers, to the Coordinator Professor T. Uzodinma Nwala, without whose unusual exertions this project would have been impossible. We salute other Officers of Alaigbo Development Foundation, and the members of the Conference Editorial Committee (Dr. Uzodinma Nwala, Dr. Chinweizu Chinweizu, Prof Nath Aniekwu, J. C. Chukwuokolo, Dr. Onyemauchechi Gbujie, Dr. S. Okechukwu Mezu, Dr. Ugorji Ugorji, Prof. Chinyere Ohiri-Aniche, HRH Princess Alu Ibiam). We acknowledge the cooperation of the participants from Nigeria and abroad who made contributions to this first ever gathering of this magnitude at a problematic juncture in the history of Igbo people and their civilization. Though they did not attend the conference, this compendium includes, as a memorial, papers by Dr. Catherine Acholonu and Dr. Adiele Afigbo, recent Africanists who have joined our ancestors. It includes also a paper about Dr. Gordian Ezekwe who labored like so many others for the Igbo cause.

Igbo Nation: History, Challenges of Rebirth and Development is a typical example of traditional Igbo society in action, everyone has one's say, each individual's right to self-expression is recognized but at the end there is a conclave and a group plan, a stand and/or a position is adopted by consensus enforceable not by law but by the perceived fairness and rectitude of the decision. Even though the papers cover a gamut of positions and beliefs, a common trend and thread flow through the discourse even when they appear discordant. Except as otherwise stated, the opinions stated represent those of the respective authors and do not necessarily represent the philosophy of Alaigbo Development Foundation or the general belief of Igbo people or the publishers.

Whether the Igbos were the original inhabitants of the world or not, their presence in every corner of the earth, yesterday and today, is recognized and felt. Ndi Igbo are gregarious, adaptable and progressive. They feel at home wherever they are and their Igbo language appears to have informed the development of every known language on earth. They are fearless, pushful and cannot be pushed around by anyone. The more they are persecuted, the more assertive they are. They are very intelligent, confident, courageous and daring and walk like princes and princesses as if they owned the earth and will risk their life, their job to challenge perceived oppression or injustice even in a strange land.

This is a chronicle of the Igbo past, the challenges Igbos have faced across the centuries, how Igbos have survived discrimination, pogrom, genocide and how now they stand on the threshold of a new renaissance that will make their numbers and business, intellectual and scientific acumen manifest the world over. They probably constitute the single largest ethnic group in the world and geographically, Ndi Igbo regard Igboland as the center of the earth. Present state of Igbo studies and research tend to lend credence to the postulation that Ndi Igbo were part of the original inhabitants of the earth before their migration to other parts of the world as we know it today. It took generations to postulate the theory of gravity which is so common place and so self-evident. A careful look and study of the world cartography shows that at the pristine stage of evolving creation [*eri mgbe – time immemorial*] the world was one single contiguous undivided mass of earthland with Africa at the center and Africa the genesis of human evolution before the so-called continents of North and South America, the other islands (Australia, Arctic Region and Antarctica) floated away due to seismic upheavals. These floatings carried away some of the original Igbo inhabitants who then struggled and succeeded in surviving in sometimes very hostile conditions and became the dark colored inhabitants of the Americas, Asia and Australia and New Zealand. Many marvel at the coincidence of the name of the place of birth of Jesus, namely Nazareth ("small Naze") and the town Naze, five miles from Owerri in Central Igboland? Over several centuries in isolation, these Igbo settlers developed a unique culture, adapted languages, adapted mythologies, a syncretic religion, indigenized crafts, sculpture and dance and a horticulture that suited their new geographic and climatic environment.

In the works of two major Igbo scholars we see so much evidence of the place of Igbo culture and civilization within the matrix of human culture and civilization in general. The late Catherine Acholonu, an outstanding authority in pre-history, has, through the study of ancient languages and cultures shown how several elements of Igbo language and general culture find their equivalents in the language and culture of far-flung civilizations as those of the Europeans, Chinese, English, Hebrew, ancient Canaanite, Greece, etc. Similarly, in the ancient Igbo civilization depicted in Chinua Achebe's novels, particularly, *Things Fall Apart*, every other ancient civilization finds its own image. It is no wonder then that Ndi Igbo rank even higher than the Jews in being the true global citizens, found in every nook and crany of the earth, yet adapting as if that very part of the earth is their natural home.

The JigSaw Earth Theory which we deign here to postulate believes that the earth was initially one land and a contiguous mass until seismic eruptions created the oceans, seas, lakes and rivers, separated the American continent, north and south, from mainland Africa and created the Mediterranean sea separating the European land mass from Africa, creating in the process also Australia, the Eastern Horn of Africa and the Asiatic continent. All the jigsaw parts put together can recreate the contiguous land mass that existed *Mgbe Eri*. The process transplanted some Igbos, the original inhabitants of mangrove Africa, to various parts of the present universe where they influenced the language and culture that developed in those areas. The Igbo language and people far from being on the verge of extinction are facing today an irrepressible renaissance. Ndi Igbo should look beyond Nigeria and Africa and see the world as their new theatre of operation.

S. Okechukwu Mezu November 30, 2014

SECTION FIVE: ECONOMICS, COMMERCE AND INDUSTRY

Commerce and Industry in Igbo Land.
by
Chief Ralph Obioha

Discounting the slave trade which had its own traction as an odious practice by the white man, other trading activities existed before the arrival of first the Portuguese followed by the Spaniards and eventually the Anglo-Saxons. These could be termed overseas trading with principal imports being mostly spirits, textiles, salt, utensils etc. The entire Igboland was covered by the nature's gift of palms bearing the fruits of palm oil, palm kernels and other by products. It became obvious that these abundant palm trees shall constitute a veritable source of wealth and industry in Igboland. The derivable products from the palm tree ultimately were referred as cash crop. The palm produce naturally attracted the attention of the Europeans and it became the foundation of trade and industry in Igbo land.

Before the arrival of the Europeans, the Igbo commerce were conducted on a well established market system which formed the Igbo four day week calendar market days of Eke, Orie, Afor, and Nkwo. These market days defined to a very large extent those that can be called Igbo. The size and magnitude of these markets before the arrival of the white man can only be imagined but examples abound at Eke Ututu (Imo State) Nkwo Igbo Ukwu, (Aambra State) Orie Orba (Enugu State) Afor Oru (Imo State) Eke Oha Aba (Abia State). It was said that over 200,000 people trade at these markets at any given market day. As white men came they set their sights at the palm produce which their people at home needed for food, fuel, detergents, lubricants etc.

Before 1912, not much can be claimed for any form of industry i.e mechanical factory in Igboland. The first mechanical factories were introduced by the United African Company (UAC) by a certain manufacturer from Hull, England. U.A.C. operated these Pioneer Oil Mills and the colonial administrators established inspection agency that doubled as a marketing Board to regulate this thriving sector which became its primary source of revenue. The pioneer oil mill was a simple steam operated mechanical machinery that greatly reduced the intensive human work load required to produce palm oil and its other by products. It also greatly improved the quality of palm oil it produced. The oil mill uses the husks and fibers from the palm fruits as fuel to fire the boiler which produces the steam that powers the engines of the palm mill, single long rod, with several belts attached to various mechanical engines perform various activities such as pressing the oil, separating the chaff, cracking the kernels and even producing electricity. Simple but effective and this became the birth of Igboland introduction to industrialization.

As earlier stated, UAC was the original owners of these industrial marvel but the demand for palm oil and kernel was so huge that UAC had earlier introduced a much simpler labour intensive hand press oil mills that were affordable to the Igbos. What maybe considered affordable today was very hard to achieve in the 1920's. The major challenge was the required capital to purchase the hand press mills then at paltry 27 pounds 11 shillings, a very huge amount in those days. Any body with that kind of resources was considered a very rich man. The hand pressed oil mills became the main artisan factories established in thousands of locations throughout Igboland. These hand press oil mills constituted the bulk of palm oil producing machineries in Igboland reaching an output of over, 98,000 metric toner of palm oil in the SPO (Special palm oil) and TPO (Technical Palm oil) categories annually in 1930. By the down of the 1940s the export was exceeding 150,000 metric tones annually. Around this period, the pioneer oil mills were brought in by UAC that were the sole operators of the mills. While UAC monopolized the pioneer oil mills operations, emerging Igbo industrialists were eyeing these pioneer oil mills but hampered by capital were satisfied to operate on the lower scale of hand pressed mills. The UAC organized a system that suited their operational strategy by using Igbo agents to effect the local buying of both the palm oil and palm kernels as the volume of the commerce greatly increased. The leading agents were Chief L.N. Obioha who was trading out of Okigwe and Oguta, Chief Z.A. Chukwujama and Chief Bassey Okoro who covered the Mbawsi axis, Chief Umeano and Chief Clement N. Egwuatu who held sway at Nsukka area, Chief E.C.I Onuigbo and Chief Charles Onwuzo who operated at Aba, Mr. Harbor, Chief Paul Okoro, Chief Okereke and a host of others were at Port Harcourt.

Mention must be made of the role of railways as the transportation gateways for the movement of these products to Port Harcourt as the staging centre for the eventually export of the commodities to Liverpool, England. By the 1950,s leading Igbos were embolden to venture into the ownership of the pioneer oil mills and UAC was particularly not resisting the entry of these emerging Igbo industrialists. UAC had already seen the entry of leading European companies such as PZ, CFAO, G.B. OLIVANT, SCOA, MCLVER etc. At the height of the Palm Produce Commerce, Igboland was producing annual tonnage volume exceeding 300,000 metric toners and vastly increasing.

Chief L.N. Obioha undisputable was amongst the first Igbos to own more than one pioneer oil mill having by 1953 erected the first at Oguta and eventually erecting some at Urualla, Amuro, Umualaoma, Yenagoa, Ndimoko etc. To supply the fruits for these mills, the buying posts called beaches were established at various locations throughout Igboland operating on a system where the majors were appointing factors to man these beaches. Because the main revenue for the government was being derived from the palm produce trade, the Eastern Nigeria government got into the act through the Eastern

Nigeria Development Cooperation (ENDC) and became major owners of the pioneer oil mills throughout Eastern Nigeria.

Beyond the palm produce activities, ENDC was the first catalyst to industrialize Eastern Nigeria and went about it in the establishment of the major industries in the former Eastern Nigeria maintaining a balance and spread that accommodated the various ethnic groups comprising Eastern Nigeria. The flagship was the Nkalagu Cement Company with another one, the Calabar Cement Company at Calabar. At Enugu, the Eastern Nigeria Government established three industries namely Niger Gas, Niger Steel and Eminite all at Emene designated then as the industrial Zone. At Umuahia two industries were established, the Ceramic and the Golden Guinea Breweries. At Port Harcourt, the huge Bulk Oil Plant was in existence handling Palm Produce for export. At the same Port Harcourt in partnership with Dunlop a huge rubber industry was established, so also with Americans a huge glass factory. WAGI. At Owerri, a shoe factory was established at Aba, mostly public and private companies came to play with gigantic factories established there namely, Aba Textiles, PZ Industries, Nigeria Breweries, Guinness Breweries and a host of other factories.

As it was widely acclaimed, the Eastern Nigeria economy was regarded as one of the fastest growing in the world. But it was suddenly disrupted by the civil was which caused a lot of devastation in the industrial base fast developing in Igboland. The solid foundation laid for the industrialization of Igboland suffered a major set back which regrettably persist till date.

By the time the civil war erupted, leading Igbos have already established thriving industrial ventures. At Onitsha, Chief M.N. Ugochukwu has established the giant Ugo Foam Industries producing mattresses and pillows. At Aba, Chief Nnanna Kalu has laid the foundation of a paper Mill which he completed soon after the war. Chief S. N. O. Madu erected the first mechanized Palm Mill in Aguata Division. The entrepreneur spirit of Igbos was manifesting in all areas of human endeavor. Still held down by scarce capital, many young Igbo men and women left the homeland and took residence in every nook and cranny of Nigeria, established businesses and enterprises. Chief L.P. Ojukwu took control of Lagos and made his impact there with very little to show at home.

Palm Produce remains dominant in the Igboland commerce and industrial activities. Heeding Dr. M.I. Okpara's hold initiative to return to Land, Chief J. N. Nwachukwu established the first vast palm plantation at Mbawsi with a pioneer oil mill which effectively made the area a major theatre of palm produce activity. Chief Wabara of Ukwa was a major player in the palm produce industry and commerce and has strong influence in the Azumini area. Sensing that operating individually, UAC and other European players will squeeze them out of the growing palm produce business, leading players namely Chief L.N. Obioha, Chief Z.A. Chukwujama, Mazi Okike, Chief

Bassey Okoro, Mr. Ukwa, Mazi Harbor formed a company, Eastern Nigeria Produce Trading Co (EPTC) to challenge UAC dominance.

The Eastern Nigeria government under Dr. M.I. Okpara promoted policies that were clearly intended to enhance the continued growth of solid economic activities in the region. He put in place several schemes that had direct impact on the growing economy of the eastern region. Dr. M.I. Okpara established farm settlements that acted as centers of animal husbandry and agricultural extension assistance. The eastern government introduced small holders scheme that encouraged the massive re-planting of the palm belt the region inherited from nature. Other progressive schemes such as pioneer status were introduced to lend assistance to deserving entrepreneurs in the region.

Just as the visible results of Igbo commerce and industry were about to explode throughout Nigeria, a devastating civil war erupted and shattered what took Igbos half a century to erect. In one full swoop everything came to a stop. The civil war that lasted 30 months literally wiped out the already established fundamentals that have set the ball rolling for Igbo industrial and commercial take-off. The devastation and annihilation of all Igbo commercial and industrial set-up were total and starting from ground zero was the only option. The big question was where the capital will come from considering the obnoxious and wicked policy decreed by Federal Government led by Yakubu Gowon that all Igbos with previous bank account status will only be allowed to draw 20 pounds irrespective of whatever bank balance they may have maintained. This monetary policy fiat has only one agenda which is to ensure the total pauperization of Igbos.

Nature's gift to Igbos immediately came to the rescue. The palm belt which we were endowed with will once again give us a lifeline. Just before the war, leading Igbo industrialist with the Eastern Region government of Dr. M.I. Okpara in the lead were laying the solid foundation to take the palm produce operations to the next level. Once again, led by Chief L.N. Obiaha, a giant Palm Kernel Crushing plant was established at Arondizuogu. At nearby Umunze, Chief M.N. Ugochukwu erected a similar plant with combined crushing capacity of 400 metric tones of palm kernel per hour and both plants were operating on 24 hours basis. The significance of this palm kernel demand made it possible for the entire local people in Igboland to earn money, no matter how small, by their sale of palm kernels they had cracked by themselves. More middle level Igbos got into the palm produce business with its associated transport business. A policy which intention was to put Igbos down instead fired them up to venture only where eagles dare. With pittance in their pockets, Igbos spread their wings and soon were on a flight to all parts of Nigeria, Africa and the world in search of opportunities.

The coming of *Ekene-Dili-Chukwu, Chi De Ebere, Osundu* transport companies were ferrying Igbo far and wide. Later *ABC transport, Peace Mass,*

Ifesinachi, The Young Shall Grow joined the transport sector. Igbo entrepreneur spirit was at work again. Chief Ferdnard Anaghara erected a large industrial complex at his home town Urualla in the rubber and palm kernel industry Chief Tony Ezenna, (Orange Drug) brought home the giant pharmaceutical factory to Onitsha to firm his philosophy of

Aku-ru-uno is the way to go.

A new generation has arrived and by the late 1970s an outbreak of young industrialists took the stage, Chief Dike Udensi was a quintessential young industrialist cum businessman with a reputation for massive importation of goods in textiles and commodities. Chief Dike Udensi erected a crown jewel, the first Igbo privately owned brewery, Dubic breweries at Aba. He opened a gate and he was immediately followed by a joint venture of Chief Tagbo Onyekwelu, Chief C.C. Onoh, Chief Jim Nwobodo, Chief Alex Ekwueme and host of others to build a brewery, Monarch breweries at 9th Mile, Enugu, Chief Joe Nwankwu built one at Agbagama Cannon Breweries, Chief D.N Nwandu built one at Onitsha, Life Breweries, Chief Alex Ekwueme built one at Oko, Pal Breweries, Chief Ralph Obioha following the footsteps of his father, Chief L.N. Obioha built one at Arondizuogu SAFARI Breweries. These were giant industries employing over 100,000 Nigerians and creating collateral engagement for over 500,000 people in supplies, transportation and services.

By early 1980s, a set of young Nnewi men and women were fast transforming that enterprising town into a hub of giant industrial complexes. They specialized in the manufacture of motorcycle and car spare parts and Chief Cletus Ibeto and Mr. Chika Okafor led the way. Combined were the famous Nkwo Nnewi mega spare parts market, the town Nnewi can be described as major industrial centre. A huge vehicle assembly plant built by Chief Innocent Chukwuma had its opening performed by President Goodluck Jonathan.

The governments of Chief Jim Nwobodo and Chief Sam Mbakwe contributed immensely to the industrialization of Igboland. Chief Sam Mbakwe erected six mega factories in the then Imo State namely, Aluminum Extrusion Industry at Ikeduru. Paint Industry at Mbaise, Clay Bricks factory at Ezinachi (Okigwe), Modern Poultry Industry at Avutu, Obowo, reconstruction of Golden Guinea Breweries and Concorde Hotels at Owerri, Chief Jim Nwobodo on his own part erected the Premier Breweries at Onitsha, Nike Resort Hotel at Enugu, Ikenga Hotels at Nsukka and Awka, Building Materials Factory at Abakaliki, Aluminum Roofing sheets factory at Nsukka, the huge Flour Mill at Emene and made spirited efforts to modernize Nkalagu Cement Factory.

The return of the military by the middle of the 1980s spelt some doom for Igbo industries. Thriving were the brewery industry which as earlier stated were located in Onitsha 2, Umuahia, Aba 3, Arondizuogu, Abagana, Oko,

Enugu, Awo Omama. From nowhere, the Federal government decreed the banning of the main raw material, malted barley, which is the main input for the brewing of beer. Except for the multi-nationals like the Nigeria Breweries and Guinness Breweries, the privately owned breweries started to shut down and by the middle 1990s all of them were forced to close by this act of federal government policy. A lot of meaning was read into this unreasonable policy.

The same federal government disbanded the marketing Board, the sole government agency that effects the stabilization of palm kernel prices and the subsequent collection of the commodity in huge tonnages for massive processing. This single decision of the Federal Government nailed the coffin of the two giant factories at Aroundizuogu and Umunze.

Industrialization continued in Igboland in a rather small scale. Dotted around our highways one will observe the presence of aluminum roofing sheets production & small scale palm kernel pressing mills, paint factories and sundry others. But the 1990s brought a new set of entrepreneurs who set their sights on large scale operations, even though most of these were outside Igboland. We should mention a few of them, Sir Stan Ekeh, Dr. ABC Orjiakor, Prince Author Eze, Engr. Emeka Okwuosa, Dr. Ernest Azudialu, Chief Emeka Offor, Dr. Ifeanyi Uba, Capt. Emma Iheancho, Chief Tony Ezenna, etc

One may question what caused the near extinction of industries in Igboland. It is traceable to the Federal Government policy somersaults that were insensitive to the strategic agro-based industries whose core back-up were the faceless local farmers who produce the raw materials. This is particularly the case with the palm produce industry. The military governments failed to appreciate the delicate linkage between the cash crop potential of a vital agro based operations and what the government considered a huge subsidy in sustaining such a pivotal sector in the lives of millions. In the palm belt, palm products provided apart from edible oil used for food, they provided cash, provided building materials, provided livestock feeds provided fuel but above all provided key employment at the most local level.

Once the Marketing Boards were dismantled, the palm produce was reduced to an artisan operation. With the astronomical increase in prices of diesel and other fuels, the astronomical cost of industries generating their energy needs rendered all industries operations kaput especially those requiring high energy input. One by one, the factories started to close shop leaving in its wake an Igboland littered with closed and deserted factories. If one looks back at the dexterity of Dr. M. I. Okpara's well planned economic strategy, his major emphasis was on the palm produce. He recognized it as our lifeline and as one source of product that will touch the lives of millions. He laid the foundation for the huge palm plantation estates at Calabar, Ohaji, Ngwa, Yenegoa and Elele covering thousands of hectares. He established the small holder scheme and encouraged replanting of improved seedlings to replace the ageing palms that carpeted our entire Igboland. He calculated that this vital nature's gift to the Igbos was for a purpose and must be cultivated. Today, Malaysia that took the palm seedling from us to their country is earning more from it than what we earn from crude oil Dr. M.I. Okpara had a vision and military leaders are bereft of it.

Much emphasis has been laid on palm products for the simple reason that it is one product that touched the lives of every Igboman and as the Yorubas claim Cocoa as their cash crop, and the Hausas claim groundnut as theirs, palm produce has been and will always be God's gift to Igboland.

This article will be incomplete if recognition is not given to the main work force in Igboland that made it possible to show palm produce as the mainstay of the Igbo economy. Igbo women were the backbone that provided the hard labour required and performed by our hard working womenfolk. They were the primary processors of palm produce. It was women and children that collected the palm fronts cut the palm fruit bunches, they sorted out the fruits they steamed the fruits, they thrashed the fiber and they pressed the oil. They will still crack the kernels to get the nuts. It is indeed a hard manual labour. The womenfolk were the real engine of the palm produce operations. Special mention must be made of two outstanding Ibo women Chief Mrs. Mary Nzimiro and Chief Mrs. Josephine Nwodo that stood shoulder to shoulder with men to conduct big produce marketing operation.

The Igbo industry is a trademark recognized not only in Nigeria but worldwide. It can be said that it is in the Igbo DNA. The Igbos can squeeze water out of rock. Their working spirit is indomitable and the Igbos leave nothing to chance to accomplish any enterprise they embark on. In commerce, i.e. buying and selling, the Igbos are second to none. No one can say with certainty how they acquired this business acumen to excel in the business of buying and selling. The Onitsha market is reputed to be the largest in West African and is followed by Aba Market. The volume of transactions and exchange of money, banks will testify it as phenomenal. It is rumored that Onitsha market generates business in excess of N700 million per day and the markets at Aba generate a turnover of N500 million daily. So in commerce, the Igbos are holding their heads high maintaining their advantage in this sector of the economy. But bear in mind that only 12% of this huge amount is earned by Igbos through trading activities as the balance 88% goes to the Federal Government in form of custom duty and the rest to manufacturers overseas. Buying and selling of imported goods translates only to the margin received as profits made at point of sell. The bulk of the profits go to the manufacturers overseas as opposed to the bulk of profits accruing to the producers of the primary products.

It is simple economics to look homewards. The Igboland economy is on its knees. It is in search of a visionary leader like Dr. M. I. Okpara to return Igboland to its place of sustainable economic growth based on our nature's gift of one of the freest raw materials endowed to a people. Untended for years, the palms have grown wild and will require a massive replanting of new hybrid seedlings to start once again and reap its great potentials. Relying on the buying and selling of imported goods that we can easily manufacture here is short sighted and unsustainable. The way to go is to develop the raw materials here and process those raw materials both for local consumption and for export.

Yes, the AMA breweries at 9th Mile is considered the largest brewery in the whole of Africa in terms of creating jobs, it is nothing to write home about because it is so automated that its workforce is not more than 200 workers. What will lift the Igbo economy is a master plan that will create an agro based platform that can create jobs and opportunities in millions and not hundreds. In the 50s and 60s, we had such a plan and platform. Three agro products, namely oil palm, cashew and cocoa can achieve the rejuvenation of Igbo economy. Palm oil trees grow as a belt over Igboland. Cocoa is viable in the Abia State areas of Umuahia, Ikwuano and Bende. Cashew flourished at Okigwe Udi and Nsukka areas. This excessive reliance on the receipts from hydrocarbons will in the end be our undoing since it is a delectable earning which is not under our own control. Have we as a people considered our future as what plans we have for even the food security of our people?

Let us pause and return to basics. The God we worship did not make any mistake to cover us with palm trees free of charge. He made no mistake to give us the soil that flourishes cocoa, cashew and rice. Let us cultivate these nature's gift and build our industrialization on the raw materials coming out of them. That ultimately will be our safe berth and sustainability.

Economic Blueprint for Attracting Business and Commerce in Igbo land

By

Felix Oti

As the saying goes; "a road once traveled, can always be travelled again". In the first Republic, under the leadership of Drs. Akanu Ibiam and Michael Okpara, the then Eastern Region was economically self-sustaining, building upon the foundation laid by the colonial masters. Some of the economic programs embarked upon by the Michael Okpara administration of the First Republic were borne out of foresight, and, to a large extent, to prove to the British colonialists that granting independence to Nigeria was not a mistake.

Through a vehicle, the Eastern Nigeria Development Corporation's (ENDC), the Michael Okpara administration was able to create agricultural cash crop estates for oil palm, rubber, cocoa, cashew rice, pineapples, banana, plantains and cassava that laid the foundation for food production. Some of the farms and their locations included rubber plantation in Amaeke Abam, Ndi-Oji Abam, Arochukwu, Ozuitem, Ikwu, Imo River waterways, Ubani Ibeku. Also established by the administration were oil palm plantations at Kwa Falls, Calaro, Ikom and Umuekwune.

The administration also made infrastructural development a priority, as many rural roads and railways were constructed throughout the region for smooth and easy transfer of people and farm produces from the local farming communities to the cities. Development of social services was equally accorded great importance as electricity and water supply were provided to all the communities, either directly by the government, or through collaborative community efforts. In the area of industrialization, companies and factories set up by the administration to create jobs and generate tax revenues necessary for continuous provision of social services and infrastructures included the Niger-gas plant and Niger Steel Industry, both in Emene; the Pepsi Cola plant in Onitsha; the establishment of the Shoe Industry at Owerri, and the Aba Textile Mill. One cannot forget the construction of the state of the art Nkalagu Cement Factory, Golden Guinea Breweries and Modern Ceramic factories in Umuahia. Plans were also in the pipeline to construct machine tool, plywood, cement manufacturing plants in the region. Aware that revenue generation is not limited to establishment of agricultural estates and manufacturing companies, the Okpara administration also embarked on the development of tourism geared towards both attracting foreign currency, and providing conducive rest and business facilities for both business and recreational travelers, by building 5-star hotels in Enugu and Port Harcourt, and a network of catering Rest Houses.

Today, all the agricultural estates are lying waste and overgrown with weeds; the factories are dilapidated and in disuse; infrastructures are either non-existent or in advanced state of decay. The vision and mission of the Okpara administration was never built upon by subsequent administrations, even after the civil war. Igboland remains a region with a "potential" that may never be realized. Elders of Igboland still recall, with nostalgia, the aggressive economic development drive of the Okpara administration, and wonder if it can ever be replicated. For the region to get back to the successes of the first republic, it must strive to be a player in the current global economic dispensation, where trade borders are seamless, technology is cheap, and venture capitalists – both local and foreign – are aplenty. To be able to know where you are going, you have to know where you are coming from, how to get there, and what you need to get to your destination. In the case of the Igbos of Southeastern Nigeria, it is obvious where they are coming from, economically.

Where are Igbos coming from? Today, the region is badly in need of good governance, reliable infrastructure, rail system and seaports, steady water and power supply, agricultural and manufacturing industries, security, improved educational infrastructures and modernized academic curriculum, agricultural, biomedical and scientific research facilities, a stable government across the region, and business-friendly laws. For Ala-Igbo to experience the success of the past, the people know they must go back to the drawing board; back to what made it successful and the investment darling of the First Republic.

Where are Igbos going? In terms economic development, Igbos would want, and do desire, to be at par with countries like Taiwan, Hong Kong, Israel, and Singapore, just to name a few. The four factors of production – resources, labor, capital, and entrepreneurial spirit - are in abundant supply in the region. What are lacking are a vision and a mission to better harness these factors, a strategy or plan to implement that mission to achieve that vision. The big question is: do Igbos have the stomach and determination to embark on this arduous task of economic development? Though the history is there, if the will is not there, the way will not be discovered either.

What do Igbos need to get there?
First, you have to know what you have to be able to identify what you need. In terms of natural resources, the region is abundantly blessed. Underground in the five Southeastern states of Nigeria and parts of Edo and Delta states lay the following natural resources and their uses:

a) Salt: found in Abia, Anambra, Ebonyi, and Imo states, is used universally as a seasoning

b) Gold: found in Abia, Anambra, and Ebonyi states is used for monetary exchange, investment, jewelry, medicine, food & drink (vitamin E), industry, electronics, coloring

c) Lead: found in Abia, Anambra, Enugu, Ebonyi, and Imo states is used for automobiles, mostly as electrodes in the lead-acid battery. It is used in solder for electronics

d) Zinc: found in Abia, Anambra, Enugu, and Imo states is most commonly used as an anti-corrosion agent, as a white pigment in paints, and as a catalyst in the manufacture of rubber.

e) Gypsum: found in Anambra, Delta, Edo, and Imo states is used as a finish for walls and ceilings, like cement blocks in building construction, fertilizer & soil conditioner, surgical plaster ingredient, a major source of dietary calcium, mushroom cultivation, dough conditioner, shampoos and conditioners.

f) Coal: found in large quantities in Enugu state, power generation as fuel or for cooking, chemical fertilizers and other chemical products.

g) Limestone: found in Abia, Anambra, Edo, Enugu and Imo states, is the main raw material in cement and mortar manufacture, for road construction, in glass making, used in paper, plastics, toothpaste, paint, tiles as either cheap fillers or white pigment, in sculptures, petroleum reservoirs.

h) Phosphate: found in Anambra and Imo states; Inorganic phosphates are mined to obtain phosphorus for use in agriculture and industry.

i) Lignite: found in Anambra, Delta, Edo, and Imo states, is brown coal for power generation in coal plants

j) Marcasite: found in Imo state is used to make or coat jewelry.

k) Iron-ore: found in Anambra, Delta, and Edo states is the main source of metallic and steel iron,

l) Clay: found mostly in Anambra and Edo states, is used for medical (anti-diarrheal) and agricultural uses, and as building materials

Aside from the listed solid minerals, there are still the oilfields at Ukwa/Ngwa Obigbo, Imo River, Obuzo, Owaza, Ngboko, Nkali, Obinagbo Odogkwa, Obeakpu, Akwete, and Isimiri. And, in Imo state, we have fields in- Ohaji, Egbema, Nmahu, Ozzuh, Izombe, Oguta, Njaba, Oru, and Awo –Omama. With modern exploration technology, even dry and abandoned oil wells, or previously hard to explore areas, could now be re-visited and explored with the assistance, and/or in partnership with foreign experts.

As the oil sector becomes increasingly deregulated by Nigerian governments, opportunities exist in both the upstream and downstream sectors for private investments in local refineries. This will not only create direct jobs but, equally, created residual businesses for host communities, and generating more tax revenues for the states. These revenues could be ploughed back into the communities to improve business-friendly infrastructures, thereby attracting more business investments. All of these natural resources could be developed to any stage desired for either local use or exported to generate revenues; what is lacking is necessary deregulatory laws that would open the door for private investment in, and ownership of, solid mineral businesses, strong commitment by the people and elected government officials to do so, and the requisite vehicle to drive a development plan.

Southeastern Nigeria Development Corporation (SENDC): The first step would be for the southeastern governors, industrialists, and academicians locally and in Diaspora to commit to the following foundational proposals:

a) Agree on a proposal to set up and fund a Southeastern development trust corporation.
b) For the region's state governments and legislators to agree on setting aside a certain percentage of the states' monthly federal allocation as contribution for regional economic development.
c) For industrialists to, equally, agree to contribute a certain percentage of their net profits to this development fund.
d) Academics to commit to drawing up a technical education master plan, and the establishing of vocational training departments/schools in state universities to be funded by indigenous banks and other financial institutions.
e) For all stakeholders to agree on setting up a well-represented corporation to draw up and implement an economic development plan for Igboland, something akin to NDDC, or the ENDC in the First Republic.
f) A broad-based and effective public relations/publicity campaign structure that will be responsible informing on, and promoting, the benefits of doing business in Igboland.

Attracting investors

As the saying goes: "if you build it, they will come"; apart from a quick return on their investments, investors look for ease of entry into any market, unencumbered movement of capital (investment and profits), uninterrupted access to internet technology, accurate and on-time information, cordial relationship with host communities, and ease of exit. The existence of cheap modern technology has made it possible for any government, region or community to put in place the technological and infrastructural resources required for efficient and effective conduct of business in any part of Nigeria. Governments and people of the Southeastern zone must ensure the following:
1. Removal or relaxation of restrictive international business laws, and replacing them with business-friendly ones which would include tax breaks for certain class of investors, generous lease agreements, build-operate-transfer (BOT) joint-venture agreements, ease of purchase/financing/sale of business entities, ease of issuance of investment and/or partnership licenses.

2. A safe and secure environment devoid of fear of armed robbery, kidnapping, financial fraud, economic sabotage, disruptions and intimidation by community groups and powerful political figures
3. Steady power and water supply, efficient telecommunication and internet services; independent power-generating and switching capacity
4. Good rural and urban inter-connecting roads and bridges, airport/airline, seaports, and rail systems for timely, effective and cost-efficient movement of raw materials, finished goods and labor force.
5. Assurances of commitment to prudent fiscal management, and transparency in dealings with investors.
6. Establishment of a business ethics watchdog responsible for resolution of problems between investors and host communities.

In Igboland today, there is abundance of venture capitalists and investor, locally and in Diaspora, new business and investment consulting experts; abundance of cheap but educated labor force, and a highly trained technical and vocational workforce within the zone. Some of these same resources could be sourced easily from outside the region. Equally not lacking is a requisite entrepreneurial zeal – the willingness and commitment to take a risk at success – among the people of the zone.

These days, governments are financially incapable of providing for all the needs of the people alone. Governments and the governed frequently come together to create a third vehicle – public/private partnerships - for the development of a community, state, region, or nation. For Igbos to get to where they want to be, we must take the bull by the horn, set a developmental goal and timetable for our land, and make the necessary sacrifices required to achieve that goal. It takes planning, time, and commitment from everyone.

SECTION 6: INFRASTRUCTURE/AGRICULTURE/NATURAL RESOURCES

Bringing Back the Focus on Agriculture
by
Mazi Sam Ohuabunwa

When Dr Michael Okpara was the premier of Eastern Nigeria (1960-1966), Eastern Nigeria became a promising economic giant and the fastest growing of the four regions of Nigeria. The growth was anchored on three strong pillars of Agriculture, Industry and Commerce. The Port Harcourt industrial axis spread through Trans Amadi into Aba industrial road, before bifurcating into Owerri and Umuahia. The Agric base built on oil palm tree, cocoa, rubber, cassava, yam and rice permeated all zones of the tropical rain forest, from the shores of River Niger in the present day Bayelsa, through the Imo River Basin unto the Paddy shores of Cross River spreading out to the outlying areas of Abakaliki, Nkano and Nsukka. Eastern Nigeria was then an agricultural and industrial region.

There was a surfeit of cash crops which led to a boom in the international market that fetched the foreign exchange with which the industrial estates and a competitive economic infrastructure was built. The industrial estates produced both capital and consumer goods which ranged from automobiles, machinery parts, tyres, glass bottles, ceramic wares to beverages, drinks, soaps, cosmetics, leather shoes and textiles. Eastern Nigeria competitiveness was further enhanced by the development of a strong commercial network.

In addition to small and medium industry (SMI) complexes in Aba and Onitsha, these two towns were transformed into major trading centers through which both the agricultural especially the industrial products were sold to the outside world. Traders and businessmen came from every part of Nigeria to buy in Onitsha and Aba. Soon the market centers attracted patrons from West, East and Central Africa.

Education and the Spirit of Enterprise – The Center Piece.

Underpinning the ability of the Eastern region to achieve its unique combination of being an agricultural, industrial and commercial hob of the nation was its high intellectual base and an unflagging spirit of enterprise. From Dr Nnamdi Azikwe (1st Premier of Eastern Nigeria) to Dr Michael Okpara (2nd premier of Eastern Nigeria) and all the political heavy weights of the time -Mbazulike, Chief Imoke, Mazi Mbonu Ojike, Dr Ozumba Mbadiwe, Barrister Raymond Amanze Njoku, Chief Nwoga, Dr Emole, Dr Akanu Ibiam, Prof. Chike Obi, Chief Nwodo, Dr Alvan Ikoku, Dr Aja Nwachukwu, Dr Obi Wali and a host of them, we had men of letters. These were well educated men, many had PhDs.

No wonder they placed so much emphasis on education. Every village had a walled primary school with proper tables and chairs (even where parents were mandated to build for their wards). Every class had properly trained teachers from the ETCs and the TTCs. Beyond the three Government Secondary Schools at Owerri, Afikpo and Umuahia, the government supported the establishment of secondary schools in every part of the region. Government gave grants-In-Aids to missionaries and communities that built secondary schools and technical colleges.

It was in Alaigbo that the first private secondary schools were built (in Arochukwu and other towns). Every effort was made to encourage bright pupils from poor homes to acquire education through the Eastern Nigeria Government Scholarship Scheme and Country Council Scholarship Scheme. I had the privilege of attending secondary school on a community Council Scholarship.

The colonial masters established a campus of the University of London in Ibadan which later metamorphosed to University of Ibadan (UI). But the first indigenous university was built in Eastern Nigeria - University of Nigeria-Nsukka with an Enugu campus. And so Eastern Nigeria produced great scholars like Prof. Eni Njoku, Prof. Kodilinye, Prof. Ezera Kalu, Prof. Njoku Obi and many others who were pioneer Vice Chancellors and who helped to establish the university system in Nigeria

All over Nigeria, people from Eastern Nigeria were in majority or second in number among the student population and the academic staff in most educational institutions including great institutions like Kings College, Lagos and College, Zaria. Alaigbo has a surfeit of professionals in all areas of endeavour. Alaigbo great engineers performed great feats during the civil war - built mobile refineries and heavy amour and in the Arts, led the way with great authors and poets like Prof. Chinua Achebe, Cyprian Ekwensi, Elechi Amadi, Chukwuemeka Ike, Chris Okigbo, Sonny Oti, Ben Enwuonwu (the Sculptor) and many others. Even in school and national sports, Eastern Nigeria led on a continuous basis.

Alaigbo was thus able to compete in all spheres of human endeavour in the Nigerian Nation and excelled. Then we began to attract national admiration and respect. The major reason this happened was our focus on education. Every father wanted to train his child to become a doctor, lawyer or engineer. Little wonder that the crop of officer corps in the Nigerian Army was made up largely of Eastern Nigerians especially in the specialist cadres like the medical and engineering corps. Eastern Nigerians could hold their own anywhere and they were respected all over Nigeria and beyond. In the Nigerian civil and public service then, wherever educated men were needed the chances were that it would be the Easterner with healthy competition from the Westerners but because we Easterners had no problem with leaving our home base, unlike our western compatriots we had an edge in National and International spread.

But what happened to us?

A lot of theories have been proposed to explain the descent and decline of Alaigbo from its competitive position in Nigeria since the end of the Nigeria Civil War. Some have blamed our woes on official policy of discrimination of the Nigerian Nation against people from the East. Some have blamed our loss of competitiveness from the physical, fiscal and psychological impact of losing the war. While there may be some credence to some of these theories, as it is indisputable that our progress was halted (temporarily) by the Civil War, it is no longer in my opinion justifiable to blame anybody for the current situation in Eastern Nigeria, especially in Alaigbo. After all, we can see across the region many men who went through the debilitating effects of the war but have risen to the top of their professions and to the top of the national hierarchy. Igbos like His Majesty Obi of Onitsha, Igwe Achebe, Dr Alex Ekwueme, Sen. Ken Nnamani, Sen Anyim Pius Anyim, Prof. Chukwuma Soludo, Prof. Uzoma Nwola, Prof. Dora Akunyili, Dr Ndi Onuekwusi, Chief Festus Odimegwu, Gen. Ike Nwachukwu, Gen Nwanguma, Gen Ihejirika, Chief Ibeto, Frank Nneji, Dr Herbert Orji, Dr Sam Egwu, Dr Nnia Nwodo, Mr Frank Nweke (Jnr), Dr Herbert Wigwe, Prof. Bart Nnaji, Prof. Anya O. Anya, Engr. Ernest Ndukwe, Mr Stan Ekeh, Chief Akwari Ukpabi, Mrs Stella Okoli, and many others too numerous to mention. These men and women amongst many others who came from the deprivation of the civil war, have risen to achieve competitive rating with the best in Nigeria and have excelled to the admiration of all. Here, we see a fine mix of a high intellectual base with the spirit of enterprise. It is therefore certain that the overall loss of competitiveness cannot be blamed on the war alone. To my mind we missed the way when we stopped paying appropriate attention to education. The problem actually started when we began the "cash and carry politics" that brought men of fair weather into the political leadership of the region.

People who did not go to school but ran into cash began to pilot political affairs, some becoming god fathers and others "Spokesmen of the Igbo nation" *A man cannot give what he does not have.* As I had shown earlier, our earlier political leaders...were thoroughly educated men who knew the value of education and its power to transform any society. They therefore, put the needed focus on education. At one time, it was said that education was the greatest industry of Eastern Nigeria but that seems to have changed.

Our schools were run down, no new schools were being built. Teachers were not being paid salaries regularly and teachers' education was relegated. While other states were giving massive scholarships to their students, not much was happening especially in the South Eastern states. The political leaders were only playing politics with education. As if the neglect by the government of schools and education was a motivation, many parents became careless about the educational pursuits of their children. It was no longer attractive to strain to become *"Nne* Lawyer" or *"Nna* Doctor" but it was more important to become *"Nne Akajiaku"*, *"Nna Omena Nwata"*, *"Nne Eriwe-Agwuagwu"* and *"Nna Eze Ego 1"*. All of a sudden our value system became corrupted because we employed political and traditional leaders who had lost their bearing. Alaigbo has become the headquarters of all forms of evil from armed robbery to kidnapping. Before EFCC decided to crack down on 419, the world headquarters was somewhere between Imo and Abia states. And yet we had governments in this region. Despite the opposition to some of these evils that we have seen recently in some states, we really need to do much more to show revulsion to these evils and muster all the resources within the reach of the government and the people to fight these evils to redeem our image. Critical to restoring the past glory of the economy of Alaigbo are four (4) key issues.

1. Educational Revolution

Education remains the critical center piece on which the restoration of our past glory will be built. It does not matter whether oil, gas, gold, zinc or iron is found anywhere, it will require men with knowledge and skills to mine and process them. Today India exports human capital to many nations and their experts remit huge sums of foreign exchange home which is used to develop India in all sectors. Yes, every state can build airports and even establish universities but they will need pilots and other professionals to fly the planes and mount courses into the universities to procure accreditation from NUC. It is well educated men with appropriate skills that will create ideas that will translate into big and successful businesses. Therefore, a *Martial Plan* for an educational revolution in the South East is imperative.

We must stop sending children away from home to go and start buying and selling. Every child must at least obtain the West African Senior School Certificate of Education (WASCE) before venturing into any trade. If need be, we must legislate this. The governments in the region must invest in education and encourage private sector participation as well. I am pleased to note what is happening in Anambra state. The government is not only returning schools to their original private owners including the churches and missions, but they are also helping to equip and support the schools. That is the way to go and I strongly urge all the other states to make education a priority.

2. Re-enactment of the Spirit of Enterprise.

Only businesses will create jobs and ultimately wealth that lift our people out of poverty. The values of industry, hardwork and enterprise must be inculcated into the youths as they go through school. Entrepreneurship must now be thought in schools from the secondary to the tertiary institutions. Our people must adopt the entrepreneurial paradigm in whatever they do. Our orientation which is derivable from a proper entrepreneurial education must be to solve problems, fill needs and create value. And this returns us to the issue of appropriate and skill based education. Our spirit of enterprise will only blossom into profitable and sustainable businesses when they are built on modern principles of entrepreneurship and enterprise development.We need to create smart businesses that can leverage technology and human brain power and artificial Intelligence. Our levels of productivity and efficiency of output must justify our efforts.

3. Return to the Basics – Agriculture and Industry

As indicated earlier, the economy of the South East was built on income from agriculture and the taxation from industry. How did they do it? And how can these be replicated, taking advantage of the progress in science and technology since then. Use must be made of Agricultural extension workers to teach farmers new farming techniques and help them solve their problems. Every senatorial zone or polytechnic and university must create the opportunity for the training of Agricultural extension workers while the Agric research centers will have to be revamped and recharged. Agricultural scientists are gradually going into extinction. What IITA is doing in Ibadan must be replicated in the South East zone. The Agricultural establishments in Umudike including the University of Agriculture should be refitted and redirected to focus on Agriculture and nothing more.

New and improved seeds and seedlings will have to be provided to farmers with Government subsidy. Indeed, seed multiplication centers will have to be developed in every LGA and given out to farmers- free if possible. Agricultural cooperatives need to be reinstated so that individual farmers can pull their resources together and undertake commercial farming while both state and Local Governments should help with support services for cooperative groups - land clearing, land ploughing and weed clearing.

Access to agricultural financing must be made liberal. We need to take full advantage of Federal Governments' agricultural transformation programmes including subsidized borrowing costs. The current guarantee being given to commercial banks by the Federal Government should be emulated by the states to enlarge the number of beneficiaries. We must also guarantee minimum crop price for farmers to ensure they do not sell at a loss. Every effort must be made to transform agriculture into a business venture that will attract the entry of serious business people with appropriate funding. Peasant farming must be de-emphasized. Commercial farming must be promoted through a combination of policies and incentives. What is happening in Kwara State must be emulated. We must rebuild the farm settlements and use them to commercialize Agriculture as full time business while focusing on our areas of comparative advantage in root crops (cassava and yam) and cereals (especially rice and maize) and tree crops (palm tree, rubber and cocoa).

4. Industrial Revolution

Coming on the heels of agricultural revolution will be industrial revolution. This revolution will be centered in the following areas of comparative and competitive advantages particularly, agro-based industries because with abundant agricultural produce, the inputs is there for a thriving agric-based industrial complexes. Production of food products for domestic consumption and exports will thrive based on cassava, maize, yams, and rice. We will not have cause to import any significant food product but will have the opportunity to export to the West and East Africa up to the Sahel regions. Other agric-based Industries will process cocoa products up to chocolates. Oil Mills-Palm oil and Palm Kernels will provide substitute for the manufacturing of margarine, marmalade and other edibles. Rubber processing will lead to the manufacture of rubber products up to Motor tyres.

With the large stock of oil and gas in the region, a petrochemical based manufacturing industry should thrive. Processing of hydrocarbons and by products of petroleum refining will yield primary and intermediate raw materials for a fledgling chemical industry – plastic, pharmaceuticals, resins and textiles. Iron ore is abundant in the South East region and steel and metallic industry has a great potential to prosper in the region. Production of auto parts, machine spare parts and full assembly of automobiles and machinery will build on the existing industry in the Nnewi-Onitsha axis.

The large population of the region creates a great market for fast moving consumables. Products like soaps, detergents, cosmetics, Alcoholic and Non-Alcoholic beverages etc will emanate from these industries for local consumption and export. More so, with as Onitsha and Aba, as existing international markets, rebuilding of the infrastructure in these two cities including rail, water supply and electricity will create a major manufacturing in the South East. If we can focus on these five (5) key areas of comparative and competitive advantage, the zone will generate income, employ millions of our youth and economically empower the component areas.

The Role of Government and Restoration of our Values

To promote this industrial revolutionof the South East, government needs to establish industrial estates in each senatorial district by providing land allocation, interconnecting Roads, water supply, electricity, security of the estate, favorable loan terms with tax concessions and holidays. Facilitate an orderly development of distribution chain.There is no way that Alaigbo can regain its past glory if we do not reconsider our current value system and cause a restoration of respect for the elders, respect for established leaders and authorities, abhorrence of all that is illegal and unlawful, condemnation of robbery whether armed or unnamed, kidnapping, counterfeiting, fraud/419, vanity, pursuit of money at all costs, veneration of titles, and tax evasion. Attention should also be paid to the disenfranchised, the poor and the needy while enthroning righteousness and good government. Whatever a man sows, that he will reap. Sow to the flesh and from the flesh reap corruption, sow to the spirit and from the spirit you reap eternal life.

In conclusion, the zeal and spirit of enterprise of the people of South East Nigeria, Alaigbo is legendary and well advertised. If the truth must be told, it is the people of the Igbo Nation that have contributed to the Economic and industrial Growth of most of Nigeria. Where the people of the South East extraction to take out their investments from Lagos, Port Harcourt and Abuja, for example, the Non Oil GDP of Nigeria will take a sharp decline.

Before the war and the aftermath, the South East Zone was the leading economic block. But we seem to have lost that position due to several factors including a decline in education, poor political leadership and governance, a dimming of our entrepreneurial spirit and the destruction of our cherished value system. We need to return. We must return to those things that made us great! We must return to education. We must reignite our spirit of enterprise. We must rediscover our Agricultural base, and rebuild our industrial estates. We must rediscover our value and retrace our steps and go back to the ways our God and creator. We must restore the dignity of the Igbo Nation, Yes, we must regain our lost glory. It is doable. All we need is an enlightened Political and Traditional Leadershipthat will help us come home and rebuild our Region and regain our past glory.

Ogbemudia's Regime and Post-civil War
Reconstruction in Western Igboland, 1970-1975
by
Daniel Olisa Iweze

Abstract

With the outbreak of the Nigerian Civil War on 6 July, 1967, Western Igboland which bordered Biafra being part of the Midwest State, was under the jurisdiction of the Federal government. The Biafran incursion into the Midwest State on 9 August, 1967 and the Federal forces re-conquest and occupation turned Western Igboland into a theatre of war and contest between the contending forces which led to devastations of economic and social infrastructure in the area. At the end of the Civil War, the Federal Military government under General Yakubu Gowon put forward the Post-Civil War Reconstruction programmes of Reconstruction, Rehabilitation and Reconciliation (3Rs), whose assignments were focused on the former Biafran enclave of East-Central State. Midwest State was excluded from the assignments of the Post Civil-War Reconstruction programmes of the Federal government, damaged infrastructure in Western Igboland were reconstructed by the Midwest State Government under Col. Samuel Ogbemudia with assistance from the Federal government and international voluntary agencies. It is against this background, that this paper examines the Midwest State government's efforts in restoring the damaged economic and social infrastructure in Western Igboland.

Introduction

Post-civil war reconstruction programme was a major event in Nigerian history. It was established by the Federal Military government under General Gowon at the end of the Nigerian Civil War in 1970 to reconstruct war-torn Igboland and re-integrate the Igbo into the mainstream of Nigerian state. Despite its importance in Nigerian historical discourse, the 3Rs have not received adequate scholarly attention from historians. There is paucity of literature that deal explicitly on the history of post-war reconstruction of Igboland. The only comprehensive existing work is that of Paul Obi-aniwhich focuses overly on the post civil war reconstruction of the core Igbo area of the defunct East-Central State while leaving out Western Igboland as confirmed by Paul Obi-Ani, *Post-Civil War Social and Economic Reconstruction of Igboland, 1970-1983*. This profound neglect of the area by historians could be attributed to the erroneous assumption that Western Igboland was not part of the former Biafran enclave and probably was never affected by the war.

With the Biafran incursion of the Midwest State and their expulsion from the state by the Federal soldiers between September and October 1967,

Major Samuel Osaigbovo Ogbmudia, a Quarter Master-General in charge of armoury in the Fourth Area Command of Nigerian Army in Benin was appointed the Military Administrator on 21 September, 1967 and later promoted to Lt. Col and Military Governor of the Midwest State on 17th November 1967. After a familiarization tour of the State and in recognition of the huge damage to the social and economic infrastructure during the civil war in the state, Ogbemudia acknowledged that the Midwest State, especially in Western Igboland, was the most unfortunate victim of the Nigerian crisis besides the East Central State (Ogbemudia, *Years of Challenge*, 117-118).

Midwest Region was created on August 9, 1963 and later re-named Midwest State on the 27th May, 1967 following the creation of twelve state administrative structure by General Gowon. Midwest Region was a multi-ethnic state peopled by Edo, Izon (Ijaw), Urhobo, Isoko, Itsekiri and Western Igbo groups. The Western Igbo which comprised the then Asaba and Aboh Divisions of colonial Western Nigeria occupy the eastern flank of the state. They were found in Oshimili, Ika, Aniocha and Ndokwa local government areas of the state (*ibid*. 1-3). The area consists of nine (9) local government areas of the present Delta-North Senatorial district of the present Delta State.

The devastations of infrastructure in Western Igboland were enormous when compared with other parts of the Midwest State, which were affected by the Civil War. Towns within Asaba, Oko, Ibusa and Ogwuashi Uku axis witnessed huge damages where the federal troops fought fierce battles with Biafran forces during the war. While in Aboh, Kwale and other neighbouring communities had minimal infrastructural damages due largely to the topography of the area and lack of development before the civil war. Most of the displaced persons/refugees in Western Igboland were from Asaba, Oko, Abala, Utchi, Ibusa, Ogwuashi Uku, Okpanam, Ishiagu, Agbor and when they returned to their various towns and communities, they met their buildings burnt down and their property looted. It has been estimated that Western Igbo people constituted about 60 per cent of the entire war victims in Midwest State (*Midwest State Government Rehabilitation*, 10).

Midwest State Government Reconstruction Programme

Ogbemudia set up a seven-Man Reconstruction and Rehabilitation Committee under the chairmanship of Mr. S.Y. Eke. It was mandated among other things, to recommend measures to bring about a return to normalcy in both the economic and social sectors of the State (Ogbemudia 115). In view of the fact that Midwest State was not one of the beneficiaries of the Federal Government reconstruction programme, Ogbemudia, revived the State's Rehabilitation Committee and renamed it the Reconstruction and Rehabilitation Committee in July 1969.

The Midwest Rehabilitation Committee was originally established in 1963, in the wake of the disengagement of Midwest State civil servants in the old Western Region. The primary responsibility of the committee was to get office accommodation for the newly created region and to resettle civil servants who were disengaged from the Western Region. The committee also handled the problem of resettling displaced persons in the State as a result of series of crises in 1966 that left about 50,000 people of from Midwest State displaced (*Rehabilitation in the Midwest State*, 5). The devastations of the war in the Midwest State brought about the widening of the scope of the terms of reference of the State Rehabilitation committee to include the reconstruction of damaged infrastructure.

The Midwest State Rehabilitation Committee was supported in the execution of the projects in Western Igboland by two American agencies: the United States Agency for International Development (USAID) and the American Friends Service Committee, the Religious Society of Friends called the Quakers. These two agencies carried out intensive rehabilitation and relief programmes in many ways which facilitated the restoration of normal life for the war victims. In October 1969, Asaba and Ibusa were chosen as the most brutalized sites for the execution of the relief programme. This resulted in the signing of agreement between the USAID, the Quaker Services and the Midwest State Committee for Reconstruction and Rehabilitation (Okocha 157).

A full quantification of the impact of the Civil War on Nigerian economy remains a daunting task. Vital documents were destroyed during the war by the contending sides and only a few fragmentary estimates from official statistics exist. Certain vital economic sectors such as agriculture, trade, industrial production and distribution were adversely affected. Approximate valuation of physical and financial losses was between £150 million and £200 million and the estimated reconstruction component of the Second National Development Plan was between £350 million and £400 million for the national economy as a whole (Aboyade & Ayida 189-190). Devastations of the Civil War in Western Igboland were immense. Appraising the enormity of the reconstruction work in the area, Ogbemudia emphasises that:*"It is much easier to win a war than to undertake reconstruction after the war. The roads, bridges and buildings destroyed must be reconstructed if life is to return to normal and if people are to go about their social, business activities in an atmosphere of calm and mutual confidence"*(Osunde, htpp//edoworld.net 2007-2011).

The Nigerian Civil War had caused massive loss of lives and property such as extensive destruction of farmlands and damage to economic and social infrastructures like agriculture, trade, commerce, transportation, post and telecommunication systems, health and education. The reconstruction of damaged infrastructure in Western Igboland by the Midwest State government could be broadly categorized into economic and social infrastructure.

Reconstruction of Economic Infrastructure

Economic impact of the war was felt in Western Igboland due partly to the economic blockade of the east by the Federal Government. Basically, it was the Biafran incursion and the subsequent Federal re-occupation of Midwest State that led to dislocation in the area as a greater proportion of human resources were involved in direct military combative activities which affected food production and the general performance of other sectors of the economy.

i. Agriculture

Agriculture, the mainstay of the economy of the people, was disrupted during the war. The produce of farmers and their livestock in the rural communities were either destroyed by bombs and shelling or stolen by the federal troops and other war destitute. This led to famine and acute food shortage because farming became risky due to military movements in the area during the war. At the end of the civil war, it became imperative to tackle the problem of hunger, starvation malnutrition and diseases. Based on this, Col. Ogbemudia urged the people to increase their agricultural production and the people engaged in farming in order to produce crops such as yam, cassava, maize and so forth.

Ogbemudia stressed the need for people to get back to farm as a means of obtaining gainful employment. The state Ministry of Agriculture was reorganized and the Farmer's Crusade project was launched at Ubiaja on February 1968. The scheme received the sum of ₦2.12 million from the Federal Commissioner of Finance, Chief Obafemi Awolowo after his four day tour of the Midwest State from August 11 to 14, 1969 (Ogbemudia 166-167).The scheme was supported with the sum of N100,000 by the State government to provide working implements, axes, cutlasses, spray pumps, chemical needed to protect the crops and planting materials. Each member of the scheme received maintenance allowance of N4.00 monthly for miscellaneous expenses before the crops were harvested and they were given temporary accommodation on their respective plots.The Farmers Crusade project had five schemes located in different parts of the State. There was maize plantation at Attache near Agbor, rubber processing equipment installed at Mbiri and Utagbo-Uno farm settlements in Ika and Aboh divisions respectively (*ibid*. 175). State-owned mechanized farms in Agbede, Warrake, and Agenegbode in Owan divison were resuscitated (ibid. 186).

The State government gave more attention to the farmers in non-Igbo areas abandoning farmers in Western Igboland whose farming activities were also disrupted. The State government established oil palm plantations in

Urhobo-East and West, Warri, Benin-East and West, Ishan, Western Ijaw Divisions, Asaba and Ika (*ibid*. 181-186). Piggery centres were established at Ogwuashi-Uku at the cost of N38,799.00 for the breeding of sows and boars. Veterinary clinics were established at Sapele, Uromi and Asaba, and a control posts at Agenebode and Obiaruku because of the increase in demand of Veterinary services in the State (Uchendu 186).

ii. Trade and Commerce

Trade and commercial activities were greatly affected during the war. Various markets across Western Igboland were destroyed. Among the markets reconstructed were the Ogbeogonogo market located at Ogbeilo village along Nnebisi road in Asaba. The reconstruction of the market was jointly carried out by the Midwest State government and Asaba Urban District Council, (AUDC) in 1970. The A.U.D.C. hired and paid for the skilled labour, while the State government provided the building materials. Ogbe-Olie market located at Cable-Point in Asaba was also reconstructed.

The reconstruction of the two markets stimulated the local economy of the town as well as other neighbouring towns such as Oko, Okwe Okpanam, Ibusa amongst others and even across the Niger. The State's Ministry of Social Welfare supplied cassava processing machines to Isheagu and Achalla women respectively. The American Friends Service Committee of the Quakers donated fishing boats to the three Oko communities: Oko-Ogbele, Oko-Anala and Oko-Amakom. This was done to support the fishing activities of Oko people who were renowned agriculturalists and fishermen. They also provided some block-moulds to Oko people. The Quakers set up a carpentry workshop in Ibusa to manufacture doors, windows, frames and other building materials (Okocha 162).

iii. Industry

The only viable industry in Western Igboland, Asaba Textile Mill was reconstructed by the state government in collaboration with Messrs Continho Caro of Hamburg reconstructed at cost of £2 million (Asineme 291). The company resumed operation on August 22, 1972, with only ten (10) expatriate staff, forty six (46) skilled and unskilled workers. It later reabsorbed some of its former displaced staff and provided jobs for some of the unemployed folks. The reduction in staff strength was attributed to the effects of the war. Some of the staff in the production section did not come back to Asaba either because they lost their lives or were displaced. However, by 1975, the work force had increased as people began to rush for gainful employment in the company (*ibid*.)The company served as a veritable source of livelihood for the people and stimulated the economy of the area and led to population growth of the town (*ibid*. 291). Apart from the Textile Mill at Asaba, there has not been any Federal or State industrial presence in Western Igboland since the end of the civil war.

Gowon's implementation of the Second National Development Plan, 1970-1974 had the objectives of promoting even development and fair allocation of industries in all parts of the country. Despite this objective, the political leadership dominated by the Hausa/Fulani and the Yoruba continued the authoritative system which was disproportionately in favour of these two ethnic groups. The Igbo were excluded from benefitting from the allocation of economic resources. The non-Igbo groups got a fair share of the political and economic resources. Apart from minor reconstruction work in Nkalagu, none of the industries in the Plan was sited in Igboland, including the Western Igbo area (Ikejiani-Clark 634). Mariam Ikejiani decried this curious exclusion of the Igbo in the nation's political economy when she observed that:

> *"All the important and expensive high technology and large employment generating heavy industrial establishments under the Second National Development Plan were sited in the Hausa-Fulani areas, with a few others sited in the geo-ethnic areas of the minorities, especially those in the then Bendel State, Rivers and Gowon's home state- Benue Plateau"* (ibid.).

Table 1 Location of Some Major Projects of the Second National Development Plan, 1970-1974

Projects	Location	Area of Location
Oil Refineries	i) Warri ii) Kaduna	Urhobo Hausa-Fulani
Single Super Phosphate Fertilizer project	Kaduna	Hausa-Fulani
Peugeot Automobile of Nigeria (PAN)	Kaduna	Hausa-Fulani
Iron and Steel Complex	Ajaokuta	Igala
Cement Factories (Existed pre-war)	i) Calabar ii) Nkalagu	Efik Igbo
Alcohol Factory	Bacita	Hausa-Fulani
Salt Manufacturing/Refinery	i) Ijoko ii) Sapele	Yoruba Urhobo
Volkswagen of Nigeria (VON)	i) Badagry ii) Lagos	Yourba Yoruba

Source: *Second National Development Plan, 1970-1974*, Federal Ministry of Information, 1970, Vol.1, p.147

Thus, all but one of the projects in the Plan were sited outside the Igbo geographical area except the Cement factory at Nkalagu in East-Central State which existed before the war. In the Midwest State, the Oil refinery and Salt manufacturing/refinery projects were sited in Sapele and Warri and none in

Western Igboland. This is contrary to the orchestrated policy objectives of the Second National Development Plan which was enunciated to promote equitable development and fair distribution of industries in all parts of the country.Inflation was a major feature of the economy of the country from 1966 to 1970. The series of crises in the period disrupted trading activities between different parts of the country. The rising inflation during the war continued up to the post war era.

The price hike was especially pronounced in Western Igboland area where many people struggled to recover from war distress. To curb the inflationary trend, the Midwest government set up the Price Control Board (PCB) in July 1970 with the responsibility to fix prices of consumable commodities. To complement the efforts of the board, the State government pegged the prices of some foodstuffs sold in Western Igboland and other parts of the State in 1971. The measure was successful because the prices of some food items dropped. The price of garri per bag, for instance, went down from £10 to £7 and the cost of a bag of rice dropped from £18 to £13. Besides, the cost of a bag of beans fell from £4.105 to £3 in 1971 (Asenime 5).

Transportation
Roads and other transport facilities in Igboland as a whole were seriously damaged during the civil war. In the post-war Development Plan of 1970-1974, Federal Government authorised the immediate reconstruction of the Asaba-Onitsha Niger Bridge and other bridges and infrastructure in the war affected areas (*Programme of Post-War Reconstruction and Development*86). In order to achieve the various policy objectives of the plan, the sum of £242.6 million was allocated as capital expenditure in the transport sector over the plan period. This was made up of £75.5 million for the States and £167.1 million for the federal programmes (*ibid*. 118).In addition, a sum of £32.9 million was set aside for the rehabilitation of various roads damaged during the civil war all over the country including: Lagos-Ibadan-Ilorin-Kano route (£5.27m); Kano-Katsina (£1.728m); Benin-Asaba (£1.3m) and Jos-Aliade-Oturkpo road (£3.9m) amongst others (ibid. 189).

Roads and bridges and other social amenities that suffered damages during the war in Igboland engaged the attention of Federal Government, with the specific aim of reactivating the national economy. Some important roads and bridges linking Igboland with the rest of the country were restored including the Niger Bridge, linking Asaba with Onitsha. The bridge was reconstructed by Dumez the company that built it. This re-established the shortest land route between Western Igboland and East Central State with the rest of the country. The two spans on the Onitsha end of the Niger Bridge damaged during the civil war were replaced with a fourteen-foot wide bailey as a temporary structure at the cost of £100,000. The estimated cost of reconstructing the two end spans of the Niger Bridge was £1.5 million (*War Damage to Roads*, 5) as seen in the table below:

Table 2 The Estimated Cost of Reconstructing the Two end Spans of the Niger Bridge in 1972

Number of Spans	13 Spans	
Estimated cost of one span	6.75m ÷13	£0.52m
Estimated cost of two spans	0.52 ×2	£1.04m
Add 25 per cent increase using	£1.04m÷4	£0.26m (1965) as a base year
Estimated cost of reconstructing two ends spans	£1.04+ £0.26m	£1.3m **£1.5million**

Source: *Report on War Damages to Roads, Bridges Water Works and Equipment in the East Central State of Nigeria. Official Document No.3 of 1970, Ministry of Works, Housing and Transport, Enugu*, p.5.

In Western Igboland after the civil war, there were the problems of bad and inadequate roads and few vehicles on the roads which made movement of people and conveyance of goods very tiring. Many workers trekked to offices while market women had difficulties getting their wares to the markets in the urban areas. Movement between the rural and urban centres was tedious, irregular and hazardous. To solve the problem of transportation, the State government set up a City Bus Service in Benin-City in 1968 and later established the Delta Bus Service in April, 1971. This was followed by the emergence of township bus services in Agbor, Asaba, Sapele which were later extended to all the Divisional headquarters and the neighbouring towns like Ubiaja, Ugo, Auchi, Warri, Gborodo and Ogwuashi-Uku. In the subsequent years, the State government established the Midwest Line (later renamed Bendel Line), which plied various routes in other parts of the country (Ogbemudia 222-223). The Oboshi Bridge which links Ogwuashi-Uku and Ibusa was rebuilt by the State government, while Asaba-Benin road and Niger Bridge which link Western Igboland with Eastern Igboland were reconstructed by the Federal government. The opening of Asaba-Lagos road after the war provided positive development and stimulated inter-state commerce and linked up prominent centres in the country which gave impetus to increase in demographic movement into the area.

A key observer believed that nothing significant was done in Western Igboland by the State government in the sphere of road rehabilitation during the reconstruction period. He maintained that while Benin-Asaba road was reconstructed by Federal government, many State and local roads were not rebuilt until 1976, when Ogbemudia's successor, George Ininh rehabilitated some roads in the area as most of the roads damaged during the civil war in various towns and communities in Western Igboland were neglected. Other successive governors of old Bendel State embarked on road development in the State including Western Igboland. By 1976, with good roads, growing urban centres emerged such as Asaba, Ibusa, Agbor, Ogwuashi-Uku and Umunede (Interview with Chief F.C. Esedebe at his residence in Ibusa on February 8, 2010). The transport business recovered quickly from the effect of the war and expanded tremendously from the 1970s to 1990s and afterwards. There is no data to show the names and number of people that ventured into motor transport sub-sector, but many individuals operated transport services especially in Asaba, Ibusa, Ogwuashi-Uku, Agbor and so forth.

Education

One of the legacies of Midwest State government during the reconstruction period was in the area of education. The war disrupted education in Western Igboland because many schools were closed down and buildings and other facilities destroyed. To tackle the problem of education in the State, Governor Ogbemudia held a meeting with the Principals of Secondary Schools, Teacher Training Colleges, Trade and Technical Schools and the officials of the Ministry of Education at Immaculate Conception College, Benin-City to deliberate on a series of problems and related issues affecting education in the State. The problems identified included acute shortage of staff, huge devastation of school buildings and resettlement of displaced pupils especially those who could not return to their schools which were either destroyed or were situated in war-torn Western Igboland area and the exodus of large number of Igbos, who were proprietors of schools, created a vacuum that had to be filled (Ogbemudia 200). The cost of maintenance of the existing schools and infrastructure and the cost of improving on the education standards was onerous. Col. Ogbemudia in an address to the Conference of Principals stressed the State government's determination to revamp the education sector in the following statement: *"We must ensure that our children are provided with the necessary educational facilities at the right time, and we must create for them that wholesome and healthy atmosphere for study which is conducive to higher and unlimited achievement"* (*ibid.*)

The rehabilitation of the damaged schools was collectively carried out by the Midwest State Government and humanitarian agencies and organisations. Schools were reopened in March 1970 and students and pupils resumed though, in trickles which improved progressively in subsequent years thanks to USAID, Quaker Services in synergy with Midwest Rehabilitation Committee. School repairs, furniture supplies, rehabilitation of school laboratories, equipment, and libraries were carried out. Based on the request from the Midwest Ministry of Economic Development, and Reconstruction, other towns and communities within Asaba and Ibusa environs such as Oko, Okwe, Isheagu, Achalla, Okpanam were included as beneficiaries of the programme (Okocha 157).

Quaker Services undertook major repairs at Sacred Heart School, Ibusa, St. John`s School, Achalla, and St. Patrick`s School, Cable Point, Asaba. Other schools rehabilitated in Asaba were Holy Trinity School, Convent Girls` School, St. Thomas`s School and St. Patrick's College. By December 1970, seven classrooms, one headmaster`s office and one store were rebuilt in each school. This development led to the re-opening of schools in Okwe and Achalla and the State`s Ministry of Economic Development provided furniture for 6,000 pupils in these schools (*ibid*.) However, despite the impressive achievements recorded by the State government during the reconstruction period, not all schools were rehabilitated. For example, Osadenis High School, Asaba was single-handedly reconstructed by its founder, Chief Dennis Osadebay, the former Premier of Midwest State. As stated by Chief John Enemoh, 72, retired civil servant interviewed at Asaba on February 8, 2010, The School of Agriculture, Anwai near Asaba was not reconstructed until Commodore Abdullahi Hussaini, Ogbemudia`s successor rehabilitated it in 1976.

Col. Ogbemudia endowed scholarship to secondary school war orphans in the area. He constituted a scholarship board to interview and screen prospective students to ensure that the scholarship awards were given to deserving students (Ogbemudia 200). The State government was assisted by the Federal government which disbursed some scholarship funds to the Midwest State government. On 13th April 1970, Ogbemudia while on a State visit to Asaba community, assured the people that orphan students should be allowed to continue with their education pending when investigation of the issue by a panel appointed for that purpose was completed. The names of affected students were screened and compiled by principals of various schools and sent to the State Scholarship Board for payment. The Ministry of Education paid the school fees to the respective schools until they completed their secondary school programme. The exercise was restricted to only secondary school level since the State operated free education at the primary school level.

One of the war orphans who benefitted from the scholarship award was Emma Okocha. He lost his parents during the gruesome massacre at Asaba orchestrated by the Federal soldiers. The scholarship award given to him in 1972 enabled him to complete his secondary school education (Okocha 162-163). The demand for scholarship was so great because a large number of displaced students who were formerly in schools in the Eastern Region before the outbreak of the war had returned to their various communities in Western Igboland. The number that sought for scholarship was greater than the available resources of the State could handle. The State government appealed to various communities to assist in rehabilitation and building their own schools to augment the government rehabilitation and reconstruction efforts. Local government councils were also encouraged to award scholarships to deserving indigenes (Ogbemudia 201). Despite the official appeal to the people for a concerted effort in that regard, the scholarship award did not reach majority of war orphans in the war torn areas especially those in the rural areas.

Prior to the civil war, education in the defunct Midwest State was in the hands of Christian missionaries. The State government undertook direct control of a few local government primary schools, two government colleges and some private schools. While the schools were adjudged to maintain good discipline necessary for teaching and learning, the State government claimed that they were not able to meet the needs and aspirations of the State both in terms of access and curricula. After the civil war in 1970, Col. Ogbemudia envisaged that missionary education with its restricted curricula and enrolment could no longer meet the goals and aspirations of the State to enable its citizens participate effectively in the processes of national reconstruction and other endeavours. Consequently, he directed the State Ministry of Education under the chairmanship of former Director of Education, Mr. E. O. Ihejirika, with Mr. S. O. Egube and Mr. J. O. Enaohwo as members, to work out modalities for the transfer of schools to the State government. The reports of the Ministry of Education were preliminary steps for the takeover of schools from the Christian Missions by the State government in 1972 and 1973 academic years (Ezewu 2).

Before the take over of schools in 1973, all schools, except Edo College in Benin-City and Government College, Ughelli, were owned and managed by private proprietors and voluntary agencies, mainly the Christian missionary groups. b Edict No. 4 of 1973, Midwest State Education Board and fifteen Divisional Education Boards were established. The Government compensated the proprietors except the Christian missionaries who did not ask for compensation.The State government's reason for the take over of schools is unconnected to the controversy between the Federal government and some humanitarian organizations during the Civil War. Federal government had accused the churches and other voluntary agencies of meddling in its affairs by giving support to Biafra. As a result, the Federal government directed all the State governments to implement the transfer of schools from the missionaries, a policy that was not popular in Nigeria prior to the war. After the take over of the schools, the number of secondary schools in the State increased from 64 in 1965 to 150 in 1974. Expectedly the enrolment figure also rose from 16,272 in 1965 to 55,289 in 1973.

Table 3: Secondary School Enrolment Figures in Asaba from 1971-1991

Schools	1971	1976	1981	1986	1991
St. Patrick's College	814	1,242	2,480	4,500	7,867
Osadenis High School	617	1,282	2,100	3,800	7,867
Asaba Girls Grammar School	450	875	1,500	2,400	6,000
St. Brigid's Girls Grammar School	500	600	650	2,000	6,450
College of Agriculture, Anwai, Asaba	200	250	600	680	2,800
TOTAL	2,581	4,249	7,330	13,380	31,517

Source: Jude Asenime, "The Foundation, Growth and Transformation of Asaba to 1991." Unpublished PhD Thesis, Dept. of History, Bayero University, Kano, 2005, p.303.

The priority attention accorded to education sector by the government in terms of huge investment during the reconstruction period is reflected in the increase in the number of schools founded and enrolment of students (Asenime 303).The school enrolment figures in some selected secondary schools in Asaba is presented above. The above data show the increased growth in the number of students from 2,581 in 1971 (at the end of the Civil War) to 31,517 in 1991. The number excluded the primary school pupils in ten schools and the Trade school, which was later converted to Electro Trade School. There is no record of the number of primary school enrolment in the period. In spite of that, the number of enrolment of primary school pupils was far greater than the number of secondary school enrolment presented above. To solve the problem of displaced students and urgent demand for higher education in the State, Ogbemudia's government decided to establish the Midwest Institute of Technology in November, 1970 and it had an initial intake of 180 students. In 1972, it was upgraded and renamed University of Benin and produced its first set of graduates in 1974 (Ogbemudia 206-207).

Health

On the eve of the civil war, medical services in the Midwest State was in a poor condition. The State had only nine (9) government hospitals with a total bed capacity of 609, which was inadequate to meet the medical care needs of the people. Some of the hospitals in the area were overcrowded with wounded soldiers and this made it difficult for civilians to receive medical attention. There was also the problem of shortage of drugs in the hospitals. To tackle the problem, the State government set up a task force on February 20, 1970 to build additional three hospitals with 240 beds and to resuscitate the existing ones. Two out of the three hospitals built were located in Western Igboland at Akwukwu-Igbo with 90 beds, Ibusa with 60 beds and one in Olue-Olgbo in Isoko Division with 90 beds. By 1970 thirty (30) hospitals were built and commissioned by the State government. The reforms in the State's Health Ministry culminated in the enactment of Edict No.20 of 1971 which provided for the establishment of the Midwest State Management Board. The Board was empowered to manage all the hospitals in the State and this brought about flexibility and efficiency in providing medical services to the people (*ibid*.) The Midwest State government recorded marginal achievements in the building of hospitals and the new hospitals were grossly under-supplied with medical personnel, essential drugs and equipment. The poor health condition in the area led to the emergence of privately-owned hospitals, clinics and maternity centres in Asaba, Ibusa, Agbor, Issele-Uku, Ogwuashi-uku and other communities in the following years.

Housing
There was acute shortage of housing particularly in Asaba, Oko, Okwe, Ibusa, Isheagu, Osssisa and Ogwuashi-Uku and other parts of Western Igboland that were greatly affected by the war. Residential buildings in many towns and communities had been destroyed and only a few were spared. When the people returned to their residences after the war, they had to construct makeshift structures to serve as interim shelters pending when they had the resources to build new comfortable houses. The prevailing critical economic crunch in the aftermath of the war left most people with no means to repair their homes. Many houses destroyed during the civil war dotted the landscape of Western Igboland communities, especially Asaba, Ibusa, Ogwuashi-Uku, Okpanam, Osheagu, Ossisa, Oko, Abala, Utchi, Ossisa. The State government did not build housing estates in the State the way the East Central State Government did at Enugu, Aba, Umuahia and Onitsha. The people had to rehabilitate their homes using local building materials. The only financial support came from USAID which disbursed the sum of £315,000 for housing projects and reconstruction of other public works in Asaba and Ibusa.

The State government in synergy with international relief agencies distributed building materials to the survivors of the war in the major towns of Asaba, Ogwuashi Uku, Ibusa, Agbor areas. Communities within Aboh and Kwale did not receive building materials since that part of Western Igboland suffered minimal infrastructural destruction during the war. Bags of cements and bundles of corrugated zinc were given to the local leaders of the communities and towns and the chairmen of various grassroots' rehabilitation committees for distribution to either those who lost their residences or were damaged during the war. The distribution of building materials were inadequate as many people in those towns and communities did not benefit from it. Some of the chairmen of the rehabilitation committee were said to have been corrupt and they reserved some of the building materials for themselves and their cronies instead of allocating them to the people. Those who did not receive the building materials had to rely on local materials to fix their homes (Uchendu 180-181).There is no data to show the names of those that received building materials to rebuild their homes. A few who received assistance included Professor (Mrs.) Kanime Okonjo in Ogwuashi-Uku, Mr. Ben Unoka and Chief John Enemoh in Asaba. Majority of the people in the rural communities especially Oko, Abala, Utchi and so on were denied the assistance of building materials as corroborated by Chief John Enemoh, Chief Mike Okwechime, Chief Fred Esedebe and Mr. Ben Unoka.

Federal government intervention in housing problem during the rehabilitation exercise came when the Ministry of Defence paid rents to civilians whose houses were used by the federal troops during their occupation of Asaba. The Nigerian military headquarters paid the sum of £2 per room, per month as compensation to the owners in line with the directive from Col. Ogbemudia (Okocha 187). Although, a paltry amount was paid as rents, they were useful in assuaging the suffering of the war victims. Not all the civilians whose houses were used by the federal troops were paid. Some of the claims put forward by the property owners were ignored and turned down by the Nigerian army headquarters, which believed that the compensation claims of the petitioners were baseless. There is no comprehensive record of those who were paid because the people sent petition to the Ministry of Defence Headquarters, Lagos collectively under the auspices of Asaba Landlord/Landladies Association chaired by Mr. George Okonta. In the petition, Mr George Okonta pleaded with the Defence Ministry that most of the petitioners were yet to be compensated.Until 1991, when Delta State was created, housing was one of the major problems in Asaba and proximate towns. From 1991 there was a great demand for houses to accommodate the newly created State Ministries, departments, parastatals and civil servants.

Electricity Supply

Electricity supply was the first major social infrastructure affected by the civil war in Western Igboland. Electricity supply disconnected in Asaba and other neighbouring towns from the Afam Thermal Station by the Biafran soldiers in 1967, was restored by the Federal Government through a new statutory body, the National Electricity Power Authority (NEPA) between 1971 and 1972. In the Second National Development Plan 1970-1974, out of the public sector expenditure of N20.050.738 million, N90.75 million (44%) was allocated to power development.[46] Despite the huge allocation to power, electricity supply from the national grid was erratic in Western Igbo area and only a few major towns such as Asaba, Ibusa and Ogwuashi Uku were reconnected after the war. Agbor was an exception, because power supply reached the town during the war period when the federal troops occupied the town (Uchendu 170). The restoration of electricity supply stimulated social and economic activities in the urban centres through the emergence of small and medium scale firms and industrial establishments. However, power supply was epileptic, irregular and did not serve many communities in the area until the creation of Delta State in 1991.

Water Supply

Water supply was disrupted during the hostilities due to the destruction of Afam Thermal station which supplied power to the pumping machines. Since water supply is the responsibility of State government, in 1974, the State government set up the Midwest State Water Board Corporation to supply water to the urban centres. Water supply in Asaba was not restored until 1977, when the Bendel State Government under Hussaini Abdullahi awarded a contract to Satani Avils Company Limited at the cost of N2,910,000 to construct a bore hole with about 2,000.000 litres reservoir capacity. The project was completed and commissioned in February 1978, and it was after the commissioning of the water project that Asaba had water supply from the Bendel State Water Board Corporation. The Board later extended its services to other towns like Ibusa, Agbor and Ogwuashi-Uku (Ukpong 83). Bendel State Water Board Corporation supplied water basically to major towns while numerous rural communities had to rely on streams and rivers.

Post and Telecommunications

The post and telecommunication infrastructure in the area were in shambles after the war and needed urgent rehabilitation but the Federal and Midwest State governments neglected and glossed over the rehabilitation of the communication sub-sectors. This utter neglect made Asaba and Ibusa people to appeal to Federal Government for assistance in restoring some projects damaged during the hostilities which they could not rehabilitate themselves. In August, 1970, the people of Ibusa, appealed to federal government to come to their aid in rehabilitating the post office in the town.

This request was not granted to them by the federal government and the post office was not rehabilitated throughout the reconstruction period (*Daily Times*, 197).Lending credence to the dismal failure of the sector, the First Progress Report of the Second National Development Plan, 1970-1974 observed that: "...*government's hopes in this area have not yet been realized. The sector has thus lagged behind developments in other sector and it is beginning to constitute a clog on overall development.*"(Ukpong 83).This same fate befell the restoration of telecommunication facilities in the area. In March 1971, the Federal Government only provided a paltry sum of £5,000 for the re-wiring/rehabilitation of telephone lines destroyed during the war that connected major towns such as Asaba, Ibusa, Ogwuashi-Uku and Agbor.

The 3Rs was a noble post-war policy, but their implementation by the Midwest State government under Col. Ogbemudia and the Federal government under Gowon, was half-hearted and fell short of the peoples` expectation because of the inherent vindictive measures that were directed against the Igbo as a whole. The fact that ethnicity was at the root of post-war reconstruction programme in Midwest State, the restoration of damaged infrastructure in Western Igboland by the state government was minuscule and selective. The desultory manner of the implementation of the reconstruction programmes by the Midwest State government compelled Asaba people under the auspices of Asaba Development Association (ADA) to petition the then Federal Commissioner for Economic Development, Rehabilitation and Reconstruction, Alhaji Shehu Shagari, imploring him to intervene by coming to their aid. To the peoples` chagrin, Alhaji Shehu Shagari informed them that the Federal government was unable to approve their war damages claim (See Shehu Shagari, *Beckoned to Serve: An Autobiography*.) The people resorted to individual and communal self-help efforts in rehabilitating themselves and reconstructing the damaged infrastructure. Professor Osy Okanya, a former Dean of Faculty of Social Science, Enugu State University of Science and Technology underscores the self-help initiative of the people when he avers that "Igbos survive within the Nigerian state not because of the efforts of the government but because of the ingenious nature of the people to survive" (Maier 269).

Conclusion

The Midwest State post-civil war reconstruction efforts, to some extent, was commendable with respect to sectors such as education, trade and commerce, industry, transportation, electricity and water supplies. These amenities effectively supported the towns and various communities on the path of recovery and stimulated development in critical sectors of the economy. However, the state government fell short of peoples`s expectation in agriculture, housing, health services, post and telecommunication. It is therefore evident that the communal and individual initiatives of the people were crucial in the restoration of their war ravaged homes and infrastructure leading to social and economic normalization thus complimenting the deficit in Midwest State government's restoration efforts particularly in Western Igboland during the reconstruction period.

References

Aboyade & Ayida, "The War Economy in Perspective" in Allison & Ayida (eds.) *Reflections on Nigerian Development*. Lagos: Malthouse Press, 1987.

Asenime, Jude."Growth and Transformation of Asaba", Unpublished Ph.D, Thesis, Department of History, Bayero University, Kano, 2005, p.291.

Daily Times, July 30, 1970.

Daily Times, August 6, 1970.

Ezewu, Edward. "Education In Delta State: The Challenges Ahead" Being a Paper presented on the Occasion of the Second Anniversary of the Administration of James Ibori, former Governor of Delta State from 1st-3rd June, 2001.

Ikejiani-Clark, Mariam I. " Igbo in Contemporary Nigeria" in G.E. Ofomata (ed.), *A Survey of the Igbo Nation*. Onitsha: Africana First Publishers Ltd., 2002.

Karl Maier, *This House Has Fallen: Nigeria in Crisis*. London: Penguin Books, 2000, p.269.

Midwest State Government Rehabilitation, p. 10.

Nigeria Observer, October, 9 1970, p.5.

Obi-Ani, Paul. *Post-Civil War Social and Economic Reconstruction of Igboland, 1970-1983.*Enugu: Mikon Press, 1998.

Ogbemudia, S.O. Ogbemudia, *Years of Challenge*, Ibadan: Heinemann Educational Books, 1991.

Okocha, Emma.*Blood on the Niger: The Untold Story of the Nigerian Civil War.* Sun Ray Publication, 1994.

Osunde, Osamade.In htpp//edoworld.net 2007-2011. Accessed on 12 December, 2011.

Shagari, Shehu. *Beckoned to Serve: An Autobiography.*Ibadan: Heinemann Educational Books, 2001.

Second National Development Plan 1970-74, Programme of Post-War Reconstruction and Development, Lagos, Government Printer, vol. ii, p.86.

Uchendu, Egodi Uchendu, "The Growth of Anioma Cities' in Toyin Falola & Steven J. Salm (eds.) in *Nigerian Cities*. Trenton New Jersey: African World Press, 2004.

_____ . *Women and Conflict in the Nigerian Civil War.*Trenton: Africa World Press, 2007, p.170.

Ukpong, I. (1979) "Social and Economic Infrastructure" in Olaleku, B., Fajana, Tomori & Ukpong (eds.) *Structure of the Nigerian Economy.* London: Macmillan Publishers & University of Lagos Press, 1979, p.83.

War Damage to Roads, Bridges, Water Works and Equipment in the East Central State of Nigeria. Official Document No.3 of 1970 Ministry of Works, Housing and Transport. Enugu: Government Printer.

A Revolutionized Agricultural Development in Southeast
and South-South (SESS) Geo-political Zones of Nigeria
by
Prof. Dennis Odionyenfe Balogu

Abstract

Agriculture still employs approximately 68 percent of Nigeria's workforce and accounts for its 48% gross domestic product (GDP) with a wide range of climate variations that permits the production of wide-range of meat animals and cultivation of a variety of cash crops. The livestock produced include cattle, sheep, goat, and fish. The cash crops include cocoa, citrus, cotton, groundnuts, palm oil, palm kernel, and rubber while the staple food crops include, yams, corn, rice, cassava, coco-yams, cow-peas, potatoes, millet, plantains, bananas, fruits and vegetables. Major production improvement programmes have focused on cultivation of larger piece of land. However, increasing population density, limited cultivatable land, and further encroachment of housing and village expansion have minimized chances of expanded farming in the Igbo areas of the South-East and South-south Geopolitical regions. Apart from the governments of former Eastern Nigeria and Mid-Western Nigeria of Dr. M. I. Okpara and Chief Dennis Chukwudebe Osadebey, respectively, no other governments have enacted agricultural development policies that had clear consideration of the Igbo environment, tradition, culture, agricultural productivity and economic well-being. Federal Government's agricultural policies and programmes since 1970 have been geared toward encouraging production practices of increasing hectarage cultivation of mostly, grain products. These policies appeared to have not considered the peculiar conditions attainable in the Southeast/South-south regions and may have contributed to low interest and low productivity of agriculture. Hence, invigorative efforts to revolutionize agricultural productivity in the Ndi-Igbo areas of the South-east and South-south regions (SESSR) should include the following components of planned strategy for sustainable food and agricultural development: (1) Revisit the issue of excised Ndi-Igbo peripheral and perimeter farm lands to the benefit of neighbouring states during the 1967 creation of East Central State as civil war military strategy; (2) development of new agricultural policy that is specific to SESSRs; (3) Grand design to undo the destruction of arable land due to erosion and reviewing methods of allocating sustainable land use for agricultural purposes; (4) reviewing appropriate production and processing technologies for improvement of agricultural yields and food security. (5) Consideration of Low-input sustainability in production and processing of foods. (6) Making agriculture socially and economically attractive to new generation: (7) Consider zoning of agricultural products and available cultivable land; (8)

Diversification of agricultural productivity in both plants and animals: (9) Ensure that decision makers and farming communities understand the importance of introducing appropriate technologies for both food production, food processing and food preservation and the identification of specialized bulk and retail markets for South-East and South-south agricultural products. In all, the objectives include creating training and employment opportunities of the Nigerian youths and the unemployed, increasing local food productivity in order to reduce Nigeria's dependency on imported food, improve the nutritional status of the less privileged in the society, and improves Nigeria's chances of gaining Food security status. Source of funding the activities will be discussed and the implication of employing the synergism of public, private (institutional) partnership for improving food production and processing success levels.

1.0 **Introduction**

Agriculture still employs approximately 68 percent of Nigeria's workforce (Balogu, 2014) and accounts for its 48% gross domestic product (GDP). With a wide range of climate variations that permits the production of wide-range of meat animals and cultivation of a variety of cash crops. The livestock produced include cattle, sheep, goat, and fish. The cash crops include cocoa, citrus, cotton, groundnuts, palm oil, palm kernel, and rubber while the staple food crops include, yams, corn, rice, cassava, coco-yams, cow-peas, potatoes, millet, plantains, bananas, fruits and vegetables. While about 90 percent of total food production in Nigeria comes from small farms, 60 percent of the Nigerian population earn their living from the small farms (Oluwalayo, et al., 2008). But generally, major production improvement programmes have focused on cultivation of larger pieces of land. However, increasing population densities, limited cultivatable lands, and further encroachment of housing and village expansions have minimized chances of expanded farming in the Igbo areas of the South-East and South-south Geopolitical regions. Apart from the governments of Premiers of former Eastern Nigeria (1960 – 1966) and Mid-Western Nigeria (1963 -1966) of Dr. Michael Iheonukara Okpara and Chief Dennis Chukwudebe Osadebey, respectively, no other governments have enacted agricultural development policies that had clear consideration of the Igbo (and its neighbouring) environment, tradition, culture, agricultural productivity and economic well-being.

The Federal Government of Nigeria's agricultural policies and programmes since 1970 have been geared toward encouraging production practices of increasing hectarage[1] cultivation of mostly, grain products, tuber

---

[1]**Hectarage** is area measurement in hectares of mostly lands used for either agriculture or forestry. **Acreage** is area measurement in acres.

crops, cash-crops such as oil-palm, cocoa, rubber, ground-nuts. These policies appeared not to have considered the peculiar conditions attainable in the Southeast/South-south regions. The peculiar conditions include (1) land constraints that make it difficult for farmers to survive from income from 'large hectarage' farm production alone without the development of policies that will target sustainable technologies for intensive cultivation in small farms; (2) Having one of the highest population densities in world, means that there are limited space for expansion of farm land and increased agricultural hectarage; (3) Sustained diminishing interest in production agriculture since the end of the civil war which may have contributed to low interests and low productivity of agriculture, in the Igbo areas; (4) Generally, Nigeria's sustained increases in population with highest densities found in Ala-Igbo (Igbo areas) means that farmers are continually losing precious farmlands to residential areas; (5) The ever-increasing unemployment rates in the country with increasing numbers of university graduates who believe that government has the obligation of providing graduate-level employment. Hence, invigorative efforts to revolutionize agricultural productivity in the Ndi-Igbo areas of the South-east and South-south regions (SESSR) should include but are not limited to the following components of planned strategy for sustainable food and agricultural development:

2.0 Policy Development
2.1 Nigeria National Policy

It was a welcome understanding that the Federal Government of Nigeria under President Yar'Adua gave high priority to the achievement of food security in the President's program. Yet the future looks glimmer for Nigeria with less interest shown by its youths in farming and other agricultural professions. Nigeria's population continually increases with the country's population which was 115 million in the year2000 is now (2014) estimated to be 176 Million with projections up to 258 million in the year 2051. And the fact that its agricultural productivity continually decreases should pose great concern to knowledgeable Nigerians. In fact, Nigeria spent over N170.2 billion on imported food between 2001 and 2006 alone (Sanusi, 2013, Balogu, 2014). For this reason, the President Umaru Yar'Adua's Federal government panicked and announced the allocation of more than N82 billion (unspent) for the purchase of foreign rice alone. Although the plan did not materialize due to public outcry, it showed the extent of Nigeria's dependency on imported food for which Nweze (2003) defined as a 'dangerous indication of the dwindling farm productivity" that would jeopardise Nigeria's prospects of enhancing its food security.

It is therefore, imperative that new and revamped strategies must be used to prevent over-dependence on imported foods. The strategies would include but not limited to: (1) Legislative strategy which will include (a) allocating state governments with responsibilities of championing production of certain cash/major crops and staple food stuffs for the benefit of the entire country; (b) Widening the responsibility scope of the Ministry of Agriculture to includes target-driven agencies that focus on specific food and environmental related issues such as production, value-added processing and storage, resource conservation, animal and plant protection and regulations if it has not yet been done; (c) Environmental management geared toward soil conservation, environmentally-friendly irrigation programmes including run-off water channelling and planned reforestation. The current trend in the world when climate change has become a challenging issue includes the adoption of sustainable development factors in environmental and infrastructural undertakings. (2) Re-culturalization training of the youths toward the improvement of agricultural and gardening skills through curricular enrichment reviews that stress food production and food security from elementary school, through secondary school to tertiary education levels. Sustainable agricultural development should include environmental cleanliness, especially, water and air, forestry conservation and preservation. Obviously, with the advent of boarding schools and majority of parents living outside the farming areas of the country, most of the youths have acquired very limited exposure to farming and food production but have sharpened appetite for foreign-looking processed food products. (3) Development of national problem-solving research and extension programmes in higher institutions and proper channelling systems for research outputs to business and production communities need to be addressed. These programmes will be geared toward tapping into the expertise of agricultural professionals in State and Federal Agricultural Institutions to conduct state-wide or region-wide and federal agricultural and food processing consultations, training, extension information dispersion, formation of cooperatives, and marketing. (4) Operational and Production Strategies in Nigeria's sustainable agricultural development would involve long and short term strategies. These would include (a) Increasing the total acreage under food cultivation from the current four million to eight million hectares in the next five years; (b) provide easy and proximal access to market for all farmers: the lack of a ready produce market for small farmers discourages large acreage farming and entry of the farming business by the youths who have little interests in marketing their products by the road-side. (c) Providing affordable prices for fertilizer and seeds, and providing comfortable environment in farm communities. A synergistic effort between Nigerian agricultural professionals abroad and home would obviously improve the countries agricultural outlooks through sharing production ideas and consultations.

2.2 **New Agricultural Policy for South-East and South-South Regions:**

Although the forced land allocation for Ndi-Igbo appeared too small for their representation in Nigeria, there are substantial evidence to show their close relationship with all the adjoining Ethnic Groups with "I" initials (Ibibio, Iddo (Edo), Idoma, Igala, Igbira, Igbo, Ijaw, Ikoi (Ekoi), and Itserkri). Without the antagonism that has been associated with the Civil War, it would have been easy to suggest that the lines of demarcation between Ndi-Igbo and their close neighbours would have been somehow, blurred.

2.2.1 **Relative Agricultural Potentials**: The total area of South-East and South-south Geo-political regions is about 12.5% of the total area of Nigeria but it contain some of the most densely populated states in the world. Land is very precious and cost of acquiring land for farming may be cost-ineffective. This issue should represent one of the primary agenda topics that ought to be addressed collectively by the representative governments of the South-east and South-south Geo-political regions or at the minimum, by the state governments with substantial Igbo indigenous inhabitants. Almost All South-East and South-south Geo-political Regions are located within Rain Forest Areas This urgurs well for round-year cultivation of most of food crops and nearly all the crops could be cultivated with little or no irrigation requirements. However, the land mass allocated to Ndi-Igbo appears to create problems with the large farm cultivation of crops and livestock production system.

2.2.2. **Land Allocation:**
Although the land allocation for Ndi-Igbo would appear two small for their representation in Nigeria, (Figure 3) there are there are great opportunities for structuring very successful agricultural and food security programmes in Ala-Igbo (Igbo-land) with careful strategic planning, scientific, technological and intensively innovative intervention of Ndi-Igbo farmers, business men, and state governments. Such plan should also seek collaboration between Ndi-Igbo and their close relatives in adjoining states. There is substantial evidence based on behaviour and beliefs to show that Ndi-Igbo share close relationship with all the adjoining Ethnic Groups with "I" initials (Ibibio, Iddo (Edo), Idoma, Igala, Igbira, Igbo, Ijaw, Ikoi (Ekoi), and Itserkri). Without the antagonism that has been associated with the Civil War, it would have been easy to suggest that the lines of demarcation between Ndi-Igbo and their close neighbours would have been somehow, blurred. Moreover, the types of crops and livestock produce by Ndi-Igbo are more or less similar to those produced in the adjoining states and ethnic groups.

2.2.3 **New Policy for SouthEast and Southsouth Regions:** The new policy ought to consider changes in socio-economics, educational undertakings, and politics of the regions. While attending schools and gaining higher education have exposed people of the South-east and South-south regions to new opportunities, higher economic-earning expectations, and higher social strata, they have also increased the peoples' cost and standard of living to uncompromisingly higher levels. Hence their new expected employment should include those that would support their higher expected standard of living. Regrettably, the output and expected income from agriculture and farming as they are practised today fall below expectation of the new generation of Ndi-Igbo and Nigeria in general, thus putting the prospect if improving national food security in jeopardy (Nweze, 2003; Ndifon et al., 2012; Balogu, 2014). It is imperative that the new policy should review several items that should enhance opportunities for the new generation-farmers. These items include but are not limited to the following:

a. Land issues: There should be opportunities through State Legislation to designate specific land areas as **'agricultural or farming land only'**. The Federal Government of Nigeria , State and Local Governments should insist on the allocation of designated areas for building residential homes, forests for conservation, forests for preservation, riparian areas, hunting, parks and farming areas. The current recklessness in the building of residential areas in the most arable and fertile lands to the detriment of farming and other land-use projects should be prohibited. Because the population densities of the South-east and South-south regions are among the purposes of efficient use of available land. Building policy should include deciding location and the sizes of houses at different quarters in cities and local governments. The method of allocation of land for residential housing should result in efficient use of land to maximise social and economic benefits. With regards to farming and gardening, as much as possible, flat pieces of land which have high silt sediments and humus should be left for food production.

b. A well planned agricultural and forest products' systems should be enacted. Under this plan, the kind of crops and production intensity should be defined to ensure environmental sustainability.

c. High-yield, short growing season crops, should be recommended and considered for food cultivation in the limited available land in the South-East and South-south regions of Nigeria. Other efficient methods of using available land resources to maximize productivity, such as mixed farming (Bourn, et al., 1994) should be studied and recommended.

d. Efforts should be made to enforce anti-erosion regulations at all time.

e. Development or the acquisition of agricultural appropriate technologies that would be efficient, affordable, and portable, and constructed for achieving desired objectives.

3.0 Issue of Land Allocation and Population versus Agriculture.

Farmland is one of the most indispensable factors in farming. Ownership, land accessibility and hectage or acreage available mostly determines the kind of farming and level of productivity. Table 1 and figure 1 show the area and percent area that are occupied by each of Nigeria's Geo-Political Regions, and their relative population densities. These factors would determine the level of availability of arable land for production agriculture and environmental management. While the Northern Nigerian Geo-Political regions occupy the highest percent land masses which ranges from 21.08 percent for North-West to as much as 33.61 percent for the North-East Geo-political region. On the other hand, the South-East Geo-Political Region occupies barely 3.17 percent. Obviously, this land distribution did not favour the South-Eastern states which are the off-shoots of the former East Central State. The objectives of the sudden creation of twelve states in 1967 by the Federal Military Government of Nigeria were more for their military advantage than for the economic and cultural nedds. Hence, the creation of East Central State had the clearest definition of strategic military initiative in 1967 to strangulate the efforts of secessionist Eastern Nigeria. So, the Federal Military Government carved away several Igbo land areas, peripheral farm lands, forests and wilderness to the favour of other newly created non-Igbo states. This action greatly weakened the ability of the former Government of Eastern Nigeria to prosecute the civil war to a successful end. But the war had ended since 1970 and it is now important that war-time strategies which continue to undermine the citizenship of Ndi-Igbo in Nigeria should be reverted. Prior to 1967, the people of the South-east (in former Eastern Nigeria) had enough agricultural and forest lands to lead and agrarian life. Otherwise, it would have been very hard or near impossible for an indigenous population that occupies only three percent (3%) of a country as large as Nigeria to have as much influence as Ndi-Igbo in Nigeria. The issue of signed-out Igbo land should be addressed to enable Igbo states to make their own contributions toward the attainment of food security by Nigeria.

Table 1: Relative Regional Population and Area*.

Geo-Political Region	Population	Area (Km^2)	Density (Population /Km^2)	Area as % of Nigeria
North-East (State Average)	23,320,614 (3,331,515)	303,824 (40404)	78	33.61
North-Central (State Average)	18,861,056 (3,143,509)	218,847 (36,475)	87	24.21
North-West (State Average)	31,438,295 (5,239,716)	190,561 (31,760)	165	21.08

South-South (State Average)	21,014,647 (3,502,442)	85,303 (14,217)	247	09.44
South-West (State Average)	27,581,992 (4,596,999)	76,761 (12,794)	359	08.49
South-East (State Average)	16,381,729 (3,276,346	28,655 (4776)	686	03.17
TOTAL	138,598,333	903951	154	100.00

*Table was developed with the Data of 2006-03-21 Nigerian Census Provisional Results

Figure 1: Relative Percent Land Allocation to Geo-Political Regions

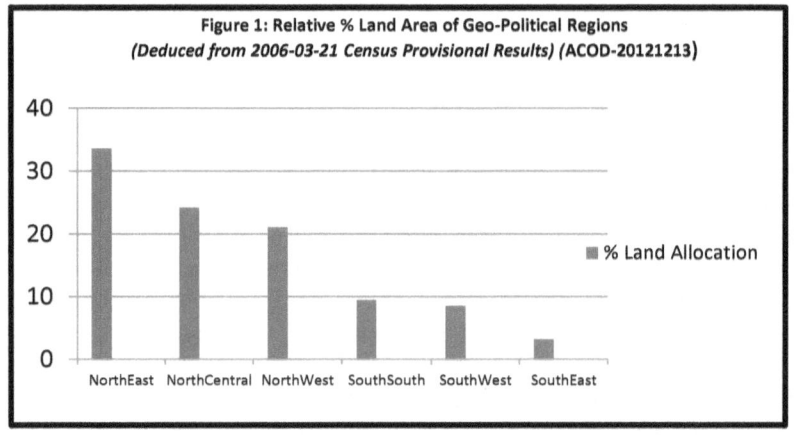

4.0 Erosion and environmental management

The development of a grand design to undo the destruction of arable land due to erosion and reviewing methods of allocating sustainable land use for agricultural purposes are of paramount importance in South-East and South-south regions (SESSR) of Nigeria. Geographically, the SESSR of Nigeria are in the part of tropical Africa that has very fragile and erosion-susceptible soils. On the average, it has about only six inches (15.24 cm) of topsoil which ought to be managed very carefully. Prior to independence in 1960, very thick rain forest covered the land mass that was susceptible to erosion. Unfortunately, during the **Nigeria civil war of 1967-1970, there were massive construction of military defensive trenches and combat barricades by the** warring armies of the Federal Republic of Nigeria and that of the secessionist Biafra.

Also, there were massive construction of access-roads for easy and convenient movement of military combatants and armoury, introduction of heavy motorized bush-clearing equipments and weapons, rocketing and bombing that tore through the forest grounds which drastically disrupted and exposed the Southeast topsoils. Over the years, these soil surface disruptions created tracks and forced gutters for run-off water that quickly washed-off the topsoils and eventually became very deep gullies that continued to spread. Without intervening remedies in the past 40 years, these gullies have transformed the whole South-east as one of the most eroded areas of Africa with the farm-friendly humus topsoils totally eroded in most areas. Although, initiation of activities for reclamation of the topsoils in the South-east and South-south regions would ultimately involve the attention of the State Governments, but it is the **Federal Government of Nigeria that would bear the ultimate responsibilities of restoring the topsoils stopping erosion of Eastern Nigeria** because it was the activities of the civil-war that initiated the massive erosion problems that is being experienced by the South-east and South-south regions.

It will also involve the employment of experienced agroforestry personnel, forest range managers, agriculturalists and environmentalists to work synergistically to restore the topsoils, and repair the damage to the Southeast and South-south environment. Indigenous perennial plants such as the oil bean trees, and adopted cover plants Kutzu plants, and dual-purpose wind-brakers, such as palm-trees could be used to checkmate erosion in the most erodible areas. A mixture of some grazing pasture grasses such as *Andropogon gayanus, Panicum maximum* and tropical legumes (Ademosum, 1976; Abayomi, et al., 2001) would be helpful in providing topsoil cover against erosion agents.

5.0 Appropriate Food Production and Processing Technologies

The act of reviewing appropriate production and processing technologies for improvement of agricultural yields, processing, preservation and food security is an important task to be accomplished before implementing a successful food production and processing plan. There are continuing clamour for the introduction of agricultural/farm mechanization and appropriate food processing technologies for the crops produced (Balogu, 2014). Appropriate mechanization should encourage individual ownership of farming equipment that is affordable and economically beneficial. For the South-east and South-south regions, with relatively small cultivable land, small affordable agricultural mechanization and processing technologies would be preferred, cost-effective and beneficial. Soil tilling equipment, small harvesters, and food processing machines would be preferred.

Preservative processing such as fermentation, dehydration and concomitant packaging technologies that will need the employment of physical labour would be more economically beneficial than the acquisition of expensive automated equipments which would require larger amounts of raw food materials to operate and fewer physical labour. Indigenous or Local automotive engineers who are currently located in the South-East and South-south regions could be contracted to develop farm and food processing machineries that could serve South-East/South-south farmers and out-of-region farmers who share the peculiar circumstances with the farmers in the South-East and South-south regions. Making contacts with automobile developers such as Engineer Izuogu of Imo State and Innoson who have assembled vehicles and other machineries in Nigeria could be very useful.

6.0 Sustainable food production and processing in South-East and South-South

With the paucity of cultivable land mass with about only six inches of fertile topsoil coverage, low-input sustainable agriculture would be much recommended for the South-east and South-south regions. This system would not only reduce erosion, increase and sustain higher agricultural productivity, but it will also contribute toward reducing factors that enhance climate change. A modified method of the campus greening project of Ibrahim Badamasi Babangida University, Lapai which was recently published and presented at the conference of European Association of Sustainable Environment, Germany could be used in an intensive agricultural production plan such as the one being recommended to the South-east and South-south regions of Nigeria. The plan sought cover all campus ground with either green plants, concrete or asphalt for the purposes of carbon sequestration and reduction of the erosion of the top soil (Balogu, et al, 2013; Balogu, et al, 2014). Through the adoption of sustainability in agricultural production, Nigeria would have contributed its quarter in international sustainable environmental pursuit.

6.1 Improving Productivity Recommendations: With regards to the small-farm land holdings in the South-east and South-south regions, low-input sustainable farming and mixed-crop farming would be most desirable. In addition to this, **the adoption of a semi-vertical integrated management system that includes a small-self managed post-harvest processing for farm crops would help in increasing small farmers' income from agriculture.** Under this plan, it is expected that more farmers would be operating on part-time basis in order to give themselves the opportunity of engaging in non-agricultural employment to supplement their incomes. In order to increase agricultural income, producers should engage in intensive farming of early-maturing crops to allow for two harvest periods on the same piece of land per growing season.

The adoption of parallel or serial multi-crop species intercropping would be highly recommended. Specifically, high yielding, short-term but labour intensive crops would be most desired to help provide employment for the large number of unemployed citizens. Because of the existing circumstances that includes limited acreage, it would not be out of place to recommend the development of new or modified technologies that interface in production agriculture and post-harvest management. The application of new or modified technologies that maximize the efficient use of cultivable land and space for food production and food processing would be very appropriate. South-East and South-south could introduce region-wide policies for the allocation of land for agriculture and modify location and space for housing in order to increase available cultivable land. In extreme circumstances, innovative combination of technology and management skills could be adopted for both vertical and horizontal expansion of cultivable land and space for both crops and livestock production.

7.0 Ensuring that Agriculture Stays Attractive to New Generation

New generation of Nigerians should be cultured into appreciating agriculture and through training, pride of being a farmer and food producer could be re-inculcated into the youths and farming. The current practice of recommending farming for only the poor and jobless reduces attractiveness of agriculture. Farming should be seen as a profession or hobby for all those individuals who find specific interest in farming. The importance of agriculture in food security, national security, national economy and environmental sustenance should be thought to citizens beginning from primary school to tertiary education levels.

Celebration and competitive culture within the agricultural profession should be re-introduced. The new yam festivals (that include cultural singing and dancing) among farmers and farming villages; competition such as:

(1) the producer of the biggest yam or cassava tubers competition;
(2) the fastest climber of palm trees, palm-wine producer (tapper) with sweetest fresh wine ought to be re-introduced to stimulate the interests of the young people.

Farm communities should be provided with adequate living facilities and modern infrastructure to avoid migration of young farmers from villages (Oshiokaya, 2003) to large cities where the convenience of electricity, portable water, good roads, access to food ingredients and beverages abound.

8.0 Consideration of Zoning of Food Production and Cultivable Land

In view of fact that Ndi-Igbo belong to agricultural regions of multiple state governments with independent administrations, it augurs well to suggest that each of the contending states to select and concentrate most of their funding efforts to producing one major/cash crop and one prime food crop or livestock. Other minor crops should also be produced small but intensive scale to maximize profitability for the available cultivable land. This would help advance effective and productive utilization of available state and Federal agricultural funds. States and farming communities should vigorously pursue available funding opportunities for agricultural production and processing. Lagos State Government recently disbursed the sum of $7.35 million, (N882 million) funds from the World Bank Assisted Second National Fadama Development Project (FADAMAII) for the benefit of about 1,700 farmers in cooperatives and local infrastructural development (Akoni and Olowoopejo, 2009).

State Governments in the South-East and South-south regions should aggressively pursue national and international funding opportunities for the benefit of technology acquisition of increasing food production, processing, preservation and storage. This could be done by planned cooperative strategies that will aim at finding and adopting measures that collectively improve productivity (Okuneye and Adegbite, 2014) identity markets and maximize farm incomes. Governments of the Southeast and South-south Regions could borrow from the establishment of a Cooperative Bank of Eastern Nigeria in 1954 which was committed to lending money to farmers who are organized in cooperatives for improved agricultural productivity.

As at the moment, most of the cash-crops or major crops in Igbo-land (Ala-Igbo) are qualitatively and widely distributed among the South-East, South-South and their neighbours groups with adjoining states. Table 1 shows the wide distribution of livestock, cash crops and food crops production in the pre-dominantly, Igbo states and their neighbours. In order to increase productivity, the governments of the South-East and South-South regions should consider allocating specific crops' production to specific states as the "flagship" producers for each of the crops for the entire regions. This policy would encourage consolidated state budget allocation, implementation and with visible food yield results. It has the advantage of publicising farmers' efforts, improving productivity, enhancing prestige, dignity and economic well-being of the farmers.

Table 1: Suggested Qualitative Model for Improved Production Cash/ Food Crops and Livestock

STATE	**CASH CROP (S)	FOOD CROP (S)	REMARKS
ABIA	Oil Palm, Poultry, Cassava, Maize.	Horticultural Crops Cocoyam, Plantain	Erosion Controlling - Food Trees, Oil-Bean, Cashew, Ugwa (Ugwha)
Anambra	Oil Palm	Cassava, Potatoes Plantain, Fish	Erosion control Food trees, Oil bean (Ugba),
Benue*(Idoma)	Yam, Rice, Cassava	Vegetable, Fish	
Delta	Rubber	Cassava, Fish Farming, Snail	Vegetable
Ebonyi	Rice, Yam,	Potato, Beans, Vegetable	Vegetable
Edo* (Iddo)	Rubber, Cocoa	Cassava	
Enugu	Poultry, Livestock	Vegetables, Yams, Beans (Tofi); Cassava	Cashew, Ugwa (Bread Fruit), Livestock,
Imo	Oil Palm, Poultry	Plantain, Banana, Cocoyam, Pepper, Garden Eggs; Maize	Oil Bean, Cashew, Ugwa (Bread Fruit),
Rivers	Oil Palm, Fish Farming	Vegetables, Plantain, Cassava	Maize
Akwa_Ibom*	Oil Palm, Cocoa	Cassava, Vegetable	Plantain, Banana
Bayelsa*	Fishing	Vegetables	
Cross-River*	Oil Palm, Livestock	Cassava, Vegetables, Potato,	Pineapple, Bush Apple

*States inhabited by ethnicities that are regarded as "Igboid" or close ethnic relatives of Ndi-Igbo. These group include the following: Ekoi (Ikoi) in **Cross-River State**; Ibibio in **Akwa-Ibom**; Ijaw in **Bayelsa** and **Rivers State**; Itsekiri in **Delta;** Edo (Iddo) in **Edo State**, Igara in Nassarawa, **Igbira** in Kogi State, Idoma, in **Benue State**.

**Food crops or cash crops are used as matter of semantics. Depending on localities, all the crops may be all cash-crops or food crops.

9.0 Diversification of Agricultural Productivity in both Plants and Animals:
Diversification of cash crops, food crops, and livestock production would be of importance to ensuring that farms are kept productive round the year. There should be the need to centrally produce seeds and seedlings for both annual and perennial crops at the state-level, which should be distributed to farmers during every planting season. While Nigerians' staple foods are not limited to rice, cassava, yams and beans, the provision of seeds and seedlings

banks should be extended to cocoyams, banana, plantain, ugwa (ugwha), tofi beans, maize, fruits and vegetables that have sparing effect on the use of the desired staple foods. Hence, there should be a planned breeding and seed multiplication research and production institutes, seeds and seedling banks that serves the purpose of providing farmers with all seeds and seedlings of all indigenous and adopted crops or plants when and as needed. There should also be the need to ensure that public and private decision makers and farming communities understand the importance of introducing appropriate technologies for food production, food processing and food preservation and the identification of specialized bulk and retail markets for South-East and South-south agricultural products. Using cooperatives' doctrine would be beneficial for the small farms. Because of the paucity of land space, all farms should consider strategically intensive multiple cropping systems with round the year planting plan to ensure higher annual total crop yield to support the farmer economically. The overall objectives therefore would include (1) creating employment opportunities of the Nigerian youths and the unemployed; (2) Increasing national food productivity in order to reduce Nigeria's dependency on imported foods; (3) Improve the nutritional status of Nigerians of all cadre and especially, the less privileged in the society; (4) And improve Nigeria's chances of enhancing its Food insecurity status. The sources of funds and cost implication of the activities should be discussed. Also, for these efforts to succeed, the synergism of public, private (institutional) partnership would be advocated for improving food production, food processing, preservation, and food safety.

10.0 Marketing and Brokerage

For most farmers, the challenge of selling their products is always of primary consideration when deciding annual farm sizes. Most farmers would be pleased to have bulk-purchase systems that would allow farmers to sell their products as soon as they are harvested. A reliable market system allows farmers to be aware of the price of purchase per unit weight (Kg). A very good example of bulk- market for farmers could be a processing company that purchases specific agricultural products for either further processing, preservation, storage or packaging.

1.0   Summary

The South-East and South-south Regions could still be agriculturally competitive with revised agricultural policies that put in perspective, the peculiar conditions of South-East and South-south Regions. Hence, invigorative efforts to revolutionize agricultural productivity in the Ndi-Igbo areaa of the South-east and South-south regions (SESSR) should include the following components of planned strategy for sustainable food and agricultural development: (1) Revisit the issue of excised Ndi-Igbo peripheral and perimeter farm lands to the benefit of neighbouring states during the 1967 creation of East Central States as civil war military strategy. This would return extensive agricultural and forestry land to Southeast for improved planning and production; (2) development of new agricultural policy that is specific to SESSRs; (3) Grand design to undo the destruction of arable land due to erosion and reviewing methods of allocating sustainable land use for agricultural purposes; (4) reviewing appropriate production and processing technologies for improvement of agricultural yields and food security. (5) Consideration of Low-input sustainability in production and processing of foods. (6) Making agriculture socially and economically attractive to new generation: (7) Consider zoning of agricultural products and available cultivable land; (8) Diversification of agricultural productivity in both plants and animals: (9) Ensure that decision makers and farming communities understand the importance of introducing appropriate technologies for both food production, food processing and food preservation and the identification of specialized bulk and retail markets for South-East and South-south agricultural products. In all, the objectives include creating training and employment opportunities of the Nigerian youths and the unemployed, increasing local food productivity in order to reduce Nigeria's dependency on imported food, improve the nutritional status of the less privileged in the society, and improves Nigeria's chances of gaining Food security status. Source of funding the activities will be discussed and the implication of employing the synergism of public, private (institutional) partnership for improving food production and processing success levels. Newly developed or modified technologies in concert of the situation would be very helpful in making the regions' agricultural sector very productive. Federal, State and Local Government should show real interest in the agricultural sector.

Refernces

Abayomi, Y. A., O. Fadyomi, J. O. Babatola, and G. Tian. 2001. Evaluation of selected lugme cover crops for biomass production, dry season survival and soil fertility improvement in a moist Savannah location in Nigeria. *African Crop Science*, 9 (4): 615 – 628.

Ademosum, A. A. 1974. Utilization of poor quality roughages in the derived Savanna zone. *IN:* Loosli, J. K., Oyenuga, V. A., and Babatunde, G. M. Eds. Animal Production in the Tropics. Proceedings of the intenational Symposium on animal production the tropics, held at the University of Ibadan, Nigeria: 26-29 March, 1973. Pp 152 – 166.

Akoni, O. and M. Olowoopejo. 2009. Lagos Disburses N88Million to farmers. *The (Nigerian) Vanguard Newspaper*; Thursday, March 26, 2009.

Balogu, D. O., M. Yakubu, N. G. Obaje, E. Gbodi, R. L. Njinga, A. Mishra, U. U. Elele, B. Jibrin, N. Kumar, T. V. Balogu, I. K. Musa, M. N. Maiturare, and I. A. Kolo. 2014. IBB University Greening Project: A Sustainable development model for African institutions. Development Journal of Applied Sci. and Tech. Research.3 (1):09- 25.

_____ ., D. O., M. Yakubu, E. Gbodi, R., L. Nginga, A. Mishra, U. U. Elele, J. Babangida, N. Kumar, I. K. Musa, M. N. Maiturare, and I. A. Kolo. 2013. IBB (Ibrahim Badamasi Babangida) University Campus Greening Project: A Model for African Greening Environmentalists. International Green Education Event, 2013 *In*: European Organisation for Sustainable Development, Karlsruhe, Germany. *Website* – www.eosd.org.

_____ . 2014. Appropriate Technologies: Food Processing and Preservation as Key to Food Security in Nigeria – Opportunities for Technology Transfer. Second Inaugural Lecture, Ibrahim Badamasi Babangida University, Lapai, Niger State, NIGERIA (March 20, 2014).

_____ . 2008. Strategic and government policy-driven planning and intervention for agricultural development and increased productivity for achieving food security in Nigeria. Paper prepared for presentation at the Annual Conference of the Nigeria in Diaspora Organisation and 4th Science and Technology Conference, Tinapa, Calabar, Nigeria. July 2009.

Bourn, D., W. Wint, R. Blench, and E. Woolley. 1994. Nigerian livestock resources survey. World Animal Review, 78 (1): 49 – 58.

Ndifon, H. M., E. I. Agube, and G. N. Odok. 2012. Sustainability of Agricultural Cooperative Societies in Nigeria: The case of South-South Zone, Nigeria. Mediterranean Journal of Social Sciences Vol. Vol. (3) (2): 19 -25.

Nweze, N. J. 2003. Cooperative promotion in rural communities: The project approach. *Nigeria Journal of Cooperative Studies*, 2 (2): 76-89. *In:* Ndifon, H. M., E. I. Agube, and G. N. Odok. 2012. Sustainability of Agricultural Cooperative Societies in Nigeria: The case of South-South Zone, Nigeria. Mediterranean Journal of Social Sciences Vol. Vol. (3) (2): 19 -25.

Okuneye, P. A. and D. A. Adegbite.(2014 – Downloaded).Agricultural Cooperaives. http://www.unaab.edu.ng.

Oluwalayo, A. B., Sekumade and S. A. Adesoji (2008). Resource use efficiency of maize farmers in rural Nigeria: Evidence from Ekiti State, Nigeria. World Journal of Agricultural Science, 4(1) 91 -99.

Oshiokoya, T. W. (2003). Financial intermediation Resource mobilization and agricultural credit rural subsistence sector. The Nigeria experience sustainable agriculture in Africa, proceedings of the agricultural seminar and research workshop selected paper, University of Edmonton, Africa World Press, Inc. Trenton, New Jersey. P. 121.

Infrastructure and Education as
the Basis for Industrialization
by
Prof. Bath Nnaji

Introduction

I would like to commend the organizers of this Colloquium for conceiving it. It is an idea that is long overdue especially since some people in Nigeria have begun to think that the time of Igbos has passed and that they are of no consequence anymore in the scheme of things in Nigeria. In particular, I applaud the effort of Professor Uzodinma Nwala and his team who maintained constant vigilance over those of us invited to speak here. I thank you for working tirelessly to enliven the spirit of our people. I believe that we are now at a point where all hands must be on deck to find a path which will lead us as a people to economic, social and political empowerment, while reverting to the social values which have guided our people for generations. The very inclusion of intellectuals to speak here implies that we are interested in re-adopting our traditional values in which our society attached value to creativity. In fact, every great society must have the architects and the builders. Igbo land traditionally, has the ideas, men and the implements. You cannot have one without the other. We have however more recently neglected to even consider the architects and the builders among us. In the last two decades, some of our people threw all the Igbo values to the wind, especially the one having to do with *Igwe bu ike*. Many of our brothers and sisters decided that it is better to mortgage our entire people, our mothers and fathers, our commonwealth, our conscience, our dignity and moral values in pursuit of wealth and power.

In the mid-90s, I participated in the Vision 2010 Committee. The Committee decided not to spend its time lamenting Nigeria's past inadequacies, but rather to concentrate on where we are, where we want to go, and how to get there. We all found it quite refreshing. It was not because we wanted to forget the past, or that we were ignorant of the importance of history in shaping the future. It was rather that Nigeria can get bogged down with the past and forget about looking for how to navigate the challenges that exist in order to land us safely into a brighter future. For this reason, I will not spend too much time castigating our previous inadequacies.

Interestingly, more Nigerians and in particular, the Igbos are moving from rural communities to urban centres. They are abandoning the traditional indices of wealth for those that can be obtained from the townships. Still, over two thirds of Nigeria's population resides in rural areas. With the oil induced income gap between the rural and the urban dwellers, it has become very difficult to justify why anyone would want to stay in the village where there is no infrastructure for advancement. A World Bank study on Nigeria states that "increasingly, poverty in Nigeria is wearing a rural face."

We can look at our large rural population with the perceptive of the glass being half – full or half – empty. The large rural population can be an asset. Many evolving countries engage in various kinds of gimmicks to attract their people to the rural settings to decongest the urban areas and stimulate development of the rural areas. Igbos and in fact Nigeria can take advantage of the existing situation and take development to the people. By empowering our people in their rural setting, we can quickly help Nigeria achieve the much vaunted double digit growth of our GDP. Our people must be empowered to see themselves as productive entities in the country's growth engine. The people of the Southeast have a special role in this. They must work to become the engines, the levers, and the mechanisms that make the system operate and produce. For the purpose of achieving progress in infrastructure, I will concentrate on the Southeast rather than all the locations where Igbo people live. This is because it should be much easier to cause joint venture activities among the Southeast governments than when you include Rivers and Delta States which have other mixtures of ethnic nationalities. Perhaps when we achieve results, it becomes easier to reach out for regional integration. Let me be clear that this posture has only to do with infrastructure. Other issues such as politics, language and culture should not have this sharp division.

With a population of more than 167 million people, Nigeria is the largest country in Africa. Interestingly, the people of Southeast constitute a significant proportion of the population and are the ones that have the propensity to go into uncharted territories to work with the locals for development and economic advancement. Nigeria is a mono-product economy that depends heavily on the oil sector, which contributes 95 percent of export revenues, 76 percent of government revenues, and about a third of the Gross Domestic Product (GDP). The people of this region can look at this state of affairs as a great opportunity to improve themselves and by extension, the country. Since this country is in severe need of economic diversification, the Southeast can take it as a challenge. We should recognize that in order to achieve this, a number of critical things should be in place. We need enabling infrastructure, we need adequate educational system for all rather than for self. In the case of enabling infrastructure which is the major bane of industrialization, it goes beyond what we physically view as infrastructure. It can include physical security, transport, ICT, telecommunications, water, health, education, finance, power and technology. We do not need to take all of these together because tackling some critical ones will address the others. Therefore we should focus on power, education, health and security.

Infrastructural Needs - Physical Security

First is the need for physical security. I was saddened when a very prominent son of the Southeast told me how he built a wonderful and conducive residence in Anambra where he planned to live and retire but that he could no longer live there because of rampant kidnapping in the Southeast and the trauma that follows when someone falls victim. The Southeast governments can join together to address this.

It will also help if the National Conference results in regional governments which will take responsibility for security, education and agriculture rather than the Federal government. Infrastructure for security of lives and property is therefore a critical element in development. Such infrastructure would include equipment for the police, vehicles, radio communications, training, uniforms, weapons and ammunition, criminal tracking devices, appropriate salaries and welfare packages so that the police will not transform from being your protector into your oppressor in order to make ends meet.

Health Care Delivery

In the area of health care, a lot of our people are walking time bombs. Many Nigerians do not undergo basic medical checks, partly because of the cost and partly because of superstition. Many still believe that only native doctors – *'dibias,'* that perform incantations have an answer to their illnesses. Wealthy Nigerians go abroad each year or many times in a year for medical checks. Unfortunately, this is a serious drain on the economy. There are thousands of Nigerian doctors who happen to originate from the Southeast but now in America and Europe, who can run and effectively manage world-class hospitals specializing in a variety of illnesses. It is not expected that the government will be the sole provider of these hospitals. There can be public and private sector partnership hospitals; and there can also be purely private sector hospitals. With the availability of quality healthcare in the Southeast, we should have created a thriving industry similar to what is obtainable in India and at the same time ensured that our people and our industrialists are able to live here economically and in good health.

Let me use the case of Obuaku Medical City project to illustrate the type of medical care industries that can occur when we join together and apply our will. This project is being developed by doctors from this region. This project is ready to be started as early as this 2014. They are discussing with a partner that will develop the place to a world-class standard. They need power and state government full support for other infrastructure including addressing security concerns in the area. They have identified a partner who is also a developer with financial resources. They have over 300 physicians mostly of Southeast origin, all over the world ready to relocate to Nigeria. Their goal is to create a planned medical city that will serve as a medical tourist city for Nigerians and Africans. It will resemble Dubai Healthcare City that has 120 medical facilities and 4000 healthcare professionals. It will also resemble Texas Medical Centre (TMC) in Houston which is the largest medical complex in the world built on 134 acres of land. Obuaku Medical City is planned to be no different from Texas Medical Centre which now serves as the eight largest business district in the United States, right after Philadelphia and Seattle.

The goal is to make Obuaku City have the largest concentration of medical professionals and experts anywhere in Africa just like TMC, but this time it will be our sons and daughters who are leading experts in the world in different branches of medicine like cardiac surgery, ophthalmology, neurology, brain surgery, pediatrics, obstetrics and gynaecology, dentistry, etc. Many of these doctors currently work at John Hopkins, Duke Medical Centre, Texas Medical Centre, Mayo Clinics, Roswell Cancer Institute, etc while some are in private practice. Texas Medical Centre is the largest employer of labour in Texas. Obuaku Medical City could be same in the Southeast, if not the entire country. In 1998, the Chukwu octuplets, (Igbos), the first set of octuplets in the United States, ranging in weight from 11.3 – 28.6 ounces, were admitted to Texas Children's Hospital. All of the seven surviving octuplets went home within six months of their birth. Same can happen in Obuaku Medical City. Think of not having to travel abroad for medical checks and treatment of serious aliment as the Indians are able to do now.

Education

The country's educational system has severely degenerated. Many teachers received educational training during the 'handout ' era and were not able to realize that it is necessary to read books apart from the ones recommended by their teachers and the ones in the syllabus. They in turn have imparted this poor practice to the pupils/students they teach and in the process engendering a belief in these same principles amongst their own students. They understand the handout syndrome. You therefore have students being taught by these teachers who do not have the building blocks for imparting knowledge. We also have schools that lack minimum level of equipment and therefore cannot teach basic skills required by students at the various grade levels. Thus there has been a proliferation of private schools, especially by people who are frustrated with the quality of service coming from state-owned schools. There was such a time that if you attend a government college, you receive first class education. This is no longer the case. The minimum that state governments and federal government should do is to ensure that schools under their care meet minimum international standards of quality. Otherwise those schools should be privatized so that either private groups or religious institutions can take them over and elevate their quality.

Another aspect of education that has diminished or disappeared is vocational education. In developed countries workers trained in vocational institutions like electricians, plumbers, mechanics and other artisans represent a significant percentage of the workforce. In the past in Nigeria, these workers took different levels of City and Guild Certification. The Nigerian Railway Corporation relied on this skilled labour force to operate efficiently. In fact, there is an area in Ogui, Enugu called 'artisan quarters' just to emphasize that artisans working for the railway live there. Today, the institutions that produced these workers who formed the bedrock of operational society infrastructure are few and far between. There is a significant need for reestablishment of such educational processes. It is not everyone that can pass through or even would like to obtain tertiary education as currently instituted.

We need to set a higher standard for students at all levels in our region. Primary school graduates should be able to read, write, add, subtract and speak grammatically correct English and Igbo. The High School graduates should be capable of algebra, trigonometry, essay writing, poems and typing. Articulation and diction is a crucial part of this level of education. They should have good working knowledge of general science. It is no longer possible to function properly in the world without general knowledge of science. University graduates should be superbly articulate and engaging in addition to their specialization. They must have good working knowledge of computers regardless of their major. This is how we can plan for human capital that will support us as the "African Tiger" of the future. This requires community effort and getting our state governments to cooperate. I believe that tasking the "haves" in the villages to contribute to school improvement and setting up community school boards to support the primary and secondary schools will be very helpful. They can ensure that schools have libraries, computers and relevant facilities. This is done in many parts of the developed world, and I have been a Board Trustee of one of such high schools in America.

Can we not as a group decide that we are going to have highly technical universities to prepare for our emergence as a developing economic sub-group of Nigeria? Is it not possible for all the Southeast states to establish Southeast University of Technology for the sole purpose of producing high quality engineers just like the Massachusetts Institute of Technology (MITS), or the Indian Institute of Technology? What is stopping us from adopting the University of Nigeria, Nnamdi Azikiwe University, Federal University of Technology or other centres of academic excellence for the production of first class doctors, engineers and business graduates? What does it take for a few of our people to band together to adopt a particular faculty, or even a department and transform it into a first class programme? In America, an individual, group, company or foundation can endow a professorship in an area to attract national or international attention on that subject or discipline. Then the university will go out and recruit a world class scholar to occupy such a chair (professorship). This is an effective way of improving the quality of education. I believe that these are all achievable. Recently I went out to contribute my own quota to my alma mater – St. Patrick's College, Emene. I got a few friends and our alumni to begin the process of rebuilding the school after the Enugu State government transferred the school back to the Catholic Church. I rebuilt and equipped the science building and helped to attract 100 computers for the students from the Federal Ministry of Communication, and provided them a transformer. I am also working with Enugu State University of Science and Technology to establish an endowed professorial chair in energy studies.

Transport

There is nothing stopping the Southeast governments from working together to solve the crisis situation in road infrastructure. Interestingly, some of the state governments of the Southeast geopolitical zone have done a lot by fixing their state roads. Some still have not done much. We should aim to have smooth movement within the entire Southeast. State governments should not allow the federal roads to go into the level of disrepair we have found many of such roads. New roads to the rural areas should be constructed to open up and connect the communities to development. Southeast states should collaborate with other states outside the region to connect the Southeast to the seaports so that the zone can develop without having its citizens going out to other areas to build industries because of lack of critical infrastructure like good roads, seaports and other basic amenities. The Southeast states can also collaborate on regional rail infrastructure to connect the major cities and capitals of the zone for effective and easy movement of goods and people.

Electricity

After food and water, electricity is perhaps the next most important infrastructure for humans. In a developing economy, this need is particularly acute since there is no way to stimulate development without adequate supply of electricity. The unavailability and unreliability of electricity has prevented Nigeria from leapfrogging into the class of emerging nations. People have had to contend with the hazards imposed by the unreliability of electricity supply. There are so many aspects to the electricity situation in Nigeria today. First, for those who can afford it, they have generators which means they have to invest large sums of money to procure these devices. Then they have to power these generators with expensive diesel. When we built the Abuja emergency power plant in 2001, the price of diesel was N26 per litre by the time we started the conception of the Aba Independent Power Plant (IPP), in 2005, the cost of one litre of diesel had risen to N48. Today, the price unfortunately is in the range of N140 – N150 per litre. Even those who use lamps requiring kerosene have had to pay more. For those who live in the urban areas, many have resorted to having small generators popularly called "I better pass my neighbour" – which produce tremendous decibels of noise as well as the highly toxic carbon monoxide. Many people in this country have all manner of ailments resulting from pollution due to over exposure to carbon monoxide from the generators placed in close proximity to people. On the roads, we are constantly struggling with fuel tankers and trucks hauling refined petroleum products and other goods to various destinations in Nigeria. It is estimated that every day, Aba receives at least 150 fuel tankers loaded with diesel required by industries and generators in the commercial city and environs.

In addition, any household with appliances like television and refrigerator would need a power stabilizer and for big companies with giant equipment, they also need matching giant stabilizers. Such measures are taken to ensure that poor quality electricity would not damage the equipment or appliances. It is particularly challenging for businesses since every business would try to maintain its core business as well as its small power company and deal with the logistics of supplying fuel on daily basis. Yet, these businesses are supposed to compete with their counterparts in developed economies where electricity is simply available from power plants that supply the product at a rate that is affordable, effortlessly and up to standard voltage that will not damage equipment and appliances.

In Nigeria, the cost of self production of electricity with diesel for large companies is in the range of N35 per kilowatt hour (kWh). For smaller companies it is close to N45 per kWh, and for households it can range from N45 – N60 per kWh. It costs a Nigerian company more than double what a company in an emerging or a developed nation pays for the same unit of electricity. I will use Aba to illustrate how to address the severe power deficiency in the country and particularly the Southeast. The growth of economic activities in Aba brought about population growth which attracted breweries and other companies to Aba as well. Soon after, the emerging industrial city began to recognize its acute need for electricity. Unfortunately, the country has sorely inadequate electricity supply to offer. Therefore, some industrialists approached us at Geometric Power to help develop a power project in Aba to address the electricity needs of the city. This was in recognition of the fact that Geometric Power had built a 22 megawatts power plant in Abuja though comparatively small but it has been able to guarantee 15 megawatts of reliable power in the Central Area of Abuja. Furthermore, the then Minister of Finance Dr (Mrs) Ngozi Okonjo-Iweala, came to Aba with the former President of the World Bank Mr. James Wolfenson to meet with small and medium scale industrialists in the famous Ariaria Market.

As we all know, the Ariaria Market, hosts thousands of industrialists who produce everything from leather to garment, plastics and a vast array of other products. The main objective of the visit of the World Bank chief and the minister was to determine what could be done to help stimulate the growth of their (i.e. Ariaria Market traders and entrepreneurs) businesses and improve the quality of their products so that such products can become internationally marketable. The industrialists were asked to name the biggest impediment to their achieving growth and quality. They replied that with reliable electricity, they could go from one production shift to two or three per day. They can run machines which could not be powered otherwise and for which they now use manual processes. They also assured that they could manufacture products with uniform high standards rather than having variations in quality of the same design.

Aba's location is also a critical element for rapid economic growth. It is 50 kilometres away from Port Harcourt and Onne Ports. Thus it can be viewed as part of the seaport metropolis. One can postulate that in no distant future, with adequate infrastructure, Port Harcourt and Aba will turn almost seamlessly into a megalopolis. It is also likely that Aba will expand northward toward Umuahia and westward toward Owerri. This expansion will be spurred by the availability of adequate power supply in the Aba and Port Harcourt areas. This expansion will lead to a significant population growth and what could be a major economic boom powered by adequate infrastructure – oil in the riverine areas and manufacturing in Aba. We can imagine the same economic expansion happening in Nnewi and Onitsha and this will lead to industries lining up the entire Aba –Onitsha road, the

Onitsha-Awka –Enugu Express Way, the Enugu –Umuahia and Enugu – Abakiliki roads. In fact, the entire Southeast can become a vast workshop of manufacturing activities where all manner of products are produced to international quality, ready for export to various parts of the world with the emblem "Made in Nigeria." This is the picture that made the construction of the Aba IPP rather compelling.

From 2004, our company began to look for a formula that would allow for reliable generation and supply of electricity in a given electricity district based on our Abuja project experience. This coincided with when a couple of Aba industrialist had approached me to discuss how we can replicate the Abuja project in Aba. It was also about the same time that the then Minister of Finance Dr Ngozi Okonjo-Iweala met small-scale shoe and leather product manufacturers in the famous Ariaria Market. The Minister in conjunction with the Federal Government gave tremendous encouragement to our company to come to Aba and build a power plant for the commercial city. We requested from the president that in exchange for not asking for the Standard Sovereign Country Guarantee, SSCG, which all the other international oil companies that build IPPs request, that we should be given the Aba territory to supply directly to the consumers. The Federal government consented to this and signed an agreement with our company.

We therefore began the journey to build a power plant unlike any other in sub-Saharan Africa. It is a project that required the construction of 141 Megawatts (MW) power plant, over 110 kilometres overhead lines, 4 brand new substations, a 27- kilometre gas pipeline, an estate to accommodate up to 250 workers, 5 access roads to the power station and substations, and a four-storey office block at a total cost of over $500 million or N80 billion. The unique steel tabular poles employed in the design of the power lines clearly make a statement. For example, the bigger poles and pillars of the network are designed to withstand all but the most extreme of the forces of nature. They are sunk to a depth of 9 meters requiring 120 bags of cement to raise the concrete support for the base of the poles. At the top of the overhead lines, we have fibre-optic cables intended for data transportation and data gathering at various poles within the network. This will help in detecting leakages at various points in the network. The 33 KV line design with its associated steel tabular poles, is the first of its kind in Nigeria. Today, the Aba IPP is the single largest investment in the Southeast.

In summary, despite the numerous constraints we had to face in the integrated power project, the pieces came together very well. The ultimate goal of all units of the infrastructure is to ensure that Aba residents, commercial enterprises and industries, enjoy reliable electricity upon the completion of the project. We cannot say that this project has been easy. We have had to contend with the challenges of being a pioneer private sector power developer in Nigeria. We have survived kidnapping of our expatriate worker, youth and traditional rulers' agitations akin to the Niger Delta; meltdown of the world financial system, the super criminal activities in Aba during the reign of "Osisi ka nku," etc.

Currently, the company that purchased Enugu Electricity Distribution Company is claiming ownership of Aba. This is in spite of the fact that we have an Agreement that predates the power reform. In addition, we have a license based on the same Agreement that the bid documents issued to them as bidders contained in black and white the existence of the Aba ring-fence given to Aba Power Limited; that Aba Power Limited has built all the assets discussed earlier; that the purchasers of Enugu DisCo, only paid $126 for the entire Enugu while our company has spent more than $500 million to build power assets in Aba alone, and that we have the first right to purchase the Aba ring-fence upon privatization. The Bureau of Public Enterprises stated that they have sold the assets of Enugu Disco. One former Supreme Court Justice who heard the story lamented what corruption has done to our nation. Even a layman would know that the shares purchased by the bidders was based on asset valuation.

This can only happen to Igbos. We are the ones that people take advantage of; we are the ones that outsiders set against each other and we gladly go to battle against one another to please others and to display our connections and power. What a pity. Igbos must decide whether showing connections is better for them than having reliable electricity. We have asked the courts and the Federal Government of Nigeria to decide but Igbo also have to decide.

Developing the Aba IPP can be likened to going to the land of spirits to fetch fire. It has been an enormous task to bring the various aspects of the project into a focussed and cohesive endeavour. All in all, we have been able to persuade investors to invest in the project. Diamond Bank in particular has taken the challenge of leading the financing of the project with the tremendous vision of the founder, Dr Paschal Dozie, its CEO and other executives of the bank. Such initiative we believe will in the future become a benchmark for progress as well as how a bank that understands the mission of a project can take the initiative to chart a path in collaboration with a project sponsor such as Geometric Power. It also underscores the very idea of supporting banks owned by citizens of the region.

The Aba IPP is virtually complete. Soon enough, we will begin the technical commissioning of the project starting with gas pipeline, and then the power plant which will be fired unit by unit. Geometric Power is already developing a new power plant in partnership with General Electric Company (GE) of USA. GE is the world's biggest producer of power equipment. This plant which is being built in Ogwe, Asa in Ukwa West LGA is 500mw phase one of 3-phase-project resulting in 1080 MW plant to add to the 141 MW power plant now in Aba at the same footprint. This is to ensure that as Aba and the region grow, there will be constant and reliable power.

Conclusion

We know that if we are consistent in advancing the building blocks, for infrastructure, that we will unleash the creative instincts of our people to drive and to achieve success in productive ventures. Infrastructure will provide the tools with which our great people will apply their ingenuity to create numerous industries that will diversify the economy. We know that infrastructure can help turn the informal sector into formal sector in the Southeast. The shoe producers who make shoes with inconsistent quality and stamp them "Made in Italy" instead of "Made in Aba, Onitsha or Nnewi" will produce consistently quality shoes no matter the number that the whole world will be proud to wear and the producers will be proud to stamp 'Made in Nigeria" on them. We know that the garment makers who produce low grade fabrics and other clothing materials can be converted to manufacturers of sown clothes to be worn in America, Europe, Asia and even in Africa. We know that the Southeast can easily become a vast workshop of entrepreneurs but this can only be guaranteed by the availability of efficient and effective infrastructure. We know that this is a place where all Black people can suddenly be so proud to be part of, all because we CHOSE to do the right thing, all because we CHOSE to work for our common destiny. Let us as a people work together regardless of our differences in order to lift our region into an industrialized part of this nation.

May the Almighty God give us the ears to hear, the eyes to see and mouth to convince our brothers and the common sense to take the right decisions.

Educational Challenges in Igbo Land: Today and Tomorrow
By
Obiageli Ezekwesili

"Let us think of education as the means of developing our greatest abilities, because in each of us there is a private hope and dream which, fulfilled, can be translated into benefit for everyone and greater strength for our nation."

John F. Kennedy

Ndi be anyi dalu nu o! I want to start by saying how blessed I feel to be part of this gathering today, and also how grateful I am for all your support and devotion towards the total emancipation of the Igbo Nation. It is indeed a source of joy to witness such a large gathering of willing and likeminded kinsmen and women. Therefore, I want to thank Professor Uzodinma Nwala and colleagues of the Ala Igbo Congress for making this gathering a reality and most importantly the Almighty God for giving us life and the well being to see this day.

Introduction
A little history will highlight the challenges of education in Igbo land. Only a few decades ago it was "ok" to apply for a bank job with just Standard Six or First School Leaving Certificate. Shortly afterwards (about two decades later), the standards were upgraded to B.SC or HND with some professional topping like ACA, ACCA, CIBN etc. However, since the beginning of the new millennium, MBA and M.Sc. holders are not any more guaranteed a place in the world of work. With globalisation and revolutions in technology breaking down barriers between countries and organizations and as global competition for talents heightens, there are striking consequences for the citizens of every society and community. The adaptive demand of businesses for strategic skills and knowledge globally, is simultaneously lifting the educational requirements across nations. However, within nations, its effect touches the very fundamental issues of the socio-economic structure of society and how to keep educational opportunity fwithin the reach of the common man. The central thesis is that poverty is making it harder for the poorer segment of society to climb the social and economic ladder through education. We therefore need to mobilize key stakeholders in Igbo land to collaborate and tackle seriously the educational challenges in Ala Igbo. Competitiveness of the next generation of citizens of all nations will be much more severe - both domestically and externally- and so only those citizens that have been deliberately prepared and equipped with a strategic edge over their global contemporaries will thrive. Education should be regarded as

an important human and capital/economic development strategy not just for developing the Igbo nation but also for restoring the dignity of our people.

Placed within a historical context, the Igbo nation's great achievements before the civil war were due to educational advantage that followed from a deliberate and targeted "catching up" strategy. It was after all through such noble vision that Igbo icons like Late. Dr. Nnamdi Azikiwe, Michael Okpara and Akanu Ibiam for example, not only received world class education but also excelled in knowledge, expertise and leadership. Even in the then military establishment, it was attainment of an exceptional standard of education that differentiated our brother the Late Dim. Odimegwu Ojukwu and secured his rapid elevation to a position of prominence. There were thoughtful leaders in Igbo land who galvanized the human capital development strategy of that era. It was after all a strategy that promoted academic potential irrespective of economic capability. It therefore ensured that no one who had the potential to excel intellectually was left behind in Ala Igbo.

Sequel to the civil war, the Igbos continued our reliance on education through yet a new round of "catch up" to recover from the profound economic, political and social devastation brought about by the civil war. However, the difference in era was all too obvious. Whereas there was strategic policy in the pre/post-independence Igbo nation approach to developing human capital through education, the post-war era approach was individually oriented with each surviving family investing its sole effort in providing educational opportunities to their children. In the context of the exigencies of the Igbo families' reintegration into the wider Nigerian society, a majority of those without means made pragmatic choice to defer the pursuit of education by their children. This was particularly so for male children who were deployed to trading activities in a quest for rapid wealth to rebuild a shattered household. With this phenomenon came a tidal wave of preference for informal apprentice/entrepreneurship training over more formal classroom education.

There were visible disadvantage in this turn of event as over time, less number of Ndi Igbo (males in particular) were prepared for the formal private and public sectors of Nigeria. The collateral effect was that Igbos lost their policy influence even though by virtue of their trading and entrepreneurship activities, they were often most affected by changes in policy direction and choices of public investment. The upside however that is evident today is that within the indigenous trade and production segment of the Nigerian economy, our people vigorously compete and in many cases dominate in specific sub sectors. Yet, this relative success in enterprise has had serious downside risks which if not mitigated, can completely divert the majority of our people from our primary source of competitive advantage. It could lead to the trapping of potentially world class Igbo talents in small scale business ventures that are easily vulnerable to the political machinations of the economy controlled by those in leadership positions within our multi-ethnic country, Nigeria.

For example, a statistical record of five years primary school enrollment conducted by UNESCO showed that all Eastern states (except Anambra) recorded a double digit decline in enrollment rate over a five year period. While our Western Nigeria contemporaries had single digit declines for the same period, except for female enrolment in Oyo state (see Appendix 1). Additionally, the educational infrastructures in our rural areas are so dilapidated and discouraging that only a handful of students could sit during classes. It is therefore necessary that we plan, and in planning, recognise the organic nature of our education system, which guides for systems approach by considering each level's specific needs and its interconnection to the whole system. It also requires a detailed diagnosis of the educational challenges, trends and plausible strategies that could raise our educational standards and strategically position the Igbo youths in Nigeria.

Diagnosing the Problem

A problem diagnosed is 50% solved, because problem diagnosis enables effective planning and allocation of resources. Consequently, during my time as Minister of Education between July 2006 and April 2007, we analytically and carefully identified that (a) enrolment, completion and progression rates at all levels of education are low; (b) not only are numbers in school low, but the quality of learning outcomes is poor because of ineffective system of staff deployment; (c) the curriculum is not appropriate for the needs of a modern society which seeks to create a competitive and efficient economy; (d) schools are not well managed, and are not operating as effective education service deliverers; (e) the education sector displays serious inequities in terms of gender (females are under-represented in both pupil and teacher numbers), geographical zones, states, local governments, and schools; (f) and there is a sharp divide between rural and urban areas and between the Northern and Southern states.

Furthermore, insufficient attention was being directed towards early childhood care and education. Teachers are insufficiently prepared for dealing with children of this age. Infrastructural support is inadequate and many teachers are not aware of the diverse social networks and possible learning and communication opportunities available. Based on (b) and (c) above, basic education is failing to provide many pupils with adequate levels of literacy, numeracy and Life Skills. Teacher training and development at both pre-service and in service levels is inappropriate in its approach. These factors also contribute to low quality learning outcomes. Throughout the education sector there is infrastructural decay, a lack of teaching/learning materials and inadequate facilities.

Governance and management structures are overly bureaucratic, too centralized in a way that leads to duplication, ineffectiveness and a lack of decisive action. Quality assurance mechanisms are weak despite a plethora of inspection services at all levels of the system. This contributes to the failure of many pupils to reach minimum standards. The education sector both suffers from, and helps to create, socio-cultural problems. This is most clearly evident in the prevalence of examination malpractice and cultism. Dissatisfaction with the public education system is leading to the expansion of private schools with a consequential exodus of influential stakeholders from the state sector to these economic status determined opportunity for quality education thereby leaving behind the majority children from poorer homes in failing public schools.

Growing Towards a Better Trajectory.

Every worthy human activity must be driven by Purpose. It is thus critical to determine from the outset what Purpose will be served by an emergent, concerted and deliberate attention to Education by Ala Igbo. Perhaps, the best approach for determining purpose is to ask some salient questions. The first question is "what type of a future do we envisage for Ndi Igbo not just within Nigeria but also within the global context? What type of Education can herald, construct and sustain that future?

Paolo Freire distinguishes between the "banking system of education" and a liberative education system. He describes the banking system of education as one, which turns students into objects rather than subjects. The students in this type of learning process assume the postures of receptacles and are deemed to be good students conditional on how well they are able to faithfully regurgitate what was handed to them. This type of learning process gives little or no room for originality, creative imagination or critical thinking.

In the "banking system" type of learning, reality is simple, one directional and static. The teacher holds the key to this reality and claims to open it up to the student in as much he or she is docile enough to continue acting as a container. This educational methodology has been used largely in the colonial and missionary enterprise. Those who receive this type of education can hardly contribute meaningfully to social change or the development of thought. They can at best be good managers and maintainers of the status quo.

Liberative education stands in opposition to the banking system. It takes off from the living experiences of the students. They are subjects in the learning process not objects. In this case, knowledge is constructed not imparted. Students are encouraged to critically analyse issues and make their own contributions rather than swallowing whatever information is handed to them. In this educational methodology, reality is complex and progressive. No one presumes to possess its totality. Liberative education enables students to know who they are and imbues them with the relevant tools to chart the course of where they want to arrive in life either individually or collectively. It is only a collaborative education model that nurtures the self-awareness necessary for self-actualization and the confidence required to harmoniously work with people of other affiliations and persuasion to build an equitable society.

Research across several countries has revealed that whereas universalization of access to basic education is foremost, its drawback is that it is not sufficient to improve economic conditions of individuals and their societies. It has become clearer through research that for education to help in promoting rapid economic well-being of larger number of citizens of any country, there must be a deliberate focus on the quality and relevance of the education provided. Quality and relevant education in the context of this paper can be summarised as the form of education that offers opportunity to graduates of the learning process all the relevant socio-economic and political knowledge and skills that are consistent with emerging and future solutions for the known and unknown problems of their communities, countries and the world at large. Central to this therefore, is a system that resolves the knowledge, competence and skills mismatches between education outcomes and labour market needs while inculcating the affective capabilities required for excellence in diverse and rapidly evolving societies.

Our education reforms, whether at the national level or within states, must be anchored on building skills for our economic diversification. The necessity and urgency for this is of course to ensure that we generate the jobs that our economy must create in order to guarantee political and social stability seeing that the nearly two million youth who join the labour market annually with cheerless prospects constitute a credible threat to the nation. We obviously are already experiencing some of the fallouts of disconnect between economic growth and job growth.

The mismatch between the skills and competencies of graduates of our tertiary institution and the demands of the economy is the reason for over 40% unemployment level among the youthful segment of our population. As a matter of fact, in a small experimental initiative to underpin the Tracking Assets for Progress initiative that was part of the reform in 2006/2007, we traced about 120,000 graduates of tertiary institutions who graduated between then and a decade before to learn more of linkages between our education system and our economy, competiveness and jobs. That exercise threw up scary pieces of data. Of the lot, 68% were still unemployed, 16% were underemployed, and only about 16% were well employed in profession or enterprise. One key substrate of the exercise was that the skills and competency disconnect from the world of work was prevalent across certain courses of studies as well as accentuated within certain institutions.

If education only meant the possession of certificates, then I can say that the Igbo people have an overflowing number of people with academic certificates. Nevertheless the possession of these various brands of academic certificates does not seem to reflect sufficiently in issues concerning Igbo collective existence. If by embracing education, we think in terms of enrolling in schools, we can aver that relative to several other states in the federation, the Ndi Igbo states are not doing poorly considering the number of nursery, primary and secondary schools (both those owned by the government, organisations and individuals) scattered all over Igbo land – viz, the overflowing number of students in these various institutions; the higher entry requirements of candidates from the five states for any national competition in education. But, we know that education indexed to global standard, quality and relevance demands much more than even our most talented students are achieving.

One recent measure that helps nations plan their education within such global parameters is World Economic Forum's first *Human Capital Index* has identified the most successful countries in the world when it comes to maximizing the long-term economic potential of their respective labor forces. The Index, which measures countries on their ability to develop and deploy healthy, educated and able workers through four distinct pillars: Education, Health and Wellness, Workforce and Employment, and Enabling Environment. These four pillars should provide an instructive set of organizing framework through which the five Ala Igbo states can strategically evaluate the states of their education systems and sectors. This is particularly so because the common feature of the countries that performed in the top rung of the ranking was the absence or negligible natural resources endowment.

World Economic Forum Human Capital Index 2013: A Ranking of Countries' Ability to Develop and Nurture Human Capital. Therefore, if these top performing countries could attain their present economic status through human capital maximization strategies, then the absence of natural resources like oil and gas in most of the states of the Igbo nation (at least for now) is a condition I absolutely consider an advantage. It should propel the Ala Igbo states to earnestly launch a human capital anchored economic development model even without natural resources receipts from the centre. Thus the knowledge-driven strategy is proven to yield excellent results that are more long lasting as seen in the economic history of countries that occupy the upper rung in global economic rankings. A human capital led economic development strategy is more relevant to the republican, rugged individualism, self-driven, incentive sensitive character of Ndi Igbo. It is in fact the approach that is most capable of restoring the dignity and protestant work ethic of *Ndi Igbo*.

Top 20		Selected Countries	
Switzerland	1	France	21
Finland	2	Korea	23
Singapore	3	UAE	24
Netherlands	4	Spain	29
Sweden	5	Chile	36
Germany	6	Saudi Arabia	39
Norway	7	China	43
United Kingdom	8	Russian Federation	51
Denmark	9	Greece	55
Canada	10	Brazil	57
Belgium	11	Mexico	58
New Zealand	12	Turkey	60
Austria	13	Tunisia	67
Iceland	14	India	78
Japan	15	South Africa	86
United States	16	Iran	94
Luxembourg	17	Egypt	111
Qatar	18	Pakistan	112
Australia	19	Nigeria	114
Ireland	20	Yemen	122

Six Point Proposal for Ala Igbo Accelerated Human Capital Development.

Whereas there are a myriad of initiatives that will be necessary to revamp the education system of any state or country comprehensively, there are some interventions that hold the biggest levers. There are four major initiatives that I consider potential game changers for purposeful education in Ala Igbo. First is, launch a program focused on raising teacher quality across the levels of education in Igbo land. Research has shown that it is the quality of teachers in the classroom that constitutes the single most important factor that determines the performance of students. More than 60% of the learning outcome of pupils and students can be determined by the quality of their teachers. The teaching profession has taken a devaluation which is worst manifested in the Ala Igbo states which have less number of mega economic magnet cities to attract top level talents. Countries like Finland, which have generated the highest value for money in education expenditure, did so by giving priority attention to their policy, system and structures for training teachers. Can the Ala Igbo Congress bring stakeholders across sectors – government, private and civil society, communities; home and abroad to revive the system for systematically producing a new pipeline of "onye nkuzi" of the highest professional variant better than we had in the era that produced the pioneers of intellectual excellence among our people? The pride and prestige of the teaching profession was one of the features of our value laden society of the past. A resurgence of vastly eroded values of dignity and integrity in Ala Igbo can indeed be achieved through an initiative for the teaching profession. To transform our children and youth to critical and creative thinkers, we must first transform their teachers. Can the "Igwebuike" ethos be reenergized among us for the launch of a "Teach America" type program across the five states?

Second, adapt and adopt publicly funded (community aided) low-cost early childhood education (a new design of *ota akara* programs) with a target on reaching as many three year olds of the poor in all communities as possible. Adding this layer to the public cost of funding basic and secondary schools may intuitively seem daunting but it is proven that savings can be generated from tighter management of existing education budget to enable states give more children of the poor this life defining head start. Research shows that by improving public financial management of resources that are poorly spent or lost to corruption in public schools, states in Igbo land could be pioneers in universalizing early child education with enormous benefits both now and in the future. Yet again, evidence from Finland demonstrates that such head start for all gives them and their society a lifelong competitive edge over late starters. That program over the last thirty years has been exhaustively analysed to show that the fiscal implication are very reasonable. Can we identify 5-10 extremely rural communities in the five states and use as experimental models for testing the modernized forms of "ota akara" schools designed as global content programs? If we did and they delivered expected outcomes in line with current research, would we not be motivated to working with various Town Unions to replicate the program across the entire sub region and ultimately for the entire country?

Third is the design of public private partnership models of entrepreneurship, technical and vocational education by adapting the existing apprenticeship models of training in multiple sectors of endeavours among *Ndi Igbo*. When I led the 2006/2007 education sector reforms the signs were emerging that we urgently needed to launch a massive skills building intervention targeted at the young people who were either not accessing formal education or not completing basic education /higher education or were stranded after graduation from general courses at various levels of education without prospects of employment or enterprise. To that end, working with the private sector, we designed and introduced a new layer of national certification known as the National Innovation Diploma is awarded to graduates of skills based institutions which are accredited by the National Board of Technical Education. The Innovation Enterprise Institutions and the Vocational Enterprise Institutions are private institutions that will offer vocational, technical, technology or professional education and training at post-basic and tertiary levels to equip secondary school leavers and working adults with vocational skills and knowledge to meet the increasing demand for technical manpower by the various sectors of the nation's economy. Ala Igbo can lead the way and launch a study of the apprenticeship program of Ndi Igbo people in the informal sector of the economy. Following from the study, can a multi-stakeholders group not be constituted to help facilitate the design and upgrading of a number of VEIs and IEIs in key domains and sectors to bring the thousands of graduates of apprenticeship training in Igbo land with nationally recognized certification of NID?

Fourth, choose two out of the State/Private Universities in the Ala Igbo states and launch a massive upgrading of faculty and facility to transform into top ranking global institution within the next five years. The strategy would include identifying priority departments in sciences and technology around which networks of the Igbo diaspora and counterparts at home can mobilize both internal and external support for raising the standard of these universities to global centres of excellence and their graduates to world class talents. We can link such an initiative to an ancillary program to address the declining rate of students in science, mathematics and technology in secondary schools. Can Ala Igbo move from this Colloquium to organizing a "call to action" meeting on this" low hanging fruit" of a few universities upgrade through strategic mobilization of partners for education within and without the sub region? Five, of the three sectors in our society; namely- government or public, private sector and civil society, the first- that is government - still remains the strongest both in structure and financial capacity to change the state of education in Ala Igbo. To that extent, I suggest that Ala Igbo takes the lead in engaging directly with the five states of the sub-region to commence discussions on the South East Zone Education Reform Program. Such a program will require each of the governments to sign on to peer program designed along the lines of the World Economic Forum program – Human Capital Index. Working in partnership with the states, Ala Igbo can mobilize the diverse talents in the field of education and other relevant professions to support the necessary reform programs to which each government will commit to leading in their states.

Six and finally, let me reiterate a salient point, that the consistency of change has challenged the bed rock of all we have learnt in the past, and to be able to maintain the edge one needs to lean, learn and unlearn to lead. Most of the blue chip jobs today are "Virtual" and those that are not, are highly technical for the average educated person who can do a little more beyond read and write. Thus we face marginalization in the new labour market and some evolving spheres of life. To paraphrase Barack Obama we need to remind our children, these new jobs are about what you know and how fast you can learn what you don't know. They require innovative thinking, detailed comprehension, and superior communication. But before our children can even walk into an interview for one of these jobs; before they can ever fill out an application or earn the required college degree; they have to be able to pick up a book, read it, and understand it. Nothing is more basic and no ability more fundamental. Nowhere will the innovation and change of the kind that President Obama so profoundly elucidates take hold as in the government of countries like Nigeria. As technology forces common democratic and plural values to define citizens' engagement with the nation state, there will be a race to the top from the present bottom in the governance of our country. It may not appear to be so now, but the prognosis of a reinvented country is more likely that the more pessimistic school would have us believe.

Strategic thinking mandates preparing ahead for such a future that would inevitably come. Ala Igbo's best asset would be human capital. For, in a multi ethnic federation like Nigeria, equity demands inclusivity so that all ethnic groups are sufficiently represented in governance for peaceful development. For each of these groups, establishing a systematic approach for developing a pipeline of competent and capable people who can creditably operate the public sector will help accelerate development outcomes not just at the centre but at the levels of local and state governments. The policy leadership process of a New Nigeria would arguably be one which rewards competence above the present norm of a race to the bottom. Part of Ala Igbo's focus on the challenges of education of the future must therefore be to build a pipeline of candidates for public sector leadership both at the technical and political levels. Perhaps, ensuring that two or three of the Universities in the sub-region have strong content of public policy training in relevant departments can be a good start in this direction. There is no legacy more worthy of Ala Igbo than the one Benjamin Franklin celebrated in his famous statement that *"an investment in knowledge pays the best interest."* Ndi Igbo surely need no better *incentive*.

Appendix 1

PRIMARY SCHOOL GROSS ENROLMENT RATE BY STATES AND GENDER					
	(1992-1996)				
YEAR	1996			1992 – 1996	
	M	F		M	F
ABIA	64%	62%		-11%	-10%
ANAMBRA	58%	57%		-5%	-5%
ENUGU	42%	35%		-19%	-17%
IMO	68%	61%		-11%	-11%
LAGOS	47%	55%		-9%	-9%
OGUN	88%	84%		1%	-3%
ONDO	74%	78%		0%	1%
OSUN	107%	107%		-2%	-1%
OYO	91%	93%		-13%	-2%
NIGERIA	75%	65			

Prof. Gordian Ezekwe: The Hall of Fame Medalist for Scientific and Technological Development
by
Alex O. E. Animalu, FAS, NNOM, IOM,

1. Introduction and outline

In 2002, I edited with Anthony Maduekwe of UNESCO, Abuja a report by Nigerian Society of Engineers sponsored by UNESCO, on the Status of Indigenous Technology in Nigeria based on surveys made in the six geopolitical zones of Nigeria. The indigenous technologies were classified under six categories: Pottery & Metal-working, Food Production & Processing, Shelter & Crafts, Transportation, Defense and Medicine. From the report, it became clear that one single person who has made the most significant contribution in all these areas was Professor Gordian Obumneme Ezekwe (May 10, 1929 – June 25, 1997) in his various capacities as a Professor of Mechanical Engineering at University of Nigeria, Nsukka(1975-1976); Director of Research of Projects Development Institute (PRODA), Enugu(1976-1989); Minister, Federal Ministry of Science and Technology(1989-1991); Vice-Chairman & Chief Executive of National Agency for Science and Engineering Infrastructure (NASENI) (1992-June 26, 1997).

On 13th September, 2010, late Professor Ezekwe was invited for post-humus induction into the Hall of Fame for Science (and Letters) sponsored by the Nigeria Liquefied Natural Gas (LNG) Limited in partnership with the Nigerian Academy of Science and Nigerian Academy of Letters: *"in recognition of your [Ezekwe's] life's work – an oeuvre bearing the indelible stamp of your achievement, personality, intellect, and world view, accompanied by its own history of reception, influence, and protégées".* As the invitation was addressed care me, I promptly approached Ezekwe's surviving family who gratefully graced the occasion and later responded to a request for materials to enable us capture and share through this biography, Prof. Ezekwe's world view, determination, passion and love for science, engineering and education. I am therefore writing this biography, not because of being most qualified, but because of my intellectual association with Gordian while he was at PRODA (1976-1989) after he commissioned me in 1977 to do a Proposal for the Development of Science Laboratories as part of the 10-year Research and Development of PRODA at its present permanent site. This request followed the elevation of PRODA (created in 1971 by East Central State Government "to foster the scientific revolution augured by the principle of self-reliance practiced by the people during the Civil War") to a Federal Establishment in 1976 by the Federal Military Government under General I. B. Babangida.

An insight into Gordian Ezekwe's world view followed from his keynote address entitled *"The Influence of External and Internal Politics of Nigeria's Technological Autarky"* presented at the inauguration of the Society for Promotion of Indigenous Inventions and Creativity (SPIIC) in February 1979 and later his October 1993 public lecture at Lagos to the Nigerian Academy of Science entitled *A National Science and Engineering Infrastructure: The Agenda for Self-Reliant Growth of Nigeria* subsequently published in Vol.12 January 1995 Nos.1&2 pages 1-21 of the *Discourses of the Nigerian Academy of Science* when I was the Academy Secretary for Physical Sciences. These demonstration of intellectual comradeship has produced an inner compulsion that goes beyond the numerous tributes to Professor Gordian Ezekwe at his interment rites to the subsequent dedication to him of my year-2000 published book entitled *"Education, Science and Technology Agenda for Nigeria in the 21st C"* with the following "Farewell Eulogy":

Our hearts are heavy with sorrow
Our voices are choked with tears
As we sing this dirge to you
Our great scientist and engineer!
There you lie motionless
On this hallowed ground, Abagana,
Land of your birth.
Where, 30 years ago, fate or was it your ingenuity
Guided your home-made rocket
To decimate in smoldering flames
Deadliest weapons of the Nigerian Civil War
As the convoy made its way into the Igbo heartland.
Having survived the war, you turned your ingenuity over
To the Nigerian nation.
You led PRODA and NASENI
To show us the way to industrialize through self-reliance.
You have done well, Gordian!
Farewell, gentle and inspiring spirit,
As you fly back to your Creator
In the weld of light!
Rest in Perfect Peace.

The *International Colloquium on the Igbo Question in Nigeria* is accordingly an appropriate forum to go down the memory lane in order to highlight certain hot issues in Education, Science and Technology in Nigeria in which Professor Gordian Ezekwe was directly involved in defining where we are coming from, where we are, and where we should be going as we face the challenge at the centenary of Nigeria's precarious amalgamation into a nation of over 400 ethnic groups for administrative convenience of the British colonial enterprise on the eve of the 1st World War (1914-1918), the Holocaust of Igbo ethnic nationality as Biafrans during the Nigerian Civil War (1967-70) and the subsequent marginalization of Igbos in Nigeria's political-economy.He played a unique role as an engineer in management during the Nigerian Civil War (1967-1970) and thereafter.

2. Roots and Educational Career

Professor Gordian Obumneme Ezekwe (B.Sc., Ph.D., Honorary D.Sc., Honorary D. Tech.: Member, Institution of Mechanical Engineers UK, Chartered Engineer; Fellow, Nigerian Institute of Science and Technology; Fellow Science and Engineering Society of Nigeria; Fellow, Nigeria Society of Engineers; Fellow, Academy of Science and Fellow, Academic Institute of Federal Polytechnics), was born on May 10, 1929 at Abagana to Chief Ezekwe Ugbo and Mrs. Maria Nwugo Ezekwe. Gordian grew up in a family environment characterized by discipline, comradeship, agriculture and industry. His father, Chief Ezekwe Ugbo, an influential warrant chief instilled in his children a sense of hard work and humility. Although Chief Ezekwe Ugbo was a polygamist married to 17 wives, his children were united to such an extent that an outsider could not tell that they were not from one mother. The children fitted in wherever they found themselves in life tolerating and accommodating people.

In 1938, Gordian enrolled as a pupil at St. Mark's Catholic School, Abagana, later went over to St. Bonaventure's Catholic School, Nimo in 1940 and in standard 5 he passed the entrance examination into St. Patrick's College (SPC), Ikot Ansa, Calabar, Cross River State. At SPC, he was discovered by the principal, Rev. Fr. Maurice Hayes who was also known as the 'Dean'. Rev. Hayes made sure Gordian was elected the Senior Prefect to whom he delegated the responsibilities of "running" the College. Gordian was discovered because he had unfathomable imaginations, universal thought patterns, admirable indefatigability, administrative ability and advanced independent convictions that set him apart from his peers. Although he was one of the youngest pupils in his class, he was elected the Senior Prefect. He earned the Cambridge School Certificate in Grade One (1947) with exemption from London Matriculation (1947). He passed the entrance examination to University College Ibadan (UCI) to study Surveying with scholarship. Gordian began studies as one of the pioneer students in the prestigious University College, Ibadan (UCI) under Dr. Kenneth Mellamby as first principal. He apprenticed at Survey Camp, Niger State and at the University College Workshop and later passed the London Inter B.Sc. in September 1950. As there was no higher degree in Engineering at the time in Nigeria, he proceeded overseas to University College, Swansea U.K. (1951-1954) where he earned a Metro-Vick Apprenticeship Diploma Manchester (1953) and the

BSc. Hons (First Class) in 1954. Thereafter, he was employed by Associated Electrical Industries, Manchester (1954-1956) and Chadderton Power Station, U.K. (1956). He then gained admission to study for a Ph.D. degree at King's College, London (1956-1959) and earned the Ph.D. in Mechanical Engineering in 1959, becoming the first Nigerian to accomplish the feat in that field. On his return to Nigeria, Gordian was immediately employed by the Nigerian College of Arts, Science and Technology, Zaria as a Lecturer in Mechanical Engineering (1959-1962). In 1962, he transferred to the Ahmadu Bello University, Zaria as Lecturer. While in service, he was Visiting Lecturer at the University of Sheffield, UK in 1964, and was promoted to Senior Lecturer at ABU, Zaria in 1964. Following the political crises in Nigeria, Gordian transferred to the University of Nigeria, Nsukka as Senior Lecturer in 1967. At the outbreak of the Nigerian Civil War (1967-1970), Gordian served as Head of the Rocket sector of the Biafran Research and Production Agency (RAP) beginning from December 24, 1967, and later served as Deputy Head of RAP, with the following responsibilities listed by Oragwu (2010:77): "Production of rocket tubes and rocket launchers; production of rocket war-heads; mass production of bomb and ogbunigwe casings; testing nad loading of rocket fuels and propellants in tubes and devices; conversion of palm oil mills into "mini" petroleum refineries; design and development of the "flying" ogbunigwe casings and launchers, etc.." Known today as Ifite-Ukpo Junction about 3 kilometers from Abagana is the place where on March 31, 1968, the 'catastrophe" of Federal troops occurred when the Biafran army ambushed and destroyed a 96-vehicle column of Nigerian soldiers with locally hand made bombs called the *Ogbunigwe* or bucket bomb. It so happened that Professor Gordian Ezekwe was responsible as leader of the mechanical engineering and metal fabrication unit (code named LD2) for the production of the *Ogbunigwe* casings (Oragwu, 2010:77). Then sometime in mid-1968, Gordian's personality and career defining moment occurred (as recorded by Sam Chukwu and Jeff Unaegbu (2013: 67) in a biography of Prof. P.N. Okeke:

"The 39-year old Dr. Ezekwe was standing inside a shoe factory, waiting anxiously. One of his acolytes, Pius Okeke, had collected some disused fuel to remix it in a hollow vertical cylinder with an opening at the top. This cylinder was part of the machinery right there in the shoe factory at Owerri which rocket scientists had commandeered. In mixing the ingredients required for making solid fuel for rocket. The Biafran rocket scientists were cautious not to allow pieces of iron into the then molten mixture at moment of preparation. Therefore, Okeke had cautiously poured in the constituents through the opening at the top of the cylinder and closed it, expecting that when they were well mixed, he would then open it to allow the homogenous mixture to cool a bit before they are poured out into moulds. Now, Dr. Ezekwe was a man who did an excellent job of supervising his workers. He believed in

assigning people to specific tasks and then supervising them by being there with them as they went about the tasks. To him, the physical presence of a monitor was very important (He was once a Senior Prefect and knew that this strategy worked soundly). Well, in this particular occasion, he was standing at the bottom of the mounted cylinder, waiting for the fuel. Okeke was standing at the top rungs of a ladder from where he could put more ingredients into the mixture through the opening. Unknown to him, there were fragments of iron in the mixture. The iron may have come from the original shoe making process in the factory or from contact with the ground in former explosive moments. These iron fragments caused frictions during the process and gave off little sparks within the container. Okeke began to hear unusual noise within the machine. These sparks soon caused a fire which produced heavy pressure in the hollow container. The pressure caused a thunderous blast off of the mixing inflammable fuel because it could not burst the container. Everything went up and out of the cylinder to the roof like a fierce volcano and then, for the call of gravity, journeyed downwards. Meanwhile, the shock waves had sent Pius Okeke flying like a kite horizontally away from the ladder and dumped him a considerable distance away. The hot fuel splashed heavily and directly on Dr. Gordian Ezekwe before he could get away. The great scientist was burnt badly. He was rushed into a helicopter and flown off to Umuahia where the best Biafran hospital was located. Doctors scampered around trying to neutralize the acid effect of the fuel on his skin. He had to spend many months in the hospital before he could fully recover..."

3: Reckoning Challenges of the Nigerian Civil War

A major rupture of neo-colonialism in Nigeria occurred during the Nigerian Civil War (19671970), because the Civil War reproduced the situation that gave birth to the Industrial Revolution itself in the former Eastern Region of Nigeria that declared itself the Republic of Biafra. As recounted by Professor Ikenna Nzimiro in his 1972-published book entitled *Class Contradictions in the Nigerian Civil War*: "The scarcity of money to buy arms from abroad, the shortage of certain vital products of daily consumption such as salt, kerosene, petrol, medicine, drinks and military weapons compelled the Biafran scientists to come together and set up one of the best organized science groups".

This organization, known as Research and Production (RAP) which was introduced in 1968 under the Biafran Military Head of State, Lt. Col. Chukwuemeka Odumegwu Ojukwu and the Science and Technology (S&T) Group leadership of B.C.Nwosu (nuclear physicist) and deputy leader Gordian Ezekwe (engineer) successfully blended military (Weapons Production) and civilian (Industrial Production) activities as sketched below. Research &

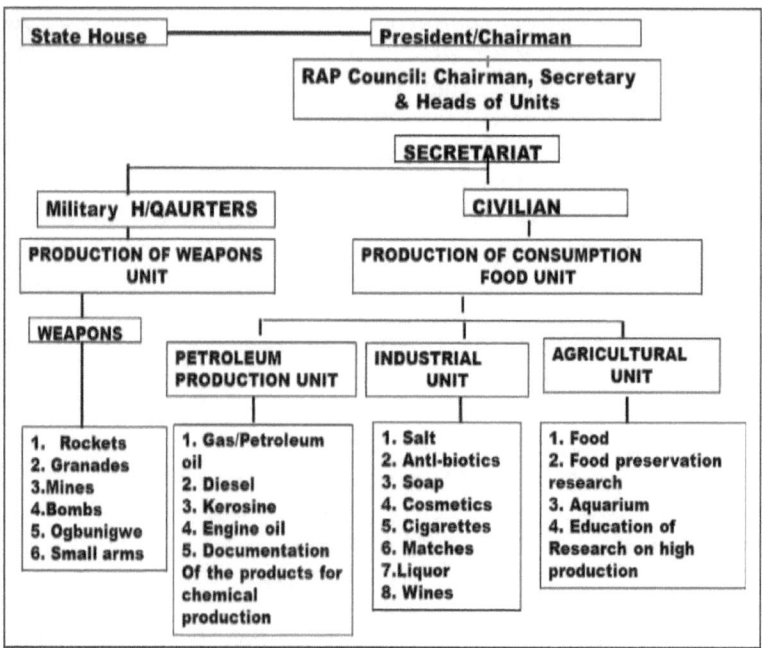

Production (RAP) Organization of the Biafrans during Nigerian Civil War (Source. I. Nzimiro *(1972)*)

RAP became a reproduction on African soil by Africans of what Felix C. Oragwu called **Technology Pull-War Push (TP-WP) Partnership** paradigm on p.7 of his 2010-pulished book (*Scientific and Technological Innovations in Biafra – The "Ogbunigwe" Fame 1967-1970*) or, what is the same thing, **Military-Industrial Complex** ideology used by the imperialist countries for sustaining the momentum of the Industrial Revolution. Two most poignant images (see Fig.1) of the Nigerian Civil War that attracted international attention in 1968 are the bodies of victims of bombing in front of Aba's Principal Hospital and the frightful image of starving children of Biafra described by Michael Mok in the *Time Life Books, New York* (1969) entitled: *Biafra Journal; A Personal Account on A People in Agony*: these images propelled creativity of the Biafran scientists (see, Fig. 2).

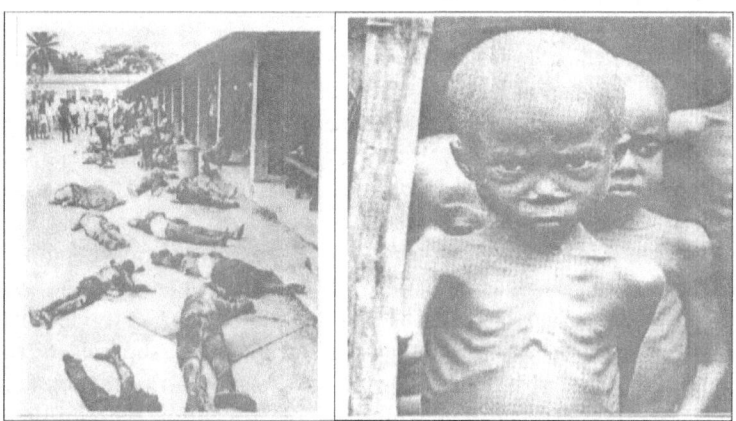

Fig.1 (Left) Bodies of victims of bombing in front of Aba's Principal Hospital (Right) Children at a refugee camp near Aba suffering from kwashiorkor – protein deficiency – have bleached hair and shriveled limbs (after Michael Mok, *ibid*. p.80)

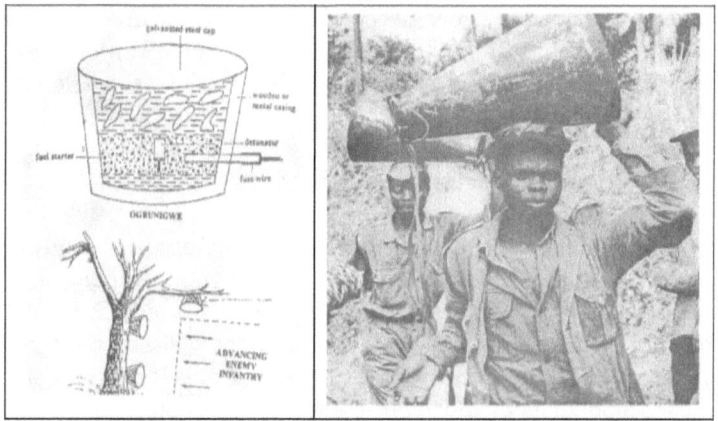

Fig. 2 (Left): Configuration & positioning on a tree of the home-made bomb called "Ojukwu kettle" or "ogbunigwe" (mass killer) created by RAP (E. Arene's *The Biafran Scientists* p.54);

(Right) "Ogbunigwe" being carried to the battle field Courtesy 1969 Time Inc., *Time Life Books* entitled *Biafra Journal* p. 42 by Charles Osborne, Library of Congress Catalogue 69-20394.

4. Post Civil War Career

At the end of war in January 1970, Gordian Ezekwe was a member of the Planning and Management Committee assigned the responsibility of reopening the University of Nigeria, Nsukka. He also resumed work as Senior Lecturer in the University, serving as the Head, Department of Mechanical Engineering, UNN, a position he held from 1970 to 1973. In 1972, he was promoted to Reader. He served as the Dean of the Faculty of Engineering, UNN (1973 - 1976). In 1974, he served as Visiting Fellow to the University of Oxford. The next year, 1975, he was promoted to Professor of Mechanical Engineering, University of Nigeria, Nsukka, becoming the first Nigerian Professor of Mechanical Engineering. In 1976, he served as the Acting Vice Chancellor, University of Nigeria, Nsukka. That same year also, he was appointed by the Federal Government as Director of Research at the Projects Development Institute (PRODA), Enugu. At PRODA, he supervised the production of ceiling board from agricultural waste, lager beer from sorghum, ceramic glazes and colours from local minerals, electrical porcelain insulator etc. As CEO in PRODA, he founded the SEDI-E in 1979. In January 1990, he was appointed the Minister of Science and Technology, a post he held until December 1991. In January 1992, he was appointed the first executive Vice Chairman of National Agency for Science and Engineering Infrastructure (NASENI), until his death on June 25, 1997. Prof. Ezekwe pioneered about 24 inventions including the Cassava Peeling Machine and the Industrial Cooker. Prof. Ezekwe's versatility is best measured in the form of his intellectual range and ability to make important contributions to discourses in science, engineering, management and politics.

4.2 The influence of external and internal Politics on Nigeria's Technological Autarky

G.O. Ezekwe, as Director of Research, Project Development Institute (PRODA) Enugu in lecture delivered to Society for Promotion of Indigenous Inventions & Creativity, University of Nigeria, Nsukka, in February 1979 maintained that the so-called machinations of the industrialised countries, which was highlighted in the 1950's by the term "neo-colonialism", has been one of the regular scape-goats to which our people attribute our slow rate of industrial advance. This attitude may have been generated in the years immediately following de-colonization by the then prevailing theory of a global division of labour, which originated from Europe, to the effect that it is more efficient for certain countries, notably those situated in the tropics, to concentrate on raw-materials production while other countries, notably situated in the temperate zones, should concentrate on material processing and equipment manufactures. More recently, the multi-national corporations emerged by a process of the capable and aggressive business organizations in the industrialized countries swallowing up others, making themselves paramount and practically establishing monopolies in their own areas of production. Some of these multinationals have since extended their influence to Nigeria and the flooding of the Nigerian market with their automated products is seen by many people as a great inhibitor in the process of industrialization through the establishment of home-based industries, quite apart from the threat which these Multinationals pose to national Governments themselves.

Gordian Ezekwe believed that the crude-oil politics of recent years has introduced a new element into the cat-and-mouse game of the industrialized and developing nations. Nigeria, like other aspirants to industrial strength, must initially import a large quantity of machinery from the industrialized countries which will enable her to take off, an importation which is mainly paid for by earning from crude-oil sales. The oil exporting countries exercise power over the price at which oil is sold to the industrial countries. But these countries in turn have the power of manipulating the true purchasing value of the oil-exporters earnings; and also over the prices which the oil-exporting countries must pay for needed machinery and equipment. The net result is that the oil-exporting country benefits no more than before, in real terms, despite increases in the price at which she sells her oil.

According to Professor Ezekwe, another aspect of the international monetary business which retards the industrialization of a country such as Nigeria is the tendency of some citizens of the developing country to deposit monies generated by their countries in secret bank accounts in the industrialized countries, thus depriving their own countries of the use of these monies for national development, while providing capital for the use of the developed country. Such deposits, which must be ill-gotten in many cases, cannot be said to be unjustly procured by the developed country but such a country had nevertheless prepared the ground, by the secrecy which are guaranteed, for attracting illicit deposits.

Some of the internal hindrances to our technological development that are even more detrimental than the external influences include: inappropriate social philosophy; (b) wrong working habits; (c) excessive corruption and (d) excessive indiscipline. Professor Ezekwe believes that we are presently operating a free-for-all social structure which has not struck a good balance between the individual-wealth incentive and the commonwealth objective. The wealth that an individual possesses consists of two types: (a) the wealth which is personal to him and which he can distribute by making a will; and (b) the wealth which he shares with the rest of the population, such as the utilities, the schools, the hospitals, the roads, the communication services, the markets, the retirement benefits for all, the free medical care, free education, etc. The present social structure has elevated the personal wealth to a disproportionate status, in comparison with the commonwealth. This has resulted in the present situation where most Nigerians engage in easy-money endeavours while shunning creative activities which take longer to yield dividends and require a harder and more sustained effort.

Professor Ezekwe castigates the emergence of the oil-economy in Nigeria which has encouraged this situation by infusing monies into the economy in large quantities which are available for appropriation by individuals without these individuals doing creative work in exchange. Thus many professionals have left their professional roles to join in commerce, to the detriment of the creative activities for which they were trained. Farmers left their villages for the towns, to the detriment of industry-needed raw-materials production. Professor Ezekwe advocates a social structure where recognition of the individual is achieved more by contributions to the commonwealth than by the acquisition of personal wealth. As happened in China, it is the concerted effort towards maximizing the commonwealth that nationalism really is; and it is a thorough-going nationalism that will lead to the attainment of national goals.

Gordian Ezekwe sees some of ills of society as being the by-products of the inappropriate social structure. "Each of them again does havoc to our march towards technological strength and industrialization. Consider our working habits. First, there are broadly two groups of Nigerians; those who are self-employed and those who work for wages. The former exert themselves no less than people of hard-working countries, though their efforts are often in non-creative endeavours. The latter are employees of Governments and other employers and they rank amongst the laziest on earth. They consist of two broad groups again, those called "workers" and those called "officers". The officers are supposed to be the leaders but they do not soil their hands. The workers do not soil their hands either except when the officers are watching them. This contrasts sharply with Britain where corporation workers engaged on road repairs will work unsupervised from 7 a.m. to 5 p.m. with only a break for tea and one for lunch. It contrasts sharply with China where even their Chairman Mao carried earth on a dam-site. Our poor appreciation of the indispensability of work has been very pointedly illustrated by the Udoji Commission reducing our working week to that of countries who have automated machines working for them while they themselves have difficulty devicing what to do with their time. The reduction of our working days to five in a week has meant that we are in effect working only 4 days; because of the Monday morning feeling and the Friday afternoon mosque and home-trip preparations. We have to realize that until we have enough machines working for us, we must work long hours. Even when we have machines working for us, we will still need to do some work to attend or drive them and to service and maintain them. Work is also needed to build the machines in the first place, excepting if we are sure that we will always have enough effortless foreign exchange to purchase them from outside, which we now know is not so."

He draws attention to the detrimental effect of bribery and corruption on our technological development including certificates-buying which has the effect of putting untrained people into jobs requiring certain competences, thus resulting in inefficiency and damage of needed equipment. Thus "driving-licenses buying results in man-power needed for development being slaughtered on the roads. Kick-backs in purchasing for Governments result in scarce capital being in-effectively used, etc. But perhaps most importantly, the demoralizing effect of these practices on those who do not like them or cannot participate in them results in lowered productivity in such people. Thus, since people who take part in those practices will devote some of their working time to hatching their plots instead of working, and those who do not take part in the practices are demoralized by them, it follows that bribery and corruption lowers our productivity all round."

"Indiscipline," according to Professor Ezekwe "is again one of the terrible by-products of the inappropriate social structure. It manifests itself everywhere, in the offices and workshops, in the schools, markets, motor-parks and roads, and it leads to poor productivity. Since a programme of technological advancement is a kind of war which is fought against technological backwardness, the nation that can fight it successfully must be disciplined so that all actions are towards the same common purpose. Technology is the child of science and science is the means of achieving order. Indiscipline is disorder. Therefore indiscipline and technology are incompatible." In sum, "although there are external factors which militate against our technological ambitions, the adverse internal factors are of greater influence than these external factors. The social structure which we presently operate is not appropriate for a fast technological progress and it should be scrapped and replaced with a commonwealth-oriented one."

4.3 A National science and engineering infrastructure: The agenda for a self-reliant growth for Nigeria

In an academic public lecture delivered in October 1993 in Lagos, Professor Ezekwe stated that success in the sustainable economic development of any nation is practically impossible today outside the context of the development of a science and technology capacity and the practical application of it to the required extent. He believes that an "indigenous technological capacity can be developed and made functional in fifteen to twenty years time, which is able to harness and apply the country's abundant human and material natural resources to the self-reliant mass production of needed materials and goods, the creation of productive and profitable employment, and the generation of national wealth."

"Over the years," Professor Ezekwe notes, "the country has achieved a high record in infrastructural development; roads, airports, sea ports, communications, educational institutions, health institutions, power supply, water supply, petroleum refineries, steel rolling mills, dams for irrigated agriculture etc. But these installations and establishments, as necessary and indispensible as they are, have by and large served mainly as general purpose assets and facilitators of trade and of consumer goods production. They only form a part of the wider infrastructure which is required for the entrenchment of a scientific capacity and the local production of the capital goods needed for a self-reliant industrialization. That they are not a sufficient infrastructure for a national economic take-off and sustainable growth is demonstrated by the fact that despite our processing them, we are not able to replicate them without resort to excessive and costly importation from overseas, nor are we able to service and repair them without resorting to imported materials and spare parts. The important but few science and engineering infrastructure projects which government mounted, such as the steel projects and petro-chemical industry, were commenced late in the day, despite the fact that in the 1970's, which saw the extravaganza of FESTAC 77 and the Scout Jamboree, money was not the handicap; and despite the fact that steel development was a prominent item in the first National Development plan 1962 – 1968."

Because, these projects, have been started late, and were not pursued with the vigour which their importance deserved, the creation and commissioning of the Ajaokuta Iron and Steel project has therefore lasted several years and is not completed yet resulting in great opportunities for progress towards a national economic self-reliance being missed. It is therefore understandable that the blame for Nigeria's lack-luster performance in post-independence national economic development efforts has been placed by many on our national development planners and implementers, whose vision of the national economy appears to be one of a consumer of industrial products from other countries and not that of a producer of such manufactures.

Ineffectiveness of Past Policies and Strategies

Professor Ezekwe also calls attention to ineffectiveness of past policies and strategies. "Despite the fact that, presently, many countries world wide suffer economic hardship to various extents, the case of Nigeria is particularly note worthy. Between national independence in 1960 and now, Nigeria has seen a calamitous deterioration of its education system[3], almost lost its food self-sufficiency, seen its national currency lose value by about 2500%, its manufacturing industries remaining consumers and not generators of foreign exchange, the degradation of the aquatic and terrestrial environment getting out of hand, and unemployment of even university graduates being rampant, while many of its learned professors have joined the private sector or emigrated to other countries. These losses have occurred despite, or because of the emergence of a crude oil economy in the early 1970's; and despite many policies and strategies which various Nigerian governments had adopted in order to arrest the decline and reverse the trend."

The Nigerian economy has not undergone the remarkable self-sustaining growth which has taken place in some comparable third world countries, such as India, Pakistan, Malaysia, Indonesia, or even in some less materially endowed ones like Korea and Taiwan. Naturally, this fact should make Nigeria to seek and identify the differences which exist between our national economic development strategies and those of the successful third world countries. There are of course many differences between each of those successful countries and ours; to wit, cultural differences, environmental differences, natural resources differences, GNP differences, differences in affinity to already highly industrialized countries, trade policies and practices etc; but there is no doubt that the dominant factor has been the difference in the approach to the domestication of science and technology, and the self-reliant application of it to productive activities."

Professor Ezekwe reiterates that like the creation of individual wealth, national wealth and well-being can only be achieved through national productivity, that is, "the sustainable local mass-production of goods and services for local consumption and for export, in order to minimize capital transfer to other countries due to excessive importation. He asserts that in the modern production system, goods and services can only be profitably mass produced by the employment of machines. This mechanization makes the difference between high volume and consistent quality production, on the one hand, and subsistence production, on the other hand; and therefore between wealth and poverty. Therefore, a national science and technology development programme would not have achieved its economic development purpose if it fails to provide, from mainly local resources, and in the required large quantities, the production processes, tools, machinery and equipment which are required for diverse production and service activities, including those for agricultural production and processing, education and training, health-care delivery, earth-working, transportation, power supply, water supply, communication, industrial production, defense etc. But Nigeria's science and technology development practice has so far operated as if scientific and technological knowledge is only an end in itself, instead of a means to the self reliant mass production of diverse goods and services for local consumption and for export. Because of this defect, upwards of 80% of the foreign earnings from crude oil sales is spent continuously in importing engineered goods from oversea countries in order to execute government projects, service utility undertakings, provide social services, and provide inputs to agriculture and consumer goods industries."

Professor Ezekwe sees the "local mass production of production tools, machinery and equipment, should therefore presently rank as the first of the major objectives of our science and technology development efforts.

However, mechanization demands the ready availability in the local market of capital products of diverse types which are required for machine and equipment design and production. These capital products in turn require an engineering infrastructure for their successful mass production. Therefore, in addition to the development of high level manpower, which our many educational institutions have been established to successfully do if they are well equipped and maintained, the establishment of a national engineering infrastructure should be a prominent component of our science and technology development programme. Our failure to lay emphasis on a national engineering infrastructure in the past thirty years, and to pursue it energetically, has been the missing link between our national development plans and the achievement of their targets; and is in fact the great difference which exist between our past national economic development strategies and those of the third world countries that have succeeded. An engineering infrastructure absorbs the qualified high-level manpower and other workers and engages them in productive work, and provides to them the physical facilities and working environment for the practical application of their scientific and technological knowledge. The engineering infrastructure enables them to apply their acquired knowledge to the development of technologies which will be employed by education, industry and agriculture in mass producing expert manpower, capital products and consumer goods. It can therefore be seen that it is our neglect of a national engineering infrastructure that has set the country back in its national process." It is therefore clear that if Nigeria is to be able to reverse the deterioration of the national economy, it must launch into the urgent establishment of a science and scientific research infrastructure, and an engineering infrastructure. At the best conditions of working, this enterprise is expected to require some fifteen to twenty years to produce the desired effect.

Science, Scientific Research, and Engineering Infrastructures.

In the same lecture, Professor Ezekwe maintained that "every productive activity requires its own special infrastructure to be able to succeed. This infrastructure consists of specialized manpower and material assets. Infrastructure for productive work is required at the individual level and at the national level. Thus, a mass-transit businessman must have his individual-level infrastructure, consisting of the required special manpower and material assets. Vehicles drivers, bus conductors, office staff and other personnel form the special man-power, while his material assets will include motor vehicles, vehicle parks, office space and equipment. However, the businessman cannot operate if the nation has not provided the general infrastructure of roads, petrol stations, bus stops, road marshals, vehicle maintenance workshops, motor spare parts etc. In fact, the complementary socio-economic infrastructure which the nation, through government, provides for the successful execution of productive work and services by citizens and commercial bodies, is so pervasive that much of government expenditure is taken by it. The list would include roads, sea and air ports, postal and telecommunication services, markets, power and water supply, educational institutions, hospitals, housing, transportation, etc. Without government providing the many types of infrastructure which various types of activities require, the productive efforts of individual citizens and commercial enterprises would be, at best, ineffective."

Professor Ezekwe then questions the use of various consumer loans obtained by the governments of Nigeria. What (a) "if the loans for the establishment of hotel were used for an engineering materials development complex, or a building materials industry; (b) if the loan for family planning was applied to the establishment of a rubber products industry, which would mass produce the condoms and other rubber products from Nigerian rubber, and export some of the products; (c) if the loan for furnishing school laboratories was used in setting up laboratory and introductory technology equipment manufacturing centres. Loans and other importation expenditures incurred in the last ten years on this subject would have set up enough of the laboratory equipment factories to make the country self-sufficient in laboratory apparatus production; (d) if the loan for water supply was used for setting up a hydraulic equipment development complex to generate industries for water supply equipment and accessories."

Conclusion

Professor Ezekwe, finally, advises that since the work of science and engineering infrastructure development will take many years and span the tenure of governments, it demands a strong political will which will not permit the programme to be suspended or abandoned at any time, or its finances diverted to more politically expedient expenditures. While some manpower training must be undertaken in overseas institutions and industries, especially initially, Professor Ezekwe recommends that the University-based research centres must give a pride of place to the local training of their staff and other scientists, engineers, technologists and technicians.

References

Ezekwe Nigerian Academy of Science (1992) & Faculty of Engineering, University of Lagos (1992): *Engineering Infrastructure, The Missing Link*

Government of the USA: *Technology Policy 1990*. Executive Office of the President Office of S & T Policy, Washington DC.

Federal Government of Nigeria. *Report of the National Committee on Engineering Infrastructure*. Federal Ministry of Science and Technology, Lagos, 1991.

Federal Government of Nigeria.*National Agency for Science and Engineering Infrastructure Decree 1992*; Government Printer, Lagos, 1992

Federal Government of Nigeria: *National Policy on Science and Technology,* Federal Ministry of Science and Technology, Lagos, 1986.

Federal Government of Nigeria: *National Policy on Science and Engineering Infrastructures.* National Agency for Science and Engineering Infrastructure, Lagos, 1993.

Federal Government of Nigeria.*Higher Education in the Nineties and Beyond.Report of the Commission on the Review of Higher Education in Nigeria,* Fed. Govt. Press 1992

Government of Tanzania: The National Science and Technology Policy of Tanzania. Ministry of Planning and Economic Affair, 1985.

Igwe: *Policies and Strategies for Commercialisation of Inventions and Research Results in Nigeria.* NISER, Ibadan, 1990.

Kuku.*North-South Co-Development in Science and Technology: Nigeria as a Crucial Factor.*

Nigerian Academy of Science. *Report of the Nigerian Academy of Science and Scientific Research Infrastructure.* Nigeria Academy of Science 1992

Nwokolo: *Science for Survival: The Nigerian Option.* Nigerian Academy of Science, 1993.

Anya: *Science and the Crisis in African Development.*Ida-Ivory Press Lagos, 1993.

OAU Lagos *Plan of Action for the Economic Development of Africa 1980 – 2000.* April 1980.

Government of Malaysia. *The National Science and Technology Policy.*Ministry of Science and Technology, 1986.

The Republic of China Medium and Long-Term Technological Development Plans.*Science Bulletin* Sept. 1992. ROC National Science Council.

UNESCO Percentage of GNP Devoted to R & D. *UNESCO Statistical Yearbook* 1988.

Makhubu: "The Contribution of Women to Science in Africa" in *Science in Africa. Achievements and Prospects.*University of Swaziland.

SECTION EIGHT: SECURITY

Security of the Ndi Igbo in Nigeria: The Way Forward.
by
Col. JMO Ezeoke

Introduction.

In the recent times, the primary issue which has dominated the attention and overall emotions of Nigerians has been the issue of security of life and property occasioned directly by the catastrophe that the nation has been plunged into by the Boko Haram organization. The victims now tend to cut across all the ethnic nationalities that make up the Nigerian nation.

It is however important to call our attention to the fact that a particular group - Ndigbo- have over the years particularly since 1966 been at the receiving end of the brutal and murderous animosity of the other ethnic nationalities in Nigeria. The paper seeks to examine the numerous security challenges Ndigbo have continued to face in the Nigerian nation particularly since 1966, and proffer recommendations against their continuation.

The Igbo Experiences.

Without contention, Ndigbo are the unparalleled agents of development in Nigeria. Their industry, peace-loving gregarious nature, effectively provided them with the disposition to play an effective developmental role ever where in Nigeria from Kano, Nguru, Zaria, Kaduna, Gombe and Jos to Akwanga, Makurdi, etc. in the Northern part of Nigeria and in Lagos, Port Harcourt, etc in the south. In return, what did Ndigbo, with all their gregarious propensity get?

In the early days of Igbo emigration from Igboland to the North, a disgusting divide between Sabon Gari and indigenes' city area was created whereas non-Igbos in Igboland were allowed and encouraged to live among Ndigbo. The existence of the divide between Sabongari and the native city, for instance, made it easy to locate and brutalise Ndigbo whenever the passion to attack and kill them was generated. Apart from challenges of physical security, Ndigbo have also been denied social and financial security in the country. In 1953, there was a murderous attack on Ndigbo in the North for reasons best known to the Northern political elites. The Igbo Union, the umbrella organisation of Ndigbo then was able to mobilise Ndigbo to stand-off the attacks. The celebrated cross-carpeting of some Yorubas from NCNC to AG in Ibadan still reverberates till date because of the ethnic divisiveness it foisted on the country. Then some Yoruba elements could not understand why and how an Igbo man should be premier in Yoruba land. The equally celebrated University of Lagos Vice-Chancellorship tussle between an erudite Igbo man Eni Njoku and a Yoruba man remains a strong pointer to the dangers Ndigbo have continued to face outside Igbo land. Any wonder then that with the failure of the Nzeogu-led coup of January 1966, that Ndigbo, became prime targets for elimination, with the active and effective prodding of the Northern elements in the Nigerian army and their elite political mentors.

Ndigbo were thus condemned to the fiery wrath of a vengeful army and motley murderous Northern Nigeria crowd and Igbos were murdered in their thousands in the most gruesome and gory manner between May and October 1966. In consequence, the Biafran/Nigerian imbroglio erupted and sadly ended in the defeat of Biafra. There was glee at the defeat of Biafra, and Igbo lives and properties became eeasy prey and murderous hunting sport for some Nigerians. In their parlance Ndigbo were a conquered people and should take anything thrown at them. Infact this was a statement credited to a one-time Inspector–General of Police. A retired General of the Army brazenly described Ndigbo as arrogant and incorrigible individuals during the Oputa panel hearings. If highly placed personalities see or speak in this uninformed manner about Ndigbo, then all should imagine what their foot soldiers are fed about Ndigbo - Absolute cannon fodder perhaps!

Ndigbo have severally been butchered since after that war without any restitution and without even as little as an apology. The incidents are numerous. The numerous Kano riots targeted Ndigbo and their properties were looted. The most incredible and horrific incident was the beheading and the parading of the head of one Chris Akaluka along the streets of Kano on a spike. Very recently, also in Kano, a woman and her child were murdered on the allegation that the piece of paper she picked up on the ground to wipe the bottom of her toddler was a page from the Koran. The Boko Haram menace is already taking its toll. However, it is almost obvious that that criminal organization is also being manipulated to target Ndigbo. It is on record that during a killing spree, two individuals from Adazi were killed in Adamawa state. Like is standard, the indigenes of Adazi gathered to discuss how to move the bodies home for burial and these murderous group came again and an additional fifteen Igbo individuals were massacred. In total derogation of the situation, the elected governor stated that the seventeen individuals killed themselves while quarrelling among themselves for money. That callous, rude and heartless statement was made by someone who is married to an Igbo lady.

Igbo Effort at Security.

It is an historical fact that no external kingdom ever conquered the Igbo kingdom until the colonialist by thrift and trading subterfuge penetrated the Igbo heartland and overwhelmed Ndigbo. Even at that, it was not smooth sailing venture for those imperialists. The coinage, *"onye nd'ilo gbara gburugburu n'eche ndu ya nche ngbe nile"* was the most articulated jingle in Biafra and it encapsulates the Igbo world view with respect to security.

Biafra was the first modern display of Igbo capacity to defend himself. After so much brutalization in Kano, Ndigbo in one bold display of the eternal capacity to defend themselves bared their fighting fangs and the murderous emotional surge of the Northern looters in Kano was put in abeyance for a very long period until very recently. In all, it is a known fact, even to the numerous Igbo traducers in Nigeria, that Ndigbo at any turn are capable of defending themselves when the Nigerian nation does not afford them such protection. This is the core of my recommendation. Ndigbo must be prepared to defend themselves at any turn until the stereotypes spurn about Ndigbo by other members of the Nigerian nation are erased.

Precedents on Self-help Security.

The situation of Ndigbo in Nigeria as regards their security is not new in history except that Ndigbo are experiencing the security void in a country in which they are supposed to be a major stakeholder. The Jews in diaspora experienced similar injustices where they were either settlers or captives of the host nations. Yet, at the height of the cruelty particularly as experienced in the Nazi Germany, the Jews organized for their self- preservation and protection. That probably did not translate to much because of the superior capacity of the Nazis but it was quite stunning to the Germans. We should not go against the laws of the land but we must stand firm henceforth to defend ourselves against all unconscionable brutalization of Ndigbo from any quarter. We should remember that at the height of the slave trade cruelty, the Igbo slaves who were sold in Haiti went up the hills of that country and from there launched an offensive against their oppressors. That action eventually led to the early independence of Haiti.

Security of Ndigbo in the Nigerian Nation.

Various security agencies abound in Nigeria, all charged with various responsibilities cumulatively aimed at ensuring the safety of lives and properties of citizens and the survival of Nigeria as a nation. Ndigbo are expected to be so protected like all the other nationalities that make up the Nigerian nation. Sadly, this is obviously not so. At will, and without recourse to the laws of the land, Igbo ventures are targeted and destroyed in all parts of the country. The destruction of education forced our youths into commercial ventures. But in all parts of the country they are not allowed the conducive environment to engage in that into which the society has forced them. The case is frighteningly desperate in Igboland where the the police engage in all manner of brutalization, intimidation and even murder just to coerce them to bring out money for no reasons at all.

Abuja has also grown in notoriety. Estates, malls, shops etc belonging to Ndigbo are destroyed at will with the support of security agents. The whole scenario creates so much frustration and desperation for these people exposed to these abuses and serial lack of any form of governmental protection of their lives and properties. It will be improper however, to state that there is absolutely no protection for Ndigbo. The continued denial of the rights of Ndigbo deserves immediate attention.

The Way Forward.

Ndigbo have over forty years now, cried against the palpable marginalization visited on them by the Nigerian state. The massive role played by lack of security of lives and property is a major issue at every Igbo forum. Ndigbo have absolute regard for the sanctity of life and appreciate having safe environment to live out their lives. This is what they expect from the Nigerian nation. It is my hope that the following recommendations will bring Ndigbo some respite from their traumas and fears.

a. Ndigbo must think home. The issue of being major development catalysts in other lands and not being appreciated should be checked.

b. We have had series of calls for state police. Ndigbo should throw their weight behind this and ensure it is upheld. In so doing, the mentality of conquest being exhibited by "foreign policemen" in Igboland will be removed. Igbos will populate the police and we shall easily lay responsibilities at the foot of any of our sons found wanting.

c. Ndigbo must be pro-active towards safe-guarding what is rightfully theirs in all parts of the country. Ohaneze Ndigbo must play a major part in this. *Ejighi akpata atufu aba ogaranya.*

d. Ndigbo form part of the vaunted Nigerian tripod and should be recognized as such. Ndigbo must begin to ask very seriously for the siting of strategic military units in Igboland. To-date we have a nominal air-force unit at Enugu. If it is a helicopter unit, then there should be functional helicopters stationed there. We also have viable locations where combat naval units can conveniently be sited.

e. The unconscionable raid of Igbo stalls in established markets by the customs and excise personnel should be stopped by Igbo clamour. That action sends negative portrayals of genuine business men as criminals and smugglers whereas these same custom personnel walk by obvious smuggled items without raising a finger. Ndigbo must be protected by this system.

In Defence of the January 15 Revolution, Chinua Achebe, Ndigbo and Biafra
by Mazi Chike Chidolue

The truth needs to be told about the January 15, 1966 Revolution, Chinua Achebe's account of the era and the role of Ndigbo and Biafra. Major Adewale Ademoyega was not only an ear and eye witness, but also, participated throughout in the planning and execution of the January 15, 1966 coup, from Genesis to Revelation so to speak. He was one of the seven majors who held the one and only formal meeting of the coup, one of the five majors that planned and executed the coup and also one of the Three Majors that formed the inner core! The unfriendly and destructive outburst from a section of the Yoruba nation against Achebe's new book on Biafra, confirms that Ademoyega's book on the coup *Why we struck*, received scant or no attention from the Nigerian reading public. This has remained so even though it is known that Adewale Ademoyega is non–Igbo, but a full-blooded Yoruba. His 'offence' is that because of Nigeria's victory over Biafra, in that war, facilitated by the strange and most unusual collaboration and collusion of communism and capitalism made possible by the intellectual domination of Ojukwu by Britain our former colonial master, he did not join the band wagon of anti – Igbo feeling to hold the Igbos as the sponsors of the glorious January Revolution. Ademoyega's book copiously illustrates the true picture of that event. History is also taken to mean his story. Emeritus Professor Chinua Achebe has written his *There was a country: A personal history of Biafra* laying emphasis where he chose.

On the January 15, 1966 revolution, it is now known, settled and agreed that the Five Majors who planned and executed it, had as part of the operation, to free Awolowo from Calabar prison and make him their leader. With this in view, the January Revolution was not an Igbo coup as the best interests of Ndigbo will not and cannot be served by Awolowo. Major Adewale Ademoyega wrote that *"...Yet there was one arrangement we had left till the date was fixed. It was the arrangement for* the release of political prisoners, particularly Chief Awolowo. Now that our own date had been *tentatively fixed for mid January, it became necessary to gear up that arrangement. At the end of the first week in January, Major Anuforo and I arranged to meet Captain Udeaja....Having briefed Udeaja generally and got his consent, we gave him his task. He was to fly in a special plane provided for the purpose to Calabar on the morning of the D-Day, to effect the release of Chief Awolowo and bring him to Lagos on the plane..."*

The intention of the Five Majors was national as confirmed by 13 Years of Military Rule by James O. Ojiako, a *Daily Times* publication quoting Major Chukwumah Nzeogwu. *"We seized power to stamp out tribalism, nepotism and regionalism. There were five of us in the inner circle and we planned the details. On Saturday morning, the officers and men thought they were going out only on a night exercise. It was not until they were out in the bush that they were told the full details of the plan. They had bullets, they had been issued with their weapons but I was unarmed. If they disagreed, they could have shot me. It was truly a Nigerian gathering and only in the army do you get true Nigerianism....They did it for the good of their country...."* Stephan, the West African correspondent of Bavarian Broadcasting, Munich, reportedly said that although *'Ojukwu was a supporter of the coup, the first in the country's history. He sympathized with the January 1966 plot makers, but was careful enough to avoid any overplayed attachment to them. Ojukwu told me later that it had been him who had requested General (Aguiyi) Ironsi to crush the coup."* Other sources reported that according to Lieutenant Colonel Abba Kyari, former military governor of North Central State stated that *"there is no question that Major Nzeogwu, Ibo leader of 1966 coup in Kaduna, had been a nationalist, not a tribalist, who was acting for the good of all Nigeria."*

Chinua Achebe extensively discussed the prevalent national resentment of the Igbos by other Nigerian ethnic groups. Ndigbo cannot help this unjustified and conspiratorial, animosity against them. They cannot volunteer their own extinction from the planet earth. Almighty God placed Ndigbo in this part of the globe, and they will not betray the responsibility of preserving and perpetuating their specie. It should be recalled that Ademoyega pointed out that *"It would be recalled that by late 1965 the efforts of the Balewa Government to Northernise the top echelon of the army was already bearing fruit. Some Northerners were already holding most of the strategic positions in the Army. Those positions could easily be used to thwart our attempt to change the Government. Sheer caution dictated that we would be sure to neutralize those officers so that our revolution would have a chance of taking off and succeeding. Later events did fully justify our apprehension, since it was the escape of only one of those marked down for arrest that brought us intense hardship and finally compromised our success. There was no plan whatsoever to arrest or kill all the officers above the rank of Major as was later claimed by extreme Northern propagandists. Even among those earmarked for arrest, only four were Northerners, two were Westerners and two were Easterners. But the North had always had more than 50% of the intake of officers into the Army since 1961, and more than 70 % of the intake of the other ranks. Therefore if casualties were to happen, it was more likely to be in that proportion than anything else. The wicked propaganda that followed the coup was only made possible by the weakness and non-revolutionary principles of the Ironsi regime, which bore no semblance to the well ordered and well controlled government that was envisaged and could have been run by us if our plans were fully executed..."*

It should also be noted that The Aburi Accord provided a critical and crucial safety where agreement was reached, signed and sealed by Ojukwu and Gowon. When they returned to their countries, instead of implementing the accord as signed, Gowon allowed his 'super' permanent secretaries, to interpret that document which was not written in Greek or Latin language, but in plain simple English language, and ended up refusing to implement it thereby precipitating the war. If Gowon had implemented the Aburi Accord as signed in Ghana, on January 5, 1967, there would have been no war. Nigerian commentators on the civil war always fight shy of the Aburi Accord and its tremendous and strategic importance, because by so doing, Igbos are set up for the kill on the guillotine of ethnic cleansing. Every unbiased umpire will agree that the civil war was caused by Gowon because he refused to implement the Aburi Accord. Any objective and sincere inquirer on the cause of the war, should go no further than the Aburi Accord. In Biafra, we had as our mantra, "**On Aburi We Stand**", while Gowon, instead of standing on Aburi with Biafra, torpedoed and demolished the good work done at Aburi.

Certainly, some critical mistakes were made by the leaders of Biafra during the civil war. A *"secret US document called Njoku* [Brigadier Hilary Njoku] *the best Enugu has (and one of the very best Nigeria has produced).The UK defence advisor who had known Madiebo as subordinate officer First Recce Squadron for several years, said he is "perfectly charming socially, but quite worthless professionally. He is weak, ineffective commander and consistently had worst recce squadron." To affirm what he was saying, he showed the US defence attaché, Madiebo's file at the Royal Military Academy, Sandhurst. Madiebo's records were abysmal....."* If, for the sake of argument, as the professors say, we accept the above portrayal of Njoku and Madiebo as correct, a natural question arises. Why did Ojukwu appoint Madiebo Chief of Army Staff while he confined Col. Hillary Njoku, a clearly very competent officer to house arrest and complete obscurity throughout the war to the utter detriment of Biafra? He probably wanted a yes man who having failed in nearly all the military operations assigned to him, would accept whatever he said without questioning or suggesting alternatives. There are several instances where Ojukwu had shown this mismanagement of Biafran war effort. For instance, when Colonel Steiner took over command of Biafran Commando Division at the death of Major George, Col. Steiner had wanted to clear and take Calabar port. Before coming to Biafra, Col. Steiner it was said, had reached an agreement with some band of mercenaries who had promised to run the Nigerian blockade of Biafra and bring in abundant supply of arms and armaments, if Col. Steiner could recapture any Biafran port held by Nigeria. Instead of allowing Col. Steiner to operate his plan, Ojukwu ordered him to move his Commando Division to take part in Operation Hiroshima whose aim was to retake Onitsha from Nigeria. That operation was an unmitigated disaster. When Col. Steiner arrived at the Onitsha sector with his men, Brigadier Amadi who was the commander of Onitsha sector told him that he (Amadi) would be the commander of Operation Hiroshima. Col Steiner, in his smattering of English language said "Me train, you command, not possible. Me train, me command, you train, you command." This is an example of the blind, thoughtless arrogant and nihilistic conduct of the high command of the Biafran military! If Biafrans could throw out the Nigerian military out of their territory all alone, why bring in external help?

At the zero hour of that operation, while Brigadier Amadi 'led' his 11 Division from the safety and cool comfort of his Div. HQ, at Central School Nnewi, Col. Steiner led his men into battle in the characteristic commando fire and movement fashion, in keeping with the admonition of the Israeli one-eyed General Moshe Dayan to Israeli officers, whom he told, "Israeli officers lead their men into battle, they do not send them into battle." The commandos occupied the centre axis while the 11 div manned the flanks. As Col Steiner led his men pushing the Nigerian soldiers out of Dennis Memorial Grammar School and heading for the Niger Bridge, Brigadier Amadi's men were trying 'to win the fire fight' with the not more than ten bullets usually given to Biafran soldiers during operations against an enemy whose soldiers had hundreds of rounds of bullets! Nigerian soldiers discovering that the commandos' flanks were exposed, cut off Col. Steiner and his men. When Col. Steiner realized their predicament, he turned back and fought through the encirclement losing a few men. He drove feverishly to Brigadier Amadi's headquarters with his revolver corked only to find that Amadi had just left. Brigadier Amadi and some indolent members of the Biafran Military High Command concocted a ridiculous fable on Col. Steiner, which they presented to Ojukwu who ordered the arrest, detention and deportation of Col. Steiner. While Col. Steiner commanded the Biafran Commandos, at the end of every morning parade at the head quarters, he visited the medical centre, exchanging pleasantries with and giving cigarettes to wounded soldiers. He also arranged for soldiers with serious wounds to be sent to Gabon or Paris. Under his command, Biafran Commandos were the best kitted, making their morale to hit the sky. When he was deported, the Biafran Commandos were no longer the Strike Force which tread where angels fear to walk.

The other example is reported in the American Secret Files which claims that in secret cable dated 24/08/67 and sent by Dr. Martin Hillenbrand, American Ambassador in East Germany, to his counterpart in Lagos, MCK Ajuluchukwu, Ojukwu's special envoy, met Soviet Ambassador to Nigeria, Alexandr Romanov, in Moscow in June 1967. Romanov said that for USSR to recognize Biafra and supply it arms, the latter had to nationalize the oil industry. Ojukwu refused, saying that he had no money to reimburse the oil companies and that Biafrans did not have the expertise to run the oil installations. A month later, Anthony Enahoro, the Federal Commissioner for Information and Labour, went to Moscow, signed a cultural agreement with

Moscow and promised to nationalize the oil industry, including its allied industries once they got arms to recapture them from the Biafrans. Within days, 15 MIGS arrived in sections jn Ikeja and Kano airports, awaiting assemblage. There was no nationalization." These are a few examples of how Ojukwu mismanaged Biafran war efforts which cost us our war of survival!

The coup was purely a Nigerian enterprise by patriotic citizens. Ndigbo or The Igbo State Union as at the time had no hand in the coup, as confirmed by Ademoyega when he said *"It was in mid – November 1965 that we held the one and only formal meeting that preceded the coup .The meeting was held in Lagos, in the military quarters of Major Ifeajuna……The meeting was very short. There was a consensus that something had to be done quickly to save Nigeria from anarchy and disintegration and to restore peace and unity to the nation. It was agreed that only the use of force could bring immediate end to the violence being perpetrated in many parts of the country. It was, however, agreed that the use of force should be minimal. Political leaders and their collaborators were to be arrested, but wherever an arrest was resisted, it was to be met with force. Otherwise, no one was to be killed. Only the heads of government, that is, the Prime Minister, the four regional premiers and their right – hand men, were considered most essential to arrest throughout the country .And among their military collaborators, only the top echelon and those holding strategic positions were named for arrest. These included the GOC of the Nigerian Army, General Ironsi, the commanders of the two brigades, Brigadiers Ademulegun and Maimalari, the Chief of Staff Army HQ, Colonel Kur Mohammed, and the Adjutant General of the Army, Lieutenant-Colonel Pam. Others were the Deputy Commander of the NDA, Colonel Shodeinde, the Quartermaster-General of the Army, Lieutenant-Colonel Unegbe and the Commander of the 4th Battalion which was based in Ibadan and was the most politicised unit of the Army, Lieutenant-Colonel Largema. Contrary to the load of wicked propaganda that has since been heaped on us,* **there was no decision in our meeting to single out any particular ethnic group for elimination or destruction.** *Our intentions were honourable, our views were national and our goals were idealistic. We intended that the coup should be national in execution so that it would receive national acclamation. We planned that the use of force should be minimal so that our methods could at once be seen as superior to those of the politicians, who simply went on killing the very people they were called upon to govern. The need to bring more of the middle level officers (Majors and Lieutenant-Colonels) was discussed. But the few names that could be mentioned had to be dropped because their interpersonal connections would compromise the security of the planning. After ninety minutes of discussion, the meeting was over. We dispersed as if from a prayer meeting since it was a Sunday and the Lord was in our midst….*

"NNA Plan to Wallop the West

"It was at this time that I met Chief H. O. Davies for the first time. He was a famous politician who had been in the nationalist struggle since 1941. He was a Federal Minister under the Balewa Government....I soon got into deep conversation with him on the political situation in the country, I was particularly interested to know what the Federal Government's view was, apart from Balewa's public statements. Chief H. O. Davies made it clear that the Federal Government had no, solution to the political crisis." Since the Federal Government had no solution to the crisis the January boys not the Igbos had to step in.)" He said that everybody was just waiting to see what would happen next and that nobody knew exactly what that would be; but surely something was bound to happen. I left Chief Davis feeling that the Balewa Government had something up its sleeve. Otherwise, the minister would not be so emphatic that something was bound to happen...

"On January 3, 1966, I went to work with Ifeajuna. After extensive prodding, we discovered that the Balewa Government had a terrible plan to bring the Army fully to operate in the West for the purpose of eliminating the elites of that region, especially the intellectuals who were believed to be behind the intransigence of the people against the Akintola Government. It was for this reason that the government had attacked the intellectuals of the Region, especially those at Ife, intimidating and victimizing them for their refusal to support it. People like Solarin of May Flower School, Ikenne, were among those marked down. It was also intended that if the plan succeeded in the West, the next target would be the East. The Federal Government was to use loyal troops for this purpose and the 4th Battalion at Ibadan commanded by Lieutenant-Colonel Largema and the 2nd Battalion temporarily commanded by Major Igboba, but soon to be taken over by Lieutenant-Colonel Gowon, were designated for this assignment."

If the January boys had not intervened, Sardauna and the Balewa Federal Government would have recolonised and severely subjugated Southern Nigeria and placed it in a condition far worse than Southern Sudan experienced before her independence. Damola, I hope you can now see that the January coup was very divinely timely. Ademoyega continued "The operation was fixed for the third week of January 1966, when the Sardauna would have returned from his pilgrimage, and Lieutenant–Colonel Gowon would have completed his takeover of the Ikeja Battalion. In preparation of this horrible move by the Federal Government, the high echelons of the Army and the Police were being reshuffled. Major-General Ironsi was ordered to proceed on leave from mid-January. He was to be relieved by Brigadier Maimalari, over the head of Brigadier Ademulegun.... In the Police, Inspector-General Edet was sent on leave from December 20, 1965. The officer closest to him was retired and the third officer, Alhaji Kam Salem was brought in as *the new Inspector–General. The stage was thus set for the proper walloping of the West…. "Late on the 14th news reached us that the Sardauna had been having a meeting in Kaduna on that day with Chief Akintola of the West, and that both Brigadier Ademulegun and Lieutenant Colonel Largema were in attendance. It was obvious to us that they were putting finishing touches to their planned "walloping of the West". But we felt confident that we were one step ahead."*

After the revenge coup, the triumphant North did not express any sympathy to Igbos in spite of the over 200 Igbo casualties compared to the about 26 casualties of the first coup. Some accused Igbos in the North of taunting their hosts of on the loss of their leaders citing a high record waxed not by an Igbo man but by a Kalabari musician named Cardinal Rex Jim Lawson. Several resented also the fact that Igbos then occupied the Vice-Chancellorship of the University of Lagos and Ibadan University, grudging Igbos also of producing Engr. Francis C.N. Agbasi, the first Nigerian Principal of Yaba College of Technology and Mr. Clement Odunukwe who was the Senior Lecturer-i-charge (Principal) of Federal Emergency Science School, Onikan, Lagos; also, Mr. F.C. Nwokedi, the first Nigerian Federal Permanent Secretary to be appointed by the colonial masters. When Mr. P. G. Stallard was retiring, Mr. Nwokedi ought to have succeeded him as the first Nigerian Secretary to the Council of Ministers. But because he came from the 'wrong' tribe, he was skipped and Mr. S. O. Wey was given the post while Mr. Nwokedi became the Permanent Secretary, Ministry of Foreign Affairs. Modesty will not restrain me from expressing my joy, be it of local patriotism because, the last three gentlemen mentioned above, hailed from my home town, Nnewi, and Mr. Nwokedi was from my village, Edoji. These were Federal institutions in Yoruba land and those appointments followed very rigorous due process. In the case of Professor Kenneth O. Dike, unanimously elected the Principal of the University College Ibadan by the University College Council, the Chairman of the Council, Dr. Akanu Ibiam, went to London, and consulted Sir Charles Morris, Chairman of the Inter-University College Council that recommended Principals and Vice Chancellors for colonial Universities. Sir. Morris said to Dr. Ibiam: *"Why do you come to us? You have your man there (Prof Kenneth Dike).You are lucky to have a ready–made man on the spot."* In 1998, Emeritus Professor Chike Obi solved the over 300 years old Mathematics puzzle – Fermat's Last Theorem established in 1637 by a French Lawyer/Mathematician, Pierre Fermat. Chike Obi's paper was accepted for publication and appeared in the USA - based Journal of Algebras, Groups and Geometries, Vol. 15 pp 289 - 299 (1998). Despite the fact that Chike Obi's paper was published by a renowned and distinguished American Journal, some Nigerians like Dr. Olunloyo and one Ogunsola, an actuary, openly disputed without any basis, the validity of Chike Obi's proof. Others accuse the Igbos of boastfulness and excessive exhibitionism of their strenuous achievements claiming that potentials, abilities, competences and the like are God-given. The Igbos are not been known to be boastful of such achievements. Nationals like Chinua Achebe merely traced the Igbos' 'Long Walk" to acquire them. This should not make anyone furiously uncomfortable. It is significant that Duro Onabule had this to say about Chinua Achebe: *"Whatever the bad feelings of his critics, Achebe's reputation, unlike his contemporaries, is that of a straightforward man. He has never been known to be cowardly, neither does he cringe before nor collaborate with local or international establishment. Achebe's character is definite as he does not charade in the day only to be settled at night.... Even if Awolowo was not in the position to effect his belief in starvation as a weapon of war, the fact remains that he (Awolowo) publicly took that position and was widely reported in the media in Nigeria and abroad.... Is Chinua Achebe fair to Awolowo in his criticisms? The appropriate preceding question is: was Awolowo fair to himself when he publicly upheld starvation as a legitimate weapon of war, more so during a civil war in which the outside world was disgusted with television visuals of thousands of starving malnourished innocent children? Achebe's critics on his latest book, especially Yoruba, should objectively read "AWO", Obafemi Awolowo's autobiography, in which throughout, there is not a single sentence complimentary to Nnamdi Azikiwe, portrayed as an ethnic jingoist....Yet, Awolowo's criticism of Azikiwe were never mischievously interpreted as hatred for Igbos. Nobody of Achebe's status and with terrible experiences of the civil war could be expected to write his recollections without justifiable criticism of starvation as a weapon throughout the war. His critics just have to be realistic rather than being emotional."*

Nigerians seem to ignore atrocities where Biafra or Igbos are the victims like where the American Secret Files assert that Mohammed the Second Division Commander was reported to have criticized Obasanjo thus: *"We told you not to end the war the way you did so as to sort things out, you went on gaddamgaddam and finished it."* What Murtala Mohammed meant was that Obasanjo did not give him time to apply the **Final Solution to the Igbo Problem** *viz* give him time to wipe out Igbos from the surface of the earth.

Chinua Achebe is not boastful and should not be pilloried when he wrote: *"The Igbo culture being receptive to change, individualistic and highly competitive, gave the Igbo man an unquestioned advantage over his compatriots in securing credentials for advancement in Nigerian colonial society. Unlike the Hausa/Fulani he was unhindered by a wary religion and unlike the Yoruba unhampered by traditional hierarchies. This kind of creature, fearing no God or man, was custom-made to grasp the opportunities; such as they were, of the white man's dispensation. And the Igbo did so with both hands. Although the Yoruba had a huge historical and geographical head-start, the Igbo wiped out their handicap in one fantastic* burst of energy in the twenty years between 1930 and 1950…. The rise of the Igbo in Nigerian affairs was due to the self-confidence engendered by their open society and their belief that one man is as good as another, that no condition is permanent. It was not due, as non-Igbo observers imagined, to tribal mutual aid societies. The "Town Union" phenomenon, which has often been written about, was in reality an extension of the Igbo individualistic ethic."

Zik decided never to ally with Awolowo after the carpet-crossing incident of 1951 in the Western House of Assembly at Ibadan, which prevented the NCNC from forming the government in spite of the fact that the NCNC was declared the winner of that election or as Achebe would put it *"Chief Awolowo 'stole' the Government from him (ZIK) in broad daylight."* Job opportunity or who would take over from the departing British was never part of the issue at all. During the colonial era and immediately after, the Igbo relied on merit and competence for advancement and securing appointments in the public service. It is worth mentioning here again, that the first Nigerian to be appointed a Federal Permanent Secretary by the British was Mr. F.C. Nwokedi an Igboman! This achievement of Mr. Nwokedi had nothing to do with the NCNC-NPC coalition. With such men as Chiefs T.O.S. Benson, Adeniran Ogunsanya, Kolawole Balogun, Adegoke Adelabu and many others of timbre and caliber it was impossible that *"the Yoruba who could have looked for jobs were shunted aside."*, because their leader was jailed! By the way, it was a Yoruba judge, Justice Sowemimo who sent Awolowo to jail. After the war, on the Twenty Pounds Policy (£20), all the bank accounts opened in Nigeria by Igbos, but operated in Biafra, were reduced to (£20) no matter the size of the account! As the victor, Nigeria was free to pay twenty pounds or nothing for the Biafran money in spite of the *No Victor No Vanquished* bogey.

The anti-intellectual opium that has made most non-Igbo Nigerians to hold Igbos responsible for the first coup is unfounded. One should again read the words of Ademoyega who wrote: *"Today, if one were to ask "when did the preparation for the revolution really begin?" the most accurate answer would be, "from 1961", because the three of us who formed the nucleus of the revolutionary group had met in that year. Although we had not there and then planned a revolution, we had seen eye to eye and we knew that we had a common cause. It was as if the seed was sown at that time and only needed time to germinate, grow and bear fruit"* Before the coup, the whole country was in distress; but the West was the most distressed, with the widespread riot, killings and their leader, Awolowo, in prison. The West was therefore, the tribe in greatest need for a coup to change the Federal Government, and restore their liberty, not the Igbos.

It has become necessary to ask, why has the North always succeeded in first, allying with the East (Azikiwe) to deal with the West and finally with the

West (Awolowo) to destroy the East (Igbos)? Zik returned from America with the noble ambition to found a 'BIG' One Nigeria, which was not a bad idea. But the foundation for that size of Nigeria was lacking. **The summary of the feasibility report on the One Nigeria Project said – not feasible, not viable and not profitable!** Awolowo saw this and wisely decided to concentrate his efforts in working for the Yorubas. Similarly, Sardauna, in answer to a question by a journalist, said, *"I am first and foremost a moslem, secondly a Northerner, I am yet to be a Nigerian!"* Why Zik could not come to the same conclusion as Awolowo and Sardauna remains a puzzle. My great and near fanatical admiration for Awolowo has been based on this self evident fact that Awolowo served and sacrificed everything he had for his Yoruba people. The Igbos were not that lucky with Zik.

After the Awolowo unconstitutionally instigated carpet crossing of 1951 in the Western House of Assembly, at Ibadan, ZIK decided not to ever have anything to do with Awolowo in politics, which was a most imprudent decision. For it is said that in politics, there is no permanent enemy, only permanent interests! Also, Chairman Mao Tse Tung said **"There is a time to ally with the enemy, but more important is to know when to break with the enemy!** It is true that the Federal Government of NPC and Zik's NCNC sent Awolowo to jail, for which he was entitled to be bitter, it is also equally true that the Igbo led NCNC under Dr. M.I. Okpara formed the United Progressive Grand Alliance UPGA, with the Adegbenro led Action Group and other progressives, to oppose the Nigerian National Alliance NNA. Arising from this alliance, Dr M. I. Okpara (M.I. POWER) informed Akintola that he would be visiting Ibadan. Akintola told him not to come, that he would not be in. Okpara said he would at least sign the Visitors Book in his absence. Okpara visited Ibadan as a show of solidarity to Adegbenro and the Yorubas. Okpara and his team were treated to a very rousing and enthusiastic reception by the students of Ibadan University, which was chaired by Prof. Hezekiah Oluwasanmi. I was an undergraduate at Ibadan University then. During the last election to the Western House of Assembly before the coup, Okpara on behalf of the Igbos, sent Mazi Ukonu of Eastern Nigerian Broadcasting Service to Ibadan, as a continued show of solidarity with the Yorubas, where he stayed at Awolowo's house at Oke Ado to announce the correct version of the election results. All these should not have been lost on Awolowo when he decided to support Gowon to crush the Igbos during the war, more especially with his inhuman strategy of 'Starvation is a Legitimate Weapon of War"

Igbo Security: Making Igbo Life too expensive to Expend
by
Dr. Luke N. Aneke

Introduction

The sanctity of life is a tenet of most civilizations aside and apart from the biblical injunctions against the taking and wastage of lives. Most civilizations observe the sanctity of life regardless of race, creed, gender, religion and societal status. In Nigeria however, it is a different story with regard to Igbos, where for decades the periodic slaughter of Igbos in the tens, hundreds and thousands have become so inconsequential as to be accepted as normal. Naturally, the abstinence or forbearance from the exercise of any prohibition is the consequence, if any, of breaking the prohibition. If people see a serious and costly consequence, they will probably abstain from it. But if there is lack of consequences, there will be violations. When reward is attached, then, it will be done with impunity and brazenness.

Easy Expendability of Igbo Life in Nigeria

The spillage of Igbo blood has become so routine and inconsequential that it now sounds somewhat of a ridicule to talk about the consequences of such acts. As a matter of fact, the spillage of Igbo blood has become a kind of expression of patriotism in the Nigeria context. Furthermore, people have come to see the shedding of Igbo blood as an avenue to greater heights and attainments in their lives in Nigeria. Someone like Theophilus Danjuma who came to light and fame by the shedding of General Ironsl's blood, with his participation in the bloodbath of over three hundred Igbo officers from July 29 to August 1, 1966, has risen to become a military General, billionaire and one commanding a lot of respect in the society. This and other examples of positive rewards from the killing of Igbos give an observer the impression that it is not only inconsequential but beneficial, and hence the impunity and lawlessness that attend the liquidation of Igbo lives at the slightest opportunity in Nigeria.

The Jewsih Aproach

What can the Igbos do to add value to the worth of an Igbo life in Nigeria, and to establish a sense of responsibility for the action of taking an Igbo life? The situation facing us now faced the Jews in the middle of last century in the wake of their massacre and liquidation in Germany and other parts of Europe around the period of World War II. To protect themselves and forestall any organized future massacre, the Jews adopted "Never Again" as their motto, and went out of their way to make it a reality. In the quest to effect Jewish security, the Jews, as individuals, groups and organizations, went after everybody with Jewish blood on his/her hands. They searched, traced and sought out Jewish liquidators without respect to position in the society, wealth, fame or subsequent friendship to Israel and Jewish people. With their concerted efforts, many Jewish liquidators were investigated, prosecuted and imprisoned. The Jews ensured that every Jewish liquidator was exposed and his or her legacy tainted. This effort was all encompassing and involved Jewish politicians, researchers, philanthropists, activists and academicians.

A vivid and well-published Jewish effort involved the well known two-term UN secretary general Kurt Waldeim who also served as President of Austria for one term. Waldeim was an Austrian, conscripted into the German Army in 1941 by the invading Germans. After serving in the German army, he returned to civilian life after World War II, having become a lawyer. He served distinctively in the Austrian Foreign Service before his two terms as UN secretary general. No serious anti-Jewish accusations came out against him, until he ran for presidency of Austria in 1986. When charges came up against Mr. Waldeim that he participated in the killing of Jews, he flatly denied the charges, stating that after being wounded on the Russian front, he spent the remainder of the war completing his law studies at the University of Vienna. However, two prominent Jews, Eli Rosenbaum of the World Jewish Congress and Robert Edwin Herzstein, then professor of history at the University of South Carolina, in United States, championed archival research that ascertained that Waldeim served in the German army beyond 1942, and in fact till the end of the war, and had served as an intelligence officer in the Balkans in a German unit accused of ruthlessness against the Yugoslav partisans. Kurt Waldeim faced severe repercussions for these WW II activities. Although he went ahead to win the presidency of Austria, he nonetheless, paid dearly in terms of public standing, damaged reputation and impaired freedom of movement as follows:

1. His name was included in the United States' Department of Justice "watch list" of undesirable aliens suspected of WWII war crimes
2. He was banned from entry into the United States
3. During his tenure as President of Austria, he was a virtual prisoner there shunned by the vast majority of nations with no exchange of diplomatic visits.
4. He did not seek re-election as President of Austria.
5. It was also found that a 1948 UN war crimes commission recommended him for prosecution.

However, it is important to note that for all that Mr. Waldeim went through, and lost in terms of prestige and public standing, it was never established that he was directly involved in war crimes or ordered war crimes activities. His biggest offence was that he served in a German army unit that was ruthless to the Yugoslavs and that deported many Greek Jews to gas chambers, but he was not personally found to have engaged in those activities or ordered any one to do so.

The Nigerian Context
But let's compare this with the Nigeria context and atrocities by Nigerian troops and their commanders during the Nigeria-Biafra war and the crises preceding it. From the foregoing World War II example that military commanders were prosecuted and jailed for genocide and war crimes not only for participating in it but for failing to prevent genocide from happening. Hence genocidal suspects have been convicted and jailed for the following:

a) Failure to prevent genocide from occurring
b) Failure to cooperate in punishing the perpetrators of genocide.
c) Failure of duty as military commander, to restrain troops from war crimes and genocide.
d) Failure of duty as military commander to protect prisoners of war from violence and killings
e) Failure of duty as military commander to protect civilians from cruelty by troops

In fact, Yugoslav and Serbian leader, Slobodan Milosevic, alone, was charged with: Genocide, Complicity in genocide, Deportation, Murder, Persecution on racial, religious or political grounds, Inhumane acts/forcible transfer, Extermination, Imprisonment, Torture, Wilful killing, Unlawful confinement, Wilfully causing great suffering, Unlawful deportation or transfer, Extensive destruction and appropriation of property not justified by military necessity and carried out unlawfully and wantonly, Cruel treatment, Plunder of public and private property, Attacks on civilians, Destruction or willful damage to historic monuments and institutions, Unlawful attacks on civilian objects/targets.

Recent Historical Massacres of Igbos
I. Massacre of over 3000 Igbos in Kano on September 29, 1966.
As we know, killing and maiming of Igbos by other Nigerians, especially Northerners, have been a feature of Nigerian history since the 1930s. But I have chosen three episodes of Igbo massacre to illustrate the points I am making that killing of Igbos attracts no unpleasant consequences in Nigeria, and this should certainly not be so. On September 29, 1966, troops of Northern origin from the 5th battalion in Kano, joined by Hausa-Fulani civilians, murdered well over 3000 Igbos in Kano, starting their killing from Kano airport. When the killing started, Gowon sent Lt Col. Mohammed Shuwa to Kano, supposedly to try to contain the massacre or, at least, minimize Igbo casualties. However, the presence of Col. Shuwa in Kano, did little or nothing

to lessen the number of Igbo victims. Eye witness correspondents from both the *Time Magazine* and *New York Times* who witnessed the killings in Kano said: "All night long and into the morning the massacre went on. Then tired and fulfilled, the Hausas drifted back to their homes and barracks to get some breakfast and sleep." (See *Untold Story of Nigeria-Biafra war by Dr. Luke N. Aneke,* 71; *New York Times October 3, 1966, page 1, col. 3)*. So the killing of Igbos in Kano ended when the killing mob was exasperated and sapped out. They were tired; they were fulfilled; they needed some breakfast; they needed some sleep. Incidentally, of the 5th battalion Northern troops that participated in the massacre of Igbos only 32 were arrested and detained (11 Catholics, 11 Protestants and 10 Muslims). However, none of them was ever prosecuted by the Gowon government. No reason was given for their release without prosecution but it is known that 22 of the 32 soldiers were Christians from Gowon's middle belt region *(*See *New York times* December 13, 1966, page 7, column 1).

II. Massacre of Igbos in Makurdi in October 1966

After the massacre of over 3000 Igbos in Kano on September 29, 1966, all available means were used to evacuate the Igbos from Kano. Planes, trains and vehicles were used by both expatriate and indigenous employers to transport Igbos out of Kano. The first train that left Kano reached Makurdi after several hours and the Easterners on board were happy and excited that they have escaped the death and destruction of Kano. But what they did not know was that their immediate neighbours to the north were not happy they escaped from Kano. Before they knew it, a mob of civilians and soldiers halted the train engineer/driver and completed that massacre that the Kano mob missed. The few Easterners that escaped were riddled with bullets and matches wounds. After *New York Times* correspondent, Lloyd Garrison, visited the survivors of the Makurdi massacre at UNTH Enugu on October 8, 1966 and wrote: "Enugu General Hospital is always overcrowded even in the best of times, today, its surgical word is jammed with 79 of the most seriously wounded refugees. Only half are in beds. The rest lie on mattresses on the corridors. Each patient's tale seems as horrifying as the rest." Paulina Okaro (age 24, then) and Joseph Onyeabor (of unstated age) were among the Markurdi massacre survivors who spoke with Mr Garrison at UNTH. (See *The Untold Story of Nigeria-Biafra war* by Dr. Luke Aneke; See also *New York Times,* October 14, 1966, page 8 column 5).

III. War crimes violence by Theophilus Danjuma and Mohammed Shuwa

Those Igbos who were of the age of understanding during the civil war will remember that Gowon repeatedly told the world that Nigeria was trying to reintegrate their Igbo brothers who have been "deceived" by Ojukwu. He also repeatedly told the world that Igbos will have their rightful place in the

Nigeria Federation. But while he was using these tunes to seek world support for their side, his field commanders were engaging literally in war crimes against the Igbos. In the last week of October 1967, *New York Times* war correspondent, LloydGarrison, decided to visit the command headquarters of Nigeria's first division in Makurdi, under the Command of Colonels Mohammed Shuwa and Theophilus Dannjuma. What he saw was a total surprise to him: a mandatory order of **ruthlessness** on Biafrans, dated September 16, 1967 that their troops must carry out on Biafrans. The order directed that: "You are therefore required to push ahead ruthlessly to vanquish the rebels in your way. You will tell this to all your men because rebels have no honor and no respect for the dignity of mankind. You are bound to have heavier casualties than hitherto but you cannot win a war without heavy casualties" (*New York Times,* Tuesday, October 24, 1967, p 20, Column 3). On analysis of this order, the following emerges:

- That their troops must show cruelty, heartlessness and utmost violence to Biafrans.
- That both civilians and uniformed men are targets of their ruthlessness campaign. No attempt was made to distinguish between soldiers and civilians.
- That Biafrans have no honor or respect, which is a methodology, used by Hitler to dehumanize his intended victims, so that their lives will not be worth much in the eyes of his troops.
- That this order must be transmitted to the lowest ranks, "you must tellthis to all your men". That means the whole division must be involved in the ruthlessness and not just a platoon, company or battalion.
- That this ruthlessness order must be undertaken even if it means heavier casualties on their own side (this is no different from the intensions of their war songs during the war).

Those Biafrans who were in Enugu in October 1967 know very well that the first division under Cols. Shuwa and Danjuma carried out the ruthlessness order over and beyond expectation, as refugees pouring into Enugu from Nsukka region told horror stories, and manifested broken skulls, chopped-off limps and gouged-out eyes. In today's language this is simply "war crimes" and both Shuwa and Danjuma who issued the orders, and the officers and men that carried them out are guilty of war crimes, and are all candidates for prosecution at the International Criminal Court, ICC.

Individual Perpetrators of Genocide should face Consequences at ICC
The efforts of the Igbos to bring the 1966-1970 genocide charges against the Nigerian State at the ICC are good but not enough. This effort must be broadened to include individuals who participated in the genocide against

Igbos, so that they can face responsibility for their individual actions in term of jail terms, monetary compensations and forfeiture of gains related to their roles in Igbo genocide. Incidentally, the Jews have shown that the passage of time and advanced ages of perpetrators of genocide are not barriers to the eventual pursuit of justice and redress. A lot of Jewish liquidators were prosecuted in the decades of 1990-2000, some fifty to sixty years after WWII, and at a time when most of the culprits were in their 80s and 90s. People have been convicted and jailed for genocide, crimes against humanity and war crimes whose offenses were much less than those of Danjuma and Shuwa during the civil war. Military commanders have been jailed for failing to restrain their troops from violence, even when they did not order the violent acts or participate personally in the atrocities. Danjuma and Shuwa mandated their troops, in a General Order (GO), to visit ruthlessness on their opponents and defenseless civilians during the civil war. Illustrative examples include the cases of Kurt Waldheim as stated above and Erich Priebke, the former German SS officer convicted of crimes by an Italian court and who died in detention in 2013 at the age of 100. He was in charge of German troops that executed 335 Jewish and Italian civilians in Ardeanline cave near Rome on March 24, 1944. It was not proved that he ordered the executions but he was convicted for "failing to protect the civilians" from atrocities by his troops. There was no evidence that Waldheim he either participated in the atrocities or ordered it or was sympathetic to it. Shuwa and Danjuma actually ordered their troops to visit ruthlessness on their opponents.

There is also the case of the Bosnian Serb army General, Zdravko Tolimir, who was convicted of genocide in 2007 and sentenced to life imprisonment for the massacre of Muslim war prisoners during the Serbian war. Although Gen. Tolimir did not actually participate in the killings, he was nonetheless convicted because "he knew of the plans" to commit horrific mass murders, and "he failed in his duty" to protect the prisoners of war before they were led away to the killing sites.It should be noted also that a group of nine Serbian paramilitary members (The Jackals) were tried and sentenced to terms of up to 20 years in prison for the murder of 120 Albanian civilians during the Kosovo conflict in 1999. Slobodan Milosevic, a former president of the Federal Republic of Yugoslavia, and later Serbia was tried for genocide, war crimes and crimes against humanity from 2002 till his death in 2005. The charges for which Milosevic was indicted included as stated earlier: genocide, complicity in genocide, deportation and murder.

Application to Nigerian Situation and Igbo Genocide

It is important to review and assess circumstances of genocide and war crimes in other countries and regions to appropriately put the Nigerian situation in real context. It is noteworthy that the standard for conviction and imprisonment for genocide and war crimes is such that it is obvious that a lot of Nigerian military commanders during the Nigerian civil war were/are candidates for war crimes prosecution, presently or posthumously. In the last two to three decades, most military commanders were convicted at the ICC (Hague) and other tribunals, not for what they actively did or participated in, but for what they failed to do. In other words military commanders were jailed not for participating in genocides, but for failing to prevent them.(See above for charges for which genocidal suspects have been convicted and jailed e.g. failure of duty, complicity and failure to prosecute perpetrators).

Notable Examples in the Nigeria-Biafra War:
Theophilus Danjuma, Mohammed Shuwa & the ruthlessness order

As *New York Times* reported in its edition of October 24, 1967 (page 20, column 3), Colonels Mohammed Shuwa and Theophilus Danjuma, respectively commander and deputy commander of the 1st Division, issued a mandatory order of *ruthlessness* to their troops dated September 16, 1967 to carry out against Biafrans. The directive, a general order (GO), to the whole first division, mandated that officers communicate the order down to all the men from brigade to battalion to company and to platoon levels. In a classical Nazi style, the order, to facilitate troop obedience and release from guilt, dehumanized their intended victims (Biafrans) by telling the troops that "rebels have no honor and no respect". Finally, they prepared their troops for heavy casualties in case it becomes necessary to perpetrate the ruthlessness order. Where is Muhammed Shuwa today? He has fallen victim to the ruthlessness of Boko Haram. Is that a cause for celebration by the survivors of his ruthlessness campaign? Absolutely not! But it is a reminder to the apologetics and rationalizers of ruthlessness and genocide that what goes around comes around, and that he who lives by the sword dies by it. Ruthlessness is defined by different dictionaries in different ways, but they have common denominators of horror and blood. They define being ruthless as *merciless, cruel, cold-hearted, having no compassion or pity, inhuman, heartless, hard-hearted, etc*. This is the way Shuwa and Danjuma ordered a whole division under them to treat Biafrans, and they did. The question is if some military commanders are serving long jail terms for failing to restrain their troops from ruthlessness, what is the appropriate punishment for those commanders who actually ordered their own troops to exhibit ruthlessness?The answer is clear and obvious.

Kano Massacre of over 3000 Igbos on September 29, 1966:

When troops and military personnel massacre civilians, is there a responsibility for such action? Of course, yes. There is, and must be, responsibility and consequences. For example, Kurt Waldeim, as described above, was banned from entry into United States, included in a "watch list" of undesirable aliens by the United States and shunned by Western countries during his presidency of Austria. His crime was serving in a German unit that perpetrated ruthlessness on Marshal Tito's forces in Yugoslavia. There was no evidence that he personally participated or ordered accordingly. Also Erich Priebke, former German Hauptsturmführer (Captain) in the SS police force (Sipo) as already mentioned, died in detention at the age of 100 for participating in the massacre of 335 Italian civilians. He was already 83 years of age when, in 1996, he was convicted of a crime he committed over 50 years earlier in 1944. Furthermore, the "Jackals", a group of 9 Serbian paramilitary members were convicted for the death of 120 Albanian civilians and received jail terms of up to 20 years. The question is if people were jailed for long periods of time and some died in detention, for killing 120 civilian in Serbia or 335 civilians in Italy, or for merely serving in a violent military unit, why are the military perpetrators of the Kano massacre of 3000 Igbos still free and walking around?

Can we find out who they are and bring them to book physically and posthumously? Absolutely yes! As previously stated, the *New York Times* of December 13, 1966, on page 7 columns I, tells us that, of all the 5th battalion soldiers that participated in the massacre, only 32 were arrested and detained. The fact that they were arrested and detained means that their records are or should be at archives of the Nigerian War College in Abuja, and research can start from there. The same *New York Times* of December 13, 1966 (Ibid), also gives us more information: that, of the 32 solders, 11 w0ere Catholics, 11 were Protestants and 10 were Muslims. Also, that the 22 Christian solders were from Gowon's middle belt region. Again, the fact that the New York Times could break the 32 soldiers down into Catholics, Protestants and Muslims means that more information about the 32 is out there, as well as the fact that 22 of the 32 perpetrators were middle belters.

More importantly, why did Gowon, after initial arrest and detention, allow the 32 to go free without prosecution? Is it because 3,000 Igbo lives were too subliminal for a prosecution? Is it because 22 of the 32 murderers were members of his kith and kin from the Middle Belt, or is it part of the general Nigerian belief that the taking of an Igbo life attracts no consequence? It will be interesting to know Gowon's explanations because part of the charges for which late Serbian leader, Slobodan Milosevic, was facing conviction before he died was failure to cooperate in punishing perpetrators of genocide," which is applicable to Gowon's actions here.

Also, some of Theophilus Danjuma's sycophants and brown envelope friends in the media often rationalize Danjuma's killing of General Ironsi by emphasing that Ironsi failed to prosecute the "January 15 Boys". So, what is Gowon's penalty for letting go 32 Northern soldiers that slaughtered 3000 Igbos, some of who may have risen to army Generals, with the blood of 3000 civilian victims on their hands? A soldier killing another soldier is one thing, but a soldier killing civilians is a different thing. That is why those that did it in

Serbia and Italy are facing stiff penalties while those that did it in Nigeria were concealed and allowed to rise to high positions in the army, and some even becoming billionaires.

III. Responsibility for the Makurdi Massacre of Igbos in October 1966.

As discussed above, this massacre of Igbos, who had escaped the Kano massacre was, again, carried out by a mob of soldiers and civilians. The victims' train had left Kano in the immediate wake of the massacre of September 29, 1966 and was halted in Markurdi, when they were almost at home in the east. Who should be held responsible for this massacre? Of course, the troops themselves and the area commander responsible for the troops! Again, this is something that meaningful research will provide answers, since we have dates and witnesses. The Eastern Nigerian government did a registration of displaced persons in late 1966, so research of archival records can trace surviving witnesses of the Makurdi massacre such as Paulina Okaro and Joseph Onyeabor (See *New York Times*, October 14, 1966, page 8, column 5).

Accountability for the sponsors and perpetrators of Igbo massacres

The task of pursuing justice for Igbo victims of massacres and bringing responsibility and consequences to the perpetrators will not be an easy one. It will involve determination, time, money, willpower, research and strong desire to make justice prevail regardless of the power and position of the perpetrators.For example, Kurt Waldheim, who served in the German army from 1941 to 1945, initially claimed that he served in the German army only till 1942. He said he was wounded in the Russian Sector in 1941, and after hospitalization for his wounds, returned to civilian life and pursued his law degree at the University of Vienna, and that he had no knowledge of Jewish liquidation or any German atrocities during his tenure in the German army. Well, what happened? The Jews came together and worked in unison in a way that will be a challenge to the Igbos. Eli Rosenbaum Director of the U.S. DOJ Office of Special Investigations (OSI), persuaded the WJC to finance a research on Kurt Waldheim's activities during WWII. The WJC obliged, and provided money to Robert Edwin Herzstein, a Jewish professor of history at the University of South Carolina in the United States. Professor Herzstein, from his research, and interviews with Waldheim's political opponents in Austria, discovered that Kurt Waldheim did not leave the German military in 1942 as he claimed, but actually served in the Germany army until the end of WWII in 1945; that Kurt Waldheim served as a lieutenant in army intelligence with German forces in the Balkans; a picture Kurt Waldheim, in military uniform, took on May 22, 1943 with Italian General Roncaglia and two other officers at Pedgorica airfield in Montenegro; Kurt Walden's signature on documents linked to massacre or deportations with medals and citations.

Following the above discoveries by Jewish efforts, Waldheim was forced to admit some of his shortcomings during WWII. The question is whether Igbos can put their shoulders together and get to the bottom of the root causes and details of the genocides against them, at least if not for this generation, then for our children and future generations.

It is not too late to seek redress

One good thing working for victims of genocide like the Igbos is that the crimes of genocide, crimes against humanity and war crimes, do not have what lawyers call "statute of limitation" where if you don't seek redress for a particular wrong for a certain time, then, you cannot seek it again. Victims of genocide are allowed to seek redress anytime the facts are uncovered, and sanctions and consequences are sought against the perpetrators. Many of the perpetrators of the Nazi holocaust in Germany against the Jews fled to South America after WWII, but their roles in the holocaust were discovered more than 50 years later, and they were prosecuted and penalized in their 80s and 90s. So, age and the passage of time do not ameliorate the evils of genocide and war crimes. Charges of genocide and war crimes do not respect position and power. Kurt Waldheim was already a two-term UN secretary General and President of Austria when he faced American and Western Sanctions for his activities in WW II. So, whether a Nigerian suspect of genocide and war crimes is a military General, a head of state or a billionaire, should not dissuade the Igbos from seeking redress and compensations against that person. A lot has already been uncovered, thanks to individual Igbos, who at the expense of their time, effort and money have already uncovered substantial facts about the genocide of 1966-1967. It has been uncovered that: Mohammed Shuwa and Theophilus Danjuma issued a ruthlessness order to their first division troops against Biafrans (civilians and military) in a general order (G.O.) dated September 16, 1976 at their Makurdi headquarters. We know that Kurt Walden faced severe Western sanction just for serving in a German unit that perpetrated ruthlessness in Yugoslavia, even though he did not participate.

That 32 Nigerian soldiers were arrested and detained for the Kano massacre of 3000 Igbos on September 29, 1966; that there were 11 Catholics, 11 Protestant and 10 Muslim. That the 22 Christians were from Gowon's Middle Belt area and were never prosecuted by Gowon. More research can uncover the individual identities of the 32 murderers. We already know that Nazi Captain Erich Priebke died in detention for his role in the massacre of 335 Italian aliens, and 9 Serbian paramilitary members are serving upward of 20 years for the massacre of 120 civilians. Then what of the 3000 Igbo civilians massacred by 32 Northern Nigerian troops? The massacre of Igbos and the other Easterners in Makurdi in October 1966 has also been described and relevant facts including some survivors of the massacre identified.

Further research can identify these victims for interviews as witnesses. Other acts of genocide and war crimes against the Igbos, such as Murtala Mohammed's extermination campaign against mid-western Igbos, Gowon's dedicated bombing of civilian targets in Biafra (homes, churches, markets, refugee camps and hospitals) and the deliberate post-war starvation of the Igbos are all subjects of additional research. Murtala's Mid-West genocide is well covered by *Le Monde* of Paris (April 5, 6, 1968), and Emma Okocha's book, *Blood on the Niger*. Gowon's air raid on Biafran civilians and Federal Government's deliberate post war starvation of Biafrans are well covered by the *Untold Story of Nigeria-Biafra War* by Dr Luke N. Aneke. Anybody interested in research on Igbo genocide and war crimes has an abundance of materials to aid his/her research.

Conclusion

It is my belief that it is important to hold liquidators of Igbo life to some responsibility and consequences if an Igbo life is going to have any worth in Nigeria, and we can start with those already positively identified as candidates for war crimes prosecution. As I said in the beginning, the security or importance of a life is determined, in large part, by the consequences, if any, attendant to the taking of that life. As we can see, the life of a Jew is worth more today and is treated with more sanctity today than it was in the period between the two world wars, thanks to the "never again" campaign and the efforts made by Jews to ensure that Jewish liquidators faced consequences of their actions.

In the New Testament book of Matthew 10:29, Jesus Christ, discussing the value and worth of life, said that two sparrows were sold for a farthing. Those who are old enough to know the farthing know that it's the fourth part of a penny. One quarter of penny is not a lot, but it still has some value. Hence, to expend the life of two sparrows you must part with a farthing as small as it is. But taking an Igbo life in Nigeria cost the perpetrators nothing, not even a farthing. It is my hope that someday in my life time, the worth of an Igbo life in Nigeria can equate or exceed that of two sparrows. If we start this accountability campaign against the perpetrators of Igbo genocide and massacres, and have the courage, determination and zeal to sustain the tempo, then, sometime in no distant future, people will no longer wash their hands in Igbo blood, and those that will try it will face very bitter consequences. Then and only then, can an Igbo be guaranteed some reasonable measure of security in Nigeria and around the world.

Securing the South-East and Igbo Economic Interest
by
AU Max Gbanite

This essay will focus on key facets of security as it affects the South East economy. I shall look into the immediate security challenges and the way forward. The essay deals with micro security-this is simply the internal perspectives; the needed cooperation within the core-states of South East in dealing with the security challenges they face. macro security-will harp on the relationship with our various contiguous neighboring states, and this includes those considered friendly and unfriendly; and what Ndigbo residing in other parts of the federation should and must do to secure their lives and properties when faced with security challenges. Strategic security deals with perception and philosophy, how to tap into the various and numerous international organizations to make our case, when Ndigbo are threatened.

Section 14 (1) (b) of the current constitution of the Federal Republic of Nigeria says that, "the security and welfare of the people shall be the primary purpose of government." However the behavior of government (at Federal, State and local levels) has shown that those responsible for upholding the above norm are yet to comprehend the full meaning of that part of the constitution. The spate of wanton killings in the south east, and all over the country by restless youth, religious bigots, and tribal-phobic's, and even uniformed (police) agents of the government, is worrisome.

The issue of militancy, cultism, terrorism, and kidnapping and community vs Fulani cattle herdsmen is fast spreading across the nation and the state of readiness of the appropriate agencies (i.e. the police) is neither here nor there; resulting in the deployment of military to our streets to perform internal security duties, a task they the military are not indoctrinated to do. These are indeed trying times for the nation and all hands must be on deck to satisfy the responsibility of government to the people as stated under the above captioned section of the constitution.The question in the minds of Ndigbo all over the world remains: how did we allow this very high level of insecurity and moral decadence to come into our midst in the south east states (Ndigbo-axis)? I still remember vividly the first armed robber killed by police in Enugu. The incident happened at Eze Street, in 1973; and the dead armed robber was "fully armed" with a 'sophisticated-touch light and sharp matchet'. It was indeed a sight, and after that incident, Enugu city started experiencing better and more equipped robbers armed with 'sophisticated-guns'. These young men were remnants of our (Biafra) soldiers who could not get employment immediately after the civil war. Ndigbo killing Ndigbo for money, or kidnapping for same is not totally alien to our traditional sense and psyche'. In the past we were actively involved in the trans-Atlantic slave trade. However, how and where water passed under the 'water-leaf plant' in recent times needs to be looked into.

We as a people must collectively trace our moral decadence to lack of employment and job security for our youth, most of them graduates of tertiary institutions; the importation and acceptance of cultism in the universities and secondary schools in the East as part of our norms; allowing the menace of kidnapping-for-ransom and terrorism from the South South to sip into our tradition; the adaptation of the North's oligarchy style of imposition of candidates during elections; and accepting that accumulation of wealth by any means necessary is more important in today's world than integrity and good family name; allowing ritual killings for wealth to replace the culture of being our brothers keepers; the adoption of South West behavior of cultism and thuggery in settling political differences; and allowing pseudo-leaders to emerge as authentic Igbo leaders; and embracing the so-called new generation churches against core orthodox religions like Catholics, Anglican, Baptist, Presbyterian, and Methodist and Animism that helped in forming the behavioral-infrastructure that made Ndigbo pure, considerate and hard-working people. Today these new generation churches espouse miracles of riches, wealth in all forms, prosperity, and propagation of 'fire-by-fire' praying philosophy while preaching less about love for one another and lacking the guts to question gullible members on how they made their money as long as ten percent of the ill-gotten money is paid to the head-pastor as tithe. Tackling the challenges of insecurity in the South Eastern states requires a three-step strategy namely, *micro, macro* and *strategic security*. I will presently deal with the micro security issue. The macro and strategic can always be discussed at another forum.

Micro Security

As Ndigbo, we are blessed to understand each other's internal dialect. Therefore communication amongst us is not a problem. We recognize our traditional rulers; however, respecting them depends on the caliber and integrity they hold within the community. Nevertheless they remain very vital in mobilizing their various communities to rise against this scourge of insecurity. The South East Governor's forum must collectively act quickly. At this point, it is imperative to mention that most south east states have created various types of community vigilantes (pseudo security groups) to assist the various law enforcement agencies in combating crimes and other forms of insecurity within. For instance, the Enugu state government passed a law to Establish, Regulate and Operate Neighborhood Associations and Watch groups and for other connected matters, in 2006. The laws were gazetted as No. 8 Vol 16 dated 28th December, 2007. Section 14 deals with the functions of the Watch Group; and it states thus:

(1) The Watch group shall work in partnership with the Divisional Police Officer in the area they are registered, justice of the peace, town union and other stake holders to perform the following functions:

(a) To prevent crime through:
   (i) Improving security through joint patrols/vigilance with police;
   (ii) Reduce opportunities for crime by increasing crime prevention awareness campaigns;
   (iii) Development of neighborhood crime prevention programmes;
   (iv) Assisting the police in identifying and finding solutions to prevalent and especially emerging crimes.
(b) To assist the police in detecting crime through:
   (i) Promoting effective communication with police;
   (ii) Prompt reporting of suspicious and criminal activity to the police;
   (iii) Providing information/intelligence to the police on suspicious persons and prevalent crimes;
   (iv) Alerting the community about types of crimes prevalent and especially emerging crimes.
(c) To reduce the fear of crime through:
   (i) Providing accurate information about crime risks;
   (ii) Promoting a sense of security and community spirit particularly amongst the more vulnerable;
   (iii) Encouragement of mutual assistance and concern amongst neighborhood members.

(Source: ISSN 1116-297XAI Enugu State, Nigeria CAP laws 20007 No. 1)

An observation of events in a village like Iwollo-Oghe in Ezeagu Local Government Area, Enugu State may be enlightening. There is no cooperation/synergy between the Traditional Ruler (Igwe-Omasi), and the President of the Town Union. Politicians in collaboration with the Town Union President impose thugs and criminals as the neighborhood watch group on the community which the Igwe refused to inaugurate. For the program to be well structured and enduring it is imperative that the nominees come directly from the people at ward (Umunna) level.

Recommendations
The traditional ruler, his cabinet, and Town union president as first tier representatives must first analyse and examine their security challenges and how to tackle the same. The government should start with the formation of Community Public Safety Security and Intelligence Council (CPSSIC), made up of members of each community from ward level and possibly including: a ward chairman of all existing political parties in the ward, a respected elder, a

woman church leader, motorcyclist leader, a young thug, and traditional medicine (herbalist) man, and a titled man. The second tier level: the Town Public Safety Security and Intelligence Council (TPSSIC), made up of a representative from each ward CSIC, and chaired by the town's traditional ruler, with Town Union President as Vice. The third tier level: the Local Government Public Safety Security and Intelligence Council (LGPSSIC). This level will include one representative from each of the Town Public Safety Security and Intelligence Council, with the Divisional Police Officer (DPO), the State Security Service (SSS), Nigeria Immigration Service (NIS), Nigeria Customs Service (NCS), and Federal Road Safety Corp (FRSC), National Security and Civil Defence Corps (NSCDC), and Military as members. There should also be a fourth tier made up of the State Public Safety Security and Intelligence Council (SPSSIC) drawn from each of the Local Governments, to be chaired by the executive governor, with one high ranking security operatives the rank of Commissioner of Police or equivalent from all the security and Para-security agencies in the state as members. The final tier should be the Interstate Public Safety Security and Intelligence Council (IPSSIC) made up of five members from each state selected by the governor; with the GOC of 82 division of Nigeria Army, as chairman and AIG of the zone as vice chairman.

Once these various committees are established, the first tier will be mandated to hold security-stake-holder's meeting at ward level; identify their immediate security challenges; identify the potential bad person(s), shady character's, drug dealers, and illegal activities in their respective wards. That information becomes the foundation for intelligence profiling. The information gathered at ward level will be collated at the town and local government levels as well. The personality and illegal activities catalogued, gives the security agencies the opportunity to counter and respond rapidly. Each ward should create a 10-man vigilante force to be paid at least the minimum wage of 18,000.00 naira, funded by a joint State and LGA security vote fund, and/or Sure-P funds. The Vigilante unit must be able-bodied, with the capacity to mobilize everyone in the community to react to any negative vice. For instance, if a robbery is in progress, a mechanism must be in place to sound out an alarm within the community, like the IKORO, as was done in the olden days. All the neighboring community leaders must be immediately alerted to mobilize their wards. Every obstacle available must be placed on the roads to immobilize the movement of the robbers. The okada riders immediately should be mobilized in strategic places to help the police with mobility. The same principle applies in the case of kidnapping. The community must be emboldened to make life of crime unprofitable to those attempting to operate within the town. Once a ward activates its early warning system, the entire town wakes up; the town leader notifies the local government leader, who also notifies the state leader; and the inter-state tier will alert the highway police to be on alert immediately; and this can be achieved within minutes of the crime being committed.

The state government in collaboration with the local government must provide the logistics such as transmission radios (five per ward); vehicles and bikes for police and vigilante groups to use. A joint task force post must be established in every town in order to build confidence within the community. After all security is our collective responsibility. If "a stitch in time saves nine" then we must begin to remove the specs in our eyes. These vices were imported into our community from other parts of the country; therefore we can collectively take back our community from rogues, cultists, and kidnappers who are in the minority. The government should also establish a compensation package for any family who loses a member in any attempt to foil robbery and kidnapping. An award should be given by the Local Government Chairman to the town's that had the least incidents of robbery and kidnapping; and the state government should do the same to LGAs.

A **'Broken window'** approach must be applied: During the festivities, any form of fighting, no matter how little must be dealt with. The police must arrest the culprits, keep them in detention and charge them to court. Drunk drivers must be detained immediately. This saves the driver's life and that of many others. The essence of 'Broken Window' in criminology is simply to demonstrate that the community in collaboration with security agencies will not tolerate any form of mischief. The effect gives a criminal the time to reflect; if the police will arrest one for drunkenness or fighting, then what happens if one does more than that. Broken window policy was initiated by Patrick Murphy, a professor of criminology at John Jay College of Criminology, New York. Community Public Safety Security and Intelligence Council at the ward level affords the community the opportunity to partner with security agencies in combating crimes. The rule of the game is that every member of the community is made responsible for each other; we become our brother's keepers. This enables Ndigbo in Diaspora to have confidence in their community and return enmass to invest economically in their various communities.

Fulani Cattle Herdsmen and Farmers' Issue

This is the most troubling issue in Igbo land besides the internal self-inflicted issue of kidnappings and armed robberies. To fully understand this bitter rivalry for competing space, let us take a look at the following 'security-report' submitted to Sir Fredericks Lord Luggard, during his administration of the then Northern Protectorate of Nigeria, when the local farmers fought with the same Fulani cattle herdsmen.

The Fulani are ascetic, kind and generous *BUT Never* fight a war (hot or old) with the Fulani. Because they have:
1. No rules of engagement (they just hit again and again).

2. No POW's (they don't take prisoners).
3. No mercy (once they pick you out as the enemy).
4. NO fighting fatigue (they are forever fit and prepared, due to their lifestyle).
5. No need for adequate provisions & permanent abode (they live on very little and sleep in the wilderness).
6. No end to hostilities (they fight to finish).
7. No ignorance of terrain and location (their lifestyle makes every one of them a human GPS).
8. No deterrence due to casualties (they are strategically distributed all over west and Central Africa, and highly mobile).
9. No need for tranquility (they have no permanent settlements which need peace to thrive).
10. No fear of consequences!!"

After reviewing the above report, Sir Luggard set up a committee to find a lasting solution and, the result became 'the littoral grazing laws' which established the grazing routes and reserves in various parts of the North. The Southern part of the country never had such laws; as a matter of fact the first attempt was the well-thought-out program of the late premier of the then Eastern region, Dr. Michael Okpara, who established an organized grazing reserve at the highlands of Obudu; christened 'Obudu Cattle Ranch'. This noble idea reduced any kind of conflict that would have risen between farmers and cattle herdsmen then. He further created a cattle discharge port at Umuahia; this enabled all the trains carrying cattle to the East to discharge at Umuahia, before the cattles are moved alongside the roads to various points in the hinter-land. His policies never allowed cattle herdsmen to transverse farmlands, hence, reducing any possibility of conflicts. The mind-set of a Fulani when it comes to grazing is that he is doing the community a favor by clearing their forest; he does not understand that individuals can actually own them as farmlands. In the North he knows that nobody claims to own such, therefore he is bewildered to find such claims in the southern parts of the country. However, his sense of justice also allows him the responsibility to pay claims when he is confronted with facts of his wandering-cattle's damages to any farm product or property.

In the past, the same herdsmen were never armed with guns; they only carried their bows/arrows and long sticks for hunting and warding off of dangerous animals. In those days the cattle was owned and managed by wise and peaceful Fulanis. But that has changed today. The new owners of these cattle are the same Fulani but these are highly educated and influential individuals who served in various capacity, and high-positions in government (military, customs, ministries, and other Para-military agencies), and retire to become Emir's, District-Heads, and business men. They have amassed and acquired tremendous reserves of money which enabled them to invest in cattle business. They also believe that their investments must be protected from rustlers and robbers who snatch their cattle, and kill their workers; hence, they procure weapons (AK47) for the herdsmen to carry. The original intent may not be to harass the community, however, suffice it to add that amongst the herdsmen are rogues who use the same weapons to take advantage of a community. It is also important not to associate the herdsmen with the religion of Islam, because they are not. Only a few are and actually practice the religion like their educated kith and kin.

Based on the security report on the Fulani, which community in Igbo land is prepared to fight a protracted war with them? For further clarification and understanding, we should study and pay attention to what is happening in Benue State, Plateau state, and Adamawa state. How do we take advantage of this situation to better our lot and reduce the friction rather than seeking a total removal or sacking of the Fulani herdsman from our land? We must also remember the fact that we are also everywhere in Nigeria doing business, making money, building houses, and raising families. Therefore, our collective decision in the South East will be placed under consideration by others when dealing with our brethrens in their various communities.

Recommendation, Macro Security and Conclusion

The South East governors must be encouraged to convince their various state assemblies to legislate laws establishing grazing-ranch-parks within. The States may agree to collaborate by developing joint-grazing-park-zones along its borders. This creates opportunities for both Ndigbo and Fulani. If indeed a ranch like 'Obudu' as envisaged by Dr. M.I. Okpara is established with at least five thousand heads of cattle, rams, and goats in addition to other livestock like poultry farms, bush-meat, snails, could be added as part of a grazing park. The added advantage makes it easy for these animals to be monitored by veterinarians, which means that citizens are sure of the health of the animals they consume. Both local and International producers of milk, cheese, and allied dairy-products will have a collective point to place orders for the raw materials need to keep their industries going. Those in tannery business will be confident of their constant supply of raw leather to the shoe, hand bags, and related industries. The natural cow manure collected can be used in organic farming of fruits (Brazilian orchard system) within the same ranch grazing park. This enables the locals to learn animal-husbandry from the Fulani, and in turn gives the Fulani child an opportunity to go to school and be more productive to his environment. This will reduce drastically the incessant clashes between local farmers and Fulani herdsmen.

Fortunately most of our neighboring states are friendly, except for the already resolved issue between Anambra State and Kogi State over the Orient Oil Refinery. However, it is important to remind our brethren residing outside

Igbo land to remember the adage that says, *"Ebe onye bi k' ona awachii"* and *"Obialu be onye abia gbuneya, onawa k' mkpumkpu ghalu idi ya n' azu."* If we abide by these principles, we shall never have problems with our hosts. We must never live under the delusion that 'we have the right to live and conduct our business anywhere in Nigeria, because the constitution says so.' If we are protected under this noble constitution, then the Fulani is assured the same right in our own land? The issue of strategic security and deals with the international community can best be discussed at a round-table with trusted minds. For us to know where the rain stopped beating us we must recognize when and where it started. I do not have all the answers. However, the time is now to act collectively by reestablishing the economic blue-print or strategic economic security of Ndigbo. Failure to act collectively places our nation on a path of 'clear and present danger'. We must no longer place the collective development of Ndigbo in the hands of strangers. Nigeria is looking up to us to lead her to a higher level of industrialization. The time is now.

SECTION NINE: NATIONAL CHARACTER

Alaigbo Development Foundation (ADF):
Rebuilding the Igbo Hearth
By
Dr. Kalu Idika Kalu, *OFR*

Introduction

Beyond a consideration of the clearly diminished political clout of NdiIgbo since the end of the 30-month Nigeria-Biafra conflict, there has been a far more serious and lingering issue about what has befallen NdiIgbo as a distinctive cultural entity. The thrust of this paper is simply to provide a broad and practical framework, a scope of a plausible agenda for the Rebuilding of The Igbo Nation. This system will be geared to the Rebuilding of the Igbo Hearth in all its essential dynamic manifestations in the twenty-first century.

A Webster Encyclopedic Dictionary definition of the "hearth" is "the fireside, the home. The hearth is, in a sense, the cradle from which the folk lore, the oral heroics, the customs and traditions of the people are spun in the natural language, the images and the tales in the flow of socializing tutelage to the present and future generations. The ultimate purpose of this effort, this scared responsibility, is to redefine and address the factors that contributed to the rapid *Rise*, and then, the apparent *Fall* or decline, of Ndi Igbo and the corresponding erosion of the stronger elements of Igbo culture within two generations!

The pertinent questions could be couched as follows: how can Ndi Igbo re-create that socio- cultural milieu which provided the back drop that propelled the Igbo-speaking peoples in the present South-East, and elsewhere, from a relatively obscure position within the larger Nigerian polity, to the forefront in so many fields of endeavour between the mid-twenties, and right through to the mid-sixties of the twentieth century? What factors have been responsible for the relative decline of NdiIgbo since the mid-sixties, seemingly accelerating, perhaps, understandably, from the January 1966 coup, and since the end of the 'civil war,' despite the pronounced lofty ideal of "*no victor, no vanquished*" at the end of the hostilities in January 1970?

Most importantly, we would in this paper, seek to examine what organs, institutions must be re-vamped or rebuilt to create a vibrant acculturation and socialization milieu to enable an irreversible "re-invention of those positive attributes that were readily identifiable as Igbo "traits"? What will have to be done in Igboland by the individual, the family, the clan or community, and by various organs, by the various tiers of Igbo political and civil institutions, to reinvent, as it were, the confident, honest, morally-upright, thrifty, respectful, humble, hardworking, fiercely and openly competitive, and upwardly mobile Igbo man and woman?

The basic thesis is that it is only by, as it were, pausing and taking stock of the meaning and implications of the events of the post-war period, and effectively reorganizing the instruments of the community's socio-political and economic dynamics, that any group, such as the Igbo nation that has endured the multiple trauma of political conflict, displacements of genocidal proportions, and a bloody thirty-month war and post war deprivations, can hope to arrest a process of progressive retrogression of its essence as a worthwhile, thriving, cultural entity.

In these volumes, there are at least four related topics to the central theme of this paper! There is Professor Awuzie's Research, Planning and Development, and the Future of Igboland; Professor Peter Ejiofor's Language, Culture and the Future of Igboland; Igbo Language, Culture and Civilization, by Professor Chinyere Ohiri-Anichie, and Structure and Governance System for the Future of the Igbo Nation by Dr S. Okechukwu Mezu. In all, the thrust of the monumental effort is towards the rebuilding of the Igbo Nation, and putting NdiIgbo squarely and effectively back into the vanguard of the political and administrative leadership in Nigeria's continuing journey into a viable nationhood.

Three major thrusts in Rebuilding the Igbo Hearth

A systematic reexamination of the culture of Aka Ikenga in Igbo Society, in all its variants across the entire Igbo sub- cultures, the essence and the central role of the Homestead, the essence of the Hearth as a primary cultural platform and guide for the infant and the impressionable youth. The structural ties that bind the conjugal family to the larger extended family, and the immediate community and the clan. Secondly, there is the socialization process through which the character is molded around the principles of individual and family honour, pride in the Igbo identity, truth and hard work in honest endeavour as the only basis for Igbo dignity. The fostering of age grade, peer group and studious apprenticeship, with the underlying spirit of pooling together" - *Onye ahala nwanneya, nwannaya.*"! Modalities for transposing the essence of this primary doctrine unto the modern commercial, industrial enterprise economy become imperative for sustaining the revival of Igbo energies and cooperative spirit. This strategy will be formally adopted for Igbo political and socio- cultural organizations in all of Igboland, outside of Igboland within Nigeria, and in the diaspora.

Lastly, the organizing framework for the rebuilding process will between the affiliates of the AlaIgbo Development Foundation (ADF), on one hand, and on the other hand, within a structured Organogram delineating various subjects, sectors and subsectors of various disciplines for the purpose of research, policy development and liaison, in the implementation, in conjunction with various entities in Igboland and beyond. For example, a basic framework could address the issue of education, the redesigning of various curricula for all levels, from the nursery to higher levels of education; health and hygiene, basic agriculture and science, handcraft, and artisan skills, to recreate the energies of our rural enterprise upon which modern skills can be usefully grafted for sustained improvement in economic productivity.

The role of various institutions at the community, local government, state, and, perhaps, also at the zonal, interstate levels for coordinated planning and investment in common infrastructures, railways, ports, water systems, and even manpower training institutions will be subject for regional planning. The major subject areas for broad based planning cuts across all development sectors, knowledge-based research into the vast and rich resource endowment of Igboland, most of which still lies relatively untapped. The development of basic science, basic nature study that created a natural synergy between the child and his environment, and the keen awareness fostered from the names and uses of the plants and fauna, the whole universe of the growing child's environment that rooted him firmly in his culture and traditions, but which sadly, became a casualty with his new rootless urban environment, with disastrous consequences for his language, his identity and his future development!

The language, music, dance, the arts and crafts will all require a structured reactivation and codification as essential aspects of an erstwhile vibrant, but vanishing culture. Committees of experts, both active and retired, from both the public and the private sectors, those living at home, within and outside Igboland, and those in diaspora, will all have to be engaged, primarily part-time, in various distinct specialties of research, policy formulation, and in proffering practical guidance for programme implementation in concert with various tiers of administrative governance in the rebuilding process!

Universal Igbo Professional Data Bank

A major starting point will be the building of a Universal Data Bank of all grades of Igboprofessionals and skills at all levels at home, and abroad, to ensure that all hands have the opportunity to contribute to the rebuilding of the Igbo hearth. Centers for Data Collation will have to be set up for the massive data collection in all local government areas across Alaigbo, from where local and diaspora data can be collated and pooled in one or more central locations under the supervision of the (ADF) Alaigbo development foundation. Major research areas should be set up by appropriate ADF supervision, but under the directorate of a select body of relevant specialists, in these four broad areas, among others:

1. A framework for the Restoration and the Rebuilding of Igboland, politics and governance

2. Issues behind the clearly diminished political muscle of Ndi Igbo
3. Ndi Igbo have suffered as individuals, and as a people. .decline in self esteem amid lingering bravados, the rise in "passing" through name change, intermarriage, and general self-perception and self-identity i.e. Delta, Rivers as descriptive of Igbo ethnicity coming from these parts of Igboland, in clear preference for the true and natural Igbo identity!
4. Agenda for Igbo renaissance...a systematic rebuilding of the Igbo Hearthas the only tangible anti-dote to curing and reversing the festering malaise that has afflicted NdiIgbo and Igbo Homeland: evidence in the butt of national jokes and negative epithets, the atrophy of social traditions, institutions and decline in the music, dance and art of NdiIgbo.
5. Historical sequence of the emergence of the 'Igbo Question' can be traced far back from the 1920's political awakening; the Aba women's riots against perceived unjust levies and taxation; the building up of the colonial service, and Igbos increasing participation in it.

There were also massive structural changes in all segments of the colonial system; the beginnings of a fledgling legislative system in 1922; the increase in real terms, of public expenditures on education, public health, transportation, roads and rails across the length of the country, i.e. Lagos to Kaduna, Port Harcourt to Kano thru Enugu, etc. The expansion in the central government civil service also witnessed what seemed a disproportionate increase in relative terms of the numbers of Ndi Igbo, from both the East and the Mid-West regions of Nigeria. The Igbos readily embraced the new colonial regime which ushered in education, new religious institutions, modern health services and other trappings of an organized polity. For the entire nation, it was a very visible upward mobility, in every sphere of life. Senior and middle-level positions, both administrative and technical, appeared to be occupied by persons from the old Eastern Region, particularly those from Igboland. However, the rise of the Igbos in retrospect, as indicated in the Crisis series publication (1967), available data suggests that only a 15-16 percent ratio, of all federal positions was occupied by Ndi Igbo. But these data were based strictly on data from Federal institutions excluding the Federal parastatals. The problem of course was, as it still is, encouraged by the very victims of this propaganda...the Igbos themselves. The 1966-67 crises and the ensuing Nigerian-Biafra war seem to have played right into the hands of those who felt Ndi Igbo have had far more than their fair share of "the national cake".
Pressures mounted to dismantle their so called strangle-hold and dominance in the federal structure including the federal universities, the police and the armed forces. These pressures were in fact behind the reprisals which occurred during the period and the subsequent post war period till the mid eighties and up to the present. The strict and wide ranging practice of federal character seem to have been applied, to the disadvantage of Ndi Igbo perception among Ndi Igbo. From the 1970s, there remained a strong feeling

and perception among Ndi Igbo that there was a secret understanding to limit the presence of Ndi Igbo in the upper echelons of the federal government, especially in the civil service and in the Armed forces despite the no victor, no vanquish policy as espoused by the leadership of the Federal government.

The agenda of the Alaigbo Development Foundation (ADF)

The work of the Alaigbo Development Fund should consist of two basic elements. The first will be to set up the ADF structure and its organizational links to the various government, NGOs, and Private sectors affiliates:

- Ohaneze and other major Igbo organs, including Ndi Igbo Lagos, Aka-Ikenga and the major town unions all across the country.
- Government institutions
- The five South East States, appropriate representation from the Delta and Rivers States and the respective State assemblies:
- The Local governments and their secretariats
- Traditional leaders and their various communities
- Private organizations—corporations and chambers of commerce
- Universities and other institutions
- Research and development agencies (such as SENEC and others at home and abroad in Diaspora.

The second challenge of the organization of the ADF, is the link to various developmental specialized areas through which derived policies will be transmitted to various development implementing agencies; education, health, science, engineering, agronomy, agriculture, various scales of manufacturing, music, art, dance, infrastructure, governance, sports etc. The list cannot be presumed to be exhaustive in this draft presentation. It will be continually updated as the committees of experts meet to deliberate on the detailed work programme. The restructuring of Igboland and the ethos of Ndi Igbo will necessarily be a dynamic process as we strive to recreate the lost or waning essence of our culture. For example, the re-introduction of myriads of very wholesome and educative and recreational indoor and outdoor games that were very important features of Igbo life and culture will need to be revisited and re-coded. Our dances, such as the famous Atilogwu, seem to have been paradoxically transplanted to other somewhat "alien" sub-cultures outside Igboland, while, the authentic dances in Igboland become steadily "discarded" in its true original forms in Igboland itself!

The welfare system that represents a measure of civilized governance will need to be explicitly re-formalized. Social welfare schemes including the rehabilitation of the weak, the sick, and the infirm, such as our war veterans who have suffered in the past struggles of the Igbo people, i.e. those in the Oji River veterans' project, will be properly administered and fully funded in recognition of their contribution to the survival of Ndi Igbo. The old, pensioners and others with special needs, handicapped, lepers, and peoples needing specialized care require financial and other accommodations from a productive society to which they have made a contribution. Such assistance also applies to all those who have been affected by the dangerous side effects of the modern industrial system. It is indeed an integral aspect of the *"Onye ahala nwanneya"* dictum.

The major focus of the ADF functions in the re-building of the Igbo Hearth will consist of (a) building the Universal Data Bank of Igbo Professionals and Skills personnel; (b) research into all aspects of the development process as a basis for information for policy recommendations that are transmitted to the appropriate affiliates for implementation; (c) all the tiers of Igboland structures – governments, parastatals, traditional and other community civil institutions; (d) publications of research and derived policy implications.The structure will be subjected to continuous review by special committees/subcommittees to ensure continuous relevance to the needs of a dynamic Igbo community. Details of these subjects will need to be explicitly set out by the respective experts, sourced and specially mandated by the ADF from time to time.It is these experts who will, in turn, determine the scope, and assess the quality of the work to be done, and where such final products should be transmitted through the stages of final consideration and approval as basis for policy recommendations.

The Charts.

The charts presented are drafts of the linkages for liaison and administrative organization of the envisaged work programme of the ADF. The ADF Organizational Structure will have to be elaborated from the existing structure already circulated. The final form will be formalized over time after due consideration for the proposed scope of the Activities and the Personnel required for take-off in various locations. The ADF already has interim board and committee derived from the draft constitution – A board of Trustees, a council, working committees and sub-committees. All these will be subject to review as the ADF settles down to its sacred task of coordinating the Re-building of Igboland. The ADF needs to constantly ensure that it maintains an efficient and streamlined administrative bureaucracy guided by result-oriented objectives. The special nature of the mandate of the ADF that calls for diverse specialties already determines to a very large extent the quality of its membership. While the AlaIgbo Congress would provide a mass platform for disseminating its work and findings, its specialized focus on the rebuilding process necessarily delimits its membership scope to essential specialists and skilled membership that are directly responsible for its core functions.

Summary

Economic, social and political process impact all human organs and social institutions. It is evident that such impact can have debilitating effects over time, on the lives, the values, the hopes and on the sustenance of peace and prosperity of any given cultural entity, such as the Igbo race. What has been sketched in this paper can be applicable with appropriate variants to any cultural entities within the Nigerian/African context. Our contention is that is only by pausing, taking an honest and effective stock of its true state as a cultural unit within the Nigerian political context, can Ndi Igbo expect to arrest and resolve what has been variably described in different terms as the "Igbo Question", or the Igbo Dilemma, etc.

We need to answer many pertinent questions about this immediate past history of the evolution of the Igbo community, from the dawn of the modern colonial era right up to "political independence" in 1960. What were responsible for the remarkable successful adaptation of Igbo cultural traits to modern ideas that were foisted on the arbitrary entity made up of diverse cultures, languages and traditions named "Nigeria"? What factors were responsible for the seemingly inexorable erosion of continuous Igbo development as a distinct entity from the eve of the so-called "political independence" to the present? What factors in the Igbo character or group political perspectives accentuated the apparent rising resentment against NdiIgbo as a cultural unity? Were such perceptions innate in aspects of Igbo culture or was the resentment based on fears of the so-called potential for Igbo domination derived, as it were, from the relatively rapid rise in the visibility of NdiIgbo at the upper ends of the ladder of Nigeria's modern institutions of control and governance. Furthermore, were these resentments justified, or were they a throwback from the culture of Ndi Igbo, particularly in relation to cultural perspectives on economic and political competition?

Whatever reasons can be adduced for the "rise ... and fall" of Ndi Igbo within a space of two generations, the important issue is what must Ndi Igbo do to save themselves from drifting to relative oblivion, in a metaphorical sense, of course! Indeed, some "objective" observers may see the formal posing of these questions as "typical Igbo presumptuousness or unbridled pride in the sense that Ndi Igbo are really not in the "total valley" as implicitly depicted ... certainly, not from an individual perspective by comparison with other Nigerians. Indeed most Nigerians, including Ndi Igbo themselves, offer contradictory evidence adduced from successful Igbo presence in Nigeria and in particular, in the diaspora...where Nigerian-type limitations do not evidently apply.

By the same token, it can be incontrovertibly asserted that the status of the Igbo as a cultural entity, as distinct from individuals, has suffered a measurable decline in virtually all aspects. What factors explain this apparent contradiction? We need to disentangle the interwoven contributory factors that created the favorable "rise" of Ndi Igbo from the early colonial 1920s through to the 1960s, and contrast this with the factors responsible for the subsequent relative decline since the post-war.

Perhaps, the "rise" of the Igbo was possible by the distinct individualistic requirements for social advance, such as in education, skill acquisition and unique management and supervision skills that were required for the manning of colonial institutions. On this thesis, the need for group or political pressure/lobby action on the attainment of independence, following the devolution of political control to indigenous actors created a new challenge for the more individualistic Igbo political players. The changes from the pre-eminence of competitive, individual merit-based requirements to the special skills of groups political action came somewhat in conflict with the emphasis on individual merit, thus, giving special advantages to others who were "culturally better-suited" to cooperative group" behavior!

4.7 Does this thesis stack up to an acceptable explanation to the histories of the parties involved in the immediate pre-independence political struggle and thereafter, following the granting of formal independence --- the Yorubas, the Hausas, etc for example? Furthermore, and most instructively could this, in fact, in part, explain the differences in the historically established fact of the "size of traditional kingdoms created in these parts of West Africa by these major ethnic conglomerates?

These issues become very instructive as one sifts through Igbo historiography in an effort to re-identify the basic elements of the Igbo Hearth. Even more importantly, from the stand point of the core purpose of the ADF in its coordinating functions for the re-building of the Igbo Hearth, is the requirement for re-creating a vibrant Igbo culture for the modern industrial age. Clearly, we would need to identify those positive elements, the individual context factors that propelled rapid Igbo advance, to the extent that these are present and relevant for the future development of Igboland.

The research into Igbo history should yield answers that can be pointers to the appropriate policies that future responsive and responsible government would require in fashioning a new Igbo society that draws from the positive elements of our cultural past. These issues have been amply covered in some of the other presentations cited earlier on. Rebuilding the Igbo Hearth is a must in our present circumstances but we must realize that it will not be an assignment that would be accomplished over a short period of time. Indeed, this effort will necessarily be a continuing process, adapted as times change in consonance with developments within, and around Igboland.

Rebuilding of the Igbo Hearth:

In summary, rebuilding of the Igbo hearth (a) must reverse the culture of pecuniary greed, and the mindless pursuit of wealth and titles without conscience and moral scruples; (b) must reinstate pride, hard work and humility as the basis for Igbo respect and dignity; (c) must start from the basics, in re-implanting the Igbo in the Igbo child to his culture, language, and mastery of his natural habitat to the full extent that is possible; (d) must include the adaptation of new curricula that encompasses the study of history, science and basic mathematics from the primary school level in Igbo and English language; (e) must involve a total overhaul of governance principles and broad-based democratic consensus building in all political and social institutions in Igboland and among Ndi Igbo everywhere; (f) must result in the overhaul of the merit system for traditional recognition away from unbridled and inexplicable wealth accumulation to positively identifiable achievements directed at improving the social welfare and the development of the community. In this respect, all non-traditionally derived chieftaincy titles should be reviewed and discarded in favor of the democratically elected leader of the respective Igbo communities. A socially-based merit system should be designed to reward positive achievements in the New Igbo community.

Chart 1 ADF and Affiliates

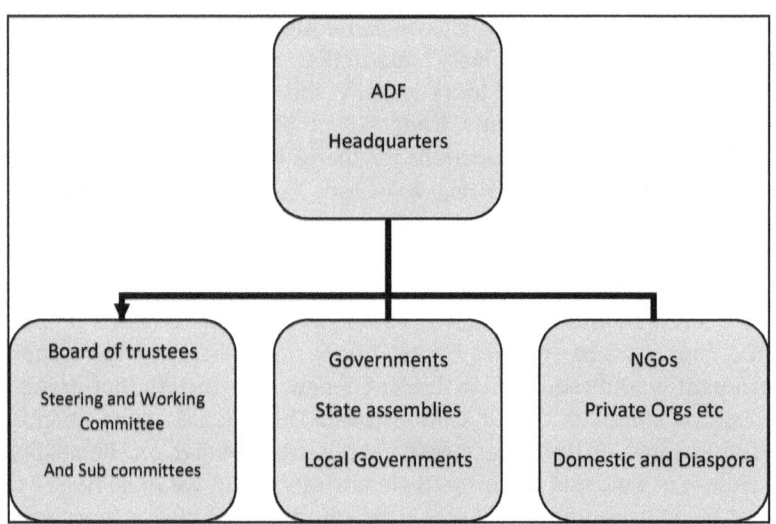

Chart 2 ADF Work Program

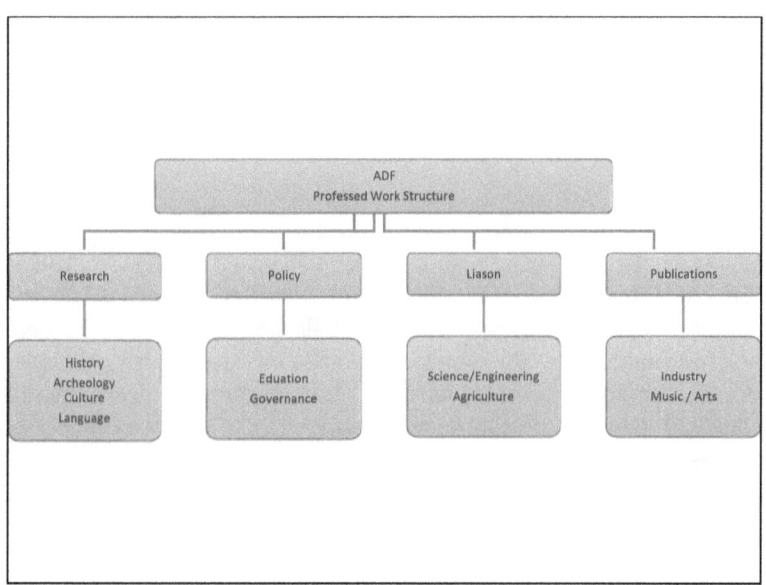

Chart 3: Elaboration of the Affiliate Structure

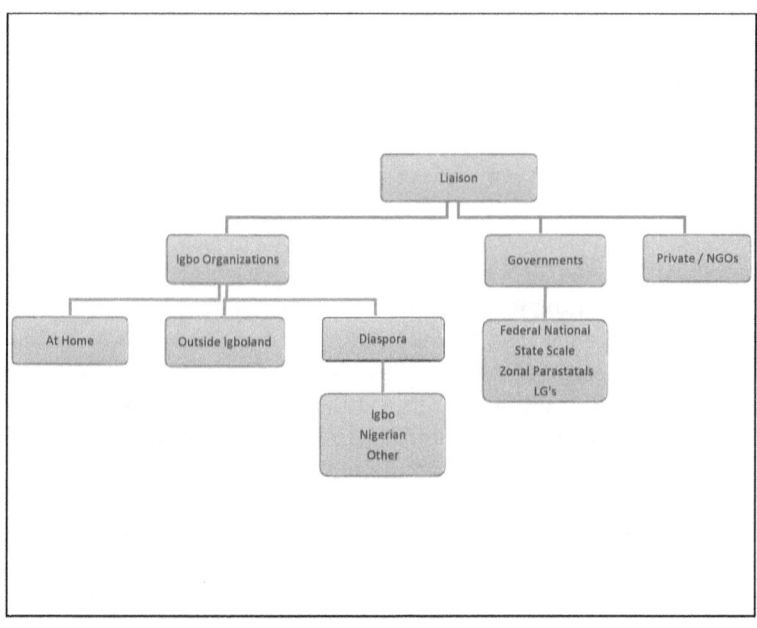

Addressing Social, Moral and Spiritual Decay in Igboland
by
Professor Vincent C. Anigbogu

Abstract

There is a growing concern about the future of Igbo community who in recent times are witnessing high levels of social, moral, and spiritual decay. This downward trend started during the civil war in late 1960s and has continued unabated. Once one of the most vibrant, cohesive, and progressive ethnic groups in Nigeria, the Igbo land is today infested with high incidents of corruption, armed robbery, kidnapping, ritual murder, political assassination, and outright betrayal of community confidence often culminating in Igbo leaders negotiating away their birthright in return for peanuts, choosing to favour the interests of other groups at the detriment of theirs. If these situations are allowed to continue unfettered, the future of Ndigbo grows increasingly precarious and their competitiveness as a people will grow dimer falling short of early post-independence promises. This paper examines the hunter and the farmer value systems derived from the biblical story of Esau and Jacob. It would urge the mentality shift of Ndigbo from the farmer mindset before the war to the hunter tendencies during and after the war which has fully blossomed to the current situation o Ndigbo. The paper concludes by examining the farmer value system that made the Jews great. Incidentally, Ndigbo shared similar value system. Therefore, rediscovering these values and using them to socially reengineer our communities could put Ndigbo back on the path of rectitude and greatness. *Osita di mma, o gabara Ndigbo nile.*

Introduction

The mentality of the Igbo man prior to 1967 was confident, hopeful, and ambitious strengthened by a strong backbone of community vision. Many of these qualities were weakened by the civil war. Gradually the spirit of greed and pomposity replaced true wealth generated through industry, innovation, and strong community accountability. Aided by external interferences, influential voices of integrity and accountability in Igbo communities began to wane, replaced by imposed leaders that do not model the age-long derived Igbo values. Money, fame, and good-life replaced real wealth of character, relationship, and common vision. Instead of– *"onye nwere mmadu ka onye nwere ego"* the contemporary Igbo man now believes that *"onye nwere ego ka onye nwere mmadu"* – a reversal of our value system.

Ezekiel 1:2 says that: *when parents eat sour grapes, their children's teeth are set on edge.* Another proverb says that: *what parents do in moderation, their children will do in excess.* Having been modeled the wrong values in recent times since after the civil war, the Igbo youth have taken it to another height- relishing in all kinds of social, moral, and spiritual vices. There is a growing concern about the future of the Igbo community who in recent times are witnessing high levels of social, moral, and spiritual decay, a trend that is being observed globally. This downward spiral started during the civil war in late 1960s and has continued to date unabated.

Before the war, the Igbo Community had well-defined cultural norms. For example, a young man or woman growing up in Igbo community would go through rites of passage that announce his/her different stages of development and the associated responsibilities in the family and in the community. These include, among others, the *"ima mmanwu"* ceremony, the admission into the age grade groups, and the *"ichi ozo"* ceremonies. Although some of these ceremonies such as the *"ima mmanwu"* ceremony, were crude in the presentation of ethics and values, others, such as belonging to an age grade, were pivotal in the effective mentorship of the youth and conveying a sense of responsibility to them. These processes defined and announced seasons in their developmental journey into authentic man-hood or woman-hood. Today such rites of passage are fading away. As a result we are producing children that do not understand the limits of personal and community boundaries and the rules of engagement within it. The dispersal of our children all over the world in search of the Golden Fleece, has added to our dilemma as they have indiscriminately copied and imported wrong values into our community. Some speak the Igbo language but their character portrays something totally the opposite - counterfeits. This is also prevalent among adults, too.

Paradigm Shift with the Civil War

The mentality of the Igbo man prior to 1967 was confident, hopeful, and ambitious strengthened by a strong backbone of community vision expressed through the Igbo Union platform established where ever one would find us. Many of these qualities disappeared or lost their true meanings with the civil war.

The civil war created realities that drastically affected and shifted the ethics and values of the Igbo Community. One of those was the recruitment and conscription of both young and old men into the Biafran army. Many families were without fatherly figures and/or a manly presence. A few of the men that did not join the army had very restricted movement. Women, due to their freedom of movement, had to become the bread winners, often traveling for days to purchase their articles of merchandise. There was also the displacement of families and communities as refugee – often housed in school grounds, church grounds, living rooms of families, etc.

The environment was no longer enabling for the continual nurturing of families and communities. The reckless behavior of soldiers did not help matter. The sense of ownership and mentorship of the community gradually faded away replaced with sense of uncertainty as men started to loose grip on their families and their community structures. There was gross indiscipline, reckless acts, assaults on young ladies and men, etc., by the untrained and untamed Biafran soldiers. The most destructive spiritual after taste of the civil was the spirit of mistrust captured by the song: *E wo, muna nwanem jelu agha, a kpiri ego, Ifeajuna ree la anyi; e wo, muna nwem jelu agha, nwanne aputa nu lee nwa nneya!* It marked the transition of the Igbo man from transformational mindset that is sacrificial and nurturing, to a transactional leadership model that is selfish and destructive- a phenomenon that is still today very strong in our community. In just three years of the civil war from July 1967 to January 1970 the family and community structures that held Ndigbo together had been fractured and the linking strings broken. Immorality and indiscipline started to fester unchecked, ushering in a new era - an epoch of sufferance, neglect, indifference, and insignificance.

The Igbo community after the Civil War

The end of the war in January 1970 was a welcomed relief and an attempt to start rebuilding our communities. After the civil war, the Igbo Community was an amorphous conglomeration of war survivors with different war experiences returning to their ravaged communities. These families were saddled with the challenge of a new beginning. Communities squatted within a few surviving family housing structures while figuring out what to do to make ends meet and to restart their lives post-civil war. The resilient spirit of enthusiasm and optimism towards a better future was strong and prevalent.

One of the saddest trends that emerged with the civil war was the unrestrained display of shamelessness by some of our women – both married and unmarried in the camps of the Nigerian army. This was one of the signs of the value shift that had occurred during the war. These women exchanged their bodies for food, drink, and cosmetics. Men equally displayed similar tendencies.

Another trend that emerged was armed robbery. For the first time in our community I heard about men robbing with guns and machete and actually killing people. Prior to this, the unusual incidents of theft involved missing chicken, goats, yam tubers, etc. Paying people to assassinate became a new development. No doubt, some of the perpetrators of the armed robbery were former military men who had not been demilitarized and re-acculturated into the community.

The third trend that emerged was the rise of the middle income group that had little to no education. These were people that traded in goods and services and prospered. This gave rise to the notion among young people that education is relevant in pursuit of wealth in so far as one is ready to hassle and bustle. Gradually the spirit of greed and pomposity replaced true wealth generated by industry, innovation, and strong community accountability. Thereafter, the spirit of 419 was introduced- making money by pure deception and extortion.

The fourth trend was the phenomenon of externally selected and imposed traditional rulers. Aided by external interferences, the influential voices of integrity and accountability in Igbo communities began to wane, replaced by imposed leaders that do not model the age-long derived Igbo values. Money, fame, and good-life replaced real wealth of character, relationship, and common vision. Instead of *"onye nwelu mmadu ka onye nwelu ego", (Central Igbo – "onye nwere mmadu ka onye nwere ego")* the contemporary Igbo man now believes that *"onye nwelu ego ka onye nwelu mmadu"* (Central Igbo - "onye nwere ego ka onye nwere mmadu") – a reversal of our value system.

Ezekiel 1:2 says that: *when parents eat sour grapes, their children's teeth are set on edge*. Another proverb says that: *what parents do in moderation, their children will do in excess*. Having been modeled the wrong values in recent times since after the civil war, the Igbo youth have taken it to another height- relishing in all kinds of social, moral, and spiritual vices. Once known for our cohesiveness and progressiveness, the Igbo land is today infested with high incidents of corruption, armed robbery, kidnapping, etc. Selfish interests now supercede communal vision; there is high betrayal of public trust by leaders who negotiate away Igbo rights in return for peanuts, or choose to favour the interests of other groups at the detriment of their own. Consequently, the future of Ndigbo grows increasingly precarious and our competitiveness as a people dimer falling far short of early post-war promises.

Restoring the Igbo Community: paradigms and mindset

Is there hope for Ndigbo? The answer is affirmatively Yes! How then? - Through deliberate and systematic paradigm shift. The Scripture says: as a man thinks in his heart, so is he! That is, one becomes what one thinks about frequently. Franklin Roosevelt once said: *"Men are not prisoners of fate, but only prisoners of their own minds."* Albert Einstein added that: *"No problem can be solved from the same level of consciousness that created it."* Obviously, the current prevalent mindset in Igboland cannot be used to address our contemporary issues. A new mental vantage point must be established. Therefore, restoring the Igbo land is possible through value re-orientation. The wealth of a people is not determined by the virtue of their wealth but by the wealth of their virtue. Virtues, therefore, are our greatest wealth while vices are our greatest curse or undoing. That is why the Scripture says that righteousness exalts a nation but sin is a reproach to any people. An Igbo proverb also says: *"Ogbanarili Chiya n'oso na ebu okuku uzo naba ula,*"meaning that he who outruns his God will sleep before the chicken. Put differently, one who is out of tune with God will die an early death.

According to Helen Hayes, *"Everybody starts at the top, and then has the problem of staying there. Lasting accomplishment, however, is still achieved through a long, slow climb and self-discipline."* We must start another climb towards the mindset or paradigm driven by self-discipline.

What is Paradigm?

Paradigm should be likened to a manufacturer's mould into which fluid substances are poured, which when they congeal, they become shaped like the mould. Moulds are shaped according to the object to be manufactured: the shape of the mould determines the shape of the object produced. Through this process one mould can produce many replicates. Likewise, cultural paradigms shape the peoples and nations into which they have been immersed. Just as one mould produces thousands of cups and plates, the same way one cultural paradigm produces thousands of peoples and many nations whether good or bad. If the cultural paradigms contain some bad character traits, these are also reproduced in the persons and nations moulded by it. The same applies to good character traits in the cultural paradigm. If a people start with one type of mould and suddenly change to another due to war or other life circumstances, the characteristics of their people would change, too, leading to different consequences.

The Biblical Story of Esau and Jacob

The shift in the mindset of Ndigbo before and after the war can be captured biblically using the story of Esau and Jacob in Genesis Chapters 25-27. When Rebecca, the wife of Isaac, took in, the Bible says that the babies struggled together within her womb. When she inquired of the Lord, Genesis 25:23 says,

[23]*And the Lord said to her: "Two nations are in your womb, two peoples shall be separated from your body, one people shall be stronger than the other, the elder shall serve the younger."*

Notice that before Rebecca delivered her set of twins, God had already made value judgment about the future of the children. He said that one will be stronger than the other, and the older will serve the younger. When she delivered, the scripture says that she delivered twin boys named Esau and Jacob. According to Genesis 25:27: *So the boys grew. And Esau was a skillful hunter, a man of the field; but Jacob was a mild man, dwelling in tents.* This Scripture says that when Esau became of age, he chose to become a hunter and Jacob chose to become a farmer. The value system of a skillful hunter is diametrically opposite of the value system of a skillful farmer. These choices and the attendant value systems were subsequently passed down to their children and children's children. It determined the strength of their descendants.

Let us examine the hunter paradigm or value system or mentality

The Scripture says that Esau was a skillful hunter according to Genesis 25:27. The characteristics if a hunter are: Hunters are wanderers – moving from one location to another; possess ability to locate a prey including tracking and trailing skills; ability to kill the prey in the first effort including approaching aiming, and shooting skills; ability to gather the prey, process it, and take preservative measures to bring it home for the family and community.Ultimately, a hunter is a consumer that looks for finished products to kill and consume; someone who meets something alive and leaves it dead or something with value and leaves valueless.

Disadvantages of the Esau paradigm or mentality

A hunter is dependent on what the forest produces. He has no control of the type or the size of the animal that appears or when it does. This makes the hunter highly dependent on the forest or any other source of animals. Hunters are very presumptive about the availability of animals in the forest. They tend to forget that natural and environmental disasters do occur and hence they hardly prepare for such emergencies, which when they occur, lead to devastating consequences on the family and community. There is no food security. The hunter relies on his physical stamina more that his intellectual or mental power. If the hunter's foot is pierced by any sharp object or he badly twists his ankles during the chase, he must quickly retreat to address the issue. In the meantime the game escapes. The hunter would not resume until the wound is healed. A hunter thinks short term in the sense that they focus on the ready-made products and not so much on how to manufacture, cultivate the product. They rarely think beyond the satisfaction of quenching their immediate hunger or taste for money, pleasure, etc. Hunters, when hungry, are dangerously careless about decisions they take regarding their future. The Scriptures says in Genesis 25:29-34

[29]Now Jacob cooked a stew; and Esau came in from the field, and he was weary. [30]And Esau said to Jacob, "Please feed me with that same red stew, for I am weary." [31]But Jacob said, "Sell me your birthright as of this day." [32]And Esau said, "Look, I am about to die; so what is this birthright to me?" [33] Then Jacob said, "Swear to me as of this day." So he swore to him, and sold his birthright to Jacob. [34] And Jacob gave Esau bread and stew of lentils; then he ate and drank, arose and went his way. Thus Esau despised his birthright.

Esau devalued his birthright to a bowl of soup, after which he ate, drank, stood up and arrogantly walked away as though nothing happened. Hunters are Slaves to Farmers. In Gen 27: 37-38, concerning his brother Jacob, Isaac said to Esau, his son: ... *"Indeed I have made him your master, and all his brethren I have given to him as servants; with grain and wine I have sustained him. What shall I do now for you, my son?"* Hunter nations are slaves to farmer nations - just think about the whole slave trade. In describing the mentality of Esau, the book of Hebrew 12:16-17 says: *"...lest there be any fornicator or profane person like Esau, who for one morsel of food sold his birthright."* The verse describes Esau as a fornicator and a profane person. A fornicator is one who takes what is precious and sells it cheaply. A profane person takes that which is noble and honorable and dishonors it. The Esau way does not add value to what they possess, rather they devalue it. Whatever Esau touches becomes of less value.

God Hates the Esau Mentality. In Malachi 1:2-4 God said to the nation of Israel: *[2]"I have loved you," says the Lord,"yet you say,"'In what way have You loved us?' Was not Esau Jacob's brother?" Says the Lord, "yet Jacob I have loved: [3]But Esau I have hated, and laid waste his mountains and his heritage for the jackals of the wilderness."* It is quite clear from this Scripture that God hates the Esau mind-set or mentality. The main reason is because it is self-centered, lacks long-term strategic thinking, and irresponsible to its environment. Check the Scriptures you would notice that every time the Esau value system ruled the children of Israel, God would threaten to destroy it and replace it with the mountain of Jacob or Israel.

The Jacob Paradigm or Value System and Mentality

Jacob was referred to as a mild man, dwelling in tents according to Genesis 25:27. Characteristics of Jacob or Israel reveal the following: Farmers are settlers, tent-dwellers, and long term planners; possess the ability to nurture- creating an enabling, protective, and preservative environment, etc.; ability to contemplate and meditate- strategically plan and execute, with monitoring and evaluation plans, etc., ability to Innovate Progressive Ideas, enterprising, entrepreneurial, scale up thinking, etc.Ultimately, a farmer is someone who looks for seed or opportunities to nurture to finished products of higher values. A framer takes something almost insignificant and makes it abundant or significant. Someone who meets something almost dead and leaves it with abundant life.In John 10:10, Jesus said, *"The thief does not come but to steal, to kill, and to destroy. But I have come that you may have life and have it abundantly."*

A Farmer can nurture many things at a time

A farmer can plant many things at a time. He could have animal farm, crop farmer in the same vicinity. In fact, the crop produces some feed for the animals while the animals produce manure for the plants. The farmer can harvest different things at different seasons. They are Independent producers. The farmer produces things in abundance and there takes what he needs and markets the rest. The farmer is therefore more independent. Farmers rely on mental strength. The farmer plans at least one year in advance as to what to plant and where to plant. Therefore, strategic and proactive planning is central to the success of the farmer. These require creative and imaginative mental skills. They think long term. He must think about planting, harvesting, processing, packaging, marketing, and sustainability. All these aspects require proactivity. The farmer as in Genesis 25:29-34 exploits the Ignorance of the Hunter because hunters are dangerously careless about their future and the farmers can take advantage of that. Hence, at the negotiating table Esau negotiates from the position of weariness (lack) whilst the Jacob approaches the matter from a position of strength (sufficiency). Jacob uses his finished consumables to negotiate for and buy future opportunities; while Esau sells his future potentials to buy what to eat in the present. This is what the civil war did to Ndigbo- turned them from part owners of Nigeria to just mere survivors.

The Farmer becomes a Master over the Hunter

As a result of the fragility and dependability of the Esau mentality, he becomes susceptible to manipulation and ultimate slavery to Jacob. In Genesis 27:28, 29, Isaac said to Jacob his son, "*^{28}Therefore may God give you of the dew of heaven, of the fatness of the earth, and plenty of grin and wine. ^{29}Let peoples serve you, and nations bow down to you. Be master over your brethren, and let your mother's sons bow down to you. Cursed be everyone who curses you, and blessed be those who bless you!*" This blessing, according to Genesis 27:37 is irreversible. It is clear from the study of the hunter and farmer mentalities why God blessed Jacob instead of Esau, despite their father's inclination to bless Esau - the first born according to tradition. God overruled that by the virtue of the fact that Jacob's productive and proactive mentality is far superior to Esau's dependent and consumption-driven mentality.

Global Implications of the Jacob and Esau Mentalities

Nations build their developmental paradigm after their national values; those values will make them either Esau Nation or Jacob Nation. Poor nations are poor because of their productivity values and rich nations are rich because of their productivity values. Values ultimately dictate policy and priority and outcomes. Just as Esau asked for a bowl of stew and not recipe to prepare one, the same way Esau nations and people always want the meal not the recipe - import finished products not technology to process raw materials into such products. Some of the poorest nations in the world are also, strangely the most richly endowed in natural resources. Their landmasses have vast deposits of gold, diamond, oil, platinum, fertile soil, fresh water reserves, and good weather. They also have large work force of citizens who are ready to sweat in the fields from dawn to dusk for very little pay. Yet the government officials spend much of their time going round begging from nations who do not have a fraction of those natural resources and labour force.

Proverbs 12:27 says: *"The lazy man does not roast what he took in hunting. But diligence is man's precious possession."* But Proverbs 12:24 says: *"The hand of the diligent will rule. But the lazy man will be put to forced labour."* One may produce gold, for example, but will have no facility for "roasting" gold; no gold refinery. They take their gold to another nation which has a refinery to refine the gold and mold expensive jewelry out of them. The raw gold producer turns around and buys the finished jewelries at very high price. These are labor intensive, hardworking nations with a development paradigm of producing raw material, but lack the commitment to "roast" what they have to the next level. You can replace gold with oil, copper, cocoa, aluminum, fish, crops, fruits, etc!

A nation becomes third world if it does not have the capacity to manage its resources from the raw primary product stage to the sophisticated secondary and tertiary stages. They become trapped in the economy where they sell their raw materials they worked so hard for at cheap prices and purchase the processed finished products at a higher price. Such a nation will always struggle to catch up on its current deficits with its competitor nations who possess the capacity to process products to various high-value stages.

You Lazy Intellectual African Scum!
In December 31, 2010 - New Year's eve- a Zambian citizen was flying from Los Angeles to Boston. Seated next to him was a former IMF employee who had lived in Zambia and other African nations - a white American called Mr. Walter. Below are excerpts from the conversation that ensued. These are Walter's words to the Zambian:

"You my friend flying with me and all your kind are lazy," he said. *"When you rest your head on the pillow you don't dream big. You and other so-called African intellectuals are damn lazy, each one of you. It is you, and not those poor starving people, who is the reason Africa is in such a deplorable state."*

"That's not a nice thing to say," I protested.

He was implacable. "Oh yes it is and I will say it again, you are lazy. Poor and uneducated Africans are the most hardworking people on earth. I saw them in the Lusaka markets and on the street selling merchandise. I saw them in villages toiling away. I saw women on Kafue Road crushing stones for sell and I wept. I said to myself where are the Zambian intellectuals? Are the Zambian engineers so imperceptive they cannot invent a simple stone crusher, or a simple water filter to purify well water for those poor villagers? Are you telling me that after thirty-seven years of independence your university school of engineering has not produced a scientist or an engineer who can make simple small machines for mass use? What is the school there for?" I held my breath.

"Do you know where I found your intellectuals? They were in bars quaffing. They were at the Lusaka Golf Club, Lusaka Central Club, Lusaka Playhouse, and Lusaka Flying Club. I saw with my own eyes a bunch of alcoholic graduates. Zambian intellectuals work from eight to five and spend the evening drinking. We don't. We reserve the evening for brainstorming."

He looked me in the eye. "And you flying to Boston and all of you Zambians in the Diaspora are just as lazy and apathetic to your country. You don't care about your country and yet your very own parents, brothers and sisters are in Mtendere, Chawama, and in villages, all of them living in squalor. Many have died or are dying of neglect by you. "Wake up you all!" he exclaimed, attracting the attention of nearby passengers. "You should be busy lifting ideas, formulae, recipes, and diagrams from American manufacturing factories and sending them to your own factories. All those research findings and dissertation papers you compile should be your country's treasure.

Why do you think the Asians are a force to reckon with? They stole our ideas and turned them into their own. Look at Japan, China, India, just look at them." He paused. "The Bwana has spoken," he said and grinned. "As long as you are dependent on my plane, I shall feel superior and you my friend shall remain inferior, how about that? The Chinese, Japanese, Indians, even Latinos are a notch better. You Africans are at the bottom of the totem pole."

At 8 a.m. the plane touched down at Boston's Logan International Airport. Walter reached for my hand. "I know I was too strong, but I don't give it a damn. I have been to Zambia and have seen too much poverty." With that Mr. Walter entered a waiting car and disappeared.

The Jewish community founded on the Jacob paradigm
In the book, *Culture Matters* by Hutchinson and Huntington, there is serious debate centered on the role of culture in national development. Four

developmental typologies have been identified by social scientists and economists. The top two groups shared one thing in common: the Judeo-Christian cultural heritage. It is becoming increasingly clear that the Judeo-Christian cultural setting is the pool within which global civilization and development have been spawned.

Group Ranking	Ethnic/Racial Groups	Economic Development Ranking	Predominate Cultural Elements
Group 1	The Jewish Community	Most Economically Developed	The Jewish Religious Culture
Group 2	Northern Europe, British Settlements	Economically Developed with the lowest Corrupt Regions in the World	Protestant Ethics & Values
Group 3	Middle and Eastern Asia	Middle Corrupt Societies	Confucian Religion with Strong Emphasis on Discipline
Group 4	Indonesia, Russia, some Latin American and African Societies	Most Corrupt Regions of the World	Mixture of Native Traditions and External Religious Beliefs

The Jews, (especially Jewish Americans) are the most well advanced group in the world economically and scientifically, the Jewish phenomenon. The Jacob mind-set is the foundation of the Jewish people and has made them one of the most successful groups in the world. Albert Einstein once said that: *"Only one who devotes himself to a cause (a vision) with his whole strength and soul can be a true master. For this reason mastery demands all of a person."*

The Jews are so devoted to the mindset of their forefathers and are fanatically addicted it. In his book, the *Jewish Phenomenon*, Steven

Silbiger shared an amazing statistics about Jewish Americas. Representing only about 2% of US population, they constitute 45% of top Forbes 400 richest people; 30% of millionaires; 20% of professors in top US universities; 30% of all Nobel Prize winners in science and 25% of all Nobel Prize winners in all fields, respectively. When the Nobel prize was announced for the year 2013, six of the eight awards went to people of the Jewish descent.

The Jews are the highest income earning group by a large margin compared to other ethic and/or religious group in America. In the publication, *USA Ethnic America, by* Dr. Thomas Sowell, the household income of different ethnic groups were studied and ranked. Below is the summary of the study and how different groups ranked:

1. Jewish – 172;
2) Japanese – 132;
3) Polish – 115;
4) Chinese & Italian 112;
5) Anglo-Saxon & German 107
6) Irish – 103;
7) U.S. Avg. – 100;
8) Filipino – 99;
9) West Indian -- 94
10) Mexican – 76;
11) Puerto Rican -- 63
12) Black – 62;
13) Native American -- 60

It is quite clear from the study that the Jewish community has the highest household income than any other ethnic group in America. Aptly summarized by Silbiger in *The Jewish Phenomenon: Seven Keys to the Enduring Wealth of a People*: "*What makes Jews Jewish is a specific religious culture and historical experience that have shaped their values and strongly influenced how they view the world.*" According to Silbiger, the seven cardinal biblical principles upon which the Jewish *Worldview* is crafted, and that have established them as a unique people, are:

Knowledge is the Real Wealth and it is Portable
One of the things strongly valued in the Jewish culture is education. This is because the Jews believe that getting wisdom, knowledge, and understanding through education in the real wealth according to Proverbs 4:7-10: *[7]"Wisdom is the principal thing; therefore get wisdom. And in all your getting, get understanding. [8]Exalt her, and she will promote you; She will bring you honor, when you embrace her. [9]She will place on your head an ornament of grace; a crown of glory she will deliver to you."*The Jew people

believe so strongly in quality education such that they enjoy the reputation in the world as one of the smartest people group. They spend extravagantly when it comes to sending their children to the best schools in the world. Where ever they are, at home, in the Synagogue or academic institutions, they turn into a place of learning. The nation of Israel has one of the highest Techno-startups and patents in the world. Ndigbo say: *"where ever you find seven dead birds under a tree, there is definitely something there that kills birds."*

The string that ties the Jewish community together is a strong family and community relationships. The Jews observe the Sabbath religiously from sunset on Friday to sunset on Saturday. The Friday evening is devoted to attending to family matters such as cooking and spending time together especially with the children. It is during this period that principles of God pertaining to life and godliness are grilled into the psyche of the children. Not only are what have been taught in school during that week discussed and evaluated, the children are encouraged to be outspoken, challenge the accounts of the Scriptures, and defend their ideological positions and to perform excellently in whatever they do. The book of Ephesians 6:4 says, *^{4}"And you, fathers, do not provoke your children to wrath, but bring them up in the training and admonition of the Lord."* On Saturday or Sabbath, the families meet at the Synagogue for fellowship and further teachings on the principles of God according to their Holy Books. As a result, the Jews have become not only tightly bound families, but communities, too. Within this they prefer to do business and other activities with one another than any other people groups. The Jews believe that you take care of your people, they, in turn, will take care of you. *"Aka nni kwo aka ekpe, aka ekpe akwo aka nni."*

The book of Proverbs 22:6 says, *^{6}"Train up a child in the way he should go, and when he is old he will not depart from it."* The Jews have successfully passed on these biblical cultural values from generation to generation. They are the longest surviving group in history outside their homeland- more than three thousand years- since the captivity of Babylon around 600 BC. *"Makana onye ajulu ada aju onweya"!* The Jews believe in Professionalism and Entrepreneurship. The Jews believe strongly in hard work and in due diligence according to the book of Proverbs 12:24 says, *^{24}The hand of the diligent will rule, but the lazy man will be put to forced labor."* The Jews combine their hard work ethics with deep thinking according to Ecclesiastes 10: 10 (AMP) which says, *^{10}If the ax is dull and the man does not whet the edge, he must put forth more strength; but wisdom helps him to succeed.* The Message Bible translation puts Ecclesiastes 10:10 this way, *^{10}Remember: the duller the ax the harder the work; use your head: the more brains, the less muscle.*

As a result of their hard work and high intellectualism, about 30% of all Nobel Prize winners in science and 25% of all Nobel Prize winners in all fields combined, respectively, have gone to scholars of Jewish descent. The Jews are the highest income earning group by a large margin compared to other ethic and/or religious group in the United States of America. When the Nobel prizes were announced in the year 2013, six of the first eight awards went to people of the Jewish descent. Constituting only about 2% of US population, they represent 45% of top Forbes 400 richest people and 30% of millionaires. This is truly phenomenal. *"Agadi nwanwa ada akanka na egwu omalu agba."*

The book of 2 Timothy 2:15 in the New Testament also admonishes us to, *15Be diligent to present yourself approved to God, a worker who does not need to be ashamed, rightly dividing the word of truth.* It is quite clear that in all our claim to be affiliated with Jews we have not fully downloaded the practical cultural patterns that give meaning and credence to the Scripture. The cultural or practical aspects of the Old Testament that have made the Jews one of the most successful groups in the world, have been lost to Ndigbo and to the Church. The greatest years of Ndigbo are still ahead when they will fully assimilate the truth of the Scriptures and make it their daily guide.

Strong communication and deliberation skill

Jewish culture promotes and encourages strong verbal skills. Children are encouraged starting at the family dinner table to ask questions, share their opinions with adults. At the age of 13, a Jewish boy or girl is considered an adult, able to make independent religious choices. At this age, they celebrate it by reading the Torah at the temple in full view of all the adults. This requires intensive preparations. Recall that by the end of 12, Jesus was already arguing and debating with adults according to Luke 2:41-49,

[41]His parents went to Jerusalem every year at the Feast of the Passover. [42]And when He was twelve years old, they went up to Jerusalem according to the custom of the feast. [43]When they had finished the days, as they returned, the Boy Jesus lingered behind in Jerusalem. And Joseph and His mother ... did not know it; [44]but supposing Him to have been in the company, they went a day's journey, and sought Him among their relatives and acquaintances. [45]So when they did not find Him, they returned to Jerusalem, seeking Him. [46] Now so it was that after three days they found Him in the temple, sitting in the midst of the teachers, both listening to them and asking them questions. [47]And all who heard Him were astonished at His understanding and answers. [48]So when they saw Him, they were amazed; and His mother said to Him, "Son, why have You done this to us? Look, Your father and I have sought You anxiously."[49] And He said to them, "Why did you seek Me? Did you not know that I must be about

My Father's business?" ⁵⁰*But they did not understand the statement which He spoke to them.*

The strong verbal skills of the Jewish people, developed from childhood has made them successful professors, doctors, comedians, performing artists, businessmen and women, and all the fields of endeavor where excellent communication skills are required. The Jewish people are extremely frugal and have excellent savings culture according to Proverbs 22:7, ⁷*The rich rules over the poor, and the borrower is servant to the lender.* It has been said that there are three ways to use money: waste it, spend it, or multiply it. Many cultures waste money in unnecessary ceremonies such as marriage, funeral, title-taking, etc. These activities often do not return dividends of lasting values. Though emotionally satisfying, these are often ephemeral. Other people spend money building edifices at locations where they are underutilized. Others buy equipment, tools and technological contrivances that they do not really need but purchased for prestige purposes. The third group, like the Jews, multiplies their money through investments. This attitude often earned them the reputation as misers and greedy to accumulate. These groups can be extremely generous in donating towards things and causes that will strengthen their communities and bless humanity. In that light Psalm 112:4-6 describes them well, "⁴*Unto the upright there arises light in the darkness; He is gracious, and full of compassion, and righteous.* ⁵*A good man deals graciously and lends; He will guide his affairs with discretion.* ⁶*Surely he will never be shaken; the righteous will be in everlasting remembrance."* While the Jews are the high contributors to philanthropy, $4.5 billion in 1997, they are misers in terms of spending money on triflings.Every Jew is psychologically driven to prove their uniqueness. In *Exodus 19:5* "*Now therefore, if you will indeed obey My voice and keep My covenant, then you shall be a special treasure to Me above all people; for all the earth is Mine."* The Jews have given true meaning to Professor Margaret Mead saying to: "*Never doubt that a small group of thoughtful, committed citizens can change the world; indeed, it's the only thing that ever has."*

Igbo connection to the Jews – Eri

Eri was the fifth son of Gad, who in turn was the seventh son of Israel. Towns and expressions pointing to the name of Eri are rather common especially in Anambra State. For example, when one wants to point to something that happened a long time ago, the expression- Eri-mgbe or Mgbe Eri – is used meaning during the time of Eri. There are cities named Agulu Eri, Umulu-Eri both meaning the farming area and descendants of Eri. There are cultural similarities between the Jews and the Igbos which are too many to be mentioned in this paper. The Igbos can emulate the Jewish people who have climbed back to significance in spite of long years of discrimination and threat of annihilation. Describing the secret to the development of Singapore, Lee Kuan Yew, the first Prime Minister of Singapore, in *From Third World to First: The Singapore Story - 1965-2000* wrote: *"This meant we had to train our people and equip them to provide First World standards of service. I believed this was possible, that we could reeducate and re-orientate our people with help of schools, trade unions, community centers, and social organizations. If the communists in China could eradicate all flies and sparrows, surely we could get our people to change their Third World habits"* (Yew 58). Let us borrow a leaf from the Jews and Singapore using the principles and values that have helped them to re-engineer and re-establish themselves by re-educating, and re-orientating our people with the help of schools, market place associations, community and social organizations, thus we can once more become one of the most dominant people group in the world.

The Concept of *"Igbo enwe eze"* and its Implications for Ndi Igbo Development
by
Dr. J. Chidozie Chukwuokolo

Abstract

Ndi- Igbo have been maligned as a people who are not capable of having an Eze in short, that from our pre-history that we are a rudderless people without respect for constituted authorities. This has helped in forming the various negative perceptions that have attracted hatred for us as a people. Several questions arise: are all these perceptions true of Ndi-Igbo? Who is an Eze in Igbo conception? How do we identify an Eze? These and more questions are what this paper sets out to answer. This paper sets out to assert that Ndi Igbo have a kingship institution that pre-dated any other in Nigeria and was entrenched before the arrival of Lugard. It also asserts that Ndi-Igbo have a critical democratic foundation that identifies their Eze with a man who identifies with their aspirations. Such a classical kingship democracy is not hegemonic and absolute. It concludes that it was to achieve certain orchestrated devious ends that the British invented the falsehood that Ndi-Igbo do not have kingship institution.

Introduction

Certainly there is no doubt that Ndi Igbo have not fared very well in Nigeria except on individual accomplishments. Since the amalgamation of Nigeria by Fredrick Lugard in 1914, Ndi-igbo became dislocated in virtually every area of living-values, politics, leadership, kingship, religion, diplomacy and indeed culturally. As if he is not done by creating an unholy marriage, Lugard saw the Igboman as a threat that needed to be uprooted if his reign would be successful; he thus employed seasoned priests, sociologist anthropologist etc to "re-invent" a civilization that dated earlier than any one in Nigeria. This was the beginning of the Igbo question in Nigeria. Lugard, Tubleman Goldie and their subsequent cohorts left the Igboman the most disadvantaged of all the ethnic groups at independence.

One of the areas Ndi-Igbo were hurt most is the aspect of organized leadership. There was as it is a complete eclipse of leadership values by Lugard such that by 1912, in his attempt to penetrate the Igbo hinterland, using his cohots, Lugard invented the dictum of "Igbo Enwe eze" (the Igbos do not have kings) as a tendentious predilected endeavor geared towards the destabilization of the almost iron-clad internal cohesion that he had met. Lugard had met an organized theocratic kingship institution headed by the Nri monarchy before he came to Nigeria in 1900. This view was attested to by "Fereira, a Portuguese visitor to West Africa, who in a story in 1505 referred to a power east of Benin "…. Whose chief among the negroes is like the Pope among us. Indeed the rule of the Eze Nri over Igbo land as well as Idu…, was similar to the primacy of the pope over medieval Europe" (Eluwa 554).That Ndi-Igbo was stripped off its theocratic kingship structure after about 407 years that Fereira had noted such a structure has more to it that could be ordinarily seen.

Unfortunately, Lugard used both the instrument of the state (the native authority and schools) and the church to disseminate the ignoble dictum-Igbo enwe eze. The tragedy of it is that Igbo scholars as A. E. Afigbo in *Igbo Enwe Eze: Beyond Onwumechili and Onwuejeogwu*, and C.A Onwumechili in *Igbo Emwe Eze: The Igbo had no kings*became the most ardent disseminators of this criminal idea. What could be deduced here is that someone could be indignantly righteous in playing complicit roles in destabilizing the facts of ones history due to mis-education. Certain questions now come to mind: why should Lugard and his cohorts tendentiously want to obliterate the truth about Igbo kingship institution? Is Igbo enwe eze factually true? Who is an Eze in Igbo conception? How do we as Ndi Igbo identify Eze? What is the implication of this dictum to the socio-political development of Ndi-Igbo in Nigeria? In other words, how has the dictum of Igbo *enwe eze* contributed to the Igbo question in Nigeria? These and more questions will be answered in this work with the intension of excavating the truth in order to create a formidable understating of ourselves. This will make for a proper situation of the Eze in Igboland so as not to malign us as a group of egalitarian republicans who have no value for constituted authority and ipso facto no history and identity. Igbo Nwere eze and we hope to use the historic-critical methods in establishing our claims. But before this, let us look at who are Ndi-Igbo?

Who are Ndi Igbo?
From the cultural histories of all the ethic groups in Nigeria, it appears that Ndi-Igbo are a unique people whose nature of leadership is not the same as the others. While the Hausa-Fulanis, the Yorubas and the Binis are monarchical oligarchy, the Igbos are a theocratic democratic pacifist monarchy. Whereas these other monarchies, could order for the killing of anybody who falls short of its dictates, the Igbos could hardly do same. Some scholars have attributed these differences in leadership styles to the historical origins of these different ethic groups. The origin of the Hausa-Fulani Oligarchy is traceable to Othman Dan Fodio, the Yoruba to Oduduwa etc, but there is hardly univocality as to who was the arch-patriarch of Ndi-Igbo. G.T. Basden has this to say in this regards: *"The Ibo Nation ranks as one of the largest in the whole of Africa… All my attempts to trace the origin of the name "Ibo" have been unsuccessful. My most reliable informants have been able to offer no more alternative than that it is most probably an*

abbreviation of longer name connected with an ancestor long since forgotten" (Basden ix).

So the question of who are the Igbos? And does the lack of obvious history of its descent really cast a shadow on whether they have kings or not become very imperative in proving our thesis. This is because it appears that this lack of evident arch-patriarch figure led these Europeans to their veiled mission of reducing Ndi-Igbo to a kingless status and to hinge their reason on this. J. A. Umeh captures it in this sense: *"The so called acephalous and stateless societies without kings which some European writers and those that follow their tagging have characterized the Igbo societies are indeed ingénous socio-political and economic units which ancient Igbos fashioned from very ancient Igbo kingdoms and states"*(Umeh 4). However, it could be said that this could have led some scholars in the search for Igbo origin to assent to the claim that Ndi -Igbo are Jews in Diaspora. This notion has gained lots of currency with the present Igbos. It should be noted that various reasons account for this notion: Ndi-Igbo and the Jews have a lot of similarities in their cultures such that one could see consanguinity as against accident in these cultures.

The following are the areas of these similarities between Ndi-Igbo and the Jews that were in practice before any contact with Christianity: "Kinglessness" circumcision of the male children on the eight day, abstinence from eating unclean animals and not eating animals with their blood, ie, removing animal blood and covering it on the sand, marrying one's deceased brothers wife, known as *shiva* in Hebrew, similarity in the mourning pattern, washing of hands and face every morning before praying and breaking of kola nut, atonement to commence the new year with fasting known in Hebrew as 'yon' Hebrew and *Ikeji* in Igbo, purification of the body at the gate through washing after touching any dead body, separation of ladies when they are menstruating or celebrating them at the commencement of the menstrual cycle of any lady (*Iru mgbede*), theocracy, serving of trade masters for seven years etc. (Emekesiri 53).

There is no doubt that these relationships can not be a mere accident: this has led most Christian Igbos to assert that Ndi-igbo are descendants of Gad, one of the sons of Jacob. They went further to argue that as the Jews had no kings but Yahweh the king of Ndi-Igbo was Chineke. This could be strengthened by theocratic system of government practiced by both societies. They argue that just like Yahweh punished the Jews when they demanded for "kings like their neighbours", Ndi-Igbo's lack of kings could be traceable to the same source. It should be recalled that in 1 Samuel chapter 8, the Jews rejected Samuel as their leader, (i.e viceroy of Yahweh their main leader) and demanded for a king as their neighbours. Accordingly, in 1 Samuel 8: 19-20, it is stated thus: *"But the people refused to listen to Samuel*

"No!" they said, "We want a king over us". Then we will be like other nations, with a king to lead us and go out before us and fight our battle."

This was regarded as an affront and rejection to Yahweh who was their king: he therefore gave them a king like other nations in Saul. The rest as they say is history. These Igbo Christians trace the root of Igbo enwe Eze to the nature of our theocratic system and avers that unless Ndi-igbo get back to their God, they will never come out of this state of leadershiplessness.

Be this as it may, several people have criticized this view of Ndi-Igbo as descendants of the Jews as mere coincidence and arising from attempts at making up of vacuum in Igbo history. For instance, Oluwole Osagie-Jacobs asserts: *"The Igbo tribe is as unique as its history. Of all the tribes in Nigeria, it is this tribe that is most difficult to place in terms of origin. Some of my Igbo friends for want of an authentic historical record believe they are Jews in Diaspora. I often call their attention to their black skin and the fact that they would be the only Jews who left Israel without Judaism ..... where as in the absence of written history or credible oral records people find recourse in hanging their early history on myths or legends, in respect to the Igbo this is an exemption. It is therefore, difficult to reconstruct the contemporary Igbo man from his past."* (Osagie-Jacobs 2).

It is very insightful of Jacobs to note that all the other Jews who had left Israel left with Judaism intact, but the Igbos did not therefore, they are not Jews. One can say that Judaism is a way of life condensed in certain values. These values are akin to the ones noted earlier in this paper. It is also possible that many years of existence could have removed or refined the Judaism in Igbo religious practices. One can hardly go without concluding that the Igbo religious worship has a lot of similarities with Judaism and therefore, Jacobs' argument does not extricate this from Ndi-Igbo the way he thought that he had done. Again, the colour argument he raised left him as a biological ignorant person. The skin colour is a product of the presence or absence of melanin. The melanin is necessary only in Tropics to avoid the damaging effects of the ultra-violet rays of the sun in the Tropic regions. But once humans leave the tropic, the services of the melanin is no longer needed, hence humans turn fair in completion. The closer one is to the colder region the whiter such a person's complexion becomes. This brings us to my skepticism on the Jewish origin of Ndi-Igbo: that there is a cultural similarity between Ndi-Igbo and the Jews, I have no doubt. This similarity to me is strong enough to argue for similar descent and ancestry. Although, this paper is not an attempt to establish the Jewish origin of the Igbo race or vice versa, yet, proper understanding of this phenomenon will help us in establishing our thesis that Ndi-Igbo Nwere Eze. Consequently, any critical analysis of Hebrew linguistics will result to the view that it is the Jews that have their ancestors to Igbo land, but not vice versa. What this amounts to is that it is in later languages that vestiges of earlier ones are found. Any language that shows elements of inclusion of its language in order is an indication of it being later part of the language in question. For example the following Igbo words are similarly found in Hebrew language but not vice versa:

Hebrew: 1) Hadith-unity, Igbo-Ha di otu,

(2) Hebrew-Kpushi/Pushi, foolish; Igbo: Nkpushi;

(3) Hebrew: Simcha-rejoice, Igbo-Sim Chia

(4) Hebrew: Puuk/Puka-come out; Igbo-puta,

(5) Hebrew, tfou-tfou- exclamiation for something abominable, Igbo-tufia-tufia

(6) Hebrew- Mezuzzah – prepare the door, Igbo-mezie uzo,

(7) Hebrew-Zobah; Igbo-Ozoba

(8) Hebrew: Amasa, Igbo-Amasa;

(9) Hebrew-Chimham, Igbo-Chimaham;

(10) Hebrew Uri, Igbo-Uli;

(11) Hebrew-Eldaah, Igbo-Edda (T.U. Nwala (ed.) Oha Ndom)

All we have tried to say is that although conclusive research has not established either that the Igbos are Jews or vice versa, my contention is that it is a fact that the Igbos are related with the Jews. However, it is not very likely that the Igbos are Jews in Diaspora, rather evidence appears more to support that the Jews migrated from Igbo land especially with argument on melanin.

Following from the above discussion, it is evident that although the problem of all societies that practice theocracy is absence of a clear cut visible king as the roles of a king and a priest are subsumed in one, yet it can not be said that Lugard and his co-travelers did not meet an organized kingship institution in Igboland. Rather, because of some devious reasons, they decided to orchestrate the idea of Igbo enwe Eze to the detriment of the entire Igbo speaking nations. Therefore, the notion that the Europeans did not meet an organized kingship institution in Igbo land and that Ndi-Igbo have similar descent with the Jews and being theocratic as the Jews made them kingless is erroneous and untenable.

Again, the idea of such people as Jacobs that the elusive leadership and answer of Ndi-Igbo could have arisen from the lack of a visible, clear arch-patriarch as Othman Dan Fodio for the Fulanis or Oduduwa for the Yorubas is non sequitor rather it could be inferred that due to the recency in arrival of both tribes in Nigeria, their history came closer to written history and ipso facto are recorded. It is obvious that the farther in time and history a thing is, the dimmer its memory becomes. The Yoruba's arrived Nigeria in the 11th century while the Fulanis arrived in the 18th Century AD. But Ndi Igbo came to Nigeria at about 50,000 BC. This could be found in the carbon dating of the works of Thurstan Shaw at Igbo Ukwu/Oreri excavations of 1959. The issue now is, why should Lugard and his group malign Ndi-Igbo the way they did? In other words, why should the British relegate the obvious kingship structure they met in Igbo land to the back drop of obliteration?

Before we do this, we shall answer the question of who are the Igbo with tracing them to the most essential values that form their binding identity. In the case of Ndi-Igbo, the Ikenga symbol is the crystallization of their supreme values. It is a symbol of justice through hard work; hence in the traditional setting, every male prays to God to bless his Ikenga. It is in keeping with this value, that Ndi-Igbo are the most hard-working of all the races of the world. The Igbo man therefore is known for his wealth achieved through hard work and justice mitigated in the extreme belief in God. One can therefore, anchor the delineation of Ndi-Igbo (the never been ruled) on this supreme value that enthrones egalitarianism and equality giving no way to unnecessary monarchism.

Did Frederick Luggard orchestrate the idea of Igbo *enwe eze*?

Perhaps it will be pertinent at this stage to ask the question above; in other words why should the British hate Ndi-Igbo as a people? It is not my intention in this subsection to emotionally express our woes for the sake of doing so or to engage in prebendal talks. Rather I intend to keep our predicament in perspective such that the facts will be laid bare and we shall understand that the Igbo condition in Nigeria started with Fredrick Lugard. It is therefore the sum total of all these tendentiously orchestrated and predilected structures to demean and retard the Igbo man that we regard as the Igbo question, Igbo predicament or Igbo condition in Nigeria.

When the British arrived in Nigeria, it should be noted that there had been over two hundred years of trade relationship with other Europeans especially the Portuguese. This trade relation culminated in the exchange of trade ambassadors between Africa and Europe Ndi-Igbo inclusive. This period was a period when each trade partner studied the other closely, it was the attendant lessons and experience of the Igbo sophistication that led the British to perceive Ndi-Igbo as a race to be checkmated immediately Europe partitioned African in 1886 in Berlin. These sophistications were gleaned from the survival structures they found in Igbo land when they came in namely the kingship structures, trade expertise, strength of character arising from self esteem etc. the British could not understand the leadership and administrative style of Ndi-Igbo epitomized by the Eze Nri kingly dynasty that almost permeated the whole of Igbo land. Accordingly, the Eze Nri was regarded with utmost awe throughout Igbo land as the viceroy of God. It should be noted also that it was easy for the British to permeate the North led by the Sarduana of Sokoto and the west led by Ooni of Ife and Alafin of Oyo but could not penetrate Igbo land due to the influence of the Eze Nri.

All their attempts to have direct contact with various village heads in Igbo land proved abortive as they were in unison as to the proclamation of

Eze Nri as their port of allegiance. The British regarded this with scorn and decided to humiliate the Eze Nri Obalike who was on the throne at the time. We shall discuss this in full details in later subsection but suffice if to say that this "arrogance" of Ndi Igbo was seen as running parallel authority to the British and needed to be checkmated.

Again, there is no place that British colonized that they got the level of resistance as they got from Ndi-Igbo. The astonishing rise and industry of Olauda Equiano brought very early to the notice of the British that the tribe of such a man must be a sophisticated one. In his autobiography, he presented the Igbo race as a sophisticated civilization such that the British sent their anthropologists to study the civilization that had similar industry as the Jews. Equiano, in fact did not mince words in comparing his people (Ndi-Igbo) with the Jews in terms of values, attitudes and culture. The result of the anthropological finding set Ndi-Igbo on collusion course with the British.

Another episode worthy of note is the popular "Aba women riot of 1929." The obnoxious tax polices of the British got through all other tribes in Nigeria without resistance but Daa Ikonna Nwanyiukwu Enyia led aresistance against this tax policy such that the British regarded it as the greatest single most eventful episode of the British Africa. The methodology used in the resistance namely picketing made it very successful and an earth quaking event that the British sent their wives and children home for some time. There is serious doubt that a pacifist society as that of Ndi-Igbo with such sophistication had no leadership structures and institutions. The quality of colonial resistance and decolonization led by Dr. Nnamdi Azikiwe himself an Igbo was untrammeled anywhere there was colonial history. The popular history of the Igbo (Eboe) landing in Virginia in the USA and the high level of self-esteem exhibited by Ndi-Igbo (as never been ruled) made the British to perceive them as both recalcitrant, and *ipso facto* enemies. Sylvia Leith-Ross captures this mood when she avers that "the Igbo as a people do not think much of the British"(Reith-Ross 16). In this atmosphere of wrong perception of Ndi-Igbo as a race that has exhibited lots of self-esteem, intelligence and belligerence, the British not only saw Ndi Igbo as a people placing themselves at par and equal competing level but also as a people that they must destroy in the Nigerian project even after independence; hence the sowing of the seed of their leadership crises. Consequently, all sorts of ploys were employed to demean Ndi-Igbo by the British. Chinua Achebe bares it all: *"Later it was discovered that a courageous English Junior Civil Servant named Harold Smith had been selected by no other than Sir James Robertson to oversee the rigging of Nigeria's first election "so that its compliant friends in (Northern Nigeria) would win power, dominate the country, and serve British interest after independence."* (Chinua Achebe, *There was a Country-A Personal History of Biafra,* 50). Even after independence, the British hate policy on Ndi-Igbo took another turn of exposing Ndi-Igbo to a volte-face of international conspiracy where other world powers saw Ndi-Igbo on a negative light as "atrocious" as the Germans under Hitler while Britain supervised the greatest genocide of black against black in World history. In fact, one of the tragedies of history is the tragic and criminal refuses of the world in recognizing Nigerian Civil war as genocide against Biafra, the British using "Professor" Kirk Green and his Irks really were seen inciting and mobilizing the North against Ndi-Igbo after the January, 15, 1966 military coup. Indeed, their ignoble roles at the time could be summarized as the "northenization" of Nigeria. We can sum up this section by averring that the British polices on Ndi-Igbo were aimed at stifling their progress economically, culturally, socially and politically. Now let us examine how this hate policy of the British has affected Ndi-Igbo in leadership.

Diachronic Perception of the Leadership Crises in Igbo Land

That there is leadership crisis in Igbo land is so hyped that it has become a dictum. Various reasons have been adduced as responsible for this quagmire. The most discussed is the view that Ndi-Igbo do not have kingship institutions. "Igbo enwe Eze", this is often juxtaposed with the often vaunted theory of cultural republicanism and individualism of the Igbo-man. According to this view, the Hausa-Fulanis and the Yoruba's have had more cohesive leadership structure because of a tradition of hegemonic monarchy that have helped to organized their affairs even before the advent of white rule. Accordingly, the proponents of this view have foreclosed any possibility of any evolving, socio-cultural leadership for the Igbos. Even none Igbos chide us for this: Abubakar Mamman Ngulde has this to say: *"The Igbo (sic) unlike the other two major ethnic groupings in Nigeria have traditionally been loosely fragmented politically. There had never been any centralized system of government but each settlement had always existed largely independent of those surrounding it in small units constituted mainly of lineages, clans and villages. There were variations in culture such as dialects, attire, art, style and religious practices amongst such villages and this is still noticed even today"* (Ngulde 24).The author above goes on to conclude that because of his perceived decentralized leadership, the Igbos can never rule this country again. At this point, it is instructive to note that though the Igbos are acephelous by nature, monarchical hegemonism is not a more conducive atmosphere for the development of a people. In effect, the socio-political institutions and structures in Igbo land are more germane for the development of Ndi-Igbo and any group of people than the oppressive oligarchy and hegemonic monarchism obtainable amongst the other ethnic groups in Nigeria. Worthy of note is that Ndi-Igbo appear to be disoriented simply because of the entrenched structures and non-democratic institutions that are in place in Nigeria. T.U. Nwala's position is both apt and instructive in this regards. Accordingly, he avers: *"There is no democracy in the Nigerian federation and when there is no democracy, the emergence of genuine leadership among the Igbos becomes a very difficult proposition. Give the Igbo a democratic environment, and give them nothing else; the sky will be their limit. Development requires an organized polity. For the Igbos, an organized polity has essential leadership institutions that evolve and function through democratic methods with inherent ethos, value-style or world view which serves as a binding force"* (Nwala 24).

It is therefore obvious that the misinterpretation of *"Igbo enwe eze"* has made people to think that Ndi-Igbo have never had recognized charismatic leaders or traditional leadership institutions. This is not true as have been mentioned earlier and the Igbo State Union (ISU) served as a veritable socio-political and cultural organization whose authority traversed the entire Igbo land during the colonial and independence era. Who becomes therefore an Igbo leader? The sort of leadership exuded by the ZC Obi's Igbo State Union provided clear leadership for Ndi-Igbo during the colonial and independence era. It was however killed by the forces antithetical to the democratization of Nigeria during the dark period of Igbo history in Nigeria. The Igbo leader is not an absolutistic figure who emerges by virtue of family lineage and inheritance or from a military commandeering stature. He emerges from his socio-cultural existential involvement as a bulwark of his people. Indeed, he identifies with their aspirations, understands their predicaments and is ready to lay his life for the yearnings of the community. This is the context whereby Dim Chukwuemeka Odimegwu Ojukwu was viewed and regarded in Igbo land as a hero. Thus seen, an Igbo leader is a democratic figure and product that usually evolves from within the existential logic of the reality of the people. It is unfortunate that those who do not understand the logic of the leadership of Ndi-Igbo disparage us as those without leadership. But Igbo *"nwere eze:"* all that is creating this issue is lack of democratic structure and institutions that conduce with the full expression of themselves in tandem with their history.

There are other theories that are put up as militating against the possibility of a credible leadership in Igbo land: the political, social and economic dislocation of Ndi-Igbo by the British over lords. This was highly accountable to the loss of the civil war. There is also the issue of very high intellectual and moral laxity of the political class where egocentricism, individualism devoid of living for one's people is the order of the day. This is a bye-product of the loss of the civil war. However, the ascendance of Ndi-Igbo before the war was as a result of a structure that enthroned meritocracy and justice in running the Nigerian polity. The reverse as it is obtainable today has made it impossible for Ndi-Igbo to find their feet again in Nigeria.

I have gone this far to evaluate the structure of leadership in Igbo land and to state that the views that are peddled hitherto against Ndi-Igbo as a fore-closure of the possibility of evolving a credible and virile leadership does not lie here nor there. It is within the understanding of the logico-metaphysical realities of Ndi-Igbo that the desired leadership could evolve. Let us look at Igbo nwere Eze and evidence

Igbo nwere eze (Igbos had kings): Evidence from History

We have in the preceding section tried to lay foundations towards the establishment of our thesis that Ndi Igbo had established kingship institutions before the arrival of Fredrick Lugard. We have also examined the rationale(s) behind the vaunted Igbo enwe Eze by Lugard and his co-travelers. In this sub-section, we shall establish that Ndi-Igbo had established kingship institutions before the arrival of Lugard and that this institution predated any other in the history of Nigeria.

At this stage, it should be recalled that we established earlier that Lugard's bias against Ndi-Igbo led into a stereotype that influenced his pattern of administration of Igbo land. Lugard used the missionaries to propagate his policy via false, illogical and invalid means. One of these means was the introduction of confusion into Igbo languages, M.A Onwuejeogwu captures this inter alia: "*Archdeacon Dennis was the first to perpetuate Lugard's idea by trying to evolve an Igbo cacaphonic written language. Dennis hurriedly took his team to Egbu near Owerri and produced an Igbo bible written in what is now called "union Igbo", a mixture of Igbo dialects, a language of confusion....in one swift move, confusion was introduced into the writing of Igbo language"* (Onwuejeogwu 27-28).

Was Dennis' manufacture of the Union Igbo an effort to establish that Igbo Language was a cacophonic one that bred no institution at all that needed a new form and perhaps "civilization" in all aspects as suggested by Onwuejeogwu.Another missionary who really perfected Lugard's policy in Igbo land was Rev. Fr. Duhaze. In an attempt to penetrate the Igbo hinterland, Fr. Duhaze and Lutz visited Eze Nri Obalike in 1906 to persuade him to co-operate with her majesty's government in their effort to bring trade, education and religion into Igbo land. They threatened the Eze Nri that unless he performs the ritual abrogating the rules of abomination of the earth goddess (isube nso ani), the colonial government would attack Nri with its military might. Although they gave this threat, the duo of Fr. Duhaze and Vogler while reporting that encounter with Eze Nri Obalike were stunned at the king's level of civilization thus: "*The reports they brought back thrilled him immensely, for although the king of Nri and the chiefs of two or nearby towns absolutely refused to allow any interference with pagan rites, they professed themselves quite pleased at their children 'learning book'..... Each town had a whole list of titles which every free-born man was allowed to take, provided he could pay the initiation fees.... the higher the title the nearer one approached to maw, or spirit: indeed the basis of respect for titled man lay in* their association with maw... The senior ozo man, if posses of initiative and personality, was acknowledged as chief" (Onyeso 42).

One would ask, if Nri kingdom was such a sophisticated one whose influence permeated Igbo land, why did Eze Nri Obalike not use his military to defend himself? A proper understanding of the pacifist structure of the Nri kingdom would answer this question. Accordingly, Eze Nri Obalike's reaction to Fr. Duhaze and Lutz was that: "*we do not believe in killing people. You have been killing the Igbo people. I shall do what you want. Go and call the Igbo leaders as I would do that Isube Nso. Isube Nso does not remove nso... one thing is clear; in two to three generations from today, you will go as you come and leave as alone*" (Onwuejeogwu 28). It is unfortunate that such pacifistic approach did not touch Fr. Duhaze and that they have not left "us alone" as Eze Nri Obalike had predicted. Instead, her majesty's government went on to convoke a meeting of the Eze Nri to attend at Awka. According to Thomas Northcorte, 'his appearance generated fear and awe among the Igbo leaders present" (Onwuejeogwu 28). They were bent on demystifying the Eze Nri before those Igbo leaders. In August 1911, the colonial authority had a forced gathering of over a hundred Igbo leaders at Nri. At the eke Nri, Eze Nri Obalike was forced to perform the ritual of Nsube nso: this was immediately followed by the district officer's remark that from that day henceforth, Ndi Igbo had no king except her majesty in England. Onwuejeogwu captures it this way:

> *Now, go to your towns!*
> *You are no more under Eze Nri*
> *You are under the king of England,*
> *Igbo have no king.*
>
> *(Kita, jebenu na Obodo unu!*
> *Eze Nri adi achizi unu,*
> *Eze obodo Ndi ocha na achizi*
> *Igbo enwero eze)*(ibid.)

The Igbo leaders, following this public demystification of the Eze Nri, went home to propagate the message that Ndi-Igbo had no kings. This is the origin of the maxim that Igbo enwe Eze: this as we have seen has its root in a tendentious political propaganda of Lugard's policy that Igbo land was anarchical devoid of any kingship institution. Subsequently, the church, the District officers and the schools refused to report the factual things they observed in Igbo land in this regards. Rather, books were written like "Akuko Onicha" in *Azundu*, Archbishop G.T. Basden's book, *Among the Ibos of Nigeria* published on London 1938 were all such books that entrenched this propaganda. The rest they say is history: up till now most Igbo scholars and even kings are seen in the public expressing that Igbo egalitarianism equates to *Igbo enwe eze*. I make bold to say that prior to August 1911, there was no such saying in Igbo land. However, there were some colonial agents whose conscience did not allow them to report falsehood: such persons were punished for daring to report things that ran contrary to Lugard's policy on Ndi Igbo. Onwuejeogwu captures this thus: *"For example, Temple who disagreed with Lugard, was denied promotion; Major Leonard and Northcorte Thomas all earned dismissal, from the service probably because of their well disposed balanced report on the Igbo. Both demonstrated that Igbo have a political institution: Leonard wrote 9 pages on Eze Nri, Northcorte Thomas wrote 14 pages"* (*ibid.*)

The Nri theocratic hegemony was established in 900 AD. Since then, a civilization was developed around the ozo, nze, dunu, obi complex where the Eze Nri is a primus inter pares. The structure was a theocratic pacificist democracy established for over a thousand years before Fredrick Lugard and Tubleman Goldie in the 1900. Indeed, Afigbo captures it thus: *"The nature of Nri hegemony was largely ritual, religious and psychological, but because.... There were no clear distinction between the religious, the political and the economic this meant that it was also economic and political. A refusal on the part of the Nri to remove pollution from a community would threaten such a community with economic* disaster (Afikpo 53-54).

If Afigbo (one of the ardent defenders of Igbo haves no king) could concede to this much, it means that the Nri had certain regulatory control of Ndi-Igbo that amounted to rulership. Eluwa captures this rulership thus: *"Indeed the rule of Eze Nri over Igboland as well as Idu land later Benin) Idoma, Igala and other lands settled by immigrants from Ado, was similar to the primacy of the pope in medieval Europe."* (Eluwa 554).

Nri by so doing, bequeathed certain legacies on Ndi-Igbo that sustained them before their balkanization by the British namely: the ritual and the commercial activities of the Igbo market days; the Igbo lunar calendar with the Iguaro; Agricultural life namely the introduction of yam and coco yam and the fertility cult of Ifejioku, the Ozo title taking which used to epitomize rectitude before its bastardization, a pacifist traditional worship that revolved around a monotheistic system of worship of Chukwu, introduction of a special democratized monarchy where the Eze Nri was first among equals. The most important of these was in the introduction of human rights to humans in 1043 AD with the Eze Nri declaring as taboo any attempt to infringe on these inalienable rights. Below is the Nri kingdom compared with 14 other kingship institutions in Nigeria as articulated by Onyeso:

1st *Nri kingdom 900 AD (dates established by Shaw with carbon 14) by Northcorte Thomas (1913) MDW Jeffries (1934) and Prof. M.A Onwuejeogwu (1974 and 1981)*

2nd Kanuri kingdom: about 900AD by Abdullah.
3rd Kano kingdom 950AD by J Hunwick (1971) R.A Adeleye (1971) and Onwuejeogwu (2000).
4th Agbo kingship 950 AD by Chief Iduwe (1985).
5th Daura kingdom 950 AD by J.Hunwick (1971), Dr. R.A Adeleye (1971) Onwuejeogwu (2000)
6th Ife Kingdom (Yoruba) 1045 AD by R. Smith (1969) R. Willet (1960) and Johnson (1921)
7th Ijebu Ode Kingdom 1080 AD by Dr. R. Smith 1969, Prof. E.A. Ayandele (1992) and Johnson (1921).
8th Old Oyo Kingdom 1145 AD by Dr. R. Smith (1969) Dr. P.M Williams (1967) Johnson (1921).
9th Benin Kingdom 1140 AD by Chief Egharevba (1934 and 1968) and Dr. R.E. Brandbury (1957).
10th Ubulu-Ukwu Kingdom 1280 AD by E.A Ikemefuna as Obi Anene (1985).
11th Owa Kingship (off-shoot of Nri) 1280 AD by Obi Efeizenwor II (1994).
12th Igala kingdom 14th AD by Dr. J.S Boston (1962).
13th Ogwashi-Ukwu Kingship (offshoot of Nri) 1500 AD by Ben Nwabua (1998).
14th Aro kingdom 1650 by Prof Kenneth Dike and Prof Ekejiuba (1990).
15th Onitsha Kingship 1750 AD by R.N Henderson (1972) Prof Ikenna Nzimiro (1972)....

Sokoto Sultanate was established barely 206 years ago, after the Fulani wars of 1804-1808 AD (Onyeso 55-56).

If this is yet still not an establishment of the entrenchment of kingship in Igbo land even before any other in Nigeria, I present to you a list of 66 Igbo towns with kings in Igbo culture area from AD 900 to 1914.

Igbo towns with kings (eze) in the Igbo culture area AD 800-1914

No. Names   Origin   Approximate date of origin of kingdoms

1. Fri Migrants into Anambra Valley   AD 700 – 800
2. *Nri* Offshoot of Eri   AD 800-900
3. *Oreri Offshoot of Nri   AD 1000
4. +Agbor+ Offshoot of Ancient Igboid migrants (Ika)   AD 1100
5. Owa Offshoot of Nri/Ika   AD 1400
6. Abavo Offshoot of Nri-Ika   AD 1500
7. Abavo Ute-okpu Offshoot of Nri/Ika   AD 1500
8. Umunede Ika/Igbo   AD 1700
9. Igbodo Offshoot of Ika/Igbo/Ishan   AD 1700
10. Akum azi Offshoot of Ika/Igbo   AD 1700
11. Obior Offshoot of Ika/Nri   AD 1500

12.	Issele-Uku Offshoot of Nri/Idu	AD 1700
13.	Onitsha-Ugbo Offshoot of Ika/Idu	AD 1700-1750
14.	Onitsha Olona Offshoot of Ika/Idu	AD 1700-1750
15	Ezi Offshoot of Ika/Idu	AD 1700-1750
16.	Issele-Azagba Offshoot of Ika/Idu	AD 1700-1750
17.	Obomkpa Offshoot of Ika/Idu	AD1700-1750
18.	Onitcha-ukwu Offshoot of Ika/Idu	AD1700-1750
19.	Issele-Mkpitime Offshoot of Ika/Idu	AD 1700-1750
20.	Ogwashi-uku Offshoot of Nri	AD 1500
21.	Ewulu Offshoot of Nri/Igala	AD 1700
22.	Ishiagu Offshoot of Nri	AD 1700
23.	Nsukwa Offshoot of E.Igbo	AD 1700
24.	Ani ogo Offshoot of E. Igbo/Idu	AD 1700
25.	Aba Offshoot of E. Igbo Nri	AD 1700
26.	Egbudu Offshoot of E. Igbo/Nri	AD 1700
27.	Ejeme Uno Offshoot of E. Igbo Nri	AD 1700
28.	Umute Offshoot of E. Igbo/Nri	AD 1700
29	Isikiti Offshoot of E. Igbo/Nri	AD1700
30	Ashama Offshoot of E. Igbo/Idu	AD 1700
31	Isumpa Offshoot of E.Ibo	AD 1700
32	Ubulu-ukwu Offshoot of Afo	AD 1300
33	Ubulu Okiti Offshoot of Ubulu-uku	AD 1600
34	Ubulu Unor Offshoot of Ubulu-uku	AD 1600
35	Idumuje Uno Offshoot of W.Igbo	AD 1700
36	Idumuje Ugboko Offshoot of W.Igbo	AD1750
37	Akwukwu Igbo Offshoot of Nri	AD 1600
38	Atuma Offshoot of Nri/Igbo	AD 1600
39	Onitsha Mmili Offshoot of Agbo/Idu	AD 1700-1750
40	Aboh Offshoot of Agbo/Idu	AD 1700-1750
41	Ogidi Offshoot of Agbo/Isu	AD 1600
42	Obosi Offshoot of Agbo/Isu	AD 1600
43	Ossomari Offshoot of Igala/Igbo	AD 1700
44	Abala Uno Offshoot of Igbo/Nri	AD 1650
45	Abala Obodo Offshoot of Igbo/Nri/Igala	AD 1650
46	Ase Offshoot of Igbo/Nri/Igala	AD 1650
47	Okpai Offshoot of Igbo/Nri/Igala	AD 1650
48	Onya Offshoot Igbo/Nri/Igala	AD 1650
49	Ibedeni Offshoot Igbo/Nri/Igala	AD 1650
50	Aro Offshoot Igbo/Akpa/Ibibio	AD 1650-1700
51	Eha Alumona Offshoot of Nri	1550
52	Egugwu Olie Offshoot of Nri	1550
53	Nsukka Asadu Offshoot of Nri	1550
54	Nibo Offshoot of Nri	1550
55	Opi Offshoot of Nri/Igala	1700
56	Ibagwa Ani Offshoot of Nri/Igala	1700
57	Akpugo Offshoot of Nri/Igala	1700
58	Nkpologwu Offshoot of Nri/Igala	1700
59	Enugu-Ezike Offshoot of Nri/Igala	1700

60	Edem Offshoot of Nri/Igala	1700
61	Eteh Offshoot of Nri/Igala	1700
62	Obukpa Offshoot of Nri/Igala	1700
63	Ichi Offshoot of Nri/Igala	1700
64	Unadu Offshoot of Nri/Igala	1700
65	Ibusa Nri/Isu (Abandoned Ezeship 1700)	AD 1500
66	Asaba Nteje/Igbo (Abandoned Ezeship 1800)	AD 1550

Sources: Extracted from:
(i) Oral traditions collected by Onwuejeogwu and other researchers, e.g. Ohadike, Okpoko etc.
(ii) Intelligence reports 1890 – 1935 (Onwuejeogwu 59-60).

I equally present to you 118 names of towns in Igboland that claim Nri root and allegiance before 1900 as again presented by Onwuejeogwu:

NAMES OF TOWNS IN IGBO CULTURE AREA CLAIMING NRI ROOT (2001)

1. Abala Uno	2. Abala
3. Abavo	4. Akabo Namkpa Mba-Ukwu
5. Akwaeze	6. Akwukwu Igbo
7. Alo (part of it)	8. Amaegu Nrobo Okpara Uzo Uwani
9. Amaezika Nkpologu Nsukka	10. Amawbia (Part of it)
11. Umuleri Ichida	12. Bebe Abbi Nsukka
13. Ebe Village Achina	14. Ebenebe Nasa
15. Egbema Ozubulu	16. Egumeri (Oraifite)
17. Eha Alumona Opi Nasa	18. Ekpweri (Kwara State)
19. Enugu Ujaji	20. Enugu Agidi
21. Enugu-Ukwu	22. Enugwu Abbi
23. Eziookwa Oko	24. Ezira
25. Igberi (Kwara State)	26. Ikot Ichie (River State)
27. Ikpo Nri	28. Ile-efi Osomani
29. Ishiagu	30. Ishi Igala
31. Isu Ochi	32. Isu Agu
33. Isu Akabo akwu Nnewi	34. Isu Awa
35. Isulo	36. Itchi Nsukka
37. Ivolo Oraifite	38. Iyagba Umudim Nnewi
39. Mbanagu Otolo	40. Mbosi Ihiala
41. Megeri (Kwara State)	42. Mgbudu Ichida
43. Ndiamazu Izuogu (Imo)	44. Ndianichie, Izuogu (Imo)
45. Nimbo	46. Nimbo Ukpabi Uzo Uwani]
47. Nkwere Isu	48. Nnokwa
49. Nsukka	50. Nawfia
51. Obiora Nnewichi, Nnewi	52. Ofrun Nrobo

53. Ogbo Akpo	54. Ogboli Issele-ukwu
55. Ogboli Atuma	56. Ogboli-Ibusa
57. Ogwashi-uku	58. Akpololo Amaichi Nnewi
59. Okpora Nrobo, Uzo Uwani	60. Okpuneze Nnewi
61. Omanenu Nkwela Ezunaka (Part of it)	62. Omanenu
63. Oraeri (Kwara State)	64. Oreri
65. Ote-okpu	66. Owa Oyibo
67. Owelle Uchi	68. Oya Afa Udi
69. Part of Okija	70. Ubulu-Ukwu (Part of it)
71. Ugbene Atama	72. Ugbene (Akwa N.)
73. Ukpabi	74. Umu Ejiofor Obeledu
75. Umu Ukabia Achalla (Awka)	76. Umu Ilozumba Obeledu
77. Umu Odume	78. Omu Okeakpukpo
79. Umu Ene Asaba	80. Umuachalaogu, Nnobi
81. Umuagu (Oguta, Imo)	82. Umuakpanshi Illah
83. Umuchi Ossomari Ogbaru	84. Umuchim Agule-uzo-Igbo
85. Umuchu, kabia (Abia)	86. Umudie Oguta (Imo)
87. Umueri Ogbunike	88. Umeri (Owerri, Imo)
89. Umeri Ogbunike	90. Umuezedi Nteje
91. Umuezedi Ifite Nteje	92. Umuezeogba (Nguru-Nsukka)
93. Umuisim Akpalu (Imo)	94. Umukabi Ikeduru
95. Umukabi Mbaise	96. Umukabi Okigwe
97. Umunkwo Uruagu Nnewi	98. Umunogha Awka Etiti
99. Umunri Ekwulu Mmili	100. Umunir Nsukwa Abatete
101. Umunri Neni	102. Umunir Oraukwu
103. Umunri Ama Okpala	104. Umunri Umuogaze Ukpo
105. Umunri Ezidike (Agulu-uzo-Igbo)	106. Umuorichi, Isikwu-Ato (Umuahia, Abia)
107. Umuosineme Awka	108. Umuri Onitsha
109. Umuebere Diba,)Oguta, Imo)	110. Uwanyana Nsukka
111. Uwanyona	112. Obiaruku (Part of it)
113. Obinumba	114. Obitim
115. Ichi	116. Inyi
117. Isoko clans founded by Nri/Awka now "Isokonized"	118. Orogon clans founded by Nri/Awka now "Orogonised" [29]

I agree with Onwuejeogwu's view that before Lugard came in 1900, that 37% of Ndi-Igbo had kingship institutions between AD 900 to 1914 thus: *"If Professor Afigbo checked my (2001) work properly on page 26, I gave examples of 15 names including appendix 1, listing sixty-four kingdoms existing in Igbo culture area, between AD 900-1914; they are verifiable. This list was made in 1967 and had undergone constant reviews. There were about 150 communities in Igbo land by 1900-1914 (Tovey & Thomas), some put it at 200. Using both figures, it means that there were between 43% and 32%*

(averaging 37%) kingdoms in Igbo culture area." (Onwuejeogwu 21).Worthy of note is that those other communities as my own, (Mmaku) that had no kings were under Nri influence.

Conclusion

I had set out in this paper to establish that Ndi-Igbo had kings before the British decided to destroy the institution through fostering the propaganda that Igbo had no Kings. This belief has contributed to the escalation of the Igbo question in Nigeria. Lugard and Goldie using the instruments of the missionaries achieved what they wanted in Igbo land namely the balkanization of Igbo unity. Ndi Igbo were never such a disjointed rudderless people. Ndi Igbo enwe eze has been wrongly equated with egalitarianism. Ndi Igbo should not accept egalitarianism and the lack of a sense of respect for constituted authority. Igbo revival lies within and not without and one of the fastest and surest means to this is the erasure of the conception that Ndi-Igbo had/have no kings. We had kings and still have kings.

References

Achebe, Chinua. *There was a Country-A Personal History of Biafra* (Great Britain; Allen Lane: 2012).

Afikpo, A.E. *Igbo Enwe Eze: Beyond Onwumechili and Onwuejeogwu*, Okigwe: Whytem ND.

_____ . *Ropes on Sand.* (Nsukka: UNN Press, 1981).

Basden, G.T Basden, *Among the Ibos of Nigeria* (London: Frank Cass & Co 1921).

Basden, G.T. *Niger Ibos.* (London: Seerly Service, 1938).

Eluwa, B.O.N. *ADO-NA-IDU- History of Igbo Origin* (Owerri: De-Bonelson Global Company Ltd, 2008).

Emekesiri, E.A.*Biafra or Nigerian Presidency What Do Igbos Want*, (London: Christ the Rock Community 2012) p.53

Equiano, Olauda. *The Astonishing Adventives of Olauda Equiano*, Enugu: ABIC Books 2007. The first edition of the book was actually published in 1792.

Eban, Abba Eban, *Heritage, Civilization and the Jews,* New York: Summit Books 1984.

Ngulde, Abubakar Mamman. "The Igbos Will Never Rule Nigeria Again", Daily Post (May 19 2013).

Northcorte, Thomas. *An Anthropological Report on the Igbo-Speaking Peoples of Nigeria,* (London: 1913).

Nwala, T.U. (ed.) *OHA-NDOM, In Memory of Daa Ikonna Nwanyi Ukwu Enyia & the 1929 Women Resistance Movement Against Colonialism*, Owerri: Liu House of Excellence Ventures, 2013.

Onwuejeogwu, M.A. "Igbo New Eze; A Anthropological Reply to A Reply", A paper presented at the Ofobuike end of year guest lecture (30th Nov. 2002) at UNIBEN.

Onwumechili, C.A. *Igbo Emwe Eze: The Igbo had no kings*, Ahajioku Lecture. MIC Owerri 2000.

Onyeso, Emeka. "Iwa Oji (Kola nut) in Igbo Cosmology", A public Lecture delivered at the Centre for Igbo Studies, Abia State Univ. Uturu (ND).

Osagie-Jacobs, Oluwole. "Ndigbo: The Elusive Leadership and Consensus", in www.FocusNigeria.com/Ndigbo.htm (Dec2009).

Reith-Ross, Sylvia. Cited in T.U Nwala, "Igbo leadership crises" Chinua Achebe Annual Lecture Series FARTS, UNN, held at the P.A.A (April 23rd 2012).

Shaw. Thurston Shaw, "Radiocarbon Dates from Nigeria" in JHS of Nigeria Vol. II, 14th June 1967.

Umeh, J.A. *Igbo People: Their Origin and Culture Area*, (Enugu: Gostak Printing and publishing Co ltd 1999).

Morality and Igbo Cohesion on the Igbo Question in Nigeria
by
Albert O. M. Ogoko

Abstract

The question of cohesion is one of the burdened concerns driving and informing the International Colloquium on the Igbo Question in Nigeria. This paper reflects on the nature and implications of the moral problems that presently characterize the lifestyle of so many in the Igbo nation leading to a situation that vitiates the realization of any meaningful progress. The moral element remains essential to progress, development and self-realization. What are these? How have we tended to forget these and how have these negatively affected sincere and conscious efforts to transform, and integrate the Igbos in the mainstream of Nigeria polity? The problems stem from economic, political and existential constraints. The task of correcting the moral chaos is enormous, but it is an inevitable task. But the gains cannot be sacrificed on any altar. Morality questions and defines or informs our thoughts and our actions and by implication our achievements

Introduction

This paper is defined by three constitutive and existential imperatives. The first is that I am an Igbo by extraction and have my whole *inmost* possibilities predicated on my spatio-temporal, socio-economic and political environment. This dialectics defines both the self and the other and the relationship between the two. Secondly, as an academic and a philosopher, I have not only to *midwife* knowledge but to reflect on the relationship between the self and the other, on what we *want,* as *end,* what we *desire* as a matter of fact - all those things that propel our drives, on the one hand and on the other, the means or instrumentality of attaining the desired objectives. This is akin to *engineering.* Because these are not modes amenable to empirical investigations, there is an interpretative understanding required to show how the reasons why we act the way we often do does or does not deviate from normal *cause-effect* principle and, *means* and *end* relationship. Some theses that inform this essay are predicated on the following assumptions that the Igbo man (a) has existential project/an ontological mandate; (b) is a responsible subject; (c) acts in concert with others; (d) is rational and orders his actions according to certain moral principles.

What is Morality?

Man is a moral being whose sole instrument is human reason. By this rational principle, man, the Igbo person, *nwa afọ Igbo,* among other ethnic nationalities and races, intuits or draws up ideas that understand to explain, justify and evaluate his or her actions. Every action presupposes a rationale that it conforms to accepted norms. To be rational entails being able to offer sound arguments, to adduce facts, evidence, etc to justify right actions. To realize this fact one may ask: *Iji kwa uche gi e me ihe? Do you act on your thought?* All our actions, therefore, are moral actions because they are judged as such. That means that in the pursuance of the means of livelihood, one *acts* in one way or other. Human conducts include all voluntary human activities called *human acts* as opposed to *acts of man,* meaning the non-volitional, non-intentional actions that one may find himself or herself doing. In this, there is a conscious process of deliberation, accenting to a desired end, a conscious choice of the means to prosecute the end and willing, and volitional motion to execute an action. In other words human conduct includes all willed or volitional actions. In such actions the agent (doer) could have done differently if he or she chose to do so. On the part of the agent, it expresses a persistent and consistent mode of behaviour that seeks to conform to expressed values in the community, the *social* approximations of what is right /acceptable or not: moral virtues, principles, codes, etc. Morality qualifies the moral agent: you and I that everyday act out lives and in those ways have our actions evaluated and qualified. So, we may refer to a particular man who is judged to have acted in a manner evil: *Nwoke Ojoo, the evil man,* or if otherwise, good*: Nwoke Oma.*

Morality, Religion and Values

All human acts carry values and are referred to as virtues. The traditional values in Igbo society include: love, truth, honesty, respect for hard work and self reliance, promotion of family name, honour and respect for elders, filial piety, hospitality, etc. Elobuike Malachy Nwabuisi opines that some of these values have been eroded by the imposition of, and continued craving for western life styles. While dishonesty, adultery, murder, among other vices prevented one from receiving titles and awards, truthfulness and honesty, courage and heroism, generosity are prized. [1-3] Values reflect sense of moral consciousness. I may not just do anything appraised by people without knowing in what manner it is valued. Elobuike defines values as ends: "their desirability is either unconsciously taken for granted ... or seen as a direct derivation from one's experience or from some external authority" or attitudes, since as expression of *likes* and *dislikes* are formed in affinity for or aversion to things, persons, and environment; and money as a means to other values. The following affect proper development of the sense of values and right attitudes to things: person's belief system which has its foundation in the person's cognitive virtues, proper emotion and behaviour. (35) While morality is not the same thing with religious observance, the former seems be reflected and be justified in the latter. This distinction is pertinent considering the proliferation of churches, and grown cases of general immorality: religious hypocrisy, worldliness, immodesty, corruption, irreligious, indecent sexual relations even in the house of God, etc. Many mechanize church activities as routine or as ritual which one is constrained to make without good reason. The idea of what is or is not moral in Kofi Awoonor's view draw from the over-all perceived and expressed relation to the providential and unassuming Supreme Being, *Chukwu okike,* mediated by a hierarchical structure of spiritual beings, ancestors, deities, and priests that maintain communion by sacrifices and rituals to ensure peace, protection, and prosperity.[49-51] Thus, according to Abanuka "religion is grounded on desire which feeds on the sense of separation from an infinite Being" and a yearning for succour and protection and maintained by rituals. [16-17]. But the reason for this relationship is existential and is understood in terms material and even spiritual interest necessary for one's survival.

The strength of such moral laws depends on the degree to which members of the society subscribe to it. Some people will rather seek to bring about the desired power, protection and riches themselves, by hook or by crook, for God may take His time to answer prayers. Recall, therefore, what characterizes our prayer points in the church and at meetings. A pervasive idea about most Christian's attitude to God, the sacramental, and the sacred in terms of serious commitment to faith and righteousness is most undesirable and not encouraging. It is in the Church that you find the corrupt, murderers, assassins, the occult grand masters domesticating the sacred, ritualists, those in political positions who have continued to embezzle public funds and others who have no interest for repentance and conversion. They are there because they are manipulating the presbytery, steal church monies and feign piety by practised social protocols. Moral question as a matter of border on one's subjective conscious experience and require no empirical parameter for validation. In a way these impact negatively on the common life pattern and ideals of integral Igbo communities. The way we live are not wholly a private issue: we relate and interact on all borders, within our homes and the wider society. Is it not said that *Nne Eghu n'ata agbara nwa ya ana ele ya?* This is a case of giving scandal. Recall, morality is 'consensual' or as customary articulate common approximations of the people on what is permissive and acceptable or not and the basis for that. Thus, rascality, virulent and self-seeking ideas, ill-informed opinions, and forms of deviant behaviour such as kidnapping, rapping, thuggery, cultism, and terrorism cannot be allowed to over turn and disrupt the socio-moral order.

Existentialism and Morality

In Igbo we say that *E be Onye bi Ka Ọ n'awachi*. This is an ontological principle of social responsibility, to *mend* and *stitch* the socio, economic and political leakages of one's environ. Reflecting on this social obligation, the late Catherine Acholonu-Olumba, notes: "Everyone bears their own cross, the loadstone of their existence. My particular loadstone is that I have no 'I' to call my own. My personality, my identity is part of the Collective Consciousness of the peoples among whom I have found myself. I desire nothing. I want nothing. I crave for nothing. I accumulate nothing." [x]

Evaluation: poor work ethics

How are we affected by negative moral order? Achebe notes "I have enough history to realize its civilization does not fall down from the sky; it has always been the result of people's toils and sweat, the fruit of their long search for order and justice under brave and enlightened leaders." (10). Among our people there are youths who want to ride expensive cars which other people laboured for many years to buy; they want to occupy privileged positions when they do no work. Visit the Local Government Areas and Development Centres in the East and you see a ghost of a dream: a massive waste pipe, a failure of grass-rooted developmental structure. It is usually on pay days, that most workers rush in, collect unearned salaries and get back for long holidays. This is immoral to get paid for doing nothing.

Leadership Problem

The Igbo states have had the misfortune of producing, more or less (except for a few, since First Republic) self-proclaimed and aggrandizing political "business men." Take a look at the party structure, the duplication of political functions, examine the comments of those who arrogate unto themselves the ubiquitous role of being "politicians" by profession, look at the massive display of ill-gotten wealth etc and you will understand that we have had less of good leaders. But the late Michael Okpara, Akanu-Ibiam, Hon. Sam Mbakwe, Ikemba of Nnewi, and a host of others are illustrious sons.

Reference to "caucus meeting", *stakeholders*, King-makers, Political godfathers seems to imply that there is a gathering of political *investors* and profiteers. Again as if these send no signal, political intrigues, varying political interests and litigations distract even a well meaning 'leader.' At other times there is a recycling of incompetence in political appointment as compensation for political membership. There is infrastructural decay everywhere.

Poverty of Thought

Achebe talked about "poverty of thought" exhibited in the biographies of Dr. Nnamdi azikiwe and Chief Awolowo in sweeping statements about their aspirations. He noted that "absence of objectivity and intellectual rigour at the critical moment of a nation's formation is more than an academic matter, (11-12). The book of ecclesiastics says that man should be mindful of his/her ignorance and ought to learn before speaking, some of our leaders paid the dear price of death either because they failed to take candid advice, or trusted the enemy, or were confident in an issue when they had no knowledge base of the problem. You think that because someone said that Igbo people are intelligent warrants you to call another a fool? Wisdom is one of the moral virtues and works with the practical intellect. According to Okere, "the intellect is man's major antenna to other reality, man's tool in mastering his environment" [131]. Worst still many Igbo hate to think critically well, logically, in a philosophical parlance, in order to make corrected inferences, our people talk carelessly and think less of the semantic import of our language. Take for instance, in a market scenario, "someone asks: *kedu ihe ichoro*? You may not be selling everything. Why on earth should someone ask that kind of question? My needs might be multiple and list endless.

Well Developed Political Ideology:

To have the right ideology one needs to know who he or she is and want and the means to achieve it. Unfortunately, some have false image of themselves. Achebe noted "One of the commonest manifestation of under-development is a tendency among the ruling elite to live in a world of make-believe and unrealistic expectation" [9]. Some of our Igbo leaders are vulgar, arrogant and care less about what they say and do, and how people see, take and read them. Quite often we hear some in political positions challenging one and say, "I makwa onye m bu?" Do you know who I am? The populace talks about these as *"Ndi odare iwu eje nga!* There are very few, if any Igbo who is not a Christian. There is too much church talking and going, yet evil, crimes, corruption practices leap the bounds everyday. If we were truly serious, our population can make the difference. We could make giving and taking bribe a taboo (Okere, 129)

Conclusion

So the researcher tried to illustrate that one cannot separate between the ideas that something is right or not from the fact that he or she acts in one way or another to satisfy certain exigencies. Choice implies a pre-deliberation which investigates and analyzes the justification of the relationship between an action or the end and the approval of the act. The concepts "Nwafo Igbo, "onye Igbo," imports a "self-hood, an identifiable pact of personality, characterized, who is predicated but not himself predicable. Quite often we hear such banal or derogatory comments addressed to an Igbo, or some retorts at your action, an obvious show of ignorance: *I bukwa onye Igbo*: yet other tribes imply so many things in connection with the name, Igbo with all its enigma.

An examination of who the Igbo person is requires a reflective understanding of the moral and metaphysical constitution encased in his being. It also critiques every supposition underlining this conception what we are that we are not supposed to be, what we are presently not that we ought to be, where we are and are not supposed to be, or ought to be are not and need be. Truly, Socrates saying that an unexamined life is not worth living "concours with the Igbo saying that" *Onye n'amaghi onwe ya, e bufee ya ama Nna ya*", and "*Onye n' amaghi ebe miri bidoro maa (wa) ya, a gaghi ama ebe o ga akwusi ima ya*". (He who does not know himself is likely to be carried beyond his father's compound, he who does not know where he meets rain will not know where it will stop. For Igbo people, *Onye ajuru, a dighi ajuu onwe ya*? Therefore each one of us has a civic, economic and political responsibility towards oneself and others. The principle is "I am" here, because you are too. "With you I am counted".

1. We must put in place a carefully articulated, culture sensitive Igbo cause system of education to train the mind and character.
2. There is also an urgent need to re-educate or de-educate to unlearn, what had erroneously been internalized even into the subconscious. A proper/reflective understanding of Igbo must begin by rejecting all projected ideologies and systems of falsified information peddled in the society. It also rejects all false or wrong manoeuvres adopted so far in the struggle
3. Our lapses, tribulations and decades of incarceration should be turned into strengths.
4. We ought to pay closer attention to our language as a means of relating to our world, articulating a world view, and putting in place an ideal conceptual scheme.

Works cited
Achebe, Chinua *The Trouble With Nigeria,* Enugu: Heinemann Books, 1984
Abanuka, B. *Myth & The African Universe,* Onitsha, Nigeria: Spiritan Publications, 1999
Acholonu-Olumba, Cathrine, *They Lived Before Adam, Pre-Historic Origins of the Igbo, The Never-Been-Ruled,* Preface, Abuja: KARAC Publications, 2009
Aristotle, *Nicomachean Ethics,* trans. by W.D. Ross, Kitchener: Batoche Books, 1999.
Bilen, Osman.*The Historicity of Understanding and the Problem of Relativism in Gadamer's Philosophical Hermeneutics.* Vol. 5, Culture and Values, CRVP,http://www.crvp.org/book/Series02/IIA-11/contents.htm,2001
Ellis, Stephen and Haar Gerrie Ter, *Worlds of Power, Religious Thought and Political Practice in Africa,* New York: Oxford University Press, 2004
Elobuike Malachy Nwabuisi, *Values and Education,* Onitsha, Nigeria: Spiritan Publications, 2000

Isiramen, Celestina, O. Preface, *Religion and the Nigerian Nation, SomeTopicalIssues*, Ibadan: En-joy Press Books, 2010

Frolov, I. ed. *Dictionary of Philosophy,* Moscow: Progress Publishers, 1984

Gratsch, J.Edward, *Aquinas Summa, An Introduction and Interpretation*; New York: Alba House, 1985

Kofi Awoonor. *The Breast of the Earth, A Survey of the History, Culture and Literature of Africa South of the Sahara,* New York: Nok Publishers International, 2005.

Okere, Theophilus, *Philosophy, culture and society in Africa*, Nsukka: Afro-orbis Publication Ltd, 2005,

Plato, *The Republic*, 2nd ed.; trans, by Desmond Lee, Middlesex England; Penguin Books, 1974,

Ricoeur, Paul "The Philosophy of Will and Action" in *The Philosophy of Paul Ricoeur: An Anthology of His Works,* ed. By Charles E. Reagan & David Stewart, Boston: Bacon Press, 1978

SECTION TEN: IGBO DIASPORA/THE INTERNATIONAL SYSTEM

Igbo Nation: A Diasporean Perspective
by
Holden Anele

Abstract

Igbo people had developed great cities abroad on the strength of the part they played, in spite of being slaves and descendants of slaves, in the United States, Haiti and the Caribbean. They defeated the great military power of France and gained independence in 1804 as Republic of Haiti. This same *Resiliency Gene* inherent in those Ndi-Igbo is still the driver behind the economic development of most major cities in Nigeria: Port Harcourt, Kaduna, Lagos Abuja, etc. There's, therefore, a crying need to rally the Igbo outside Nigeria with direct constructive engagements as the focus. This should achieve a result similar to that achieved by European and American Jews when they faced a situation similar to ours (the Igbo), eventuating in the creation of the modern state of Israel.

Introduction

There is no ethnicity, tribe, or enclave that shares a synonym with the word "Igbo". It is unique and peculiar to the indigenous people of Igboland, the south eastern Nigeria. We have a language that is very unique in world linguistics. It is a language with a unique capability to craft and integrate almost any foreign word into Igbo alphabetology. Unfortunately, we, the Igbo, appear not to appreciate our Igbo language and its versatility. As a consequence, there is a real danger of its extinction, albeit gradually. The following excerpt buttresses my point: "But following the prediction by the United Nations Educational, Scientific and Cultural Organization (UNESCO) Advisory Committee on Language Pluralism and Multi-language Education that Igbo language and by implication, culture, may be heading for extinction, and subsumed by other stronger Nigerian languages by 2025, if nothing is done, by its speakers to ensure that it is not only taught in schools, colleges and universities, but also used as language of official communications within government and business circles in the five Igbo-speaking states - Abia, Anambra, Ebonyi, Enugu and Imo - the prayers, this time around, seemed to have changed from that of (language) height gain to long life" (Abanobi, 2012:27).

Historical Background

There are many Igbo geographical settlements around the world, and which settlements have endured challenging times, hardships, sufferings of immigrants and circumstances of geopolitical factors. It thus appears that the Igbo gene (genotype) is an inherited dominant allele that, thanks to Providence, has served, and carries survival value. It possesses economic, social and intellectual resiliency which confers on it a physiological robustness toward an expression of dominance and dare, and feistiness... This Igbo resiliency gene manifested itself elaboratelyafter the Nigeria-Biafra war, when the federal government of Nigeria imposed an obnoxious and anti-Igbo economic policy. The Finance minister at the time, Chief Obafemi Awolowo, gave Igbo people £20 regardless of the amount of money they had in Nigerian banks. This is what I called Awolowo's £20 robbery. Igbo people walked away from Awolowo's twenty pounds prescription. Ndi-Igbo had to begin life afresh with nothing except their ingenuity, hard work, and determination to succeed. Today, Ndi-Igbo own many banks and financial institutions in Nigeria without the help of the federal government. Many banks in Nigeria would collapse if Ndi-Igbo withdrew all their funds. This accomplishment was by sheer hard work and Igbo resiliency gene. Most often, they never awarded Ndi-Igbo contracts, however, Igbo business people bought at exorbitant prices the contracts the government had awarded to other people, executed them and made money from them against all odds. This was the tactics of the famous Abuja contracts.

Subsequent to this apartheid retrogressive and retarded economic policy of Nigerian government was the issue of the so-called "Abandoned Property". General Gowon and his Supreme Military Council through a federal government commission gave away Igbo-owned real properties outside Igboland to other people. The person who was assigned to execute this crime against humanity was David Mark, the current president of the Nigerian Senate. He performed this job satisfactorily well to his boss, General Gowon. By this singular act, Ndi-Igbo were alienated from their properties outside Igboland principally in Port Harcourt, a town developed mostly by the Igbo. Credit must be given to Chief Samuel O. Mbakwe, who took the federal government of Nigeria and the Abandoned Property commission of David Mark to courts. It should be realized that this ugly policy was later brought to the fore in 1991 when Lagos state government wanted to reverse the ownership of one of the properties of General Chukwuemeka Ojukwu, which prompted him to undertake a "sit-in" protest on his property. Today Igbo people own more than 73 percent of real estate properties in Abuja. This fact was made known by the former minister of Federal Capital Territory, El Rufai (http://www.nairaland.com/54751/el-rufai-Ndi-Igbo-own-73-abuja). These were undeveloped pieces of land that were bought from some Hausa people whom they were originally awarded to but lacked the expertise to develop them. I must add that we must start to look inward because there may be a second abandoned property issue in Nigeria. As though the abandoned property issue did not teach any lesson, Ndi-Igbo are building ultra-modern schools in Lokoja.

There are so many incidents of injustices that were brought on Igbo people by Hausa-Yoruba administrations/cabal in Nigeria. Those multidimensional acts had no bound as they traversed every aspect of existence. They carefully never established any federal presence in Igboland except police stations and military barracks. They never established any university until 1982 when Collins Obi wrestled the Federal University of Technology Owerri from Shagari administration to enable him win the 1983 election.

Gowon-Murtala-Obasanjo administrations in Nigeria had a clandestine policy of total neglect of Igboland including repairs of federal roads. They even went very far in perpetuating academic illiteracy in Nigeria by making JAMB to have a different set of standard for Igbo candidates while lowering cut-off points for Hausa candidates. This was achieved with sinister policies such as quota system, catchment areas, state of origin, academic disadvantaged Northern states, etc. In other to head off these academic discriminatory policies of Nigerian federal government, Chief Sam Mbakwe commenced the establishment of Imo State University. At the time there was only one university in Igboland, University of Nigeria Nsukka. The federal government fought him through its proxies in the court. Eventually, he was able to establish the state university after which other states followed suit such as Bendel state university (now Ambrose Ali University Ekpoma), Lagos State University, etc. Ironically, while the federal government was busy with its cold war on Ndi-Igbo, it was simultaneously and vehemently fighting the Apartheid policy of South African government, a despicable double standard!

In the area of oil and gas, they engaged in "pseudo-gerrymandering" by appropriating and allocating some oil fields in Imo state to neighboring non-Igbo states such as Rivers state in order to "short-change" an Igbo state in revenue allocation. This practice started at the end of the war and was exacerbated by the Obasanjo administration. We should recall that during the 1983 presidential campaigns, Alhaji Shehu Shagari wanted to site a petrochemical refinery in Imo state. When Buhari administration came in place, he unilaterally sited the refinery in Kaduna while at the time, Kaduna already had the best refinery in Nigeria. Ever since then, there has been no mention of building a refinery in Imo state by the federal government. Kaduna we know produces no crude oil or natural gas.

The aviation industry was not spared either. Imo state had no airport and its citizens had to be travelling to mostly Port Harcourt in order to catch a flight. This became a very viable source of revenue to Rivers state but a great inconvenience to Igbo people. Chief Sam Mbakwe, governor of Imo state, decided to unilaterally build an airport for his people. When it was almost nearing completion, Alhaji Shehu Shagari, the president of Nigeria, dispatched his minister of aviation and took over the project with the promise to complete it in record time. Little did Ndi-Igbo know that was a terminal grandiose deceit to deny them the airport. The airport became an uncompleted project until recently. However, it remains the first and probably the only airport ever built by a state government in Nigeria with no financial contribution from the federal government of Nigeria. Currently, it is alleged that the Nigeria federal authorities are covertly working to stifle efforts and initiatives to upgrade this airport to an international status. These discriminatory and anti-Igbo policies were prevalent in every sphere of activity including military enlistments, military promotions, federal civil service, federal appointments and promotions, admissions into Nigerian Defense Academy, etc. Against all these factors, Igbo people in Nigeria have survived a tremendous deal! We survived the pogroms of the Northern Nigeria that presaged and precipitated the declaration of Biafra.

Ndi-Igbo survived the genocides Adekunle, Obasanjo and Murtala Mohammed orchestrated on Owerri and Asaba people respectively in the pretence of fighting a war as presented in *Blood on the Niger: The First Black Genocide* by EmmanuelOkocha. Their war tactics were devoid of international convention in humane treatment of enemy soldiers, and anti Geneva conventions in the treatment of prisoners of war. The federal troops were incessantly bombing market squares killing civilians mainly children and women with no remorse. In contrast, the United States destroyed Iraq in the war led by George Bush (the second) and instead of abandoning Iraq, they subsequently embarked on its reconstruction which gulped billions of US dollars. That was what reconstruction was about. Eastern Nigeria was never reconstructed neither were Igbo people reconciled and rehabilitated contrary to Gowon's Three R's declaration (reconciliation, reconstruction and rehabilitation) at the end of the war. It seemed obvious that Gowon's Three R's speech might had been written for him by Chief Awolowo.

The political reality of Nigeria is one bedeviled and clandestinely manipulated by *mafioso* organizations. The Kaduna Mafia, Bida Mafia and Langtang Group in concert with the Sokoto Caliphate have a solid resolution never to allow an Igbo man to be president of Nigeria. A document exists that clearly spelled this out and signed by the notable key Northern politicians. We should recall that Olusegun Obasanjo was also compelled to sign a document that he must hand over to a Northerner. That was the condition they brought him out from jail and made him the President of Nigeria in 1999. He did, nevertheless comply exactly with the terms of that agreement. The universal incontrovertible truth is that power is never given to anyone, rather people fight or struggle for power. Our people in politics must devise a sophisticated methodology to wrestle power from the sharks in the Nigerian political terrain.

Igbo Resiliency Genes at Work

We were not given any preference in terms of admission policies into tertiary institutions. However, we are numerically among the top graduates of tertiary institutions each year in Nigeria. We also have the capability of crippling the economy of the major Northern cities and Lagos if our people decide any day to stay home for three weeks. Even though they stole our properties, today we own far more properties in Nigeria than the number they stole. We started with nothing at the end of the war but today we are the most progressive group in Nigeria. The Hausa pogroms and massacres conducted by Murtala Mohammed could not deter us and whenever the true census is conducted in Nigeria, it will prove that Igbos are the most populous of all the ethnic groups in Nigeria.

Igbo Diasporean Communities

In 1992, I met a man in the United States at a conference and introduced myself. He wanted to know my last name. I told him I was an Igbo from Eastern part of Nigeria. He went into a history lecture I had never heard of. He told me how a ship that carried some slaves predominantly Ndi-Igbo from Nigeria came to North Carolina, before it could anchor, the slaves rather decided to jump into the ocean. None of the slaves remained alive. He also narrated that the place of this incident was named "**Igbo Landing**". (This is a historic site in the sand and marshes of Dunbar Creek in St. Simons Island, Glynn County, Georgia marking an 1803 resistance of Igbo slaves brought from West Africa on slave ships. The purpose of this anecdote is to portray the lone-purpose and ironclad determination and nature of Ndi Igbo. Ndi-Igbo used to work with a concentrated, pinpointed focus on issues that related to their collective survival. This was self-evident in the rallying-song of **Enyimba Enyi**. Whenever, this was called, Ndi Igbo rallied together and performed a task irrespective of how complex it was. That does not exist anymore. The slave trade did establish many Igbo settlements outside Africa. Their Igbo resiliency genes made most of them to overcome their arduous antagonistic environments of sub-human living conditions and flourished to attain enviable heights. There are many countries that have Igbo settlements and a lot more whose histories are traceable to Igboland. The following are quite a few of them:

The Republic of Haiti

Haitians are Ndi-Igbo that were sold into slavery to the Americas. Their physical attributes, industriousness, enterprise, anecdotal evidence and history lay claim to this. Their ancestors told them by word of mouth that they came from Igboland. This has been passed down the generations. This is one of the main reasons why they did not waste time in recognizing the Republic of Biafra. Haiti was the first to fight for independence in the western hemisphere after the United States. They defeated the great power of France and became an independent nation on January 1st, 1804.
http://www2.webster.edu/~corbetre/haiti/history/revolution/revolution4.htm).

The United States, Caribbean and South America

There were many Igbo slaves brought to the United States, the Caribbean and South America. They were more in those countries that played significant roles in the slavery including Brazil. In Brazil, there is a strong Yoruba community today that spanned and spurned from slavery. But the nature of Igbo and its acculturation propensities probably hindered the Brazilian Igbo slaves from maintaining their Igbo identities unlike the manner Brazilian Yorubas did but quite akin to today's Lagos Ndi-Igbo as they don't speak Igbo to their children. The indigenous people of Brazil speak about 170 languages. There's a high probability that one of these 170 languages could be a mutation of Igbo language. In the United States, there are many Black Americans that will identify themselves as Ndi-Igbo based on their family genealogy and computer applications in Genetics. But we have to initiate the move. If we don't identify ourselves or assert our existence and be proud of it, how can other people whose origins are from our native compounds identify themselves as our cousins? In 2009, Danny Glover and Forrest Whitaker, prominent American actors, identified themselves as Ndi-Igbo by tracing their roots to Nkwerre, Imo state.

(http://newsnigeria.onlinenigeria.com/templates/?a=1420

Equatorial Guinea

Equatorial Guinea was one of the few African countries that gave Biafra diplomatic recognition and followed it up with action. When Awolowo asked Gowon to blockade Biafra and stopped all foreign shipments coming into Port Harcourt, within a short period of time there was a grave shortage of food and medicines. Awolowo overtly proclaimed that "starvation is the best instrument of war". Within months, Biafran children started dying of "kwashiorkor". Equatorial Guinea came to immediate assistance including airlifting Biafran children to Equatorial Guinea. Few of those children came back to Igboland while many developed as adults, settled and nationalized there. Today there is a huge Igbo community in Equatorial Guinea which the continental Ndi-Igbo do not even care about. This population once produced the first lady of that country.There are many other Igbo communities scattered around the world as a result of the international slave trade, but due to no efforts to reach out to them, their great grandchildren are today lost to other ethnicities. There is no doubt that there are many generations of Igbo people in Europe especially in the United Kingdom and Netherlands being few of the key slave trade outposts of Europe.

Recommended Tasks

While we are currently fixated with getting our house in order, so to speak, and re-claim our God-given leadership role we have temporarily abdicated in Nigeria, we must not lose sight of our gateway to the world. Ndi-Igbo in diaspora is our gateway to the world. We must always be cognizant of this fact.

Undoubtedly no country and no people of the world have been through upheavals and terror more than the people of Israel, the Jews. Their success and entrepreneurial ingenuity have always as in the biblical period brought them hatred and envy very close to their extermination as a people. The Jews all over the world recognized that fact and made the passage of their culture and religion to their children a *sine-qua-non*. Therefore a Jew born anywhere in the world is still a Jew and identifies with Jewish cause: self-determination. With the unsurpassed aggressiveness and political lobbying, they used their successes in finance to achieve their self determination by making the United States President and Prime Minister of Britain to coerce the United Nations into adopting Resolution 181 in 1947. In May 14th, 1948, the state of Israel was formed. Today any politician in the United States who is anti-Israel will never win election. There is tremendous wealth that pours into Israel and it's both economically and militarily strong to withstand its antagonistic hostile neighbors.

In the same vein, we can harmonize all the people of Igbo descent around the world and lead them to the recognition of their lost history. They will gladly follow because some of them have given up searching for their ancestral roots. While we are doing that, we will also keep pace not to lose the recent Ndi-Igbo that emigrated outside Igboland such as Ndi-Igbo in Equatorial Guinea, Cameroun, Ivory Coast, Lagos, etc. The amount of wealth, cultural exchanges, enlightenment and power that will pour into Igboland will be monumentally unprecedented if this is done. That alone can force the leadership of Nigeria unto the hands of Ndi-Igbo!

A clear road map to this is the creation of a body that will have this great responsibility of designing a congruent and unequivocal *modus operandi* to raise the Igbo consciousness in diaspora outlined above and work towards their self-recognition and self-realization of who they are. For a verile Igbo Nation, the following programs are recommended:

1. Adopt the teaching of Igbo language and culture as a subject in all Igbo states and every student must take it up to final West African General Certificate of Education. It must be a mandatory first and second year courses in colleges and universities in Igbo land for students.

2. Igbo people should be encouraged to establish their businesses in Igbo land with adequate support from Igbo governors. The Igbo governors should be willing to allocate sites for industrial development where Igbo industrialists will site their factories.

3. Formation of **Igbo Diaspora Movement** that will work to raising the global Igbo consciousness and re-connecting all Ndi-Igbo worldwide to Igboland.

4. Embarking on annual celebration of World Igbo Day with the main event being in major Igbo cities. This is a day Ndi-Igbo will reflect, take stock and re-strategize as a people living in a hostile environment and in a country where they are surrounded by antagonistic neighbors.

References
Ani, Kelechi Johnmary. *Developing Country Studies* ISSN 2224-607X (Paper) ISSN 2225-0565 (Online)Vol 2, No.8, 2012
http://www.nairaland.com/54751/el-rufai-Ndi-Igbo-own-73-abuja
Okocha Emmanuel, *Blood on the Niger, The First Black Genocide.* Triatlantic Books, 2006.
http://www2.webster.edu/~corbetre/haiti/history/revolution/revolution4.htm
http://newsnigeria.onlinenigeria.com/templates/?a=1420

The Potentials of Diaspora Igbo in the Making of a Powerful Igbo Nation in a Fast Degenerating Nigeria
by
Professor Anthony Ejiofor

Introduction

It is important to explain, *ab initio*, the context in which the term Diaspora Igbo is used here. It is the scattering of Ndi Igbo which is a condition of debilitation, helplessness and a pathology that must be overcome as we match towards renaissance. Jonathan and Daniel Boyarin have described this as a unique source of power and strength. While recognizing the new waves of emigration of Ndi Igbo due to unfavorable political atmosphere in Nigeria, it is now clear that Diaspora Igbo refers to the totality of scattering of the Igbo over time and in pathetic circumstances that are largely beyond their control. Due to the effects of emigration and the Atlantic slave trade, there are descendant Igbo populations in countries such as Cameroon, Equatorial Guinea, Gabon, Angola, South Africa as well as outside Africa including the United States, the Caribbean (Jamaica, Cuba, Haiti, Barbados, Belize, Trinidad and Tobago, Puerto Rico and Honduras) and even in faraway India. Why is this narrative necessary? We must borrow from the experience of the Jews in contemporary history which has shown that there is power in Diaspora experience. With the current genealogy tracing by means of DNA testing, the roots of the Diaspora Igbo is being uncovered by descendants of the victims of the Atlantic slave trade who are researching their family history. We have an impressive list of celebrities who have traced their ancestry to Igbo land. Such celebrities include Bishop T.D. Jakes, Forest Whitaker, Paul Robeson, and Blair Underwood. One only needs to scratch the surface of history to discover that the Igbo lay claim to the vast areas of land development and people in New England, Maryland, Virginia, Kentucky, Georgia, the Carolinas, Mississippi, the Gullah tribe and what have you. In other words, the Igbo are rich and powerful and only need to cash into our ties with these people to bring rapid development to Igbo land, develop a formidable international force like the Jews did and are still doing and place the world on notice that the Igbo can no longer be kicked around. This expose will explore the potential roles these people could play in the development of Igbo land once we can mount a strategic and sustained effort at letting them know we want them "home" and that they "belong here". When we merge this cohort of "Igbo people" with the modern entrepreneurial and professional acumen packed in both fists by contemporary Diaspora Igbo, you have an explosive Igbo power ready to detonate. The detonator should be the outcome of the discussion of this subject at the colloquia. Think of the fire power we can develop in lobbying the centers of power in this world starting from

Washington, D. C. Think of the economic power we can muster in New York and California. Think of the forces we can array behind us as we take on human rights abuses of the Igbo head-on. Think of the resolutions we can push through at the United Nations to protect the Igbo anywhere on the globe.

The Jewish Template

It is fanciful among our people to claim relationship with the Jews hence we are referred to as the Jews of Nigeria. It is easy to draw many parallels between the Jews and the Igbo. Indeed the Igbo apex Diaspora organization, World Igbo Congress, was set up in principle after the World Jewish Congress model. One would expect that the parallels between these peoples should extend beyond the ephemeral and wannabe mentality and translate to the well-known success story of the Jews. There is this lingering question: Why are Jews primarily engaged in trade, commerce, entrepreneurial activities, finance, law, medicine, and scholarship? And why have the Jewish people experienced one of the longest and most scattered Diasporas in history? For the avoidance of doubt the fact that Jews are disproportionally successful in many fields of endeavor is undeniable. The statistics simply speak for themselves. Jews make up less than half of 1% of the world's population but they consistently have made up more than 20% of the Forbes 400 list of the world richest people. It is not just making money that a disproportionate amount of Jews seems to excel at. Thirty percent of Nobel Prize winners in science are Jewish, and major Hollywood studios, like Paramount Pictures and Universal Studios, are also run or owned by Jews. In virtually every industry successful Jews are disproportionally represented. Some people think that Jewish success has to do with genetics, and others surmise that it is related to their intense persecution. It is also known that strategies for success are inherent within Jewish religious teachings and Torah stories are ideas that relate directly to behaviors and attitudes that lead directly to successful outcomes. Why do we not copy these? After all, we have suffered long and intense persecution like them. We are scattered in the metropolises of this world like them (Jews usually do not live in the rural areas and are usually not farmers). We have the greatest numbers of educated people in the aforementioned endeavors. Is the blade blunt or is the barber not proficient? In Owerri parlance: *Owu Mgbeke ama ala ma owu aguba ari nko."*

It is important to state that if we want to be as successful as they are (and we have the potentials) we must do some of the proactive things they do. It has been said that all Jews directly or indirectly study the greatest book of wisdom ever written—the Torah. All Jews benefit from its wisdom in the form of attitudes and teachings that Jewish parents and communities teach and pass down. Do the Igbo have parallels here? No we don't but should. We must begin by writing our history, our books, I mean serious books in economics and business or our version of the Torah. Without an intentionally organized guide the new generation of the Igbo born by first generation (Those who left Igbo land from 1970 till date) Ndi Igbo will, like those of them scattered Igbo all over the world through slave trade will be lost to Igbo land permanently.

I cringe at the ominous thought of the often bandied about that Igbo language will be extinct in the immigrants in the US, Europe and elsewhere who are now between 15 and 40 years old. These new Igbo have nothing concrete to promote the Igbocentricism in them.

A seasoned Igbo Think Tank and Igbo Future

The Igbo must stop puffing themselves up with words like Think Tank and really get to do what think tanks do. The Igbo have a powerful cadre of intelligentsia capable of really charting a course for us in the next quarter of a century. This Think Tank must be knowledgeable people experienced in the development of roadmaps. They must develop organizations capable of tapping into our Diaspora reserve to make them think Igbo. They must have two things in mind:

1. Create opportunities for the establishment of incontrovertible Igbo lineage for all Diaspora Igbo. In the US alone the Igbo were most numerous in the states of Maryland (coincidentally where there is a predominant population of recent Igbo immigrants) and Virginia, so much so that some historians have denominated colonial Virginia as "Igbo land." With a total of 37,000 Africans that arrived in Virginia from Calabar in the 18th century, 30,000 were Igbo according to Douglas B. Chambers. The Frontier Culture Museum of Virginia estimates around 38% of captives taken to Virginia were from the Bight of Biafra. Igbo people constituted the majority of enslaved Africans in Maryland. Chambers has been quoted as saying "My research suggests that perhaps 60 percent of black Americans have at least one Igbo ancestor..." Think about this, my people. The same story is told in the Caribbean and elsewhere. We must go straight into assisting our people, the Diaspora Igbo trace their roots back to Igbo land so they can lend a hand in the arduous task ahead. Howard University among many organizations now offer **genetic testing** so Americans of African ancestry can determine where on the continent their ancestors came from. Cambridge University Press, North America, is now offering a CD-ROM containing the records of two-thirds of all slave ship voyages. Howard University, a historically black college in Washington, D.C., has assembled the largest collection of DNA records from West and Central Africa in the world, some **3,800 samples** in all. The collection concentrates on ethnic groups in areas where **most slaves** in the United States came from. We need to sink out teeth into these as Igbo nation. Here in lies the movement that help Igbo nation come alive.

2. Promote the establishment of highly targeted organizations that will tap into our proverbial business acumen to produce next generation home-bound entrepreneurs. Access to financial capital is crucial for the Igbo seeking to pursue entrepreneurial activities. The micro-credit and micro-savings revolution has opened a path to entrepreneurs who operate on a very small scale. Some societies, such as that of the United States, attach high value to individual initiative and reward successful entrepreneurs with social status as well as wealth. This is also the Igbo paradigm that must be escalated among Igbo Diaspora. Individuals with high levels of human capital tend to be more entrepreneurial than those without. However, knowledge and education alone do not spur entrepreneurship. Individuals working in economic clusters or areas saturated with like-minded and experienced professionals in specific sectors have access to valuable social capital, including networks and knowledge transfers, which facilitates joint ventures and partnerships among current and former colleagues. Research suggests that highly skilled individuals make their decisions on where to migrate based on the presence of other talented professionals, capital infrastructure that promotes education and professional growth, and the promise of good returns on one's own human-capital investments. Let me expand this concept a little more in the next section.

Suggested Commitment to Home-Bound Diaspora Entrepreneurship

Over the past decade, a number of African and Asian governments and other organizations have established programs to encourage emigrants and their descendants to invest in their home countries. Initiatives range from privately run and funded to government-led, but most involve some sort of public-private partnership. Many organizations are hybrids and promote activities in several categories, including networking, mentoring, investment, venture capital, and strategic partnerships. We must have our eyes on the next 25 years as we work to bring home all shades of Diaspora Igbo.

Networking organizations promote diaspora entrepreneurship by offering opportunities for diaspora and local business leaders and professionals to meet one another (either in person or via the internet) and discuss potential business and investment opportunities in the homeland. Some networking organizations are involved in public-private partnerships to facilitate meetings between locals and members of the diaspora, while others promote networking among diaspora business leaders to foster partnerships and opportunities in countries of origin.

Mentoring organizations are more actively involved in supporting entrepreneurship among diaspora members than pure networking organizations, in that they try to match aspiring entrepreneurs or business owners seeking to expand their operations abroad with seasoned Diaspora experts and business leaders. Some mentors offer one-off services, while others provide internships or even job opportunities in their corporations. GlobalScot, Armenia 2020, and The Indus Entrepreneurs are examples of mentoring organizations.

Training organizations help aspiring Diaspora entrepreneurs acquire the knowledge and skills to set up and run a successful business. Training programs range from transferring knowledge from Diaspora experts to country-of-origin entrepreneurs to offering lessons on business management to providing guidance on how to find financing.

Investment organizations provide initial start-up funds or subsequent capital infusions, usually in the form of pooled private and public funds or matching grants. Some investment organizations take a hands-off approach to the money they offer entrepreneurs, while others are more involved in overseeing how their money is spent at various stages of project implementation. Such an organization will develop strategies for an "Igbo bank" in the Diaspora

Venture capital and partnership organizations provide more than just start-up funds, and usually are heavily involved in business projects that they believe will be profitable. Often they form strategic alliances with other venture capitalists, business leaders, engineers, and other professionals. For these organizations, the number of strategic partnerships or projects supported by venture capital usually matters less than the quality of the proposed investment, the high potential for return on investment, and the impact of such partnerships and investments on economic growth in strategic sectors. For others, strategic partnerships are about fostering trust and long-term relationships among key institutions in countries of origin and destination.

Conclusion

According to Gloria Chuku, working largely on court and county documents as well as the recently published transatlantic slave database, Douglas Chambers uses the circumstances surrounding the 1732 death of Ambrose Madison, the paternal grandfather of President James Madison, to reconstruct the history of the Igbo slaves in Virginia. Her book is primarily about the dominant role of enslaved Igbo in the formation of early Afro-Virginia slave culture and society. The Virginia story is only a microcosm of the human capital the Igbo potential has in the Diaspora. We have a dire need to tap into this. We must build a strong bridge between the Igbo in the home land and all shades of Igbo in the Diaspora. That bridge should bring economic prosperity that will provide the needed strong economic base in Igbo land. An entrepreneur undertakes new ventures which, if successful, create wealth and jobs, Igbo wealth and jobs. Having feet in two worlds, diaspora entrepreneurs are uniquely well equipped to recognize opportunities in their countries of origin and can be especially motivated to contribute to job creation and economic growth in Igbo land. It is little wonder that development practitioners are interested in trying to harness this tremendous force for economic growth and dynamism. Igbo land must not let this pass.

Encouraging members of the diaspora to pursue entrepreneurial ventures seems a matter of common sense as an element of development policy. Peace, stability, and the construction of basic infrastructure are prerequisites for substantial diaspora investment. Governments of Igbo land, multilateral institutions in Igbo land, Diaspora organizations, and other civil society groups can help Diaspora entrepreneurs to tap the resources they need and clear obstacles to realizing their ventures — or at the very least, they can get out of the way.

References Consulted

Chambers, Douglas B. (2005). "Murder at Montpelier: Igbo Africans in Virginia". ISBN 1-57806706-5

Chuku, Gloria. 2005. Igbo women and economic transformation in southeastern Nigeria: 1900 – 1969 (New York: Routledge)

Klapper, Leora, Raphael Amit, Mauro F. Guillén, and Juan Manuel Quesada. 2007. *Entrepreneurship and Firm Formation across Countries.* Washington, DC: World Bank.

Kuznetsov, Yevgeny and Charles Sabel. 2006. International Migration of Talent, Diaspora Networks, and Development: Overview of Main Issues. In *Diaspora Networks and the International Migration of Skills: How Countries Can Draw on Their Talent Abroad,* ed. Yevgeny Kuznetsov. Washington, DC: World Bank.

Leblang, David. 2009. "Another Link in the Chain: Migrant Networks and International Investment." Presentation at the World Bank Conference on Diaspora and Development, Washington, DC, 37

Newland, Kathleen and Tanaka, Hiroyuki, 2010. Mobilizing Diaspora Entrepreneurship for Development". Migration Policy Institute 1-35

Newland, Kathleen, with Erin Patrick. 2004. "Beyond Remittances: The Role of Diasporas in Poverty Reduction in their Countries of Origin." A Scoping Study for the Department for International Development, United Kingdom.

Ofili, Echiemeze Chizekene 2013. Igbo Global Agenda: Igbo Purpose in the rapidly increasing Igbo Diaspora. Part I.

Papademetriou, Demetrios G., Will Somerville, and Hiroyuki Tanaka. 2009. "Talent in the 21st Century." In *Talent, Competitiveness and Migration.* Eds. Bertelsmann Stiftung and Migration Policy Institute. Guetersloh: Bertelsmann Stiftung.

Ramamurti, Ravi. 2004. Developing Countries and MNEs: Extending and Enriching the Research Agenda. *Journal of International Business Studies* 35 (4): 277–85.

Saxenian, AnnaLee. 2006. "International Mobility of Engineers and the Rise of Entrepreneurship in the Periphery." Research Paper No. 142, United Nations Univ., Tokyo, Japan. 1-31

United States Agency for International Development (USAID). 2008. *Global Diaspora Networks Alliance Framework.* Washington, DC: USAID.

United States Agency for International Development (USAID). 2008. *Diaspora Networks Alliance: Leveraging Migrant Resources for Effective Development.* Washington, DC: USAID.

SECTION ELEVEN: MEDIA/IT/COMMUNICATIONS

Media Ownership and Control in Nigeria: The Dialectics of Political Hegemony
by
Abia Onyike

Introduction

The essence of this paper is to examine and analyze the ownership and control patterns of the Nigeria media landscape and how the evolving dynamics impact on the politics of the nation. Even though media scholars have not been able to establish the extent to which the press influences human action, there is a general acceptance that the society is heavily impacted by the media through various forms of education, information, indoctrination and spread of ideological consciousness. Another important premise of our analysis is that even though the mass media are believed to be working for the overall good of society, the press has never been able and cannot afford to be a neutral arbiter in the discharge of its professional duties. In any class society with ethnic, religious, regional and sectional divisions, the press sometimes knowingly or unknowingly tilts towards sectional pressures and serves the interests of its owners or tends to favour the views, ideas and postulations of certain power blocks in the polity.

In the United States of America, the Cable News Network (CNN), projects the interests of the American ruling class, namely the Pentagon, the Wall Street and the military industrial complex. This is also the case in Britain, where the British Broadcasting Service (BBC) serves the overall media interests of the ruling oligarchy. Other newspapers such as *Washington Post*, *New York Times* and London *Times* are structured to promote and project news, opinions and editorials which sustain and consolidate the dominant political and economic order in the Western World. In Nigeria, the popular myths of ethnic chauvinism and their attendant sophistry find expression in the ownership patterns and control of media resources in the country which have over the years justified and defended the status quo ante. According to Chinweizu, political hegemony in Nigeria is founded on the "caliphate ideology", which is sustained by myths, lies and sophistry which adjudged the Hausa-Fulani as Nigeria's Aryan race, divinely endowed for leadership compared to the southerners who are perceived as burden bearers and servants of the Danfodio's scion. The hegemonic ambition of the Northern aristocrats was enunciated by Ahmadu Bello, the grandson of Othman Danfodio – the man who led the jihad which brought the disparate Northern nationalities under the sphere of the Hausa-Fulani dynasty. The jihad penetrated the South-Western Yoruba land through the invasion of Ilorin, Oyo and Ogbomosho, after which Islam was imposed in Yoruba land.

In October, 12, 1960, shortly after Nigerian independence, Bello was quoted by the *Parrot* newspapers to have stated that, "The new nation called Nigeria should be an estate of my great grandfather Usman Danfodio. We will ruthlessly prevent a change of power. We use the minorities of the North as willing tools and the minorities of the South as conquered territory. We will never allow others to rule us. We will never allow them to have control over their future". That was the beginning of the mythical charter of ethnic ideology in Nigeria.

The Nationalist Press and the Struggle for Independence

A random survey of Nigeria's media ownership patterns in the last 100 years (1914 to 2014) shows that 90% or more of the newspapers were owned and published by Southern Nigerians who were mainly based in the old capital territory of Lagos. However before the advent of the indigenous anti-colonial crusaders in the 1920s, the early frontiers of nationalist thought in Nigerian journalism were three distinguished pan-Africanists who were active in the Negro movement. They were Edmund Willmot Blyden, who hailed from St. Thomas, Virgin Islands, a pure Negro-of Igbo ancestry. The others were John Payne Jackson, a Liberian, who published the *Lagos Weekly Record*. He was in active journalistic practice from 1890 to 1919 when he died. Then his son, Thomas Horatio Jackson took over as the Editor of the newspaper. While Blyden emphasized cultural nationalism in his writings, the Jacksons specialized in political nationalism. Blyden argued that Africans should not emulate other races but should explore the tenets of African regeneration by bringing forth the unique contributions of African continent to humanity. Jacksons's newspaper was adjudged the most popular of the early nationalist newspapers because of the intensity of its assault on the colonial government. James Coleman thus noted that, "his lengthy editorials, always hung on the edge of sedition."

The emergence of the anti-colonial freedom fighters and their crusading journalism continued with the radical tradition marked by intense critical commentaries and incisive editorials which were tailored to advance the cause of Nigerian nationalism and humanism in general. The newspapers of that era and their publishers were as follows: *African Messenger*, Lagos (1921) published by Ernest Ikoli; Lagos *Daily News* (1925), published by Herbert Macaulay; *West African Pilot* (1937) published by Nnamdi Azikiwe; *Nigerian Tribune* (1949), published by Obafemi Awolowo; the *Northern Advocate* (1949) published by Bob Ogbuagu; the *West African Examiner* (1950) published by Nwafor Orizu. There were also other sister publications established by Zik in other cities such as the *Southern Nigeria Defender* (Warri, 1943); *Nigerian Spokesman*, Onitsha (1943); The *Eastern Nigeria Sentinel*, Enugu (1952) and the *Daily Comet*, Kano (1950).

The independence movement in Nigeria was essentially piloted by the these nationalist press, especially Nnamdi Azikiwe whose newspaper chain had become the main platform for the grooming of radical youths who were active in journalism and at the same time vibrant in the Zikist movement. Moveover, the popular Democratic tradition which the press in Nigeria espouses till today had its roots in Azikiwe's pan-Nigerian and pan-Africanist bent. Some of the leaders of the Zikist Movement included Mokwugo Okoye, Osita Agwuna, Nduka Eze, Anthony Enahoro, M.C.K. Ajuluchukwu, Bob Ogbuagu, Kola Balogun. Other prominent journalists trained by the Zik's newspaper chain were A. K. Blankson, Babatunde Jose, Alade Odunewu, Mobolaji Odunewu, Solomon Simbi, Babatunde Salami, Adisa Williams, Agbaje Williams and Sa'ad Zungur formerly National Secretary of the National Council of Nigerian Citizens (NCNC) and the political mentor of Mallam Aminu Kano. Thus, Adebayo Williams once described Nnamdi Azikiwe as "the founding father of modern Nigerian journalism, who provided the lightening rod for the cultural and intellectual revolution. A pan-Nigerian hero and a demotic genius who fired the imagination of Nigeria youths with his political derring-do". He concluded by noting that, "it was in the Nigerian press that the intellectual and political foundation of Nigerian nationalism was laid".

The Post-independence Press and the Road to Internal Colonialism.

Nigeria's politics in the run-up to independence in 1960 was characterized by extremist tribal and ethnic irredentism. The rise of separatist political parties, namely the Action Group and the Northern Peoples Congress, both of which came into being in 1951 laid the foundation for a calculated attack against the pan-Nigerian vision of the NCNC, which was led by Azikiwe. These developments followed the crushing of the militant Zikist movement by the British colonial state apparatus which rallied the Hausa-Fulani-Yoruba alliance against Nnamdi Azikiwe and the NCNC, which was dreaded by the colonialists and their local collaborators. The resultant effect of this scenario was the consolidation of feudal and semi-feudal potentates in the Northern and Western regions of Nigeria, thus preventing the emergence of a national democratic revolution. Therefore, Nigerian independence was granted as pseudo independence. This faulty foundation has continued to haunt Nigeria till date and manifested itself in several horrible incidents, namely the collapse of the First Republic, the three year civil war which pitted the Eastern Region against the Hausa-Fulani-Yoruba alliance, military dictatorship from 1966 to 1999 (minus 4 years of civilian rule from 1979 to 1983), the annulment of a democratic election in June 1993 and its attendant crises. The latest political crises hunting Nigeria since the ascendancy of President Goodluck Jonathan and the Boko Haram insurgency (which has killed over 50,000 Nigerian citizens since its inception in 2009) are all traceable to the conflicts generated by Nigeria's hegemonic political tradition.

Oil Economy and Class Struggle.

The discovery of oil in Oloibiri in present–day Bayelsa state in 1956 and oil exploration activities created an economic system in which 90% of export earnings accrued from the sale of crude oil. The huge oil and gas resources catapulted Nigeria into the status of the 5th largest oil exporter in the world and the first in the African continent. Experts believe that over $600 billion has so far been appropriated by several Nigerian governments from the sale of oil since the 1970s, yet Nigeria remains one of the poorest nations on earth.

The Nigerian economy is a petroleum-driven economy, with a monolithic structure of inequalities whose major characteristics include a unitarist and rigid administrative order. This is an abnormally for an expansive nation – state made up of over 250 ethnic nationalities. Unfortunately, 53 years after independence and 100 years after amalgamation, Nigeria still suffers from the crises of underdevelopment, namely mass unemployment, violent crimes, kidnapping, infrastructural decay, inability to generate electricity, mass illiteracy, armed banditry, assassinations, rampant road and air accidents and the instalmental killing of citizens by armed insurgents and religious extremists. Her citizens are still plagued by deadly diseases. Nigeria is one of the countries in the world where polio eradication is yet to be achieved. The other two countries are Pakistan and Afghanistan-two wretched and war-torn countries located in the fringes of the Middle-East. Nigeria is also known to have the highest percentage of infant mortality in the world, alongside Pakistan. Several studies on the Nigeria economy, politics and society, indicate that the Nigerian economic system dominated by the indigenous oppressor ruling classes was founded on intrigue, perfidy and an orchestrated policy of impunity and armed violence directed at the indigenous peoples, with a culture of sustained deprivation, dispossession and impoverishment of the lower social classes. Some of the fall-outs of the politics of hegemony in Nigeria include the environmental degradation of the oil bearing communities, the draconian decimation of the Ogoni resistance movement and the liquidation/brutal killing of Ken Saro-Wiwa in 1995, the mass murder of peasants in Bakalori in 1983 and the seizure of their farmlands, the Odi massacre and the Zaki Biam tragedy etc. These repressive measures against minority ethnic nationalities represent aspects of the hegemonic politics of the dominant power blocks in Nigeria.

Analysis of Media in Contemporary Nigerian Politics.

The evolution of the modern press in Nigeria requires a critical scrutiny in order to understand its current discordant tones in the face of national conflagration. Despite the fact that the Nigerian press is concentrated in the Lagos-Ibadan axis - an area reputed for industrialization, in comparative terms with other parts of the country, experience has shown that beyond the populist sloganeering of its leading editorial chieftains, the press has been largely influenced by the economic and political forces which hold the nation to ransom. Thus, Victor Kalu once referred to their editorials, opinions and vaunted news headlines as "the invasion of the polity by the mercantilist press and the parochial bantustan philosophy which they proffer". Beginning from the time when irredentist elements in the separatist nationalist movement invented ethnic ideology in Nigerian politics, up to the way and manner in which the Nigerian civil war was turned into a genocidal engagement to decimate and emasculate the Igbos in their self-determination struggle, the Lagos-Ibadan press is yet to rationalize its justification of the obnoxious episodes, solely on account of its adherence to Awoist principles. Such ideological fixation even in the face of human calamities of ethnic cleansing, which its intellectual leaders continue to justify till date has exposed the press as the nattering purveyors of man's inhumanity to man, in the Nigerian landscape. The vulnerability of the press has been further enhanced by the pretended excess of an enduring culture of intense rascality and gangsterism which define Nigeria.

According to Gordon Duff, the language of politics "in such societies has been replaced by the language of crime". He added that what has been misconstrued as political problems are and have long been responses for the depradations of criminal mafia organizations which control governments. Therefore, it is an irony that even though most of the National newspapers namely *The Guardian*, *The Sun*, *Vanguard*, *This Day* and *Champion* newspaper were owned by publishers from the South-South and South-East regions, the desperation to survive the harsh and uncertain economic climate of the Lagos market compels them to adopt editorial politics which promote Hausa-Fulani-Yoruba political ascendancy. Secondly the infestation of the media environment by Agbero culture as occasioned by motor-pack touts, street urchins and area boys spewed from the Oshodi – Maza-Maza-Idumota market network sometimes operate as subtle threats to dissenting voices who would prefer to save their heads than lose it in defence of patriotic ideals.

Of course the operations of the press since the return to democratic rule can be cited to explain the double standards alleged in this analyses. When General Olusegun Obasanjo was elected President on 29th May, 1999, the Lagos – Ibadan press resorted to setting an agenda which sought to demonize the National Assembly, while protecting the Obsanjo presidency and insulate it from critical surveillance. All kinds of allegations were made against the principal officers of the National Assembly, leading to the removal of Evans Enwerem and Chuba Okadigbo as senate Presidents. Within the sane period, the first speaker of the House of Representatives Salisu Ibrahim was disgraced out of office. The press turned a blind eye to Obasanjo's abysmal performance in office. The ethnic support for Obasanjo in the 2003 elections, which culminated in the Alliance for Democracy (AD) adopting "their son" as a joint presidential candidate with the PDP says volumes of the tribal conspiracy theory from which the press cannot exonerate itself. The emergence of Goodluck Jonathan as President, following the death of Umar Musa Yar'Adua in 2010, has further exposed some sections of the Nigerian press as being incapable of promoting a consistent humanist perspective in national development. Some of the newspapers in question have turned full circle to exhibit extremist partisanship against the Jonathan Presidency. These elements in the media and the pro-democracy movement do not even care that their current posture would obliterate all the efforts made in the past to launch an effective offensive against the Northern hegemonists, who are regarded as the main obstacles to Nigerian developments.

Conclusion

The Nigerian press can only succeed in the performance of its professional duties if it can re-invent itself as an unbiased umpire in a complex and plural society. Media practitioners must eschew corruption. They should borrow a leaf from the teachings of Walter Lippmann who enjoined media practitioners to see themselves as mediators and translators. By so doing, they will endeavour to guarantee effective communication between the elite and the masses. We must explore the tenets of social responsibility journalism which is anchored on the principles of objectivity, truthfulness, accuracy, fairness, impartiality and humanistic editorial pursuits.

Mass Media in the Spectrum of War Propaganda
during Nigeria's civil war years
by
Ray A. Udeajah

Abstract

Many people affected by a war carry with them a souvenir of the experience. Nigerians emerged from their civil war richer in recollections than they had been prior to the conflict. The spectrum of Nigeria's memory of the civil war is horrific and complex. The significance of the reminiscence was accentuated in the mass media. For instance, in the broadcast media, Radio Nigeria were broadcasting 'to keep Nigeria one' whereas, determined to broadcast 'for survival', Voice of Biafra adroitly attracted the attention of a universal audience and eloquently triumphed in the airwaves, winning both the sympathy and admiration of the whole world save for those of Britain and Russia. This historical survey examines the diverse events of the three-year war and identifies the experience of media propaganda during the civil war. The findings indicate that the war is an experience many Nigerians are too young to remember and their elders who participated in it prefer to forget. Above all, this study confirmed that the Nigeria-Biafra war, executed as much in the airwaves as in the warfronts, remains a bitter past that none would ever want repeated.

Introduction

Nigerians emerged from their civil war richer in experience than they had at the inception of the crisis. The spectrum of Nigeria's reminiscence of the war was accentuated in the mass media where propaganda frequently guised as either information for public enlightenment or education and public relations but rarely as manifest propaganda.

News constitutes a vital component of the life of individuals, groups, communities and nations. It comes in the form of print or broadcast, always bringing information to the people, the news re-presents the society to the world. Persons in authority, government or its agents, who wish to utilize the media to their advantage or to control events in such a manner as to win favourable publicity, often employ tactics called news management. Experts in this aspect of journalism are spin doctors: they are in the business of propaganda aimed at highlighting the good news and down-playing or concealing as best they could the bad.

Nigerians recognize that nationalists of the pre-independence era were not only aware of the potency of propaganda, but that they applied the techniques whenever the need arose. The same is true of the politicians of

Nigeria since Independence. That Nigerian politics has never been devoid of propaganda is due partly to the innumerable crises that have bedevilled it since independence, and partly because propaganda cannot be separated from politics as it is understood in contemporary society (Udeajah 2004, p. 68). Therefore, in examining the events that occurred in Nigeria between 1967 and 1970, during the Biafran revolution, attention to the obligatory element of crisis-politics, which is propaganda, seems particularly important.

In the confusing dimensions of political instability that followed Nigeria's flag independence, the military intervened. They assumed power promising to restore political order and to accomplish what civil politics was unable to tackle. The broadcast stations were among the first institutions occupied by the military when the first coup occurred. This testifies to the central importance that had come to be attached to the broadcast media.

Observers of Nigerian political environment would not easily forget the background to the coup which originated from the disagreement over the conduct and result of the federal elections of December 30, 1964 that triggered a chain of actions that resulted in the incursion of the military. The euphoria enjoyed by the Nigerian politicians did not last long because while the supposed victors of the chaotic elections were adjusting and getting used to their new status, some soldiers in the Nigerian army were busy plotting measures to stamp out corruption from the society. They planned a kind of revolution that would clean up the country and produce a clean society with honest, non-sectional government. Some five majors in the army advanced and executed the plan and sent several political leaders to the grave. That was on January 15, 1966. Many Nigerians welcomed the revolution and some even regarded the Majors as national heroes.

Dr Nwafor Orizu made a broadcast to the nation on Radio Nigeria. In the broadcast he acknowledged that he had been advised by the Council of Ministers to hand over the administration of the country to the Armed Forces. The General Officer Commanding the Nigerian Army, Major General J.T.U. Aguiyi Ironsi, made a broadcast to the nation, accepted the "invitation." General Johnson Thomas Umunnakwe Aguiyi Ironsi, the General Officer Commanding the Nigerian Army became the Head of the National Military Government.

It is evident from the coup-day broadcast that the army incorporated broadcasting institution into its political system right from the day the soldiers took over the Nigerian political theatre. Major General Aguiyi Ironsi was murdered on July 29, 1966. On August 1, 1966, Lieutenant Colonel Gowon the leader of the Northern Army rebels, announced that he had assumed the office of the Supreme Commander and Head of the Federal Military government, although there were at least half a dozen military officers senior to him.

Gowon also organized a constitutional conference to determine the future of the country. However, the irony of circumstances in Nigeria was such that while the constitutional conference was going on in Lagos, the Northern Nigerians surprised and butchered to death innocent civilians of Eastern origin. The massacre occurred in numerous places in the North. This embittered the Eastern government. As the number of Easterners killed in the North continued to increase, the Eastern delegates who returned from the said constitutional conference in Lagos refused to return to continue the deliberations on the future of Nigeria. It was feared that their security could no longer be guaranteed.

Meanwhile, the Governor of the Eastern region summoned all Easterners to return to the East. It was perceived that the Nigerian federation could no longer offer the Easterners safety, nor protection, nor guarantee them the atmosphere essential for the development of their innate capabilities. Many believed that their continued association with Nigeria was tantamount to acquiescence to intimidation by Northern feudalism.

Several attempts were made to reconcile the parties involved in the crisis but they all proved abortive. The Aburi International mediation that resulted in an agreement between the two principal actors almost succeeded. But it did not. The Aburi conference lasted for two days. As perceived by Adewale Ademoyega, all the other members of the council from Nigeria had apparently come to meet and reconcile with Ojukwu. This is because he was the only one who had not attended earlier meetings in Nigeria. Subsequently, almost all the proposals put forward by him were adopted unanimously. According to Ademoyega (1981:133), it was at Ojukwu"s instance that the Council collectively avowed not to use force to settle the Nigerian crisis. At his instance also the Council conceded a confederal status to the Regions without any adjustment of boundaries. At the end of the meeting it was agreed that the resolutions should be embodied in a Decree to be issued by Lagos with the concurrence of the Military Governors.

Neither Ojukwu nor any representative from the Eastern region attended the meeting of the Supreme Military Council convened by Gowon after the Aburi accord. Also absent from the meeting was the Governor of Western region, Colonel Adebayo. It is worth noting that at about that time, the Western region asked that the Northern army of occupation be removed from the Western region. Ajibola (1978, p. 126) reported that the Western Governor made it plain that he would not participate in the meeting as long as Northern troops remained in the West. Above all, Chief Awolowo resigned from the Constitutional Conference in protest against the continued presence of the Northern army in the Western region. Consequently, they were withdrawn. Only a small population remained.

In this context, it may be recalled that the historic Aburi meeting of the military leaders in dispute, in January 1967, opened with a condemnation of the irresponsible performance of the mass media in aggravating the national crisis. Tamuno (1989, p. 10) acknowledges this reality. However, the general concession remains that no sole factor may be deemed responsible for the escalation of the conflict.

To make matters worse, the administration of Gowon refused to pay several months' salaries to the Easterners dislocated from the other regions at the inception of ethnic killings. The population so affected trooped to Enugu in search of consolation from the governor of the Eastern region. Under pressure from such groups, Ojukwu sought to pay the workers in order to remedy the situation. In a broadcast message at the end of March 1967, the Governor of Eastern Region announced his government's edict, which stipulated among other things that thenceforth all revenue due from any source whatsoever in Eastern Nigeria, collected for or on behalf of the federal government, shall be paid to the Government of Eastern Nigeria. The thrust of the broadcast message engendered the *Eastern Nigeria Government Revenue Collection Edict* (March 31, 1967), *Statutory Corporation Edict* (1967), and *Companies Edict* (1967).

Apart from the broadcast edict, there were a number of decrees issued to effectively separate the region, in various respects, from the rest of Nigeria. Again Ajibola (1978, p. 31) observed that at every instance the reason given for the action was the same: that the region was no longer wanted by Nigeria and so had to leave and live. In keeping with this survival motive, Ojukwu announced in a broadcast message of April 24, 1967, what he termed a "Survival Budget: Covering more than fiscal measures, the budget explicitly suggested that Nigerians drift a little apart' as a means of survival.

In response to Ojukwu's seizure of federal revenue, Gowon suspended all Nigerian Airways flights to the East and halted postal and money-order transactions. What was more aggravating in that situation was that he further cancelled the diplomatic passport of thirty prominent Igbos, who he alleged, were lobbying against the federal government overseas. According to Stremlau (1977, p. 51), prominent among the people whose passports were cancelled were K. O. Mbadiwe, Pius Okigbo, Francis Nwokedi, Flora Azikiwe and a number of diplomats suspected to be engaged in arms purchases abroad.

Finally, on May 27, 1967, the Eastern Nigeria Consultative Assembly, after some two-day deliberation, passed a resolution empowering the Governor, Lt. Col. Ojukwu, to find a separate political identity for the people of the region. Although Lt. Col. Gowon announced that evening the creation of twelve states in Nigeria, three of which were to be in the Eastern Region, this was strongly rejected by the Governor of the Eastern Region. In fact, Ojukwu went on and declared the Republic of Biafra, thus formalizing the situation, which had existed since July 1966. Stremlau (1977, p. 51) recorded part of the broadcast declaration as follows: "I do declare that all the political ties between us and the Federal Republic of Nigeria are hereby totally dissolved ... And the territory and region known as, and called Eastern Nigeria, together with her continental shelf and territorial water, shall henceforth be independent, sovereign state of the name and title of the Republic of Biafra." The situation was perceived and described differently by both parties. While the Biafrans saw the act as an exercise of their right to self-determination, the Nigerians felt bad about it. Ajibola (1978) observed that the federal government's retort to Biafra's secession was to declare it an act of rebellion which would be crushed.

Whatever impressions the parties might have given the world through their respective broadcast media, the reality that confronted them was that neither of the groups was adequately equipped for the imminent showdown of war. Nevertheless, after some while war broke out between Biafra and the Federal Republic of Nigeria. It all began on July 6, 1967. Different reasons were given for the war. For the federal government, it was a "police' action intended to arrest a rebellion, whereas the Biafrans saw it as an act of genocide designed to exterminate the Biafran population. In his book named after the nation, *Biafra*, Ojukwu (1969, p. 37) stated: "We are fighting a war which for us is one of survival. We have used the term now and again, but what actually does it mean? It means that we are fighting for everything that makes our life worthwhile, so that we may breathe God's air. It is my pride and honour that I happen to be on the scene at this time, but I believe that whether I was here or not this war would have come sometimes and Biafra would still have survived ..." Months later he reminded the people of the reason for the war, emphasizing that it was the only way for the oppressed people of Biafra to survive: "Let us not forget, nor allow the world to forget the real causes of this war. We never started this war. We were attacked by Nigerians. Indeed, we are fighting purely in self-defence and for our security and survival. Despite all our efforts and contributions right through our unfortunate association with the people of Nigeria, we had been suspected, provoked, persecuted, and oftentimes killed. The climax came in 1966 when, with clock-like regularly in May, July, August, September and October, our people, in a manner most brutal, were massacred in different parts of Nigeria. In search of safety and security, we returned home and abandoned every material thing we had earned and possessed .Today we have justified our claims and our right to survival as a nation."

Broadcasting for Survival

The nation in this context is Biafra. The very mention of Biafra evokes varied images that many Nigerians are too young to remember and elderly Nigerians would prefer to forget. All the same, it should not be forgotten that throughout the period under review, the broadcast media became deeply engrossed in sectional war of words. In short, the broadcasting stations in the country were allied into blocks as media practitioners spread propaganda in favour of their regional inclinations. Teaming up with the political elite, broadcasters took sides with their regions during the series of conferences that were organized to determine the supposedly new constitutional propositions for the country. With the declaration of the Republic of Biafra and the subsequent outbreak of war, therefore, there emerged a series of slogans from the opposing camps. For instance, Radio Biafra affirmed as follows: "*The price of Liberty is eternal vigilance. Biafrans, be vigilant!*' Through constant repetition, citizens of the Biafran camp soon learnt the appropriate slogan by heart. Indeed, it was as if their lives depended on the ability to recite the war slogan. Needless to state, in that context, that the broadcast media continued their political education, even in such a war situation.

The broadcast stations within Nigeria re-echoed the messages emanating from Lagos, while Radio Biafra went it all on its own. Although the fortunes of war once altered on August 9, 1967, when Nigeria's Mid-West region became the "Republic-of-Benin', the luck did not last long to be cherished. Weeks after the Biafrans' liberation of the region, the federal might descended upon the younger state and strangled it out of existence. That left Biafra alone in the struggle for survival.

But the political actors on the path of Biafra realized early in the struggle that modern warfare is waged as much on the military and diplomatic fronts as through the power of broadcast media. Accordingly, the media were used to condition the people of the young nation, who were called upon to make the inevitable sacrifice that they were fighting in the name of survival. Biafran broadcast professionals considered it expedient to portray the Hausa-Fulani oligarchy as wicked, murderous aggressors – a fit subject for collective hatred of the Biafran state. In other words, the broadcast media in Enugu convinced the Biafran population of the blamelessness of their own government, and in particular Radio Biafra aroused in people a spirit of righteous indignation against the enemy. Thus, media conditioning eliminated the problem of motivation in Biafra. Genocide stories were used to mobilize public animosity against the invading enemy and to justify Biafra's actions of self-determination.

On August 18, 1967, in a broadcast from Radio Biafra, in Enugu, Ojukwu spoke about his seizure of Benin and the Mid-West region. The author of *Yakubu Gowon,* Clark (1987, p. 102) reported the broadcast message as follows: "Brave and courageous Biafrans: On July 6, Nigeria launched its military aggression on our young Republic of Biafra ... My purpose, to-night, is to take a look at those grim and historic weeks of our war of resistance and survival against a monstrous enemy. The sole purpose of the enemy was to destroy our identity and existence as a people, to plunder our wealth, eliminate our menfolk, desecrate our sacred and holy places, defile and befoul our women and put our children and generations unborn in perpetual serfdom to the Hausa-Fulani oligarchy ... I want to restate our aims ... Our general strategy has been to lure the enemy to our territory. When they have been fully committed and trapped for destruction, we then strike. From Benin we are now in a position to launch a decisive offensive against the enemy to bring the war to an end."

Clark (1987, 106) further noted that the following month, on September 29, 1967, Ojukwu, broadcasting from the same station in Enugu stated: "Fellow countrymen. Brave and Proud Biafrans ... We know that victory for Gowon, the mendacious symbol of Hausa-Fulani imperialism, would mean continued genocide for our people, bestiality, disease and the desecration of our religion ... Can anyone forget Gowon's dishonesty, duplicity and high-handedness over the Aburi agreement?"

Following the fall of Enugu on October 4, 1967, Radio Biafra moved from the state capital to Aba where it continued broadcasting to the public. There was no break in transmission. Indeed, people marvelled at the fact that there was continuous transmission. But they eventually realized that the instant adjustment from Enugu to Aba, without break, was the miracle of Biafra's technological expertise. The feat was without rival in the history of African nations. Radio Biafra consistently reminded the world and intensified the popular belief that survival pivoted on resisting genocide to the bitter end. The overwhelming effect of this broadcast media conditioning was evident in such songs whose lyrics clung irresistibly onto people's mind.

For example:

We are Biafrans
fighting for survival,
by the name of Jesus we shall conquer.

They may bomb us,
killing all our children, but,
by the name of Jesus we shall conquer.

The memory of those days never left the imagination of people who witnessed the events. Nwankwo and Ifejika (1969, p. 278) recorded this rhyme from their experience during the war. The broadcast messages were always dominated by slogans, namely, short, sharp, snappy phrases that were easily remembered. Biafran broadcast people realized that, in order to be effective, propaganda must deal with a few simple points driven home by endless repetition.

During the Aba adventure, the management of the dynamic station realized the wisdom of not confining all one's eggs in a sole basket. So, it was decided that the external service section be separated from the domestic body of Radio Biafra. Subsequently, the external radio station arose and moved from Aba to Umuahia and continued its transmissions from there. It was christened "Voice of Biafra".

The organization of the Voice of Biafra appeared to be the most difficult task undertaken by the Biafran government, and at the same time the most important and the noblest. Voice of Biafra did far more than men, women and children, and any other institution within the Biafran enclave. It made the world know of events that were taking place in Biafra, and thus, saved the tender state from genocide inflicted by Nigeria and her allies – Britain, Russia and to some degree, the United States of America. In fact, it was feared that supported by these world powers, the federal might would have blockaded, starved and bombed Biafra out of existence without the international community knowing what happened. But the never-silent "Voice of Biafra' saved the situation. Actually the irresistible Voice of Biafra, in those trying months, successfully gained worldwide attention and sympathy in Europe and in the United States. The volume of humanitarian relief that entered the young Republic during that period indicated vividly that the efforts of the broadcast media among other social institutional variables within Biafra paid handsome dividends. Instances of the concern of world leaders for the oppressed people of Biafra were evidence that those international politicians heard the cry for survival emanating from Voice of Biafra. Many nations like Tanzania, Gabon, Ivory Coast, Haiti, and Zambia, recognized the young nation in 1968.

However, time dragged on and the war persisted. As the fortunes of the war altered against the young Biafra, resulting in the loss of Umuahia on April 22, 1969, "Voice of Biafra' changed location and stationed anew in Osu-Ihite-Ukwa, near the famous Eke-Ututu market community. It was from there that the Voice continued its international broadcasting all through the rest of the war. To Nigerian soldiers, the existence of the "Voice of Biafra' was shrouded in mystery that defied comprehension. It was like a horizon to the invading Nigerian soldiers whose efforts to span it proved futile, despite the illusive perception of its proximity. Even years after the war, Voice of Biafra remained a mystery to many. The external services wound up immediately the civil war ended.

The domestic station, Radio Biafra, also had to change location as the war raged on and on. The surviving Eastern Nigerian Broadcasting Stations (ENBS and ENTV), which got relocated from Enugu to Aba, remained in operation in Aba until the fortunes of the combat dictated otherwise. From Aba, the radio unit moved to Okwudo and established the administrative headquarters for broadcasting in Biafran style. However, the transmitting station for Radio Biafra was re-located to Obodo-Ukwu, for known reasons. (Obodo-Ukwu is in Ideato area of Imo state). The television segment had some difficulties in re-location and, as such, had limited life span within Biafran enclave. When the war ended, it was Radio Biafra, which stationed in

Obodo-Ukwu that made the last broadcast before the arrival of invading Nigerian soldiers. According to Nwankwo and Ifejika (1969), it was from there that the populace was informed about the state of things as the tempo of the war waned.

Broadcasting to keep Nigeria one

One of the major challenges that confronted Radio Nigeria, Lagos, during the crisis was how to repaint the image of Gowon and make it acceptable to the world as capable of leading the country through such a critical period. Underlying this challenge was the overwhelming evidence of negative perceptions of the man in Nigeria and especially in the Western countries. For instance, Clarke (1987, p. 70) observes that political revolutions rarely turn out as they were designed to do. Certainly, the second military coup in Nigeria did not. Those responsible for the planning did not imagine that at the end of the day after it started, Yakubu Gowon would be Head of state.

The initial representation of Gowon in international media was that he was a Christian from a Muslim region of the country. In fact, British newspapers of June 4, 1967, courtesy of Ajibola (1978, p. 61), noted that Gowon was a prodigal son of the Northern rulers, while the army from which he derived his power was controlled by Lt. Col. Hassan, the son of an Hausa ruler. Hassan in turn was surrounded by hawks. He would agree with Gowon, but only so long as Gowon agreed with him. Above all, despite Gowon's Christian faith, he was stated to lack any talent for political rule; and above all, most Southern Nigerians believed that he was speaking for the North.

Several international journalists were interested in Nigeria, especially at the peak of the conflict. Undoubtedly, the personality of a political actor in the conflict dictated, to a considerable extent, the nature and quality of information about him that was reported to the international public. Thus, when the image of Gowon was juxtaposed with that of Ojukwu, as reflected in both *Sunday Times* and *Sunday Telegraph* of England on June 4, 1967, the spin-doctors on Nigerian side realized the enormity of the challenge before them. According to the report, Ojukwu's tutors in England said that he (Ojukwu) was "very patriotic and fore-sighted with brilliant ideas for the education of his people, well disciplined, with an Oxford accent ... if he survives, he is likely to develop into one of the outstanding figures of post colonial Africa."

What was more demoralizing to many Nigerians was the report that the army officers from the West and Mid-West were reluctant to join in any military attack on Biafra. In fact, the Governor of the West was quoted as saying that his region would not support one side against the other. The Governor of Mid-West on his part, promised to maintain his region's territorial integrity. Against these "doves' were the Northern "hawks' who propelled Gowon and his troops into hostility against the East. This perception of the conflict reflected in the British media, rendered insignificant all the efforts of Radio Nigeria to counter balance the impression.

In an attempt to reduce the obstacles undermining the morale of Nigerians, Lt. Colonel Hassan claimed that it would take only a few hours to subdue the East. In a radio broadcast in Kaduna, he tried to give the Nigerian broadcast media practitioners a sense of direction: he encouraged them to employ all their skills in order to create adequate motives for people to join in the hostility against the East. Hassan's suggestions were put to work for Radio Nigeria. Lagos reported that the federal government sent a mission to the Soviet Union, in June 1967; the objective was to purchase "sophisticated' weapons. Kaduna capitalized on this and induced many to alter their attitude in favour of the federal government, which was then supported by both Britain and Russia.

From Radio Nigeria, Lagos came also an allegation of French support for Biafra. The federal government claimed that French financiers had acquired mineral and oil concessions in Biafra. Such a deal, if made, was capable of compromising Britain's investment in Nigeria's petroleum. This is because Shell-BP was a major holder of petroleum exploration licences in Nigeria. This claim by the federal government was intended to strengthen British support for Nigeria while inciting the people against France. Underlying the claim was the assumption that the British government would not want, either by omission or commission, to forfeit its benefits from West African countries, including Biafra. Although France was pro-Biafra, French support of Biafra was nothing compared to the strong support of Britain and Russia for Nigeria. Nevertheless, the broadcast stations in Nigeria capitalized on these variables to create some kind of enthusiasm for the war.

A press briefing stunned most radio and television journalists in Nigeria; a Minister in the Commonwealth Relations Office gave it on June 30, 1967. On this Ajibola (1978, p. 41) noted that the minister, Mr. Thomas, had declared that the Nigerian government oil blockade of Biafra was against international law. After this press briefing had been reported, Nigerian spin-doctors realized more than ever before that the media must be put into maximum use to justify the actions of the federal government. Subsequently, the media stations declared repeatedly that Biafra's act of self-determination was a rebellion, which would be crushed. Initially, Radio Nigeria in Lagos simply re-echoed Gowon's claim that the war was a "police" action designed to arrest leaders of the "rebellion". The Kaduna station naively repeated Hassan's claim that it would be a matter of hours to bring the East to total submission. However, as events began to unfold and the federal troops suffered some setbacks in several fronts, the broadcast professionals in both Lagos and Kaduna eventually learnt to moderate their messages and to adapt them to the prevailing political realities.

Given this background, it would seem an understatement to observe that the broadcast media stations in Lagos and in the other regions of Nigeria sang the war song intoned from the seat of government in Lagos. Actually, Lagos was eager to rouse people to war, so was Kaduna; but the same may not be said about Benin and Ibadan. The broadcast media in these Regions hesitated for long before joining in disseminating messages of hostility against the East. Eventually though, they joined the chorus as prompted by Lagos. The overused slogan was that the sole reason for invading the East was "To keep Nigeria One".

The national broadcast stations in Lagos and the regional stations in Ibadan, Kaduna and Benin did their utmost to report the war. It must be acknowledged, however, that they had their limitations. For instance, although their crews, in compliance with the military injunction "GOWON: **Go-On-With-One-Nigeria**", managed to get to some war fronts and to obtain pictures and make reports, they lacked the survival motive that inspired the Biafran journalists to daring heights. Nevertheless, the Western Nigeria Television was able to present to the world some images of events in the war zones.

As the war progressed, practical experience overtook Nigeria's trailer-load of beliefs in its own strength. Both Gowon and Hassan abandoned the notion that the war would be a brief affair. They began to realize the strength and significance of Biafran determination. Gowon, in particular, acknowledged the enormity of the challenge. Clark (1987, p. 107) noted that in an anniversary speech, broadcast from Lagos on October 1, 1967, Gowon stated as follows: "Fellow Nigerians, I wish to call upon you all, on this seventh anniversary of our independent existence as a nation, to rededicate yourselves to the task of building a strong, united and prosperous Nigeria: a Nigeria in which every citizen regardless of his or her religious belief or ethnic origin will have equal opportunities with his fellow Nigerians... The government does not underrate the task before it and I hope that I can count on your support in this fight for survival of our fatherland and in the work of national reconciliation which lies ahead."

There was no doubt that the federal government, after the bitter experience of losing the Mid-West region to the Biafran forces, corrected its underrating of the forces of its opponents. When Gowon realized the strength of the East, he quickly sent his men from one world power to another shopping for more formidable arms. Britain and Russia came to his rescue and offered all they could to help Gowon fight the war. And, as if to make things more explicit, in addition to the formidable ammunition it sold to Nigeria, Russia sent its naval ships to pay 'a friendly visit' to Lagos in March 1969, while the war was in its inferno. The visit was a testimony of Soviet presence in the war against the tender Republic.

However, so many harms had been done to Nigeria's image in the world, particularly in Europe, that Nigerian broadcast media people were asking themselves questions. They wondered why they were not yet able to counter effectively the propaganda of the Voice of Biafra, or at least, make the world see the other side of the picture. The lamentation of the people was thus reported in *Nigerian Opinion* of August (1969, p. 134): "Much as it is true that Federal Government external propaganda has been weak comparatively, it is true still to say that it is at its weakest point in France". It went further to indicate that linguistic factor played a significant role in making the Biafran image in the international scene. Inadequacy of this component was observed to be one of Nigeria's great handicaps, especially among French speaking audience.

Perhaps, it was a desperate bid to remedy the losses engendered by linguistic incompetence of majority of its personnel that induced the federal government to invite Russia to visit with its naval ships and planes. What Nigeria lost in linguistic roundabout, it hoped to gain in the Soviet swing. Whatever way the matter was perceived, Biafra ended up a victim of the brutal genocide. Finally, on January 15, 1970, Gowon again broadcast the following message to the nation: "Citizens of Nigeria, it is with a heart full of gratitude to God that I announce to you that today marks the formal end of the civil war".

Responsibilities of the Broadcast Media during the Civil War

When the Nigerian conflict escalated into war none of the parties involved in the conflict realized the war would last for so long, nor did they imagine it would entail so many losses of human and material resources. But, unfortunately, it did. As the war raged, the broadcast media in each side of the divide were effectively utilized to spread an ideology chosen to lead the people in accepting the political challenge and in actively participating in the war. In other words, the broadcast media disseminated information intended to make the political acts related to the war acceptable to the general public.

The broadcast media on the Federal side were confined to rationalizing the existing war situation. Their primary task was to transform the unconscious actions of Nigerians into conscious ones by desired activity that was considered laudable and justifiable (Ellul 1965, p. 75) by the military government of General Yakubu Gowon. Briefly, the media mobilized the populace to fight in order to keep Nigeria one. Constantly, they convinced the listeners and viewers that they were to be the beneficiaries of the resultant conquest of Biafra. Thus, the task of the broadcast media within the Nigerian enclave, during the war, was to communicate the message of integration. In addition, they had to mobilize the citizens not only to accept the regime"s justification of the war but also to mobilize them to volunteer to fight in order to reap the rich benefits of success in the combat. It seems reasonable to state that the Nigerian government would not have sustained its forces in the war for six months without the broadcast media of radio and television, which tended to counterbalance the power of Radio Biafra. However, as soon as the destabilizing effects of Biafran broadcasts were perceived in Lagos, electronic forces were mobilized in all the media stations under the Gowon administration. Only by so doing were they able to save the situation and eventually aroused some patriotic sentiments in the citizens. Consequently, they promoted some kind of unity in a grossly pluralistic country.

The broadcast media, on the part of Biafra, tried to stretch the energies of the Biafran populace to the utmost by inducing them to fight on and on. Under the influence of the admonitions emanating from the media the gallant soldiers made substantial sacrifices. In fact, Radio Biafra on several circumstances induced the Biafran youths to bear heavy ordeals. It would take everyday life of a Biafran, his normal framework, and plunge him into enthusiasm and military daring. The Voice of Biafra opened to each Biafran unsuspected possibilities. It suggested, time without number, extraordinary goals, which were to appear completely within reach.

The broadcast media within the compass of the Nigerian civil war were effective in mobilizing the population; especially the less educated and informed citizens. Among these classes of people, the electronic media relied on some key words of magical import which were believed without question, even though the hearers could not attribute any real content to them and did not fully understand them. Among the Biafrans such words were independence, liberty, survival, genocide, and vandals. Both Radio Biafra and Voice of Biafra used such evocative words to appeal to the masses and their effects were very rapid and spectacular. It is on record that despite the threat of starvation, bombing and blockade, the Biafran soldiers maintained high morale all through the war. By accusing the Gowon administration of genocide, the Voice of Biafra succeeded in gaining the sympathy of the international community. In fact, broadcast programmes from Biafra aroused the people of the world on the subject of food shortage within the young nation.

Policy towards International Communications

Most communications from outside the compass of each part of the conflict were never harnessed for political or any use whatever. This is because social scientists (Davison 1965, p. 8) understood clearly that there were always some communications that produced dissonant ring, and as such, must be controlled. Given the war circumstances, therefore, high-powered censorship was applied on both sides of the divide. This phenomenon of censorship constituted a major obstacle to international communications within the war-torn countries. Both out-going and in-coming information got censored during the war. In addition to censorship, there was the prohibitive cost of maintaining the channel through which whatever authorized information was could be harnessed. As a result the availability and utilization of international communications scored low marks in the war context.

The situation was even more pathetic on the Biafran side than on the Nigerian side. However, greater harmony was achieved by stimulating awareness on the part of those who were in touch with international audiences of the political side effects of what they said and did. Sensitizing them on such side effects pre-disposed the Biafran broadcasters in many cases to emphasize the desirable ones and reduce those that were found less desirable.

Piquant news commentaries emanated from the broadcasting stations operating in Biafra. Remarkable among them were such news-talks intended to downplay the intimidating image conveyed by British and Russian political personnel that visited Nigeria during the war. Whenever such a visit was perceived to be to the detriment of Biafra, Okon Okon Ndem would conjure the right word to evoke appropriate emotions. Commentaries that engaged passion undermined whatever impression Nigeria and its foreign partners might have designed. In order to achieve their set objective, Biafra broadcaster employed all known strategies. Even name-calling was not uncommon in the war situation. For instance, when the British secretary of state for Commonwealth affairs, Lord Shepherd, visited Logos and made remarks that betrayed his bias in favour of Nigeria, Okon Okon Ndem with his unique voice re-echoed the Biafran leader's remark that "This particular Lord will not be our shepherd. Wilson of Britain visited and, in his remarks betrayed his bias in favour of Nigeria, Okon Okon Ndem did not hesitate to say: "This "lord' will not be our shepherd." Conversely, he assured gallant Biafrans that God was on their side. Biafran soldiers found the assurance very motivational. In a similar commentary, Radio Biafra advised thus: "Don't mind that small island in the sea that calls itself Britain". Another commentary referred to the British Prime Minister, Harold Wilson as "Crime Minister". The reason invariably was that Wilson was Gowon's partner in the crime of genocide against innocent Biafrans.

Some news commentaries also came from the broadcasting houses on the side of Nigeria. Okoi Arikpo was eloquent up to a point. So were others like him in the vanguard of Nigerian propaganda machinery. But all of them put together could hardly make half the impact equivalent to that of Okokon Ndem of Biafran fame. Close associates of Gowon acknowledged that he was always worried about the thundering voice of Okon Okon Ndem. On several occasions he actually ordered Russian planes to heavily bombard Biafra in desperate bid to get Okon Okon Ndem, or Radio Biafra, or Voice of Biafra, or all of them. But none of them was got. Russian fighters only succeeded in terrifying and killing helpless citizens. In actual fact, the presence of Okon Okon Ndem was a great boost to Biafra; his performance in the war of words was an eloquent testimony to the entire world that the war was not merely an Igbo affair. All Biafrans were involved. The area one came from did not matter, because all Biafrans were one. Okon Okon Ndem further taught Nigerians that mere use of the broadcast media did not at all constitute propaganda. The new wisdom is that when persuasion is the goal, passion must be engaged and emotions aroused. Okon Okon Ndem's tonic commentaries were addressed to the masses.

Although both sides in the conflict tried to out-do each other in the dissemination of propaganda, none was technologically well-equipped to jam the opponent's broadcasting stations all through the duration of the war. Briefly, the airwaves had some ample dose of broadcast propaganda, sometimes white, but frequently clad black and grey.

Significant Effects of War-induced Broadcast Communications

The fortunes of the combatants on both sides of the battle line continued to change from time to time. Tamuno and Ukpabi (1989, p. 11) acknowledged that despite federal Nigeria's capture of Nsukka, the University town, and Enugu, the capital city of Biafra, Voice of Biafra, and Radio Biafra became as peripatetic as ever. As the propaganda war of words intensified, the Biafran forces continued to fight undaunted by insufficient supplies of firearms and cash, and were unbowed by malnutrition, disease and starvation. Meanwhile each side in the conflict sought to convince the world that its cause was right. The propaganda campaigns mounted by both sides used every avenue they found convenient to win the war. In such circumstances, the irresistible voice of Radio Biafra in those trying months successfully gained worldwide attention and sympathy, especially in Europe and in the United States of America. As noted by Tamuno and Ukpabi (1989:11), in such verbal battles, Radio Biafra proved equal to the combined efforts of Radio Nigeria and the Broadcasting Corporation of Northern Nigeria, Kaduna.

The bottom line remains that the efforts of the broadcast media together with other social variables within Biafra paid handsome dividends. This was evident in the volume of humanitarian relief that entered the young Republic. In early 1968, when the Biafran government intensified its campaign to awaken international concern to the plight of the civilian population, the impact was a great solace to starving Biafrans. The simple objective was to convert the resultant, growing interest into political pressure that would force Nigeria to accept an unconditional cease-fire and thereby halt the federal military offensive. For a while it appeared that a cease-fire and negotiated settlement might be possible. This was because representatives from the two sides met in formal discussion. The Commonwealth Secretariat and the Consultative Committee of the Organization of African Unity (OAU) sponsored the talks in Kampala and Addis Ababa respectively. The organization tacitly acknowledged Biafra"s independence of the federal authority. Stremlau (1977, p. 109) agreed that this was the high point of Biafra"s attempt to penetrate the international political system. Instances of the concern of world leaders for the oppressed people of Biafra testified to the fact that the world heard Biafra"s survival broadcast messages. African countries like Gabon, Ivory Coast, Tanzania and Zambia recognized Biafra for the same humanitarian reason. In fact, the Biafran charge of "genocide" against federal Nigeria, from deaths associated with malnutrition and disease hit the federal propaganda machine on its most tender spot. Federal spokesmen who denied such charges were hardly believed by outsiders.

Assessing the overall performance of the broadcast media during the war, Tamuno and Ukpabi (1989, p. 18) note that the media on both sides tended to mix facts with propaganda, in fair and unfair proportions, in their bid to win and retain the support of audiences inside and outside the area of location. According to the scholars, the resultant media blitz, occasioned by the Nigerian civil war, competed effectively with the claims of other major events, in such trouble spots as Vietnam and the Middle East, for prime time. Hence, the major newspapers, magazines, radio and television stations throughout the world sought to bring home to their respective readers, listeners and viewers the grim facts of the Nigerian civil war. For some, such reports represented a war of words. For others, the issues at stake were so grave that interested pressure groups worldwide sought to influence governments, agencies, institutions and individuals deemed capable of influencing events on both sides of the battle-line in Nigeria.

On January 12, 1970, however, Radio Biafra made its last broadcast under the name. The time was 4.30 p.m. Earlier in the afternoon of that historic day, Biafra"s Chief of General Staff, Major-General Philip Effiong had announced in a broadcast to the nation that General Ojukwu left the country two days before. General Effiong further stated that he was mandated to effect "an orderly disengagement of troops'. On the basis of that mandate he affirmed that a delegation was ready to meet representatives of the federal government anywhere "to negotiate a peace settlement on the basis of the OAU resolutions," Irukwu (1983, p. 176) reported. He further noted that in a message broadcast over Radio Nigeria the following night, Gowon welcomed the proposition; he declared thus: "we have arrived at the end of the tragic and painful conflict".

Broadcasting in the Spectrum of War Propaganda

Propaganda is a phenomenon as old as humanity itself; it is one of the oldest forms of communication. It is rooted in persuasion. Propaganda is a kind of psychological motivation. According to Jefkin and Ugboajah (1986, p. 75), propaganda ranks among the three major methods for winning people over in an argument. The other two methods are coercion (force), and corruption (bribery). Actually, persuasion is supposed to make a person or group of persons, or an entire population do what the communicator intends them to do. Hence, Ugboajah and his colleague describe the phenomenon as "mind management". Thus understood, propaganda is a systematic attempt to influence opinion or attitude in the interest of some cause, in this context, the civil war. To be successful, propaganda must be carefully planned and properly executed. The objectives must be clearly defined. In the case of Biafra, the goal was unquestionably that of survival as a nation, while that of Nigeria was to t keep the country united. Throughout the civil war years, both sides in the conflict relied on propaganda to maintain morale, stir up patriotism or demoralize the enemy. The prevailing propaganda tended to indulge in fallacious stories aimed at depicting the enemy as evil. The broadcast media provided some ready avenues for issuing war propaganda in the Nigerian and Biafran situations.

A crucial observation that remains to be made in this analysis is that broadcasting constituted but an outlet of a macro-system of propaganda that prevailed in the war situation. Although very powerful in its effect, it is only in the context of modern scientific system that broadcast propaganda could effectively perform. As understood by Ackoff (1974, p. 15), a system's performance depends on how it relates to its environment. Thus, the performance of the system of broadcast propaganda would be better evaluated and appreciated as part of the larger system that contained it. Fundamental to broadcast message that were disseminated during the Nigerian civil war was the existence of some organizations that determined the content of the media programmes.

Prior to the outbreak of the war, all the broadcasting stations in the country were government-owned. They were operated by civil servants and managed by politically appointed directors. By this arrangement, the broadcasting system was controlled by relevant authorities of both federal and regional Ministries of Information. This organizational set-up remained in operation within the Nigerian enclave throughout the war years. Since a typical civil servant in Nigeria was indolent, and nonchalant to responsibilities, this unhealthy attitude tended consequently to manifest in the performance, in terms of propaganda, of Nigeria's broadcasting media stations. Indeed, the overall performance rate of broadcasters deteriorated considerably, following the 1966 crisis. As Fashina (1984) observed, the work force of the country at that period was sick from the root to the branches. The broadcast operations were regrettably going downhill because Nigerian civil servants were wont to shirk their responsibilities. Furthermore, subsequent to the mass return to the East by the Easterners, some deplorable vacuum was created in the Nigerian civil service in the other regions. The federal propaganda machinery, under the circumstances, tended to make use, in sporadic fashion and at random, of a radio programme here, a newspaper article or a poster there. It only organized a few meetings and lectures and wrote a few slogans for the screen. In fact, it was apparently a perfunctory propaganda. Morale, the essential stimulus, that mobilizer of sentiments in organizations, was apparently lacking. Nigerian propaganda was a matter of individual whims or the use of unsophisticated tricks. Little did the organizers realize that science had entered the propaganda spectrum. Consequently, the propaganda activities left much to be desired.

This phenomenon was promptly recognized and eliminated only in the Biafra system. Initially, responsibility for Biafran propaganda rested, like its federal counterpart, with the Ministry of Information. It was a direct descendant of the Eastern region's ministry and its staff of seventy civil servants. This inheritance did not satisfy Biafra's aspirations and needs. Stremlau (1977, p. 111) observed that the ministry's work was considered inefficient, pedestrian, and not sufficiently in tune with the hopes and fears of the Biafran people. In order to remedy the situation, a Directorate of Propaganda was established. It took off and operated temporarily within the ministry. But it eventually made a successful bid for more power at Umuahia and got it. In an interview with Stremlau, Uche Chukwumerije, the Director of Propaganda in Biafra, acknowledged that the directorate had plenty of money to accomplish its objectives. It quickly expanded to forty-one committees with at least four or five people per committee. However, there were some committees with as high as eleven or twelve members.

The senior positions in the directorate were occupied by scores of displaced faculty members of the University of Nigeria, renamed University of Biafra, Nsukka. This cadre of intellectuals led Biafra to a golden age of propaganda. Stremlau (1977, p. 111) identified some of the university lecturers that served the Biafra public relations as Dr Ifeagwu Ekeh (Humanities), Commissioner of Information; Dr Michael Echeruo (English), Head of War Information; Dr Ifemesia (History), Director of Research and Documentation; J. Onuoha (Physical Education), Head of Public Enlightenment, and Dr Anya O. Anya (Zoology), Editor, *Biafra Newsletter*. Moreover, the twelve-man Propaganda Analysis Committee was entirely staffed by University personnel. Cyprian Ekwensi, the internationally renowned author and Nigeria's former Director of Information Services, headed the Overseas Press Service Unit. That the team obtained its initial mandate during an assembly in Princess Alexandria Auditorium (PAA) in Nsukka, goes to explain the infernos Nigerian bombers inflicted on the institution on the outbreak of hostilities.

Undoubtedly, Biafran propaganda was founded on scientific analysis of psychology and sociology. Step by step, the propagandists built their techniques on the basis of their knowledge of man, his propensities, his desires, his needs, his psychic mechanisms, and his conditioning. Following reliable principles, (Ellul 1965, p. 4), they structured their procedures on the basis of their cognizance of groups and the laws of group formation and dissolution, of mass influences, and of environmental limitations. Before embarking on active propaganda operation, they considered it necessary to make a scientific, sociological and psychological analysis first, and then to utilize those elements of science for successful execution of their task.

To complement the messages from Radio Biafra, domestic activities were initiated at village level. This action was carried out by the Political Orientation Committee, which organized hundreds of university students and secondary school leavers, who would introduce, explain and justify government policy to small groups of peasants. They would lead criticism of Nigerian atrocities as described by Radio Biafra and provide exaggerated praise of Biafran military successes in order to raise morale. The daring spirit of Biafran forces bore laudable testimony of the success of such propaganda operations. The content of Biafra's propaganda was determined by the Psychological Warfare Committee, which usually met every Tuesday, to review and plan the major themes to be introduced each month. As perceived by Stremlau, the themes so determined were used for domestic and international audiences. According to Stremlau (1970, p. 115), three elements that remained endemic to propaganda during the final year of the conflict were: "an emphasis on alleged Nigerian atrocities; the impossibility of any compromise with the implacable enemy; and the indomitable will of the Biafran people."

Stremlau further noted that foreign distribution of the directorate's daily and the Overseas Press Service, which had also been established shortly before the evacuation of Enugu, handled weekly output of propaganda. As has been noted earlier, Cyprian Ekwensi, the internationally renowned author and the former Director of Information Service in the Eastern Region, became the Head of Biafra's Overseas Press Service in January 1968. Ekwensi's responsibilities included the censoring of all non-official news stories transmitted from Biafra and forwarding of the Directorate of Propaganda's daily news bulletins and other materials to a Geneva public relations firm, Mark-press News Feature Services. Mark-press, owned and operated by an American, William Berbhardt, had its headquarters in Geneva. It served primarily as a transmission point for materials that had been written in Biafra by Biafrans. Stremlau (1977, p. 117) affirmed that between February 1968 and January 1970, Mark-press relayed a total of 740 news bulletins from Biafra (via the Lisbon telex link) to 3,200 newspapers, parliamentarians, church leaders, and other opinion makers in Great Britain, Western Europe and North America. By comparing random selections of Radio Biafra transcripts and subsequent Mark-press releases, one discerns very little difference in wording. The Directorate of Propaganda's role in generating international concern for Biafra's plight can only by surmised. Uche Chukwumerije, who ran the directorate, referred to the Berhardt office (Mark-press) as merely a "mail drop".

As international concern for Biafra got roused, the number of journalists, religious leaders and parliamentarians, who were flown into the Biafran enclave increased significantly. The Directorate of Propaganda managed those visits through the Internal Publicity Department. It ensured that public demonstrations, meetings with Biafra officials, or press conferences focused attention on the need to preserve the Biafran nation as a prerequisite for the survival of the Igbo people. Prior to the influx of foreigners, Ojukwu's personal involvement in propaganda effort had been limited to the strategy sessions within the Psychological Warfare Committee. However, in early 1968, he began to take a direct interest in the daily operations of the Internal Publicity Department. Later in the struggle, at the pinnacle of Biafra's diplomatic offensive, other leaders like Sir Akanu Ibiam and Hon. Dr Nnamdi Azikiwe became involved in the propaganda strategy.

There is no gainsaying the fact that Biafra was well ahead of the federal government in presenting its case overseas. For instance, Stremlau (1977, p. 174) reported that during the peace negotiations, the federal Ministry of Information's booklet, *'Framework for Settlement'*, which featured Enahoro's address, was not available in Nigerian embassies for weeks. By contrast, 3,200 copies of Mbanefo's address were mailed to editors and opinion makers in Europe and America within hours of its delivery. Biafran propaganda was addressed both to individuals and to the masses at the same time. It was total in the sense that it utilized all of the technical means at its disposal, namely, press, radio, television, posters, meetings, and door-to-door canvassing. Biafran propagandists utilized all of these media because they recognized the principle of propaganda as expounded by Ellul (1965, p. 10) who advocated that each usable medium had its own particular way of penetration. Each was understood to be specific but localized and limited. Each, in isolation, could not be effective in achieving the desired objective. For example, a word spoken on the radio was not the same, would not produce the same effect, and could not have the same impact, as the identical word spoken in private conversation or in a public speech before a large crowd. This was the wisdom that informed and animated Biafran propaganda; it was all encompassing. It was total.

Biafran propagandists were accordingly known to be relatively more involved in their job than their Nigerian counterparts in the field. A plausible explanation of the reality, which made them highly determined to achieve results could be that they had their fate in their own hands, and were entirely dependent on their own strength for survival. Consequently, they were fully committed to the attainment of anticipated goals. Those responsible for Biafran propaganda realized that to have a team of demoralized civil servants and broadcasters at that critical period of Biafra's history would be suicidal for the young nation, and would not augur well for the citizens.

Conclusion

Our analysis of mass media in the propaganda programmes that characterized the Nigerian civil war years has confirmed that there were abundant elements of propaganda in the messages broadcast by both parties in the conflict. Broadcast communications functioned among and through such a nexus of mediating factors and influences that typically rendered mass communication a contributory agent in a process of reinforcing persuasive power of political actors in modern war theatre. To affirm therefore that the broadcast propaganda of Biafra was more successful than the Nigerian counterpart would be only a simple acknowledgement of the ingenuity of the intellectual men and women who organized the larger system of Biafra Directorate of Propaganda. Biafrans who survived the war understood that they were indebted to those personnel of the University of Nigeria, Nsukka, who sustained the macro system of Biafran propaganda. At the end of the war, Gowon contrived the Gordian knot. By acknowledging that there was "no victor no vanquished," he implied that both parties in the conflict were victorious, each in its own way. Precisely, Nigeria was victorious in the battlefield whereas Biafra was victorious in the airwaves.

References

Ackoff, R. (1974). *Redesigning the Future: a system approach to societal problems*. New York, USA: John Wiley.

Ajibola, W. A. (1974). *Foreign Policy and Public Opinion*. Ibadan: Univ. Press. See also Federal Republic of Nigeria (1966). Constitution (Suspension & Modification) Decree No 5. *Official Gazette*, 53 (51). May 24.

British Broadcasting Corportion (BBC) News Report as in Ajibola (1974: 126). *Foreign Policy and Public Opinion*. Ibadan, Nigeria: University Press.

Cambridge (2010). Advanced learner"s dictionary, (3rd ed.) Cambridge: University Press Chukwumerije, U. (1977). Interview with Chukwumerije, as in Stremlau (1977). *The International Politics of the Nigerian Civil War, 1967-1970*. Princeton, USA: University Press.

Clark, J. D. (1987). *Yakubu Gowon: Faith in a United Nigeria*. London, England: Frank Cass. Davison, P. (1965). *International Political Communication*. New York, USA: Frederick A Praeger.

Eastern Nigeria (1967). *Edict on Revenue Collection*. Enugu, Nigeria: Government Printer. See also *Statutory Corporation Edict* (1967), and *Companies Edict* (1967). Enugu, Nigeria: Government Printers.

Ellul, J. (1965). *Propaganda*. New York, USA: Vintage.

Emeka, L. (1999, March 12). Interview with Lawrence Emeka, Nigerian Press Council, Enugu, Nigeria.

Fashina, S. (1984). "Theories of Motivation and the Nigerian Situation", In Ejiofor and Aniagoh (Eds.). *Managing the Nigerian Workers*. Ibadan, Nigeria: Longman.

Irukwu, J. O. (1983). *Nigeria at the Cross Roads.* London, England: Witherby.

Jefkin, F. & Ugboajah, F. (1986). *Communication in Industrializing Countries.* London, England: Macmillian.

Katz, E. & Wedell, G. (1978). *Broadcasting in the Third World: Promise and Performance.* London, England: Macmillan.

Larson, C. U. (Ed.) (2013). *Persuasion: Reception and responsibility (13th ed.).* Boston, M. A. Wadsworth

Nigerian Opinion (1969, August-October). *Nigerian Opinion: A Monthly Magazine of the Nigerian Current Affairs Society,* vol. 5, No. 8-10.

Nwankwo, A. A. & Ifejika, S. U. (1969). *The Making of a Nation: Biafra.* London, England: C. Hurst. *Observer* (1967, June 4). *British Observer.*

Ojukwu, C. O. (1969). *Biafra.* New York, USA: Harper & Row.

Otubanjo, F. (1989). "National Security". In Tamuno & Ukpabi (Eds.) *The Civil War Years: Nigeria since Independence*, vol. iv, Ibadan: Heinemann.

Stremlau, J. J. (1977). *The International Politics of the Nigerian Civil War 1967-1970.* Princeton. USA: University Press.

Sunday Telegraph (1967, June 4). *British Sunday Telegraph. Sunday Times* (1967, June 4). *British Sunday Times.*

Tamuno, T. N. (1989). "Men and Measures in Nigerian Crises: 1966-1970". In Tamuno & Ukpabi (Eds.). *The Civil War Years: Nigeria since Independence*, vol. vi. Ibadan, Nigeria: Heinemann.

Udeajah, R. A. (2004). *Broadcasting and politics in Nigeria: 1963-2003.* Enugu: Snaap. *West Africa Magazine* (1966, June). London: England.

Watson, J. Hill, A. (2006). *Dictionary of media and communication studies (7th ed.).* London: Hodder Arnold.

SECTION TWELVE: LANGUAGE AND CULTURE

Ajo Onudu Asusu Igbo na ihe a ga-eme ya
nke
Okammuta (Prof.) Pita Ejiofor

Umi okwu (Abstract)
Asusu bu njirimara kacha njirimara e ji ama agburu obula. Ndi Igbo nwere isi oma na Chineke na alaanyi bu Naijiria bulitere asusu Igbo elu, dowe ya na asusu Awusa na Yoruba n'oche eze. Ma, o bu ihe mwute na ndi Igbo na-eleda asusu ha anya. Okpurukpu okwu akwukwo a na-ekwu bu na, beresq ma ndi Igbo ha gbanworo ajo agwa ha na-akpaso asusu Igbo, na asusu Igbo ga-anwu pii na mgbe na-adighi anya. Akwukwo a jiri ihe amaihe di icheiche gosiputa na, ka ndi Igbo na-ekwe "Igbo Kwenu, kwenu", na-ekwu n'qnu na asusu ha di ha mkpa, omume ha niile na-egosi na ha achoghi asusu Igbo ndu. Akwukwo a "miiri obara" asusu Awusa, Igbo na Yoruba, wee jiri ihe ano metutara asusu, wee nyochaa ha, mara ka ha si eku ume ndu. Ndi a bu etu ndi agburu ato a si jiri asusu ha emeputa ejije onyonyoo, etu redio mbauwa siri jiri asusu ndi a agbasa ozi, etu uloakwukwo mbauwa na-ewu ewu si akuzi ha, na etu ndi Igbo si asu ya n'ime ezinulo ha ma n'ogbako ha.

N'ule a niile, o nweghi nke asusu Igbo chitara aja na ya. O no ka o nwuolarii n'ihina a dizighi agunye ya na mgbaonuogu obula. Ihe gbagwojukarichara anya bu na otutu mahadum juru n'ala Igbo, ebe mmuta kwesiri iju eju bara abara, afughirii na nnukwu ihe na-acho imebinari ndi Igbo. Anyi kwusiri ike, daa ya oku, na o bukwaghi Goomenti Etiti maobu ndi agburu ndi ozo di na Naijiria na-egbu asusu Igbo, na o bukwa ndi Igbo na-ememila asusu ha. Anyi kwukwara na o bukwaghi ndi ozo ga-azoputara ndi Igbo asusu ha, kwukwa na e nyechaala ndi Igbo ikike niile ha ga-eji kwalitekwa asusu Igbo ma ha choo. Anyi sekwara aka na nti na mbo izoputa asusu Igbo adikwaghi ka egwuregwu nkita na ibe ya, nke o na-abu ogu nne na-agbara nwa ya. O bu ogu ndi Igbo ga-achichipu anya wee luo. Akwukwo a na-akpokuzi ogbako a, ka o gaa ngwangwa, hu ndi Govano niile na-achi ndi Igbo, were ikpere ala rio ha, ka ha wubaa n'mbo izopta asusu Igbo tupu ihe mere Biafra emee asusu anyi.

Ndubanye: Chineke kesiri ndi Igbo ike
O nwebeghi ndi ha na ndi Igbo mekoro ihe, ekpupughiri ha okpu, ka ndi bu dike e ji eje mba. Q bu Napoleon nke Frans, mgbe ndi Igbo menyere ya egwu na Haiti? Q bu ndi ocha chiri Naijiria, ha na Jaja nke Opobo na Azikiwe ha gbariri. O bu ndi chigburidere ndi isi ojii ka ohu, rue na Olauda Ekweano (Ezifeh, 2014) awaa anya, gbakapu, gbatakwa onwe ya, gua akwukwo; a na-ekwu na O guru akwukwo, o dee akwukwo, soro n'onye isi ojii mbu dere akwukwo n'uwa. Ogbe ndi Igbo (Igbo*Village)* di na Stanton, Vajinia, weputakarichara dike ndi Igbo bu, makana o bu ndi Amerika hiwere ya, ka ha siri hiwe Ogbe ndi English, Irish na German (agburu ato ha na ndi Igbo

tokarichara ntuala Amerika), iji gosi na, bxraagodx n'oge ndi isi ojii niile darukarichara ala, ndi ocha were ha mee ohu, na o bu ndi Igbo senitakarichara isi na ndi ohu ahu na mmepe e mepere Amerika. Ekele diri ndi Steeti Vajinia hiwere ogbe a. Ihe bi eziokwu bu, na Chineke kesiri ndi Igbo ike, nye ha okpukpu aka, oguguisi, akonuuche na uba mmadu *(population)* n'udi puru iche. A si m kwuo, asi m na o bu ubochi Monde ka Chineke kere ndi Igbo.

Onu ogu ndi Igbo.

Chineke jiri uba mmadu wee choo ndi Igbo mma n'udi puru iche. Iji maa atu, asusu diiche iche n'uwa di 6809 (Roy-Campbell, 2012), ma onu ogu ndi Igbo (nde 30) buonu ogu nke 41 na ndi kachasi uba. E dee ya n'uzoozo, o buru na onu ogu ndi Igbo kariri onu ogundi na-asu asusu6,768 di n'uwa (Ejiofor (a, b) 2013). Ozokwa, n'ime agburu di ihe dika puku abuo (2000) n'Afrika, naani agburu abuo ka onu ogu ha kariri nke ndi Igbo. Ndi a bu Fulfulde na Hausa. N'Odida anyanwu Afrika niile (ECOWAS), naani otu agburu ka onu ogu ka kariri nke ndi Igbo, ya bu nke ndi Hausa. E wepu Naijiria, onu ogu ndi Igbo kariri onu ogu mba *(countries)* obula di n'ECOWAS. N'ime agburu kariri 250 na Naijiria, naani otu agburu (ya bu Hausa) ka onu ogu ya kariri nke ndi Igbo.

Agumonu Naijiria 1952.

Cheta na, n'agumonu ikpeazu ndi ocha guru na Naijiria n'afo 1952 (Apendis1), tupu Naijiria enwere onwe ya na 1960, ihe ndi ocha gutara bu na:

Hausa di	5,488,542;
Igbo di	5,483,660;
Yoruba di	5,046,861.

Ihe o putara bu na, ihe ndi ocha gutara bu na, ndi Hausa jiri 64,882 karia ndi Igbo; ndi Igbo jiri 436,861 karia Yoruba! Ugbua ndi Naijiria jizi aka ha agu, amazinighi m ugboro ole ha kwuru Hausa maobu Yoruba jiri karizi ndi Igbo (Cheta na Festus Odimegwu jiri iwe gbaa arukwaghim dika Onye isi oche Boodu Agumuonu Naijiria).

Iwunjiko Naijiria. A hapu onuogu, Iwunjiko *(Constittution)* Naijiria, Nk 55, dere ya, o doo anya, na asusu e nwere ikike iji na-aru oru n'Olu Omebeiwu Gooment Etiti Naijiria bu English, Hausa, Igbo na Yoruba. Ebumnuuche Najira Maka Agumaakwukwo *(National Policy on Education)* kwue na a ga-eme ka nwata akwukwo obula na Naijiria kweta ka o mua asusu Bekee na asusu olu nne ya, wee tinyekwa otu n'ime asusu ato ndi a: Hausa, Igbo na Yoruba. Na bekee, o si:

> *"The Government considers it in the interest of national unity that each child should be encouraged to learn one of the three major languages*

*other than his own moher tongue. **In this connection, the government considers the three major languages in Nigeria to be Hausa, Igbo and Yoruba"** * (oda oku bu nke m).

Nchikota ya.
Olee ihe ozo Chineke na alaanyi ga-emekwuru asusu Igbo? Ihe bu eziokwu bu, na Chineke na alaanyi bu Naijiria buniri agburu Igbo elu, dowe asusu Igbo (na Hausa na Yoruba) n'oche eze na Naijiria. Lezie anya na Fig 1.1 ka I hu udi ukpoeze Chineke na ala anyi Naijiria kwekebere asusu Igbo (na Hausa na Yoruba). Olee ihe a huziri?

Fig 1.1

Ebe e wetara: Ejiofor (2013b), ib 14

II. Nwa agu atawa ahihia, odum ekpowe oke mbe.
Chinua Achebe. Ma nwa agu hapuziri iri anu di ndu, ya na ewu tawa ahihia. Leenu ihe otu nwaafo Igbo ji agara, owa na-ekpupuru okpu, bu odezuluuwa Chinua Achebe (1999) kwuru na 1999, mgbe o nyere Nkuzi Odenigbo **(Lecture)** n'Owere. Na bekee, o si:

> *"Let us think a bit about the **completely unsatisfactory situation of the Igbo Language today.** If you take the Igbo situation and compare the Yoruba or Hausa situations in Nigeria, in Africa and the entire world, **there is no other way we can describe that of the Igbo except one of shame and tears.** How are the mighty fallen! Why is it that the Igbo, who were an example of progress in the whole world, could fall behind in the primary thing a country is known by - their language"*

Achibishopu Obinna. Lekwanu ihe nuzpepa bu **Daily Sun** kwukwara na Akbishopu Uka Katoliki Owere bu Antoni Obinna kwuru n'afo 2009, ebe e dere: *"Uje, Uje….Akbishopu Obinna akwaa akwa ariri maka onwu asusu Igbo tinyerela n'ukwu ….."* (Hu **Daily Sun**, 2009; p1).

President Umaru Yar'Adua. Leenu ka onyeisiala Naijiria bu President Umaru Musa Yar'Adua (2007), onye Hausa, siri dokwa ndi Igbo aka na nti n'Owere maka asusu Igbo, n'okwu o jiri mepe ogbako mmuta n'Owere n'afo 2007. N'asusu bekee, O si: ***"I wish to equally acknowledge that human knowledge must have provided the impetus for this projection, that is, by 2025 the Igbo language would have been subsumed by other stronger languages."*** (ida oku bu nke m). Hukwua Chika Amobi (2012), ***"Igbo Language to die by 2025"***
Chimamanda Adichie. Ada anyi bu Chimamanda (2014), kpakpando ala Igbo na-achawaputa ugbua, kwukwara otu okwu ahu n'Awka, na Jun 25, 2014, otu

onwa taa kpomkwem, n'okwu o kwuru n'ogbako iji cheta otu nari ubochi Govano Anambra Steeti bu Chif Willie Obiano (Akpokuadike Aguleri) rigotara n'okwa.

Mu Onwe m. Mu onwe m kwukwuru mgbe m nyere Nkuzi Odenigbo n'Owere na Septemba 7, 2013, na ileghara asusu Igbo anya, ga-aputakwara ndi Igbo aju ihe jogburu mmeri e meriri anyi n'ogu Biafra (Ejiofor, 2013 (a)). Lee etu otu nuzpepa siri dee ya.

Ugboguru, o na-ami anyi?
Nka o bukwa ka e wee si na onye a si, onye a asighi; o nwere onye no ebe a amaghi na asusu Igbo na-anwu?
Asusu otutu umu ntakiri anyi adizighi asu;
Asusu otutu ndi Igbo anazighi asu n'ezi na ulo ha;
Asusu anyinwa bu ndi okenye anaghi asu ma anyi zukuta;
Asusu anaghi akuzi nke oma n'ulo akwukwo;
Asusu anyi anaghi agu agu, ma obu dee ede;
Asusu na-emezi otutu ndi Igbo nwe ya ihere.
Olee ebe ozo asusu di etu a na-eje abughi n'ili? Ndi Igbo ufodu aputakwuala ife na-ekwu, si ejizila onwu asusu Igbo eyi ha egwu, na o nweghi uru asusu Igbo bara na *"21ˢᵗ century"*. Hei, ndi be anyi; ma, Hausa bakwara uru na *"21ˢᵗ century"*, Yoruba bakwa uru na *"21ˢᵗcentury"*. Efik bakwara. Ya mere na, ebe obula, ndi Igbo ana-ememina asusu Igbo. Ma ihe otutu ndi Igbo amaghi bu, na asusu na-aga n'ili, agburu nwe ya ana-eso ya: ka asusu Igbo na-efu, ka aha Igbo na-efu.

Ilele asusu Igbo ahu.
Iji choputa onudu ahu ike asusu Igbo, anyi gara "ulo oru" asusu, "miri obara" asusu ato ndi Naijiria: Hausa, Igbo na Yoruba, nyoo ha n'onyokomita, were Igbo tinyere Hausa na Yoruba, mara ka isi na anya dizi asusu anyi. Ahu anyi lele ha di ano:
a) Etu e si jiri asusuato a emeputa ejije onyonyoo *(home video);*
b) Etu e si akuzi asusu ndi a n'uloakwxkwq mbauwa (countries);
c) Etu e si eji asusundi a agbasa ozi na redio mbauwa; na
d) Etu ndi nwe asusu ndi a si echukwa ya, na-asu ya.

"Obara" Nke Mbu: Mmeputa Ejije Onyonyoo Na Naijiria.
N'ihi nnukwu mkpa ejije dizi ugbua "na *21ˢᵗ century*", nke onye obula maara na e ji ejije azu, jiri ya egbu; Gooment Etiti hiwere olu oru aha ya bu *"National Film and Video Censors Board"* n'afo 2004, ka o kwalitewe imeputa ejije na Naijiria, ya na ka o na-enyocha ejije obula e meputara maobu tubata, tupu o nye ikike ka e rewe ya na Naijiria. Mgbemgbe, ulo oru a na-edeputa n'akwukwo *newsletter* ya bu *The Classifier,* aha ejije niile e

meputara ndi o kwadoro ka e resiwa oha na eze; dee aha ndi mere ya, ebe o nyochara ya, na asusu e jiri meputa ya. Ka anyi guputazia ihe e dere na *The Classifier* nke Julai 2010 ib 21-28.

Tebulu 4.1
Mbukota Onu ogu EjijeUlooru National Film And Video Censors Board (NFVCB) Kwadoro N'Onwa Eprel Na Mee, 2010

Asusu Ejije	Onu ogu Ha	%
Bekee	31	13.25
Hausa	98	41.88
Yoruba	94	40.17
Bini/Edo	11	4.70
Igbo	0	0.00
Mbuko	**234**	**100.00**

Ebe e wetara: *The Classifier, Official Newsletter of the National Film and Video Censors Board, Vol 2 No 2, July 2010*, ibe 21-28

Unu ahulanu ka isi na anya dizi asusu anyi. Ole ka Igbo nwere? **0/234 (zero "over" 234).** Atututaghi ma o bughi otu n'ime 234! Chetakwa na ndi Igbo sokwa na ndi kacha ewu ewu na Noliwudu.
Ajuju m buruzia: Olee ihe ndi Igbo nu na Noliwudu jiri nuru, na-ele, ndi ogbo ha ndi Hausa na Yoruba na-akwalite asusu ha, ma ha na-emere onwe ha ejije n'asusu bekee? Anyi banye na nke a, anyi agaghi ala taa. Naani ihe m ga-ario bu, onye obula arukwala umu anyi ndi Noliwudu ajo aka, nihina ike mposi anyi ghekwa oghe. Lekelerii nkenke abu a:

Awo ikpo Awo ibe ya Wikpom
    Umunne m nwoke na umunne m nwanyi ndi Igbo,
Iwe unu adikwala oku maka ndi Noliwudu Igbo,
Ka awo gharakwa ikpo awo ibe ya wikpom,
Ite akpokwua akwukwa oji ka unyi.

Etu ndi Noliwudu anyi esighi kwe asu Igbo,
Ka otutu nne na nna esighi asuru umu ha Igbo,
Ka otutu mahadum esighi kwe akuzi Igbo,
Ka otuto ndi nkuzi si apia nwata ihe na o suo Igbo.

Etu ndi Noliwudu anyi siri jiri bekee eme ejije,
Ka ndi okenye anyi siri jiri bekee eme ogbako,
Ka otutu ndi uka anyi siri jiri bekee efe Chineke,
O buzirii Gooment ala Igbo ekweghi akwado asusu Igbo.

O bukwanu ya bu na asusu Igbo nuzi na *"Going ... Going ...."* Ebe niile n'ala Igbo, otu ihe ahu: a hapu Igbo a na-asu oyibo; a suwa Igbo asuwa, a na-**agwutuku** ya na bekee, bekee akazia Igbo; onye kulie ikwu okwu, o were nganga kwua na ya enwezighi ike ikwu ihe ya choro ikwu n'Igbo; a na-aso Igbo hu otu onye agburu ozo, a suwazia bekee. Ma emeputaghi ejije n'asusu Igbo emebiwegoro anyi nnukwu ihe. Iji maa atu, oge ulo oru tiivii **nnuuruonwe** kacha n'Afrika bu DSTV bidoru iwaakuko *(channel)* n'asusu ndi Naijiria n'afo 2010, ebumnuuche ya bu ibido iwaakuko ato maka asusu ato ahu, ma naani iwaakuko abuo ka ha bidoziri; **Channel 156** maka Hausa, **Channel 157** maka Yoruba. Mgbe a juru ha ihe ha ejighi bido nke Igbo, ha kwuru na ha ahughi ejije e mere n'asusu Igbo ha ga-eji mepee *Channel* Igbo (Fayose, 2010). Uzokwa, na 2013, mgbe otu ulooru ahu tuwere ndi bu ukaibe na mmeputa ejije n'Afrika ugo di icheiche, imeputa ejije n'asusu ato ndi Afrika so n'ihe iri atq ha tuwere ugo. Asusu ato a bu asusu Hausa, Yoruba na Swahili. Asusu Igbo esoghi na ha.

"Obara" nke Abuo: ikuzi Asusu Ato a n'Uloakwukwo Mbauwa". Anyi chikotara ebe a ihe eserese gosiputara etu e si akuzi asusu Hausa, Igbo na Yoruba n'uloakwukwu mbauwa na-ewukaricha ewu na nkuzi asusu. Ndi a bu

***School of Oriental Studies (SOAS)** na London,
***Institut National des Langues et Civiliizations Orientales (INALCO)**(National Institute of Oriental Languages and Civilisations)* di na Paris,
***African Academy of Languages (ACALAN)** ndi **African Union** (AU, a na-akpobu OAU ruru na Bamako, Mali), na
*Mahadum niile di n'Amerika; wee tinyere
*Mahadum di na Naijiria.

SOAS, London. Ka o di n'afo 2010 , asusu ndi Afrika di isii n'ime asusu ndi uwa SOAS na-akuzi (SOAS, 2010). N'ime isii ndi a, asusu ndi Naijiria so na ha bu Hausa na Yoruba. Igbo adighi ya. Chetakwa na naani asusu abuo kariri asusu Igbo n'onu ogu n'Afrika.
INALCO, Frans. Ka o di n'afo 2006, asusu ndi Afrika di 13 n'ime asusu kariri 90 ndi uwa niile INALCO na-akuzi. N'ime 13 ndi a, asusu ndi Naijiria so na ha bu Hausa na Yoruba. Igbo adikwaghi ya (Alao, 2006). Chetakwa na naani asusu abuo kariri asusu Igbo n'onu ogu n'Afrika.
ACALAN, nke African Union di na Mali. Asusu ndi Afrika a na-akuzi na ya di 12. N'ime ndi a, naani Hausa ka o na-akuzi. Yoruba jihuu nwayoo na-abata. Igbo adikwakwaghi ya. Chetakwa na o bu ego Naijiria anyi soro nwere ka e ji akwalite AU nwe ACALAN. Chetakwua na Iwunjiko Naijiria mere asusu Hausa, Igbo na Yoruba nhatanha. Ka ihe a niile na-eme, ndi Igbo adighi aju ese.

Mahadum diga n'Amerika. Ka o di n'afo 2012, n'ime mahadum niile di n'Amerika, iriabuo na abuo (22) na-akuzi asusu ndi Naijiria. N'ime ha, 18 na-akuzi Yoruba, 11 na-akuzi Hausa, 4 na-akuzi Igbo (Hu Apendis 3). O bu eziokwu na nke Igbo pekarichara, ma anyi ga-akupukwara obodo Amerika aka. (E deziri ugbua na mahadum 47 na-akuzi Yoruba)

Fulbright Foundation na Embasii Amerika. Bido n'afo 2002, Embasii Amerika (tinyere Fulbright Foundation na 2006) jikoro aka onu na-akwalite umu akwukwo Naijiria na-agu asusu Bekee na mahadum di na Naijiria, ndi chiri ubu ndi nkuzi na ha guchaa. Ha na-enye umu akwukwo ahu skolashipi otu afo ka ha bia Amerika, wee muta isu asusu bekee nke nma. Ndi ahu ga-akuzikwa asusu olu nne ha n'Amerika. Ma ndi Fulbright na Embasii dere na **naani ndi ha na-enye skolashipu ahu bx ndi nwere ike ikuzi Hausa maobu Yoruba** (Fulbright, 2012). Unu ahulanu. Ajuju anyi buruzia: Olee ihe ulo akwxkwo nwere agba n'uwa jiri leghara asusu Igbo anya? Amaghi m, ma echiche m bu na onye ga-abanye n'ihe o ohuru ga-emegodu nnukwu ima imi n'ala *(feasibility studies)* tupu o banye. Ulo akwukwo ndi ahu ga-achoriri ka ha mara ka e si akuzi Igbo na Naijiria tupu ha ebido kuziwe ya na be ha, ka ha wee jide n'aka na ha ga-enweta ndi nkuzi na umu akwukwo. Nke a putara na anyi ga-achoputakwu etu e si akuzi asusu Igbo na Naijiria. N'ihi oge adighi, m ga-akwusi nchacha a na mahadum.

Onudu Nkuzi Asusu Ato a na Mahadum Naijiria.

Ulooru Goomenti Etiti Naijiria bu *National Universities Commission,* mere nchocha n'afo 1999/2000 ka a mara Ngalaba Mmuta *(Program)* niile di na mahadum niile di na Naijiria. Ha weputara nchoputa ha na 2002. N'ihe gbasaara Ngalaba Omumu Asusu, ha choputara na:

Mahadum ole nwere Ngalaba Omumu Asusu Yoruba di	7
Mahadum ole nwere Ngalaba Omumu Asusu Hausa di	4
Mahadum nwere Ngalaba Omumu Asusu Efik/Ibibio di	1
Mahadum ole nwere Ngalaba Omumu Asusu Kanuri di	1
Mahadum Ole Nwere Ngalaba Omumu Asusu Igbo	**0**

Unu ahulanu ebe mmiri siri baa opi ugboguru. Ulo akwukwo mbauwa maara na ndi Igbo anaghi akuzi asusu ha, mara na ha bu ndi mbauwa choo ibido kuziwe ya na ha agaghi enweta ndi nkuzi na umu akwukwo, wee ghara imepe Omumu Asusu Igbo na mahadum ha. Onye ekwughi na ya no, o bu ndi ozo ga-ekwuru ya? Onye kporo ite ya mpempe eju, o bughi umunna were ya kpowe nti ka o na-ekwu? Ndi Igbo mere asusu Igbo oke, puusu wee na-eri ya!

Aga m ajukwano: Olee ihe mahadum di n'ala Igbo ejighi nwe Ngalaba Asusu Igbo mgbe ahu? Onye obula makwanu ihe kpatara ya: Olee ihe mahadum na-akuziri ihe ndi mmadu achoghi? Ha mepee Ngalaba Igbo, inweta umu akwukwo na ndi nkuzi arawa ha ahu, ma umu akwukwo ma ndi nkuzi anatawa mkpari, a kpowa ha "igbotic", "Igbo, Igbo, BK".

Imiri "Obara" Nke Ato: Etu E si Jiri Asusu Igbo eme Mgbasaozi na Redio Mbauwa.

Anyi maara nae nwere **BBC Hausa Service,** nwee **Voice of America** Hausa Service. Ma ihe otutu nwere ike na ha amaghi bu na e nwekwuru **Hausa service** na Radio ndi Frans, Jamani, Chaina na Saut Afrika. O nweghi nke nwere **Igbo Service**. (Ana m anu na e nwere redio na-agbasa ozi maka Biafra, ma na nne ji nke ahu iche).

Fig 4.1

Nchikota Onudu Asusu Ato ndi Agburu Naijiria n'ebe Redio Mbauwa na-ewu Ewu.

Olee ihe redio mbauwa ndi a na-ewu ewu ejighi agbasa ozi n'asusu Igbo, ma ndi Igbo so n'agburu anu kacha agburu n'Afrika? Echiche m bu na o bu ihe ulo akwukwo di elu hara ka ha hakwara: onye ka ha na-agbasara ya, o bx ndi Igbo enwegh[nganga n'ebe asusu ha di?

Mgbasaozi na Redio Naijiria. Iji tanye onye obula n'anya, leenu ihe mekwara na Naijiria afo ato maobu ano gara aga na mgbasa ozi. Redio Naijiria (FRCN) weputara ezigbo atumatu maka iji kwalite asusu ndi agburu Naijiria sitena ihiwe FM **Radio Station** maka ha. O hiwela **Radio FM Karama** na Kaduna, ga na-asu, na-akwalite Asusu Hausa awa 24 kwa ubochi. O hiwela **Radio FM Amuludun** n'Ibadan, ga na-asu, na-akwalite Asusu Yoruba awa 24 kwa ubochi. Rue taa, e nwebeghi nke obula e hiwere maka Asusu Igbo. Mgbe m juru, a gwara m na ha ka na-akwado nke Enugu akwado. Ndi Igbo adighi aju ese.

Imiri "Obara" Nke Anu: Ka Ndi Agburu Ato A Si Asu Asusu Ha.

O nweghi uru o bara ikowa maka nke a, makana oge adizighi. Onye obula maara na ndi Hausa na Yoruba na-asu asusu ha, ma ndi Igbo adighi asu nke ha.

Ibido Mechiwe

Nsogbu ndi Igbo nwere na Naijiria Erika, dika ndi Igbo ejikoghi obi onu, enwezughi qnxqgx Steeti na LGA ka ndi zoonu ndi ozo, enwebeghi **President** onye Igbo, uzo awalaawala (PH-Enugu-Onitsha) idakasicha; enweghi odu ugbommiri **(River Port)**, enweghi ezigbo ndustri, enweghi oru, wee tinyere asusu Igbo na-anwu anwu. I lee nsogbu ndi a niile anya, I hu na, bereso otu, o nweghi nke naani ndi Igbo nwere ike ikwusi ma o buru na ndi aburu ndi ozo enyereghi ha aka. Otu ahu bu onwu asusu Igbo. Ihe niile a ga-eji kpotekwa asusu Igbo n'ura onwxu o na-araha di n'ala Igbo. Ma anyi achoghi iji ha rua oru. Anyi akpoghi nsogbu asusu Igbo nwere ihe obula. Olee ihe a ga-eme.

Ihe a ga-eme
1. Ekwubuola m ya n na Nkuzi Odenigbo **Lecture** m nyere n'Owere na Septemba 2013 (Ejiofor 2013a), kwukwa ya na nkuzi m nyere n'Ogbako Goomenti Enugu Steeti chikowara na Disemba 2013 (Ejiofor 2013b), na naani dibia ga-agwq oria asusu Igbo bu ndi Gqvano ala Igbo. Ha aputakwaghi, o nweghi ebe e ji azu eje. A dighi aghara isimkpuruaka agba ufiu. Ya bu biko, ugbaku a gaa rio ndi Govano na-achi n'ala Igbo, ka ha jiri ike niile Chineke nyere ha wee zoputa asusu Igbo.

2. Unu riochaa ndi Govano, riowanu ndi nne na nna ndi Igbo, ha bido suwara umu ha Igbo na be ha, ka ndi Hausa na Yoruba si eme.
3. Unu riochaa ndi Govano, jisienu ike mee udi ogbako a na Steeti niile di n'Amerika na mbauwa **(countries)** ndi ozo ndi Igbo bi.
4. Unu riochaa ndi Govano, ndi agbataobi **(neighbourhood)** obula n'obodo oyibo na obodo mepere emepe bidoro umuaka ha, klas mgbede **(evening classes)** maka ikuzi Igbo mgbe olidee **(holidays)**.
5. Unu riochaa ndi Govano, riowanu ndi VOA ka ha bido mgbasaozi n'asusu Igbo. Ha biko were ya kwukwua ndi nnanna anyi ugwo maka mbo ha gbara n'imepe Amerika.
6. Biko nyerekwuanu aka n'uzo obula ikwalite "Otu Suwakwa Igbo". Nke a bu afo asato ndi Otu a na-aga ebe di icheiche na-enye nkuzi maka ajo anodu asusu Igbo. O nweela ihe di iche kemgbe ahu, ma ikwu eziokwu, ndi Igbo ebidobeghi nje m a choro. Bidokwuanu otu a n'Amerika na mba uwa di iche iche.
7. Bikonu, onye Igbo obula we baa na mbo a na-agba izqputa asusu Igbo. Were onwe gi bido.

Mmechi
Na mmechi, ihe na-eme n'uwa egosila, na otu uzo kacha uzo e ji ejiko mba bu asusu, gosikwa na e jikwa asusu ekposa nwanne na nwanne. Ejikqghi obi uno na-emebi ndi Igbo nnukwu ihe na Naijiria n'oge a. N'Ogbako Iwunjiko e nwere n'Abuja, anyi huru ya. Na be anyi na Naijiria, onye Igbo si Steti ozo rukata oru bekee, otu ubochi Steti o na-aruru oru achuo ya, chuo ya achitakwaghi akwa. E bidochaa ezigbo otu jikotara ndi Igbo, obere oge gaa, esemookwu adaa, e jewe uloikpe. O buzi na ndorondoro Naijiria. O banyekwuola n'uka? Egwu dikwa.

O nwekwara ike buru na ejikoghi obi unu a gbanyere mgborogwu na ndi Igbo ekwezighi asu asusu Chineke nyere ha. E kwere m na ndi Igbo bido taa kwalitewekwa asusu Igbo ka ndi Yoruba na Hausa si eme, na ndi Igbo ga-ejikotakwa onu. E jikotaraa onu, agamnihu abiakwa n'ala Igbo.

Ndi Igbo, Suwakwanu Igbo ugbu a. N'ihi gini? Asusu bu ndu mba. Ndewonu.

Staunton Virginia: Fraidee, Nkwo; Julai 25, 2014.

Edensibia

Achebe, Chinua (1999) "Tomorrow is Uncertain: Today is Soon Enough" Odenigbo Lecture.

Alao George (2006), "Teaching an African Language and Culture in a Changing European Environment: Achievements, Challenges and Perspectives". www.lingref.com/cpp/acal/36.paper1412.pdf

Arinze, Segun; "Ethnic War Rocks DSTV", *Sunday Sun*, April 4, 2010; p25.

Amobi, Chika. "Igbo Language to die by 2025" *Daily Sun*, August 28, 2012.

Adichie, Chimamanda. (2014) "Conscience and Integrity, Central to Igbo Culture" Lecture delivered in Awka to mark the First Hundred Days of Willie Obiano as Governor of Anambra State.

Ejiofor, Pita (2006), *Ibeku ndi Igbo Maka Asusu Igbo*. Valid Publishing Company, Awka.

_____ . (2012), *Ibeku ndi Igbo Maka Asusu Igbo*. Valid Publishing Co., Awka.

_____ . (2013 (a)). *Oganihu Igbo: Onudu Asusu Igbo*. Catholic Archdiocese of Owerri, 2013 Odenigbo Lecture. Ejiofor, Pita (2013 (b)). *Asusu Igbo: Ogbatauhie Na Uzo Agamnihu*. Government of Enugu State, Ministry of Culture and Tourism; Valid Publishing Company, Awka.

Ezeifeh, Ifeanyi (2014) From Slave Boy to Abolitionist: the Incredible Story of Olaudah Equiano. Homeland Publishers. Umuoji.

Fayose, Segun "AfricaMagic Igbo: Multichoice Cites Insufficient Content", *Saturday Independent*, May 8, 2010.

Mustapha, Abdul Raufu (2006) "Ethnic Structure, Inequality and Goernance of the Public Sector in Nigeria", CRISE Working Paper No 18, Queen Elizabeth House, University of Oxford, 21 St Giles, Oxford OX1 31A, UK.

Roy-Campbell, Zaline Makini (2012)

(http://en.wikipedia.org/wiki/listof languges by number of native speakers (ebudatara 27/9/2012).

_____ . (2012) "The State of African languages and the Global language Politics: Empowering African Languages in the Era of Globalization (extracts)" *http/www.lingref.com/cpp/acal/36/paper1401.pdf*

ebudatara 16.10/2012

Yar'Adua, Umaru Musa (President) (2007), "An Address by the President and Commander-in-Chief of the Federal Republic of Nigeria, His Excellency, Alhaji Umaru Musa Yardua GCFR at the 2009 Conference on Extinction of Igbo Language Held at Alvan Ikokwu Federal College of Education Auditorium, Owerri, Imo State on 17th July, 2009. Ndi Edeghi Odee

1999 Constitution of The Federal Republic of Nigeria.

"Going...Going: Archbishop Obinna Laments Imminent Death of the Igbo Language, Advocates Compulsory Teaching in Schools", *Daily Sun*, January 19, 2009.

National Policy on Education (Revised) (nd).

National Universities Commission (2002), Ranking of Nigerian Universities According to Performance of their Academic Programmes in the 1999 and 2000 Accreditation Exercise.

School of Oriental and African Studies (SOAS) *Undergraduate Prospectus*. 2011 Entry.

Preserving Igbo Ancestral Language and Upholding
the Linguistic Human Rights of Igbo Children
by
Professor Chinyere Ohiri-Aniche

Abstract

For the past three decades, international agencies, linguists and other researchers have called attention to the violation of the linguistic human rights of many indigenous and minority peoples, as well as the endangerment of most of the world's languages. The Igbo and their language are beset by these twin problems. Researches show that increasingly, the Igbo no longer use their language, nor do they hand it over to their children, thus steadily leading the language to extinction. For instance, Ohiri- Aniche (2002) found that 8% of Igbo secondary school children in Igboland and 20% of them residing in other parts of Nigeria did not speak Igbo. In 2007, she found that in Imo State, 7% of the children aged 6 to 11 years and 9% of them aged 5 years and below could not speak Igbo. For Igbo children residing in Lagos State, the comparable figures were 35% and 52.5% respectively. This dwindling competence in Igbo among the children is not surprising, considering that increasingly, the language of the Igbo home is shifting to English.

Thus, in the 2002 study, 19% of Igbo parents in Igboland and 43% outside Igboland conversed with their children mostly in English or a mixture of English and Igbo. In the 2007 study, 50% of parents in Imo State and 80% in Lagos State spoke mostly English or a mixture of English and Igbo with their children. The failure of the Igbo to hand over their ancestral language to their children, in the first place, constitutes a gross violation of the linguistic human rights of the children as defined in UNESCO (1987) and the United Nations(1994). More importantly, it is the surest way to the extinction of the Igbo language, and ultimately, the Igbo race.

If the Igbo wish to rescue their language that now has more than 24 million speakers from the league of the 90% of the world's languages which linguists predict would not by the next century, then they have to take some drastic actions and firstly revert to the active use of the language in their homes in Igbo homeland and in the diaspora and secondly to start handing it over to their children within and outside the Igbo homeland. *Taa bu gboo.* [Today is early enough].

Introduction
The Language situation in Nigeria

Nigeria has about 400 indigenous languages according to Crozier and Blench (1992). In the late 19th Century, Britain assumed colonial powers over the territories that became amalgamated in 1914 into one country called Nigeria. English became the official language and has remained so, even after Independence in 1960. Three of the indigenous languages – Hausa, Igbo and Yoruba have sizable populations and are known as the major languages of the country. Thus, the Constitution of the Federal Republic of Nigeria (1979, revised 1989, 1999) provides for these three languages to be used alongside English in the National Assembly. The other Nigerian languages have much smaller numbers of speakers varying from 2 million to even 1 speaker!

Table 1: Native Speakers of Three Major Nigerian Languages

Language	Native Speakers
Hausa	34,000,000
Yoruba	28,000,000
Igbo	24,000,000

Source: Wikipedia (2014)

Table 2: Some Nigerian Languages with less than 10,000 Speakers

Language	Native Speakers
Koma	3,000
Kugbo	2,000
Bali	1,000
Kafanca	970
Bassa – Kontagora	10

Source: Crozier and Blench (1992)

The severe language endangerment problems facing the country's languages means that many of the small languages are fast becoming extinct. For instance, Haruna (2007) reports that Bubbure, a language spoken in Bauchi State has only one known speaker, while Holma spoken in Adamawa State had 4 aged speakers in 1987.

The Changing Fortunes of Igbo Language within and outside Igbo Society

Scenario 1: Igbo is almost dropped as one of the three major languages in Nigeria in the draft revised 1999 Constitution. In April 2005, when the 1999 Constitution of the Federal Republic of Nigeria was being reviewed, a draft appeared which did not list Igbo as one of the three major languages of Nigeria, alongside Hausa and Yoruba. In the wake of general outcry by the Igbo, the then Attorney General and Minister of Justice had to issue a statement denying that Igbo had been removed as one of the three national languages. The incident was attributed to a typing error (*Guardian Newspaper*, Sunday April 24, 2005, Front Page).

Scenario 2: Igbo is not one of the priority languages of the African Academy of Languages (ACALAN)

The African Academy of Languages (ACALAN) with headquarters in Bamako, Mali is a specialised institution of the African Union. In 2004, ACALAN adopted five key projects, which would form the substantive programmes of the Academy for the next decade or so. These projects are:

- The Year of African Languages in 2006
- Stories Across Africa
- Joint Masters/ Ph. D. Programme
- The Terminology Project
- The Translation and Interpretation Projects

Faced with the estimated two thousand languages that exist in Africa, ACALAN naturally had to choose which languages to start working with. For now, it appears to have opted for so –called "cross border languages", that is languages spoken in two or more countries. Thus, in Nigeria, Hausa and Yoruba are the two languages that have so far been involved in the Academy's programmes. (See Newsletter of the Language in Education in Africa Project Number 8 – July, 2005, page 4).

Scenario 3: Igbo is not one of the languages chosen for the Fulbright Foreign Language Teaching Assistance Programme (FLTA)

In the past few years, students of English in Nigerian Universities, but with Hausa and Yoruba backgrounds, have benefitted from one year Foreign Language Teaching Assistance Programme (FLTA) tenable in the USA. There, the students teach their indigenous language and also get a chance to improve their English language competence. Following inquiries, the American Consulate in Lagos explained that languages were chosen for the Programme based on their ranking by US Institutions. For Nigerian Languages, Yoruba had the highest ranking, followed by Hausa, while Igbo ranked low. Thus, Hausa and Yoruba were chosen for the FLTA Programme.

Scenario 4: Igbo is not one of the Nigerian Languages assigned its own movie channel on DStv

No development has irked Igbo people in recent times as the fact that Hausa and Yoruba languages have been assigned their individual movie channels on the DStv, while the Igbo language is not assigned any channel. A pertinent question here, however, is whether there are Igbo language movies available for such a channel. Table 3 below displays the number of home video movies approved by the National Film and Video Censors Board for the months of June and July, 2014

Table 3: Home Movies Approved by the National Film and Video Censors Board For June And July 2014

MONTH	LANGUAGE	NO OF MOVIES APPROVED
JUNE 2014	ENGLISH	16
	YORUBA	25
	HAUSA	19
	IBIBIO	2
	IGBO	NIL
JULY 2014	ENGLISH	29
	YORUBA	30
	HAUSA	12
	BINI	10
	IBIBIO/EFIK	4
	IGBO	NIL

Source NFVCB (2014)

Many an Igbo has complained bitterly of the above four scenarios where the Igbo language is steadily being downgraded as one of the major languages of Nigeria, and indeed of Africa by external agencies. The next four scenarios will, however, show where Igbo children are discomfited or thoroughly embarrassed with regard to their ancestral language by internal Igbo forces

Scenario 5: An Igbo child is unable to communicate with a villager

In December 2004, a four year old Igbo girl is taken to Abia State from Lagos. A villager comes to ask after her father, speaking in Igbo. She replies in English that he was sleeping. Not understanding her, the villager repeats her question. At this, the little girl bursts out in anger that she had said he was sleeping. She runs into the room and for the rest of the family's holidays, she withdraws into her shell, avoiding all visitors.

Scenario 6: A nursery school pupil bursts into tears at being spoken to in Igbo

A new teacher at a nursery school in Enugu State wants to familiarise herself with the pupils and starts chatting to them in Igbo. When she asks a five year old pupil his name, the little boy bursts into tears: " I do not understand that language and my mummy says I should not speak it".

Scenario 7: An Igbo child is an alien amidst relatives

A bus-load of Igbo relatives and friends are travelling home from Lagos to Nsukka for a celebration. There is boisterous communication in Igbo and merriment among the co-travellers. A seven year old boy is, however, excluded from it all, cocooned in his incomprehension of the Igbo language – yes, of the songs, jokes etc that were going on. From time to time, he could be heard exclaiming "O o Chineke mu!" meaning "Oh my God" – apparently the only Igbo he could speak.

Scenario 8: The children of an Igbo traditional ruler do not speak Igbo

Some visitors on a courtesy visit to a traditional ruler, an 'eze' in Imo State were surprised that none of his children could communicate in Igbo. He and his 'Loolo' (wife) were communicating with their children in English – the language of their home.

Scenarios 5 – 8 above clearly show instances where the Igbo adults, especially parents, have failed to bring up their children to speak Igbo. This marginalization of Igbo children with regards to their ancestral language is not only a gross violation of their linguistic human rights, but is also an important contributory factor to the dwindling fortunes of the Igbo language within and outside the Igbo society.

Violation of the linguistic human rights of Igbo children

Increasingly one observes children whose parents are Igbo but who do not speak the Igbo Language. In systematic studies on indigenous language competence among children, Ohiri –Aniche (2002) and (2007) found an alarming number of Igbo children both within and outside Igboland who are unable to speak Igbo. The 2002 study surveyed 270 secondary school students in such Igbo towns as Awka, Onitsha, Owerri and Nsukka as well as in Lagos, a town outside Igboland. The study found that 8% of the students living in Igboland and 20% of those living in Lagos could not speak Igbo, or did so with difficulty. The 2007 study which was conducted in Owerri, Imo State and in Lagos inquired into the Igbo language competence of three age groups: children aged 1 – 5 years, children aged 6 – 11 years and adults. It was found that 7% of children aged 6 – 11 years in Imo State and 9% of them aged 5 years and below were unable to speak Igbo. For the Igbo children residing with parents in Lagos, 35% of them aged 6 – 11 years and 52% of them aged 5 years and below were also unable to speak Igbo.

The inability of these children to speak Igbo is not surprising since in an increasing number of homes, parents now bring up their children to speak English, rather than Igbo. Similarly the language of communication in many of the homes is shifting from Igbo to English.

The failure of the Igbo to hand over their ancestral language to their children as well as endow them with an unalloyed Igbo identity clearly constitute a violation of the human and linguistic rights of the children. Right from its inception, the 1945 Charter of the United Nations recognised language, alongside race, sex and religion as basic human characteristics which all signatory countries agreed to uphold. Subsequent UN human rights efforts such as the Universal Declaration of Human Rights 1948, the International Covention on Economic, Social and Cultural Rights, 1966, the United Nation's Convention on the Rights of the Child, 1989 and many others have all had sections dealing with language as an important human right to be protected. Some of the coventions and declarations specifically touch on the linguistic rights of children. Skutnabb-Kangas (2000:541-543) discusses two such examples. The first is the Recife Declaration (1987) which was the outcome of an international seminar on Human Rights and Cultural Rights held in Recife, Brazil under the joint auspices of the International Association for Cross-Cultural Communication and the UNESCO. Two articles of the Declaration pertinent to our discourse are the following:

Every social group has the right to positively identify with one or more languages and to have such identification accepted and respected by others.

Every child has the right to learn the language(s) of his/her group fully.

The second example is from the **UN Draft Universal Declaration on Indigenous Rights** (1994). This Declaration which was adopted in 1994 has as its article 14, the following:

Indigenous people have the right to revitalize, use, develop and transmit to future generations their histories, languages, oral traditions, philosophies, writing systems and literatures, and to designate and retain their own names and communities, places and persons.

Clearly, the Igbo are not exercising any of these rights. The curious thing is that no one is preventing them from carrying out any of these activities which are necessary for the health and vitality of their language. This negligence on the part of the Igbo has set the Igbo language on the road to endangerment and ultimate extinction.

Igbo language endangerment

Many people remain sceptical whenever Igbo is mentioned as an endangered language and one that might not survive beyond the present century. They feel that a language that has at least 24 million speakers (*Wikipedia* 2014) or about 35 million speakers if one includes those that speak it as 2nd or 3rd languages (Prah, 2001) could hardly be considered endangered. It is true that endangerment is usually associated with small languages. For instance, Brenzinger et al. (1991) define an endangered language as one that has less than five thousand speakers. However, there are other signs of language endangerment. For instance, the UNESCO (2003) Language Vitality Index gives indices for determining the likelihood of the future survival of a language. These are:

Intergenerational transmission
Absolute number of fluent and committed speakers
Proportion of speakers within the total population
Shifts in domains of actual use
Materials for language use and literacy
Government and institutional language attitudes and policies, including official status and use
Interaction and social effects between language attitudes and policies
Nature, type and quality of language documentation.

Clearly Igbo language will be hard-put to survive for much long as it has fallen short of many of the indices which make for language vitality.

Consequences of Igbo Language Endangerment

The endangerment of the Igbo language has some of the following consequences:

(a) The importance of Igbo as a major language in Nigeria and indeed, in Africa, becomes diminished.
(b) The cohesion of the Igbo as a major ethnic group in Nigeria is threatened with this weakening of their main binding force. This is why the solidarity cry *"Igbo Kwenu"* now receives weaker and weaker response.
(c) The identity of the average Igbo, especially of the children, becomes shaky and far from one of pride and honour. The identity crisis of the Igbo nowadays is manifest in many ways, such as:
(d) Not wanting to be identified as an Igbo, especially through speaking Igbo
(e) Not dressing as an Igbo
(f) Discarding Igbo surnames for non-Igbo ones, etc.

Politically and socially, the Igbo become less a force to be reckoned with. The Igbo lose the wealth of their intangible cultural heritage. As an orate culture, the wealth of Igbo knowledge in all its ramifications is encapsulated and preserved in the language and has been transmitted orally to future generations. Allowing the language to decay and die will amount to wiping out 6000 years of accumulated cultural wealth. Indeed, the United Nations has been keen to prevent the loss of cultural heritage in any part of the world. Towards this, in October 2003, the 3rd UNESCO General Conference approved the **Convention on Intangible Cultural Heritage**. Following this, the then Minister of Culture and Tourism in Nigeria inaugurated a National Committee on Intangible Cultural Heritage. At the inauguration ceremony, the Minister explained UNESCO's definition of oral and intangible assets to mean: "People's learned processes, along with the knowledge, skill and creativity that informed and developed them." (See The Guardian Newspaper, Saturday April 16, 2005, page B25). As the Igbo use their language less and less and fail to hand it over to their children, the ultimate consequence will be the extinction of the language.

The Igbo cannot exist as a distinct people if and when the Igbo language had ceased to exist. History is replete with examples of past robust groups that are now only known in historical terms. For example, the Incas and Aztecs once had flourishing civilizations in South America, but from the arrival of Spanish conquerors in the area about five hundred years ago, many of the native languages and cultures went into decline, eventually becoming extinct.

Conclusion

This paper has argued that the failure of the Igbo to hand over their ancestral language to their children constitutes a gross violation of the linguistic human rights of the children. This, as well as the penchant of the Igbo not to use their language in different spheres of life - the home, the school, in politics and governance, print and electronic media, entertainment industry, etc., is leading the Igbo language steadily into extinction. The paper further argues that the extinction of the Igbo language will ultimately lead to the annihilation of the Igbo as a distinct people on earth. The unfortunate thing is that the Igbo have themselves to blame for this fate.

Suggestions

Can any measures be taken to prevent the extinction of the Igbo people and their language? The answer is yes, provided the Igbo choose to recognize the looming dangers and develop very strong popular and political will to remedy the situation. This will now lead them to undertake some right actions, such as bringing up their children to speak Igbo and using the language in all spheres of life, and doing so with pride. The paper ends with the following three Igbo sayings:
   (a) *Ekwe kuo, ama agbaa* (When the wooden slit drum sounds, a warning is given)
   (b) *Onye kwe, chi ya ekwe* (If one believes/agrees, his or her personal god will also believe/agree)
   (c) *Taa bu gboo* (Today is early enough)

References

Brenzinger, M. et al. (1991). "Endangered Languages in Africa" In R.H. Robins and E.M. Uhlenbeck (eds.) *Endangered Languages.* Oxford/New York: Berg Publishers.

Crozier, D. and R. Blench (1992). *An Index of Nigerian Languages.* Dallas: Summer Institute of Linguistics

Guardian Newspaper (2005) "Our Hands Are Clean, Says Govt" *The Guardian*, Sunday April 24, 2005 (Front page)

Guardian Newspaper (2005) "Committee for intangible cultural heritage". *The Guardian*, Saturday April 16, 2005, page B25.

Haruna, Andrew (2007). "On the Moribund Languages of Nigeria: The Need for Documentation" Paper presented at the 21st Annual Conference of the Linguistic Association of Nigeria in Uyo, Akwa Ibom State, 19th -23rd November, 2007.

Language in Education in Africa Project "Interview with Salam Diakite" *LEAP NEWS 8*, July 2005 (pages 4,5).

National Film And Video Censors Board (2014). *Half of A Yellow Sun* Among 77 Approved Films For June 2014 by Censors Board.
http://www.nfvcb.gov.ng/news.asp?newsid=121

National Film And Video Censors Board (2014). Censors Board Approves 89 Films For The Month of July, 2014.
http://www.nfvcb.gov.ng/news.asp?newsid=123

Ohiri-Aniche, Chinyere. (2003). "Language Endangerment Among a Majority Group: The Case of Igbo." *Lagos Education Review*. Vol. 9 No. 1, June 2002.

Prah, Kwesi (2001) "Language Harmonization and Orthography: Implication for Higher Education in West Africa." In: Ford Foundation *Pipeline Issues in Higher Education in West Africa*. Lagos: Ford Foundation.

Skutnabb-Kangas, Tove (2000) *Linguistic Genocide in Education-or Worldwide Diversity and Human Rights?* New Jersey: Lawrence Erlbaum Associates.

UNESCO (1987). *The Recife Declaration: Resolution on Linguistic Rights*. Cited in Skutnabb-Kangas (2000).

UNESCO Ad Hoc Expert Group on Endangered Languages (2003). *Language Vitality and Endangerment*.

United Nations (1994).*The Draft Universal Declaration on Indigenous Rights*. Cited in Skutnabb-Kangas (2000).

WikipediaThe Free Encyclopaedia*List of Languages By Number of Native Speakers*
www.En.wikipedia.org/wiki/list_of_languages_by_number_of_native_speakers

Igbo Language before, during and after the Biafra War.
by
Dr. Crescentia Ugwuona

Abstract

Language, an irreducible fulcrum, from which any nation revolves, is invaluable in the discussion of any socio-political situation in any nation the world over, and Igbo nation is not an exception. The focus of this paper is therefore on the status of Igbo language, before, during and after the Biafra war in Nigeria. The persistent challenges in the Nigerian federation as well as the predicament of the Igbo nation in the federation since the amalgamation of Nigeria, 1914 call for urgent need for Igbo linguists and intelligentsia to address the issue. This paper therefore examines the status of the language at this various levels to see how it affects the socio-political development in Nigeria specially the Igbo nation. The work which is basically expository draws on various researches on Igbo language. From the study, it is glaring that the entire Igbo nation should retrace their steps and embrace their identity through their God-given language as a means of overcoming the challenges they face both in Nigeria and in the Diaspora. In this way, her citizens can live a life of dignity; and co-exist peacefully with her neighbours and the world at large. This study is a step in the direction of evaluating the status of Igbo language in Nigeria before the Biafra war till date. It suggests ways of arresting the threats and challenges that loom with respect to the language.

Background of Igbo Language

Igbo as a language is as old as the Igbo people. The Igbo language is primarily indigenous to the Igbo people and is one of the three major languages in Nigeria. The Igbo people occupy the Southeastern part of Nigeria. They are found predominantly in states such as Enugu, Imo, Abia, Anambra and Ebonyi states. They are also found in parts of rivers, Delta and Akwa-Ibom, States. Currently, the Igbo are found globally. Various estimates have been presented on the number of languages in Nigeria. These range from 250 to 500 (see Ikekeonwu) 2009, Emenanjo 2003, and Ugwuona 2013). The current population of Nigeria (see the 2006 census) is put at about 140 million people.

Igbo language belongs to the new Benue Congo language family. Greenberg (1963) classified it in the Kwa group along with other clusters such as Akan, Gbe, Yoruba-Igala, Nupe-Ebira Edo and Idoma. Native speakers are estimated to be between 25-40 million people and 150 million people the world. That implies that 150 million people are potential speakers of the language globally.

Igbo language seems to manifest the greatest dialect diversity, many of which vary in inherent intelligibility. It is probably due to this fragmentation of the Igbo people and their language that brought about Igbo language internal conflict, where the dialects vie for ascendancy due to political, economic or socio-economic reasons. The Igbo language fragmentation is captured properly in the words of Uwalaka (2001) thus: "....practically, every village was independent, and so great was the isolation of each small community that the inhabitants of each neighbouring village speak in entirely different dialect." The above statement suggests that even before the coming of the colonial masters, as well as the amalgamation of Nigeria in 1914 by Sir Fedrick Lord Luggard, the dialect consciousness with its concomitant political, and socio-economic motives are already there.

In terms of the origin of the Igbo people, there have been several conjectures and reconstructions of the origin of the Igbo language. One of the most wide spread is the hermitic theory leading some to draw attention to the Israel hypothesis, such as: the Eri migration, archaeological evidence, glaring similarities between the Igbo tradition and Jewish custom. There are other claims of other origins such as, to Igala people to the Northern part of Igbo land (Nsukka), Ibibio, Ogoja, and Ekoyi peoples to the South East of Igboland, Ijaw people to the South West, and Bini to the West. To lighten the heart of the Igboman over this issue of origin a few modern historians especially Isechei (1973), Nwadike (2002) and the archaeological findings at Igbo Ukwu, and some other places do establish that the belt formed by Awka, Orlu, Okigwe and Owerri is known as the core or nuclear Igboland. From here started a migration to the South and to East.

However, the archaeological findings and excavations at Igbo Ugwu, Afikpo, the 4500 years old pottery uncovered at the University of Nigeria Nsukka, and a rock shelter at Ibagwa in Nsukka area which yielded both ancient pottery and tools of stone, all point to the fact that Igbo people as well as their language is autochthonous. In addition Isichei (1973), a great historian also testifies to the above fact and quotes one of the informants, an elder man from Mbaise as saying "we did not come from anywhere and any one who tells you we come from anywhere is a liar. Write it down". The decline of the autochthonous language of the Igbo people largely started with the attitude of the Igbo people towards their language, the arrival of the colonial masters, the 1914 amalgamation of Northern and Southern Nigeria, and the subsequent Biafra war. Babayide (2001) captured this faulty amalgamation thus: "the political phenomenon called Nigeria came into existence in 1914 as a result of amalgamation of the southern and northern protectorates of the British territory around the River Niger area. The name Nigeria is said to be morphologically derived from a blend of Niger and area. Lord Lugard, the then colonial administrator considered this merger necessary for ease of administration. Thitherto, different and separate autonomous kingdoms had existed. In effect, Nigeria is an artificial structure initiated by foreign colonial master Lord Frederick Lugard, who had neglected to consider the religious, linguistic and ethnic differences of the peoples involved.

Brief History of the Development of Igbo Language

In this section, I discuss the state of the Igbo language under three broad periods: Igbo language before the Biafra war with its subheading such as: the Isuama period 1700-1900, the Union Igbo period 1900-1929, the central Igbo period and the great Igbo orthography controversy. This will be followed by Igbo language during the Biafra war and Igbo language after the Biafra war.

The Igbo Language before the Biafra War (1500 -1700).

Igbo language is as old as the Igbo people. The earliest and special form of writing of the Igbo people and their neighbouring groups (Cross River) was Nsibidi. Nsibidi as Nwadike (2002:17) observes served various function such as identity label, public notice, private warning, declaration of taboos, amorous dealings, reckoning of taboos in the localities where it operated. This form of writing, described as formalized pictographs – (Nsibidi) was popular among secret cults (among the Cross River peoples, Aro) in the pre-1599s (Okwudishu 2010).

Nsibidi was also said to have been used extensively in recording proceedings in the count. It died a natural death probably because of its limited use. It was not until 1904 that its existence was learnt by T.D. Maxwell a European, the then acting district commission in Calabar. Oraka (1983) noted that apart from Nsibidi writing, the Igbo people acculturated themselves effectively by formal methods.

The Isuama Dialect (1700 to 1900)

Isuama dialect was used in Igbo studies in the 19th century. The earliest attempt to commit Igbo to writing was done via the Isuama dialect. This dialect was not universally spoken in the whole of Igbo nation then. It was the dialect spoken by the Igbo ex-slaves who were resettled in Sierra Leone. The dialect was later adopted for literary works both in Freetown and Onitsha. Considering the history of the ex-slaves who were resettled in Sierra Leone, it was glaring that their spoken Igbo can be captured as a pidgin Igbo. Asuama was a sort of an Esperanto which the different dialect groups of the Igbo ex-slaves used for the purpose of mutual intelligibility. Regardless, Ajayi Crowther of the church missionary society (CMS) Niger mission who with his men established a mission at Onitsha adopted it for their evangelical work. In effect, Crowther was assisted by schon, a linguist who from his base in London had worked on Igbo for a good number of years and had produced a grammar of the Igbo language in 1875: Oku Ibo, grammatical elements of the

Ibo language. In 1875 at a conference Crowther and his translator were summoned to resolve that: "... The standard and reading dialect is strictly to be that of Isuama, it being the one which all other dialects will learn to speak, while the Isuama will yield to no other one, hence, translations in this dialect will be universally received by the nation" (Hair 1967: 94 as cited by Uwalaka 2001).

The adoption of the Isuama dialect as the standard Igbo for the Igbo nation then provoked different reactions from different people of Igbo nation and the subsequent failure. Part of the reason for this is that the Isuama dialect was altogether foreign in Igbo nation and not universally spoken across the whole Igbo land. The other reason (Ugwuona 2004) relates to the over democratic and indomitable spirit of the Igbo people. In 1882, Crowther wrote vocabulary of the Ibo language, the first comprehensive dictionary in Igbo. In 1883 Crowther and Schon jointly revised it and added more words. They eventually came out with vocabulary of the Ibo language part II, an English - Ibo dictionary. By this time, Igbo had some 50 books and booklets published in it (Oraka 1983). In 1885, Roman Catholic Mission (RCM) reached Igboland but did not seem to be interested in the study of the Igbo language. In 1891, Bishop Crowther died and the Isuama Igbo period died with him.

However, a lot of work on Igbo studies were achieved during the Isuama period (see Oraka 1983, Nwadike 2002, Emenanjo 1995, Achebe 1971 and 1972, and Okwudishu 2010 for details). In effect, by the late 1880s, the Isuama experiment had died a natural death.

The Union Igbo Period 1900 – 1929

Union Igbo was intended to be the brand of Igbo which every Igbo man would understand and speak. In other words, it ushered in the development of an Igbo version aimed at merging or writing of at least five major dialects of an Igbo (Arochukwu, Bonny, Uwana, Onitsha and Owerri) that would be a central or compromise language, playing the role of a literary medium for the Igbo people. The most important and popular work published in union Igbo was the Holy Bible. Other solid work during this period include materials on Igbo culture proverbs, folktales, riddles and custom, translation works, anthropological report of the Igbo speaking people of Nigeria, revision and enlargement of existing Igbo grammar books, among others. In spite of all these achievements listed above, union Igbo has some critisms as we can see from the words of Achebe (1971).

Union Igbo is a heavy footed and clumsy Esperanto. ... The inability of the Union Igbo to cope with drama and poetry... rules it out decisively as a language of creative literature. Ward (1941) also reorganizes the short comings of the Union Igbo thus:

- It makes use of some few constructions which are only used in a very limited area;i.e. the perfect suffixes-*wo* as in *woro* were recorded only in Afikpo and Okana and used by two of the informants at Awgu.
- It makes too frequent use of the participles *we* (used in a few dialects, eg Onitsha, to continue a narrative but not to begin it). This is the form used for the Bible and introducing a sentence.
- Union Ibo has made use of somewhat restricted range of grammatical forms, this must have tended to exclude the variety of constructions and idiomatic expressions that make Igbo a lively and vigorous language. The above problems imply that the Union Igbo has not settled the dialect problem of the Igbo people.

The Central Dialect & the Great Orthography Dispute 1929-1962

This period overlapped with the orthography period with the failure of union Igbo to satisfy the purpose for which it was structured, the search for a viable dialect to be adopted in the production of Igbo literature continues. Consequently ward in 1941 looked for a dialect of Igbo which would be accepted over a considerable area of the Igbo nation, and which might form the basis of a growing standard Igbo. Ward then selected what came to be known as the central dialect; that is, the dialect of the central area of the Igbo people in contradiction to that of the Onitsha area. The dialects are those spoken in old Owerri province. Ward asserts that some of the Northern dialects including Nsukka, Eke, Udi as well as a number of borderline dialects show more affinity with the central dialects variation than with Onitsha dialect. Uwalaka (2001) believes that Wards approach to the Igbo language internal conflicts resolution appeared to be a realistic one, given that no artificial creation of standard dialect was involved.

The discussion of the development of Igbo before the Biafra war in Nigeria cannot be complete without a look at the issues of orthography controversy between 1929 and 1961. It is almost the worst aspect of the dialect/or orthography controversy in Igbo nation. The early work on Igbo language was done with the Lepsius orthography in 1854. It was this orthography that Crowther and the entire C.M.S mission adopted. In 1922, the Phelps–Strokes an American philanthropic organization whose main interest was the education of the black peoples issued a report known as the Phelps-Strokes. This report contained a strong recommendation that the African child should be educated in his mother tongue. In 1926 the education ordinance/ code was enacted, requiring that only the vernacular or English be medium of instruction. In June of the same year, the International Institute of African languages and cultures (IIALC) was launched. Its first publication "The Practical Orthography of African Languages appeared in 1927. This orthography was a radical departure from the Lepsius alphabets used by CMS. The replacement of the Lepsius orthography with the IIALC orthography adopted and renamed Adams ward orthography in the Eastern Nigeria, was not accepted by the CMS conservatives. This sparked off a controversy with the government. The Roman Catholic Mission (RCM) and the Methodist on one side, and the CMS (Anglican) conservatives on the other side (Okwudishu 2010). In effect, an advisory committee that included representatives from the missions agreed to set up a translation Bureau at Umuahia in 1930. In 1933, Omenuko by Pita Nwana was published after winning an all-Africa literacy contest in indigenous African language organized by international institute of African languages and culture. The first edition was in the protestant orthography, but it was soon issued in the other orthographies. Longman Nigeria published an "Official Orthography Edition" translated by J.O. Iroaganachi between 1939 and 1944, a combined effort of Adams and Ward advocated the use of a new orthography known as the central dialect and the development of a common language. The result was chaotic and acrimonious. The Anglicans insisted on the Onitsha dialect, the Methodists embraced the central dialect. In 1948, the RCM created a new diocese at Owerri. RCM readers were then issued in two dialects the Onitsha and Owerri. The orthography controversy lasted for about 70 years. The gravity of the dispute could be better appreciated from the pamphlet published in 1957 by the protagonists of the old or the Lepsius orthography titled **Investigation into the new Igbo Orthography.**

What seems to be the case in the orthography dispute was that support or opposition to a particular orthography was not always due to linguistic considerations rather religious, political, and socio-economic considerations complicated the dispute. There is no doubt that Hausa and Yoruba language did not experience the kind of controversy that engrossed the Igbo language. Little wonder the challenges the Igbo nation face in Nigeria. Besides, there is dearth of literary work on Igbo language studies especially during the wake of the orthography dispute and the civil war. The Igbo orthography dispute continued to rage until 1961 when the government set up a committee headed by Dr. S.E Onwu to bring a lasting solution to the orthography conflict. With the orthography controversy apparently over with the setting up of Onwu committee in 1961, Igbo language studies under the SPILC moved into a new age that is, the age of standard Igbo.

Igbo Language during the Biafra War

During the civil war, serious work was not done on Igbo language and literary studies had to wait till after the Nigeria Biafra war. Following the settlement of the dispute and the events of the Biafra war (1967-1970), the SPILC directed its tools to ensuring authentic development of the Igbo Language as well as the Igbo culture. It is interesting to note that the events that followed the Nigeria – Biafra war helped the development of the Igbo language.

Though the war brought a halt to printing and publishing in the language (Uwalaka 2010), it engendered an Igbo cultural revival, a new self awareness of the Igboness of the Igbo indeed an authentic Igbo renaissance that parallels that of Europe. Hence, there was a new interest on Igbo mother tongue and the birth quarrels over the orthography and the dialect question was somewhat laid to rest.

Igbo Language after the Biafra war 1970 – 1999.
This period coincided with the period of standard Igbo or modern Igbo era. The period was heralded by the standardization committee set up by SPILC. By the late 60s, Igbo language had been made a requirement for the award of B.A. (Hon) degree in the University of London see (Chijioke, 1995, Okwudishu 2010). (a) to adopt words from different Igbo dialects the terms of reference of the committees include: (b) to enrich the Igbo language; (c) to adopt loan words where there were no Igbo equivalent.

The major objectives among other things was to create a standard Igbo which could be understood by all Igbo nations, hence, it was expected to be more flexible than the Isuama, Union Igbo, and central Igbo dialects since it embraced almost all the dialects of Igbo Language. Between 1971 and 1978, SPILC made the following educational developments/achievements:

i) Conducted its annual seminars which were well attended by people from different parts of Nigeria and the Diaspora;

ii) Approved the recommendations of the standardization committee on the spelling of the Igbo words;

iii) Influenced the decision to establish a department of Igbo language and culture at Alvan Ikoku College of Education;

iv) Recommended the rearrangement of Igbo alphabet;

v) Made F. C. Ogbalu the head of department of Igbo language and culture at the Anambra College of Education, Awka;

vi) And influenced the decision to establish another department of Igbo at Federal Advanced College, Okene in the then Kwara state

vii) Influenced the inclusion of Igbo language among the subjects for the advanced level examination from 1979, among others.

Okwudishu (2010) asserts that apart from efforts at language development during these years, Igbo language was taught as a school subject from 1940 to 1942 when it was included in the secondary school curriculum. It was first taken as an examination subject in 1942 for the senior schools Cambridge certificate. It was also introduced into grade II teachers college and between 1946 and 1947, about ten Igbo students were sent to the School of Oriental and African Studies (SOAS), London by the government and the missions for the study of Igbo language. There are other achievements and development of Igbo language between 1970 to date (see *Journal of Igbo Studies* from 2005- date for details). In effect, Igbo language is considered to be endangered judging from the present status of Igbo language in Nigeria.

Igbo Language at Present

It is interesting to note that the introduction of linguistics and Igbo into our Nigeria universities and colleges of education has contributed immensely to the development of Igbo language presently. This has also made it possible for serious studies and research in Igbo language in the Universities.

Igbo language studies at present enjoy a number of impressive studies and publications. It is patient to appreciate the forebears of Igbo language study that is, those who gave life to Igbo language studies such as Pita Nwanna of *Omenuko*, F.C. Ogbalu of *Azu Ndu*, Prof. I.U. Nwadike of *Igbo language in education*; Dr. S. Okechukwu Mezu, *Umu Ejima* (Igbo adaptation of Plautus' *Menaechmi*); Oraka of the Foundation of Igbo Studies, Prof. C. I. Ikekeonwu the Director of NINLAN Aba Campus, Dr. C. U. Aebedo of Ogwu, Dr.B.M. Mba et al. of *"Igbo Adi"* (Igbo-English dictionary) forth coming, Prof. Nolue Emenanjo in collaboration with I.U. Nwadike and Dr. S.E. Ikeokwu of the *Journal of Igbo Studies (*vols 1 to 8) in the University of Nigeria Nsukka among others.

In spite of the above achievements, much progress has not been made considering the Igbo language experience from 1500 to date. Igbo language is considered to be endangered judging from its present status in Nigeria from the follwing stand point.

- Lack of seriousness in the use of the language in the media
- Abusive borrowing and hyperadaptation by educated native speaker
- Preaching the communication in Igbo language without practicing - so "who is cheating who?"

In addition, Ohiri Amuche (2008:9) observes that among the three major Nigerian languages, Igbo has been documented as the most endangered and is currently under severe threat of extinction. The United Nations reports that Igbo language may extinct in the next 50 years. All these largely justify Aniche's observation. In effect, the bitter truth of no language, no culture and no culture no identity looms over the Igbo nation in Nigeria. Little surprise that Ndigbo have been facing enormous challenges in Nigeria and the contemporary world partly because of their negative attitude towards their God-given talents and endowments especially their language.

The Re-birth and Way Foward

Under this ugly situation, how can the Igbo nation expect any meaningful and effective involvement in the power system in the country, Nigeria. Every ethnic group nation exists with prestige and status only with its language embedded as a vital aspect of it. Maintenance and development of ones language are necessary conditions for the development of any ethnic group and the subsequent involvement in power nationally and internationally. Language is one of the aspects of culture that endowns man with the power of civilization without which man is powerless. Power is the context of this paper relates to effectively using ones given languages to influence a greater part of this sphere. Further more, just as the people of Igbo nation came out of a patricidal Biafra war, financially empty handed almost, and few owing at most a bicycle, but now the greatest operators of inter ethnic vehicular transportation, Igbo people should make the Igbo language acquire much power of language infection in Nigeria and the world over. All these will go along way in improving the present political structure as well as involve the people of Igbo nation effectively in socio-political situation and make them relevance in the power system in the Nigeria federation.

Conclusion

We, ourselves, our families both those at home and across linguistic borders should show interest in the language. In addition more efforts in publications and extensive media outreach in Igbo language should be made. In line with Ikekeonwu, the opening of an international airport in Igboland (Enugu) is likely to attract foreign business men and women, contractors, investors, among others to the South East. Basic textbooks on the learning of Igbo language and culture could be published and placed at the point of entry (the airport) to help the visitors effectively chart their daily interactions with the indigenes. These and other suggestions raised in this paper would certainly go along way in overcoming the enormous challenges facing Igbo nation in Nigeria and in the contemporary world.

References

Achebe, C. (1971) "The Bane of union: An appraisal of the consequences of union Igbo for Igbo language and literature." In *Anu Magazine*. Vol. 1, No. 1 Pp 33-41.

Afigbo A.E. (1981). *Ropes of sand*. Ibandan: Caxton press.

_____ . (1975). "The place of the Igbo language in our schools. A historical explanation" in Ogbalu and Emenanjo (ed). Pp 70-85. Ibandan: Oxford University Press.

Babajide A.O. (2001). "Language attitude patterns of Nigeria. In Igboanusi," (ed.) *Language attitude and language conflict in West Africa*. Pp 1-13 Ibadan: Enicrownfit Publishers.

Bamgbose, A. (1971). "The English language in Nigeria" in J. Spencer (ed.), the English language in West Africa. London Longman

Chijioke, M.U. (1995). "The development of Igbo language study: A historical perspective." In A.E. Afigbo and F.C.Ogbalu (eds.). Onitsha: University Publishing Company.

Hair, P.E.H (1967). *The early study of Nigerian language*. Cambridge: Cambridge University press.

Ikekeonwu, C. I. (2009). Language and gender in Nigeria: perception, patterns and prospects. An inaugural lecture of the University of Nigeria, Nsukka.

Isichei, E. (1973). *The Ibo people and the Europeans*. London: Macmillan.

Mezu, S. Okechukwu. (1974). *Umu Ejima: a play in Igbo*. (Igbo adaptation of Plautus' *Menaechmi*). Owerri: Black Academy Press, Inc.

Nwadike, I.U. (2002). *Igbo language in education: An historical study*. Obosi. Pacific Publishers.

Ohiri-Anichie, C. (2008). "5% of Igbo children do not speak the language." *Ndigbo Journal*. Vol. 1

Okwudishu, A. U. (2010). "Igbo Language studies: Yesterday, today and tomorrow." In *Journal of Igbo studies*. Vol. 5 (1-13).

Olebra, N. (2008). "Language, culture and power," In *Journal of Nigeria languages and culture*. Vol. 10, No 2 Pp 1-14 Enugu: SAN Press Ltd.

Oraka, L.N. (1983). *The foundation of Igbo studies*, Onitsha: University Publishing Company.

Ugwuona, C.N. (2004) Language choice and attitudinal differences on Igbo language: A case of Nsukka Urban. A M.A. Thesis. University of Nigeria, Nsukka.

Ugwuona, C.N. (2013). A sociolinguistic study of language contact in Ubolo speech community, Enugu State Nigeria. A doctoral thesis University of Nigeria, Nsukka.

Uwalaka, M. A. (2001). "The anguish of Igbo as a mother tongue: internal and external conflict," In Igboanusi, H. ed. *Language attitude and language conflict in West Africa*. Pp 50-68. Ibadan. Enicrown fit publishers.

Ward, I.C. (1929). *Igbo dialects and the development of a common language*. Cambridge: Heffer & Sons Ltd.

Mammy Water in Igbo Culture: *Ogbuide of Oguta Lake*
by
Dr. Sabine Jell-Bahlsen

Water is Life

Without water there is no life on earth as we know it. Life originates from water, and our bodies largely consist of water. When a space craft travels to another planet, it will report either on the absence or potential presence of water as an indicator of possible life on there. The awareness of water being connected to the life giving force is well-known to humankind since time immemorial and also to modern scientists. The awareness is largely lost on urban dwellers of the industrial world in the USA, Europe and in Africa. The knowledge of the connection between, and the sacredness of *water and life* is firmly anchored in the culture and custom of rural Igbo communities. This is attested in proverbs such as, *Ndu mmiri, ndu azu* – "So long as there is a living body of water, there will always be live fishes in it."

Sources and Background

Professor Ikenna Nzimiro of Oguta not only introduced me to Igbo culture but encouraged me to expand his own original research to cover the Oru-Igbo group of towns and focus specifically on the senior town of Orsu-Obodo, Oguta II, in 1978. I lived there for an entire year then, began to learn about the divine pair of water deities, *Uhammiri* and *Urashi*, and have continually expanded and updated my research ever sincefocusing 1) on the significance of *Mammy Water* in Igbo culture, and 2) on the importance of this religious belief beyond Nigeria.

What I have learnt from Oru-Igbo culture on water as a divine force and on the female side of the universe is ever relevant. Although many events and statements I have recorded and documented in my book took place in the past, I am presenting my findings in the "ethnographic present." This is to acknowledge the continued vitality and relevance of Igbo culture, its achievements, and the veracity of its wisdom, especially on the existential and spiritual significance of water. Culture matters (Harrison and Huntington 2000) and is part of one's history and individual and collective identity, productivity, and progress. Socio-economic relations and political economy are basic to a culture. Moreover, culture is defined as the sum total of a people's material, economic, political, social, artistic, philosophical and spiritual achievements transmitted from one generation to the next.

Researching *Mammy Water*

Mammy Water is a Pidgin English name with different spellings applied to diverse water deities with many local names throughout West Africa including Igbo communities in Southeast Nigeria. The colonizers were conquerors of territories and more interested in the earth (*terra*) than in water they could not control. As a result, the earth goddess, *Ani/Ala* is much more widely known and documented among researchers than the Water Goddess. Moreover, an academic controversy on the authenticity of the Water Goddess took off from the foreign image associated with the English name, *Mammy Water*. The well-known *Mammy Water* icon depicts a woman with long hair, snakes and often a mermaid fishtail not part of the original print. The chromolithograph itself has been traced to a German artist, is known as "snake charmer," and may have been designed for export to India. This print was introduced to Nigeria in the early 1900s, spread quickly, and gained popularity among different ethnic groups who share similar ideas on the connectedness between water and life or female fecundity. The image with its recurrent features is immediately recognizable, has frequently been copied and applied to a host of diverse yet related water deities, both male and female, some androgynous, and still others conceived of as a pair.

Foreign researchers were slow to accept the notion of an indigenous African water goddess. They have largely taken their clues from the foreignness of the imported image and its foreign name. This discourse follows three major strands of thought: 1) A psychiatrist and some psychologists associate *Mammy Water* with mental illness, e.g. fear of *Ogbanje* (Wintrob 1970) 2) Sociologists and social anthropologists often emphasize the imported nature of the image and its name, and associate these with an oedipal desire for foreign wealth, goods, or powers beyond the reach of the indigenous communities (Fabian 1978, Bastian 1993, 1997) 3) Art historians have also focused primarily on the imported character of the artwork and suggested that because art may transcend linguistic borders, and due to the image's frequent adaptations and imitations, the icon itself may have become the source of a new creation within a conglomerate of indigenous spirit worlds (Salmons 1977, Drewal 1988, Paxon 1980). My own research takes the opposite approach: I am taking my clues primarily from ethnography rather than from imports. Ethnographic research relies primarily on first-hand participant observation, interviews, and oral literature. Structured interviews nterviews come first. Second and equally significant are casual conversations and stories. Third and most important are statements, songs and other utterances directed at spirits, ancestors or deities addressed in prayers, invocations and songs. The English language serves as a *lingua franca* for communication in my research and its presentations, while my mother-tongue is German. Most of the relevant oral sources are in Igbo, and all original verbal statements, prayers and songs were carefully tape recorded, transcribed and later translated into English. My ethnography has continually grown and is complemented by social science, history, literary and humanities research. My understanding of *Mammy Water* prioritizes local beliefs and cultural practices, rather than the imported icon and name. Dr.

Chinwe Achebe corroborates this view when she explains: *Nne Mmiri* is a female deity with variants of local names, e.g. *Idemili* . . . With the arrival of Europeans to this part of the world, "*Nne Mmiri*" became known as "*Mami Wota*" - a translation which enabled the local inhabitants communicate the existence and exploits of this female deity to foreigners. (Achebe 1986: 15) *Ogbuide,* the Goddess of Oguta Lake is one such "local variant." The female water deity is also known as "*Mammy Water,*" yet only under certain circumstances such as in conversation with foreigners or outsiders, and under special conditions of vocation and priesthood.

Ogbuide/Uhammiri

Ogbuide, the Goddess of Oguta Lake is a major representative of the female side of the universe, recognized since time immemorial as "mother," and credited with giving life, nourishment, protection and support ("Nwapa interview" in: Jell-Bahlsen 1998). Yet, she is also venerated with awe. *Ogbuide* has multiple names and titles, just like the people who worship her. *Uhammiri* is her ancient local name, while the name *Ogbuide* may be traced to a wave of immigration from Benin. The goddess' title, *Eze Mmiri* is used in prayer when addressing her directly and in respectful phrases such as *Eze Mmiri di Egwu*—"the Water Monarch is great / awesome," offered as a greeting to the goddess as well as to her priestess. One of her praise names is *Ogbuama*; she sparkles like the rainbow and is extremely beautiful, a "killer beauty."*Ogbuide*'s priesthood is traditionally hereditary and male. However, additional male and female individuals may attain this priesthood through vocation associated with healing and initiation. They are known as *Mammy Water* priests and priestesses. Some are diviners and/or herbalists. They may lead a group of fellow worshippers who are often former patients. These groups known as *Ndi Mmiri* meet regularly once in the 4 or 8 day Igbo market week to hold services for the goddess on *Orie* day. Each group has its own music, costumes and dances. Their performances are artistically versatile and psychologically significant. The water goddess is situated in the pre-Christian pantheon of Gods and Goddesses. The Supreme Being, *Chukwu*, is beyond shape and gender. Members of the pantheon of deities below *Chukwu* may act as mediators, but also hold divine powers of their own. There are two complementary sides, with largely male ancestors who founded human custom and civilization on the one hand, and the nourishing, yet more volatile forces of nature on the other. Among the latter are the female earth goddess and the female water goddess (Jell-Bahlsen 2008). The water goddess' preeminent position in the eternal cycle of life is outlined by Dr. Chinwe Achebe in her book, *The World of the Ogbanje* (1986). In this circular notion of life and time, the human being must pass through water twice: once before being born, and again after death. The requirement of crossing water after death is a recurrent theme in ancient Egyptian beliefs and images, and also in Greek mythology where humans must cross the river *Styx* before reaching the underworld, *Hades*. Yet, the notion of crossing water again before re-incarnation links water not only to death, but also to the birth of new life. Furthermore, the water goddess' role at this pre-natal transition is crucial: she is believed to control the cross roads and challenges humans before their re-incarnation to either live up to their destiny, or change it with her help which will then require gratitude, service and obedience to the goddess later in life.

Ogbuide is primarily venerated as *the* life giver. People pray to the goddess for children. Oguta's renowned novelist, Flora Nwapa has cast doubt on the lake goddess' ability to grant children (Nwapa 1961, 1966). However, Nwapa had her own agenda, pursing issues of modern womanhood and specifically emphasizing a woman's worth beyond producer of children (Jell-Bahlsen 2007). Thus, some of Nwapa's texts may seem provocative to people who worship *Ogbuide*. This has also been misunderstood by some researchers to suggest that "Uhammiri has no children." (Wilentz 1992). This preposterous proposition is spread by Christian proselytizers who aim at discrediting native beliefs in favor of their own. Yet, a careful reading of Nwapa reveals that she did not intend to discredit *Ogbuide's/ water's /woman's* power to give and protect life. In Nwapa's novels, the individuals who negate the lake goddess' gifts are liars and negative characters who harm the novels' heroines. Nwapa's questioning of *Ogbuide*'s gifts was a critique of some of Oguta's customary norms and ideas, but not intended to unravel the entire culture (Jell-Bahlsen 2007).

Ogbuide's husband is the river god, *Urashi*. The divine pair ideally works together to achieve procreation and a productive life. This ideal of complementary duality (Nnaemeka 2012) or "complementary binarism" (Osuagwu 2013) is a core concept of Igbo culture and expressed in many proverbs (Nnaemeka 1998, Ilogu 1974). Of course, human marriages are not always as harmonious as portrayed in the divine ideal. Flora Nwpa challenges this idealized harmony when she portrays *Uhammiri* and her husband *Urashi* as constantly quarreling in her children's book, *Mammywata* (Nwapa 1979). *Ogbuide* is *the* major reference point in the daily life of the rural Riverine Igbo communities around Oguta Lake. Society's norms are attributed to the lake goddess. The clues for the major traditional economic activities of farming and fishing are ritually connected to the flooding and falling waters of Oguta Lake and its adjoining rivers and creeks. *Ogbuide*'s rules once guided all communal activities, daily life, codes of conduct, and especially reproductive behavior. The lake goddess' requirement of post-partum sexual abstinence for an entire 2 year period of breast feeding is one example. This rule results in birth-spacing and moreover, in the formation of named male and female age-grades every three years. This institution in turn facilitates keeping track of personal and communal history and also supports communal projects.

Ogbuide is perceived as a nourishing and loving, but also a strict mother. The harbinger of children and wealth, *Ogbuide's* wrath is feared; she is volatile and may change a person's destiny; she harbors both, fortune and doom; she brings life but could also take life and bring illness and death — especially to those who are ungrateful for her gifts, or do not follow her rules. Although credited with enforcing custom, the water goddess' domain is transition and change. She is dynamic and may change her appearance, just like Igbo custom is dynamic and may be adapted to new circumstances rather than being a static entity as portrayed in the colonial system (Obiora 1993). Examples include the faking of female circumcision (Nwapa 1961, 1966), the abolition of prenuptial female promiscuity at Orsu-Obodo, or the dethroning of a "sacred" king at Oguta during colonial times. Due to this inherent flexibility, the *Mammy Water* priestess' group of worshippers may even include and protect twins and mothers of twins otherwise scorned by Igbo custom (Uchendu 1965).

The image popularly known as "Mammy Water" features a woman with long hair and two big snakes (Figure: the *Mammy Water* icon). Local worshippers immediately recognize these snakes as royal pythons. Pythons were once held sacred in many parts of Igboland, the Niger Delta and Benin, and if accidentally killed, buried like a human. Pythons were regarded as messengers of God, and especially of the water goddess. In the Oguta area and elsewhere, local stories attest to the python's special position in the culture and the power ascribed to this creature. Like the goddess on whose behalf they act, the python is associated with the gift of life, but also with death. Pythons figure prominently on antique war drums and shrines (Cole and Aniakor 1984). A python may carry a message from God, or punish (Chinua Achebe 1986). Situated and vacillating between the worlds of the living and the dead, the python is associated with healing and appears on a *Mammy Water* healer-priestess' sign board (Jell-Bahlsen 2008:202 figure 73) - like the snake on the Greek asclepiad used by medical doctors worldwide to advertise their practice and recognized by patients to this day, who perceive the snake as a powerful icon associated with life and death. On the asclepiad, the snake represents divine force enabling life over death. (Jell-Bahlsen 2008: 198, figure 71).

Another line of thought interprets the enigmatic creature negatively. The ideas of a sacred python, a female Goddess, female empowerment, duality or complementary binarism, of water the life giver, of circular time and reincarnation are alien to Christian and Muslim ideologies alike. The snake was once associated with the divine power of pro-creation, life, death and re-incarnation in many cultures around the world. However, some people regarded this creature as an icon of sin and evil. Today, the Water Goddess and other traditional beliefs and their followers are violently attacked by fanatics in a rapidly changing Nigeria where pre-Christian Igbo beliefs, custom and cultural achievements are being destroyed, by people ignorant and hostile towards their own history and culture. Yet, the famous African-American author, Maya Angelou, has observed "No man can know where he is going, unless he knows exactly where he has been." Responding to "The Slaughter of the Gods," a report on the destruction of Igbo masquerades, anthropologist Simon Ottenberg remarked, "A society that completely denies its past is a lost society. Or is it that Igbo society is a lost society so that it then completely denies its past?" and historian Adiele Afigbo warned: "To embrace new ways of doing and being is one thing, to completely turn your back on the old ways of doing and being which kept you going for millennia and which brought you to the point where you were able to embrace new ways, is an entirely different thing. It signifies death of the essence."

Conclusion

There are important lessons to be learnt from Igbo culture in general and from its religious beliefs in particular focusing on life, nature and more specifically water. Even without believing in water as a divine force, one ought to respect those who do. Water is increasingly recognized as more valuable than both, petroleum and gold. Some even predict a third and final world war over water. This resource of tremendous value must neither be wasted nor polluted. Even without worshipping water, we owe her respect. Our failure to respect coastal shorelines, courses of rivers, and the purity of creeks and lakes has devastating consequences, e.g. when a Typhoon recently caused major damages in the Philippines where coastal mangroves protecting the area had been destroyed in favor of large-scale commercial shrimp farming. On the other hand, pristine waters can turn into a major source of income through tourism as in many instances in Europe, or at Oshogbo where the River Oshun and her sacred sites attract tourists from all over the world. There is a perceived urgency for an awareness of the indebtedness to one's own history, culture and natural resources such as water as a source of prosperity, well-being and life itself.

References

Achebe, Chinua. *Anthills of the Savannah*. New York: Anchor Books, 1986.

Achebe, Chinwe, C. *The World of the Ogbanje*. Enugu: Fourth Dimension Press, 1986.

Bastian, Misty L. "Married in the Water: Spirit Kin and Other Afflictions of Modernity in Southeastern Nigeria." *Journal of Religion in Africa,* 27 (2), 1997

_____. "Bloodhounds Who Have no Friends: Witchcraft and Locality in the Nigerian Popular Press. In: *Modernity and Its Malcontents: Ritual and Power in Postcolonial Africa.* (Ed.) Jean Comaroff &John Comaroff. Chicago: University of Chicago Press, 1993: 129-166.

Cole, Herbert and Chike Aniakor, eds. *Igbo Arts. Community and Cosmos*. Los Angeles: Fowler Museum of Art, 1984.

Drewal, Henry. "Performing the Other: Mami Wata Worship in West Africa". *The Drama Review*, T118, 1988: 160-185.

Fabian, Johannes. "Popular Culture in Africa: Findings and Conjectures." *Africa*, 48, 1978: 315-334.

Harrison, Lawrence, E. and Samuel P. Huntington, eds. *Culture Matters. How Values Shape Human Progress.* New York: Basic Books, 2000.

Ilogu, Edmund. *Christianity and Igbo Culture*. Leiden: E.J. Brill, 1974.

_____. "Ofo - A Religious Symbol of Igboland." Lagos: *Nigeria Magazine* no. 82, 1964.

Jell-Bahlsen, Sabine. *Mammy Water in Igbo Culture. Ogbuide of Oguta Lake*. Enugu, Ezu Books, 2014.

_____. *The Water Goddess in Igbo Culture Ogbuide of Oguta Lake*. Trenton, NJ: Africa World Press, 2008.

_____. "Interview with Flora Nwapa."*Flora Nwapa: Emerging Perspectives*. Ed. by Marie Umeh. Trenton, NJ: Africa World Press, 1998: 633-654.

_____. "Flora Nwapa and Oguta's Lake Goddess; Artistic Liberty and Ethnography." *Dialectical Anthropology* 31, 2007: 253-262.

Nnaemeka, Obioma. "Keynote Address." *Igbo Studies Association* Meeting, Enugu 2012.

_____. Ed. *Sisterhood, Feminisms, and Power*: *From Africa to the Diaspora*. Trenton, NJ: Africa World Press. 1998.

Nwapa, Flora. *Efuru*. London: Heinemann. 1961.

_____. *Idu*. London: Heinemann, 1966.

_____. Flora.*Mammywater*. Enugu, Nigeria: Tana Press, 1979.

Obiora, Lesleye Amede. "Reconsidering African Customary Law." *Legal Studies Forum* 17 (3), 1993: 217-252.

Osuagwu, Chidi. "*Ndu m Ikenga ndu m ihite*; Obowu Identity recovery and rectification in post-invasion Africa." 2013 Ezumezu-Wiyi Lecture, Otoko Obowu, 16 August 2013.

Paxson, Barbara. "Mammi Water: Ideas and Images of a New World Transcendent Being." Seattle: Univ. of Washington: Master Thesis, 1980.

Salmons, Jill. "Mammy Wata". *African Arts*, 10, Spring 1977: 8-15.

Uchendu, V.C. *The Igbo of Southeastern Nigeria*. New York: Holt, Rinehart and Winston, 1965.

Wilentz, Gay. "Flora Nwapa, Efuru." *Binding Cultures*: *Black Women Writers in Africa and the Diaspora*. Bloomington: Indiana University Press, 1992.

Wintrob, Ronald M., M.D. "Mammy Water: Folk Beliefs and Psychotic Elaborations in Liberia." *Canadian Psychiatric Association Journal,* 15, No.2, April 1970: 143-157.

Ofo in Igbo Culture
by
Professor Richard C. Okafor

Abstract

According to the Oxford University Press (1973), a symbol is "something that stands for, represents or denotes something else...especially a material object representing or taken to represent something immaterial or abstract" (p.2218). Primarily then, the purpose of creating a symbol is so that it will express something of a sort to the understanding of those who should know when they express the intended purpose they communicate. Symbols serve to transmit a message in a condensed manner as well as to focus the mind on an idea or ideal. They are, therefore, cultural shorthand. People who use a common symbol are mostly invariably linked in a common bond. Any time they look at their symbol, they seem to be in a mystic communication or communion. And so a symbol is forever in a lucid oration. The right audience has only to tune in or listen.

It is significant that Igbo symbols are made from, on, or with materials available in the Igbo environment and culture area. One of the most important symbols of the Igbo is the *Ofo/Owho/Oho*. It is not a common tree and the Igbo regard it as a special tree created by God for their social, ritual and ceremonial functions. For example, *Oji ofo adi ato n'uzo/n'ije* (The traveller with *ofo* can never be lost away from home); *Ofo ka idide ji awa ani* (The tender worm uses its *ofo* to pierce the earth). This paper discusses *Ofo* in Igbo culture and its use as a symbol of uprightness, justice, innocence and truth in a dynamic Igbo culture.

Introduction

Culture is the totality of a people's way of life by which they can be differentiated or identified from other groups of people. It has two components - material and non-material. The material aspect of culture includes tangible things like food, housing, tools, clothing, utensils, weapons, medicine, etc., while the non-material aspect includes religion, ideas, beliefs, languages, values, traditions, etc. Therefore, culture can only exist where there are people who live in an environment. Described as *man-made part of the environment* (Herskovits, 1955), it is central to life in a human society. People express their culture through their language, dress, music and dance, drama, spirit-manifests, marriage, musical instruments, religion, traditional festivals and ceremonies, myths and legends, sports and games, religion and rituals, arts and crafts, traditional markets, agriculture, architecture and settlement patterns. An important characteristic of culture is its dynamism such that it can cope with changing and changeable environments - what it was yesterday, it is not now and what it is now, it will not be in the future.

This dynamism is encountered through cultural contact, acculturation, Western education, Christianity and Islam, and other acculturative agencies like trade, travels and Information Technology.

Since culture is the cumulative experience of a people in their years of systematic attempts to master their environments so that they can enjoy a higher quality of life, culture and environment are intertwined. In Nigeria, there are many vegetation zones - the mangrove swamp, the rainforest, the deciduous forest and the savannah. Because of this, their fauna and flora vary. Nigerians, including the Igbo, have learnt through many thousands of years to master their environments and their resources. Invariably, there is also a close link between culture and agriculture. Botanists have identified 600,000 plants worldwide yet very few of them account for three-quarters of human menu worldwide. These include yams, rice, maize (corn), cocoyam, beans, groundnuts, Bambara groundnuts, coconuts, banana, cassava, breadfruit (*ukwa*), *oji* (kolanut), bitter kola (*aku inu*), pear, apples, *oha/ora, okro, egwusi, ogili*, bitter-leaf (*onugbu*), *ugu, uda, uzuza, ogbonno*, etc.

With respect to the construction of houses, various species of plants feature as structural and roofing (thatch) materials, e.g., palm tree, (*nkwu*), raffia palm (*ngwo*), iroko and grass. Several species of woody plants are used for ceremonial and customary purposes that are of immense value to the people, e.g., kola nuts, palm-wine, breadfruit, oil bean, etc. Some other species are sources of traditional religious worship. Among these are *ekpili, ngwu* and *ofo*.

Ofo in Igbo culture

Much of what I have written here on *ofo* in Igbo culture is based on the Focus Group Discussion (FGD) Methodology. This means that much of the information I obtained on *ofo* was based on interviews, interactions and discussions with people. However, I also obtained some information from some related literature and fieldwork.

Ofo/owho/oho/offor tree is not a common tree. There are not as many of them as other trees. Consequently, it is not commonly found. It germinates on its own and is not harvested until it falls down from its branches. Because of these attributes, some people regard it as a special tree created by God for the Igbo for their social, ritual and ceremonial functions, hence Ilogu (1974) states:

The *ofo* stick is very important in Ibo religion and life...It is a stick of varying sizes from about two inches long, and a half an inch in diameter, to something near five inches long and one and a half inches in diameter, becoming thinner towards the tail end. It is made out of a branch of the *Detarium Senegalense* tree. One of the special features of this tree is that the branches fall off from the parent trunk when they are fully grown. No cutting of the *ofo* is done. It is believed that *Chukwu* (the great God), purposely created this tree to be sacred, and by the manner its branches fall off unbroken, he (*Chukwu*) symbolizes the way families grow up and establish new families and lineages. Therefore, the *ofo* made out of these branches is the abode of the spirit of dead ancestors, hence the authority and the sacredness of *ofo*, as well as the special place given to it as the emblem of unity, truth and indestructibility for the individual or the group possessing the *ofo* (p. 18)

Ofo Tree at Umuezedume, Umuagba Owa, Ezeagu LGA, Enugu State

In Ogwofia, my hometown, for example, there are not more than six known *ofo* trees in the entire community. And because of the sacredness attached to it, the *ofo* tree is not usually felled down. But, when important situations arise for felling it down-construction of buildings and roads-it is cut down, after performing appropriated rituals and sacrifices. One of my informants, Mr. Innocent Eloike, informed me that in 1987 at Isulo, Orumba, in Anambra LGA, an *ofo* tree was cut down, during the construction of a road. It was, however, pushed aside the road and no firewood was collected from it as a sign of respect for a tree that is a symbol of truth and justice among the Igbo. In Owa, before an *ofo* tree is cut down, a ritual ceremony, called *ikpuo ishi* (shaving its hair), is performed by killing a cock for it by the oldster of the community after appropriate rituals and sacrifices have been performed.

Ofo is a tree with long branches and tiny leaves. Its botanical name is *Detarium senegalense*. Its fruits are brown in colour and as round as *ujulu*

(native mango). Among the Igbo, *ofo* is a symbol of justice, as the Cross is the symbol of Christianity and the Crescent of the moon, that of Islam. A symbol is part of material culture. It is an emblem, that which by custom and convention represents something else. Symbols are also close systems of communication. They serve to transmit a message. Each people have their own symbols but there are some that can only be interpreted by a few individuals-diviners and secret societies.

There are two types of symbols among the Igbo-the mystical and the authoritative. The mystical symbols include the *ofo* and *ogu* while the authoritative symbols include the *abuba ugo* (eagle feather), red cap, elephant tusks and the ankle-lace. Physically, *ofo* is a short ritual staff, which naturally falls down from a branch of tree without being cut. An *ofo* is usually made up of about six or more *ofo* pieces tied together with a rope and smeared with ground pepper, blood and feathers of cocks killed during ritual offerings. With the passage of time, the layers of theses make the *ofo* to grow fatter and fatter. Artistically, it may be very unimpressive, but it communicates several moral and mystical concepts of the Igbo. It is a person's or community's bastion against the forces of evil, oppression or malice, malevolence and wickedness, provided that one has "clean hands and a pure heart." It stands for the inevitable and unalterable prevalence of the forces of good over those of evil. It stands for hope that provided a person is without blemish; his enemies shall not have the last laugh over him. *Ofo* derives its protective power from virtue (Emeka, 2004). According to Ilogu (1974:19): "It is used by the Ala priests to remove the evil effects of abominations after proper sacrifices have been offered." A sacrifice is, above all, a way of entry into relations with the ancestor, the dialogue of Thee and Me.

Ofo also symbolizes the collective love and force of the ancestors standing guard over the present generation and the continuity of the culture. Such forces can be very terrible when on the offensive or in action. Mbiti (1969) refers to the departed as the "living-dead" whose personal immortality is expressed or externalized by the living through sacrifices, the pouring of libations and other rituals. These are symbols of communion and fellowship and remembrances; the mystical ties that bind the "living-dead" to those on earth.

Let's examine the various roles played by *ofo* in Igbo life. First and foremost, the oldster in the family, community or clan holds *ofo*. The holders are usually persons who have taken the pre-*ozo* title-*iwa alo*-or the *ozo* title. In Owa, Ezeagu LGA of Enugu State, part of their paraphernalia are the *okobo* (box stool), the *ofo*, which is kept inside the *okobo* and the *akpulu alo*-a piece of ritual staff.

(A) Ofo on top of an *Okobo*
(B) Ofo sticks

A family's ofo is held by the oldster (*ogaala, onyi-ishi, okpala/okpara, di-okpala, diokpa, duuru, okenye*) who may not necessarily have taken a title, and, therefore not entitled to have an *okobo*. Because the head of each level of the lineage is charged with holding the *ofo* of that group, he becomes not only its political and social leader but also that 'family's' priest and uses the *ofo* in blessing the people at all public worship. At the death of such a head, the next *okpala/okpara* inherits it. To transfer such an *ofo*, a ceremonial-washing is performed by a priest in which a cock is killed and its blood smeared on the *ofo*. Just as the 'family's' *ofo* domiciles in the home of the oldest male, the *ofo* of the village, town or clan is likewise is likewise held by the oldsters in those communities. The chief priest of a village shrine is also a holder of the *ofo*. The *ofo* of the lineage or clan and therefore must be displayed when all the living are assembled for important 'family' discussion. Poverty or wealth is, therefore, not the determinant of this status but age. And so, age is the guardian of a family's *ofo*.

Anuehe Eneje (a.k.a. *Wa nkwu a na-agbo igu*), the Chief Priest of *Anu Amofia* (earth goddess/shrine), Ogwofia Owa, Ezeagu LGA, Enugu State, seated on his *okobo*, holds a buffalo's horn *(mpu atu)* for drinking palm wine, and the *akpulu alo* and *ofo* in front of him. The first thing that an ofo holder does in the morning is to wash his hands and pray with his *ofo-igo owho/ofo ututu*-before any interaction with the people. In addition, he uses *oji* (kola nuts) and *atawa/utaba* (tobacco snuff). Such a prayer could read as follows:

> God, the Creator of heaven and earth,
> I thank you for making me wake up healthy this morning
> And for the gift of a new day
> I come with greetings and pleadings
> It is kola I bring. It is all I can offer
> While you take it as a whole, we take it in lobes
> Our forefathers chose kola for offerings and hospitality

Of all the food on earth, only the kola is not cooked by water and fire
But by the spoken word
Whoever brings kola, brings life, health, peace, prosperity, fruitfulness of the womb, and children

> So, our fathers, hear my voice
> God, hear my voice
> Let our enemies not laugh over us
> But, let whoever comes to kill me, kill himself
> I pray for the good of family, both at home and abroad
> What is good is what we want
> Ward off evil, bring good
> Let diseases, evil, hunger, accidents and death flee away
> What should consume the head should preferably wear a helmet for one head
> Is more valuable/precious than ten head pieces
> Let the kite perch and the eagle perch
> Whichever denies the other the right to perch, may its wings break
> Let today be better than yesterday
> I offer this kola nut with a child's hand while you receive it with an elder's hand
> On that I break the kola nut

As he says this prayer, he throws bits of the *oji* on the *ofo*. Thereafter, he strikes the *ofo* on the ground, meaning so be it. All those around will partake of the kola nut, but women do not partake of the particular lobe of the kola nut used for the prayer. It should be mentioned here that, on normal occasions, when kola nuts are passed round to qualified and entitled persons to break them, after the most rightful breaker has broken his kola nut, others would say in unison, *ofo solu ibe ya lee*, that is may our prayers work together.

Members of a family group usually pay some homage to their oldsters as a sign of love and respect, and to incur/merit God's blessings to attain old age. They normally bring some presents and even money to these oldsters, who use their *ofo* to bless them, thus:

> It will be well with you
> Your enemies shall not prevail over you
> God will protect you in your work
> And our ancestor shall shelter you, etc.
> Therefore, he strikes the *ofo* on the ground.

Ofo is also used to curse. Any offence against a people (like the destruction of lives and Government property that took place in Anambra State in 2004) would attract a curse from a people to the perpetrators of such heinous crimes, by striking an ofo on the ground. Between 10 to 13 November, 2004, hoodlums unleashed an unprecedented violence on Anambra State, destroying and burning down public buildings including the

Governor's Office, that of his Deputy, the State Independent Electoral Commission Office, the State Broadcasting Service complexes in both Onitsha and Awka, the State Government-owned Ikenga Hotels amongst others. Apart from reported deaths, several government-owned and private vehicles were also vandalized and burnt in the mayhem.

In my hometown, Owa, there is a festival for the veneration of or paying homage to the ancestors called *Ndu Ihu*. During this festival, members of the 'family' invite their oldster to their compound to pray for them. Nine tubers of yams (*ji neteghuna*), one cock, palm-wine, kola nuts and *atawa/utaba* (tobacco snuff) are presented to the oldster for this ritual ceremony. The oldster performs this ceremony with his *okobo, akpulu alo, ofo* and a cock. The cock is killed and its blood and feathers are smeared on the ofo and shared according to local prescription. The palm-wine, kola nuts and the *atawa/utaba* are equally offered to the participants. At the end of it, the oldster is given one tuber of yam, while the owner distributes some to other participants and keeps the rest for his household.

To declare one's innocence, a person either says *E jili m ogu ofo* (I have a clear conscience) or *E ji m ogu na-eji m ofo* (I hold ogu on one hand and ofo in another, that is, I am wholly innocent). Ogu is also a symbol of innocence and could be represented by either a piece of broomstick or a stick of *Neubolda laevis* (*ogilisi* or *akoka*), or an ordinary stick.

In Ogwofia Owa, Ezeagu LGA of Enugu State, a dispute between two persons could be settled by *wa-dibie/nwa dibia* (diviner) with two *ogu* that identify each of the disputants. Payment of some money is made for this money. The *ogu* picked by the diviner determines who is right. If foul play (*akabe*) were established, the claimant would go to the oldster for justice to be done to him (*ku emefuo ashushua*), and the offender to be condemned. Different types of *ogu*, as mentioned supra, are used to identify each claimant. In Nsukka, at the end of such a ceremony, the oldster would say:

Woke shi nu ya ji oho	A man says that he holds the *oho*
Wanyi shi nu ya ji oho	A woman says that she holds the *oho*
Manu oho kwunyilu onye-okale	Let the *oho* stand for the innocent or
Manu ofo ma onye ji ya	But, the *ofo* knows the offender/culprit

It has to be noted, however, that where there are witnesses in any dispute between persons, such witnesses are given the *ofo*, which they hold in their hands while giving testimonies in a case. It is the folk belief that anyone who swears falsely with the *ofo* would suffer for it or even die as a result.

Ofo is, however, used in oath taking when all forms of arbitration and settlement have failed. Such an oath taking is administered by the *wa dibie/nwa dibia* (diviner) who uses the *ofo* as one of his paraphernalia for administering the oath. It is generally believed that the ancestors, whose spirits the *ofo* represents, are always helpful in determining a successful result of the particular subject for which a client seeks divination. Here, the expression *okwa ihe ejilu n'ogu bu ihe a ghulu n'owho?* (Is it what I swore on the *owho* that was mentioned in the *ogu?*) is applied.

Ofo is also used to ward off trespassers in a farm or an economic tree. The owner ties a rope round the farm or tree and attaches *ofo*, which he removes each time he enters the farm or wants to harvest fruits from the economic tree. Failure to do this brings to him the same wrath as would befall a trespasser. And, so, people avoid tampering with a farm so warded off.

Ofo is used for warning as is implied in the saying *Ome ihe jide ofo* - whoever acts should be upright. This proclaims a well-known Igbo philosophy of social action, which means that a person must always think, speak or act from the stand of justice and uprightness. Besides, this widespread and acceptable mystical symbol in Igbo culture is one of the names given to the Igbo, as personal names, title and praise names:

Offor	- A just man
Oforbike	- *Ofo* is my strength
Oforkansi	- Innocence or being on the right side prevails over charms or poisons
Ofordille	- A just person is powerful
Oforka / (Oforkaja)	- It is better to be on the right side than to offer sacrifice
Ejiofor/Ejimofor	- The upright one; one who upholds justice
Oguejiofor	- A justified war/battle

Furthermore, *ofo* is used to empower or to give mandate to people among the Igbo. This is explicated in such pithy statements as the following:

Ogugo owho bu idude ji awa anu ibe - The earthworm penetrates the soil through uprightness. In other words, a just person will always succeed.

Oji ofo adi ato n'uzo n'ije - The traveller with *ofo* can never be lost away from home.

Ofo ka idide ji awa ani - The tender worm uses its *ofo* to pierce the earth

Ide ji ofo awa ani - It is through the power of *ofo* that the flood burrows the hand ground

Ihe n'owho yi - *Ofo* is not for nothing. It is not a trifling matter

Oji ofo ga ana - An upright person must be free of any accusation

Oji ofo ka onye ji nshi - A holder of *ofo* (i.e., An upright person) is more powerful than a person armed with charms

Isi-aka nwata bu ofo ya - A child's thumb is his/her *ofo*. As long as one is innocent, justice could prevail on the side of the lowly.

It might be necessary to give another dimension about the *ofo* as a symbol of nationalism, historiography and solidarity as reported by Professor Canon Edmund Ilogu in his book, *Christianity and Igbo Culture* (1974)

One particular feature of Ngwa traditional religious ceremony is the annual *Ofo* ceremony performed at Okpala Ngwa, the traditional headquarters or the seat of the *Okpara* (priest elder) of the Ngwa people. At this ceremony the eight traditional *Ofo* (religious sacred wooden staves in which the spirit of the ancestor is believed to live) belonging to the eight ancestor-founders of the eight sub-clans of Ngwa, are presented and "washed," that is to say, cleansed and revitalized. It is a ceremony for re-enacting the solidarity of the people under the covenant of their unity through common ancestry and the protection of one clan god. This annual ceremony is continued even now and some Christians who, fifty years ago, would not witness it, do so today as identification exercise with the rest of their fellow clansmen. This further emphasizes the dual nature of existence of most Ibo people-one traditional with little interruption from outside cultural influences and the other, mainly town life, manifesting the impact of outside cultural influences. This dual existence can also be detected in the people's religious life-one phase is Christian life, another phase is traditionally Ibo with its religious life (pp.: 109-110)

Finally, the fruits of *ofo* are licked and the seeds are used for the preparation of soup for swallowing *fufu* among some Igbo communities like Mgbowo, Abakaliki and Owa, to mention but a few. Today, the impact of Christianity has tended to affect the *ofo*, especially the killing of a cock and the spraying and smearing of its blood and feathers on it during some traditional rituals and sacrifices. However, Christian principles do not oppose some of the principles that make the *ofo* important, that is, the belief in uprightness, justice, equity, innocence, truth, hope, unity and indestructibility. An 'Ode,' *Interger Vitae*, by Horace states:

A man of upright life
Pure and clean does not need a poisoned arrow or spear to guard him
Virtue protects him.

The fruits of *ofo*

Culture is dynamic and, consequently, can cope with changing and changeable environments. It is experience that implicates change and continuity. Provided that it is open to constructive new ideas, culture offers the best accommodation for a high quality of life while maintaining the equilibrium in human society. Therefore, the use of *ofo* as a symbol of uprightness, justice, innocence and truth will still be pervasive in a dynamic Igbo culture.

References
Basden, G.T. (1966). *Among the Ibos of Nigeria*. London: Frank Cass & Co. Ltd.
Eloike, I.O. (2001). Oral Interview
Emeka, I.N. (2004). Symbols. In R.C. Okafor and L.N. Emeka (Eds.) *Nigerian Peoples and Culture* (pp. 411-428). Enugu: New Generation Books.
Herskovits, M.J. (1955). *Cultural Anthropology*. New York: Alfred A. Knopf, Inc.
Ilogu, Edmund (1974). *Christianity and Igbo Culture*. Enugu: NOK Publishers.
Mbiti, J.S. (1969). *African Religions and Philosophy*. London: Heinemann.
Okafor, J.C. (n.d.). The Role of Plants in Igbo Culture. Enugu.
Okafor, R.C. (1994). Sacrilege Against the Earth (*Nso Ani*) in Igbo Culture, *Nigerian Field*, 59: 105-110.

SECTION THIRTEEN: WOMEN/YOUTH/CHILDREN/HEALTH

The Youth in the Posterity of Igboland: Victims or Villains?
by
A. N. Aniekwu

Abstract

Empirically, it would seem that the successors of our past heroes in social, business and political life, are not able to sustain the attainments and successes of their progenitors or parents. Yet it is in the hands of these ones that the posterity of our people lie. There is a compulsion to ask the million dollar question, what went wrong? The estates and business empires left behind by these pioneers have crumpled despite the sophisticated western education their children received.

This work essentially looks at the plight of the youth as our future leaders, with a view to gauging their preparedness to sustain the growth and development of the Igbo Nation. The trajectory of this inquiry leads this work to interrogate the actions of the youth and the inactions of the pioneers in getting to this point. The work further reviews these missing links and tries to reestablish a connectivity through some recommendations that may help us locate the points of divergence between what we wish for our children and what they have become.

Introduction

The post Biafra war era in Igboland witnessed many successes especially amongst Igbo business men who despite the losses and trauma of the Civil war still managed to build large enterprises relying on self-help. Chief Augustine Ilodibe was easily Nigeria's biggest transporter with his "Ekene Dili Chukwu" transport business. There were others that built large scale business enterprises in construction, such as Chief R.O. Nkwocha, Chief J. U. Nwankwu, Chief D.O Nkwonta, Chief F.G.N Okoye, etc. Others thrived in industry and real estate such as Chief John Anyaehie, Chief Nnana Kalu, Chief Ferdinand Anaghara, Sir Louis Odumegwu-Ojukwu and Chief Onwuka Kalu, just to mention a few. Those that focused on commerce (import and export) thrived as well, such as Chief G.E Chikeluba and his partners at the GMO Group. Unfortunately, most of these worthy pioneering Igbo sons have all passed on and the estates and business empires they left behind have mostly crumbled. The same is reflected in the lives of our political heroes, thus begging answers to the questions of what went wrong and why with all the modern instruments for managing businesses available in our modern society, the sophisticated business management education that has thrown up 20-year old billionaires, they could not salvage the businesses or even grow them further as are the cases in the West. Businesses which began as family enterprises such as Ford, Daimler Benz, Toyota, Heinz, Guinness, etc and those that trailed the political path like the Kennedys', the Kenyatta's, the Bush family, the Sinawatra of Thailand, etc, have all acquired Worldwide fame as public brands.

It is evident that the points of departure between the essence of our great Igbo leaders and their children are numerous. Most of the benefits our past heroes had that made them successful are no longer available to their children. The normal family upbringing that is rooted in our traditional values are no longer available to them; the quality of education they receive is one of the worst quality in the World; they are exposed to an intense bombardment of decadent and negative foreign influences and information; the protection and provisions that the Society culturally provide for a group that is being nurtured for succession is totally lacking; while the example they are presented with as role models through the lifestyle of their elders and parents is the worst that a youth can be exposed to.

A study of these aberration reveals that the problems may lie more in what the elders or society failed to do and are still not doing, than in what the youth are doing. Have we unwittingly denied our children the necessary survival tools they require for success in a hostile world through wholesale consumption of western ideals and propaganda? Have we neglected to groom our children in our obnoxious quest to remain relevant? Is it too late to begin the process of restoration? The work further reviews these missing links and tries to reestablish a connectivity through some recommendations that may help us locate the points of divergence between what we wish for our children and what they have become.

The Burden of the youth

From generation to generation the youth has remained the treasure and strength of society. The youth of any nation constitute the engine room of its production and developmental processes. They provide the brawn and grit for the national development workforce and military services. Their strength can be utilized for good (example, productive activities) or bad (example, thuggery). The meaning of youth and the way society regards youth, varies across time, space as well as within societies. For developing nations and most particularly for African countries the definition of youth poses a persistent challenge given the socio-economic and political realities within which youth are defined and characterized in policy formulation and design (Odinkalu, 2013). The youth leader of one of the political parties in Nigeria was a man of over 60-years old. The African Youth Charter defines youth as individuals aged 15 to 35.

The African Population is estimated to be more than a billion people of whom over 60% are young men and women under the age 35. The majority of African youth continue to face: unemployment, underemployment, lack of skills, relevant education, access to capital, unmet need for health-related information and services including those related to diagnosis, treatment and care of those living with HIV and above all, prevention of new HIV infections among them. This situation is even more accentuated among youth in rural areas. The greater proportion of youth does not have the opportunity to fully develop its potential and contribute effectively to the realization of the declared Vision and the Mission of Africa's leaders (UNESCO, 2011).

In today's Nigeria, the youth have been demonized and marginalized to the fringes of our society in every respect. Most of the benefits our past heroes had that made them successful are no longer available to the youth. The example they are presented with through the lifestyle of the elders is the worst that a youth can be exposed to. Social indiscipline is shown by what seems to be a total disregard for set rules and regulations. Timing is a typical example of social indiscipline where a programme seldom, if ever, begins on time. Officials and important people assume that no matter what time is specified in a programme, the actual time is whenever the most important personality attending the event arrives. Other serious manifestations of indiscipline is the increasing incivility among young people. This is shown in the election violence perpetrated by idle youths or in student cults at universities. Given that the youth are the future of any nation, unruliness in this group is a cause for concern. It raises questions about what leadership will be like in the near future.

The consequences of this disconnect is that youth unemployment, delinquency and alienation ultimately creates opportunities for their abuse by political elites and business interests. During elections, disgruntled and abandoned youths are recruited by unscrupulous politicians who practice sit-tight' politics in order to cause violence and political thuggery, destruction and vandalism of public property, and assault on the lives of citizens. The response to the spread of violent crime and the breakdown of law and order has been the tendency of some state governments to create their own vigilante groups for self-protection, which tend to exacerbate rather than reduce youth violence. Some transnational corporations are also known to have engaged the services of such groups to protect their property. This trend has further undermined the formal security services such as the police, and has led to the privatization of public security.

Rape cases among the youth are rampant while street children are also a common feature in Nigeria. Homeless children living on the streets are found in most cities. Numerous factors have caused children to turn to the streets, including instability in the home, poverty, hunger, abuse and violence by parents, and displacement caused by clashes in the community. HIV and AIDS have also had tremendous impact on the numbers of orphaned street children. Nigeria is a source, transit and destination country for women and children trafficked for the purposes of forced labour and commercial sexual exploitation. Within Nigeria, women and girls are primarily trafficked for domestic servitude and sexual exploitation, and boys by religious leaders for forced begging; forced street hawking; labour exploitation in agriculture, mining and stone quarries; and domestic labour, etc.

The youth

Nigerian population is estimated to be 170,123,740 as at July 2012 (NPC, 2013) which makes her the most populated nation in Africa. 62% of the population are under 24 years old. The period of Adolescence is between the ages of 10 – 19 years (where as Youth: 15-24 years, Young people: 10-24 years and Children: 0-18 years) (UNFPA 2003). Nigeria's dwindling economy and persistent low human development index of 0.42 (UNDP 2010) has made it difficult to reap the full demographic dividend of the youth bulge. Hence, there is urgent need to put measures in place so as to optimally harness the youth potentials.

There is a consensus of opinion that countries with young age structure are prone to conflicts (Urdal and Sciubba. 2007 and Population Action International, 2007). Given this paradox of youth bulge and radicalism most literatures underscore highly the importance of harnessing the potential of youths effectively and efficiently. But unfortunately, the youth often fail to develop a sense of responsibility necessary for their effective participation. Many factors have been identified for this among which are general apathy, wrong perception of the role of the youth, youth unemployment and abuse of technology. All of these can be summarized as lack of proper education and guidance especially at the family level.

Youth education

Education is the key to creating, adapting and spreading knowledge both for individuals and for Countries. Basic education increases people's capacity to learn and to interpret information. But higher education increases the technical training needed to build a labour force that can keep up with a constant stream of advances, which compress product cycles and speed the depreciation of human capital. And outside the classroom, peoples' working and living environments are the setting for still more learning, well beyond the ages associated with formal education. Recognizing these benefits, many countries have made great strides in expanding enrolment at all levels of education, and a good number have made primary and even secondary education universal (World Bank, 1999).

Basic education with the proper content is very critical for enhancing people's capabilities to harness knowledge while investments in higher education offer the appropriate labour force for enhancing and advancing knowledge base. Besides teaching new and better skills, tertiary education and technical training produce people who can monitor global trends, assess their relevance to the country's prospects and help formulate an appropriate national strategies.

Nigeria's poor human resource base is considered to be its biggest handicap in attracting foreign capital, improving productivity and reducing poverty. The country has 35,000 primary schools with an enrolment of 12.9 million pupils, and 6,400 secondary institutions with an enrolment of 5.1 million. At the tertiary level it has 62 colleges of education (with 86,000 students), 47 polytechnic institutes (120,000), and 42 universities and interuniversity centres (325,000). But its combined primary, secondary and tertiary gross enrolment ratio of 45% is only slightly higher than the average for Sub-Saharan Africa of 42% in 1999. The adult literacy rate remains low at 63%, compared with an average of 73% for developing countries; the average for Sub-Saharan Africa is around 60% (Economic Commission for Africa, 2002).

The country confronts two main problems in human resource development, unemployment among the educated youth and the dwindling federal budgetary allocations to educational institutions. The growing unemployment among recent graduates, particularly at the tertiary level, stems in part from the mismatch between educational output and requirements of the labour market. The quality and relevance of education have declined as academic resources, staff, equipment and facilities have become increasingly in short supply (Hartnett, 2000). As the national population grows, enrolments have outpaced budget allocations. The average enrolment per university in the federal sector rose from 8,300 in 1991/92 to 13,200 in 1998/99 (Dabalen and Oni 2000). But much of the growth has occurred in areas with little labour market demand, while enrolment in such critical areas as Engineering, Medicine and Administration has grown relatively slowly. For example, between 1987 and 1997 the share of science students among university graduates dropped from 29.4% to 24.5%. Under the National Rolling Plan for 2001–03 the federal government had intended to increase science enrolments to more than 54% of the total by 2003 (Nigeria, Ministry of Finance 2000).The declining funding for education poses a major obstacle to solving the problems of poor quality in education and thus of the unemployment among the educated youth. Public spending on education in Nigeria has lagged behind that in other Sub-Saharan countries for many years. As a share of the federal budget, education spending fell sharply from its peak of nearly 15% in 1994 to around 1.8% in 2003 (Fig. 1). This trend reflects a gross lack of understanding or will to embrace policies that are necessary to launch the Country into the global community (Aniekwu and Ogbeide, 2002). The UNESCO recommendation of 26% of National budget allocation to education, which is necessary to correct the imbalance and position the country to benefit from the current global trends in commerce and industry, has never been attained.

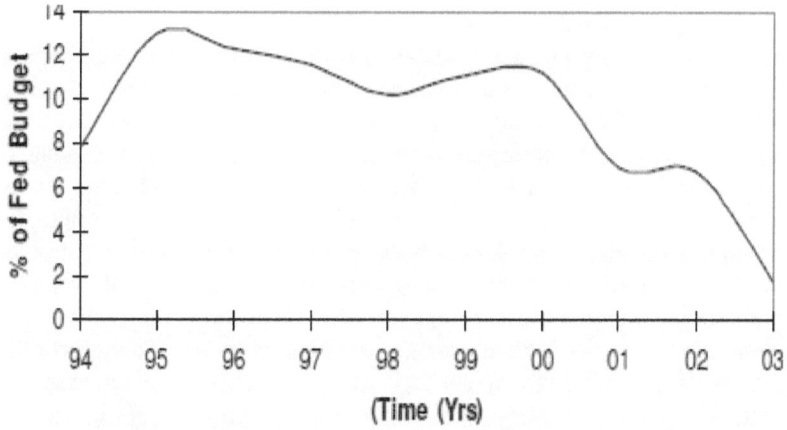

Figure 1. Budgetary allocation to education 1994 – 2003

The long term implication of this situation is extremely disturbing because a time will come when the population who have been so denied their opportunity of meaningful training will be directly responsible for the continued functioning of the country in general. This will obviously amount to a regression.

The Family and the youth

The mother and father as well as the immediate members of the family are the first group of teachers at this level. Later the peer group influence follows. The education at this stage centres on the personal needs of the child such as food, body care, evacuation, sleep etc. This is usually done by petting, rocking, singing and reassuring appellation to soothe and communicate pleasure. This process of education includes all other agencies of learning outside the formal learning system. These agencies include the home (family), church or mosque, peer-group, mass-media. Informal education can also be received in the market, farm, along the road and so on. Though, not deliberately, planned like the formal education, informal education provides learning opportunities for the child to develop his natural potentialities within a given limit. It enlarges the child's scope of learning and helps to build up the comprehensive experience of the formal education system. What the child learns from his/her mother, father, elderly ones, peer group, associations fall under the informal education. In this form of education the children and adults can learn from one another or from the society, consciously or unconsciously. Informal education is still relevant today. It provides some raw data to the child, which could be refined in the formal school system. The child should be guided so that the child learns nothing negative through this form of education.

The Igbo apprenticeship system

Under this apprenticeship system which is traditional to Ndigbo, teenage boys stay with their rich relations or neighbours under a tutelage arrangement in which they are exposed to the rudiments and practice of a particular trade. The apprenticeship arrangement, which is usually sealed without any formal agreement, lasts between 5-10 years, after which the apprentice is settled by his "oga" *[boss]*. This is partly responsible for the dominance of Ndigbo in the country's commerce sector and has absorbed so many of our youth into gainful engagement instead of joining the ranks of the unemployed. Ndigbo are very egalitarian and perform best when they are independent and are indeed used to being independent. The apprenticeship scheme bails out a high percentage of Igbo youths from joblessness. This practice is entirely traditional to Ndigbo and indeed most of our past heroes received whatever business education they had through this arrangement. It is one of the customs of our forefathers that has remained relevant in today's Nigeria and the world at large. It not only assures our youths of an independent life after the training, but also in these times that most young people who graduated from the University are still roaming the streets unemployed, assures the recipients of having an enduring business when you finish from 'igba-boyi' *[apprenticeship]*. The scheme particularly allows those who could not afford formal education to learn a trade and still become useful members of the society. We can build upon this.

Critically, this Igbo concept can be fundamentally reviewed and statutorily instituted. The business mentor or 'oga' undertakes the responsibility to teach the 'boyi' the rudiments of the trade; he takes care of his well being, housing, accommodation, clothing, healthcare, etc. over the period. The 'boyi' on his part undertakes to serve his 'oga' diligently. At the end of the agreed period, the 'oga' settles the 'boyi' with an amount that will enable him to begin his own trade. However, this scheme has been subjected to various abuses by both the 'oga' and 'boyi'. Some 'ogas' have been known to abuse their 'boyis' treating them like domestic slaves. Some perpetuate quarrels with their 'boyis' as they near their 'freedom' by concocting stories of theft, insubordination etc against them so that they won't settle the 'boyi' as agreed. Some 'boyis' also are known to have stolen from their 'ogas', shown acts of disloyalty and even sometimes contributed to major financial setbacks for their 'ogas'. Given the clamour for the child rights act, this very useful practice should be refined.

Because this scheme is semi-formal relying on existing family ties and relationships, there are not usually written terms of engagement. Each of the parties interprets the relationship as they deem right. In the context of today's world, there is a strong argument for the formalization of these types of apprenticeships to prevent abuse, so that the relationships can add more value to the lives of both the 'ogas' and the 'boyis'. Such arrangements should guarantee the 'boyis' some minimum level of education even while they are 'serving their ogas'. The idea of a "Market Place Education", similar to the nomadic education of the Northern herdsmen lends good appeal and appropriate government agencies can be set up to develop this idea.

This is particularly needful because while their mates may be studying theoretical aspects of business in the universities, the apprentices are actually undergoing practical training and acquiring needed skills in customer service, accounting and finance, business management, stock keeping and logistics etc. Others receive practical training and gain much needed experience in trades such as plumbing, furniture, hair styling and so on. This could also be reviewed to make the 'ogas' receive some kind of support from the government for giving the opportunities to the 'boyis', something that should actually be government's responsibility. These kinds of support may include but not limited to access to business funding, information etc. There may also be a need to define the lower and upper limits of the tutelage in other to provide a forcastable, fair and formalized framework.

Igbo traditional child care practices

The practice of caring for children in Igboland has always been a collective effort whereby the responsibility of training and upbringing of a child is not just that of the immediate or extended family but also involves neighbours and indeed all adults. Thus traditional early childhood care practices exist in various informal forms in both rural and urban societies in Nigeria. The aim is to produce individuals with behaviour-patterns, abilities and skills necessary for effective citizenship in the community. The objectives of such communal child-rearing practices are to develop the child's latent physical skills, character, and intellectual skills and inculcate respect for elders and those in position of authority. Other objectives include a need to develop in the child a sense of belonging and to participate actively in family and community affairs and to understand, appreciate and promote the cultural heritage of the community at large. Some of these traditional type cares evolved into non-formal day care centres where children are clustered in groups (usually according to their street or mothers' market stalls) and an elderly person oversees their affairs while their mothers are in the markets or farms.

The age grade system and the youth in the Igbo society

The Igbo Age Grade System is a social phenomenon which is organized around persons within a certain age bracket, who come together to constitute a particular age grade. The ages of the members of one particular age grade are not necessarily the same but they are all born within the age brackets of 5 - 10years. This grouping constitutes the groups for sharing assignments and rewards in the traditional Igbo setting. For example, there will be an age grade that goes to war, while another age grade will be responsible for supplying them with sustenance and weapons. There is the age grade for maintaining the roads and other infrastructure in the town, while another age grade will take care of protecting the village, etc. This way special bonds are formed between the members of that group that separate the members from others. The members of an age grade are like a family and bear allegiance and trust to each other. The responsibility they owe to themselves and to the community in general engenders a sense of competition with others while bequitting them with pride when they succeed. The sense of pride in accomplishment, team spirit and teamwork, the sense of responsibility and a sense of accountability and a the sense of primacy of public good are all inculcated into members through participation in the activities of their age grade. In fact, one can say with a reasonable level of confidence that each one of our past heroes not only knew and belonged to an age grade but they also knew who their members or mates were.

The age grade is a social tool for nurturing youths into responsible and contributory members of the community. The age grade also serves to transmit moral values and socialize her members to value the path of hard work and performance of duties, as well as accountability in responsibilities and public office. Members discuss matters that are peculiar to them and as a result are self moderating while developing a sense of belonging and participate actively in family and community affairs to make their situations better. They administer discipline erring individuals, contributing towards its development through communal labour, constructing and maintaining the public infrastructure and among other efforts protect their communities from external attacks or invasions from their neighbouring communities.

This age old system of socialization was very important in the Igbo society and helped to mold the lives of our progenitors. However, this system has been systematically rendered irrelevant as we gullibly and whole heartedly embraced the western self-centred culture and have rendered the age grade system literally defunct. Thus the modern youth are growing without any moderating influences even from their own peer and have no sense of community. The support that society usually offers to growing youth through the traditional institution is thereby eroded, leaving the modern youth directionless.

Conclusion

It is apparent that all is not well with our handling of our youth and they in consequence may not be in the position to manage our posterity creditably. The youth did not receive the same kind of education their parents received. In the formal education sense, they received far more superior education than their parents. Some of them received advanced business degrees from some of the best universities in the world, whereas some of their parents did not have any formal education. However, it would seem that the estates and business empires left behind by these pioneers have crumbled despite the sophisticated western education their children received. Even some with Ivy league Masters in Business Administration (MBA) degrees, were not able to sustain their legacies nor grow them further as is the cases with many such enterprises elsewhere in the Western World.

It is evident that the points of departure between the essence of these great builders and their children are numerous. Chief amongst these differences is that the training, albeit traditional and informal, that these pioneers received prepared them better for survival within the Nigerian polity than their offspring. Their participation, training and networking in the informal traditional system grounded them in the uniqueness of the Nigerian environment which does not yield easily to classical business theories. Even the contemporary success stories are mainly from persons who have had reasonable exposure to the informal traditional system in addition to their western style education. Thus, it would seem that the absence of the traditional training accounted for the inability of our youth to sustain the legacies they inherited. Ndigbo as a people must try to protect the good things it have.

References

Basden, G. T. (1982). *Among the Ibos of Nigeria*, Onitsha: University Publishing Co. Hastings, A. (1976). *African Christianity.* New York: Cassell and Collier Macmillian Publishers

Dabalen, A. and Bankole Oni. (2000): "Labour Market Prospects of University Graduates in Nigeria". Paper prepared for a World Bank– sponsored study on tertiary education in Nigeria. Nigerian Institute of Social and Economic Research (NISER), Ibadan.

Economic Commission for Africa, (2002): Tracking Performance and Progress: Nigeria Untapped Potential". *Economic Commission for Africa*, Addis Ababa Pg 153 – 182.

Hartnett, Teresa (2000). "Financing Trends and Expenditure Patterns in Nigerian Federal Universities: An Update." *Background study for the Nigeria University System Innovation Project*. World Bank, Education and Training Unit, Washington, D.C.

Nigeria, Ministry of Finance 2000)

Odinkalu, Chidi. (2013), Education and Nigeria's Future, *Premium Times.* Published, September 25, 2013.

Population Action International, 2007)

(UNFPA 2003).

(UNDP 2010

(Urdal and Sciubba. 2007

United Nations Educational, Scientific and Cultural Organization (UNESCO), *Education for All Global Monitoring Report 2011, The hidden crisis, armed conflict and education*, UNESCO, Paris, 2011.

World Bank (1999). *Acquiring knowledge. World Bank Developmental Report 1998- 1999.* The World Bank, Washington DC. pp. 27- 46.

The Nigeria-Biafra War and the Igbo Question:
Travails of the Biafran Woman
by
Ada Agbasimalo and Godwin Okaneme

Abstract

The world has known wars and these wars are very often fought with weapons of war that have technological sophistication which come with devastating effects. Whichever way one chooses to look at it, war portends evil, although many are wont to argue that war is a function of balance of power, which is an active ingredient of international politics and diplomacy. Others would argue that war settles scores and brings about renewed peace. This however can only be possible if the cause of war is identified and nipped in the bud to avoid reoccurence. It is only through this way that the effect of war can be doused by the resultant sustainable peace. The aphorism that when two elephants fight, it is the grass that suffers is always true during war situations as women are among the vulnerable groups that suffer much during wars. It is in the light of this that this paper discusses the travails of the Biafran woman during the Nigeria- Biafra war. The paper takes the strong view that despite the unfortunate reality that Igbo women suffered so much during that ruinous war, they have through sheer hard work and determination come to be counted among women of substance in contemporary Nigeria. This unassailable claim will be elucidated by giving some notable examples

Introduction

So much literature has been written on the subject matter of the Nigeria/Biafra war which is one of the most gruesome events in the history of Nigeria as a nation. Unfortunately most works on the war have more or less been tainted with political, religious, social and ethnic colorations thus preventing in most cases an unbiased and objective reportage of what really took place. These distorted views of the events of the war indeed mirror the Nigerian society where issues of national importance are approached purely from parochial and sectarian perspectives. Objectivity in such issues becomes lacking.

Furthermore most of the literary works on the Nigeria/Biafra war have been penned by men and highlighted whereas there is a dearth of literature developed by women on that war. Even where such literary works exist, their value has been feared to be downplayed, except in a negligible number of cases where personal self survival efforts have been known to push the works to limelight. One of the major reasons for this paper is to bring to the fore, some of the war experiences of the women of Biafra, a lot of which is considered shameful, embarrassing and not to be talked about but which has already been documented in book format to conscentize the public on the senselessness inherent in wars, and showcase the strength and resilience of the Biafran woman and the beauty of her survival.

This paper discusses briefly the travails of the Biafran woman in the course of the gruesome war. It is a fact that while men take direct bullets from wars, women and children suffer most from the residual effects of raging battles during wars the world over. The Nigeria-Biafra war was no exception as the women of Biafra suffered untold hardship, including loss of human dignity. They went through physical and psychological torture ranging from hunger and starvation, rape and loss of esteem, loss of children and husbands as well as the total destabilization occasioned by the war. It is however to the sheer credit of these women that they emerged stronger at the end of the war and have stood tall among equals, who might not have had direct experience of war.

Background History of Nigeria

The nation called Nigeria existed as a number of independent ethnic nationalities with linguistic and cultural differences prior to the amalgamation of the Northern and Southern protectorates in 1914. The actual building of Nigeria as a multinational state could be said to have begun in 1914 with the aforementioned amalgamation. The amalgamation was simply done for administrative convenience and economic interests of the British government and her officials who were the nation's colonial masters. After the 1914 amalgamation episode with its concomitant negative effects, no other viable constitutional development took place in the new political entity called Nigeria until 1922, when for the first time, provision was made for elected members to sit on a Nigerian Legislative Council. In 1940, Nigeria was divided into four administrative units, namely the colony of Lagos, the Northern, Eastern and Western provinces. These administrative divisions brought about increased powers for the colony and the provinces and strengthened the separate units. Sir Arthur Richard's constitution of 1946 inaugurated and deepened Nigeria's regionalism, achieving a semi political breakthrough by integrating the North with the South at the legislative level.

After the Second World War in 1945, there was a high level of political awareness in Africa. Nigeria was not left out as political parties were formed in the country on regional and ethnic basis and the outcome of this was very obvious. It brought about wholesale regionalism in the nation's body politics. With the Macpherson's constitution of 1951, a greater measure of autonomy was granted to the regions with stronger regional legislatures, leaving only residual powers to the central government. It could be argued that with this development, a very strong possibility of three countries emerging out of Nigeria became evident, as Nigeria politically took a clear turn for the autonomy of administration and economy, and regional strength. In 1953, the central cabinet was divided over the acceptance of a set date for securing self-government with the end result being the Kano riot which claimed the lives of many Nigerians, majority of them, Igbos. This created a big gulf between the regions. For the first time, the North talked openly of the possibility of secession rather than endure what they considered as humiliation and maltreatment of the Northern region. The West also threatened to secede over the non-inclusion of Lagos in the West in the new constitution. The 1954 constitution confirmed and rubber stamped the wishes of Nigerian leaders to remain apart as much as they possibly could. There were two options of government to choose from – the unitary and federal options. The federal option was overwhelmingly chosen. The constitution equally hastened the political process in the country leading to the convening of constitutional conferences in 1957, 1958, 1959 and 1960 culminating in the grant of independence to the country on October 1, 1960.

If the post Independence text below is truly credited to Sir Ahmadu Bello, then Premier of Northern Nigeria, then there is indeed cause to worry: *"The new nation called Nigeria should be an estate from our great grandfather, Othman Dan Fodio. We must ruthlessly prevent a change of power. We must use the minorities in the North as willing tools, and the south as conquered territories and never allow them to have control of their future."*

The Nigeria –Biafra war: A Historical Exegesis

As a result of ethnic, tribal and sentimental leanings, a clear and unbiased historical account of the Nigeria-Biafra Civil War as it really happened has become hard to come by as many who had written on the war in the past had approached the subject matter from ethnic perspectives. That is not to say however, that there are no dispassionate and unbiased accounts of the unforgettable and regrettable event, most of which are found in accounts of personal experiences. It is an undeniable fact that the war was a survivalist one fought for the purpose of Igbo self-preservation and continued existence. It is also a fact that the Biafran war may have been averted if there was egalitarianism and respect for human rights in the country. Achebe (2012:95) captures the scenario quite clearly. According to him:

To fully comprehend some of the competing positions during the Nigeria-Biafra War, it may be useful to begin with an examination of the local and international response to Biafra. Beginning with the January 15, 1966 coup d'état, through the counter–coup (staged mainly by Northern Nigerian officers, who murdered 185 Igbo officers) and the massacre of thirty thousand Igbos and Easterners in pogroms that started in May 1966 and occurred over four months the events of those months left millions of other future Biafrans and me feeling terrified. As we fled "home" to Eastern Nigeria to escape all manner of atrocities that were being inflicted upon us and our families in different parts of Nigeria, we saw ourselves as victims. When we noticed that the federal government of Nigeria did not respond to our call to end the pogroms, we concluded that a government that failed to safe-guard the lives of its citizens has no claim to their allegiance and must be ready to accept that the victims deserve the right to seek their safety in other ways including secession.

Achebe's explanation cited above is one clear way to explain the emergence of Biafra as a political entity. As Achebe and his people fled, Agbasimalo (2012), captures the discussion in a train, of two other fleeing men: *"But only people from the Eastern part of the country are in this race for dear life, targeted for selective killing. It all looked well-thought-out. First the soldiers from the East, in their barracks, then the civilians in their homes, only at night, then on the streets, in institutions and everywhere, including East-bound trains. And the bodies of our brothers and sisters littered the streets, many mutilated,"*

The above seems to perfectly complement Achebe's account on the reason for seeking self-preservation and continued existence. Biafra thus came into being from the foregoing, as a result of ethnic bias and unparalleled hatred of the Igbos by other ethnic nationalities in Nigeria, practicalized by the killing of Igbos in the North and other parts of the country by people who were supposed to protect them as their hosts and fellow countrymen. The Igbos, known for their egalitarian nature saw the affront as a threat to their continuous existence. Their bravery was not in doubt and when Col. Emeka Odumegwu Ojukwu, the then governor of the East Central State made a clarion call for the people to rise up and defend themselves, the people had no option but to heed the clarion call of the people's general. Thousands of able-bodied youths in an unparalleled show of solidarity poured into the Biafran military camps voluntarily for recruitment as soldiers, to fight the survivalist cause. University lecturers and students, civil servants and business persons, none were left out in this patriotic crusade. Though several Igbos lost their lives in the course of the 30 months war, the Biafran soldiers demonstrated uncommon bravery and unquestionable patriotism in their resolve to defend their fatherland and ensure invader casualties as well. Their resoluteness and ingenuity were second to none.

One cannot discuss the Nigeria-Biafra War without mentioning the despicable and condemnable role of the Nigerian government and the military in the 30 months Civil War. In Agbasimalo's (2012) account, one of the sufferers who managed to escape, asked: *"Where are the authorities? Why have they kept mum? Are these killers not the same people with whom we have lived and interacted all these years?*

Furthermore, the use of hunger as a weapon of war directly employed by the Nigerian government against Biafra is evil and oppressive. Perhaps, it is quite obvious that many more people died of starvation during the war on the Biafran side than of bullets and other war paraphernalia. It is morally reprehensible to employ starvation and economic blockade as a direct weapon of a war and even more so for a civil war. Biafra women came to the rescue as Agbasimalo (2012) reports: *"Food scarcity heightened. The enemies had blocked the channels through which assistance came in. Women picked up their baskets and combed the hinterland, the distant markets, in search of food, walking along serpentine pathways through bushes and villages, wading across shallow streams. Moving in groups, they left home in the afternoon and reached the market town at dusk. By a bush corner, under the shade of a tree, in abandoned homes or uncompleted buildings, they found a place to lay their heads. And in the wee hours of the morning, before the farmers and traders came in with their green plantain, yam tubers, cassava products, smoked fish, local salt and other items, the women were already at the market place. Within two hours, Deze's mother, Dora and her group were done with buying. On their way home, they looked out for smaller markets where they resold the items purchased from the distant market, targeting some profit and consciously reserving some of the food for the family's needs."*

The mass killing of children and women during the war, especially occasioned by this economic blockade has heightened the call to charge Nigerian leaders during the war for genocide. Perhaps the Igbo intelligentsia may have to create more intellectual awareness on this.

The Igbo Question

It is the considered opinion of this paper that the poem Agbasimalo 2012), quoted below answers to a considerable extent, the Biafran question: "Lamentation"

They stripped us and savored our nakedness
Went in and out of our women like needlework
Threatened our male descent seed

They defecated in the backyard on our sacred places
Urinated over our kitchen furnace, like inebriated bulldogs

Virgin places are denuded
There are no more secrets
There is no more privacy

The glory is gone
For they had the gun
We had only our pride
To ride

Jubilation

Yesterday I could not touch them
Today they have become my plaything.
Ha! Ha! Ha!

Affirmation

Not for much longer... Not anymore!!!"

Although the war ended over four decades ago, the painful memories linger in the consciousness of millions of Igbos. Perhaps Nigeria and the world should note that this is not a consciousness that can be erased easily through sloganeering and rhetoric. It calls for conscientious human considerations aimed at redirecting the paths of injustice. But this has not been done rather the absence of serious and conscious efforts made since the end of the civil war to reintegrate Igbos into the mainstream of the Nigerian nation, stares in the face, in spite of the no victor no vanquished gimmick, and the promise of the three Rs – Rehabilitation, Reintegration and Reconstruction. But after inflicting war injury on the Igbos, they were left on their own to rehabilitate themselves and reconstruct their ravaged homeland, while the multi millions were used to develop areas where war was not fought.

Nearly forty-five years after the end of that civil war, Igbos are still being massively discriminated against and marginalized in the scheme of things in the country. In clear terms they are treated as second class citizens as well as near undesirable elements, clearly reminding them very often that they lost a war and must therefore be treated as prisoners of war at all times. Of a truth, marginalization of Igbos has been heightened to an unbearable level in Nigeria. Though it is claimed in some quarters in the country that the Nigeria-Biafra war was a war of unification and reintegration, the positive effects of that claim years after the war ended, are yet to be seen. The Igbo man or woman cannot feel free in other parts of the country as they are molested and killed frequently under very flimsy and innocuous circumstances. The unfair and inhuman treatment meted out to Igbos makes the building and maintenance of an egalitarian social structure difficult and almost impossible in Nigeria.

The Travails of the Biafran Woman

Women are unique and special beings. From nature they are set apart to be so. They are so divinely endowed that life without them is miserable and almost unbearable not only for the male folks but for humanity as a whole. Perhaps this explains why Iwuchukwu (2006:207) stated emphatically that: *"Though the African culture with all its appurtenances-symbols, norms and values seems to play down the status of women, yet the African women's roles as compassionate lovers, wives and mothers have made them become most influential and indispensable in life and society. They are the main stay of our total being, of our churches, our educational, cultural and social institutions.*

Obioha (2007:304) views women and their status in society more vigorously. According to him: *"The efforts since the last two decades of the 20th century to de-patriarchalize our society and give women a better status have continued to grow and bear fruits despite numerous oppositions posed by their male counterparts. The male chauvinists who want to maintain the status quo of well regimented patriarchal systems and structures."* It is with regards of the low recognition accorded women especially in our clime that Okoye (2009:84) lamented thus: *"Women especially in this part of the world are regarded as inferior to men, portrayed as being senseless, morally debased, devilish, childish and weak. Women in turn have made little or no effort in trying to change this perception until recent times when women have begun to take their rightful places in society."* Okoye's postulation has since been set aside by the giant strides women in Nigeria have made in recent times.

The Biafran woman is a symbol of courage and unbridled resilience. Were it not for the women of Biafra and their courage and rare doggedness, the Biafran race and nation would have been faced with the challenge of complete annihilation during the Biafra War of survival of 1967-1970. We know of no other group of women in history who suffered more than the women of Biafra as several saw their spouses leave for war, never to return. Many of them were abducted and forcibly converted to camp bed mates while many others were raped right in their homes by the rampaging and ruthless morally depraved Nigerian soldiers. A huge number of the women helplessly watched their children suffer and slowly die from starvation. They witnessed their families pine away. The agonizing scenario was too strong for these women to bear but their uncommon strength and courage, that which distinguishes them as Biafran women, provided the spirit and resilience that helped them pull through. Such uncommon tenacity that sustained them through this harrowing ordeal that lasted throughout the period of the war also allowed them to rebuild and nurture self to new maturity levels, from their forced zero position. That was the true Biafran woman, whose travails are being discussed. The Biafran woman this paper discusses is that one who the war sent into the valley of circumstances but who persevered and gradually worked herself up to the mountain top of success. Agbasimalo (2012), in 'The Forest Dames' paints a true life post-war picture of the experience of a young Biafran girl:

"Passing out from the NYSC was exciting for Deze who, fully kitted in her green and white uniform, marched enthusiastically with the rest, raising her

cap in obedience to the commander's voice. Looking proudly into the future with high hopes, she could not but recall how lucky she had been. Cold shivers made her shudder as she remembered the time when the gun ruled and caused death to become the people's companion. She cast her mind back to the days spent in the forest when the jaws of ferocious animals were bound and their appetites put on hold. She found herself thanking God profusely. Those were also the days when the evil forest turned benign and played host to defenseless women, allowing them to penetrate it, even at night. She could not help thinking about those who were not so lucky. She found herself fighting back tears. But the tears streamed down her cheeks all the same as she wondered how forest dame Sofuruchi was coping with rejection in her new environment. More tears rolled down for Ojonma, whose return from the end-of-war military camp roadblock was still being awaited. Through her wet eyes, she could see young Uwadiegwu, Madam Rosa's daughter, in agony; the others too, many of them. Will they ever return?"

That is part of the Igbo question. Biafra is synonymous with Igbo. This paper also looks at the situations that spat on the faces of the husbands of the Biafran women, during that war. Agbasimalo (2012) paints another disturbing true life picture:

"One of the aggressors had ordered the woman to stop eating and follow them. Trembling, she picked up her baby and got up to go with them but was rebuked and ordered to leave the baby there. Ogechi left her baby in obedience. As she was led away, her five-month-old baby, who was still on breast milk, cried as if she knew what was going on. The woman's husband looked on, speechless. His wife was gone with the invading soldiers and he now had to take over the care of their baby,"

This work also brings to the fore situations where Biafran women helplessly watched their children drop dead. Again Agbasimalo (2012):

"The raid was swift and, before they knew it, the "birds" had departed as quickly as they had come, leaving the people further traumatized. Orjay's wife sensed that the baby strapped to her back was now lifeless. She did not feel her daughter's heartbeat anymore. She had felt the baby slump. With tears in her eyes, she drew her husband's attention to this development..."

***

"I'm sorry, Mrs. Ejema, we did our best for Sunday but he just did not make it," Dr. Harrison said softly to Julie, who flung herself on the ground and fainted. She did not need any interpreter to tell her the doctor's message. She had lost the equanimity provided by her belief in fate and providence. Who could blame her? Sunday was her only son and she really had expected him back. The news of his death was therefore shattering. She had wished for death but, instead, received immediate medical attention from the visiting team. She regained consciousness. Now she sat up with her back against the wall, feet astride, head rolling from side to side against the wall, her lower lip clenched between her teeth."

This work decries the trauma most Biafran women, young and old, suffered – Agbasimalo (2012:
"By one corner, another mother was crying. Her baby had just been buried. Meanwhile, some women surrounded another, creating a barricade.
"Push, push!" the women urged. And, a baby's cry was heard. Deze was scared. She hurried to the back of the building. The stench oozing from there was equally intense. She looked the other way and saw several fresh graves.
"Oh my God! Eeh! Eeh!' She was screaming and running farther away, her hand clutching her head. People looked at her and wondered what was wrong. They had become inured to their misfortune"

This paper is not oblivious of great Igbo women who lived and died before the emergence of Biafra, especially those in the forefront of the struggle to free the people from colonial domination, as far back as 1929. 'Oha Ndom (2013:3), edited by Uzodinma Nwala, describes these women as: 'The mothers of the fathers of anti colonial struggle."Notable among them are Daa Ikonna Nwanyiukwu Enyia (leader), Nwanyereuwa, Nwannedia, Nwugo, Nwada, Mabel Uwaluuche Ejekwu, Mary Okezie, Madam Chinwe, Ahebi Ugabe, Ihejelimebi Ibe, Elizabeth Effiong, etc. These women are largely unsung as their names, instead of lining the annals of history, lie there almost forgotten but luckily found in foreign archives. The heroic acts of these women weigh more than that of the regular Nigerian women mentioned as heroines of old. The fact that these women have almost gone into oblivion due to the Igbo lethargy or non-interest in Igbo affairs is part of the Igbo question.That Igbo women are high achievers is not in doubt. However, in an article of this nature, it will be difficult to name all of them. This paper has selected just a few of them for mention.

Chief Janet Mokelu: Was the first female parliamentarian and member of the House of Representatives in the history of Nigerian politics. A very dynamic pioneer nationalist, she played a very dynamic role in the struggle for Nigerian independence and was woman leader of the National Council of Nigerian Citizens (NCNC), the major political party that won political independence for Nigeria.

Flora Nwapa: Was Nigeria's first ever female novelist and the first female novelist in the English Language in all of black Africa to be published internationally. Famous for her great novel titled 'Efuru', she was also a teacher and an astute administrator. Flora like Mokelu and the rest was sparsely celebrated.

Buchi Emecheta: At a very young age, overcame many hardships to obtain her education at a time when educating girls was not a priority in Igbo land. Determined to rise from poverty, she took a degree in Sociology while working and raising her 5 kids all alone. She continued to write and eventually became one of the female writers to reckon with, writing books for both young and old.

Professor Zulu Sofola: Whose real name was Nwazuluoke Sofola, nee Okwumabu, was internationally known by her theatre name of Zulu. Born to Igbo parents of Issele-Uku, Delta state and married to an Ijebu professor, Tunde Sofola, Zulu was Nigeria's and Africa's first and most celebrated female playwright and dramatist. She was also first Nigerian and African female to earn a PhD in Theatre Arts. She was Nigeria's first female professor of Theatre Arts.

Chinyere Kalu (Nee Onyenucheya): Who hails from Akwete-Ndoki in Abia state and married to Kalu Okoli of Ohafia, is Nigeria's first female pilot. In 2011, President Goodluck Jonathan appointed her as Rector and Chief Executive Officer of Nigerian College of Aviation Technology, the largest aviation training institute in Africa.

Chioma Ajunwa Opara: Also known as Chioma Ajunwa is a police officer and a well known athlete who specialized in long jump. She is the first athlete in Nigeria to win an individual Olympic gold medal at the 1996 Summer Olympics in Atlanta, United States of America. To date, Chioma remains Nigeria's only individual Olympic gold medalist. She is from Ahiazu Mbaise in Imo state.

Dr Ngozi Okonjo-Iweala: Is the former and current Finance Minister and Coordinating Minister of the economy in the current government of Goodluck Jonathan. She is also the first woman to hold that position. She is a great economist widely known for championing tremendous economic reforms in the country and also a former World Bank managing Director.

Dame Virginia Etiaba: Is a great school teacher and disciplinarian who became the first female governor in Nigeria's political history, when she took over the mantle of gubernatorial leadership in Anambra state from November 2006 to February 2007. Elsewhere in Nigeria, these women would have been celebrated to high heavens but the Igbo question is: Why were they not? High flying Nigerian women abound but cannot all be mentioned here. Institutions of higher learning, the banks, ministries and parastatals, even the religious sector and market and business sectors overflow with right thinking Igbo women of high worth, in spite of the marginalization experienced. The Biafran/Igbo spirit is that of doggedness and hope for a better future.

Conclusion

The uniqueness of the Igbo person whether man or woman is not in doubt. Igbo women have clearly demonstrated this unique trait in clear and unmistakable terms. From a near-hopeless scenario they found themselves in, at the end of the civil war in 1970, these women of valour have weathered all storms and risen to stardom within a short space of time. The Igbos have indeed become men and women of excellence who have hugely excelled in all areas of human endeavour.

It is instructive to note the astronomical rise of the Biafran woman to stardom within a short space of time after the civil war. It is a show of rare courage and resilience exemplified by hard work and positivism. Such courageous displays are commendable. The Biafran woman deserves encouragement more than any other thing. She deserves praise as well, for her ability to shake off the smear of destitution and work herself to stardom, standing shoulder high with equals who did not have a direct war experience. In fact she is a role model in the society.

References
Achebe, C. (2012), There was a country: A personal Hisory of Biafra, London: Penguin Books Ltd.
Agbasimalo, A. (2012) "The Forest Dames" AuthorHouse UK limited.
en.wikipedia.org/wiki/list of Igbo people (Dec 04 2013).

Iwuchukwu, R.C (2006), "Gender, Culture and Traditional Practices in Igboland", in Journal of Nigerian Languages and Culture, Volume 8, November, 2006.
Nwala, Uzodinma (2013) "Oha Ndom" Owerri, Nigeria.
Obioha, P.U (2007), "Between Radical Feminism and African Family Values: Problems and Prospects", in Journal of Nigerian Languages and Culture, Volume 9, Number 2, September 2007.
Okoye, C.L (2009) "Sex Bias and Language Use in Igboland: A socio-linguistic Study" in Journal of Nigerian Languages and Culture, Volume 11, No 2, November, 2009.

SECTION FOURTEEN: THE NATIONAL CONFERENCE

The Ndi-Igbo Interest in Nigeria
by
Dr. Chinweizu Chinweizu

Key point

In any negotiation of the future of Nigeria, the minimum Ndi-Igbo objective should be to secure enough autonomy for Ala-Igbo so it can operate as a distinct economic zone, be developed by Igbo enterprise, and attain such economic power as would deter any forces outside Ala-Igbo that might want to threaten the lives and property of Igbos anywhere in Nigeria.After some 20 years of calls for a Sovereign National Conference (SNC), we now seem to be on the brink of an official renegotiation of the Nigerian Federation. Whenever and wherever the renegotiation of Nigeria commences, it is vital for Ndi-Igbo and their mandated negotiators to be clear about thef undamental and non-negotiable Ndi-Igbo interest: i.e. their minimum need that must be guaranteed in any Nigerian arrangement.

Three vital questions need to be answered:
a) What is the Ndi-Igbo objective?
b) What is the game plan for achieving it? and
c) What leadership team is best able to achieve it for Ndi-Igbo?

(And I don't mean the Onye-Igbo objective, the Igbo individual's personal objective with which we too often confuse the group objective. When we talk of the Igbo position or Igbo whatever, we should, but don't usually, distinguish between Igbo as Onye-Igbo and Igbo as Ndi-Igbo. Because we don't make that distinction, our politicians tend to act as if their individual, personal interest, their Onye-Igbo interest, is the same as the Ndi-Igbo interest, the Igbo nation's group interest. We need to remove this ambiguity from our political thinking and discourse.)The proper time for working out a game plan, and selecting the team to play it, is after Abuja has called a conference and specified its agenda, so I shall here focus on the first question.

Abuja and ACF gimmicks

Since November 2011, Abuja and its Califate-ACF (Arewa Consultative Forum) masters have come up with sundry gimmicks to keep their "One-Nigeria" racket going and to evade a thorough and complete renegotiation of the terms of association which they have imbedded in their fraudulent 1999 constitution. First, in Nov. 2011, they set up a Constitution Review Committee that would presumably follow instructions and stay out of the Abuja-imposed "no go-areas"; then, in Jan. 2012, they tried to divert attention from the rising interest in the Sovereign National Conference (SNC) by hurriedly imposing a huge fuel price hike on January 1, but that backfired as the ploy only heated up the political space and threatened to spark an uprising. So they quickly defused the crisis by reducing the price hike and getting the strike called off. Then at the National Assembly (NASS), in February, they threw the bait of states creation to catch and sideline some of the still restive opposition; and now, in March, alarmed by the unfurling of the regional integration flag of the SW zone, the ACF seems to be gearing up for a conference of some sort to discuss the future of Nigeria. Whether it is called the SNC or not is largely irrelevant. What matters is that some sort of negotiation seems to be on the way and Igbo politicians, as usual, are divided, confused and unprepared. As their objective, some Igbo politicians want Igbo Presidency in 2015; some want creation of more states in the SE zone. For either of these to happen, they need the Califate-serving status quo to continue. There needs to be a public examination of these private and personal desires to see if they serve the permanent interest of Ndi-Igbo, the Igbo nation as a whole.

As it is, too many Igbos are committed to the idea of "One Nigeria", and haven't started to think outside the One-Nigeria box in which their minds and emotions are trapped. Some insist that "it is in the long term strategic interest of the Igbos that Nigeria works." But is it so? That claim needs to be thoroughly examined. I myself think there is another and better world possible for Ndi-Igbo outside this Lugardian prisoners-of-war camp called One-Nigeria, and we should explore it. But that is a task for another occasion. What we need now is to determine the Ndi-Igbo Interest and how it should be met, and then see the minimum Ndi-Igbo should aim to get out of any negotiations about Nigeria. But first, let's consider States Creation, Igbo Presidency as well as Constitution review and amendment, to see what, if anything, they offer Ndi-Igbo.

States Creation

States creation just amends and reinforces the chop-chop, *lootocratic* status quo. It is no way to solve the problems of Nigeria or Ndi-Igbo. To make that clear, let's ponder some questions:

Will more states end the insecurity of Christian and Igbo life and property in Shariyaland (the zone of Shariya states in the Far North)? How many of these states will be self-sustaining? How many of the present 36 states are self-sustaining? Whose resources will be used to sustain the thieving politicians who will run the proposed states? How would more states protect us from the James Ibori's of Nigeria? How would more states solve the problem of resource control? How would more states solve the problem of true federalism? How would more states bring economic autonomy to the federating units?

In my view, states creation at this time is just part of the ACF bag of tricks to divert attention from the SNC that should negotiate the terms of our continued association. The National Assembly (NASS), which is considering the creation of more states, is itself part of the problem, not part of the solution. It is operating on the military-imposed 1999 constitution that is a fraud, a pseudo-democratic façade behind which Dan Fodio's heirs can continue to exploit Nigeria as an enlarged Sokoto empire. The 1999 constitution has to go, and a peoples' constitution has to replace it. And an appropriate platform to negotiate the guidelines of the peoples' constitution, such as the Sovereign National Conference of the Ethnic Nationalities (SNC-EN), is the only democratically valid way forward.

Igbo Presidency

One of the usual bananas dangled before Igbo politicians by the ACF is Igbo Presidency. But since the ACF is desperate to get back the presidency as soon as possible, and assuming that GEJ will seek and get a second term in 2015, the best the ACF can genuinely offer to Igbo Presidential aspirants is the Vice Presidency in 2019. After taking their turn for eight years, maybe the ACF will concede the presidency in 2027 to some Igbo person they can trust and control, like they did to the Yorubas through OBJ in 1999. But ***should Igbos trust any Igbo politician who is acceptable to the ACF?***

Those hooked with the bait of Igbo Presidency are like a foolish man jailed for life who refuses to contemplate a jailbreak because he has been promised a night, at some unspecified future date, in the arms of the prison Commandant's daughter. Those who bite this bait are like that black slave in the USA, Josiah Henson, the real-life prototype of Uncle Tom, who had his chance to escape from slavery but refused to take it out of slave-mind loyalty to his slavemaster.

Constitution review and amendment

I presume that any Igbo person on the Constitution Review Committee is representing, not just himself, but Ndi-Igbo, the Igbo nation as a whole. If so, we need to educate and instruct him on the vital interests he should secure for us. And then we must ask if, with its "no-go- areas", a Constitution Review and Amendment process can serve the Ndi-Igbo interest.

Security: The Paramount Ndi-Igbo Interest

The core problem Ndi-Igbo have in Nigeria is the chronic insecurity of Igbo life and property that began with the pogroms of the 1950s and has continued till today with the Boko Haram terrorism. With Boko Haram, Ndi-Igbo are painfully back to the acute insecurity problems of 1966. Our politicians have proffered no answer to the problem. Some, in their political wisdom, advised Igbos in Shariyaland to stay there and, presumably, put their faith in a FGN that cannot protect its own police posts and even its national police headquarters let alone the millions of Igbo homes and property scattered all over Shariyaland. That advice is suicidal madness. We need something that would permanently banish this chronic insecurity nightmare from the lives of Igbos.

As somebody has pointed out, "In every state throughout the federation, if you remove the indigenes or local government, the Igbos are the largest investors. From Cameroon to Gambia the story is not different." We must note, however, that outside Nigeria, from Cameroon to Gambia, Igbos safely go about their business without being made targets of pogroms, suicide bombings, checkpoint assassinations, etc. (For over 50 years Igbos inNorthern Nigeria have been special victims of these crimes and the perpetrators have never been prosecuted, let alone punished. This is part of why these crimes continue to be perpetrated with impunity against Igbos.) As a result, Igbos are safer outside Nigeria than in their alleged country Nigeria. **Something is wrong with that and it has to be permanently corrected.**

At the root of the insecurity problem of Ndi-Igbo in Nigeria is the fact that they don't have the power to defend themselves wherever they reside (whether in Igboland or outside it) and have to rely for security on a Federal Government (FGN) that has proved, for over 50 years, unwilling or unable to protect Igbo lives and property. To be of any use to Ndi-Igbo, any Constitution amendment or renegotiation of Nigeria must permanently solve that problem.

How might this be done?

This vital security need could be met if Nigeria obtained a Federal Government that has the will and the means to deter or punish attacks on Igbos anywhere in Nigeria. But since such a will cannot be guaranteed by any constitution, the next best thing is to focus on why Ndi-Igbo are dispersed all over Nigeria and then change that underlying source of the problem. If so many Igbos did not feel compelled to disperse outside Ala-Igbo to earn their living, that problem of insecurity would disappear or at least be minimized. So what is needed as the ultimate remedy is a situation where most Igbos can stay in Ala-Igbo and earn their living.

But regardless of insecurity everywhere else, there is another issue to be considered: **Why should Igbo enterprise be spent in developing other parts of Nigeria while leaving Ala-Igbo in economic distress?** Rectifying that anomaly is the basic political task and requires a constitution that will allow, and even encourage, Igbos to develop Ala-Igbo, and thereby help keep Igbos at home to develop their society and culture. As a by-product, this would reduce their exposure to massacres and expropriation, especially in Shariyaland. Obtaining such a constitution is the primary task, I think, our politicians should focus on. What is needed is a constitution that guarantees economic autonomy for Ala-Igbo. On that there can be no concession whatever. From this perspective, the task of guaranteeing security of life and property for Igbos translates into that of guaranteeing, in the constitution, the economic autonomy of Ala-Igbo.

In effect, we need a constitution that would allow Ala-Igbo to function as an autonomous economic zone so that Igbo enterprise can develop the Ala-Igbo economy and society in ways that will reduce the pressure for Igbos to emigrate to other parts of the country to earn their living. Within such an autonomous economic zone, Ndi-Igbo could develop enough economic power to deter any Arewa forces that might contemplate attacks on Igbos anywhere in Shariyaland. Such Arewa forces will desist only when they can see and feel an Igbo power that is much stronger than their own. And that power, at the minimum, must be an overwhelming Igbo economic power located in Ala-Igbo. The quiet message would then be: If you threaten or attack Igbos in Shariyaland, Ala-Igbo will deploy its economic power and devastate your Arewa economy. Such a prospect should deter most of these attacks on Igbos. Constitutionally securing the economic autonomy to build Igbo economic power in Ala-Igbo, I propose, is the main project to which Ndi-Igbo and their politicians should now dedicate their efforts.

The paramount Ndi-Igbo interest is security within the borders of Nigeria, and the minimum objective it sets for Ndi-Igbo in any constitutional negotiation is a guarantee of economic autonomy for Ala-Igbo.

What sort of constitution might provide the requisite autonomy? I believe the 1995 Constitution of Ethiopia is a model of what Ndi-Igbo need. Its preamble states:

"We, the Nations, Nationalities and Peoples of Ethiopia:

Strongly committed, in full and free exercise of our right to self-determination, to building a political community founded on the rule of law and capable of ensuring a lasting peace, guaranteeing a democratic order, and advancing our economic and social development;

Firmly convinced that the fulfillment of this objective requires full respect of individual and people's fundamental freedoms and rights, to live together on the basis of equality and without any sexual, religious or cultural discrimination;

Further convinced that by continuing to live with our rich and proud cultural legacies in territories we have long inhabited, have, through continuous interaction on various levels and forms of life, built up common interest and have also contributed to the emergence of a common outlook;

Fully cognizant that our common destiny can best be served by rectifying historically unjust relationships and by further promoting our shared interests;

Convinced that to live as one economic community is necessary in order to create sustainable and mutually supportive conditions for ensuring respect for our rights and freedoms and for the collective promotion of our interests;

Determined to consolidate, as a lasting legacy, the peace and the prospect of a democratic order which our struggles and sacrifices have brought about;

Have therefore adopted, on 8 December 1994 this constitution through representatives we have duly elected for this purpose as an instrument that binds us in a mutual commitment to fulfill the objectives and the principles set forth above."

It further provides for a federal government of nine ethnic-based regions and guarantees that all Ethiopian languages will enjoy equal state recognition, although Amharic is specified as the working language of the federal government. Is it possible to amend the 1999 Constitution into something like this Ethiopian constitution? Let us explore that question.

The first issue is whether that is possible when "no-go-areas" are imposed on the review and amendment process. I doubt it, given that the covert purpose or hidden agenda of the "no-go areas" is precisely to protect the Arewa advantages entrenched in the 1999 Constitution, such as, the preponderance of states, LGAs and NASS constituencies unfairly allotted to the Arewa dominated North.

Secondly, we must note that this 1999 constitution doesn't recognize entities like ethnic groups, autonomous areas, nations and nationalities. It is based on the false premise that we are in Nigeria simply as individuals. That is historically and socially incorrect. We came into Nigeria, not as individual immigrants, but through our pre-colonial groups [ethnic nations, empires, kingdoms, chiefdoms, autonomous village groups etc.] which were conquered by the British. And, in practical life, we still are treated and treat one another as members of these precolonial groups. Hence the phenomenon of "tribalism". Our constitution-making needs to recognize these behavioral and historical facts.

A constitution is unlikely to grant autonomy to entities it doesn't recognize. So, for Ala-Igbo to get the autonomy that Ndi-Igbo need for their physical safety, the constitution, as happened in Ethiopia, has to be one negotiated between the ethnic nations and nationalities. In Ethiopia, the 1995 Constitution was created by ethnic nation movements that were in the EPRDF, Ethiopian Peoples' Revolutionary Democratic Front, a coalition of the rebel ethnic group forces that had, in 1991, overthrown the Derg government of Mengistu and its Marxist State.

I submit that the 1999 Constitution cannot, by a process of amendments, be transformed into a constitution of the Ethiopian type. It takes a new political beginning to make that sort of basic change. [As happened in China in 1949; Cuba in 1959; Iran in 1979; the USA in 1787; South Africa in 1994; Ethiopia in 1995; etc] Most such transformations take place at the conclusion of a revolution. In fact, the change from one type of state or constitution to another is tantamount to a revolution. Examples?

From monarchy to a republican Commonwealth (Cromwell's revolution in England, 17th century);

From monarchy to a republic (the French Revolution in the 18th century);

From empire to soviet republics (the Russian Revolution of 1917);

From a racial electocracy (Apartheid) to a non-racial or multi-racial electocracy (South Africa in 1994);

From a unitary Marxist Republic to a Federal Democratic Republic of ethnic nations (Ethiopia in 1995).

Now to the Question of the ACF Banana Baits.

Will even two consecutive 4-year terms of an Igbo presidency give Ala-Igbo the economic autonomy that is the minimum condition for the security of Igbo life and property within Nigeria? I don't think so. Has GEJ's tenure at the Presidency yielded the resource control that the Ijaw have been clamoring for? Has Obama's tenure done anything significant to improve the lot of the African-Americans? We have to understand that occupying an office, even the most powerful office in the state, does not confer on the occupant unlimited freedom to effect whatever changes his constituency desires. The President is simply a captive of the system he is President of, and can only do what the system permits, not what his supporters demand. When GEJ confessed sometime ago that his government is infiltrated by Boko Haram, he was, in his own way, admitting that strategic places in the Nigerian state apparatus are heavily populated by persons loyal to the ACF sponsors of Boko Haram. And that even he, the President and Commander-in-Chief, is more or less a one-man hostage to them and the system they have entrenched.

Will the creation of more sates produce the security we need? Would even the conversion of every present LGA in Ala-Igbo into a state --which is most unlikely-- do that? I don't see how it can. Do you?

Will any constitution review and amendment, even if without restrictions and no-go areas, provide the Ethiopian style constitution that Ndi-Igbo need? Not bloody likely. Constitutions are quite conservative instruments. The interests entrenched and served by a constitution are most likely to hold their ground against assailants demanding fundamental changes. The task is as difficult as laying siege to a fortress on a mountain, or trying to dislodge defenders entrenched in a narrow mountain pass. That is why bloody revolutions are usually needed to effect such changes. As the 1999 constitution does not even recognize the existence of ethnic nations/ nationalities, it would require much more than amendments to introduce new entities into its framework. A complete rethink is necessary. So what is required to produce any constitution that could satisfy the minimum requirements for Igbo security is not an amendment or series of amendments, but a fundamental change of the framework and principles on which that constitution was devised and, in particular, a change that would recognize ethnic nations and the concept of autonomous areas. So what Ndi-Igbo need is a totally new constitution based on new principles. Without that, constitutional amendments and the negotiations over them would not yield the minimum Ndi-Igbo requirement. Nor can Igbo Presidency or more states in Ala-Igbo, or more contracts and oil blocs for Igbos, meet the security need.

Ndi-Igbo would therefore do well to instruct Igbo politicians not to fall for such banana baits and thereby end up serving the ACF objective of perpetuating the pro-Califate system—a system that cannot guarantee the security of the Igbo nation, Ndi-Igbo. Any Igbo politician who does so would be sacrificing the Ndi-Igbo interest for some personal Onye-Igbo interest; would be selling the security of present and future generations of Ndi-Igbo for some ephemeral mess of ACF pottage that is personal to him. Such an act would be tantamount to a heinous death-penalty crime (*mpu*), the sort for which, in pre-colonial Ala-Igbo, ***Mmadu n'agbana n'osu*** (a person would flee into the ***osu*** community and adopt ***osu*** status in order to escape punishment).

All rights reserved. © Chinweizu 2012

Nigeria's National Integration and the Dilemma of *Ndigbo*:
A sober reflection
by
Prof. Michael O. Maduagwu

Introduction

This contribution discusses the serious dilemma facing Ndigbo, the Igbo people, in Nigeria today. Ndigbo have been the most ardent promoters of Nigerian unity and national integration. That Nigeria achieved independence as one geographical entity as it stands today must be largely attributed to the compromising character of Nnamdi Azikiwe among the three giant founding fathers, including Ahmadu Bello and Obafemi Awolowo. It was indeed ironical that it was Ndigbo who were forced by circumstances to seriously attempt to secede from Nigeria in the ill-fated Biafra war, 1967 – 1970. Re-integrated into Nigeria after the 30-month brutal war in which millions of them perished, Ndigbo once more fully embraced the Nigerian nation-state. Thus, shortly after the war, they returned to their former places of residence all over Nigeria, including the furthermost parts of northern Nigeria. Today, 44 years after the civil war and 54 years after Independence, Nigeria's national unity is still being threatened. Worse still, Ndigbo have continued to be at the receiving end of the inability of the Nigerian policy makers to achieve genuine national integration. The plight of Ndigbo, especially in northern Nigeria, has been exacerbated since the eruption of ethno-religious crises in northern Nigeria in recent years as well as the emergence of the terrorist group known as Boko Haram. Furthermore, Ndigbo also feel that they are the most politically marginalized of the three major ethnic groups in Nigeria. What then should be the appropriate course of action by Ndigbo in Nigeria today?

Being practically everywhere in Nigeria, Ndigbo are by far the primary promoters of Nigerian unity and integration than the other ethnic groups. But they have continued to pay high price for this through unjustified loss of lives and property especially in Northern Nigeria. The insecurity of lives and property of Ndigbo in northern Nigeria today is reminiscent of pogrom they suffered in 1966 following the first military coup which eventually led to their mass flight to their home region and the subsequent secession and civil war. As a result of this, there has been renewed agitation for self-determination by many Ndigbo. Should Ndigbo therefore re-embark on self-determination even if at a Conference Table or should they continue to lose their lives and property unduly while working for the promotion of Nigeria's unity? This is the dilemma of Ndigbo in present-day Nigeria. In discussing this, the paper first revisits the issue of whether the Amalgamation of 1914 was really a mistake. It then elaborates on the Ndigbo dilemma and proffers the choice before them. The paper argues that it is in the best strategic interest of

Ndigbo to remain in Nigeria and contribute towards developing it into a more egalitarian society for future generations.

Is the 1914 Amalgamation really a Mistake?

Nigeria is endowed with a large population and a vast area. It is also a multi-ethnic country. Apart from the three major ethnic groups, the Hausa-Fulani, the Igbo and the Yoruba, there are also several other ethnic groups, usually called minorities but some of whose populations are as large as many other African countries. Sociologists have estimated that there are between 250 and 400 different ethnic-linguistic groups in Nigeria (Otite 1990).

The religious diversity in Nigeria should also be noted. There are two major religions in the country, Islam and Christianity. In general terms, adherents of these two religions seem to be on par and, due to historical factors, equally concentrated in the Northern and Southern parts of the country, respectively. Thus, Islam could be said to be mainly practiced in the North while Christianity could be said to be mainly practiced in the South. Today, however, each of the two religions have large numbers of followers in Northern States. The membership of the two religions in the North often follow ethnic lines, with the Hausa-Fulani being Muslims while the minority ethnic groups are Christians. This usually complicates inter-ethnic conflicts as has been manifested in Plateau and Kaduna States in recent years.

Having effectively colonized this territory from about 1861, the British ruled it, first as three separate Protectorates, then as Northern and Southern Protectorates and finally as one country with the Amalgamation of Northern and Southern Protectorates on January 1, 1914. Till today, many Nigerians still blame the inability of Nigerians to mould various ethnic nationalities into a nation-state on British colonialism. The British have been accused of having applied *divide-and-rule* in governing Nigeria, implanting in the minds of the Nigerians the feeling of separate identities. Even the Amalgamation was essentially for economic reasons rather than for nation-building.

However, the continued complaint that the British forcefully brought strange bed-fellows into one country should be re-examined. Nigerian historians have now established that centuries before the coming of the British there had been close contacts between the various peoples of the territory, which the British later called Nigeria. Those contacts manifested themselves especially in trade, marriages but sometimes also in wars. The conclusion of our historians has been aptly summed up by the statement credited to Uzoigwe to the effect that "if Nigeria was a historical accident, then it was an accident anxiously waiting to happen" (Quoted in Erim 1996: 17).

In the light of this, we must regard as unfortunate the statements of some of our foremost nationalists who had regretted the bringing together of our peoples by the British through the Amalgamation. It was Obafemi

Awolowo (1947: 47) who described Nigeria as "a mere geographical expression", while Ahmadu Bello (1962: 133) had burst out in anger during one of the sessions of the constitutional conferences of 1953 that "The mistake of 1914 has come to light". But 54 years after Independence and 100 years after the Amalgamation there are still some Nigerian scholars and elites who regret the unity of Nigeria and who blame all our woes on the so-called forced unification of separate peoples into one country.

The Dilemma of Ndigbo

Nevertheless, Ndigbo are facing serious dilemma today in Nigeria. They had been at the forefront in the fight for Nigerian unity. Of the three main Nigerian nationalists, the other two, Obafemi Awolowo and Ahmadu Bello were avowed regional leaders who placed their regions first before Nigeria. Nnamdi Azikiwe, on the other hand, was first an avowed nationalist before circumstances turned him around. As is well known, he was prevented from becoming the first premier of Western Region in 1951 and he had to return across the Niger "whence I came", as he told us in his autobiography. Nevertheless, Zik's nationalist temperament continued to influence his politics all his life to the extent that he was quick to make compromises at crucial moments for the sake of Nigeria's unity. Today, some Ndigbo blame him for not have doggedly championed the Igbo interest like his other compatriots.

Following the unfortunate turn of events after the first military coup d'état in 1966, in which thousands of their people were brutally murdered especially in the Northern Nigeria, Ndigbo seceded from Nigeria. Rather than allow them to go, the other two major ethnic groups, Hausa-Fulani and Yoruba united to suppress the secession. What an irony of history that the champions of Nigerian unity became the "villains" of Nigeria's near disintegration!

The tragic Nigeria-Biafra war almost led to total decimation of Ndigbo. It was nothing short of genocidal war as has been vividly re-affirmed by the foremost Igbo icon, Chinua Achebe in his last literary legacy, *There Was a Country*, before his demise. Towards the end of the war, Zik, who had in fact withdrawn his support from the Biafran cause, travelled from London to meet the Nigerian authorities to plead that the surviving Ndigbo should be granted amnesty after the war. Did Zik influence Gowon's declaration of *"No Victor, No Vanquished"* and his policy of "Reconciliation, Rehabilitation and Reconstruction"? There is no concrete evidence for this, but Zik alluded to his role in securing amnesty for Ndigbo after the war in his *Civil War Soliloquies*.

Be that as it may, 44 years after the civil war, how reconciled and how rehabilitated are Ndigbo? How far is their geo-political area reconstructed? The truth is that Ndigbo have not yet fully recovered from the reality of defeat. At the Oputa Panel Ndigbo catalogued several atrocities they have suffered in Nigeria since before and after Independence. Even with the purported Gowon's policy of 3Rs there were deliberate policies that bring home the reality of defeat to Ndigbo. The Federal Government banking policy after the civil war nullified every amount any Igbo person had in banks and they were paid only the then Nigerian Twenty Pounds. Shortly after that Nigeria carried out indigenization policy and of course Ndigbo, not having any resources, could not participate. Despite the reconstruction policy, the federal highways in the then Eastern Region have remained the worst in the whole of Nigeria even with the bulk of crude oil ferried across the country from that part of Nigeria. Despite the proclamation after the war of "No Victor, No Vanquished", the property of Ndigbo, including houses, furniture, shops, factories and landed properties were seized by the Rivers State Government and declared "Abandoned Properties" with the acquiescence of the Federal Government. No compensations were paid to the owners. Politically, Ndigbo also feel that they are the most marginalized of the three major ethnic groups in Nigeria since independence. For one thing, they have only ruled Nigeria for mere six months by default, when Aguyi Ironsi became the military head of state after the unfortunate first military coup in 1966. Then of the six geo-political zones, the South East, despite its population, is still the only zone with only five States while the other zones have six each and one zone has even seven States.

Yet, the above catalogue of woes pale when compared with the continuous loss of lives and property and indeed the general insecurity of Ndigbo in the North at any flimsy excuse especially since 1999. Whenever there is ethno-religious crisis in any State of the North between the Hausa-Fulani and other indigenous peoples or Christian minorities, Ndigbo become the main target of violence by the Hausa-Fulani Muslims. In fact, even when Hausa-Fulani Muslims feel that Islam is being attacked in foreign countries they vent their anger on Ndigbo in the North by attacking them, destroying and looting their property. The climax of insecurity of Ndigbo in Nigeria today, particularly in the North is of course the ongoing Boko Haram terrorism. As usual, when this insurgency started about 2009, Ndigbo in the affected States in the North were the main targets. They were killed in their numbers, their property destroyed and several thousands of them had to flee home.

Given this scenario, what should be the appropriate course of action for Ndigbo in Nigeria today? Should they continue to bear the brunt of the promotion of Nigeria's unity and national integration or should they, as being suggested in some quarters, re-embark on self-determination or independence from Nigeria, even if by peaceful means as eventually happened in Ethiopia and Sudan, to cite only recent African examples? The next Section addresses this issue.

The Way Forward for Ndigbo

At different fora in recent years, especially with the increased loss of lives and property by Ndigbo during the incessant ethno-religious crises that erupted in many parts of the North after the return to democracy in 1999, as well as the emergence of the Boko Haram terrorism, many Ndigbo have been agitating for either outright separation of Ndigbo from the rest of Nigeria or at the very least self-determination of Ndigbo. Today, many Ndigbo are convinced that they are not safe in the other parts of Nigeria except in their homeland. This is particularly so with regard to the North.

After a sober reflection, I have come to the conclusion that the interest of Ndigbo will still be better served both in the short but especially in the long run if they remained in Nigeria than if they separate, assuming separation could even be achieved at a conference table. If for nothing else, the temperament of Ndigbo, their enterprising nature, their adventurous nature, their sheer doggedness in the midst of challenges, their adaptive nature – all these endowments make it almost impossible for Ndigbo to be circumscribed in their little home enclave. They must venture out not only to survive but also to achieve meaningful existence. Is there any part of Nigeria, town or village you will go to today, especially in the far North and you will not find an Igbo man? In fact, just as it is in the strategic interest of Nigeria that the West African Sub-region remains safe and secure so should it be in the strategic interest of Ndigbo that Nigeria survives as a nation. Therefore, rather than attempting to set back the hand of the clock, it would be better for Ndigbo to continue to apply their intellectual and material resources to the development of the Nigerian project. This is not to say that they should neglect the development of Igboland. Quite the contrary. As the saying goes, charity begins at home. Ndigbo, both at home and in the Diaspora, should join hands together to develop Igboland in such a way that it becomes the "Singapore" or "Hong Kong" of Nigeria. And why not?

Someone may ask: why should Ndigbo continue to invest in the development of Nigeria in the face of political marginalization and, in particular, in the face of insecurity of their lives and property especially in Northern Nigeria? My answer is that this is where the intellectual and political astuteness of Ndigbo should come in. How was it possible for the blacks under the leadership Mandela to eventually succeed in getting their white minority but powerful arch South African enemies to turn around and now live in peace with them in a united South Africa? How was it possible that the African American leaders spearheaded by Martin Luther King Jnr. were able to fight for the emancipation of their people until they become accepted as equal citizens in the United States to the extent that a black man eventually became the President of the United States? Ndigbo should build on their traditional democratic values, egalitarianism and respect for the rule of law to work towards the eventual enthronement of justice and fair play for all in Nigeria. If this becomes the long term political goal of Ndigbo, sooner or later, a new Nigeria will emerge where they will no longer be targets of violence and marginalization.

To start with, Ndigbo, through their political leaders and the elite, should champion legislations at the National Assembly that would curb the incessant attacks on their people in any parts of the country. After the horrible experience of Holocaust during the Second World War in Germany, the Jews vowed "Never Again!" Ndigbo have shed enough blood in Nigeria. The time is over due to enact laws for the effective protection of the lives and property of Ndigbo anywhere in Nigeria. The primary duty of any government is the protection of lives and property of its citizens. Therefore it must be the responsibility of both the Federal and State Governments to ensure that the lives and property of Nigerians are effectively protected anywhere in Nigeria. Henceforth, any attack on Ndigbo, in particular during communal or ethno-religious crises anywhere in Nigeria should not go unpunished. There must be laws for appropriate compensation of victims of communal crises in Nigeria as well as appropriate punishment for the perpetrators. If such laws are enacted and effectively enforced, they will go a long way in reducing the frequent attacks on Ndigbo especially in the North.

In the meantime, Ndigbo need to liberate themselves from the psychology of defeat. The civil war is long over and Ndigbo owe no one any apologies for seeking safety in their homeland when it seemed they were no longer welcome elsewhere or trying to defend themselves when attacked. Ndigbo have no reason to be tiptoeing anywhere in Nigeria today as if they were aliens or barricading themselves from their people when they are in positions of authority. Having been fully re-integrated into Nigeria, they should be bold at all times to demand their rights when denied. While those in authority among them should not succumb to the temptation of nepotism, they should also not continue to cowardly deny their compatriots what they truly deserve under the guise that "*ha ga-asi*" (people will talk). Unfortunately, this has become the bane of Ndigbo perhaps since after the civil war.

Conclusion

It is argued in this contribution that in the long run it is of the strategic interest for Ndigbo to remain in Nigeria than to re-embark on separation even if on a conference table. The character of Ndigbo is such that they require a large territorial space for survival and self-fulfillment. The paper does not advocate that Ndigbo should fold their hands and continue to lose their lives and property especially in Northern Nigeria. Rather, they should employ political engineering to work for national integration and a more egalitarian Nigerian society where justice and rule of law would eventually triumph. Mandela and his compatriots achieved that in South Africa and

African American leaders achieved same for the blacks in the United States. Finally the paper admonishes Ndigbo to put behind them the unfortunate civil war experience liberate themselves from the psychology of defeat which seems to have continued to haunt them in Nigeria.

References
Achebe, Chinua (2012), *There Was a Country: A Personal History of Biafra.* New York: Penguin Press
Awolowo, Obafemi [1947], *Path to Nigerian Freedom*, London: Faber and Faber Ltd.
Azikiwe, Nnamdi (1970), *My Odyssey: An Autobiography*, London: C. Hurst and Company
Bello, Ahmadu (1962), *My Life*, Cambridge: Cambridge University Press.
Erim, E. O (1996), "Pre-Colonial Antecedents of the Foundations of the Nigerian Federalism: Theoretical Considerations" in Elaigwu, Isawa J and Erim. O. Erim. *Foundations of Nigerian Federalism: Pre-Colonial Antecedents,* Abuja: National Council of Inte-rgovernmental Relations.
Otite, Onigu (1990), *Ethnic Pluralism and Ethnicity in Nigeria*, Ibadan: Shaneson Ltd.

Draft Igbo Agenda in Nigeria Project
by
Nze Professor M A C Odu

1. Preamble

Certain weighty statements have to be made on the Nigeria Project to clarify the import of this document.

1.1 Ndigbo were in the forefront of Nigeria's leadership elite during colonialism and shortly after independence. The political elite of Ndigbo set their sights on Nigerian leadership and did precious little to provide appropriate cognateness for growth of Ndigbo as a major segment of Nigerian populace. Ndigbo failed to address a united front in the Nigeria Project on account of individual pursuits of wealth and importance that precluded Igbo unity. Attempts to foster Pan-Igbo unity was frustrated by leadership who had an agenda to lead Nigeria and its heterogeneity and perhaps Africa without ensuring that there is a solid Igbo home-front to create and fall back to, when the need arises; thereby negating the Igbo proverb that admonishes leaders to organise and beautify the home before daring distant lands. Leadership of Nigeria especially in technology and bureaucracy, naturally devolved on Ndigbo as independence approached. It is on record that University of Nigeria led in public service intakes as soon as its products hit the labour market.

1.2 Disaffection and envy arose in the consciousness of neighbours and developed into a crescendo when a coup di etat was planned. Ndigbo received a shock from neighbours when their concept of nationalism became their undoing with the interpretation of the military intervention of the majors received skewed colouration to their detriment. The downward slide of Ndigbo commenced. Nigeria commenced a process of clipping the wings of Ndigbo and shortchanging the delivery of quality service in the public sector of Nigeria project. Quota arrived to whittle delivery of services further and entrenched mediocrity and sharing on the basis of population rather than competence. An army of technocrats received replacements from a new quota power elite and the Nigeria Project started floundering. That descent to the abyss of productivity has continued till this day of writing. Greed and Avarice accentuated the decline of the Nigerian Project that was initially result oriented. Our real sector growth was impaired by sharing of resources meant for capital creation and real sector development among power elite who had no ranking concept of difference between private and public owned resources. The northern Islamic elite made free of national resources for welfare of their people in consumption terms only. The Nigeria Project bled at the altar of ineptitude of its new cannibals. The result was that when Ndigbo received pent-up avalanche of hatred with concomitant hostility of various kinds, no recovery plan could be conceived and implemented by Igbo leadership. The military incursion into leadership in Nigeria could not elicit appropriate response from Ndigbo. Fear of skin pain among the leadership led to the collapse of Ndigbo. Ikemba Odumegwu Ojukwu's response to the motley of disdainful experiences following the Pogrom of 1966 and thereafter was naïve in perspective and unwholesome to the future of Ndigbo in the Nigeria Project. No foundation had been laid for Igbo resurgence or even survival ever since. Ndigbo have consequently lost out of relevance and are compelled with this document to accept that fact.

1.3 It is the bounden duty of the elite of every race to redirect their race when it is evident that the trajectory of that race has gone awry and no longer congruent to aspirations of her majority. Our daring spirit has not redounded to our advantage because there is a severe lack of leadership for a race of people numbering close to fifty million and more, with only one language shared in a vast territory now constricted by envy and fear among neighbours to five states neglecting cousins carved disdainfully into neighbouring states.

1.4 Ohaneze Ndigbo by fits and starts has remained the apex Igbo organisation to champion much-needed resurgence of Igbo Spirit not necessarily for national leadership but for self realization and eventual relevance to the aspirations of Igbo majority. The organisation of Ohaneze Ndigbo so far leaves much to be desired. Personal interests of its leaders have shortchanged its impact through its history. Penchant for gain with position and power has whittled down its restorative impact on the Igbo psyche. The corporate destiny of Ndigbo has been a subject for trade. Ndigbo have failed to rise to relevance through the new attempt at building a new republic from 1999 till date. There has been a subtle and deliberate consensual block to Ndigbo resurgence in Nigeria Project.

1.5 The Nigerian Project has continued floundering on the altar of ineptitude of beneficiaries of the project to garrison resources for pervasive benefit for current and future Nigerian humanity. It is vital now to sue for destiny to return to Igboland from a national level into which it was erroneously ceded by military adventurists whose intervention has turned out to be destructive in the main. This has to be conducted on a national plane with agenda from all contending parties as template. Ndigbo must not be found wanting in articulation of an agenda for its own survival in Nigeria Project.

2. True Federation is no longer negotiable

2.1 A strong central government in Abuja has not redounded to commensurate benefit to the existing zones of the Federal Republic of Nigeria. Power should be devolved to the zones which must now contribute to the maintenance of a central government on terms that will be agreed upon.

Abuja Nigeria's Capital Territory has become an unmitigated disaster in terms of positive evolution of Nigeria Project. It produces nothing but provides access to limitless profligacy and greed of the three arms of government.

2.2 The Legislature replete with inexperienced law makers hive for themselves as much portions of the commonwealth as they can conscript by increasingly disastrous legislation and get away with it. They net in capital for further forays in power with legislative swindling, resulting in weaker and weaker economy bereft of real sector growth.

2.3 Power has for decades eluded the productive sector and little has been done to change the steep downward slope to diminishing productivity and gross national product. Education in functional terms has gone to the dogs.

3.4 Competence is sliding at all levels of society and crime is rising on account of failure of Nigeria Project to even envision a future for an ill-prepared work force in a fast developing world. In the meantime resources evenly spread out in the four winds of Nigeria are not being applied toward increasing productivity. They are being looted for investments offshore. The Federal Government currently and through these near five decades have festered and fostered poverty on Nigeria.

3. Agenda Items

3.1 Item No. 1 on the agenda

Ndigbo have come to the conclusion that the slide must be checked by devolution of power to the zones that have been largely accepted as political power blocks in the Nigeria Project even though our defeat in Biafra War resulted in our diminution to a weaker status. Ndigbo must accept that fact as the outcrop of conflict and carry on without any further distraction.

3.2 Item No. 2 on the agenda

The Presidential System of Government is no longer acceptable to Ndigbo. A parliamentary system shall be in force at the centre and the zones. Candidates with appropriate experience in various spheres of life above sixty years of age shall contest for both national, zonal, state local government assemblies to make laws for the various levels of government. Legislation at any level is a job for experienced citizens.

3.3 Item 3 on the agenda

Natural Resources within each zone or state of the new Federal Republic shall belong to the zone and shall be exploited for the benefit of the zone or state. Laws shall be made by a National Assembly for contributions to the centre by zones for the upkeep of our central organisations and international obligations and common services.

3.4 Item 4 on the agenda

Ndigbo will not seek to contest for the presidency of Nigeria for the next sixteen years. It is a distraction which has resulted in the fractionalization of our corporate spirit. The body language of our co-travelers in Nigeria Project is eloquent enough. We shall however use our population to full effect, and determine through voting whoever will gain ascendancy to a diminished central government.

3.5 Item 5 on the agenda

Ndigbo shall present to contending parties to power at the centre requirements for the development of Igboland, which shall be drawn up by a committee of Ohaneze Ndigbo and approved by Ohaneze Ndigbo worldwide. These requirements must be acceded to in writing by the contending parties before Ohaneze directs Ndigbo to cast their votes for an approved contender for office at the centre.

3.6 Item 6 on the agenda

Ndigbo shall obtain from Nigeria Project an undertaking not to tamper with Investments of Ndigbo in any zone or state in Nigeria by blatant or subtle means in return for her distance from power during these sixteen years of corporate immolation. Nothing shall preclude Ndigbo from giving support to states which provide safe anchorage for Ndigbo investments in their states during our period of corporate immolation.

3.7 Item 7 on the agenda

Ndigbo shall demand Trader Education Project from all governments of the New Federal Republic as a matter of course. Arrangements will be initiated by Ndigbo for the anchorage of this project and presented in a shopping bag to contenders for national leadership.

3.8 Item 8 on the agenda

Ndigbo shall require central support for its farming people. A massive cooperative movement shall be embarked upon to assure Ndigbo of food security. To this effect, a Cooperative Bank shall be reignited to power production and development in the rural sector and assure food security into the far future in all parts of Igboland. The central government shall be required to lend initial support.

3.9 Item 9 on the agenda

Ndigbo shall require liberal importation of industrial hardware for establishment of industries in all parts of Nigeria where raw materials exist. Liberal terms for establishing these industries will be sought for and should be granted in return for employment opportunities to be created for incipient zones or states in which such industrial concerns shall be located.

3.10 Item 10 on the agenda

Ndigbo shall insist on the completion of Third Niger Bridge, development of Oguta Inland Port and dredging of its access to the sea for purposes of shipping and international trade and tourism which shall be vital for commerce and industry in Igboland. Onitsha Port should be completed for Inland Water Transport, now that sections of River Niger have been dredged ready for inland transportation of people and goods. Special concessions shall be sought for operating cargo ships and barges on River Niger and its tributaries from operators. A Free Trade Zone is necessary for Igboland and should be contemplated immediately.

3.11 Item 11 on the agenda

Ndigbo would require one more international airport at Oba in Anambra State for purposes of commercial and industrial establishments that will be powered into existence by local entrepreneurial skills domiciled in the area.

4. Conclusion

4.1 A Sovereign National Conference is implied in all of these proposals. Other zones are encouraged to come up with their own agenda to make the conference an easy task to accomplish.

4.2 If Ohaneze Ndigbo receives assent to these demands in writing it shall support a party with a good and qualified candidate for presidency of Nigeria as a zone and as a single language community in the Nigeria Project. The proviso of course shall be the full implementation of all the demands within the administration which Ndigbo shall support.

Humbly presented as material for deliberation at all levels of Ohaneze Ndigbo. Nze Prof. M A C Odu, Member from Imo State, Sunday June 16 2013

SECTION FIFTEEN: THE WAY FORWARD

Ndi Igbo in Nigeria: Challenges and the Future
by
Dr. Dozie Ikedife

When I was the President General of Ohaneze Ndigbo in my Presidential address at the 2008 Igbo Day Celebration, the theme for which was *Ofu Onu, Ofu Obi*, I expressed my belief that if Igbo people of Nigeria could achieve the status of *Ofu Obi, Ofu Onu*, they shall have no reason whatsoever to talk of marginalization in Nigeria again. Their God given ingenuity will be harnessed synergistically to the benefit of themselves, Nigeria and the rest of Africa.

We need prefects, whips, *Ndi nche*, to help us re-enact the age old discipline within the Igbo society. We are where we are in the Map of Africa by God's design, not by accident. God's design can never be thwarted by men. What challenges do we have in Nigeria? There are many. I shall not bore you with a long list. They are palpable everywhere. Ndi Igbo who are one of the Principal stocks of Negroid race occupied part of the ancient nation called Biafra. When the European (Portuguese) explorers first came in contact with them in the 15th century (1470s) as they travelled east wards along the coast of West Africa, the Biafrans were at that time identified as settled people with stable collective gerontocratic administrative structure. Then these explorers identified three main nations in the vicinity (1) Biafra. (Biafra) located in the present Eastern region of Nigeria, Southern Cameroon down to present Gabon (2) Zamfara in the region north of Biafra and (3) Bini nation on the western side of Biafra. These were the three known nationalities in those areas. Further North-West we had the Shongai Empire. Then the Biafrans had stable settlement and stable government. The British explorers and traders came much later. About 450 years later a false marriage of amalgamation of many incongruous people was foisted on us in 1913, operative from 1914. It is obvious that our ancestors did not negotiate or consent to or sign the amalgamation document. By coercion and manipulation this shotgun marriage held for 46 years while the British were the watchful masters. But even under their watch sporadic ethnic clashes were manifested here and there from 1953 till independence in 1960. More violent clashes and genocidal manifestations of disparate people of Nigeria become the order of the years thereafter. It is still there to date in one form or the other.

Progressively manifestations of hate overwhelmed demonstrations of love. The Biafrans were visited with immeasurable doses of attempts to obliterate them off the face of the earth. To the extent that now the Bight of Biafra was removed from all new maps of West Africa. The old ones still have them. After the June 1966 Coup d' etat a more blatant and systematic genocide followed. General Gowon and the rest of the north were shouting *araba, araba, awale awale* - divide, divide Nigeria. The Biafrans in Nigeria took the queue, escaped into Biafraland and declared the state of Biafra. On the advice of Britain, Gowon did 180 degree turn and sang a different refrain- "to keep Nigeria one is a task that must be done" and declared war against Biafra. With the active support of Britain, Russia and Egypt, Nigeria inflicted a merciless annihilatory war on Biafrans and in the process committed many war crimes against humanity contrary to the Geneva Convention. This is meanwhile buried just in a shallow grave and will be visited in time. The war-induced manifestation of Biafran technology and ingenuity was also "killed". "In Biafra Africa Died" (Apologies to Rev. Dr. Emefiena Ezeani).

The Biafrans (indigenous People of Biafra with Nigerian nationalities) today face a lot of challenges. The challenge of Existence or Survival; The fear of loss of identity. God made no mistake by creating us as Ndi Igbo and Biafrans and planting us here. How much do our neighbours love us? How well do they understand us? How willing and ready are they to co-operate with us to take our destinies in our hands- together? We have the challenge of rediscovering ourselves and to regain the self confidence the Igbos and Biafrans had before the war. We must achieve *Ofu Obi, Ofu Onu*. The broom tied together or separated analogy is very applicable. *Igwe bu ike*.

In the mean time let us have proper enumeration, evaluation and computing of the losses. If the rest of Nigerians want us they must demonstrate it in no uncertain ways, at least by apology, reparation and accommodation. If they do not then they must let us be. The Biafrans have always had the Indigenous system of governance; one for all and all for one, with collective leadership. One of the many interpretations of the expression *"Igbo Enwe Eze"* may mean "Ndi Igbo ... have no Kings" (a wrong interpretation) King or no King, the Biafrans must have common interests which must include survival - survival within or better, outside Nigeria. To this extent the indigenous People of Biafra through Bilie Human Rights Initiative Incorporated have gone to a Federal High Court to pray for an order declaring among other things, the following-:

(a) An Order declaring that the Claimants (the Biafrans) have the right of self-determination pursuant to Articles 19 – 25, Cap 10, Laws of the Federation of Nigeria, 1990, and are therefore free to exercise their unquestionable and inalienable right to self-determination to freely determine their political status and pursue their economic and social development according to the policy they have freely chosen.

(b) An Order declaring that the ethnic nationalities that make up Nigeria are not held as slaves under Section 2(1) of Constitution of Nigeria 1999 and therefore have the right of self-determination to decide their political status by the rule of law.

(c) An Order declaring that the Defendants (Federal Republic of Nigeria) are liable to pay to the Claimants (the Indigenous People of Biafra) by way of compensation or reparation the present value of all money, properties and assets of the Claimants seized by the Defendants pursuant to the Abandoned Properties Act of 1979 in violation of the Claimants right to own properties in any part of the country since the properties were not seized in war time but nine years after the war, based on the post-war discriminatory policies and laws made by the Defendants to suppress the Claimants from generation to generation.

(d) An Order directing the Defendants to comply with the provisions of Article 20 (30 of the Africa Charter on Human and Peoples' Right (Ratification and Enforcement) Act Cap 10 Laws of the Federation of Nigeria 1990 and consequently give all assistance to the Claimants in the exercise of their right to self-determination.

(e) An Order declaring that the Defendants by registering Nigeria as a member of the Organization of Islamic Countries (OIC) have turned Nigeria into an Islamic country contrary to Section 10 of the constitution of Nigeria 1999 and therefore the Claimants being mostly Christians have the right to dissociate themselves from the Defendants and refuse to be called the citizens of an Islamic country.

The future is bright. We shall re-discover our self, our spirit of honest endeavor, sense of honesty, fair play, justice and equity as symbolized by *Ofo na Ogu*. We were doing quite well before the amalgamation. We have been bruised, battered and bloodied and almost completely exterminated within "the geographical expression called Nigeria" (apologies to late Chief Obafemi Awolowo). Security of life and property is fundamental in any nation. Sacrificial lamb should not here be translated to mean a "sacrificial people," the Biafran People. The game we are playing today is not a game of survival. It is a suicidal game. Any wife or husband beater has no right to insist on the marriage continuing. Divorce is an option that could be exercised by either partner. That option is fundamental. If nothing else it engenders mutual respect.

Our economy, which, like any other survival economy is beyond our geography. It must extend much farther afield. For instance look at the following countries – Taiwan and China, United Kingdom and America, Japan and Australia – countries with viable economies.

We have been pushed to the wall. Let Nigeria be wise and draw examples from Union of Socialist Soviet Russia (USSR), Yugoslavia, Czechoslovakia, Indian sub-continent, Sudan, United Kingdom, Timor and others. But let us do a better job of it, bloodlessly. It is better to be neighbours and respect each other than pretend to be brothers that hate, kill, exploit, suppress, and draw circles of exclusions.

Summary:

If Ndi Igbo and Biafrans could achieve the status of *Ofu Obi, Ofu Onu* or just viable consensus their God-given ingenuity and industry will in synergy propel Nigeria and Africa into the mid stream of the 21st century, into a place of pride among the advanced countries of the world. If Nigeria does not accept Nde Igbo and Biafrans on basis of equity, equality, justice and fairness - then they should let us be. Whatever is the case we must remain united as a people.

The Road Map to Igbo Restoration and Reconstruction
by
Dr. Uduma Idika

Ndi Eze, Nze na Ozo, Ndi Ichie na Ndi Nna; umu Igbo – ndi Nwoke na ndi Nwanyi nile - onye obula zaa nke ana-etu ya. Udo diri unu nile, dikwara ndi Igbo nile.

From the platform of IGBOBRIO (The Igbo-Hebrew cultural restoration organization) we consider this occasion not only as unique but also as divine because as the Igbo proverb says *"Ukwa chaa, ya adaa n'ala"*. This is the reason for our confidence and participation.

Igbo Root and Igbo Character

The Hebrew (IBOS) or "Jewish race" - a concept first used by Adolf Hilter in 1933 - claim to have descended from a progenitor called Abram (Ibiam). Father Abraham is eternally remembered for his monotheistic vision. Abraham's vision of one supreme God has eternally defined divinity as well as the fusion of divinity and humanity in such a manner that man has anchored his evolution and civilization around Abraham's concept for more than four millennia. Also, his vision provided a unique characteristic for Abraham and his descendants "for- ever," the covenant of circumcision on the 8th of birth.

This covenant and its expressions among generations of Abraham's descendants contain the seed of opposition by the other peoples of the earth toward the descendants of Abraham who became identified as Jews over time. This opposition continues to grow and be expressed generation after generation in spite of, or even because of humanity's acceptance of Abraham's vision of divinity and humanity. The claim of unique relationship with God by Abraham and his descendants understandably remains objectionable to other peoples despite varied attempts at the same assumptions. The second attempt by another Hebrew leader, Moshe (MOSES) to expand and explain Abraham's vision still emphasized the uniqueness of the Jews and by implication contained further seed of opposition to the Jews. Moses' revelation on Mount Sinai and the giving of the law to Israel became the defining corner stone in the evolution of the character of the Israel – spiritually, psychologically and sociologically. This is the root of Igbo culture (omenala). On this same account, the two other religions – Christianity and Islam – that claim to be fathered by the same vision and principles of Abraham and Moses have sustained the greatest oppositions to the Jews everywhere, including Igbo till this century. This conflict is not moral, it is not political and it is not even religious. The conflict is psychological and cultural. And so may not be easily resolved because of the sublineal and resilient nature of culture.

As it is the experiences of the Jews across the nations and communities of the earth, this is the crux of the conflict between Igbos and "others in Nigeria." You can now appreciate the reason why ACF [Arewa Consultative Forum], during the "Oputa Human Right Violations Panel" presented a news paper publication of 1940s, where in addressing Igbo students in US, Nnamdi Azikiwe reminded them the claim that they are Jews. The unstated aim of the ACF was to let Igbo know that Igbo claim of unique or Jewish identity is offensive, unacceptable.

It must be noted in brief that the fusion of humanity and divinity provides the Jewish minds direct access to the source of all provisions, individually and collectively. Thus, although the Greek philosophers provided the theoretical framework for democracy, the Jewish vision provided the psychological and spiritual basis. This is the root of Igbo perpetual opposition and resistance to domination and subjugation. This is the under lining character trait of the Jews – the Hebrews – Ibos.

Historical Interventions and the Root of Igbo Burden

Some of the major historical encounters and exposures of Igbos have been such that tended to strengthen this specific characteristic of the people – they continuously feel unique and different from other peoples. But let quickly point the fact that the uniqueness is never felt in terms of superiority but separateness and distinct. It is this separate identity that kept Israel (i.e. European Jews) for two thousand years of exile or in Diaspora without dissolving completely into Europeanism. And, as Odumegwu Ojukwu said, it also kept Igbos as an "Island within the raging sea of Islam" in Nigeria. Let us briefly examine some major historical encounters of Igbos in the light of Igbo (or Hebrew) unique characters.

(a) Conquest of Samaria and Emigration: The Assyrian conquest of the kingdom of Israel between 738 and 702 B.C.E. was unique in one major sense. It was fueled by extreme hatred and brutality and aimed at wiping out the people of Israel and their identity. In consequence, the people were carried into exile (of no return) and strangers brought in to *occupy their land and its resources*. And to the exile Hebrews, it was a horrific and psychological trauma resulting from loss of their original ancient national home bearing their national land-marks; loss of their authentic religious and spiritual center and the sacred documents of their ancient creed. Also the encounter of the fleeing Hebrews with the Edomites – their neighbors on the southern end of Judah; and descendants of Esau - bore another mark of hatred and thus strengthening the psychological feeling of separateness among them. By that encounter, many of the Israelites who could have escaped alive to Egypt were brutally hedged and murdered by the Assyrians, on the invitation of the Edomites [kith and kin of the Israelites].

Again, after staying in Egypt for more than a century, those Hebrews could have lost their national identity and permanently dissolve into their Diaspora surrounding. But one of their unique religious institutions, the prophet, resisted that tendency. Thus, prophet Jeremiah who was also swept to Egypt, by a later wave of conquest of the kingdom of Judah by the Babylonians, began to rebuke the Hebrew communities in Egypt for joining in the worship of a popular fertility goddess in ancient Egypt called, Ushim.

(b) Encounter With the Oduduwa Immigrants: The Igbos and their kindred tribes and arrived in the territory called Nigeria today between the 6th and 5th centuries B.C.E. [according to some African historians, including Basil Davidson]. They evolved a large and powerful empire of Ado that lasted for a millennium or more before the arrival of a new immigrating group expressly, escaping the ravages of early Islamic jihadists of the 7th century C.E.

As the new immigrants were not violent and destructive, the Ado people had no qualms in accommodating them in their territory. With time there were population mixes between the two groups – with each group managing to retain its unique characters. That was before the treachery orchestrated by the Yoruba group, aimed at taking over the Ado stool and royalty, ignited a major friction. For reasons yet to be fully revealed by research, the Ado royalty disintegrated stimulating a migratory trend from Southwest across the Niger (Osimiri ide) to the Southeast and South-south territories. The nature and pattern of those migrations that spanned more than three centuries became the pivot and the foundation of acclaimed concept of *"Igbo Enweze"*. The migrations were in small family or clan units and had no central co-ordination. Thus, each immigrant group across the Niger became autonomous and almost self reliant, giving vigor and expression to their instinct of republicanism, and completely resolving the patriarchal throne of Ife and the stool of Ado king, *Ogene"*.

(c) European Encounter: It is doubtful whether there have been an encounter as impactful on the destiny and troubles of Igbos as the European encounter. It was the voyage of Mungo Park, a *(Marano and Converso?)* Jew in the late fifteenth century that opened the coast of West Africa to the European markets. Two decisive events have characterized Igbo encounter with Europe more acutely. Namely, *slave trade and colonialism*. Let us briefly consider the impacts of each encounter on Igbo destiny.

The trade link that opened between Europe and the Athlantic Coast of Africa in the 15th century was majorly based on exchange of African forest products and European ornamentals. Due to the demands of the new world, *America*, the nature of the trade between coastal Africa and Europe changed within the first century. To exploit the potentials and opportunities found in America, Europe needed to expand agricultural production. Human labour was the most critical factor in agricultural production of the preindustrial age. But Europe's population of 13th to 16th centuries was never adequate for that challenge. Some socio-political and religious factors that resulted series of population expulsions on the reasons of race, religious or political differences meant significant emigrations out of Europe. The devastation of the *"Black death"* epidemic was blamed on the Jews.

Consequently, Europe turned towards Africa for the supply of the manpower needed to exploit American agriculture. But the nature or condition of slave trading known to man from the ancient times was insufficient for the American demand. This meant the *birth of slave cartel* from coastal African soil. Also, owing to traits largely associated with Igbo's, Igbo land quickly became the focus of the illicit human cargo trade. The traits include but never limited to *resilience, endurance, intelligence, agility and resourcefulness.* It should also be noted that the *republican* nature of the Igbo communities made comprehensive campaign against slave trade almost impossible. It is estimated that one out of every four slaves bought in Africa was Ibo.

Most historians writing about the Impacts of slave trade on Africa often focus on African depopulation and the socio-political and economic dislocations. Attention has rarely been paid to the psychological and spiritual devastations of African people. But there lay the worst impacts of slave trade. The fears and anxieties induced in our communities by slave raids survived up to the third quarter of the twentieth century in Igbo land. It accelerated communal suspicions more than any other social factor. The **Aros,** the most ebullient Igbo group centrally involved in slave trade smeared their image. In the process, they barter a positive destiny of providing a most needed rallying point or leadership for Igbos, after their migration from the Southwest.

On the religious angle, Aros also introduced a religious concept that almost blurred the Igbo-Hebrew *religious identity.* For purposes of profiting in the business of slave trade, Aros adopted and popularized an idol venerated by an Aborigin community in Calabar area. The concept *"Chukwu"* which originally was **"Tshuk"** was not an original Igbo concept. As the Aros adopted and popularized it as the most powerful oracle, it became corrupted among Igbos as Chukwu, because, Igbo language had not evolved *"tsh"* which they could not pronounce. In consequence, the concept *Chukwu* which now implies the great God in Igbo language provided a powerful and logical tool for the religious black mail against Igbos. Thus, the missionaries quickly pointed at the concept "Chukwu" as evidence that Igbos venerated multitude of gods. Because, if Igbos have one *"big God"* they must also have other *"smaller gods"*.

This assumption, though a black mail, quickly gained currency and influenced the attitudes of the early missions and their local converts towards Igbo nation. The Socio-religious devastations arising from this root remain immeasurable. This is the root of the gospel of community or city or family deliverances that have turned Igbo communities and families into bits since 1990s.

Before the oracle, Chukwu became exaggerated and popularized by Arochukwu, Igbo concept that described the Almighty are **"Obasi or Obasi bi n'igwe and Chineke".** These two concepts are of Hebrew origins, with minor linguistic corruptions and both were adopted by Igbos in obedience to the *third commandment* of Moses which almost forbade Israel from mentioning the revealed name of their God. The word **Obasi** was corrupted from a Hebrew word "Abasha" (which literally means "father in heaven") similarly **Chineke** is a coinage of two Hebrew words: *chi or chai and "neke or leke*. In Hebrew, "chai" means "life" while neke means distribution or distributor. Thus, Chineke in Hebrew means the giver or distributor" of life. Igbo ancestors knew that they venerated only the mighty God, the owner of the whole universe. But local or individual deviations should not be confused with national or general thrust of the people.

Finally, in our evaluations of the negative impacts of slave trade on Igbos. Let's ask one or two important questions. First, why Christian Europe and America did not introduce Christianity simultaneously with their trade in coastal Africa in the 15th century? Why did they have to wait for more than three centuries of slave cartel before introducing Christianity? Was Christianity introduced to enlighten the "Savage"people and preparing them for blissful eternal life or as a tool to deflect the steam of a bad business – *slave trade* – gathering to bust upon Europe and America with terrific consequences? We shall return to these questions. The summary of our conclusions here is that the *slave trade* comprehensively disintegrated Igbo Nation – *physically, politically, socially and psycho–spiritually*. There are few communities of humanity that could absorb these measures and still survive.

Another major impactful encounter of Igbos with Europe is **colonialism.** The "positive" and negative impacts of colonialism across the communities of Africa or the third World countries are still elaborately told and written. However, because of the tendency to use a *"universal"* standard for the assessments, and because it is the victor that writes history, some critically vital and specific impacts on groups, or communities, of Africa are rarely considered. For instance, the common assumption for the *non-workability* of the *Nigerian system* is that it is of colonial origin, but what in the colonial enterprise produced this Nigerian system? The amalgamation! The amalgamation forcefully yoked together several incompatible tribes. Why the

British colonial office did desire the amalgamation for the peoples of this territory? Our primary text books say that it was to augment the deficit of the northern protectorate with the surplus from the south.

However, after considering the turn of events in Nigeria from the period of amalgamation and the volume, frequency and vehemence of oppositions and protests from especially southern Nigeria, and after noting the ferocity and rapidity of the British desire for the policy, kirk Greene in his unpublished essay of 1968 on the Nigerian system *made a salient* observation. Namely: that the British Crown, Frederick Lugard and the Secretary of State, have not truly disclosed the reason for the policy. Was the British economic interest the only reason for which the rational British completely ignored the popular expressions of colonial subjects? Were there no other alternative measures by which the economic differentials between north and south could have been managed? How much was the difference when the major sources of revenue were cotton, groundnuts, hides and skin from the north, while cocoa was from the West and palm from the East? Black gold was yet to enter into the economic circle.

In recent times some have began to suggest **"Igbo containment"** as the main factor in the British colonial policy of amalgamation. Indeed, Frederick Lugard never concealed his bias against southern Nigeria and most particularly Eastern Nigeria. The republican nature of Igbo communities and Igbo trait of "hard to rule" have also been mentioned as reasons. But were Igbo republicanism and hardness still of major administrative relevance after the British military conquest Igbo land? Could the "rational and holy England sustain such magnitude of hate towards colonial subjects because of minor political behavior? These evaluations are necessary because, right from the beginning the disastrous consequences of amalgamation were not obscured in the minds of the local citizens and their leadership and other citizen of the British Empire. All that should know knew of the coming disaster. Today, we have come to realize that England had a *deeper resentmen*t against the people of Eastern Nigeria. It was based on a deeper factor for which the whole of Europe had battled for more than eight centuries earlier.

Discrimination against the Jews had always been a regular factor in the history of Israel. But hatred against the Jews by the Christian Europe assumed a most dangerous dimension from the time of the first crusade of the 11th century. This European bigotry evolved a specific concept known as **"anti–Semitism"**. Anti-Semitism was a social evil which every European knew about, but no one was willing to challenge until it erupted into the disaster of the World War II.

From the 16th century till the World War II, anti–Semitism was so pervasive that many European leaders were literally hiding under it to explain away the failures of their socio-political and economic policies. It was under that atmosphere that the **"Jewish identity"** of the peoples of Eastern Nigeria was revealed in the late 19th century. The first Anglican missionary in Igbo land, Rev. Barsden wrote a conclusive report (after twenty years of research) that he has discovered one of the missing tribes of Israel – the Niger Ibos. As the Church of England received the report she applied to the king for permission to publish the report as a major discovery. But King George V rejected the application on the claim that it will hinder both the colonial and missionary ventures in the region. The king reminded the Church (if she had forgotten) that Judaism had remained Christianity's greatest opposition, just as the Jews had remained the greatest problem of Europe. Thus, to think of another group of Jews in West Africa, another territory of British interest was a major disaster.

The report was not published but the information became useful to the colonial and missionary authorities in their dealings with the peoples of Eastern Nigeria. *This was the deeper reason that led to harsh attitudes, policies and treatments of the peoples of the East.* This was the reason behind the obsessive desire for Igbo containment, the reason for the amalgamation. Also, the discovery itself became a "**gag rule**". Even the Anglican Church would not mention it in any public forum – neither in their ecclesiastical rendering nor their petition to the God of Israel. In consequence, Igbos were forced into various straight jacket administrative systems with little regard to the systems they were familiar. Examples abound. The excessive use of the brutal force in the expedition for **the destruction of Arochukwu "long juju"** which almost saw a total disintegration and humiliation of *the ebullient Aros*. Obnoxious taxations were introduced in the East such as the women tax law that resulted in the Aba Women Riot of 1929; the arbitrary fixing of prices of commodities by the colonial marketing board that made the eastern produce – *palm* – sell cheaper than those from the north and the west. Population counts were manipulated to ensure that east was technically denied her natural numerical majority, which would also have meant political majority. Even church workers and missionaries were induced to adopt "unchristian tools" to win converts. Some locals were forced or induced to convert. Falsifications of religious creeds and dogmas were useful and there must be no comparative evaluations of the peoples' traditions and customs with those prescribed by the church. Every aspect of the peoples' culture was regarded as fetish and rejected.

In all essentials therefore, the man of the east was encaged and denied of his basic socio-political and economic rights. The peoples of the east saw themselves terribly and psychologically burdened and distressed. These became the inner motivations for their relentless desire for freedom from the grip of the colonial masters.

Igbo and the Nigerian Project

Every political historian knows that granting of "**independence**" to colonial territories in Africa and elsewhere within the second half of the twentieth century was not based on the good will of the European colonizers. The wind of change that was blowing across the globe and most powerfully Europe made colonial adventure obsolete. Many of the nationalist movements that sprang up in the colonies, including Nigeria were beds of comfort providing soft landing spots for the crashing colonial enterprises. But the colonial masters would not be expected to allow their fortunes drain away. They adopted several measures and strategies – directing and manipulating programme and processes to their desired end. In the Nigerian front, from the time of amalgamation, the colonial authorities began to create political units in such a manner that granted political majority to the north at the expense of the south's numerical majority. Population censuses have to be manipulated and falsified. For instance, the first organized census of colonial Nigeria, in 1919 gave the people of the east a significant majority with north following at a distant second position and the west a much further distant third. But, the second count after a decade, the population of the east significantly dropped whereas those of the north and west increased. By the result of that count northern Nigeria became numerically first, the west second and ironically east the third. Although the result in the east was an abnormal demographic result, no questions were asked instead major political delineations or constituencies were to be created based on that census result. This is the root of the structural jacket inside which the east has been suffocating. But the implications were not quite obvious in the colonial regional arrangements.

Similarly, the local administrative policy in the east, popularly known as *warrant chieftaincy* was intended to further balkanize the political foundations of the people. This policy which has been name–coated variously from 1929 till date has been used to foist on the communities in the east *charlatans, opportunists, adventurists and criminals* as leaders. Additionally, it has completely alienated the people from those in political control and has greatly promoted *leadership caricature and leadership vacuum in the east.* It is also on record that the colonial economic policies were comprehensively anti-east. The removal of the capital territory of the south from Calabar to Lagos was a major economic stroke. The colonial marketing board arbitrarily fixed the prices of eastern products – *palm oil and palm kernel* – cheaper than the products from other regions. What factors in the international markets could have made hides and skin or cotton and cocoa – all with limited uses sell at higher prices than "oil" in the age of industrial revolution and high energy demand? The massive outflow of Easterners to other regions was induced by economic hardship. Same was the reason for their massive entrants into the menial colonial white collar jobs. There was virtually no major economic infrastructure or institution established in the east. The people of the east more than any other had hoped that independence would free them from the strangulations of foreign domination and that it would mean the people being in control of their destinies. But their hopes were erroneous. These structural imbalances running for more than nine decades makes the East perpetually subjugated in a united Nigerian. It is on this account that one is tempted to question the wisdom of some eastern politicians insisting on a united Nigeria. The past fifty years of independence and "unity" is clear evidence that the East will remain enslaved in a united Nigeria. Confederation as envisioned by the Aburi Accord should be the minimum accommodation if the Ast is to recover and survive.

The Twilight of Independence and Death of Democracy

The colonial authorities knew that the euphoria of self-rule for the colonies was mere cosmetic dressing and not real. Colonia authorities were not yet ready to relinquish the economic control of their colonies. Therefore they devised means to ensure the protection of their interest while maintaianing the need for **"Igbo Containment"**. Therefore, the government of James Robertson could not differentiate between electoral supervision and brutality, intimidation and harassment of political opponents, massive vote rigging and other irregularities to ensure electoral victory for NPC. Following the independence elections, Tafawa Balewa found it necessary to write a letter in his tribal language to the governor General, James Robertson, praying him to assist the north in frustrating the demands of the NCNC for a coalition government. He also requested for assistance, if conditions would warrant it, for the north to seek for separation.

Nevertheless, we must also look inwards for reasons for our afflictions in Nigeria. What was the beauty or eternal value to be derived from an awkwardly united Nigeria? What made the ceremonial office of President more attractive than the premiership to the number one Igbo Politician (Zik)? Why were Eastern Nigerians made the scapegoats of the military intervention which was precipitated by political crises in the West? What were the offenses of more than 30,000 Easterners – majority of whom were private citizens – massacred in various locations in Nigeria? Who was there to promote the safety and welfare of easterners? Was Britain standing idly watching the early independence crises in Nigeria? Or was Britain by the corner fueling the tempo and direction of crises for her policy of "Igbo containment" as the bloody war of survival broke out? Why did the American government ignore America's historical experience and maintain a state policy of **"kill Biafra quick?"** Why was Britain interested in the brutal suppression of Biafra and not diplomatic mediation for peace? When the military conflict ended, none of the big powers cared whether or not the terms of agreement were implemented by the Nigerian government? Why did they look away while a new dimension of war of economic deprivation was waged against Eastern Nigeria for more than four decades? There are still many other questions to ask. Unfortunately no one is there to answer them. But, we must not fail to ask about the sociological and psychological impact on the Igbos of the policies following the end of the war.

i. The deceptive policy of 3Rs: **Reconciliation, Rehabilitation and Reconstruction**
ii. N40 (£200 *ex gratia* payment to those whose economic foundations and infrastructure were totally damaged by the war.
iii. Nigerianisation of major economic institutions and structure when Esterners were unable to participate.
iv. Prolonged socio – political and economic war from 1970 to 2013 in form of state and local government creations, quota system, and the *concept of federal character*. What impact did these have on the attitude and evolution of the people of the East, especially the Igbos?

The Expressions of Igbo Burden.

Centuries of the historical experiences of the people have affected their character traits. These include:

Loss of identity and cultural disorientation. In Nigeria today, it is only the people of east that sustain the least affinity to their cultural identity. The various languages of the people are in steady decline. Some of the attempts at reviving the culture and the languages are more like caricature than real. Of course, the culture received the greatest assault from the colonial and missionary adventurists. And their local converts have sustained the devastations on the culture. The burden imposed on the people by cultural disorientation becomes pungent in realizing that it is culture that provides a given society the necessary grove for socio-economic and spiritual growth and development. For as, Rick Joyner stated *"people and their community are like plants and their culture is like the soil holding the plant.* When a people are uprooted from the roots of their culture they wither and die just like any plant removed from the soil". The reason for the widening social dislocation in Igbo society today is because Igbo cultural compass – *omenala* – has been removed. There are no more socio-cultural standards of behavior for our citizens. It is the culture that provides and defines the moral codes and ethics. Even the legal system cannot be strengthened where the cultural grooves have been destroyed or removed.

Leadership vacuum: The twentieth century witnessed the greatest impact of leadership in the world more than any of the previous centuries. But unfortunately Igbos recite with uncanny and ironic relish the concept *"Igbo – enweze"* as if it were something most glorious. Attempt has been made here to indicate when and how the concept evolved in Igbo Society. The burden of Igbo *enweze* continues to weigh heavily on the social fabric of Igbo society. Igbo *enweze* is a false concept orchestrated for colonial blackmail and purposes. If it is true that Igbos do not have **"Eze"** the concept would not have evolved in Igbo language. You cannot develop a concept for what you do not know. The truth is that in the intervening historical assaults on the Igbos, "Eze" has lost its true meaning and essence. The word *"eze"* is of Hebrew origin, meaning the *"helper"*. In Jewish philosophy of Social-humanism, the leader (or king) is not an over lord, dominating and ruling the people. Rather, the leader or eze is supposed to be a helper or a servant of the people. Thus, when you say **oha na-eze,** you mean exactly the people and their helper. Hence, Jesus said to his disciples *"your leaders shall be your servants"*.

Two, Igbo *enweze* can be seen as true because as the colonial adventurism dismantled Igbo leadership system and structure and enthroned essentially community rejects, antagonist and strangers, the concept of "Eze" took a new meaning and a new essence. It was in the essence of eze as helpers that Igbo ancestors adopted it as the title of their leaders. But when the colonialist imposed exploiters and opportunist upon the people, "eze" lost its original meaning. Thus, Igbo enweze became a true testimony of the reality in Igbo nation. When eze was a helper or the servant of the people they were rarely chieftaincy tussles as they exist in every community today. And whenever eze reassumes its original meaning in harmony with Igbo spiritual and cosmic and social personality and destiny, then the people shall again experience the expressions of Igbo wonders and exploits. The leadership vacuum is one of the greatest burdens of Igbo nation. As the Holy Scripture says, "where there is no vision [leadership]} the people will perish. The enemies of Igbo have worked so hard to ensure this evil, particularly since after the civil war and with the proscription of the **Ibo State Union.** As a result, sell-outs, sycophants, opportunists and criminals are serially imposed upon the people. The field of Igbo nation has remained devastated. What a burden!

Igbo Jackets of illusions*:* Another great burden, with impacts that are more psychological and subliminal are here described as *Igbo jackets of illusion*. "These illusions are the aggregate of Igbo historical and environmental experiences particularly on the unholy union. Their impact are mostly in preventing the people from the thorough grasp of the extent and dimensions of Igbo troubles. Some of the illusions include:

a) **The Omnipotent and invincibility of Igbo:** The belief of the great powers of the world in the great intelligence of the Igbos is as wide spread as it is pervasive. But the belief has become an illusion because potential powers are of no value if they are not properly activated and applied. An elder and former patron of and "IGBOBRIO" late Chief Frank Ikem Owelle, described it as *"the Paradox of highly intelligent Igbo, the object of caricature in Nigeria"*.

b) **The belief that the Igbo problem shall resolve somehow**: This illusion and complexity arising from the current theology of faith and confessions, instead of hard work and efforts, as means to solutions in Igboland have caused a great many of the people to become complacent. Complacency and passivism have become twin maladies of our people. And as **Abba Eban** said of the European Jewry before the recreation of the state of Israel, *"Igbos seem to take pride lamenting over what has befallen them instead of evolving and executing actions and program for solution.* "Thus Igbo nation has unwittingly become a community of reactionaries. We have only reacted to the actions and initiatives of others. We have taken no benefits of hindsight strategies in many of the things we do as a people. A great burden!

c) **The belief that someone else will solve Igbo problems**: Sometime ago, the former Libyan strong man, late Col. Muammar Gaddafi made a statement suggesting dissolution as the answer to the problems of Nigeria, many other Nigerians, especially from the North were mad at Gaddafi, but some Igbos already began to build their castles of hope for freedom on his statement. Again, the prediction by a section of the international media that *the Nigerian Union may not survive beyond 2015* has also become a great source of hope to many Igbos. There are a lot of such other funny calculations making rounds among the people that are not based on their own initiatives, plans and actions. But, if one may ask, "should America or whoever we think is capable take the initiative and challenge of dissolving the unholy union, will they do so just for the interest of Igbo? Of what benefit will there be for America or any other nation to want to solve Igbo problems without Igbo initiative? Initially, some thought that the Balfour Declaration of 1917 was a British benevolent policy to help the Jews establish a national home in Palestine. But later, it became clear that Great Britain was acting on a self interest strategy for her war efforts. Meanwhile, the leadership of the Zionist Movement caught into it for the interest of Israel. Because the leadership was sensitive and focused it anchored on the Balfour Declarations and made it part of their dreams and strategic tool. In this regard, and in the expectations of Igbos, history has little example to show. *Every man's destiny is in his hands*. You can barter yours with a plate of porridge or protect it with a grip of eternal oath.

d) **Ultra Nationalism**: It has often been said that Igbos are the only true nationalists in Nigeria. But Igbo pride in this assertion is a delusion. The world history and Igbo experiences of a century in the Nigerian union should have been the best lesson. Of course, some friendly representatives of the U.N.

advised Israelis against such illusions when Israel had to negotiate relationship with the Arab Palestinians. Besides, an Igbo proverb says *"an'esi n'ulo mara nma puwa n'ama"*. Our patrotic zeal can only be best expressed towards Igbo nation. This is the principle that has made late Chief Awolowo a scion, a demi-god, to the Yoruba nation.

e) **Igbo Economic Domination:** One of the particular reasons for this illusion is the great numbers and the great striving of Igbos. Their presence is everywhere felt, striving immensely for success. The vibrations and/or commotions they generate in the process often overshadow their true economic status, *as the master servant or economic master slave of Nigeria*. But what can provide a clear economic status of Igbos is the absence of anyone (from south – south and south – east) in the club of 20 richest Nigerians as well as the absence of a major industrial outfit in Eastern Nigeria. What is the true value or earning capacity of entrepreneurship particularly in an economy over exposed to superior foreign competition? This in addition to the stifling economic policies obviously implemented from the erroneous perspectives of the illusion of Igbo economic domination or as a direct affront against Igbo economic interests.

The Home Truth

A careful survey of Igbo historical landscape provides a vivid expression of people whose experiences largely consist of what they have suffered, what they have endured, escaped or overcome - enemies so virulent and so determined to vanquish or exterminate the people. The historical landscape reveals a people whose experiences are filled with their **reactions** to other peoples' initiatives and actions. But this is strange to the authentic character of the Jews for instance. It is also a deviation from the vision and expression of Abrahamic covenant with the Almighty. They are also strange to the impulse that impelled Israel to an historic exodus from Egyptian slavery to the land of Canaan. These are the reasons why these character burdens have become so heavy on Igbo - because they have cut asunder both the psychological and socio-cosmic thread of Igboness. To cure these maladies, a new thinking and acting personality on the basis of Igbo initiatives must be encouraged to emerge. A new generation that will recapture the true essence of an Abrahamic vision and the vision of exodus from Egyptian slavery to the land of freedom must be stimulated to emerge. This is the greatest leadership challenge for this generation of Igbos.

The Road Map to Igbo Restoration

There are no other cosmetic arrangements that can redeem Igbo from the present socio-political, economic and spiritual strangulation except the emergence of a new generation with traits anchored on initiative, fore-thoughts and pre-emptive action. So the Road Map to Igbo Restoration must begin with a psychological rebirth of the Igbo whose future shall be determined and colored by Igbo actions, not reactions; Igbo initiative and force - not Igbo responses alone. The Igbo must thrust into the future with a grip on life and upon Igbo destiny - no longer Igbos managing to escape and surviving the on-slaught of aggressors and enemies! It must be a new generation decisive in initiating and executing programs and projects for the development of the people and the environment.

It is in this context that we can appreciate the challenges of late Professor Afigbo when he said that the greatest challenge before the present generation of Igbos is a redefinition of Igbo identity. To paraphrase Abba Eban, in order to be itself 'Igbo' the national society has to be different from everything else. The driving force must be a quest for identity …. Its ideas and priorities must be collective not individual. What matters is a man's service to the emerging nation not his prowess in self advancement ... the Igbos must live at last with the unique taste of national solidarity and creativity. Like the Jewish consciousness, Igbo consciousness must go beyond the mystic hope of oncoming salvation. It must be anchored on a practical faith for restoration and reconstruction of Igbo nation - a faith that sees both internal and external limitations and obstructions as launching pads to great national adventure; a faith that will turn a devastated desert into a fruitful garden; a faith that will cause a rebirth of a sovereignty lost for 2000 years. Thus, the road map to Igbo restoration and reconstruction must begin with a rebirth of Igbo identity and consciousness. Some practical steps required to speed up the process of restoration and reconstruction include:

i. Construction of restoration platform or platforms.
ii. Recruitment and training of cookers.
iii. International engagements.
iv. Strategies segmentation of the programme.

Construction of Restoration Platforms.

There is need for organization of a platform or platforms with the capacity as well as legitimacy to champion the programs of Igbo restoration. Solution to group or community problem in the modern society no longer require the role of a sole benefactor or hero. Experiences have shown that such singular heroes often turn despots. Therefore the leadership of the restoration program must operate on an organizational platform and be accountable to the people from whom they derive there mandate and authority.

For practical purposes, the size and dynamic nature of Igbo society, emergence of a single organization may be unrealistic. But there is need to discourage formations of numerous in-effective "splinter-groups". Many of such splinter groups should be encouraged to merge in such manners that their synergy will produce effective force of action. Also, the encouragement should be by persuation, enlightment or education which may be undertaken by such 'mother organization like Igbo Zurume Association and Ohaneze Ndi Igbo. For the later organizations to undertake this role, they must remove their cloak of elitism and become truly the people's organization. Well articulated and co-ordinated platform or platforms will facilitate the process and speed of the restoration.

Charting a New Political Direction for Ndigbo
by
Dr Uma Eleazu

Abstract

Ndigbo participation in Nigerian politics has in the past been shaped by our orientation towards Nigeria as a nation. Following our foremost leader Nnamdi Azikiwe, Ndigbo accepted Nigeria as their country and attuned their political and economic behaviour to the political space created by colonialism. In the first Republic, the dominant logic was that Nigeria was perched on a tripod and so no one will rock the boat by daring to remove any of the legs of the tripod. This turned out to be false. In the second Republic under Shagari, we played second fiddle in the hope that the tripod theory could be recreated. We lost. In the meantime, the Hausa-Fulani Caliphate was busy consolidating their hold by creating a new leg for the tripod in our backyard (South-south). To achieve this, the North has gone back to its traditional clientage based association (read patron/vassal relationship). Since after the civil war Igbo politicians have had to find a Northern patron in order to make "progress."

Yorubas played the politics of the underdog (opposition) and have succeeded in gaining more of what there is to be got in politics – by hook or by crook. Their under dog strategy has paid off. The North frittered away their chances and now want power at all cost to see if they can recover lost ground. Both the West and the North play group politics, while Ndigbo and to an extent Efik/Ibibio play individual politics.

The paper argues that it is time to reorient politics in Alaigbo. There are two aspects to this. First, how we govern ourselves in Alaigbo to produce a strong home based political elite that can lead Ndigbo to confront Nigerian politics. Secondly we need to develop a new logic for being in Nigeria. Finally, if things fall apart, how do we govern ourselves in an independent Alaigbo Republic?

1 The historical background
1.1 A country takes shape

Nigeria came into being as a result of European interest in Africa. Around the fifteenth century, white men came looking for slaves. They introduced guns and gunpowder to West Africa and the technology of warfare changed. There was massive movement of peoples and resettling at different times and in different areas. According to historians, the dominant empires in these parts were the Benin, the Biafran and the Zamfara empires. At that time any oppressed tribe(s) exercised their right of self determination by voting with their legs. If a people's territory was overrun by a more powerful group, the people simply moved en masse. So boundaries between empires were very fluid. Contacts with Europeans started with trade in slaves among equals, then later degenerated into punitive wars to hunt down and enslave people who were then transported to the Americas.

By the Nineteenth century changes in the economy of many European countries changed and as the industrial revolution progressed so also the object of trade changed. Europeans no longer were looking for slaves but for vegetable oil, elephant tusks, and other forest resources such as timber and rubber; minerals especially gold and copper, thanks to the industrial revolution which first gathered momentum in England. Our forefathers responded by settling down once more to an agrarian way of life and to produce the new commodities of world trade.

Unknown to most African peoples, the Europeans gathered in Berlin in 1884/5 and divided up Africa among themselves, (so called Scramble for Africa) and established "spheres of influence". They wiped the map of African clean and gave new names to their spheres of influence. Whatever they called their sphere of influence in the African booty became its name. That is how we got place names such as Gold Coast, Niger Area; Upper Volta, Porto Novo; Ivory Coast; Guinea Coast, Fernando Po, Sierra Leone, etc. In our own case "Niger-area" later was shortened to NIGERIA. That is where the trouble began. Nigeria was awarded to the British Crown as her "sphere of influence."

Before then, this chunk of territory referred to as Nigeria had in its bowels parts of the old Benin empire, parts of the old empire of Biafara, and parts of the old Zamfara empire enclosing the seven Habe states. Within these empires there were different peoples - the Yorubas. Edo, Itshekiri, Urhobo, Igbo, Efik-eburutu; Ibibio, Ijebu, Oyo, Ilesha, Anang, Tivi, Nupe, Hausa, Fulani, Kanuri, Jukuns, Mbembe and many other ethnic groups.

Each of these peoples governed themselves in their own way – now trading and then warring among themselves or against any invaders. Before they knew it, the European invaders clamped everyone into the colonial grid of the British or French or German Empire. Before colonialism, these peoples lived under a plethora of political systems with different political cultures.

By the 1890s, the Niger-area comprised of three disparate units variously called Oil Rivers Protectorate, Niger Coast Protectorate, Lagos Colony and Protectorate extending to Ilorin and Northern Protectorate (in some documents called Lower Soudan). The Northern protectorate was a massive chunk of land acquired by the Royal Niger Company partly by deceit and partly by conquest. Goldie the owner of the Royal Niger Company had little resources to manage the territory he had acquired for the Empire. Besides the area was not very productive as the southern territories thus proving costly to maintain as a colony.

On the other hand, trade in the Niger Coast was more profitable because the people had quickly adapted to palm oil trade. British and African traders met on equal terms in the "market place." Initially the area was not run as a colony with white settlers, thanks to the mosquitoes. Instead, the British maintained diplomatic relations with the kings of the area by appointing a British Consul. Macgregor Laird was such a consul to the Bight of Biafra from 1846 to 1849. There was even what was known as Court of Equity for the settlement of commercial disputes among the traders white or black (see Dike, *Trade and Politics in the Niger Delta*).

After the Scramble for Africa, things changed dramatically for the African peoples. Each European power was expected to prove "effective occupation" in the area it had acquired. To do that the Colonial Office had to evolve a policy for governing their territories. In 1898 the Selbourne Committee was appointed to look into the matter and advise the Colonial Office in London, on the desirability of merging all the territories acquired in the Niger area into one administrative unit and "to make plans for the future administration of the area".

Bearing in mind the reluctance of the colonial office to spend British taxpayers money on colonies, the Committee recommended that (a) the charter of the Royal Niger Company be revoked; (b) that unification though desirable should wait until communication infrastructure improved; and (c) that the Niger Coast protectorate and the Lagos Colony and protectorate (which by then included all Yoruba land except Kabba and Ilorin) be merged to become Southern Nigeria Protectorate while the Northern territories become the Northern Protectorate. These recommendations were accepted and Nigeria came into being on 1st January 1900 with two protectorates under different administrations (Mackintosh, *Nigerian Government and Politics*).

The years between 1900 and 1912 saw a steady increase in the revenue of the Southern protectorate and a corresponding increase in British Treasury subvention to the Northern Administration having abolished the Royal Niger Company's charter which used to bear the cost. Also by 1913, the railway project had reached Kaduna from Lagos. To release the burden of administering the North from the British tax payers, the idea of unification was brought back to the front burner. Captain (Later Lord) Lugard was brought back from Hong Kong to undertake the task of unification. That is how the Amalgamation came in 1914.

According to one British author, "There was scarcely any discussion in London concerning the fundamental significance of amalgamation. Even in 1912 ... British officials never seriously discussed how conflicting policies in the two Nigerias might be harmonized; how the rapidly growing individualism of the south, with its cash crops, its rapidly expanding mission schools, its growing wage earning and clerical class, its African entrepreneurs and petty capitalists, could be blended with northern feudal conservatism, Muslim law and self sufficiency" (*ibid.*)

1.2 How Nigeria was Governed: The Roots of Discord

In spite of the Amalgamation, and Lugard assuming the title of Governor General, the Lieutenant Governors of each half continued developing their area as they saw fit and so each of the two territories developed along two parallel policy lines until after the war (world War 11): indirect rule in the North and Direct rule in the south. A feeble attempt to install "Warrant Chiefs" in the East failed woefully (See also Stockwell, *Federalism and Nation Building: the Nigerian Experience 1946 -1964*). If politics is defined as "Who gets What, When and How" (Lasswell, 1962), one can argue that in the immediate years preceding the Amalgamation, there was really no politics for the locals. The British administrators on the ground took orders from the Colonial Office in UK. If they built railroads or highways, it was to assist evacuate goods from the interior parts of the country to the coast, and vice versa. If they built roads or maintained law and order, it was all to further the goals of imperial governance. For trade to thrive, there must be law and order. The infrastructure they built were the necessary paraphernalia of the extractive colonial economy.

Although a Nigerian Council was established in 1922 for the Southern protectorate, there was no counterpart of it in the Northern Protectorate. This Nigerian Council provided for four unofficial members. (Three to represent Lagos and one to represent Calabar.) The Lagos members were to be indirectly elected through the Lagos Town Council while the Calabar member was by appointment, otherwise the Council was made up largely by colonial officials - the Heads of the various services and Government Departments.

Although there were sporadic agitations here and there over local issues of maltreatment of some natives, there was really no organized opposition to colonial rule. In most areas the chiefs did not realize that the Treaty of Protection they signed meant that they lost their right of independent action even in ruling their own people. They were now subjects of a foreign monarch.

The need to elect people into the Nigerian Council and the Lagos Town Council provided the first opportunity for the local people to "play politics". By now (1922) a class of African intelligentsias had been growing in numbers in Lagos and Calabar, made up of Sierra Leoneans, Jamaicans, and Brazilian blacks from the days of Back to Africa Movement in the 1890s etc. These were later to be joined by Yorubas and other Nigerians who had studied abroad in UK, USA and Sierra Leone or those who had found employment in the white man's businesses. It was from among these that what could be called a Nigerian identity, and later nationalism took root.

For people like Herbert Macaulay and Edward Blyden, their orientation was that of the Pan African Movement which had challenged the moral basis of slavery in the New World and later colonialism in Africa. They rightly criticized the arbitrary lines drawn by imperialists on the map of Africa and so started agitating first for a say in how these territories were being administered and later for self determination and independence for each of the territories. At the Pan African Congress held in Paris in 1919, it was agreed that Africans were to go and challenge colonialism in the territories they found themselves. But at that time what came to be called African Nationalism was yet in its infancy and patchy. Thus Nigerian nationalism became the affair of those peoples who had been enclosed in the area called Nigeria challenging British rule within the boundaries created by imperialism. A new country called Nigeria had come to stay encompassing various ethnic nationalities and peoples who perforce had to live together under an alien rule (Coleman, *Nigeria: Background to Nationalism*).

Odious as colonial rule was, it had some unintended consequences, it created a new reference point for political consciousness and economic space for both economic and political action. From the late 1920s to the 1930s, the colonial frame work provided new opportunities for its inhabitants. New economic opportunities in the white man's world, coupled with new means of transport widened the horizon for many, especially those from the south. The new wealth represented by the white man's money galvanized trade among the people. Within this area, the *pax britannica* provided relative security. A new class of people emerged who started seeing themselves as Nigerians in addition to being Efik or Igbo or Yoruba. The Nigerian context became a kind of "common market" and "common social milieu"with free movement of goods, services and personnel. They could interact on the business level but not yet mix as to their respective cultural values (See also Deutsch & Foltz. Eds. *Nation Building*).

However, there was one snag, British policy in the northern protectorate had created a situation that did not accept this "common market" idea. This was because the Indirect Rule policy was interpreted by some British officials in the North to mean that the Emirs were allowed to run their affairs according to Muslim law while they the "political officers" attached to the Emirs were to merely advise the Emirs on matters that were considered repugnant to British sense of Justice. They kept out (Christian) Missionary activities from the north, which they considered "disturbing elements". Under the Township Ordinance 1917, in almost all major northern towns they created "Sabon Gari" to house non northerners (See *Nigerian Government Gazette,* October 1917).

When in 1931, Sir Hugh Clifford, became the governor of Nigeria, he decided to tour the country to acquaint himself about the country. What he found shocked him. He wrote in his report: "I did not fail presently to detect that the very existence of the township and a location inhabited by Africans who did not belong to the Northern Provinces (Sabon Gari) was a modern innovation which many of the political officers to those provinces were inclined to regard with intense disfavour. These things represented an alien encroachment upon a domain in which the political officers had been supreme until these disturbing elements obtruded themselves upon his peace" (Eleazu *op.cit.*)

He was even surprised to note that these political officers extended their hatred and distrust to "traders and missionaries of his own race" feeling that the presence of the white traders would lower what was called "the prestige of the white man". This policy is important in understanding the attitude of the Northern politicians to Nigeria till the present time.

Part Two: Towards independence for the "New Nation"
2.0 Constitutional change and proto Nationalism

The people we have come to regard as the founding fathers of Nigerian Nationalism were really anti-colonialists. Some of them challenged colonialism on moral and religious grounds, some on economic grounds and others on humanitarian grounds but rarely on ethnicity ground. All over Africa, they wanted, as Africans to throw off the yoke of colonialism first and then sort themselves out later. As mentioned earlier, the introduction of the 1922 Constitution which established the Nigerian Council provided the immediate impetus to form a political party to "fight" for the three elective seats provided for Lagos. Herbert Macaulay and other leading intelligentsias in Lagos, mainly the vocal, educated residents of the Lagos colony formed the Nigerian National Democratic Party (NNDC). Though they described themselves as "national and Democratic", they had no intention of going outside Lagos, not even to fight for the one Calabar seat to be equally elective as those of Lagos. In fact, in fielding candidates for the Lagos Town Council, they selected only those they regarded as real Lagosians as opposed to those they termed Ara-oke, that is up country Yorubas and others from the rest of the protectorate. This did not go down well with the growing number of other "Nigerians" who were fast becoming the majority of Lagos residents.

In 1932 a new political movement called The Nigerian Youth Movement (NYM) was formed by the more youthful araokes, challenging the leadership of NNDC as being conservative and reactionary. The objective of the NYM was more "nationalistic" in tone. It declared in its Nigerian Youth Charter thus:". . . (t)he development of a united nation out of the agglomeration of peoples who inhabit Nigeria. (Also) It shall be our endeavor to encourage the fullest play of all such forces as will serve to promote complete understanding and a sense of common nationalism among the different elements in the country ...." (Sklar, *op. cit.*)

Like the NNDC, the NYM concentrated on the politics of Lagos colony. It even managed to win all three seats in the new Legislative Council (introduced in 1931) as well as majority of the members of the Lagos Town Council in 1938. Nationalist activities were attenuated during the World War 11 years. However one incident gave birth to a new political organization. This was the formation of a pan Nigerian Movement to protest the treatment of King's College students who were asked to vacate their dormitories to house war prisoners in 1943. This movement eventually metamorphosed into a political movement known as National Council for Nigeria and the Cameroons (NCNC). It was later to become the foremost political movement in the inter war years agitating for Nigerian Independence. After the war, Britain was more eager to rebuild war torn Britain than spend much money on colonial territories. Moreover, current world opinion had swung against the domination of one people by another. So Britain decided on their own to fast forward the political development in their empire. By now the NCNC had overshadowed the NYM and many of the younger men flooded into the NCNC leaving a rump of Yorubas in the NYM under the leadership of Chief H O Davies and Chief Obafemi Awolowo. The NCNC was led by Herbert Macaulay and Dr Nnamdi Azikiwe. Up to now, ethnic politics was not pronounced.

2. 1 Fast forward to 1946–1960: Towards Self Government

Between 1946 and 1960, the British Government introduced further constitutional changes which necessitated the nationalists to prove that they really represented the wishes of the people and that power could be transferred to them.The Richards Constitution restructured the country into Eastern, Northern and Western Groups of Provinces. The Macpherson Constitution (1951 to 1954) turned each group of provinces into semi autonomous Regions. Each region had its own constitution and electoral laws as well. It also created a Central Legislature in Lagos whose members were indirectly elected through the respective Regional Assemblies. It was in 1953 that Chief Anthony Enahoro moved a motion in the Federal House of Representatives for Independence for Nigeria in 1956. This sparked off a big row between the Northern members and their Southern counterparts. The North did not want Independence then. They thought they were being hurried by the "more educated southerners". In the end the British Administration allowed the Eastern and Western Regions to have "internal self-Government" in 1956.

Because the British did not want Nigeria to break into three parts as the East African Federation was already breaking down into Kenya, Tanzania and Uganda; they proposed for Nigeria a Federal State made up of the three regions. All the London constitutional conferences that the leaders of the various Regions attended in London between 1954 and 1958, were to hammer out conditions that would allow us obtain independence as one country. There were also issues like formula for revenue allocation, federal or regional police formations, and protection of minority rights. The last of such conferences was in 1958. It should be noted that the Eastern and Western Nigeria which were virtually independent delayed their full independence to wait for the North till 1960.

2. 2 Features that shaped the Nigeria Federation:

For the purpose of this essay, it will not be necessary to follow all the twists and turns that gave rise to ethnic nationalism and the politics of bitterness and violence in the years immediately following Independence. However we shall mention in brief the major events and factors that shaped the struggle for power and which eventually led to civil war and near disintegration of the country.

1. First was a structural imbalance in the sense that one of the three autonomous units (Northern Region) was larger that the other two both in area and population. Based on this, the number of seats allocated to it in the Central Legislature was also more than the other two put together. (North 174 seats; East 73; West 63 and Lagos 3 seats). This was based on the 1952 Census which many Southerners were leery about. Many southerners did not believe there were that many people in the northern region to warrant such lopsidedness. They bided their time to wait for the 1962 census to confirm or redress the imbalance.

2. Secondly, there was the structure of the parties. Only the NCNC had a following in all three regions, the Action group was dominant in the Western Region but with a sizeable NCNC presence. The Northern Peoples' Congress was the dominant party in the North. But it so happened that in each region there were minority ethnic groups who feared and loathed the dominance of the larger ethnic groups that dominated the political parties. These minorities formed their own parties and sort alliance of protection from the bigger groups, playing one against the other or demanding their own region. So we had in the North the party of the talakawas (commoners) the Northern Elements Progressive Union, as well as the United Middle Belt Congress., in the East we had the COR States movement and the Niger Delta Congress while in the West, the NCNC was championing the rights of the Mid West which eventually became a region. The Eastern Minorities tended to ally with the NPC in any election. Elections, especially federal elections became a three cornered contest in which NPC will try to win all the seats in the north and thus could afford to form a government without any seat from the south. The NCNC as well as the Action Group would want to use the UMBC or NEPU to checkmate the NPC in the north while retaining the seats in their region. In the run up to Independence, the 1959 Federal elections did not produce a clear winner, and so the NPC was forced to form a coalition

government with the NCNC. The Action group became the Opposition Party in Parliament

3. The third factor had to do with the understanding of the politicians of what constituted "Loyal Opposition". There was talk of National Government in which no party will be left in the cold. Chief Akintola, deputy leader of Action Group and Premier of the West, liked the idea. Chief Awolowo the leader of the party, and leader of Opposition in the Federal House did not like it. So there was a split in the Action Group which degenerated into fratricidal contests. Awolowo was accused of treason along with other leaders of the faction of the Action Group that supported him. He was tried and jailed. Akintola formed a new party, NNDC and allied with NPC seeking to oust the NCNC in the coalition government at the centre. All hell was let loose in the West and a State of Emergency was imposed in the west following a fracas in the State House of Assembly.

4. The fourth factor was the Census of 1962. A lot depended on its result to solve once and for all the structural imbalance mentioned earlier. The census was anchored by a British official. The first set of figures showed that there were more people in the South than in the North. That would have meant a redistribution of the seats in Parliament. The Northern Government rejected it. There was a recount in 1963 which confirmed the earlier figures for Eastern and Western Regions but now inflated the Northern figure in a way to maintain the status quo in parliament. As would be expected the other Regions rejected the results. And so it has been, we have never had a reliable head count in Nigeria because of its political implications.

5. With Awo in jail, Akintola back tracked and accepted the census figures thus setting the stage for a show down between NCNC and NPC Coalition in the House. Akintola descended on the faction of AG that was demanding Awo's release from prison, and the western region was in tumult all throughout 1962 to 1965. 1964 saw a federal election which was a fiasco because of the boycott by UPGA (a coalition of the NCNC and a faction of the Action Group, UMBC and NEPU), followed by Western regional election (1965 Sept) which degenerated into a mini civil war in Yoruba land, the stage was set for disintegration. In the meantime there was disagreement between the President, Dr Azikiwe and the Prime Minister over declaring another Emergency in the Western Region because of the mayhem which had been let loose in that region. For reasons of political strategy, the Sardauna, Premier of the North did not allow the Prime Minister, Balewa to act because he was comfortable with his alliance with Akintola and wanted the NCNC to be dropped from the Federal Government Coalition. There was even talk of removing Dr Azikiwe as President and replacing him with the retiring Chief Justice Adetokumbo Ademola. In the meantime the situation in the western region was deteriorating by the day. It was more like Hobbes' state of nature

where "the life of man was nasty, brutish and short". That was the situation in January 1966 when the Army struck (10).

3.0 Political Dynamics in a Praetorian State.

To understand the need for a new direction for the Ndigbo, we need to examine the socio-political as well as the socio-economic environment in which the game of politics in Nigeria was being played. The socio-political environment is not the same as the institutional structure of politics although as we will be discussing shortly, the one affects the other.

First the socio-political environment created and left by the military is one characterized by authoritarianism which manifested itself in intolerance of people's views, arbitrariness in decisions that affect people's lives; a command-obedience culture which brooks no discussion, sooner or later this was to turn into a culture of impunity and blatant disregard of set rules or behavioral boundaries. These in turn have led to corruption and all kinds of criminal activities and violence.

As soon as political activities started, political parties organized themselves into cabals under god fathers (like platoons under their platoon commanders) fighting to get their hands on to state power which hitherto was held by the military officials; not because they want to serve the people but for self aggrandizement, irrespective of what the law says. Because of the enormous wealth that comes from holding a piece of the state power, it is also a political environment fraught with violence; electioneering is a "do or die" affair. Anyone who wants to make it in politics must be part of a "structure" or start his own if he has the where withal. As one observer put it

> "The main features of military rule(in Nigeria) were arbitrariness, command and obey syndrome, intemperate language, total absence of debate on issues of state policy, intimidation of civil society, total disregard of civil rights, absence of rule of law and due process, and emasculation of the judiciary through ouster decrees."(11)

The politicians of today have unconsciously adopted this military mode with its culture of intolerance and impatience in matters that normally would require simple due process. Any wonder "Honourable" members are quick to remove their agbada or jacket to settle issues with their fists on the floor of the House instead of mounting an intelligent and coherent debate. Disagreement over issues of public policy are taken personally. The political institutions that set the rules or boundaries for the political game are those enshrined in the 1979 constitution and later modified in the 1999 constitution. Patterned along the lines of the American constitution, ours have all the outward trappings of a federal system but not the spirit or the culture that animates it. Whereas the framers of the American constitution were afraid of "Big Government" while at the same time desiring "a more closer union", they designed a system that on the one hand protects individual rights to "life, liberty, and the pursuit of happiness" and on the other, gave the union government enough powers to protect those rights, and at the same time instituted "checks and balances" from the federating units that could counterbalance arbitrary use of power at the centre.In our own case the military was interested in protecting the various decrees they had made to curtail or sideline the Igbos and protect the power elite that supported the Federal side during the Nigeria-Biafra war. To recap for the benefit of those too young to know -

1   On the eve of the onset of hostilities, Gowon created twelve states out of the former three/four Regions, ostensibly to whittle down the power of the Northern Caliphate oligarchy in the affairs of the Federation, but in reality it was a strategic move to isolate the "minority" ethnic groups in the Eastern region from supporting the secession. It didn't quite work out so they sold Bakassi to the Cameroon government to gain access into Biafra through that border.

2   There were other state creation exercises to 19 and then 21, 30 and finally to 36 states and each turn they pushed the Igbo into smaller space; and through boundary adjustments, carved out some Igbo people into states where they would be in the minority. Some changed the spelling of their names and claimed not to be Igbo.

3   Each state was subdivided into Local Government Areas without regard of 'ancient boundaries' or cultural affinities. On the whole the five Igbo states were given 95 LGAs where Kano State had 44 and Jigawa 40 or so. It did not stop there, allocation of money for local development "on the basis of equality of LGAs" already had built in marginalization against Ndigbo.

4   They created a central Federation Account, abolishing the fiscal arrangements agreed upon by our founding fathers at the London Conference of 1958. Thus all royalties, corporate taxes, customs duties etc accrued to the federal government. This was followed by innocuous revenue allocation formulae – land mass, population, school enrolment etc when it is known that no authentic census had really established the data base for the formulae.

5   The many states created became dependent on the monthly allocations from Abuja. A situation where the government does not depend on the labour or industry of its populace to survive creates a non responsive government to the welfare of its people.

Turning to the socio-economic environment, the end of the civil war almost coincided with the oil boom which brought in much needed funds to the Federal Government. All of a sudden the military government had so much money that it thought it could literally do anything it wanted. "Money was no longer the problem but how to spend it" the Head of State, General

Gowon, was quoted as saying in 1972. Nigeria went all over the world on a shopping spree. Government purchases were done through Supply Contracts. Supply Contracting became the easiest enterprise to start, though entry was limited to those with the proper connections within the military or the power elite groups that were behind the military. Those who did not belong to any of the power elite groups (mostly easterners, especially Ndigbo) had to look for an "Arrangee", that is somebody who knew someone who knew somebody who knew the Oga of the ministry or parastatal dishing out the supply contract papers (invariably an Alhaji or Chief). Trust the enterprising Igbos: housewives became emergency contractors, artisans and technicians re-designated themselves as Engineer so and so, petty traders became importers and exporters, manufacturers Representative, clearing and forwarding agents, etc, even students in schools turned part time merchants and joined the Government Spending Spree, all fueled not by productive wealth creating activities, but by inflow of petro-dollars into Government coffers.

Ala Igbo was emptied of its more energetic but hungry youths who now went to Lagos (and later Abuja) where the power elite that controlled the funds were to be found. Even farmers left the land in search of fertilizer supply contracts. The Nigerian economy suddenly became a typical extractive economy - an economy that has built in institutions that can create enormous wealth for the state without regard for the productive activities of the populace or other sectors. Invariably, those who controlled state power also come to control the enormous wealth thus created. This was the position the Military found itself in the 1970s and even the civilians that took over in 1979 and beyond followed suit. The culture of arbitrariness mentioned earlier, coupled with the rent income created incentives for life and death struggle to control the source of power to take charge of the "Honey Pot"- State power.

In 1978/79 when the military allowed political activities, it was the entrenched interests in this extractive economy that formed political parties to protect their interests, their scions in the army having ensured the exclusion of the Igbos and other marginal groups such as the Ogonis and Ijaws who were on the receiving end of the spoliation of extractive capitalism. As long as the source of the wealth was not threatened, extractive economic institutions and the political systems will seek to protect their hold on power. Quite often, they can engage in white elephant projects while neglecting basic welfare programs. The result is that the marginalized and the deprived groups engage in one kind of insurgency or other non legal activities to gain access to state power. Politics becomes a matter of life and death. This is the situation confronting Ndigbo in Nigerian politics today.

3. 1 Why New Direction?

So given the nature of political dynamics governing the economy of Nigeria, what and how should ndigbo confront Nigerian politics. In this writer's opinion, the time for Big Tribe politics is gone. A new logic is required, one based on existential fact of Igbo interest in Nigeria. Why do we as Ndigbo need a new direction in Nigerian politics?

Two reasons at least can be adduced. First, the environment of politics in Nigeria has changed dramatically since the end of the civil war and the long military occupation of the political space. Secondly, the generation that fought for independence and for whatever it is worth, who were groomed by their education and political socialization could be regarded as democrats have all passed on or are in the departure lounge of life. More importantly, we now have a generation of Ndigbo who have only a smattering knowledge of Igbo history, culture and values and who have tended to buy into the dominant logic of what others have said about Ndigbo. Besides, this new generation who were toddlers or a little older during the civil war and were the most affected by the dislocation of family, economic and political life of Igboland by the war, must be presumed to have suffered both physically and psychologically in the struggle to survive in post civil war Nigeria in which the igbo person was now an under dog. Besides this new generation coming up may think that the Igbo has always been under dogs in Nigeria, because since the return to civilian rule, especially since 1999, the Igbo seem not able to put its acts together to pull ala igbo out of the socio political mess we find ourselves.

3.1 The New Political Morality

So we need first of all to consider what has happened to the Igbo psyche since the war. When one considers the extant fractiousness and normlessness among the youth, one finds that it is not unconnected with the way the civil war ended. For example, when it became apparent that the fall of Biafra was imminent, there was no high level meeting of the leaders, (the war cabinet or the top commanders) to plan a tactical or strategic withdrawal; no call for a truce even though the Red Cross was calling for such so as to allow food to get in; there was no plan B to allow for a negotiated surrender. The man who embodied the struggle made his own arrangements as it were and left "to seek peace in Ivory Coast". General Effiong (brave man) was left to confront a very desparate situation and with no option than to surrender to General Obasanjo. What was left of the Biafran army simply dissolved into the bush. Some committed suicide rather than be Nigerian again. Others had to fight their way back to their villages and began picking up the pieces of their lives. For the generality of the Igbos, it was like the proverbial scattered sheep without a shepherd. Most people felt that their leaders had woefully disappointed them. It was now "to thy tents, oh Israel." And in local parlance, *onye na nke ya, onye na nke ya*." The epithet "*Igbo enwe eze"* took on a new meaning – aversion to centralized authority of any kind.

However coming back to Nigeria they had to deal with this leviathan the military created. On individual basis, it was now *ike keta o rie*, and the measure of *ike keta* was *money*.

Erstwhile moral values were superseded by the need to survive, no matter how or what one did, anything goes. Within the Igbo enclave, it was dog eat dog, and outside it, the ethos was blatantly mercenary, and many went for the money; stealing, armed robbery, prostitution, obtaining money by false pretenses' (419), emergency contractors, you name it, were all employed to survive. Conventional wisdom became "man must survive". The Federal Government did not help matters. The shoddy manner it treated returnees to their posts, Awo's "beggar thy neighbor" policy of giving out only twenty pounds to those who had bank accounts, no matter the pre-war balance in their account, seizure of property in the name of abandoned property; all helped to create an atmosphere of discontent and lack of direction in Igboland. Efforts by the late Dr M I Okpara to popularize and revive the spirit of *onye a hala nwanne ya* did not catch on before his demise. That is why it has been so difficult to rebuild the Igbo State Union spirit.

Also this is why even those "elected" to public office see it first as a place to rehabilitate themselves. There is now hardly that "**Onye ahala nwanneya** spirit that built the Igbo State Union. Worse still the generation born after the civil war has never known, nor have they shown any interest in Igbo unity. They have grown up with a different set of outlook, some would say un-igbo values. Make money, take chieftaincy title and you have arrived. No one asks how the money was made. So the stinking *nouveau riche* became "leaders" and got themselves elected to public offices which afforded them opportunity for further primitive accumulation of capital.

3.2 Charting new directions

It is against this background that we consider the possible paths into the future. Certainly, there are many of the younger generation who are dissatisfied with the way things are. They blame the older generation for not giving them good leadership; always quarrelling over inconsequential issues instead of leading them to take their share of the national cake. How do we organize them for action in rebuilding the Igbo hearth? What of the Igbo in the Nigerian diaspora - clustered in Lagos, Abuja, Kano, Ibadan and virtually in all major town and cities in Nigeria? What should be their orientation to Nigerian politics? What of the Igbo in other African countries. Europe, America and China, how can they be made to become part of rebuilding Ala Igbo?

But the more important group is the Igbo group at home. I believe that if the place we call Ala Igbo suddenly becomes developed – with good infrastructure - power, roads, rail lines with fast trains, good drinking water, good schools for the children and health facilities within reach of the average family, an Igboland that is a pride for all black people; many of our diaspora compatriots will return to make the place even more attractive. This scenario is possible and that is for me the function of the **New Direction of Igbo Politics**. *It is possible even with the same marginalized situation we have found ourselves to create a modern marvel of development in what is now South East Geo-political Zone. It will require Visionary Leadership from the five states to plan and execute it. So we must decide on a number of steps to be taken:*

1. We must come together and develop a constitution on how we can create an inclusive political/economic community where the individual will have the freedom to pursue his interests within the law; where political leadership will come from below and public service is seen as such - *Service* - to the people. A constitution that sets limits or boundaries beyond which sanctions follow.

2. The constitution must provide for democratic institutions, meaning institutions that allow participation in decision making either directly or through representatives elected by the people themselves. It follows from this that local government must be small and local and given powers over issues dear and close to their daily welfare.

3. Limiting the cost of Governance must be paramount so that available resources will be devoted to economic and social development. We must begin to see the Zone as an economic unit within the Federation and plan its development as such.

4. There is need for a lot of political education to re-socialize people into the symbols of Igbo nationhood - Igbo literature and language; Igbo history (*Aham efule*), art and culture; text books to be written and used in schools. Our educational system should be such as to inculcate the known and celebrated Igbo traits such as creativity and ingenuity, hard work and honesty, respect for those in authority as well as other people's feelings, of course not neglecting the hyper-wired globalized world in which we now live.

With our home based politics and economy taken care of, we can raise our head in the conclave of other nationalities making up Nigeria. The second scenario envisages the South East Zone becoming by default an independent State of Biafra as a result of the action or inaction of the present political arrangement and its drivers (read manipulators). In both scenarios, the concern of this writer is how internal self government will be organized so as to achieve the purposes for which governments are instituted among men. Since everything revolves on **Leadership**, how do we groom and elect competent and credible leaders in Ala Igbo? This requires a little excursion into socio-political philosophy. A people's values and interests tend to animate their social action. Ndi Igbo are known to be republican and democratic when it comes to political orientation. We value hard work and integrity and we are very achievement oriented. At the same time we are a people who like to talk things over in the village square, even if, *ndi kwe, ndi ekwghi* and in the end *oha kara ka nma*. The task therefore will be how to devise institutions and processes that can allow these two features – republicanism and democracy to come into play. In pre colonial times, we had our eze, obi, igwe; and there were also traditional rules and procedures by which one arrived at the position of an eze, obi, or igwe. Alongside these positions were usually a council of Ndi Ichie (Elders' *nkpuke* or *imeobi*) and also a set of rules defining their roles and responsibilities vis a vis the *Eze, Obi* or *Igwe* on the one hand, and towards the demos (oha) on the other. Each village/town/*ama/ogo/mba* had its autonomy. This autonomy however did not preclude cooperation with contiguous communities when necessary. We practiced what political scientists call consociational democracy – a type of democracy that recognizes that a majority can be wrong and so allow a minority to veto or withdraw from a proposed line of action. Can we recreate and modernize this tradition and build it into our Governance system based on the careful identification and grouping of those who belong together to form the lowest base of the governance structure. We can call it the CLAN level. The Clan Governing councils at this level should not be partisan. In addition to these territorial units of government, we can also recognize and charter some municipalities as local governing entities.

It is at this local level that government and local interests tend to coincide and also here we should give as many as possible, opportunity to participate in decision making. Election at this local level tends to be more meaningful because local issues affect the daily lives of the people and the candidates are also local people whose character and abilities are known fairly well. It has been shown that in many countries, especially in the US and UK, that turnout of voters is usually higher at the local than at the state or national elections.

The same pattern can be followed to create Counties made up of a number of clans with cultural affinities to become the next level of government. Then at the top we can have the Zonal or Regional Government. If we were to find ourselves within one region, this would give us three levels of government thus abolishing the states as currently exists. Although there will be representative bodies, (County Councils and Regional House of Assembly) these need not be on a political partisan basis. At each level Traditional Ezes, Obis or Igwes authority will be built into the representative bodies.

After all, democracy is about representation and participation in decision making. The institutions through which participation and representation are made possible usually evolve following the nature of cultural values and societal interaction among the participants. The so called mature democracies did not start full blown with one man one vote or two political parties. These evolved as part of the struggle for participation and/or being represented in decision making by the various classes in those societies. There is a lot of political education to be undertaken and changing of mindset in the process of rebuilding Igbo society and politics. Some how, we have to learn how to govern ourselves once again. In addition to these institutional aspects, we will also need to inculcate a more legal-rational approach otherwise known as Rule of Law. Many of our current political leaders either do not know what it means or are simply not ready to abide by the rule of law. This also should extend to the bureaucracy – the public services. In other words, governance in Ala Igbo will eschew arbitrariness and the culture of impunity and corruption which has characterized politics in Nigeria. Service to the citizen and loyalty to the Igbo nation should be paramount. Whether we become independent or stay as part of Nigeria this should be the ethos that will animate governance. Responsiveness to the needs of the citizenry is what makes a government democratic, not just the shell of borrowed institutions.

Igbo politics in the Nigerian Diaspora:

Turning now to the second scenario, that is being part of a Federal Nigeria. This calls for a clear definition of what constitutes the Igbo interest in Nigeria and how to pursue and protect those interests. As noted earlier, colonialism was an economic phenomenon. It was the quest to maximize their economic interests in Nigeria that led the British to amalgamate their spheres of influence into what has become the country called Nigeria. As the British were exploiting their colony, Nigerians also found the enlarged economic space useful for their operation. Some took advantage of it to pursue their "happiness" anywhere within Nigeria. In this pursuit class interests and class conflict were bound to emerge even though at times we tended to define these conflicts in ethnic terms. If one looks at the economy of the country today, one finds a high degree of economic modernization and diversification which has outrun the traditional agrarian and pastoral economy.

Economic opportunities have encouraged a lot of migration out of the rural areas into the growing modern urban areas. This has in turn brought the different ethnic groups into close commercial contact and competition. Unfortunately, the language and ethos of the market place is not the same as the language of the political market place whose stock in trade is power. As a result the hatred generated by unrestrained violent language of politics negatively affect the ordinary peasant in search of his livelihood in markets outside his/her cultural base.

With that in mind we notice also that many ndigbo have investments all over Nigeria but without a corresponding investment by other Nigerians in

Ala Igbo for the simple reason that neither the federal nor the state governments have seen it fit to develop the necessary infrastructure that will attract investments into the area. Presently, Lagos State houses all the major businesses. Of recent the major oil companies have been moving their headquarters back to Lagos from the former Eastern region due to the activities of the "militants". The reason for such concentration of economic activities is not far to seek: the infrastructure - sea port, road network, rail, international airport and until recently the seat of government, and the head offices of major banks, the Stock exchange are all in Lagos. Outside of Lagos no other part of Nigeria has that kind of concentration. Igbo virtually dominate the SME business sector in Lagos.

There are sectors that are dominated by Igbos: distributive trade, land transport, small scale industries, maritime business and the fact that they are the shopkeepers of Nigeria. The Igbos are not yet strong in the manufacturing sector except at the lower end of "finishing touch" or assembly type manufacturing. People have tended to gravitate to trading and petty contracting partly to raise initial capital and partly because of lack of motive power – electricity and gas in Igbo Land. Currently, the hospitality industry is an emerging one and Ndigbo are positioning themselves in the hotel and tourism sector. No doubt this can easily be linked into the transport aspect of tourism. In effect, Ndi Igbo have adapted positively to the economic opportunities offered by Nigeria and this has to be protected in any constitutional negotiation.

The edge that Aba once had in medium scale industries has been wiped away by the decline of Aba as a major trading centre. A study of the economic history of Aba and Nnewi speaks volumes on the necessity of building a strong economic home base. In their heyday, traders came from as far as the two Congos to buy locally manufactured goods for resale in their own markets, - shirts, singlets, Tshirts, hand bags, shoes, etc. Igbos in the African diaspora are already making waves. In the circumstance any association with Nigeria should be such as would allow us maximum room to extract from the rest of Nigeria the resources to rebuild the politics and economy of Igbo land along the lines earlier suggested.

One problem however, is that the Igbo man is a good businessman but bad political man. He seems not to understand the use of political power. So he goes on merrily making his money, investing here and there without thinking of using political power to protect that investment. In places like Lagos and Abuja, there is no reason why Igbos cannot organize to control the local governments even if through surrogates. We have to create the political structure for this to happen.

3.4 Conditions for Remaining Part of one Nigeria:

What kind of association should we go for now that they are talking of National conference? What we need is a very loose Federation giving more powers to the Regions. Our experience with the American type of presidential system seems to show that it is too expensive for our low income, low education population. It does not accord with our native instinct to "truck and barter." Therefore an inclusive political system that allows maximum discussion and debate at various levels is nearer our cultural orientation to politics. My personal preference is for the British type parliamentary system.

The Exclusive Legislative List in the 1999 Constitution needs to be whittled down to about 12 or 10 major areas - Foreign Affairs, Money and Banking, National Security, etc. In fact most subjects will be on the concurrent list so as not to stifle economic development of any area. One would therefore suggest a Local Government system that allows a large assembly (an elected local council) and a professional local administration tied to the main civil service of the region to carry out the decisions of the Local council as well as delegated administration from either the county or Regional Government. The same should apply to what I call the County level except that they too will have delegated powers from the Region and Federal levels. At the Regional level, there will be the parliamentary system made up of elected members with the leader of the party with a majority of members in the House of Representatives would become the prime minister. This will be almost the same as in 1956 to 1959 constitutional structure.

At the Federal level, we can have a modified Presidential system headed by a college of six Presidential Counselors elected one from each Region. One of them becomes the President General for a term of two years and steps down, then it rotates until all six have had their turn. Election for a presidential Councilor will take place only in the region where a vacancy occurs. Certain functions of a sensitive political nature can be put directly under the Presidential Council. They act as arbiters at critical junctures in the affairs of the state of Nigeria. Effective power will still be in the Cabinet and the Parliament.

There will still be a parliament of a single chamber and the party with a majority in it will form the Government. Ministers will be appointed from within the House or from outside the House subject to the approval of the Presidential Council. This replaces all the argument about zoning and rotation. Details of this arrangement can be worked out if interest in it is shown. It is a combination of what has worked in Switzerland and the Federal Republic of Germany. The Legislative powers of the Central (federal) Government should be whittled down leaving the Regions with residual powers not specifically granted to the federal government.

References

Coleman, James S. *Nigeria: Background to Nationalism,* Univ of California Press 1958.

Deutsch, Karl. "Integration of Political Communities" in K Deutsch and Foltz eds. *Nation Building.* N.Y.: Praeger Books, 1960

Dudley, B. J., *et al.* in J P Mackintosh, *Nigerian Government and Politics.* NWU Press, 1966

Dike, K.N. *Trade and Politics in the Niger Delta,* OUP, 1956.

Eleazu, Uma. *Federalism and Nation Building: the Nigerian Experience 1946 - 1964.* London: Arthur Stockwell, 1976

IDEA: International Institute for Democracy and Electoral Assistance; Series 10 on Democracy in Nigeria, *Continuing Dialogue for Nation Building in Nigeria.* 2000.

Jones, G.I. *Trading States of the Oil Rivers,* OUP 1956

Mackintosh, John P. Ed. *Nigerian Government and Politics,* George. London: Allen & Unwin, 1966

Nigerian Government Gazette of October 1917. Government Printer, Lagos

Sklar, Richard. *Nigerian Political Parties: Power in an Emergent Nation;* Princeton U Press, 1963

The Igbo Nation in the 21st Century
by
Professor Umelo Ojinmah

Eddie Onuzuruike, had titled one of his books *The Stable Tripod* [1] on the premise that the stability of the Nigerian nation rested on the three assumed major tribes: The Hausa/Fulani, the Yoruba, and the Igbo. Though debatable, events past and present have convinced me that the Igbos are gradually either being made, or making themselves irrelevant in the vital affairs of the nation, Nigeria as will be shown by a cursory look at the other two legs of the fabled tripod.

The Hausa/Fulani

The Hausa/Fulani are arguably also the ethnic group that has most benefited from the enterprise called Nigeria. Politically they have dominated all the other ethnic groups and have in the process amassed formidable economic and social benefits there from. Today, they are in the top echelons of every rung of the economy, the civil service, the army, the navy, the air force, the police, and the academia. At the grassroots, they have the most redoubtable organised leadership/followership that makes mobilisation a snap. With about the highest literate/enlightened ratio of rulers occupying the stools as Emirs and traditional rulers, the Hausa/Fulani have succeeded in positioning their people well for the 21st century.

The Yoruba

The Yoruba are Nigeria's most homogenous ethnic group and have used this asset to their advantage. Each succeeding generation of Yoruba leadership has built on legacies bequeathed by the previous. There is a quiet revolution going on in Yorubaland. The fruits of this will blossom in the next five years or so. They have a stranglehold in the areas of organisation, agriculture, civil and formal education. Having been primed from 1966-1972 to replace and appropriate positions vacated by the Igbos, and having been financially empowered to bullishly appropriate the commonwealth of Nigerian economy in the early years after the Nigeria/Biafra war, they have systematically entrenched themselves in all the Federal ministries and parastatals both domestic and foreign. Also, their very cohesive organisational and administrative structure engenders easy mobilisation and information dissemination. More than any other ethnic group in Nigeria, the Yoruba are politically fortified for the 21st century.

The Igbo Nation

The foregoing therefore makes it imperative that the Igbo nation must wake up. It is unfortunate as our elders say that "the people we started running with are now beckoning on us to hurry up", but life throws some curves sometimes. It is true that the plight of the Igbo nation today is traceable to the war years 1966-1970, however, the greatest undoing of the Igbo nation is their lack of unity and cohesion. We grew up hearing that "*Igbo enwe eze*". Our elders had the most sophisticated democratic system in Nigeria. When a decision of major import is to be undertaken, it is tabled at the *Ilo* or *Obi* where the elders will discuss it and at the end a consensus is formed which is binding on every one. What can be better than that? That is democracy in action. But there is a major snag now. What worked in the days of our forefathers, when people knew who they were and titles and hierarchies had not been bastardised hardly works now. Many people have commented on the Igbo-man's arrogance and haughtiness: no one can forget in a hurry the crass display of affluence on major roads in Nigeria in the 1980s and 1990s by a few Igbo men who had dabbled into the cocaine trade and 419 (something that members of the other ethnic groups had been doing for donkey years without making noise but quietly using the resources to develop massive infrastructures and industries). The actions of these few men drove many Igbo youths into abandoning school and following suit to the detriment of the future of the Igbo nation.

When you consider the two ethnic groups, the Hausa/Fulani and the Yoruba, discussed above, you hardly can find a rich upstart standing up in a meeting of the elders to challenge them. No matter how rich he/she is, people do not see that happen. Today in Yoruba land, despite the rising profile of Asiwaju Bola Tinubu as a leader, he still venerates Awolowo. Even as he aspires to replace him in Yoruba consciousness, he treads carefully, anchoring his credentials for leadership on service to the Yoruba nation. The same thing is happening among the Hausa/Fulani ethnic group. Those aspiring for leadership use the mantra of past venerated leaders. No one can forget in a hurry Chuka Okadigbo's (May his soul rest in peace) insults on Dr Nnamdi Azikiwe. No one can also forget how Dim Odumegwu Ojukwu was demystified at local election in a bid to "cut him to size". If Ojukwu had been a Yoruba or Hausa, no young man, no matter what the inducement was, would have challenged him in an election in his Senatorial zone. Yes, we say "*Igbo enwe eze*", and that slogan haunts the Igbos. Can Ndigbo mention one person in the whole of the Igbo nation that will issue a call and Ndigbo will answer? There is no such person. Even our umbrella organisations that used to be our strength have been bastardised. When two young men make their first millions they form a "pan-Igbo" organisation so that their names will be heard for one day. That is the plight of the Igbo nation.

A few years ago, some Igbo politicians were nursing presidential ambitions and jostling for prominence. A group under the auspices of Igbo Think Tank called them to a meeting at Enugu to broker some measure of understanding. We felt then that four or five Igbo men jostling for the same position was untenable as they still will have to face the larger Nigerian nation. So, we told them (I don't know if it is proper to mention their names here as one of them is now a Governor and one is dead) to allow Ndigbo choose from among them who best will represent the collective Igbo interest and that they should accept that whoever is chosen will be supported by the rest. They walked out of the meeting and started pursuing their individual campaigns and interests. Of course they all lost despite spending huge sums of money. The Igbos have been likened to snakes. They are vulnerable because they go alone. *Igwe bu ike*, our elders say, but not so with Ndigbo of today.

Lessons

Igbo leaders have not learnt much from the experience of the war. It is sad to notice the quantum of selfishness exhibited by Igbo political leaders. None of them has an eye on posterity. When one considers the systematic way Yoruba Governors are positioning their various states economically, through massive investments in agriculture, vocational and regular schools, youth empowerment programmes that are functional and meaningful; when one looks at how the Northern Governors are investing in the same youth empowerment programmes and education; one cannot but bemoan what the fate of Ndigbo will be in another five to ten years. It is amazing that we claim to be intelligent and yet with our eyes open we are walking into cactus.

Economy

Igbos are the hub of the Nigerian economy by dint of hard work and self deprivation. We started business after the war with nothing. But the indomitable spirit of Ndigbo has made them to survive. But all we have done is survive. For Ndigbo to move to the next level requires concerted efforts and purposeful leadership. Can you imagine if ALL the containers brought in by Igbo traders are only opened in Onitsha or Nnewi? Can you imagine if Igbos are united and they decide that no container will be opened except it is brought to the East. Yes, it will add a little to the cost of goods at the beginning but can you just imagine what the East will be like? Can you imagine if half of the factories owned by Igbos in Lagos are located in the East? If you manufacture quality goods no matter where you are, customers will come there. After all, Nigerians fly to China, Brazil and other far flung places to buy goods. So what is wrong if people come to Nnewi, Onitsha or Aba, for that matter to purchase goods? In the golden era of Ariara market, people came from Cameroun and Ghana to buy things there.

Politics

Further undoing of the Igbo nation is the attitude of our sons and daughters. I stated earlier that events, both past and present have further convinced me and many others that the Igbos are gradually either being made or making themselves irrelevant in vital affairs of the nation, Nigeria. Politics is one such vital area. It is true that we have a few of our sons and daughters occupying one political position or the other, but most of such appointments and positions are individual based. Apart from the position of Secretary to Federal Government and Deputy Senate President which were tokenishly given to Ndigbo, all others were either given to the individual or fought for by the individual. It is not so with the other two major ethnic groups. They dictate what they want, what Ministries should be reserved for them, what portfolios should be *given to their people*. The Igbo nation lost an opportunity to borrow a leaf from their Yoruba neighbours. Despite the fact that the Yoruba nation rejected PDP as a political party, yet they have strategically gotten from PDP government massive patronages in all areas. The key is unity. They have leveraged on their cohesion to block out PDP from their domain, which means that for the government at the centre to have an inroad into their domain it must discuss with the party in control, and this makes it possible for the political leaders to articulate what best positions to request for the benefit of the region.

Ndigbo lost this opportunity with what Chief Chekwas Okorie did with APGA after it was registered. At the conceptualisation level, it was decided that when the party is registered, it would be grassroots based. The Igbo Think Tank led by Barrister JSPC Nwokolo and Dr. Charles Amanze conceived and registered APGA and contrary to public opinion, Chief Chekwas Korie was mandated by the Igbo Think Tank to coordinate the registration exercise. Neither Dim Odumegwu Ojukwu nor any of the benefitting Governors were members of the Think Tank. Other prominent members included the present Deputy Senate President, The Right Hon. Senator Ike Ekweremadu, Professor Chinedum Nebo, before he even became the VC of University of Nigeria Nsukka, Chief Victor Umeh and eight others including my humble self.

The decision was that the certificate will be photocopied and given to all autonomous communities and the various Igbo Unions in Nigeria, with the mandate to select the candidates for the various elective positions. The thinking then was that if that was done, it would be impossible for any party to defeat a candidate chosen by the people. Furthermore, with predicted electoral victory in Igbo land Ndigbo will have a bargaining chip when it comes to discussing with the government at the centre just like the Yoruba nation does. All that planning was jettisoned when Chief Chekwas Okorie, without the mandate of The Igbo Think Tank, the original conceptualizers and powers behind the formation and registration of APGA, went and submitted both the certificate and flag to Dim Odumegwu Ojukwu as the flag bearer and presidential candidate of APGA. That singular act destroyed all the planning and hope of APGA as a party destined to revive the fortunes of Ndigbo.

As intellectuals, many of us have refused to comment on the absolute destruction of the dream of renaissance of the Igbo nation through systematic and pragmatic thinking which Igbo Think Tank had done by the conceptualising and registration of APGA, which the action of Chief Chekwas Okorie had occasioned and the subsequent tussles between him and Chief Victor Umeh. It was obvious to many of us that the profundity of the thinking to leverage the Igbo nation from its present marooned political state (Igbo nation not Igbo men and women) was lost on them beyond what was in the project for their individual pockets and egos.

Today, when we see APGA posturing itself as if it was a serious contender in the Nigerian project, we are more saddened than amused. Saddened by the gigantic opportunity for cohesion and bargaining position that the Igbos have missed as a people, which our leaders seem not to be aware of, despite our fabled intelligence. Maybe, just maybe, someday soon, a governor or respected Igbo elder will remember that "beauty starts from home", and will call other brother governors and political leaders to an *"Nkpuke"* meeting. Not the meeting whose agenda will be on CNN before it holds; and there, tell them the real truth about governance and people oriented programmes that focuses on the future not on today. That is our hope and prayers. That the Igbo nation will wake up before they become completely irrelevant in national discourse. Despite the individual wealth of many Igbo men and women, today it is possible to discuss who will rule Nigeria for the next ten years without any Igbo input. The other ethnic groups know that all you need to do to shut up the Igbos, is call two or three of them to a "caucus meeting" and bestow on them some palliative appointments and they will take up megaphones to tell the Igbo nation that we are still important in Nigeria. As we pray to God to deliver Ndigbo, it is pertinent to remind ourselves that any person who falls into a pit and decides to lie down and sleep there rather than holler and seek rescue may end up dying in that pit. The mere fact that northerners have the statistics of all Igbo investments in the north and Abuja, as illustrated by the words of the Deputy Secretary-General of Arewa Consultative Forum (ACF), Alhaji Abubakar Umar reported in the recent article in *This Day,* speaks volumes.

http://www.thisdaylive.com/articles/acf-threatens-to-retaliate-maltreatment-of-northerners-in-south-east/183966/

1. Onuzurike, Eddie. *The Stable Tripod.* Abuja: Roots Books & Journals Ltd, 2008.

The Psycho-theoretic substrate for the Economic and Technological Resurgence of Ala Igbo
by Goddyn Ehiogu-Nwosu

You see things (that are) and you say, why?
I dream things that never were (but can be), and I ask, Why not?

George Bernard Shaw (paraphrased)

This paper would have rung hollow without due tribute to some of the giants of Biafran scientific and engineering community (RAP: Research and Production), among whom were: *Engineering:* Profs. Mark. O. Chijioke, Mr. Kanu Okoronkwo, Mike Nwachukwu, Willie Achukwu; *Physics:* Profs. B.C. Nwosu, Felix O. Oragwu, Cajetan Okeke; *Chemistry:* Profs. Chimere Ikokwu, Emma Okafor, Nwaji. Eugene O.Arene. *Microbiology:* Profs. Njoku-Obi, Steve Emejuaiwe, *etc., some of whom are alive and well. We can now see far into the distance of possibilities because we stood on the shoulders of these giants.*

Introduction

This colloquium, an august event in the context of its goal, shall remain a source of pride for all Ndi-Igbo. It's an event whose psycho-cathartic impact is long overdue for the long-suffering Igbo man and woman who had pined for 44 years (in the wilderness) for a bold "statement" such as this. In deed, *"Weeping may endure for the night, but joy shall surely come in the morning". (Ps 30:5)* In life, as in business, we get what we negotiate. Otherwise, and by default, we end up with what we deserve, a prescription for dissatisfaction. Today voices are rending the air for a "negotiated confederal arrangement", and this is as it should be.

The Theory and the Pragma

Ndi Igbo collectively, can, *in theory* do whatever they need to do to stanch the surging tide of dysfunctionality, mediocrity, and stagnation in Nigeria in any chosen sphere of human endeavor. The *theory* derives from the fact that our people have already laid the foundation (47 years ago), for the translation of academic theory into practice/product. The time has arrived for us to take the necessary steps, albeit tentative, to translate theory into a co-ordinated economic and technological take-off.

The Nigeria-Biafra war (July 1967 – January 1970), in hindsight, appears to have been a "necessary evil", so to speak. Landlocked and blockaded by air, land and sea, Biafra had to turn inwards, intellectually and pragmatically, for solutions to the lopsided superiority of the Nigerian side in the battlefield and in the arena of international politics. Biafra, in so doing, discovered bottled-up intellectual and technological strengths that helped sustain it until the cessation of physical hostilities. Serendipity had come to the rescue.

The foregoing is a stated "necessary" part of that "evil", the imposed suffering. Biafra could achieve feats under duress (just as Hitler's scientists and engineers were compelled by adverse desert conditions - lack of water) to come up with the Volkswagen (the people's car), an automobile with an air-cooled, desert-friendly engine. Ala Igbo during Biafra fashioned-out petroleum refineries that met most of its needs. The introduction of the famous *Ogbunigwe* was a natural result of the need to apply knowledge of theory to pressing challenges, and the efficacy, elegance aside, was there for all to appreciate. The "Abagana debacle" suffered by the enemy was, and still is, testimony to the power of harnessed theory. Uli Airport, built by Biafran engineers, was a wonder under the then-prevailing circumstances, thanks to the ingenuity of the oppressed and the pressed.

S.W.O.T analysis

Let us adopt a S.W.O.T analytic approach to tackling the development bog-down of Ala Igbo. Ala Igbo has its well-known **S**TRENGTHS, **W**EAKNESSES, **O**PPORTUNITIES, and **T**HREATS. These attributes are explored briefly and contextually, and a "road map" for a plausible, pragmatic strategy for a robust turnaround advanced.

STRENGTHS: Ndi Igbo generally display dynamism (a go-getter attribute), and thus industrious and achievement-oriented; culturally proud and family-oriented.

WEAKNESSES: Any race, or society, always possesses its own identifiable weaknesses, and for the Ndi Igbo, being politically naïve appears to be one of these. The perceived lack of strategic thinking also appears to be a defect. Detractors within Nigeria tend to see the Ndi Igbo as incurably attracted to money and will 'cut any corner' to acquire it. Too bad for these detractors!

OPPORTUNITIES: Opportunities for growth and advancement within Nigeria are in direct proportion to the general level of preparedness (educational, commercial, technical, multi-linguistic) of the individual. This is serendipity. The propensity of the Igbo to easily relocate to foreign lands speaks to their achievement orientedness. They simply go where the perceived opportunities are, to the chagrin of their detractors.

THREATS: Threats can be viewed as non-hospitable, or non-welcoming, conditions to the execution of a laid-down strategy, potentially thwarting efficacy. Here in this country, there is a phenomenon of an impulsive and almost intractable dislike of Ndi Igbo outside their homesteads. The seemingly "programmed" murders of the Igbo since 1945, be it in the North or elsewhere attests to this.

Strategy for moving forward

A common name in Ala Igbo is *Umunna wu ike (There is strength in communalism)*. While this is true, there is also a slightly countering reality: *recalcitrance (Igbo a nagh e new eze)*. Every Igbo is a king in his own right, in society. How, given these seemingly opposing tendencies, can we move forward? The answer seems to lie in our history of collectivism: Ndi-Igbo citizens in the former Imo State under the then governor, Sam I. Mbakwe, contributed monetary levies toward the building of the Imo Airport in Owerre. Prior to this, communities, pre-the Nigeria-Biafra war, were always embarking on, and completing, one communal project after another, rarely with any external (government) help; communities usually contributed money to sponsor the higher education of a son in Nigeria, or abroad. So Ndi Igbo already have a track record as a guide, and with this in mind, this paper recommends (1) creating a **Fund** for the economic development of Ala Igbo. This is beyond principles. The mechanics and *modus operandi* will be worked out. However, a core tenet is that this is an **Economic Self-Development Fund** structured in such a way that, overseen by a Board of Trustees elected by each state, subscriptions to tranches for each state should be co-ordinated and effected through chosen banks. (2) that this **Fund** explore the workability of creating a **Micro-Finance Bank** (in the real sense in which Dr. Muhammad Yunis, the founder of Grameen Bank/Bangladesh) had envisioned it. Crafted in a way that accountability and responsibility co-opt our cultural values and expectations, this should be a worthwhile and workable initiative. (3) that this **Fund** can be a source of funding for the establishment of *educational orientations/outreach* to high schools in Ala Igbo in order to enlighten the children on the various scientific achievements of Ala Igbo scientists between 1967 and 1970. The expected psychological/academic lift of such an initiative should not be underestimated.

It is apparent that, from the SWOT inventory, our strengths as Ndi Igbo overshadow and overwhelm what some consider a weakness. Our strengths have even become multiplied simply on the strength of the "survival instinct" built into us, somehow. Moreover, the perceived "threats" have always been opportunities in disguise to the well attuned and prepared. In fact, from the physics of motion (dynamics) we learn that without the frictional force that not only impedes our motion but also, paradoxically, provides traction, we humans, or other animals would have been unable to walk.

The foregoing has intentionally been kept simple and brief, with no forays into high-brow academic treatises. These few suggestions are here in order to stimulate "possibility thinking," as it were. According to Emerson, "Do the thing and you'll have the power," and by Gandhi we're also enjoined to realize that, "The mere act of Thinking Big makes one big". This colloquium is just the first of other planned colloquial initiatives (from what I have been told). So, there'll be opportunities to re-visit, discuss, and digress on the opportunities presented.

Research, Planning and Development:
The Future of the Igbo Nation
by
Prof. Ukachukwu A. Awuzie

1. Introduction

The answers to the question of what the Igbo nation needs in order to develop politically, economically, educationally, culturally, can be given in many ways. But the only solution we are proposing here, today, is the timely adaptation and effective application of the organic synthesis of the global contemporary culture of research and planning as a means of accelerating her developmental processes. With the present situation of Igboland, and given the global synergy of modern scientific and technological culture, the imperative to evolve systematic ways of discovering, identifying, explaining and pursuing basic developmental aspirations for the progress and empowerment of the Igbo people, is quite crucial. In the present world that is often described as post-modern, any country or society that wants to survive, develop or grow must invest in, or sponsor strategic research and planning as potent vehicles of development.

Indeed, sustainable development programs today are anchored on research and planning, or as it is popularly known, research and development (R&D). Evidently, the key term of our discussion that is linked to planning and development is research. In this context, the term research is, technically, the systematic, objective, and consistent investigation into and study of materials, sources, etc., in order to establish facts and reach new conclusions.' This is the modem scientific way of advancement in the study and knowledge of any type of reality. As such, research procedures involve planning and, among other things, the analysis and reporting of controlled observations with a view to arrive at the development of generalizations, principles, theories or explanation of phenomena. It discovers, corrects and interprets new facts in search of a solution to well defined-problems. It is also concerned with modifying, revising or verifying accepted theories or conclusions based on new information (Adewumi 12).

Perhaps the difference, we observe, between the traditional and modern societies is on the pattern of thought and its systematic application for the effective control of nature and the environment. Nigeria and other African countries remain marginal on the technological barometer because of this lack of concrete commitment to invest in R & D. Over the course of human history and civilization, peoples and nations distinguish themselves by the ways in which they organize their knowledge along scientific and technological paradigms.

Comparatively, while most of the Nations within the African continent are associated with cultural forms and features that are grounded on the religio-mythical cosmologies, the Western nations that conquered and colonized most of the African nations, for a considerable period of time, operated with modern cosmologies based on astronomy, physics, mathematics and philosophy. Evidently, the success of the West in military, commercial, industrial, medical, political, and artistic advancements in the course of history, is attributed to the overriding rational framework of this cultural orientation and the investments they make in R & D.

In this paper, we shall take a look at the concept and give a broad understanding of, and the relevance of R & D in technological progress. Secondly we would show the spasmodic features of R & D in Nigeria; as a feature of this, and in terms of how it impacts the Igbo nation in the South East, we shall indicate that R & D is even, in contrast to the efforts being made at the Federal level, comatose in the entire Igbo nation in Nigeria. Our final comments would then be to recommend a renaissance of R & D in the educational institutions and industries in Igbo heartland and provide suggestions about how this can be done.

2. The Role of Research and Planning as Vectors of Development
The Concept and the Process of Research and Development (R&D)

Research is basically a "systematized curiosity," a methodic inquiry, a process of investigation that is sustained by a desire to produce goods and services that will satisfy the needs of the society. Development on the other hand is a complex term. It can mean different things in different domains of discourse; but aligned to research, it delineates the concept of innovation; and as such it predates the contemporary applications that see it as a post cold war phenomenon. Indeed development and innovation are processes that signify major shifts within various civilizations. Watershed events [like the discovery of fire, wheels, the renaissance, telephony, photography, telegraphy, cinematography, pasteurization, vaccination, radio transmission, radiology, television, laser beams, and sundry developments that stitch people together and constitute major demand and supply chains and market possibilities], are major "developments" in the history of civilization.

As a feature of modern market political economy, R & D has tended to absorb a sizeable proportion of corporate and public investments in the developed countries. R&D comprises all the creative work undertaken on a systematic basis in order to increase the stock of knowledge, including knowledge of man, culture and society, and the use of this stock of knowledge to devise new applications (OECD, 2002). In the modern market economy, R & D is mainly carried out by researchers in higher educational institutions (HEIs), research clusters or institutes (public and private), and industrial firms. As a process, it is constituted through the procedure of ideation, research, funding, production [prototyping and mass-production or manufacturing] and post-production marketing and distribution of goods and services. Therefore the process of R & D is not complete until the goods - the products of the research are commercialized.

Thus, as a productive venture, R & D is expected to lead to new product(s) or improvement of existing product(s), new processes of developments or improvement of existing processes, generation/creation of new knowledge, patents, copyrights and publications. Publication is a sign of good quality of invention and research outputs while patents, copyrights, and funds from companies are signs that those inventions have market potentials. [1] Equally, R & D is normally typified as in involving three main activities:

- Basic research - experimental or theoretical work undertaken primarily to acquire new knowledge of the underlying foundations of phenomena and observable facts, without any particular application or use in view. It analyses properties, structures and relationships with a view to formulating and testing hypotheses, theories or structures and relationships with a view to formulating and testing hypotheses, theories or laws.

- Applied research - on the other hand, is also original investigation undertaken in order to acquire new knowledge (OECD, 2002). It is pragmatic, in the sense that it is usually, directed primarily towards a specific practical aim or objective. It is undertaken either to determine possible uses for the findings of basic research or to determine how new methods or ways of achieving specific and predetermined objectives work.

- Experimental development leading to Commercial marketing of utility distribution and usability (Siyanbola 2-3).

Research and Planning as Vectors of Development

Planning, as a cognate concept of R&D, refers to the act of organizing and deciding in advance what is to be done, how, when and where to do it, who is to do it in order to achieve the goals or objectives of the system. B. Adeyemi defines planning as a way of projecting our intentions; that is, a method of deciding what we want to accomplish. S. Ejiogu also holds that to plan, means to project, forecast, and design, make or chart a course (Ejiogu 37). Research and planning lead to strategic thinking and support the successful management of projects, providing focus and structure to activities and thereby enhancing the likelihood of successful outcomes. Indeed, there is a water-tight relationship between research and planning because planning involves the utilization of information derived from research for the sake of decision making and its adequate implementation. Proper use of research in planning helps to clarify the nature of the records necessary to substantiate interdepartmental performance reports reflecting key development indicators. Development happens faster and is stable if there is a detailed scheme, program or method worked out beforehand for the purpose of achieving set objectives. Sustainable development hardly, or in fact does not take place if there is no research or proper planning for it.

In recent times, research and planning have become essentially necessary for both individual and societal progress. The adaptation of research and planning helps to equip both individuals and societies with useful information that are capable of radical transformation of their lives for the good. Historical logic testifies to the fact that almost all the nations that have insisted on the application of systematic research and strategic planning, have reaped enormously from this venture. In fact all the developed nations of the world today, attained impressive heights in agriculture, energy production and conservation, medical science and information technology through the extensive application of research and planning.

Ultimately, most countries of the world now invest in R & D as a means of advancing their scientific and technological knowledge that guarantees durable economic growth and competitiveness in industrial activities. Thus, for most of these nations in their frenetic search for new frontiers of scientific and technological empowerment, R & D activities must be creative, innovative and exist within a strong national innovation system (NIS). Equally, for this reason, it is necessary that scientists and engineers possess entrepreneurial skills with focus on market-driven research or applied research. (Siyanbola 1).

Nevertheless, Nigeria, and the Igbo nation, like many other developing countries as it were, remain locked-in, or focused on the last stage of commercialization in the process of R & D - at the receiving end of goods and services, patented and produced in other countries. This is a fall-out of the oil boom whereby the country has become a dumping ground for finished products, instead of being in the avant-garde of research, development and productivity.

3. Nigeria's Adventure in the Field of R & D

The greatness of a people is not often measured by the endowment of talents and natural resources, but by the systematic way of applying their talents in harnessing and maximizing their natural resources and deploying them pragmatically and fruitfully in social drawers where they are needed. The consistent application of research and planning has speeded up the processes of human civilization framework and transformed its paradigmatic modes and forms from their primitive stages to the contemporary levels of sophistication. But the question that confronts us now is: why has it not materialized in the Nigerian case? Briefly, let us look at the few attempts made so far in the field of R & D in Nigeria

Some Initiatives toward the Promotion of R&D

As a nation, Nigeria is not lacking in formidable talents. Indeed the country is blessed with massive endowments of mind and means: over the years, the country has struggled to articulate a road map for its R & D terrain. It was realized early that the educational structure bequeathed by the colonial government was not research/technology oriented. Thus, realizing the strategic importance of R&D to its development, in the 1970s the country's leadership created institutions for the coordination and promotion of R&D activities in Science and Technology (S&T). This effort led to the establishment in 1970 of the National Council for Science and Technology (NCST) responsible for ordering national priorities in scientific research and coordinating and supervising both basic and applied research activities. In 1971 the Agricultural Research Council and the Industrial Research Council were established, and followed by the Medical Research Council and the Natural Science Research Council in 1972 and 1973 respectively.

Further information on the repositioning of R & D as a dominant feature of national policy is given on the website of the National Bureau of Statistics, where it is stated that in 1973, virtually all the research departments in the various ministries were made autonomous research institutes. These research institutes are:

- The Cocoa Research Institute of Nigeria [GRIN], Ibadan
- Federal Institute of Industrial Research Oshodi (FIIRO), Lagos
- The Forestry Research Institute of Nigeria [FRIN], Ibadan
- Hydraulic Equipment Research Institute (HERO, Kano
- Institute for Agriculture Research (IAR), Zaria
- Institute for Agricultural Research and Training IAR&T, Ibadan
- Lake Chad Research Institute (LCRI), Maiduguri
- National Agricultural Extension and Research Liaison Service (NAERLS), Zaria
- Natioal Animal Production Research Institute (NAPRI), Zaria
- National Agency for Science and Engineering Infrastructure (NASENI), Lagos

- Nigerian Building and Road Research Institute (NBRRI), Lagos
- National Cereals Research Institute (NCRI), Badeggi, Niger State
- National Centre for Genetic Research and Biotechnology (NCGRB)
- National Institute for Freshwaters Fisheries Research (NIFFR), New Bussa
- Nigeria Institute for Oil Palm Research (NIFOR), Benin city
- National Horticulture Research Institute (NIHORT), Ibadan
- National Institute for Medical Research NIMR), Yaba
- Nigeria Institute for Oceanography and Marine Research (NIOMR), Lagos
- National Institute for Pharmaceutical Research and Development (NIPRD), Abuja
- Nigeria Institute for Trypanosomasis Research (NITR), Kaduna
- National Root Crops Research Institute (NRCRI),Umudike, Abia State
- National Research Institute for Chemical Technology (NRICT), Zaria
- Nigerian Stored Products Research Institute (NSPRI), Yaba
- National Veterinary Research Institute (NVRI), Vom, Jos
- Projects Development Institute (PDI), Enugu
- Rubber Research Institute of Nigeria (RRIN), Benin City [NBS]

[It can be noted from this list that the South East region, the heartland of the Igbo nation was systematically excluded, except for the installations at Umudike and Enugu. But we shall return to the politics of this later]. The most radical change was the creation of the National Science and Technology Development Agency [NSTDA]. In January 1977, the NCST was replaced with the National Science and Technology Development Agency (NSTDA) with a revised mandate for the promotion and development of S&T including initiation of policy in relation to scientific research and technology. The objective was to make scientific research relevant to economic development.

In 1980, a full-fledged Federal Ministry of Science and Technology (FMST) was established to take over the responsibilities of NSTDA. In 1984, FMST was merged with Federal Ministry of Education; and regained its autonomy in 1985 and was again merged with the Federal Ministry of Industry in 1992. FMST was however reactivated in 1993 with mandates to, among others, promote basic science research; scientific and technological research for agricultural, industrial, medical, and energy applications; administration of technology transfer programmes; coordination and issuance of policy guidelines to all S&T research institutes in Nigeria; advising the President on S&T matters?

In 1993 as well, a new agency called National Agency for Science and Engineering Infrastructure [NASENI] was established. The research institutes in the defunct Ministry of Science and Technology were transferred to their sectoral ministries. By 1993, the Ministry of Science and Technology was reactivated with a Secretary of cabinet minister rank as its chief executive with the following mandates:

Promotion of Scientific and Technological Research.

Promotion of Agricultural, Industrial, Medical, Road, Building, Energy Research and Basic Sciences Research.

Promotion and Administration of Technology Transfer programmes.

Coordination and issuance of policy guidelines to all research institutes in Nigeria. Approval of the institutes' research programmes and sanction their capital and recurrent expenditures.

Advising the President on the appointment of the governing council/board for each institute. (Cf. 2012 National Bureau of Statistics. All rights reserved, Accessed May 16, 2014).

Signs of Poor R & D Intensity in Nigeria

R & D intensity refers to the practical seriousness or commitment or investment that a company, government or venture capital or private equity actually makes to R & D. In other words, it is the incentivized dedication to practical objectives of the research project. In this regard then, even though Nigeria has, over the years, outlined good paper policies on R & D; they remain just that - paper policies, on paper. The practical budgetary and rational commitment and investment has been lacking. Records show and indicate that the percentage budgetary allocation to the general basic research through funding and infrastructural development in Higher Education, the various research institutes and the S&T ministry in Nigeria from Year 2007 and 2012 has been close to abysmal. From a height of 1.04% of the national budget in 2007, allocation declined each year to a lowest point of 0.56% in 2010. Marginal increase in allocation was witnessed in 2011 with the allocation in 2012 standing at about 60% of 2007. Comparatively, Nigeria ranks amongst the lowest in S&T funding having 0.01% of GDP as against Germany, 2.5% of GDP, India 2.5% of GDP, Russia 5% of GDP, United States of America 2.8% of GDP. The current funding system whereby government is the main source of funding for R&D will not translate to the realization of the desired contribution of the sector.

It is important to note that Nigeria as a nation has failed as far as the promotion of R&D is concerned. The Nigerian failure has obviously affected the Igbo nation that has been technically sidelined in matters of R&D. Nevertheless, the Igbo people know that the dynamics of the present world is driven by science and technology. They are aware of the fact that their only means of survival in the present situation of the country is to cling to the powerful tools of science and technology. This, for instance, is the only tool and weapon of advantage with which a small nation like Israel is still soaring high in the midst of ever-growing conflicts and hostilities existing between her and her Arab neighbors. The situation of the Igbo nation in the Nigerian State bears notable marks of similarity with that of Israel among the Arab nations.

4. The Case of R&D in Igboland: Potentials for Scientific and Technological Advancement

If the adaptation of scientific and technological culture, through the instrumentality of research and planning, is the secret of modem civilization framework, our stake in the present paper is that Igboland, in her present situation, cannot develop in any significant way, without avidly seeking and embracing the new scientific culture through research and planning. Therefore, we shall now demonstrate the fact that given the remarkable Igbo potentials for scientific and technological advancement, her feature hope of survival in the Nigeria State lies in the maximization of her talents in the area of research and planning as the potent vehicles of development and empowerment.

In the pre-colonial era, the Igbos excelled in Agriculture, commerce and industry (Afigbo 124-139). Within the traditional society, there was a substantial evidence of a competitive agricultural life that gave rise to the Ikenga cult of the recognition of individual achievement. The agricultural practice was not brought to its highly expansive and mechanized stage because of the lack of sufficient fertile land. As Igbos occupy a relatively limited landmass in comparison with other ethnic groups in Nigeria, most of the young people, who could not engage in Agriculture resorted to trading. Equally, as some Igbo scholars have noted, ecological differences contributed immensely to the development of local and regional trade amongst the Igbos. Particularly, as Ikerionwu states, "the inhabitants of northern and central Igboland, whose soils were over-farmed, resorted to trade" [2]. It could be said that it was in commerce that the Igbos exhibited their excellence and industry. This Igbo entrepreneurial prowess, has constituted as a potent source of envy for which Igbos are persecuted in various parts of Nigeria, especially, in the North. Indeed, the indubitable Igbo entrepreneurial spirit is recognized by so many non-Igbo scholars such as Kate Meagher and Olanrewaju Olutayo. Remarking on this as an essential reason for the persecution of the Igbos in the North, Kate Meagher states: "The conventional view is that Igbo involvement in the informal economy has been a divisive rather than a uniting force. High levels of migration and Igbo dominance of lucrative trades in other ethnic regions of Nigeria, particularly in the Hausa areas of the north, have been represented as important triggers of ethnic riots, both in the run-up of the Civil War, and during serious outbreaks of violence during the 1990s." (Meagher 31-46). Added to this high sprit of enterprise in business, the discovery of Igbo-Ukwu finds in recent times, testifies to the Igbo early engagements in craft and industry. The bronze and other associated archeological finds in Igbo-Ukwu town, given their high level of technical skill, prove that the Igbo effort in technological advancement is one of the earliest in the West African rainforest area [3].

As a people, the Igbo have great potentials for high-technological advancement as was evidenced during the Nigerian-Biafran War. Many studies on the history of Igbo origin that tend to link the Igbos to the Jews of Israel have established that the globally acclaimed technological prowess of the Jews is also seen in the Igbos (Ezeani 56). Pressed with the urgency of sheer survival during the war, the Igbo, out of their resourcefulness developed quite reputable and effective indigenous technologies: mobile refineries, cluster bombs known as *Ogbuniwe*, armored tanks, rocket launchers to mention but a few. In the work, *In Biafra Africa Died*, Emefiena Ezeani commenting on the ingenuity of the Igbos during the war, described Biafra, nay Igbo, as the Japan of Africa that was killed in infancy: "Biafra was, by chance, that spark of African modern technological ingenuity and inventiveness that might have, if allowed, taken African development on a different course today. Biafra was the home of the `can do' attitude forced upon Biafrans by the necessity of war and crystallized in their culture of enterprise and ingenuity. Biafrans in a space of two years and under intolerable war conditions, mined oil, refined petroleum in refineries locally fabricated and kept their vehicles moving despite a total blockade. At a time when 20th century rocket science was only a few decades old Biafrans fabricated their own rockets, powered it with their own refined rocket fuel and launched them with devastating effects on the Nigerian army" (Ezeani 56).

Though Biafrans lost the war, the Biafran scientific and technological achievements could be counted as a victory over Nigeria. For if Nigeria boasts of winning the war with ammunition supplied by the West and Soviet Nations, Biafra should boast of resisting world powers with home-made ammunition. In fact, the one time governor of the old Anambra State, Chief C. C. Onoh quoting Soviet Union Government Official puts the Igbo (Biafran) might in a good relief: "... a country that is not yet two months old that can manufacture ogbunigwe (monster bombs) and rockets must be feared" (*ibid.*) All these were possible, thanks to, Biafran Research and Development Directorate in the

Politburo which tapped the Igbos 'can do' attitudes: adventurous, enterprising, bold, cosmopolitan, ubiquitous, visible, and ingenious.

Similarly, even before the war, the Igbo prowess was manifested in their leadership of the decolonization struggle, not just of Nigeria, but of the African continent. Dr. Nnamdi Azikiwe, that great son of Igboland, - historically regarded as the doyen of pan-African nationalism did not just play strategic roles in the liberation of Nigeria but also inspired many other African nationalist leaders, who not only admired him but tried to emulate his sterling leadership qualities. Zik inspired Dr. Kwame Nkrumah while in Ghana in the 1930s as the editor of Accra Morning Post, and also greatly influenced the nationalist spirit and dedication of Nelson Mandela. Robert Omote, writing about players in pre-independence Nigeria, said that the Great Zik himself in an unguarded moment interjected that "it would appear that the God of Africa has created the Ibo nation to lead the children of Africa from the bondage of ages..." (Omote 34). According to Ihejirika, the prominent role played by the Igbo in Nigeria's liberation struggle was manifested in the fact that many of them were incarcerated for their anti-colonial activities during the struggle for independence. And in his affirmation of this prominent Igbo role, Chinua Achebe, noted: "the British had thrown more of them into jail for sedition than any others during the two decades or so of pre-independence agitation and troublemaking." In the bid to elaborate further this fact Ihejirika states: "With a population of over 50 million according to census figures, the Igbo rank among the five largest nationalities in Africa and perhaps among the top ten in the world." [4] The Igbo high potential for advancement is evidenced in the world-renowned citizens in various fields of human endeavor she has produced. Almost every version of the history of Nigeria shows that the Igbo of Nigeria have proven to be the *sui generis* among the Black race, as exemplified by the likes of Equiano, Blyden, Azikiwe, Ibiam, Okpara, Ikoku, Ojike, Mbanefo, Ironsi, Orizu, Sir Odumegwu Ojukwu, Dike, Uchendu, Emeka Ojukwu, Achebe, Ekwensi, Okigbo, Afigbo, Nwapa, Oputa, Chike Obi, Arinze, Okere, Ukaegbu, Anyaoku, Nwabueze, Okonjo-Iweala, Emeagwali, Adichie, Nnaji, and hundreds more who recorded their firsts in Nigeria and among the Black race." (Ihejirika 1). In fact, stretching further, this almost innate Igbo character of resistance and innovation, it should be noted that their women laid the foundation of the resistance against British colonialism during the famous Aba Women Riot of 1929. Equally, it is indisputable that the little progress that Nigeria has made in the recent times was engineered by the sons and daughters of Igbo nation. Name it: the debt relief that Nigeria got from the Paris Club was negotiated by Dr. Ngozi Okonjo Iweala; the Naira policy was initiated by Prof. Chukwuma Soludo as the CBN governor; the war against fake drugs was fought, at the risk of her life, by Prof. Dora Akunyili as helmsman of NAFDAC; and the cell phone revolution as is well known today was engineered by Ernest Ndukwe as the Executive Secretary of the National Communication Commission. All these are facts of common knowledge among Nigerians.

Most importantly, as a matter of global achievements record, Igbo contributions in science and technology is recognized all over the world. In the most recent times, some Igbo scientists, technologists and professionals have proved their mettle in the world record of great contributions to humanity. Among the Igbos who have raised their heads above the shoulders of others in their respective areas of specializations are: Ezekiel Izuogo (scientist and inventor of the first Indigenous African automobile technology, the Z-600), Augustine Njoku-Obi (developer of Cholera Vaccine), Damian Anyanwu (inventor), Philip Emeagwali (American computer scientist and mathematician), Augustine Asogbue and Okechukwu Anthony Mezu (NASA scientists), Peter Nwangwu (Famous pharmacology research scientist), Bartholomew Nnaji (Robotics scientist), Cyprian Emeka Uzor (Father of modern Chip Interconnection Technologies, World-class scientist and prolific inventor holding over 100 US patents), etc. These are veritable indices of Igbo potentials for great accomplishment in every aspect of human endeavor. This means that, given a very conducive environment, with proper organization and equipment, most Igbos can fly high and even higher in any given profession beyond any imaginable expectation.

5. Some Obstacles and Causes of the Present Atrophy for R&D in Igboland

There is no gain saying that the present situation of Ndi-Igbo is quite deplorable in spite of their capacity for greatness. Nevertheless, the Igbos, collectively as a nation, have set themselves within a downward trend of self-negation. The post-war era has seen the Igbo cultural civilization gradually spiraling and receding into a state of dismemberment, anarchy and self-destruction. Indeed, an objective assessment of the present situation shows that politically, socially and culturally, the Igbos have lost the tight grip of collective search for survival and the erstwhile ambitious move toward the consolidation of cultural development.

In a recent paper, delivered to Ala-Igbo Congress titled: **Ikenga Run Amok—Towards a Diagnosis and Healing of the Ndi-Igbo Crisis,** Chinweizu chronicled the trauma and malaise of the Igbo nation and its present atrophy thus: During the 20th century, the Igbo World was shaken to its foundations by a series of political and cultural earthquakes, including being conquered militarily twice in seventy years - by repeated British military expeditions and patrols and in the Nigerian

Civil War, which added a host of political, economic, cultural and social dislocations to those already inflicted by the British; by Christian missionaries who blew up sacred groves and shrines, burning religious artworks); by political traditions of democratic gerontocracy which were devastated by experiments in autocracy and indirect rule; by her economy reorganized for exploitation by foreign interests, particularly through the deliberate ruination of local crafts and manufactures by cheap imports. The cumulative result is that Ndi-Igbo today show symptoms of a people who have almost lost their culture, whose society is close to disintegration, and who, for lack of a firm anchor in their ancestral culture, are adapting haphazardly to bewildering circumstances. Consequently, Igbo cultural identity is in jeopardy and the result is the anarchy of social chaos. For a more systematic appreciation let us analyze these sets of trauma thematically:

a) **Lack of Awareness:** Generally, the Igbos are still poor, rapidly fading into oblivion in terms of development. Every factual and empirical description shows that Igbos have failed abysmally where it matters most: development. In this light, the Igbos, according to Chieke Ihejirika, now fits the pattern of Egu, the baby caterpillar which holds firm while young, but falls when it matures. The Igbo predicament in terms of underdevelopment is a sad story and a living example of a sleeping giant. She remains a reference point for an ethnic nation lacking in substantial development, particularly since after the Nigerian-Biafran War.

b) **War Aftermath:** It must be said that the four decades of post-Civil War existence of the Igbo nation have been quite harsh and difficult. Among many others, the experience of the war seemed to have stricken the Igbo with a rabid sense of despair, self-forgetfulness and, consequently, has set the entire Igbo nation spiraling downward into self-abnegation. Just as the properties of the Igbo people in other states were declared as abandoned property, the entire Igboland is still suffering the same fate of an abandoned area in the Nigerian State.

Indeed, with the tragedy of the civil war and post war experiences, the average Igbo person seems to be confused, disoriented and without a clear focus. As Ekwuru observes, the war dealt a heavy blow on the Igbo collective personality. It destabilized the cultural spirit that constitutes her cultural personality (Ekwuru 1-38). Nonetheless, scholars like Kate Meagher and Tom Forrest retain that the Nigerian Civil War, in terms of its effects on the Igbo personality was a mix of blessings. For, according to them, even though it remains a traumatic experience, it intensified the role of self-reliance in the development of Igbo enterprise (Meager 31-48). With the defeat of the war, the Igbos lost the collective sense of the pride of Igboness. It brought the Igbos to the steady trend of self-marginalization and the dual system of technical depopulation and de-Igbonization (Uwalaka 44-47). It is a developing phenomenon that we are technically being depopulated through the politics of steadily diminishing census figures. And, on the other hand, most Igbos, for certain socioeconomic reasons known to them, have decided drop their Igbo names in order to align themselves to the other ethnic groups.

3. Systematic Marginalization

It is important to observe that the issue of neglect and abandonment of southeastern Nigeria did not start with the defeat of Biafra. It has been a steady posture of hate and disregard of the Nigeria State toward Igboland. Long before Nigeria gained political independence, Dr. Nnamdi Azikiwe in his presidential address delivered to the Igbo State Union Assembly held at Aba on the 25th of June, 1949, among other things, indicated as follows:

> On the economic plane, I cannot sufficiently impress you because you are too familiar with the victimization which is our fate. Look at our roads, how many of them are toned, compared, for example with the roads in other parts of the country? Those of you who have traveled to this assembly by road are witnesses of the corrugated and utterly unworthy state of the roads which traverse Igboland, in spite of the fact that four million Igbo people pay taxes in order, among others, to have good roads. With roads must be considered the system of communications, water and electricity supplies. How many of our towns, for example have complete postal telegraph, telephone and wireless service compared to the towns in other parts of Nigeria? How many have pipe-borne water supply? How many have electricity undertakings? Today these disabilities have been intensified. (Azikiwe, "Presidential Address to IboState Union," 1949).

Today, as the Great Zik said, these disabilities have continued unabated. In the present moment of the 21st Century, many sections of the Igbo nation are characterized by abject poverty. In terms of basic amenities and infrastructural development, Igboland remains the most neglected area in terms of federal presence. Even with their notable communitarian self-help development efforts, following their principle of *onye ajuru anaghi aju onwe*, a greater part of the Igbo live in a deplorable condition of abject poverty. Pipe-borne water, regular supply of electricity, modern well equipped hospitals, effective and functionally relevant schools are notoriously absent or are in short supply. Indeed, about 70% of its citizens live below the UN benchmark of 2 dollars a day, and there is that sense of bitter disappointment across the land. Her current state of underdevelopment, despite her blessings, may mean that, social forces or under currents, actions or inactions in our modus operandi, have facilitated her abysmal descent into chaos.

4. Bad Political Leadership

The Igbo political landscape is bereft of collective consciousness. Consistently, with systems of technical and structural exclusion and marginalization, the Igbos are psychologically adjusting themselves to the political position of second class citizens in their own country. They are happy to play the second fiddle in any government appointment (Igbokwe 71). Evidently, "the consequence is that the Igbos appear to be marginalized in all important aspects of Nigerian life. So whether one thinks of political, military, bureaucratic or economic power, etc, the Igbos are no longer major players in Nigeria.[26] As it stands now, the Igbo role in Nigerian politics is dwindling and unsteady. Igbo politicians have lost the sense of unity of purpose and collective interest. Joe Igbokwe thinks that the "Igbo political elite have routinely acted against their own self-interest" (*ibid*.) The situation today is that Igbo political capital in Nigerian politics is lessening as a result of apparent lack of unity of purpose and interest in their political will, vision and struggle. This is not all, with very few exceptions, Igbo politicians are known to be corrupt, selfish and unpatriotic of Igbo collective interest and agenda. Commenting on this horrible situation within the context of the Nigerian politics, the Committee of Concerned Igbo Intellectuals in London puts it this way: "...the culture of state looting and deconstruction which governed the practice of politics at the Federal level soon permeated the States. And where heretofore communal property was held sacrosanct in Igboland, most of the post war politicians (military and civil) have, even in Igbo states, not thought twice before diverting public resources to private pockets, and soon by the multiplier effects produce new business millionaires who would now join the political bandwagon and ensure the calcification of this heretofore foreign, if not errant, political behavior and culture. The situation is now further compounded by the emergence of 419 chiefs and millionaires." (In *The Igbo Network*).

With the present culture of corruption, Igbo leaders seem to have become a curse rather than a blessing to their people. They struggle to occupy leadership positions by force, without the collective will of the people. They occupy the State Government houses for years without leaving any substantive legacy. This aberrant political culture has left the Nation in a continual trend of socio-economic decline and moral degeneracy. The present state of affairs creates both social and economic difficulties leading to mass exodus of Igbo youths to other parts of Nigeria and the outside world. The presumed Igbo leaders in their constant looting of the public treasury, have emasculated the Igbo collective personality, bringing shame to their people, while rendering them highly impotent in engineering any substantive developmental process and socio-cultural transformation.

5. Poor Educational Structures

Furthermore, with a lot social havoc caused by present political misdirection, the educational sector is in shambles. It is not an understatement to say that Igbo educational system has lost its pristine integrity and credibility and has degenerated into a shadow of what it should be. Right from the nursery, through the primary/secondary to the tertiary levels, Igbo institutions are far below standard in acquisition of knowledge, language and technical skills. To say the least, our schools no longer serve as places of learning as students leave those schools in the end, quite diminished in quality and value than when they came in. If we call for a proper assessment along those social paradigms that guarantee the right educational development of the child, the darkness in the Nigerian schools would reveal that an average adolescent cannot develop well academically in Nigeria.

Proper screening of the Nigerian educational institutions in the light of the indices for safe development of the child like: healthy social environment, good education, robust economy, strong institutional infrastructure, service-driven politics, security and all other factors that ensure child quality education, will show that there is no proper education going on in our schools. Least wonder then, such an erudite scholar like, Nduka Otonti, in his objective assessment of this situation, says: "There are a given details about the poor financing, the inadequacy or even non-availability of basic infrastructure, the lack of books, laboratory and other teaching equipments, examination malpractices, secret cults, indiscipline, ad nauseam" (Otonti 213). Obviously, the socio-political crises of bribery and corruption have infiltrated into the educational system. Today, the notion of education in Nigeria, has been reduced to an institutional system for the acquisition of certificates. As such, there is a mad rush for primary, secondary and university education, with the sole aim of acquiring certificates. "We of course know," says Nduka Otonti, "that this quest for certificates is probably the greatest driving force of the Nigerian educational enterprise and has given rise to innumerable abuses and malpractices"(*ibid*. 144)

Considering the deplorable situation of Nigerian educational institutions, some scholars like E. T. Aworo and R. M. Morakinyo in "A

Study of exam malpractices in secondary schools in Akure" have gone to the extent of declaring tertiary education in Nigeria a colossal waste of resources since they consume so much and profit so little. Such an extremist position seems to be an objective judgment when one considers the fact that in the 2007 ranking of African and World universities, in terms of quality, none of the over 20 tertiary institutions within Igboland then, according to Eso (2008), was rated among the first best 30 universities in Africa. In fact, by the rating of the report, the best university in Nigeria, the Obafemi Awolowo University, came 33rd, while the second, the University of Ibadan stood at 72nd and the third, the University of Benin rested at 87th positions respectively. Equally, in the global rating, the three Nigerian universities mentioned also stood at the 6199th, 6971st and 7442nd positions respectively (Eso, "The State of Education in Nigeria"). Similarly, The latest ranking of the first 100 of Nigerian universities, in 2013, according to research abilities, by the National Universities Commission did not see any of the universities in Igboland (public or private), among the first ten. The best in and around us here, the Federal University of Technology Owerri, stood at the 12th position. UNN was at the 14th position, UNIZIK was 16th, Michael Okpara 29th, while my own very dear IMSU was 39th. (NUC 2013, "Top 100 Universities in Nigeria"). This is a clear evidence that Igbo tertiary institutions have lost their integrity and credibility, and have degenerated into the status of public social entertainment bodies. While this is most true at the tertiary level, it is equally true at the primary and secondary school levels.

Given these catalogues of woes as a result of the dysfunctional structures of our socio-political and cultural lives, we must agree that something has gone wrong in our collective posture as a people. In fact, we are compelled to agree with Ihejirika that, "for a people reputed to be smart, enterprising, cosmopolitan, competitive, etc., the Igbo seem to have failed abysmally where it matters the most in the post-war Nigeria. They seem to have abandoned the basic values and characteristics that distinguished them as a nation. They have failed to cater to their collective future as a race, and hence have seriously jeopardized their survival as a cultural entity in a multicultural country." (Ihejirika 2). Actually, to call attention to the Igbo innate potentials for greatness, is the major reason behind this paper. What gives rise to her failure has been the neglect of those values that have served as cultural inspirational symbols for great accomplishment. Nevertheless, it is a truism that Igbo great achievements arise in the moments of daring challenges and necessity. And I believe that in the face of the present ever increasing challenges of our collective survival and development, the Igbo creative instinct of substantial collective action of empowerment and emancipation must be re-ignited.

5. The Capital Value of Research Investment: Towards a New Vista of Development - The Role of Igbo Governors

For an Igbo renaissance in R & D [because time and space constraints do not allow), we make the following concrete suggestions on: The Role of Igbo Governors; Human Capital Development through Education and the Erection of Industrial Clusters and Platforms of Collaboration through ICT-Intensive processes. Igbo states have had spates of good governance and lots of failed leadership. Sam Mbakwe and Rochas Okorocha come easily to mind as examples of good governors. However, for our purposes here, we recommend the following as roles of governance in R & D deployment. We suggest that for a resurgence of the Igbo industries, our Igbo governors must evolve policies and strategies to support diffusion of knowledge and deployment of new technologies as well as research and discovery. These strategies include:

- Direct and Indirect Investments in Basic R & D
- Direct and Indirect Investments in Applied R&D
- Human Capital Development
- Enacting Policies That Foster Innovation
- Facilitating Government/Academic/Non-Profit and Industry Collaborations, [RENs, RIs]
- Promoting Technology Transfer, and [discouraging brain drain, reverse brain drain and FDI
- Creating Favorable Tax, Regulatory, And Visa Policies (Alic, Mowery and Rubin, 2003).

Human Capital Development through Education

The fastest way and veritable platform to actualize the Igbo dream of development is to invest in and boost research capacities of educational institutions from the cradle. "Learning would make him unfit for slavery," so said Hugh Auld during the era of the slave trade in the United States. Before the abolition of slavery it was a criminal offense in the United States for slave owners to educate their slaves. What slaves needed were some doses of biblical instruction, to oblige them to be "obedient to their masters" and never to revolt in the face of inhuman treatment meted out to them. We learn from the autobiography of Frederick Douglas - the black American who was one of the most eminent human rights leaders of the 19th century, how the wife of Hugh Auld defied the state law by teaching the boy to read. The revolutionary attitude of this white woman led to conflict with her husband who declared that 'learning would make the boy unfit for slavery (Ndiokwere 283).

From the captivating story of the self-making of Frederick Douglas, through the liberating action of education, we can say that learning will make the Igbos unfit for any kind of domination or marginalization by others. Education is the key to any durable form of liberation, emancipation and collective empowerment. Studies upon studies have shown that Nigerian, nay Igbo educational institutions are far below standard in acquisition of knowledge, language and technical skills. As we all know, the Nigerian educational system, even with the changes of the recent times, has not radically diverted from its original colonial package meant to produce servile laborers and not thinkers and inventors. There is need to change from the educational system which lay more emphasis on the acquisition of ready-made facts and bits of information, which scholars call banking education, to the one which leads to the understanding of principles, the questioning of accepted facts and dogmas, the acquisition of skills for invention and development, which most scholars call liberative system of education. For any type of meaning and consistent development activities to take place, an adequate system of education must be adopted and massively promoted. As Nduka Otonti puts it: "Education is by common consent a crucial tool in development. Indeed, it is probably the most sensitive instrument not only for effecting but also for monitoring progress in the realization of the nation's goals and objectives. Specifically, education not only helps individuals to acquire literacy and technical know-how but also is the vehicle for the diffusion of culture and ideas" (*op. cit.* 103).

As this author further notes, although, we have produced so many educated men and women who have amassed wealth of information and strings of degrees and certificates, we have failed to produce a significant number of them with proper scientific attitude and critical turn of mind. It is against this backdrop that it is both imperative and urgent to invest in a liberal system of education in our schools. The new system of education for which we are advocating, must go beyond mere system of churning out educated illiterates. The Igbo people are endowed with an innate capacity for the search of excellence in everything they do. That is our mark of distinction and other ethnic nations know that. Right from, the beginning, Igbos have trained themselves to be the best. They have no system of half-measures. They maximize their powers to the highest limit. This is what Uzochukwu Njoku articulated very well in his write-up: "...one of the driving forces of Igbo consciousness is achievement, success, excellence and influence. ... Before the advent of the Europeans, the Igbo hunter strives not just to be onye na achu nta (one who hunts) but specifically to be known as Di-nta(master of hunting). In the same way, the wrestler strives to be Di-mgba, the palmwine tapper Di-ochi.The advent of the Europeans led the Igbo to re-define the areas of achievement and influence to consist in taking after the Europeans. This could explain how the Igbo (though late comers in Western education) could match with the Yoruba within a short time and cover up whatever gap that existed earlier and also have overtaken them in the embrace of Christianity" (Njoku 4).

The Igbo people by nature have a natural proclivity toward the best. Therefore what is needed for the education of our people is nothing short of the best system of education. There is, therefore, the need to equip and upgrade our educational institutions, from primary to tertiary levels, and thus increase their abilities to generate functional and creative systems of knowledge. One way to do this is to equip the libraries to be up to date with latest research technologies. Equally, there is need for an active community participation in education.

Educational Research Models and Objectives

The educational system that we are advocating for, should be research-orientated. The educational system must lay much emphasis on research and planning as potent vehicles of development. Igbo children, right from the nursery through the primary, secondary and tertiary levels of education, must be thought to search for the root-causes of things. The potent words of Vigil that, *"Felix qui potuit-rerum cognocere causas,"* meaning, "Happy is he who is able to know the causes of things," should be imprinted in their minds as a motivating factor. In order to inculcate the need of research in our younger generations and achieved the desired research-oriented culture, Igbo scientists and technologists should champion, with the help of entire Igbo communities, the cause of revamping on Igbo science culture that was lost with the intrusion of the European presence. Igbo science and technology should take the pride of place in the planning of curriculum for Igbo educational system. In advocating for a more science-oriented program of studies in Igboland, these Igbo scholars, Ezeudu F. O. Nkokelonye C. U. and Ezeudu S: A. put it thus: "Research is needed to find out industrial possibilities of local scientific activities. For instance, the industrial production of "gari" and manufacture of diesel oil from palm oil is desirable in achieving global recognition. Ndi Igbos have professional and supportive staff here and there but painfully lack a "core staff" who can render selfless service without the dreaded double standard of ethics and morality. The actual need to take Igbo science across globe is the development of people with high sense of patriotism able to serve *pro dei et patria* (for God and Fatherland). Development of people with a sense of public obligation and willing to perform public service with humility, integrity, and honesty is a serious challenge. Many highly-talented Igbo youths in Diaspora are the bedrock of foreign economy; whereas their talents and expertise are badly needed at home" (Ezeudu 135-136).

What these authors are advocating for, is not only the implementation of the program, but the establishment of Igbo Educational Research and Development Council (IERC), to see to the planning and execution of such program. The IERC will substitute and continue the work of the former Biafran Research and Production Board (RAP), which galvanized the activities of Igbo scientists and technician for the great technological accomplishments during the war. It is on record that the local arms industry developed by RAP led to the production of Biafran handmade grenades - *ogbunigwe*, rockets, guns and so on, that helped immensely to sustain the Biafran army for three years. Indeed, the RAP has already laid a solid foundation for modern scientific and technological based industrialization, and IERC will continue from there. In view of this, and in order to accelerate the development all the educational institutions in Igboland, the IERC should design their programs to suit the needs of Ndi-Igbo. The need to adapt internalized research programs is the magic of successful development. This is what has helped countries like Japan, Singapore and Taiwan. Japan is what it is today, particularly as one of the world's greatest economies because her school curriculum was designed to reflect the needs and aspirations of the country. Japan in her search for scientific and technological advancement, refused to copy the Western cultural models. Hence, her unique model of the inculturation of modern technology was put in an ideological maxim: Western technology and Japanese spirit. With this ideology, Japan extracted the scientific and technical aspects of the West without copying and imbibing their cultural spirit. This was successful due to the establishment of an educational policy for research. The aim was to conduct research and surveys to make an even greater contribution than before, in order to plan and design the nation's education policy. The contents of the curriculum of Japanese academic institutions are never drawn without due consideration of the findings of this institute. The same Japanese strategy is what has made countries like Singapore and Taiwan, to be counted among the so-called Asian Tigers. Their universities and research institutes are among the best in the world today. We can appreciate their speedy development in the areas of research and planning if we only remember when Taiwan products were regarded as fake and imitation. But today, these nations are models of the type of development that the Igbos should emulate. As the Igbo Council of Europe upholds, Singapore and Taiwan are nations whose successful development models represent a nexus that showcase the possibilities that can be unleashed when the collective will, human resources and other potentials are well harnessed (*ibid*. 180).

Therefore, the timely establishment of IERC will lead to the founding of more research institutes in Igboland. And consequently, the presence of research institutes will boost the sponsorship of Igbo scholars to engage in extensive research projects in accordance with the need of our people. Right now, apart from Michael Okpara University of Agriculture Umudike, I cannot think of any other functional research institute in Igboland. Indeed, as the most practicable and realizable option within a very short time period, I would strongly suggest that all the state universities in Igboland should develop research bureaus or have research clusters or institutes attached to them.

Effective ICT Approach to Education and Research

In line with the need to establish research institutes, there is, equally, the need to make our educational institutions - from the nursery to the tertiary - ICT compliant. As some Igbo scholars are suggesting, efforts should be made to integrate Igbo science into the globalized world of 21st century, in order to enable students to internalize scientific attitude of life. Science and technology schools should give students basic concepts, abilities and skills they need in order to cope with the global system of information Technology 4^0 The necessity and urgency for ICT approach to learning were underscored by Ezeudu et al, in their statement that: "World knowledge base doubles every two years at least. Advancement in ICT opened new trends and approaches in teaching and learning. No one can afford to use yesterday's tools to do today's business and hope to be in business tomorrow. Teachers all over the world are re-engineering their classroom operations to meet the challenges posed by ICT so as to remain relevant in the labor market. ...The era of teachers without ICT skills is gone. Knowledge without Internet is poor and unacceptable today. Everyone is adjusting to fit into the new information superhighway and be relevant in the global trend. Anybody not part of the global trend is left behind. Everyone has to adjust to a world that has become science and technology driven. ICT approach, therefore, has implication for human resource development and technological gap management" (*ibid*.)

Since ICT compliance, has been generally adjudged, to be the biggest driving force behind economic growth in the contemporary society, having lifted more than 10 percent of the world's population out of poverty in less than ten years; development in ICT as a key driver to a people's growth, will kick-start considerable amounts of investment, and generate significant fiscal revenues and employment opportunities. The potential impact of information and communication technologies (ICTs) on development or the positive effects of the Internet and other forms of ICTs to create new economic, social and political opportunities for developing countries is known all over the world. As local information technology (IT) service industries have become engines of job creation, especially for youth and women, it has the unimaginable dynamics of promoting both trade and competitiveness. Therefore, it is our studied view that the most effective way to inculcate the rudiments of research and planning culture in the younger generation is to invest in and develop a robust complete ICT-based education in all the levels of our school system. Inevitably, this will not only help in scientific and technological advancement, but equally, will help Igbo future leaders to meet the challenges of the 21st century. Building in the culture of ICT early enough in our youths will therefore help the Igbo nation to effectively live out her dream of prosperity, peace and stability. This paper is strongly convinced that Igbo nation's development drive needs to be anchored on strong and massive investment in IC

Investing in R & D

Furthermore, with the effective establishment of IERC, State budgets and investments, within the Igbo nation, should also give more attention to education and investment in research. The trend, for instance, in Imo State with more than 200 modern, well equipped functional hotels and guest houses, but not up to 20 up-to-date libraries should be discouraged and reversed. Ghana is known to be investing more than 30% of her annual budget in education. That is the reason behind the high quality one finds in Ghanaian tertiary institutions. There are more schools than recreation centers in their cities. The scriptural assertion that whatever one (person, nations, tribes) sows (invests in, gives attention to) is what he/she will reap, is a truism. ("Letter of St. Paul to the Galatians," 6:7). Dear friends and colleagues, let us be frank about this. If we sincerely want a brighter future for our youths, then we must give them more libraries than hotels and relaxation centers, more books than dancing clubs and other unnecessary entertainment gadgets. Indeed we must turn them into builders of innovative IT gadgets, instead of rabid consumers of things produced by children elsewhere!

If the vision and mission of the people are to be realized, we must invest in our youths, in the search for durable development in Igboland. There must be deliberate and systematic effort to accelerate social development that gives high priority to youth empowerment. Clearly, Ndi-igbo will build a strong future, if her youths are properly mobilized and equipped to drive and accelerate the desired Igbo integration and development agenda. Evidently, in the new Igbo world of our dream, our youths have a very significant role to play. The estimated over 60 million population of Ndi-Igbo has over 60% as young men and women under the age 35. Studies have shown that a demographic bonus creates the window of opportunity to accelerate investment that could serve to leapfrog socio-economic growth and infrastructural development within a decade. Clear examples that serve as points of reference are countries of South East Asia and the emerging new world economies of India, Brazil and China. Evidently, the youth-led and focused networks and organizations in those countries serve as sources of technical supply and support, for policy research and data analyses based on established priorities and initiatives.

Conclusion

Dear people of Igboland, I have abundantly made it clear in this paper that the Igbo people are great in every sense of the word, and are blessed with remarkable talents and spirit that make them the envy of other ethnic nations. The Igbos have a proclivity toward the maximization of their potentials and the mastery of every profession. This is why I maintain that they have an inbuilt psychological and genetic tendency for excellence. Achievement is in our DNA. Therefore, that the Igbos have not yet achieved a collective development of the entire Igboland, in spite of their great endowments, is because they have not seen it as a necessity for survival in the Nigerian State. Presently, the Igbos are still distracted and confused, scattered all over the world, using their talents and resources to develop other States of the federation and other nations of the world. It is not surprising, therefore, that the average Igbo of present day Nigeria, thinks that every part of this nation belongs to every Nigerian, and that he or she must be accepted in every part of the nation as a worthy citizen. But this basic Igbo mindset has been proved wrong by the consistent tragic events that have been associated with the Igbo presence in other ethnic nations of Nigeria. The simple message that is communicated to every Igbo today, is that his or her citizenship as a Nigerian does not extend beyond the ethnic boundaries. Therefore, the only place that every Igbo can call a home is Igboland. That is why it is imperative upon every Igbo to seek for ways of quickening the development of his or her homeland.

The Igbos must act to give rise to a new wave of Igbo renaissance. And the time for this necessary action is now. The time of procrastination is gone. This is the time for action. Our love for the Igbo question and indeed for the progress of the Igboland should be demonstrated through concrete actions, and no longer in speeches and rhetoric. Beautiful talks and wonderful ideological projections are very easy to come by. But action, they say, speaks louder than words. We have to begin with ourselves gathered for this conference to seek for means of implementing whatever we have articulated as the best way to develop our land and move our people forward. Let this conference not just end as one more academic gathering for mere intellectual musings.

We have raised enough academic awareness about the situation of Ndi-Igbo and the need for concrete actions for the development and empowerment of our people. Let us now begin to put our words into concrete actions. Let the collective vision for the future development of Igboland, that have been articulated in words over a long period of time, lead to concrete steps of actualization. Let us now commit ourselves in every sense of the word, to see that our beautiful words lead to the application of strings of fascinating actions. There is, therefore, the need for immediate switchover to a new vision of creative thinking and the adaptation of the new culture of systematic research and strategic planning as the vectors of scientific knowledge. It is only through these means that we shall guarantee the consistent processes for the development of Igboland and the empowerment of our people.

Works Cited

Abiodun Egbetokun. R&D and the Challenge of Wealth Creation in Nigeria" in

Academia.edu http://www.academia.edu/3091928/20/5/2014.

Adeyemi B. A.and P. A. Fasina, *A Multifaceted Approach to Research Methods, Osogbo*, Jehova Press, 2004.

Afigbo, A. E. *Ropes and Sand*. Nsukka: Uiversity of Nigerian Press, 1981.

Committee of Concerned Igbo Intellectuals London. "The Igbo Leadership Conundrum and the Quest for a Resurgent Igbo Polity: A Discussion Paper on the Way Forward," in The Igbo Network.

Ekwuru, E. George. "The Residual Effects of the Biafran War on the Igbo Cultural Personality," in *Unicorn: International Journal of Contemporary Studies*, Vol. 1, No. 1, 2013. Ezeani. E. In Biafra Africa Died, 2nd Ed., London: Veritas Pub. 2013.

Ezeudu F. O. Nkokelonye C:U. and Ezeudu S: A. "Science Education and the Challenge Facing its Integration into the 2list Century School System in a Globalized World: A Case of Igbo Nation," in *US-China Education Review*, Vol. 3, no. 3, March 2013,
pp. 172-182. file.eric.ed.gov/fulltex/ED5411825.

J.B. Adewumi, *Introduction to Educational Research*, Florin: Gbenle Press, 1988.

Adesina, S., *Educational Management, FDP Educational Series*, Enugu: Fourth Dimension Pub., 1990.

R_and_D_and_the_Challenge_of_Wealth_Creation_in_Nigeria 3/22]

Omote, Robert, "Echoes of Ethnic Politics" Guardian, February 21, 2010

Agbo Agbo, "The Dearth of Quality Research (II) an edition of his column, Pushing Out, in *The Nation*, Thurs, Jan. 2 2014.

Aworo, E.T., Morakinyo, R.M., (1997), "A study of Exam Malpractices in Secondary schools *in Akure* Loca/ Government Area of Ondo State unpublished research report.

K. Eso, "The State of Education in Nigeria," A paper delivered, at Redeemer's University, Ogun State, August, 2008.

Dioka, J.T. *Today's Man and World*, Owerri: IMSU Press, 2006.

Eluwa, B.O.N., Ado-na-Idu: *History of Igbo* Origin, Owerri: De-Bonelsons Pub, 2008.

Emefiena, Ezeani, In Biafra Africa Died, 2nd Ed., London: Veritas Pub. 2013.

Igbo Council of Europe. Igbo-Ukwu. http://igbocouncilofeurope.org/igbo-community/igbo-ukwu/

Igbokwe, Joe. *Igbos: Twenty Five Years after Biafra*. Advent Pub. Ltd, 1995.

Ihejirika, C. A Quest for Survival and Prosperity, A paper delivered at an Igbo Conference Lincoln University.

Igbokwe, Joe. www. nigeriavillagesquare.com/joe-igbokwe.

Ikerionwu, Daniel Ikechukwu. "The Place of Ndi-Igbo in Nigeria's Social and Economic Development," in www.academia.edu/2565774/.

J.B. Adewumi, *Introduction to Educational Research*, Florin: Gbenle Press, 1988.

Ndiokwere, N. I., Search for Greener Pastures, Igbo and African Experience, Nebrasaka: Morris Pub, 1998.

Meagher, Kate. "The Informalization of Belonging: Igbo Informal Enterprise and National Cohesion from Below," in African *Development,* Vol. XXXIV, no. 1, 2009, pp. 31-46. Cf. www.ajolinfo/index/ad/article/100/45734.

National Science Board. Research & Development, Innovation, and the Science *andEngineering Workforce: A Companion to Science* and Engineering Indicators; 2012.

Njoku, Uzochukwu. "The Education Question and Igbo Way Forward: Re-examining the View of Justice Oputa," in Nigerian World Feature Article. http:/nigerianworld.com/articles/2004/jan/091.html.

Nnamdi Azikiwe. Presidential Address Delivered to the Ibo State Union Assembly held at Aba on Saturday, 25 June, 1949. Cf. Igbo Network.

Ogu, Ben. *The Burden of Self-Imposed Marginalization: An Igbo Experience.* Edu-Edy Pub., 2009.

Omote, "Echoes of Ethnic Politics" Guardian, February 21, 2010.

Ejiogu and P. A. Fasina, *A Multifaceted Approach to Research Methods*, Osogbo: Jehova Press, 2004.

Siyanbola Willie Owolabi, Olamade Olumuyiwa Owolabi, Yusuff Shola Adeleke, and Kazeem Abubakar. Strategic Approach to R and D Commercialization in

Nigeria in International Journal of *Innovation, Management* and Technology, Vol. 3, No. 4, August *2012.*

Siyanbola W.O., Isola O.O., Egbetokun A.A. & Adelowo C.M. *R & D and the challenge of wealth creation in Nigeria.* National Centre for Technology Management, (Federal Ministry of Science and Technology) Obafemi Awolowo University Ile-Ife, Nigeria.

Ukege, B.O. *Education for Social Reconstruction.* Ibadan: Macmillan Pub., 1966.

Uwalaka, Jude. *The Struggle for an Inclusive Nigeria: Igbos to be or not to be?* Enugu: SNAAP Press LTD., 2003.

About the Contributors to volumes one and two

Acholonu, Prof. Catherine (26 October 1951 – 18 March 2014) is an Igbo writer, researcher and former lecturer on African Cultural and Gender Studies. She wrote poetry and essays on Nigerian literature and culture, and histories of Igbo people. A former Senior Special Adviser (SSA) to President Olusegun Obasanjo on Arts and Culture, she was a foundation member of the Association of Nigerian authors and best known for her work - *They Lived Before Adam: Prehistoric Origins of the Igbo The Never-Been-Ruled*

Afigbo, Professor A. E., (*NNOM*), (22 November 1937 – 9 March 2009) **formerly of the Department of History and International Relations, Ebonyi State University, Abakiliki is best known for** *Igbo History and Society (A Collection of His Essays),* ed. Toyin Falola, 2005. He wrote on the history and historiography of Africa, Igbo history and pre-colonial and colonial history including *The Warrant Chiefs: Indirect Rule in Southeastern Nigeria* 1891–1929, *Ropes of Sand: Studies in Igbo History and Culture,* etc.

Agbasimalo, Amb. (Mrs) Ada is an academic product of the University of Nigeria, Nsukka and the University of Lagos. She is the author of the following books: *Bow You Must, Waves of Destiny* and *The Forest Dames*. She is also a Justice of Peace, having been recognized as an Eminent Peace Ambassador of the United Nations. Previously Genevieve magazine gave her the award of the Extra-ordinary woman (unsung) while the Nigeria Association of Women Journalists (NAWOJ) gave her the award of Excellence and Integrity.

Agbo, Joseph. Senior lecturer in the department of philosophy and religion, Ebonyi State University, Abakaliki, Nigeria. He holds an M.A degree in philosophy from the University of Ibadan, Nigeria (1997), B.A. Philosophy, University of Lagos Nigeria, and he is currently concluding his Ph.D thesis at the University of Nigeria Nsukka. He is a social crusader, an incurable believer in the Biafran cause and one who believes in the global historical destiny of the Heebos (Ibos)

Ajiaebeli, Dr Nnamdi, a historian by training and profession, lectures in the Department of History and International Studies, University of Nigeria Nsukka. His research interest and specialty covers Nigerian History and African Diaspora History (with a focus on Igbo Diaspora in the era of the Atlantic Slave Trade and Slavery). He has published extensively on local and international journals.

Amucheazi, Prof. Elochukwu is Vice- President, Professor of Political Science, former Chairman of MAMSER, and Chairman of Council, Anambra State University. Current Secretary Igbo Leaders of Thought.

Aneke, Dr. Luke Nnaemeka, *MB, BS* (Nig), *MD* (New York), *LLB* (New York) New York-based practicing physician and Health Law consultant. Author of 800 page *Untold Story of the Nigeria-Biafra War*, Triumph Publishers, New York City, 2007. At the colloquium, he presented a paper on "Igbo Security, Emulating the Jewish Approach."

Anele, Holden who wrote "Igbo Nation: A Diasporean Perspective," is Chairman, Political Action Committee, TRF United States

Aniekwu, Prof. Nath is a Professor of Construction Management at the Civil Engineering Department, University of Benin, with degrees in both Agriculture and Engineering and has consulted widely for both local and international organizations.

Anigbogu, Vincent C. is a Professor and Director General Institute for National Transformation International, Abuja, FCT

Animalu, Alex O. E., *FAS, NNOM, IOM* **is** a longtime associate of Prof Gordian Ezekwe and *FAS, NNOM, IOM,* Emeritus Professor of Physics, Univesity of Nigeria, Nsukka.

Apeh, Dr. Apex A. is of the Department of History and International Studies, University of Nigeria, Nsukka.

Awuzie, Professor Ukachukwu Aloysius, *fnia*, B.Arch. and Master of Landscape Architecture (MLA), the first Nigerian Professor of Land scape Architecture. He has a lot of academic publications to his credit. A registered Architect and a Fellow of the Nigeria Institute of Architects and Member International Federation of Landscape Architects (IPLA), he is the National Chairman, Association of Architectural Educators (AARCHES) in Nigeria 2007-2012 and twice the Dean College of Engineering and Environmental Studies and Member, Governing Council of Imo State University. Professor Awuzie is known more in Nigeria for his performance as the President of the Academic Staff Union of Universities (ASUU 2008-2012). He was Chairman ASUU, Imo State University, Owerri (2000-2004) and currently Vice Chancellor, Imo State University.

Balogu, Prof. Dennis Odionyenfe, Ph.D., M.P.A., is Professor of Agriculture/Nutrition and Physiology, Faculty of Agriculture; Director, Centre for Applied Sciences and Technology Research; and Head of Department of Food Science and Technology, Ibrahim Badamasi Babangida University, Lapai, Niger State, Nigeria. Earlier, Balogu was Professor of Agriculture and Acting Director/International Affairs Officer, University of Arkansas at Pine Bluff, Pine Bluff, Arkansas, U.S.A.

Chidolue, Mazi Chike was former Officer, 12 Commando Brigade, Biafra Army and a known commentator on contemporary Nigerian issues.

Chimee, Ihediwa Nkemjika is a historian, lawyer and a Lecturer in the Department of History and International Studies, University of Nigeria, Nsukka. His research areas include social and political history, human rights. He has written on *Infrastructural neglect and economic imperatives in the post-war Igbo migration to the Northern and Western parts of Nigeria*. He has contributed chapters in edited books as well as to several journals.

Chinweizu, Dr. Chinweizu is the author of several books including *The West and the Rest of Us* (1975); *Decolonising the African Mind* (1987); *Voices from 20th Century Africa* (1988); and *Anatomy of Female Power* co-edited (1990). In March 2014, he received a Silverbird Lifetime Achievement Award for his Afrocentrism and uncompromising stance against colonial influences on African Thought.

Chukwuokolo, J. Chidozie is a senior lecturer in the Department of Philosophy, Ebonyi State University, Abakaliki and presently the Financial/Assistant Secretary of ADF. He is in addition an Ozo titled man from Mmaku with Nnadoziri as his title. He wrote "A Critical Examination of the Concept of Igbo *enwe eze* and its implications for Ndi Igbo."

Ejiofor, Prof. Anthony is Executive Director World Igbo Congress is a professor of Microbiology at Tennessee State University USA. He is a member of numerous professional organizations and is well-published.

Ejiofor, Prof. Pita is the Founder and National Chairman of *Otu Suwakwa Igbo Initiative* Nigeria, was the Vice- Chancellor of Nnamdi Azikiwe University, Awka(1998-2003). He was a Commissioner for Finance, and later Commerce and Industry in former Anambra State. He has carried the campaign for the rescue of Igbo Language to different parts of Nigeria, Britain and the USA. He was the 2003 Odenigbo lecturer in Owerri and the keynote speaker in the 2004 World Igbo Congress in Houston, Texas.

Ejiogu, Prof. E.C. is with the Department of Sociology/Anthropology, University of Nigeria, Nsukka. He is the author of *The Roots of Political Instability in Nigeria: Political Evolution and Development in the Niger Basin* (Ashgate, 2011). He was with the Centre for Africa Studies, University of the Free State, South Africa.

Eleazu, Dr. Uma was the pioneer Director of Research, National Policy Development Centre, Chairman Petroleum Products Marketing Ltd., Executive Director, Manufacturers Association of Nigeria. He was a member of the 1979 Constitution Drafting Committee as well as a member of the committee that drafted the present 1999 constitution

Ezekwesili, Obiageli is a chartered accountant and co-founder of Transparency International, holds a MA degree from Harvard University and the University of Lagos. Served as Nigerian Federal Minister of Solid Minerals and later Education under the Obasanjo regime. She serves on several company boards including Bharti Airtel, World Wildlife Fund among others. She has also been the Vice President of the World Bank's Africa division.

Ezeoke, Col. Justino is a retired officer of the Nigerian Army and an architect. A very uncompromising fighter for the Igbo cause whose experiences as an Igbo man has resulted in his delivering several lectures strongly advocating Igbo renaissance. He is a council member of the Alaigbo Development Foundation and the pioneer Publicity Secretary. He hails from Umuchu, Aguata LGA of Anambra state.

Ezeukwu, Ijeoma Charity author of "Interrogating the Military Incursion into Nigeria Politics and the Collapse of the First Republic in 1966," is of The Nnamdi Azikiwe University, Awka

Gbanite, Dr. Max is a strategic security consultant and defence analyst

Gbulie, Col. Ben, Rtd. Born in 1939 at Nimo, Njikoka LGA, Anambra State, Nigeria, he attended CiC Enugu, 1959, and joined the Nigerian Army in March 1960. He trained at the RMA Sandhurst, England, was commissioned in 1962. He attended The Royal School of Military Engineering, Kent as well as an Engineer Officer Career Course, Fort Belvoir, Va, USA. He took part in Nigeria's 1st *coup d'etat*. A veteran of the Nigerian-Biafra war, he is author of *Nigeria's Five Majors, The Fall of Biafra* and *Figments and Nothing*.

Idika, Dr Uduma who authored "The road map to Igbo restoration and reconstruction" is of the The Igbo-Hebrew cultural restoration organization (IGBOBRIO).

Ikedife, Dr. Dozie, *Ikenga Nnewi, CON,* is Chairman of BOT of ADF, British-trained Obstretrician and Gynacologist, ex-President-General of Ohanaeze Ndigbo, and Chairman Anambra Elders Council. He wrote on "Ndigbo in Nigeria: Challenges and the Future."

Iweze, Daniel Olisa, Ph.D., lectures in the Department of History, Bayero University, Kano, Nigeria. He holds a Bachelor and Master's of Arts degrees from Bayero University, Kano and a doctorate degree from University of Nigeria, Nsukka. His research interests are on Social and Economic History specializing on transport systems, business biographies, inter-group relations, post-civil war reconstruction and post-conflict studies. He has published articles and chapters in reputable scholarly international and local journals and edited books.

Jell-Bahlsen, Prof. Sabine is a cultural anthropologist focusing on Africa, especially Igbo culture since 1978, has published *The Water Goddess in Igbo Cosmology* (Africa World Press, 2008) and *Mammy Water in Igbo Culture* (Ezu Books, 2014), many articles and documentary films. She holds a Ph. D in Anthropology from the New School University in New York and an M.A. from the Free University in Berlin, Germany, has taught in the USA and PNG, and served as Editor-in-Chief of the journal, *Dialectical Anthropology*.

Kalu, Dr. Kalu Idika, *OFR* educated at Kings College Lagos, BS (Hon); MA, PhD Econ Dev & Public Finance (Wisc) '72; Yale Stimson Fellow; World Bank Economist (East Asia & Pacific, Japan, Korea, Taiwan and Hong Kong), 1972-80; formerly, Head of Economics, Skoup & Co, Enugu (1980-3); Commissioner, Finance and Economic Planning, Imo State (1984-5); Nigeria's Federal Minister of Finance, (1985-6; 1993–94); Federal Minister National Planning (1986-87); Federal Minister Transport (1987-9); Chairman, BGL Plc. And IPED co-founder of Justice Party, former Presidential Candidate (NNPP) and Finance Committee Chairman, ADF.

Korieh, Prof. Chima holds a Ph.D in African History from the University of Toronto, Canada. He was a British Academy Fellow at Oxford University, in 2008. He has edited or authored many books including *The Land Has Changed: Studies in Agrarian Change, Gender* and Society in Eastern Nigeria (The University of Calgary Press, 2010). He is the editor of *Igbo Studies Review*.

Maduagwuna, Prof. Michael O., MA, Ph.D. (Philosophy, Univ. of Innsbruck, Austria), is a Senior Fellow at the Nigeria's prestigious National Institute for Policy and Strategic Studies (NIPSS) Kuru – Jos. A long standing staff of the National Institute, Prof. Maduagwu was Acting Director of Research of the National Institute (2001-2002). He has travelled to several countries in Europe, the then Soviet Union, United States, Jamaica, China, Singapore and Pakistan as well as Africa. In addition to English, he speaks German fluently and has a working knowledge of French.

Mezu, Rose Ure, BA, MA (SUNY/AB), Ph.D. (Uniport), Diplôme d'Etude (Sorbonne) is Professor of English and Comparative Literature, Morgan State University, Baltimore, USA and author of over ten books including *Chinua Achebe: The man and his works; Women in Chains;* and *Songs of the Hearth; A History of Africana Women's Literature; Black Nationalists* and over ten other books. First Female Commissioner in Imo State under Mbakwe's regime, she has numerous articles published in renowned journals. A notable public speaker, Mezu's numerous awards include Black Woman Icon from NASA Glenn Space Center, USA (2012).

Mezu, Dr. S. Okechukwu, MA, LL.B, Ph.D, The Johns Hopkins University, Biafran Ambassador to Ivory Coast, was Professor, the Founder/Director of the African Studies Program at the State University of New York/Buffalo in 1970. A novelist and author of *Behind the Rising Sun;* poet, *Tropical Dawn*, literary critic, *Léopold Sédar Senghor et la défense et illustration de la civilization noire*, and political critic, Dr. Okechukwu Mezu has published several books in Igbo, English and French and his works have been translated into several European languages. He is the publisher of Black Academy Press, Inc. established in 1970 and the very first black owned academic publishing house in the USA.

Njoku, Professor Raphael is the Program Director for International Studies and the Chair of the Department of Economics at the University of Idaho Pocatello. Previously, a tenured professor of African/World History at the University of Louisville, he holds the Ph.D. degree in African History from Dalhousie University in Halifax, Canada, and another Ph.D. degree in Political Science from Vrije University in Brussels, Belgium. He also served as the editor for the journal *Notes and Records: The International Journal of African and African Diaspora Studies*.

Nnaji, Prof. Barth, *CON, NNOM, FAEng, FAS* is Distinguished professor of Mechanical and Industrial Engineering, Former Minister of Science & Technology, former Chairman of the Task Force on Power, ex-Minister of Power, (Member BOT) and holder of several honorary degrees.

Nwala, Prof. T. Uzodinma is Distinguished Professor of Social and Political Philosophy, Father of Contemporary African Philosophy, Statesman associated with the founding of some major institutions of our society- NYSC, ASUU, G-34, Rotational Presidency, six-geo-political zones in Nigeria, PDP, etc. Former Chairman, United Nations Youth Caucus and Chief Representative of ISMUN at the UN. Author of Igbo Philosophy. Coordinator of International Colloquium on the Igbo Philosophy and President of Alaigbo Development Foundation (ADF).

Nwaezeigwe, Dr. Nwankwo Tony is currently the Acting Director, Center for Igbo Studies, with concurrent appointments as Senior Lecturer, Department of History and International Studies, and Senior Research Fellow at the Institute of African Studies, University of Nigeria, Nsukka. Scholar at Igbo History and Culture, Ethno-Religious Conflict, and Black Africa-Middle East Relations

Nwagbara, Prof. F. Onyi is currently a Professor of Environmental Toxicology/Chemistry and Microbiology at Nasarawa State University, Keffi. He's also, a Visiting Professor of Military Science, Nigerian Defence Academy, Kaduna and A retired Officer in the U. S. Army. Prior to joining NSUK he was interim Dean School of Arts and Sciences, Chair of the Petroleum Chemistry and Natural and Environmental Science Programs at the American University of Nigeria, Yola and Professor at Florida A and M University Tallahassee Florida, U.S.A. Prof. Nwagbara has more than twenty two years of academic, military and technical experiences in regional and global arena as an educator/administrator, military officer, researcher and government official.

Nwosu, Goddyn Ehiogu. B.S., B.A., MBA, was an ardent participant in the defence of Igbo civilization and right to survival during the Nigeria-Biafra war, working as a research/technical assistant at the RAP Group (the Research and Production/Electronics, Group). He is the Dean/Managing principal of Bridge Institutes of Mathematics, O/A Bridge Learning Centers (Nigeria) Ltd. He is also the proprietor of FinRisk Consultants, a risk management & behavioral finance consultancy.

Obioha, Chief Ralph, former member House of Representatves, wrote on commerce and industry in Igbo land.

Odu, Prof. Mark is a member from Imo State in the 2014 National Conference and also Chairman of Central Planning Committee of Imo Co-operative Summit 2013.

Ogoko, Alberta, Senior Lecturer at the Dept of Philosophy & Religion, Ebonyi State University, Abakaliki is the author of "Philosophy: Reality & Consciousness," has many chapter contributions in books, journal articles and conference papers in epistemology, culture, history, phenomenology and national issues. He is completing his Ph.D at University of Nigeria, Nsukka, Nigeria.

Ohiri-Aniche, Prof. Chinyere obtained a B.Sc in French and Linguistics from Georgetown University, Washington D.C. in 1975, and M.Ed. in Language Teaching from the University of Montreal, Canada in 1977, and a Ph.D in Linguistics from the University of Port-Harcourt in 1991. She taught Linguistics and Language Education at the University of Lagos from 1980 to 2010. As the current President of the Linguistic Association of Nigeria, she continues to pursue the preservation, development and promotion of all Nigerian languages, including the Igbo language.

Ohuabunwa, Sam E. is a Pharmacist and former CEO of Pfizer West Africa and Founding President/CEO of Neimeth International Pharmaceuticals. He is an alumnus of University of Ife, Columbia University and Lagos Business School. He is the immediate past Chairman of the Nigerian Economic Summit (NESG) and the current President of the Nigerian American Chamber of Commerce. He is also a writer and lay minister.

Ojimba, Christian Chinyeremaka who wrote "Remembering Uli Biafra Airport (1968-1970) An historical perspective," is of the Department of History, Federal College of Education, Kano

Ojinma, Prof. Umelo is Professor of English & Literary Studies and the author of several books and co-edited many others including *China Achebe: New Perspectives* (1991), *Witi Ihimaera: A Changing Vision* (1993), *Use of English for Universities of Technology* (1997), *Bleak Moments* (2003), *Flower Kissed by the Sun* (2005), *The Pact* (2006), *Essays for the Eagle on the Iroko: Gendenkscchrift for Professor Chinua Achebe* (2014).

Okafor, Professor Richard C. is Professor of Music Education and Ethnomusicology, Enugu State University of Science and Technology.

Okaneme, Godwin is of the Department of Philosophy and Religions, University of Abuja, Nigeria.

Okorie, Chief Chekwas, *Ojeozi Ndigbo*, former member Abia State University Governing Council, former President General *Nzuko Abia na Imo*, Founder and President General Igboezue Cultural Association, Founder and Former National Chairman All Progressives Grand Alliance (APGA), Founder and National Chairman United Progressive Party (UPP), is a businessman in the Water Engineering Industry.

OkpalaEze Na Nri, Prince Emeka Onyesoh. Chukwuemeka Onyesoh is a prince of Nri, a community recognized as Custodians of Igbo Culture. A prolific writer, he believes that Southern Nigeria should get its acts together with minorities of the North who constitute over 50% of the North in order to avoid a permanent crisis of Islamic militancy in Nigeria.

Okwu, Amb. Prof. Austin S. O. was an Eastern Nigerian senior civil servant before transferring to the Nigerian Foreign Service. He served in London, Accra, Washington, D. C. and Tanzania as Acting High Commissioner 1962-1964. He was Biafra's first envoy in London and from there to East and Central Africa as Special Representative and later Ambassador and was honored by General Ojukwu with Biafra Silver Medal Award after he helped obtain Biafra's first diplomatic recognition from Tanzania and also another from Zambia. He is author of many articles and books including *In Truth: For Justice and Honor*.

Onyike, Hon. Abia. Former Deputy President, Nigerian Union of Journalists, Ex-Commissioner of Information, Ebonyi State. Chairman Publicity Committee

Oti, Felix studied Economics at the University of Arlington, and University of North Texas, Denton. He is a Senior Partner with Oti & Associates, a Personal Finance and New Business Advisory consulting agency based in Arlington, Texas USA. He also has many years of experience in new business products contract bidding and pricing from over two decades of working for Fortune 500 companies in the United States. Mr. Oti is a member of the National Association of Business Economics, American Economic Association, and National Economic Association, all in the United States. He is married with four children, and lives in Arlington, Texas.

Udeajah, Dr Ray A. is a Consultant in Political Communications. He is a Senior Lecturer in the Department of Mass Communication, University of Nigeria, Nsukka. Sections of the present article had previously featured in *Broadcasting and politics in Nigeria, 1963 – 2003*, a book by the same author published in 2004 by Snaap in Enugu, Enugu State, Nigeria.

Ugwuona, Dr. (Mrs.) Nwaeze C., Lecturer 1, Department of Linguistics, Igbo and Other Nigerian Languages, University of Nigeria, Nsukka. Her major discipline is sociolinguistics. She has taught courses on introduction to Sociolinguistics, Igbo people and their language, problems of a multilingual nation. She wrote the article, "Igbo language before, during and after the Biafra war (1500-2014) in Nigeria and the Igbo question."

Umeh, Prof. J. A. *OFR*, is Professor Emeritus and holds a traditional Igbo title of *Ogbuefi Eze-Ekwueme,* was educated at the Universities of London and Cambridge. He pioneered the establishment of first degree and postgraduate degree courses in Estate Management in Nigeria as well as establishment of the Faculty of Environmental Studies at the University of Nigeria. Professor Umeh is a sole author of sixteen books. Professor Chinua Achebe described him as "extra-ordinary phenomenon in contemporary Igbo life and letters."

Uriah, Dr Ify Ogbesowah wrote "The Asaba Massacre – The Rise from the Dead: An Eyewitness Account." Dr. Ifeanyi Uraih is a graduate of the University of Ibadan and the University of Lagos. Dr. Uraih's area of specialization is in New Product development. He is a Fellow of the Chartered Institute of Marketing, UK and Fellow of the National Institute of Marketing, Nigeria.

Uzondu, Anyadiegwu Charles, Ph.D., is a Public Health Specialist and a Development Researcher, by trainingand practice, an Epidemiologist, Operations Research Scientist, and Monitoring and Evaluation Specialist. He possesses the PhD degree in Infectious Diseases Epidemiology and the Master of Public Health (MPH) in Health Promotion and Communication. He has over ten years of experience working with International Donor Agencies in the healthcare and Development system in Nigeria. He is currently the President General of Ikwuano Development Union (Federated).

Index

A

A. E. Afigbo · *177*
A. K. Blankson · *220*
A. N. Aniekwu · *296*
Aba · *231*
Aba Power Limited · *87*
Aba Women Riot · *396*
Aba Women's Riot · *13*
Abagana debacle · *385*
Abanuka · *196*
Abba Eban · *355*
Abba Kyari · *121*
ABC Orjiakor · *29*
ABC transport · *27*
Abia Onyike · *218*
Abubakar Mamman Ngulde · *183*
Aburi Accord · *122*
Achebe · *309, 396*
Achibishopu Obinna · *249*
Ackoff · *240*
Action Group · *366*
Ada Agbasimalo · *307*
Adebayo · *226*
Adegoke Adelabu · *128*
Adekunle, · *205*
Ademulegun · *124, 126*
Adeniran Ogunsanya · *128*
Adetokumbo Ademola · *367*
Adewale Ademoyega · *120, 226*
Adichie · *396*
Adiele Afigbo · *20, 282*
Adisa Williams · *220*
Afigbo · *187, 396*
African Academy of Languages · *252*
African Messenger · *219*
Agbaje Williams · *220*
Agriculture · *15*

Aguyi Ironsi · *330*
Ahmadu Bello · *327*
Ajayi Crowther · *269*
Ajibola · *227*
Aka Ikenga · *20, 151*
Akanu Ibiam · *32, 90, 243*
Akwari Ukpabi · *40*
Ala Igbo Congress · *89*
Alade Odunewu · *220*
Alaigbo · *39*
Alaigbo Development Foundation · *20, 154*
ALAIGBO DEVELOPMENT FOUNDATION · *17*
Albert Einstein · *170*
Albert O. M. Ogoko · *194*
Alex Ekwueme · *28, 40*
Alex O. E. Animalu · *99*
Alliance for Democracy · *223*
Aluminum Extrusion · *28*
Aluminum Roofing sheets factory · *28*
Alvan Ikoku College of Education · *273*
Ambrose Madison · *214*
Aminu Kano · *220*
Aneke · *140*
Anthony Ejiofor · *210*
Anthony Enahoro · *123, 220, 365*
Anthony Maduekwe · *99*
Anuehe Eneje · *289*
Anya O. Anya · *40, 241*
Anyaoku · *396*
Anyim Pius Anyim · *40*
Archdeacon Dennis · *185*
Arewa Consultative Forum · *319*
Ariaria Market · *86*
Arinze · *396*
armed robbery, kidnapping, 419 · *14*
Arthur Richard · *308*
AU Max Gbanite · *141*
Augustine Asogbue · *397*
Augustine Ilodibe · *296*
Augustine Njoku-Obi · *397*
Author Eze · *29*

Awolowo · *120*
Awuzie · *151*
Azikiwe · *367, 396*
Azu Ndu · *274*

B

B. Adeyemi · *389*
B.C. Nwosu · *384*
B.C.Nwosu · *104*
Babatunde Jose · *220*
Babatunde Salami · *220*
Babayide · *268*
Bart Nnaji · *40*
Bartholomew Nnaji · *397*
Bassey Okoro · *25*
Bath Nnaji · *79*
Ben Enwuonwu · *39*
Ben Unoka · *58*
Biafra Newsletter · *241*
Biafra War · *20*
Biafran Military High Command · *123*
Biafran Research and Production Agency · *102*
Bight of Biafra · *212*
Blair Underwood · *210*
Blyden · *396*
Bob Ogbuagu · *219*
Broken Window · *145*
Bubbure · *259*
Buchi Emecheta · *315*
Building Materials Factory · *28*

C

C. C. Onoh · *395*
C. U. Aebedo · *274*
C.A Onwumechili · *177*
C.C. Onoh · *28*
Cajetan Okeke · *384*
Call to Service · *18*
Canaanite · *22*

Cannon Breweries · *28*
Catherine Acholonu · *20, 21*
Centre for Igbo Studies · *15*
Charles Amanze · *382*
Charles Morris · *126*
Charles Onwuzo · *25*
Chekwas Korie · *382*
Chi De Ebere, · *27*
Chief Janet Mokelu · *315*
Chieke Ihejirika · *398*
Chika Amobi · *249*
Chika Okafor · *28*
Chike Chidolue · *120*
Chike Obi · *126, 396*
Chimamanda · *249*
Chimere Ikokwu · *384*
Chinedum Nebo · *382*
Chinese · *22*
Chinua Achebe · *22, 39, 127, 182, 249, 396*
Chinwe Achebe · *279*
Chinweizu · *397*
Chinweizu Chinweizu · *20, 319*
Chinyere Kalu · *316*
Chinyere Ohiri-Aniche · *20, 258*
Chinyere Ohiri-Anichie · *151*
Chioma Ajunwa Opara · *316*
Chuba Okadigbo · *222*
Chuka Okadigbo · *380*
Chukwuemeka Odimegwu Ojukwu · *184*
Chukwuemeka Odumegwu Ojukwu · *104*
Chukwuma Soludo · *40, 396*
Chukwumah Nzeogwu · *120*
Clark · *229*
Clay Bricks · *28*
Clement N. Egwuatu · *25*
Clement Odunukwe · *126*
Cletus Ibeto · *28*
Collins Obi · *204*
Concorde Hotels · *28*
Council for Intellectual Cooperation of Nigeria · *20*
Council for National Coordination · *20*

Crescentia Ugwuona · 267
Cyprian Ekwensi · 241
Cyprian Emeka Uzor · 397

D

D.N Nwandu · 28
D.O Nkwonta · 296
Daily Comet · 219
Daily News · 219
Damian Anyanwu · 397
Daniel Olisa Iweze · 45
Dennis Chukwudebe Osadebey · 63
Dennis Odionyenfe Balogu · 63
Dike · 396
Dike Udensi · 28
Dora Akunyili · 40, 397
Douglas B. Chambers · 212
Dozie Ikedife · 340
Dr Michael Echeruo · 241
Dr Nnamdi Azikiwe · 380
Dr Nnamdi Azikwe · 38
Dr. Akanu Ibiam · 126
Dubai Healthcare City · 81
Duhaze · 185
Duro Onabule · 127

E

E. O. Ihejirika · 55
E. T. Aworo · 401
E.C.I Onuigbo · 25
East Central State · 63, 69
Eastern Nigeria Consultative Assembly · 227
Eastern Nigeria Development Cooperation (ENDC) · 26
Eastern Nigeria Development Corporation · 32
Eddie Onuzuruike · 379
Edmund Ilogu · 293
Edmund Willmot Blyden · 219

Edo College · 55
Edward Blyden · 363
Egbu · 185
Ekene-Dili-Chukwu · 27
Ekwensi · 396
Eli Rosenbaum · 138
Elobuike Malachy Nwabuisi · 195
Eluwa · 187
Emeagwali · 396
Emefiena Ezeani · 341, 395
Emeka Offor · 29
Emeka Ojukwu · 396
Emeka Okwuosa · 29
Emma Iheancho · 29
Emma Okafor · 384
Emma Okocha · 55, 140
EmmanuelOkocha · 205
English · 22
Eni Njoku · 39
Enugu Disco · 87
Enugu Electricity Distribution Company · 87
Enyimba Enyi · 206
Equatorial Guinea · 207
Equiano, · 396
eri mgbe · 21
Erich Priebke · 137
Ernest Azudialu · 29
Ernest Ikoli · 219
Ernest Ndukwe · 40, 397
Esau · 164
Europeans · 22
Evans Enwerem · 222
Eze Nri · 177
Eze Nri Obalike · 182
Ezekiel Izuogo · 397
Ezera Kalu · 39
Ezeudu · 407
Ezeudu F. 0 · 405
Ezeudu S: A · 405

F

F. C. Ogbalu · 273
F.C. Esedebe · 53
F.C. Nwokedi · 126, 128
F.C. Ogbalu · 274
F.G.N Okoye · 296
Fashina · 240
Federal University of Technology · 83
Federalism · 14
Felix C. Oragwu · 104
Felix O. Oragwu · 384
Felix Oti · 32
Ferdinand Anaghara · 296
Ferdnard Anaghara · 28
Festus Odimegwu · 40, 248
First International Colloquium · 13, 20
First Republic · 13
Flora Azikiwe · 227
Flora Nwapa · 280, 315
Flour Mill · 28
Forest Whitaker · 210
Foreword · 20
Francis C.N. Agbasi · 126
Francis Nwokedi · 227
Frank Ikem Owelle · 355
Frank Nneji · 40
Franklin Roosevelt · 163
Fred Esedebe · 58
Frederick Douglas · 403
Fredrick Lugard · 176
Fulani Cattle Herdsmen · 145
Fulbright Foundation · 253

G

G.E Chikeluba · 296
G.T. Basden · 177, 186
Gabon · 231
George Okonta · 58
Gloria Chuku · 214
Goddyn Ehiogu-Nwosu · 383
Godwin Okaneme · 307

Golden Guinea Breweries · 28, 32
Good Governance · 15
Gordian Ezekwe · 20, 99
Gordon Duff · 222
Government College, Ughelli, were owned and managed by private proprietors and voluntary · 55
Gowon · 203, 225
Greece · 22
Greenberg · 267
Gullah tribe · 210

H

H O Davies · 365
H. O. Davies · 125
Haiti, · 231
Harbor · 25
Harold Smith · 182
Hassan · 232, 233
Hebrew · 22
Herbert Macaulay · 219, 363, 364
Herbert Orji · 40
Herbert Wigwe · 40
Herskovits · 284
Hezekiah Oluwasanmi · 129
Hilary Njoku · 122
Howard University · 212
Hugh Auld · 403
hunter paradigm · 165

I

I. B. Babangida · 99
I.U. Nwadike · 274
Ibeto · 40
Ibiam · 396
Ibo State Union · 354
Ifeagwu Ekeh · 241
Ifeanyi Uba · 29
Ifejika · 230
Ifemesia · 241

Ifesinachi · 28
Igbo Containment · 352
Igbo enwe eze · 176
Igbo Enwe eze · 176
Igbo Landing · 206
Igbo Nation · 17
   History, Challenges of Rebirth and Development · 20
Igbo Security · 130
Igbo Studies Association · 20
Igbo women · 30
Igbo World Assembly · 20
Igbozurume Unity Centre · 13
Igwe Achebe · 40
Igwe bu ike · 79, 381
Ihejirika · 40, 396
Ike Ekweremadu · 382
Ike Nwachukwu · 40
Ikenga · 394
Ikenga Hotels · 28
Ikenna Nzimiro · 103, 277
Ikerionwu · 394
Ikoku · 396
Infrastructure and Education · 79
Innocent Chukwuma · 28
Innocent Eloike · 286
International Colloquium on the Igbo Question in Nigeria · 100, 194
Ironsi · 124, 125
Iru mgbede · 178
Irukwu · 239
Isaac Akuchie · 18
Ivory Coast · 231
Izu-Umunna · 20

J

J. O. Enaohwo · 55
J. A. Umeh · 178
J. C. Chukwuokolo · 20
J. Chidozie Chukwuokolo · 176
J. N. Nwachukwu · 26
J. Onuoha · 241

J. U. Nwankwu · 296
J.O. Iroaganachi · 272
J.T.U. Aguiyi Ironsi · 225
Jacob · 164
Jacob Paradigm · 166
James Coleman · 219
James Madison · 214
James O. Ojiako · 120
James Wolfenson · 85
Jeff Unaegbu · 102
Jefkin · 239
Jesus · 21
Jesus Christ · 140
Jews · 22
JigSaw Earth Theory · 22
Jim Nwobodo · 28
JMO Ezeoke · 116
Joe Igbokwe · 400
Joe Nwankwu · 28
John Anyaehie · 296
John Enemoh · 58
John Payne Jackson · 219
Josephine Nwodo · 30
Journal of Igbo Studies · 273, 274
JSPC Nwokolo · 382
Jude Asenime · 56

K

K. O. Mbadiwe · 227
Kalu Idika Kalu · 150
Kanime Okonjo · 58
Kano massacre · 138
Kanu Okoronkwo · 384
Kate Meagher · 394, 398
Ken Nnamani · 40
Kenneth Mellamby · 101
Kenneth O. Dike · 126
King George V · 350
King Jaja · 13
Kodilinye · 39
Kola Balogun · 220
Kolawole Balogun · 128

Kurt Waldeim · *131*
Kurt Waldheim · *135, 138*
Kwame Nkrumah · *396*

L

L.N. Obiaha · *27*
L.N. Obioha · *25*
L.P. Ojukwu · *26*
Lagos Weekly Record · *219*
Largema · *124*, 126
Lee Kuan Yew · *175*
Leonard · *187*
Life Breweries · *28*
Lloyd Garrison · *133*
Louis Odumegwu-Ojukwu · *296*
Ironsi, · *396*
Lugard · *176*
Luggard · *146*
Luke N. Aneke · *130*
Lusaka · *169*
Lutz · *185*

M

M A C Odu · *334*
M. I. Okpara · *29, 63, 129*
M.A Onwuejeogwu · *185*
M.C.K. Ajuluchukwu · *220*
M.I. Okpara · *26*
M.N. Ugochukwu · *26, 27*
Macgregor Laird · *361*
Macpherson Constitution · *365*
Madiebo · *122*
Maimalari · *124*
Mammy Water · *277*
Mandela · *332*
Mao Tse Tung · *129*
Mariam Ikejiani · *50*
Mark. O. Chijioke · *384*
Mark-press · *242*
Martin Hillenbrand · *123*

Mary Nzimiro · *30*
Maurice Hayes · *101*
Maya Angelou · *282*
Mbanefo · *396*
MCK Ajuluchukwu · *123*
Mgbe Eri · *22*
Michael Mok · *104*
Michael O. Maduagwu · *327*
Michael Okpara · *38, 90, 146*
Mike Nwachukwu · *384*
Mike Okwechime · *58*
Mobolaji Odunewu · *220*
Modern Ceramic · *32*
Modern Poultry Industry · *28*
Mohammed Shuwa · *132, 134, 136, 139*
Mokwugo Okoye · *220*
Monarch breweries · *28*
Moshe Dayan · *123*
Mungo Park · *346*
Murtala Mohammed · *127, 206*
Musa Yar'Adua · *249*

N

Nath Aniekwu · *20*
National Agency for Science and Engineering Infrastructure · *393*
National Assembly · *321*
National Conference · *14*
National Council for Science and Technology · *391*
National Electricity Power Authority · *59*
National Universities Commission · *253*
natural resources · *33*
Nazareth · *21*
Naze · 21
NCNC · *220, 366*
Ndi Onuekwusi, · *40*
Ndigbo in pre-history · *13*
Nduka Eze · *220*

Nduka Otonti · *401, 404*
Nelson Mandela · *396*
Ngozi Okonjo-Iweala · *85, 316*
Niger Delta Congress · *366*
Niger Steel Industry · *32*
Niger-gas plant · *32*
Nigeria-Biafra War · *14*
Nigerian National Democratic Party · *364*
Nigerian Spokesman · *219*
Nigerian Tribune · *219*
Nike Resort Hotel · *28*
Njoku Obi · *39*
Njoku-Obi · *384*
Nkalagu Cement Company · *26*
Nkalagu Cement Factory · *28*
Nkokelonye C. U · *405*
Nnaji · *396*
Nnamdi Azikiwe · *90, 182, 219, 220, 243, 327, 365, 396, 399*
Nnamdi Azikiwe University · *83*
Nnana Kalu · *296*
Nnanna Kalu · *26*
Nne Mmiri · *279*
No Victor No Vanquished · *128*
No Victor, No Vanquished · *330*
Nolue Emenanjo · *274*
North and South America · *21*
Northcorte Thomas · *187*
Northern Elements Progressive Union · *366*
Northern Advocate · *219*
Northern Peoples' Congress · *366*
Nsibidi · *269*
Nwabueze · *396*
Nwadike · *268*
Nwafor Orizu · *219*
Nwaji. Eugene O.Arene · *384*
Nwanguma · *40*
Nwankwo · *230*
Nwapa · *396*

O

Obafemi Awolowo · *203, 327, 365*
Obiageli Ezekwesili · *89*
Obioha · *313*
Obodo-Ukwu · *231*
Obuaku Medical City · *81*
Obudu Cattle Ranch · *146*
Odimegwu Ojukwu · *90*
Oduduwa · *346*
Odumegwu Ojukwu · *380, 382, 396*
Ofo · *284*
Ofo na Ogu · *342*
Ofobuike Intellectual Union · *20*
Ofu Obi, Ofu Onu · *340*
Ogbanje · *278*
Ogbemudia · *45*
Ogbuide · *279, 281*
Ogbunigwe · *385*
Ogbuniwe · *395*
Ogunsola · *126*
Ohaneze Ndigbo · *335*
oil palm plantations · *32*
Ojike · *396*
Ojukwu · *120, 226*
Oke Okpa Ebela · *18*
Okechukwu Anthony Mezu · *397*
Okere · *396*
Okereke · *25*
Okigbo · *396*
Okocha · *54*
Okoi Arikpo · *237*
Okon Okon Ndem · *237*
Okonjo-Iweala · *396*
Okoye · *313*
Okpara · *396*
Okwudishu · *272*
Okwudo · *231*
Olanrewaju Olutayo · *394*
Olauda Ekweano · *247*
Olauda Equiano · *182*
Olaudah Equiano · *13*
Olunloyo · *126*
Oluwole Osagie-Jacobs · *179*

Omenuko · *274*
On Aburi We Stand · *122*
Onitsha market · *30*
Onwuejeogwu · *186*
Onwuka Kalu · *296*
Onye ahala nwanneya · *372*
Onyemauchechi Gbujie · *20*
Oputa · *396*
Oragwu · *102*
Oraka · *269*
Orizu · *396*
Osita Agwuna · *220*
Osundu · *27*
Osy Okanya · *60*
Othman Dan Fodio · *177, 180*
Othman Danfodio · *218*
Owerri · *21*, 185

P

P. G. Stallard · *126*
P.N. Okeke · *102*
Paint Industry · *28*
Pal Breweries · *28*
Pam. · *124*
Pan African Congress · *363*
Paschal Dozie · *87*
Patrick Murphy · *145*
Paul Obi-Ani · *45*
Paul Okoro · *25*
Paul Robeson · *210*
Peace Mass · *27*
Peter Ejiofor · *151*
Peter Nwangwu · *397*
Phelps–Strokes · *271*
Philip Effiong · *239*
Philip Emeagwali · *397*
Pioneer Oil Mills · *24*
Pita Ejiofor · *247*
Pita Nwanna · *274*
Pius Okeke · *103*
Pius Okigbo · *227*
Premier Breweries · *28*

Princess Alu Ibiam · *20*
PRODA · *99*
Professor Uzodinma Nwala · *13*

R

R. M. Morakinyo · *401*
R.O. Nkwocha · *296*
Radio Biafra · *229, 230*
Ralph Obioha · *24*
Ray A. Udeajah · *224*
Republic of Biafra · *227, 229*
Republic of Haiti · *206*
Republic-of-Benin' · *229*
Resiliency Gene · *202*
Rex Jim Lawson · *126*
Richard C. Okafor · *284*
Richards Constitution · *365*
Rick Joyner · *353*
Robert Omote · *396*
Rochas Okorocha · *403*
Roman Catholic Mission · *270*
Roncaglia · *138*
rubber plantation · *32*

S

S. Ejiogu · *389*
S. N. O. Madu · *26*
S. O. Egube · *55*
S. Okechukwu Mezu · *20, 22, 151, 274*
S.E Onwu · *272*
S.E. Ikeokwu · *274*
Sa'ad Zungur · *220*
Sabine Jell-Bahlsen · *277*
SAFARI Breweries · *28*
Salisu Ibrahim · *222*
Sam Chukwu · *102*
Sam Mbakwe · *28, 204, 403*
Sam Ohuabunwa · *38*
Samuel Osaigbovo Ogbmudia · *46*

Sardauna · *129*
Second National Development Plan · *51*
Security · *15, 116*
Selbourne Committee · *361*
Shehu Shagari · *204*
Shell-BP · *233*
Shodeinde · *124*
Shoe Industry · *32*
Skutnabb-Kangas · *263*
Slobodan Milosevic · *132*
Solomon Simbi · *220*
Southern Nigeria Defender · *219*
Sovereign National Conference · *319*
Stan Ekeh · *29, 40*
Staunton Virginia · *256*
Steiner · *122, 123*
Stella Okoli · *40*
Steve Emejuaiwe · *384*
Stremlau · *242*
Sylvia Leith-Ross · *182*

T

T. Uzodinma Nwala · *20*
T.D. Jakes · *210*
T.O.S. Benson · *128*
T.U. Nwala · *183*
Tagbo Onyekwelu · *28*
Tamuno · *239*
Tanzania · *231*
Temple · *187*
The Conference of Democratic Scholars · *20*
The *Eastern Nigeria Sentinel* · *219*
The Guardian · *222*
The Sun · *222*
The Young Shall Grow · *28*
Theophilus Danjuma · *136, 139*
Theophilus Dannjuma · *134*
Things Fall Apart · *22*
Thomas Horatio Jackson · *219*
Thomas Sowell · *171*

Thomas, · *233*
Tom Forrest · *398*
Tony Ezenna · *28, 29*

U

Uche Chukwumerije · *241, 242*
Uchendu · *396*
Uduma Idika · *344*
Ugboajah · *239*
Ugorji Ugorji · *20*
Uhammiri · *279*
Ukachukwu A. Awuzie · *387*
Ukaegbu · *396*
Ukonu · *129*
Ukpabi · *239*
Uma Eleazu · *359*
Umar Musa Yar'Adua · *223*
Umeano · *25*
Umelo Ojinmah · *379*
Umu Ejima · *274*
Umunna wu ike · *385*
UNESCO · *91*
Union Igbo · *270*
United African Company · *24*
United Middle Belt Congress · *366*
United Nations Educational, Scientific and Cultural Organization · *202*
Universal Data Bank · *152*
University of Biafra · *241*
University of Nigeria · *83, 241*
UPGA · *367*
Uwalaka · *268, 271, 273*
Uzochukwu Njoku · *404*
Uzodinma Nwala · *20, 89*
Uzoma Nwola · *40*

V

Vanguard · *222*
Victor Kalu · *222*
Victor Umeh · *382*

Vincent C. Anigbogu · *160*
Virginia Etiaba · *316*
Vogler · *185*
Voice of Biafra · *224*

W

West African Examiner · *219*
West African Pilot · *219*
Western Igboland · *45*
William Berbhardt · *242*
Willie Achukwu · *384*

Willie Obiano · *250*
World Bank · *79*
World Igbo Congress · *20*

Z

Z.A. Chukwujama · *25, 26*
Zambia, · *231*
ZC Obi · *184*
Zik · *128*
Zikist Movement · *220*
Zulu Sofola · *316*

www.ingramcontent.com/pod-product-compliance
Lightning Source LLC
Chambersburg PA
CBHW022045160426
43198CB00008B/136